Selected Readings on Strategic Information Systems

M. Gordon Hunter
University of Lethbridge, Canada

INFORMATION SCIENCE REFERENCE

Hershey · New York

Director of Editorial Content:	Kristin Klinger
Managing Development Editor:	Kristin M. Roth
Senior Managing Editor:	Jennifer Neidig
Managing Editor:	Jamie Snavely
Assistant Managing Editor:	Carole Coulson
Typesetter:	Lindsay Bergman
Cover Design:	Lisa Tosheff
Printed at:	Yurchak Printing Inc.

Published in the United States of America by
  Information Science Reference (an imprint of IGI Global)
  701 E. Chocolate Avenue, Suite 200
  Hershey PA 17033
  Tel: 717-533-8845
  Fax: 717-533-8661
  E-mail: cust@igi-global.com
  Web site: http://www.igi-global.com

and in the United Kingdom by
  Information Science Reference (an imprint of IGI Global)
  3 Henrietta Street
  Covent Garden
  London WC2E 8LU
  Tel: 44 20 7240 0856
  Fax: 44 20 7379 0609
  Web site: http://www.eurospanbookstore.com

Library of Congress Cataloging-in-Publication Data

Selected readings on strategic information systems / M. Gordon Hunter, editor.

    p. cm.

  Summary: "This book offers research articles on key issues concerning information technology in support of the strategic management of organizations"--Provided by publisher.

  Includes bibliographical references and index.

  ISBN 978-1-60566-090-5 (hbk.) -- ISBN 978-1-60566-091-2 (ebook)

  1. Management information systems. 2. Strategic planning. I. Hunter, M. Gordon.

  HD30.213.S45 2009

  658.4'03801--dc22

                        2008020496

British Cataloguing in Publication Data
A Cataloguing in Publication record for this book is available from the British Library.

All work contributed to this book set is original material. The views expressed in this book are those of the authors, but not necessarily of the publisher.

Table of Contents

Section II
Development and Design Methodologies

Section III
Tools and Technologies

Section IV
Utilization and Application

Detailed Table of Contents

Section I
Fundamental Concepts and Theories

Chapter I

    Mark Xu, University of Portsmouth, UK
    Roland Kaye, University of East Anglia, UK

This chapter discusses the nature of strategic intelligence and the challenges of systematically scanning and processing strategic information. It reveals that strategic intelligence practice concentrates on competitive intelligence gathering, non-competitive related intelligence have not yet been systematically scanned and processed. Much of the intelligence is collected through informal and manual based systems. The chapter proposed a corporate intelligence solution, which comprises of three key intelligence functions, namely organizational-wide intelligence scanning, knowledge enriched intelligent refining, and specialist support. The chapter develops insight of strategic intelligence, and the solution could significantly enhance a manager's and a company's sensibility and capability in dealing with external opportunities and threats.

Chapter II

    Keith Sawyer, Alpha Omega International, UK
    John Gammack, Griffith University, Australia

Although it is widely accepted that alignment of knowledge with corporate strategy is necessary, to date there have been few clear statements on what a knowledge strategy looks like and how it may be practically implemented. The current study is representative of similar studies carried out across a range of organisations using a novel and practically proven method. This method, StratAchieve, was used here in a client situation to show how the core competencies were identified and tested for incorporation or not in the strategy. The paper concludes by considering the value of the approach for managing knowledge.

Chapter III

Implementing Supply Chain Management in the New Era: A Replenishment Framework for
the Supply Chain Operations Reference Model 34

William Y. C. Wang, University of South Australia, Australia
Michael S. H. Heng, Universitas 21 Global, Singapore
Patrick Y. K. Chau, The University of Hong Kong, Hong Kong

This chapter reviews the literature of Supply Chain Management (SCM) from several paths that can
be the basis of a proposed framework for SCM within academic and managerial contexts. In addition,
it includes the approaches of supply chain operations reference (SCOR) model, which was developed
by the Supply Chain Council and is recognised as a diagnostic tool for SCM worldwide. This chapter
also summarises the literature of performance control and risk issues in SCM and the SCOR Model and
discusses a proposed framework for the future research.

Chapter IV

Behavioral Factors and Information Technology Infrastructure Considerations in Strategic
Alliance Development 52

Purnendu Mandal, Lamar University, USA

Since behavioral and cultural factors play a major role in strategic alliances between partners, IT managers
must understand the intricacies involved in the development of resultant IT infrastructure in satisfying
both business requirements and cultural fit of the aligned partnering units. This chapter first highlights
the IT-related issues and cultural issues which are important in the process of developing a strategic
alliance between partners. Then, a case study involving a major telecommunications organization and
several retail electricity organizations is presented to illustrate the IT requirements and human-related
considerations. The analysis focuses on the requirements of pre-strategic alliance phase of the negotiation process.

Section II
Development and Design Methodologies

Chapter V

A Methodology for Developing an Integrated Supply Chain Management System 66

Yi-chen Lan, University of Western Sydney, Australia
Bhuvan Unhelkar, University of Western Sydney, Australia

Integrated Supply Chain Management (ISCM) involves the linking of suppliers and customers with
the internal business processes of an organization. ISCM solutions allow organizations to automate
workflows concerning the execution and analysis of planning, sourcing, making, delivering, returns
handling, and maintenance, to name but a few. Many of today's ISCM systems use primarily Web technology as the supporting infrastructure. Though electronic (Internet-based) ISCM systems deliver the
enterprises with a competitive advantage by opening up opportunities to streamline processes, reduce

costs, increase customer patronage, and enable thorough planning abilities, there has been significant customer backlash concerning the inability of software vendors to deliver easy integration and promised functionality. Although various researchers have suggested strategies to overcome some of the failures in operating ISCM systems, there appears to be a lacunae in terms of architectural investigations in the analysis stage. The methodology proposed in this chapter seeks to resolve these gaps and provides a fundamental framework for analyzing ISCM systems.

    Summer E. Bartczak, University of Central Arkansas, USA
    Jason M. Turner, Air Force Institute of Technology, USA
    Ellen C. England, ISN Software Corporation and Kaplan University, USA

It is widely acknowledged that knowledge management (KM) strategy is a desired precursor to developing specific KM initiatives. Strategy development is often difficult due to a variety of influences and constraints. Using KM influences as a foundation, this case study describes issues involved in developing a KM strategy for the Air Force Material Command, including issues to be considered for future strategy development such as leadership support and understanding, conflicts with IT organizations, funding, technology usage and configuration, and outsourcing.

    Michael Shumanov, Monash University, Australia
    Michael Ewing, Monash University, Australia

While the managerial rationale for adopting customer relationship management (CRM) has been fairly well articulated in the literature, research on strategy development is scant. Moreover, reports of "CRM failures" in the popular business press have done little to inspire confidence. To date, what little research has been conducted in the area of CRM strategy development has been confined to a single country (often the U.S.). Global CRM strategy development issues have yet to be specifically addressed, particularly which elements of CRM strategy should be centralised/decentralised. The present study examines the complexities of global CRM strategy using the case of a leading financial services company. Interviews are conducted in 20 countries. Global Head Office and external IT consultant perspectives are also considered. Our findings confirm that a hybrid approach has wide practical appeal and that subsidiary orientation towards centralisation/decentralisation is moderated by firm/market size and sophistication.

    Richard Welke, Georgia State University, USA
    Gabriel Cavalheiro, Ernst & Young, NL
    Ajantha Dahanayake, Georgia College & State University, USA

Commercial airlines face an extremely challenging operating and competitive environment. Increasingly, airlines are realizing that a "plan-execute" mode of operation must give way to a "sense-respond" mode of operation; in other words they must become a real-time (agile) organization, capable of sensing the occurrence of unforeseen events such as the placement of a last-minute shipping order, flight delays, and cancellations, and respond effectively in real-time to such events. To enable enterprises in general, and the airline industry in particular, to improve their sense-and-respond capabilities and ensure better resource utilization, a number of software vendors are offering event stream processing and Business Activity Monitoring (BAM) solutions. This case examines a longitudinal set of real-world implementation projects using such a solution at a major US airline (referred to as Southern International Airlines) and the results and lessons gained from this deployment.

Section III
Tools and Technologies

The rapid development of computing technology has facilitated its use in engineering design and manufacturing at an increasing rate. To deliver high quality, low cost products with reduced lead times, companies are focusing their efforts on leveraging this technology through the development of knowledge-based systems such as an IDA. An IDA, which can also be referred to as a design information system, is a part of the overall enterprise information system framework, and plays an important role in improving competitiveness in product development oriented companies. This chapter discusses the structure and development of a knowledge-based design information system that can convert this descriptive information into forms that are suitable for embedding within decision-making algorithms.

Today, information and timely decisions are crucial for an organization's success. A decision support system (DSS) is a software tool that provides information allowing its users to make decisions timely and cost effectively. This is highly conditioned by the quality of the data involved, usually stored in a data warehouse, and by a sound and complete requirements analysis. This chapter shows that conventional techniques for requirements elicitation cannot be used in DSS, and presents a methodology denoted DSS-METRIQ, aimed at providing a single data quality-based procedure for complete and consistent elicitation of functional (queries) and nonfunctional (data quality) requirements.

Chapter XI

This study proposes a new methodology that facilitates organizational decision support through knowledge integration across organizational units. For this purpose, this study develops a decision support loop and explains how to organize individual knowledge related to a specific business problem and formulate and test the organized knowledge using cognitive modeling techniques for decision support. This study discusses the proposed approach in the context of an application case involving a beverage company. The application case shows the validity and usefulness of the proposed approach.

Chapter XII

This chapter presents a new concept for supporting electronic collaboration, operations, and relationships among trading partners in the value chain without hindering human autonomy. Although autonomous intelligent agents, or electronic robots (e-bots), can be used to inform this endeavor, the chapter advocates the development of e-sensors, i.e., software based units with capabilities beyond intelligent agent's functionality. E-sensors are hardware-software capable of perceiving, reacting and learning from its interactive experience through the supply chain, rather than just searching for data and information through the network and reacting to it and can help to avoid the "bullwhip" effect. This chapter briefly reviews the related intelligent agent and supply chain literature and the technological gap between fields.

Section IV
Utilization and Application

Chapter XIII

This chapter identifies important barriers to the successful application of Computational Intelligence (CI) techniques in a commercial environment and suggests a number of ways in which they may be overcome. It identifies key conceptual, cultural and technical barriers and describes the different ways in which they affect both the business user and the CI practitioner. The authors aim to highlight to technical and business readers how their different expectations can affect the successful outcome of a CI project. The authors hope that by enabling both parties to understand each other's perspective, the true potential of CI can be realized.

Chapter XIV

E-business is far more about strategy than technology, and the strategy of e-business is very important in today's dynamic and competitive environment. This chapter describes a balanced scorecard-based framework in detail and discusses its potential e-business uses. This framework enables e-business managers to plan and allocate resources more effectively and align strategic objectives with performance results. It also provides a stable point of reference for e-businesses to understand and manage the fundamental changes introduced by e-business initiatives.

Chapter XV

An appropriate outsourcing and supply-chain planning strategy needs to be based on compromise and more objective decision-making procedures. Although factors affecting business performance in manufacturing firms have been explored in the past, focuses are on financial performance and measurement, neglecting intangible and nonfinancial factors in the decision-making planning process. This study presents development of an integrated multi-criteria decision-making (MCDM) model. This model aids in allocating outsourcing and supply-chain resources pertinent to strategic planning by providing a satisfying solution. This developed model will reinforce a firm's ongoing outsourcing strategies to meet defined requirements while positioning the supply-chain system to respond to a new growth and innovation.

Chapter XVI

Decision making is one of the basic cognitive processes of human behaviors by which a preferred option or a course of actions is chosen from among a set of alternatives based on certain criteria. This chapter presents a fundamental cognitive decision making process and its mathematical model, which is described as a sequence of Cartesian-product based selections. A rigorous description of the decision process in real-time process algebra (RTPA) is provided. Real-world decisions are perceived as a repetitive application of the fundamental cognitive process. The result shows that all categories of decision strategies fit in the formally described decision process. The cognitive process of decision making may be applied in a wide range of decision-based systems such as cognitive informatics, software agent systems, expert systems, and decision support systems.

Section V
Critical Issues

Abou Bakar Nauman, COMSATS Institute of Information Technology, Pakistan
Romana Aziz, COMSATS Institute of Information Technology, Pakistan
A.F.M. Ishaq, COMSATS Institute of Information Technology, Pakistan

This chapter examines the causes of failure in a Web-based information system development project and finds out how complexity can lead a project towards failure. Learning from an Information System Development Project (ISDP) failure plays a key role in the long-term success of any organization desirous of continuous improvement via evaluation and monitoring of its information systems (IS) development efforts. This study reports on a seemingly simple (but only deceptively so) failed ISDP to inform the reader about the various complexities involved in ISDPs in general, and in developing countries in particular. An existing framework from contemporary research is adopted to map the complexities found in the project under study and the critical areas, which lead to the decreased reliability and failure in Web-based information system development, are highlighted.

Fiona Fui-Hoon Nah, University of Nebraska – Lincoln, USA
Zahidul Islam, Independent University, Bangladesh
Mathew Tan, Agilent Technologies, Malaysia

Enterprise resource planning (ERP) implementations in multinational manufacturing companies have experienced various degrees of success. This chapter investigates factors influencing the success of ERP implementations in multinational manufacturing companies in the Malaysian Free Trade Zone. The results indicate that enterprise-wide communication and a project management program are key factors influencing the success of ERP implementations, while other factors such as top management support as well as teamwork and composition are not as critical to the outcome.

Shirish C. Srivastava, National University of Singapore, Singapore
Thompson S. H. Teo, National University of Singapore, Singapore

Most existing studies on technology training address the operational issues of training process (e.g., training needs assessment, learning, delivery methods, etc.). The strategic concerns of IT training for enhancing business productivity largely are not addressed by the current literature. This chapter explores the strategic concerns of IT training in hierarchical organizations, which are typically prevalent in developing countries. Various ideas in the literature on change management, training needs analysis, and IT adoption are synthesized in order to evolve a strategic IT training framework for hierarchical organizations. The proposed framework recognizes the differences in IT training requirements for different levels of employees and suggests a differentiated training content for different segments of employees.

Chapter XX

Timothy Shea, University of Massachusetts Dartmouth, USA
Aherhn Brown, HDR Inc., USA
D. Steven White, University of Massachusetts Dartmouth, USA
Catherine Curran-Kelly, University of Massachusetts Dartmouth, USA
Michael Griffin, University of Massachusetts Dartmouth, USA

Adopting a focus on CRM has been an industry standard for nearly two decades. While evidence suggests that a majority of the attempts to implement CRM systems fail, no single reason for the failures has been identified. Assuming that CRM implementation is an extension of a customer-oriented business strategy and assuming successful integration with Enterprise Information Systems such as Enterprise Resource Planning (ERP) systems, the authors contend that the lack of valid and reliable CRM metrics leads to the perception of failed CRM implementation. Only through the development, application, and use of CRM metrics can organizations hope to achieve their CRM goals.

Chapter XXI

Thorsten Blecker, Hamburg University of Technology, Germany
Wolfgang Kersten, Hamburg University of Technology, Germany
Hagen Späth, Hamburg University of Technology, Germany
Birgit Koeppen, Hamburg University of Technology, Germany

This chapter introduces a game-theoretic approach to supply chain risk management. The focus of this study lies on the risk of a single supply chain member defecting from common supply chain agreements, thereby jeopardizing the overall supply chain performance. The chapter goes on to introduce a manual supply chain game, by which dynamic supply chain mechanisms can be simulated and further analyzed using a game-theoretic model. With the help of the game-theoretic model, externalities are identified that negatively impact supply chain efficiency. The conclusion drawn from this chapter is that incentives are necessary to overcome these externalities in order to align supply chain objectives.

Section VI
Emerging Trends

Chapter XXII

Ketan Vanjara, Microsoft, India

This chapter initiates the concept of a customer-centric model in supply chain systems. It discusses various constraints of present-day supply chain systems resulting from their roots being in logistics management and suggests an alternative next-level paradigm of a customer-centric matrix model. This chapter further demonstrates how this model would add value to the customer by taking the example of a healthcare information management system. The chapter also delves into the limitations of and anticipated issues and challenges in implementing the suggested model. Finally, the chapter hints at some broad directions for future research and action in the field.

Chapter XXIII

    Ronald E. McGaughey, University of Central Arkansas, USA
    Angappa Gunasekaran, University of Massachusetts Dartmouth, USA

Business needs have driven the design, development, and use of Enterprise Resource Planning (ERP) systems. Intra-enterprise integration was a driving force in the design, development, and use of early ERP systems, but increased globalization, intense competition, and technological change have shifted to focus to inter-enterprise integration. Current and evolving ERP systems thus reflect the expanded scope of integration, with greater emphasis on things like supply chain management and customer relationship management. This manuscript explores the evolution of ERP, the current status of ERP, and the future of ERP, with the objective of promoting relevant future research in this important area.

Chapter XXIV

    Rahul Singh, University of North Carolina at Greensboro, USA

Organizations rely on knowledge-driven systems for delivering problem-specific knowledge over Internet-based distributed platforms to decision-makers. Recent advances in systems support for problem solving have seen increased use of artificial intelligence (AI) techniques for knowledge representation in multiple forms. This chapter presents an Intelligent Knowledge-based Multi-agent Decision Support Architecture (IKMDSA) to illustrate how to represent and exchange domain-specific knowledge in XML-format through intelligent agents to create, exchange and use knowledge in decision support.

Chapter XXV

    Huizhang Shen, Shanghai Jiaotong University, China
    Jidi Zhao, University of New Brunswick, Canada
    Wayne W. Huang, Ohio University, USA

A review of group decision support systems (GDSS) indicates that traditional GDSS are not specifically designed to support mission-critical group decision-making tasks that require group decision-making to be made effectively within a short time. In addition, prior studies in the research have not considered group decision preference adjustment as a continuous process and neglected its impact on group decision-making. This chapter intends to address this neglected group decision-making research issue in the literature by proposing a new approach based on the Markov chain model. Furthermore, a new group decision weight allocation approach is also suggested.

Prologue

INTRODUCTION

This book is part of a series of books containing selected readings on the many and varied aspects of information technology. The focus of this book is on strategic information systems. The objective in preparing the book is to provide a source of selected readings which will benefit both researchers and students. The content offers a comprehensive view of concepts and theories and their application within the context of strategic information systems. Researchers will find this book a valuable resource of ideas for their own programs of investigation. Students will gain an understanding of current leading edge research being conducted in the area of strategic information systems.

The format of this prologue is as follows. To begin, the term "strategic information systems" is defined. Then a brief discussion is presented regarding the status of information systems as a research discipline. Further, within the discipline various topic areas exist. The focus of this book is on one of these topic areas, specifically strategic information systems. This prologue concludes with an overview of this area with an emphasis on aspects related to the role of the chief information officer (CIO). The establishment of this role represents an organization's formal recognition of the strategic importance of data and the necessary systems to produce information to support high level organizational strategic initiatives.

STRATEGIC INFORMATION SYSTEMS DEFINED

Strategic information systems, "… apply information technology to a firm's products, services, or business processes to help it gain a strategic advantage over its competitors" (O'Brien & Marakas, 2008:16). Thus a strategic information system may be any kind of information system that addresses the firm's strategic objectives, usually in the form of gaining a competitive advantage. The intent of a strategic information system is to help the organization enter into a new market, positively affect market share, or serve customers better. Strategic information systems have a tremendous impact upon the firms' financial performance.

THE INFORMATION SYSTEMS RESEARCH DISCIPLINE

Much research is currently taking place to identify just what is the IS research discipline. There is much discussion about the IS field and its status as a discipline (Benbasat & Zmud, 2003; Gorver et al., 2006a; Gorver et al., 2006b; Hevner et al., 2004; Hoving, 2007; Kvasny & Richardson, 2006; Teo, 2005; Truex et al., 2006; Wade et al., 2006). This discussion suggests the field is relatively new and is currently struggling to determine a specific identity. Many theories exist within the field. Some theories have been adopted from other fields of study, while a few others have been developed specifically related to information systems.

Mora et al. (2007) propose a framework to integrate the existing and disparate theories in the IS field. They comment on the complexity of the IS field as follows:

This discipline, from its conception as a potential scientific field, has been driven by a dual research perspective: technical (design engineering oriented) or social (behavioral focused). This duality of man-made non-living (hardware, software, data, and procedures) and living systems (human-beings, teams, organizations, and societies), the multiple interrelationships among these elements, and the socio-cultural-economic-politic and physical-natural environment, make IS a complex field of inquiry. (Mora et al., 2007:1)

Parameswaran and Whinston (2007) suggest IS researchers face challenges from diverse disciplines and that this offers the opportunity to lead and participate in cross-disciplinary research.

TOPIC AREAS WITHIN INFORMATION SYSTEMS

In general, the area of research in information systems may be categorized as relating to tools, techniques, and people. Tools and techniques relate to the more technical aspects as outlined by Mora et al. (2007) above. The people category relates to the social aspects of information systems (Mora et al., 2007).

There are some emerging topic areas within the information systems discipline. Grossman (2007) comments upon the emergence of knowledge management into the IS field. Halawi et al. (2008) present a framework for assessing the success of knowledge management systems within an organization. McGaughey and Gunasekaran (2007) explore the current status of research into enterprise resource planning (ERP) systems and suggest a more business oriented focus. Welch and Kordysh (2007) reveal best practices in the implementation of ERP systems. Sujitparapitaya et al. (2003) evaluated data warehouse topologies and their relationship with modes of IT governance. Lee et al. (2004) presented a model for evaluating IT outsourcing. Nguyen et al. (2007) discuss strategies that support successful customer relationship management (CRM) implementations. Finnegan and Willcocks (2006) documented issues regarding tacit knowledge in the implementation of CRM. Arnott and Pervan (2005) suggest that currently decision support systems are an under-researched area when compared with the use of such systems in industry. King (2007) presents skills necessary for organizations to have in order to participate in global offshore outsourcing. Further, Fink and Neuman (2007) investigated how the technical, behavioral, and business capabilities of IT personnel contribute to corporate strategic agility.

Another topic area and the subject of this book is the study of strategic information systems. The planning process for the implementation of strategic information systems attempts to link the development of the portfolio of new information systems to the strategic initiative of the organization (Newkirk & Lederer, 2007). Thus, planning for strategic information systems is based upon the recognition that information systems are a strategic resource for the organization (Brown, 2004).

Further evidence of the consideration for the strategic nature of information systems is the establishment of the CIO role within the organization (Hunter, 2008). The CIO role is established so that one individual may be assigned the responsibility for the firm's information resources. Further, the CIO role is created as part of the senior management team. While the CIO then is responsible for the efficient operation of the firm's information technology the CIO is also expected to thoroughly understand the business. The CIO is thus responsible for ensuring information technology is adopted by the firm which contributes to establishing and maintaining competitive advantage as a strategic initiative (Andrews & Carlson, 1997; Arnold, 2001; Benjamin et al., 1985; Bock et al., 1986; Korn/Ferry International, 1998; Maciag, 2002; Nolan Norton Institute, 2001; Olson, 2000; Weiss & Anderson, 2004). Lindstrom et al. (2006) identified Swedish CIO concerns for the future. Of the three most important issues identified by the CIOs one related to cost control while the other two, relationship between IT and the business and computer support for the business, were of a strategic nature.

STRATEGIC INFORMATION SYSTEMS AND THE CIO ROLE

A necessary precursor to the establishment of the CIO role and the strategic application of information systems is the consideration by senior management that information is a valuable resource of the organization and should be managed appropriately. Thus, senior management must recognize that information must be managed strategically just as corporate finances and human resources are managed (Meagher, 2003). Evidence of this recognition would be the establishment of a rich information technology infrastructure, a senior management steering committee, and initiatives to ensure competent business managers as well as alignment between the information technology and business functions.

Senior management must be committed to ensuring the existence of the necessary level of information technology infrastructure (Broadbent et al., 1999). This infrastructure must go beyond the usual components of hardware, software, telecommunications and databases. Indeed, the infrastructure must include those systems which facilitate functional boundary crossing and extension of services to employees, customers, and suppliers. An example is an enterprise resource planning system.

A steering committee consisting of senior management representing the major business units within the organization must be established with the responsibility to make strategic decisions that ensure the resources allocated to information technology support and promote the goals of the organization. Karami et al. (2000) determined that the existence of such a steering committee facilitated the link between the goals of the organization and the direction set for information technology. Also, the existence of a senior management steering committee provides a stage for the performance of the role of the CIO.

Along with this formal recognition by senior management regarding the importance of information through the establishment of a steering committee, there is also the need to ensure functional managers understand the capabilities of information technology. They must be aware how technology can be employed to support their operations. This increased knowledge has been determined (Reich & Benbasat, 2000) to facilitate alignment between information technology and the goals of the organization.

In general, information technology leadership in the form of the CIO role and organization leadership in the form of the senior management team must be aligned. So, activities of the information technology unit must be coordinated with the goals and objectives of the organization (Luftman & Brier, 1999). The most important factor in this alignment is communication (Reich & Benbasat, 2000). Both information technology leadership and senior management must develop shared domain knowledge.

A concern recently investigated (Kolbasuk, 2005; Kaarst-Brown, 2005) suggests that while the CIO role has been established as part of the senior management committee, appreciation for the role has not been forthcoming. Thus, the CIO role is currently held in lower regard than other more traditional business unit management roles. This situation is evolving and through time it may be resolved. However, it is now incumbent upon the CIO to work with senior management to ensure the appropriate understanding of both the capabilities of information technology and the advantages to the organization of the establishment of the CIO role within the senior management team. Information and the technology that provides it must be recognized as a strategic resource.

In the future, the CIO role will emphasize more about "information" and less about "technology". However, the CIO must maintain a thorough understanding of information technology as well as knowledge about the organization and its functions. In both cases (Blair, 2005) it will be incumbent upon the CIO to obtain knowledge of future initiatives and how to apply leading edge information technology to support the strategic direction of the organization.

CONCLUSION

Strategic information systems are a very important component of the current operation and future direction of an organization. It is necessary for senior management to formally recognize this importance and put in place people, systems, and organizational components to facilitate strategic initiatives. This book provides erudite readings related to this important subject area.

Further, Hassan and Becker (2007) determined, using citation analysis that a gap exists between IS research concepts and the content of introductory IS textbooks. This situation must be addressed. Introductory IS courses are taught to many different majors. Thus, most future managers will probably only be exposed to one IS course. It will be important for these future managers to exploit the capabilities of IS in order to have as effective as possible operation of their functional business unit. But, as shown by Hassan and Becker (2007) the textbooks and thus the content of course presentations do not reflect leading edge research issues. This book, by providing selected readings and focusing on strategic information systems responds to addressing this gap.

REFERENCES

Andrews, P., & Carlson, T. (1997). The CIO is the CEO of the future. *CIO Conference*, www.cio.com/conferences/eds/sld018.htm

Arnold, M. A. (2001). Secrets to CIO success. *Credit Union Management, 24*(6), 26.

Arnott, D., & Pervan, G. (2005). A critical analysis of decision support systems research. *Journal of Information Technology, 20*, 67-87.

Benbasat, I., & Zmud, R. W. (2003). The identity crisis within the IS discipline: Defining and communicating the discipline's core properties. *MIS Quarterly, 27*(2), 183-194.

Benjamin, R. I., Dickinson, C., & Rockart, J. F. (1985). Changing role of the corporate information systems officer. *MIS Quarterly, 9*(3), 177.

Blair, R. (2005). The future of CIOs. *Health Management Technology, 26*(2), 58-59.

Bock, G., Carpenter, K., & Davis, J. E. (1986). Management's newest star – Meet the chief information officer. *Business Week*, October 13, No. 2968, 160-166.

Broadbent, M., Weill, P., & St. Clair, D. (1999). The implications of information technology infrastructure for business process redesign. *MIS Quarterly, 23*(2), 159-182.

Brown, I. T. J. (2004). Testing and extending theory in strategic information systems planning through literature analysis. *Information Resources Management Journal, 17*(4), 20-48.

Fink, L., & Neumann, S. (2007). Gaining agility through IT personnel capabilities: The mediating role of IT infrastructure capabilities. *Journal of the Association for Information Systems, 8*(8), 440-462.

Finnegan, D., & Willcocks, L. (2006). Knowledge sharing issues in the introduction of a new technology. *Journal of Enterprise Information Management, 19*(6), 568-590.

Grossman, M. (2007). The emerging academic discipline of knowledge management. *Journal of Information Systems Education, 18*(1), 31-38.

Gorver, V., Ayyagari, R., Gokhale, R., & Lim, J. (2006a). About reference disciplines and reference differences: A critique of Wade et al. *Journal of the Association for Information Systems, 7*(5), 336-349.

Gorver, V., Ayyagari, R., Gokhale, R., Lim, J., & Coffey, J. (2006b). A citation analysis of the evolution and state of information systems within a constellation of reference disciplines. *Journal of the Association for Information Systems, 7*(5), 270-325.

Halawi, L. A., McCarthy, R. V., & Aronson, J. E. (2008). An empirical investigation of knowledge management systems' success. *The Journal of Computer Information Systems, 48*(2), 121-135.

Hassan, N. R., & Becker, J. D. (2007). Uncovering conceptual gaps in introductory IS textbooks. *Journal of Information Systems Education, 18*(2), 169-182.

Hevner, A. R., March, S. T., Park, J., & Ram, S. (2004). Design science in information systems research. *MIS Quarterly, 28*(1), 75-105.

Hoving, R. (2007). Information technology leadership challenges – Past, present, and future. *Information Systems Management, 24*(2), 147-153.

Hunter, M. G. (2008). *Contemporary chief information officers: Management experiences.* Hershey, PA: IGI Publishing.

Kaarst-Brown, M. (2005). Understanding an organization's view of the CIO: The role of assumptions about IT. *MIS Quarterly Executive, 4*(2), 287-301.

Karimi, J., Battacherjee, A., Gupta, Y. P., & Somers, T. M. (2000). The effects of MIS steering committees on information technology management sophistication. *Journal of Management Information Systems, 17*(2), 207-230.

King, W. R. (2007). The IS organization of the future: Impacts of global sourcing. *Information Systems Management, 24*(2), 121-127.

Kolbasuk, M. (2005). CIOs get respect. *Insurance and Technology, 30*(9), 18.

Korn/Ferry International. (1998). *The changing role of the chief information officer.* London.

Kvasny, L., & Richardson, H. (2006). Critical research in information systems: Looking forward, looking back. *Information, Technology & People, 19*(3), 196-202.

Lee, J. N., Mirandam, S. M., & Kim, Y. M. (2004). IT outsourcing strategies: Universalistic, contingency, and configurational explanations of success. *Information Systems Research, 15*(2), 110-131.

Lindstrom, A., Johnson, P., Johansson, E., Ekstedt, M., & Simonsson, M. (2006). A survey on CIO concerns – Do enterprise architecture frameworks support them? *Information Systems Frontiers, 8*, 81-90.

Luftman, J., & Brier, T. (1999). Achieving and sustaining business-IT alignment. *California Management Review, 42*(1), 109-122.

Maciag, G. A. (2002). The CIO challenge: Bridging the gap between IT and CEO. *National Underwriter, 106*(33), 33-34.

McGaughey, R. E., & Gunasekaran, A. (2007). Enterprise resource planning (ERP): Past, present, and future. *International Journal of Enterprise Information Systems, 3*(3), 23-35.

Meagher, R. (2003). Putting 'strategic' into information management. *The Information Management Journal*, January/February, 51-57.

Mora, M., Gelman, O., Forgionne, G., Petkov, D., & Cano, J. (2007). Integrating the fragmented pieces of IS research paradigms and frameworks: A systems approach. *Information Resource Management Journal, 20*(2), 1-22.

Newkirk, H. E., & Lederer, A. L. (2007). The effectiveness of strategic information systems planning for technical resources, personnel resources, and data security in environments of heterogeneity and hostility. *The Journal of Computer Information Systems, 47*(3), 34-44.

Nguyen, T. U., Sherif, J. S., & Newby, M. (2007). Strategies for successful CRM implementation. *Information Management and Computer Security, 15*(2), 102-115.

Nolan Norton Institute. (2001). Say goodbye to the CIO, Welcome to the business prophet. *Information Management and Computer Security, 9*(2/3), 123-125.

O'Brien, J. A., & Marakas, G.M. (2008). *Management information systems (8th edition)*. Boston: Mc-Graw-Hill Irwin.

Olson, L. A. (2000). The strategic CIO – Lessons learned, insights gained. *Information Week, 785*, May 8, p. 264.

Parameswaran, M., & Whinston, A. B. (2007). Research issues in social computing. *Journal of the Association for Information Systems, 8*(6), 336-350.

Reich, B. H., & Benbasat, I. (2000). Factors that influence the social dimension of alignment between business and information technology objectives. *MIS Quarterly, 24*(1), 81-113.

Sujitparapitaya, S., Janz, B. D., & Gillerson, M. (2003). The contribution of IT governance solutions to the implementation of data warehouse practice. *Journal of Database Management, 14*(2), 52-69.

Teo, S. H. T. (2005). Has information systems discipline lost its way? *Journal of Information Technology Case and Application Research, 7*(2), 1-2.

Truex, D., Holmstrom, J., & Keil, M. (2006). Theorizing in information systems research: A reflexive analysis of the adaptation of theory in information systems research. *Journal of the Association for Information Systems, 7*(12), 797-821.

Wade, M., Biehl, M., & Kim, H. (2006). Information systems is not a reference discipline (and what we can do about it). *Journal of the Association for Information Systems, 7*(5), 247-269.

Weiss, J. W., & Anderson, D. (2004). CIOs and IT professionals as change agents, risk and stakeholder managers: A field study. *Engineering and Management Journal, 16*(2), 13-18.

Welch, J., & Kordysh, D. (2007). Seven keys to ERP success. *Strategic Finance, 89*(3), 40-47.

About the Editor

M. Gordon Hunter is currently an associate professor of information systems in the Faculty of Management at The University of Lethbridge, Alberta, Canada. Gordon has previously held academic positions at universities in Canada, Singapore, and Hong Kong. He has held visiting positions at universities in Australia, Monaco, Germany, New Zealand, and the U.S. During July and August of 2005 Gordon was a visiting Erskine Fellow at the University of Canterbury, Christchurch, New Zealand. He has a Bachelor of Commerce from the University of Saskatchewan in Saskatoon, Saskatchewan, Canada and a doctorate from Strathclyde Business School, University of Strathclyde in Glasgow, Scotland. Gordon has also obtained a certified management accountant (CMA) designation from the Society of Management Accountants of Canada. He is a member of the British Computer Society and the Canadian Information Processing Society (CIPS), where he has obtained an information systems professional (ISP) designation. Gordon chairs the executive board of The Information Institute, an information policy research organization. He has extensive experience as a systems analyst and manager in industry and government organizations in Canada. Gordon is an associate editor of the *Journal of Global Information Management*. He is the Canadian world representative for the Information Resource Management Association. He serves on the editorial board of *Information and Management*, *International Journal of e-Collaboration*, *Journal of Global Information Technology Management*, and *Journal of Information Technology Cases and Applications*. Gordon is also a member of the advisory board for *The Journal of Information, Information Technology, and* Organizations. Gordon has published articles in *MIS Quarterly, Information Systems Research, The Journal of Strategic Information Systems, The Journal of Global Information Management, Information Systems Journal,* and *Information, Technology and People*. He has conducted seminar presentations in Canada, USA, Europe, Hong Kong, Singapore, Taiwan, New Zealand, and Australia. Gordon's current research interests relate to the productivity of systems analysts with emphasis upon the personnel component including cross-cultural aspects, the use of information systems by small business, the role of CIO, and the effective development and implementation of cross functional information systems.

Section I
Fundamental Concepts and Theories

Chapter I
The Nature of
Strategic Intelligence:
Current Practice and Solutions

Mark Xu
University of Portsmouth, UK

Roland Kaye
University of East Anglia, UK

ABSTRACT

This chapter discusses the nature of strategic intelligence and the challenges of systematically scanning and processing strategic information. It reveals that strategic intelligence practice concentrates on competitive intelligence gathering, non-competitive related intelligence have not yet been systematically scanned and processed. Much of the intelligence is collected through informal and manual based systems. Turning data into analyzed, meaningful intelligence for action is limited to a few industry leaders. The chapter proposed a corporate intelligence solution, which comprises of three key intelligence functions, namely organizational-wide intelligence scanning, knowledge enriched intelligent refining, and specialist support. A corporate radar system (CRS) for external environment scanning, which is a part of the organizational-wide intelligence scanning process is explored in light of latest technology development. Implementation issues are discussed. The chapter develops insight of strategic intelligence, and the solution could significantly enhance a manager's and a company's sensibility and capability in dealing with external opportunities and threats.

INTRODUCTION

As the business environment becomes more turbulent and competition becomes fiercer, developing foresight about future opportunities and threats, and reacting quickly to the opportunities and threats, becomes a core competency of a wining organization. Companies that can generate competitive intelligence are leaders in their industry (Desouza, 2001). However the increasing demand for strategic information has not been satisfied by the explosive growth in data available. This is reflected in two facets: firstly, computer-based information systems are inadequately implemented at the corporate level for strategic information delivery; secondly, senior mangers who go online always feel overwhelmed with the glut of data instead of meaningful, actionable information. Research which applies computing technology to support strategic management activities concentrates on the development and the implementation of computer-based systems for decision support. Systems such as decision support system (DSS), executive information systems (EIS), or executive support systems (ESS) are examples. Strategic management process however is more than an activity of making decisions (Simon, 1965), the process begins with strategic information acquisition, formulating strategic problems, reasoning strategic alternatives, and finally making a decision. There is a distinction between supporting managers with strategic information and supporting making decisions. Information systems tend to emphasize decision-making support more than strategic information support. Senior managers' information acquisition processes have not been adequately addressed in the context of information systems development, except the field of competitive intelligence (Cobb, 2003; Pelsmacker et al., 2005; Patton & McKenna, 2005; Sauter, 2005) and Web-based information searching systems (Chen, Chau, & Zeng, 2002). Supporting strategic intelligence activity with information technology is an area remaining largely unexplored. This chapter aims to address the nature of strategic intelligence and the challenges, and to explore the possible solutions towards improving organizational strategic intelligence process.

DEFINITIONS OF STRATEGIC INTELLIGENCE

The term of strategic intelligence is often used interchangeably with other terms: data, information, intelligence, and knowledge. There seems to be no generally agreed definitions towards these terms, but they are different in the context of this chapter as follows:

Data is the raw material of organizational life; it consists of disconnected numbers, words, symbols relating to the events, and processes of a business. Data on its own can serve little useful purpose.

Information comes from data that has been processed to make it useful in management decision-making. Intelligence in most cases is referred to competitors' information (CI), or competitive intelligence or the totality of external information (Baatz, 1994). Competitor intelligence has often been regarded as a process of collecting and processing competitors' information following a CI cycle, which includes identifying the strategic needs of a business, systematically collecting relevant information on competitors, and processing the data into actionable knowledge about competitors' strategic capabilities, position, performance, and intentions. However, the boundary of competitor's intelligence has always been extended to include not only competitor's information, but also market and environment information for strategic decision. For example, Tyson (1990) defines competitor intelligence as an analytical process that transforms raw data into relevant, accurate, and usable strategic knowledge, more specifically, it includes:

- Information about a competitor's current position, historical performance, capabilities, and intentions.
- Information about the driving forces within the marketplace.
- Information about specific products and technology.
- Information external to the marketplace, such as economic, regulatory, political, and demographic influences that have an impact on the market.

Baatz (1994) refer the term "corporate intelligence" to the collection and analysis of information on markets, technologies, customers and competitors, as well as socio-economic and external political trends. Another term, business intelligence (BI) has been prevalent in the IT industry. Business intelligence is a process that its input is raw data; the data then is evaluated for usefulness to a relevant and reasonably reliable body of information; the analyzed, digested, and interpreted information thus becomes intelligence. The term "strategic intelligence" used in this chapter means strategically significant information to senior managers that is scanned, analyzed, digested, and is meaningful that could affects senior managers' beliefs, commitments, and actions. The entire process of turning original data from both external and internal environment into intelligence is referred to intelligence activity.

Data, information and intelligence are closely linked to knowledge. Knowledge refers to totality of information related to policy, problem or issue whether it is quantitative or qualitative, data or opinions, judgements, news or concepts. According to Nonaka and Takeuchi (1995), knowledge is "justified true belief"; it is a dynamic human process of justifying personal belief towards the "true." Information provides a new point of view for interpreting events or objects, which makes visible previously invisible meanings or shed light on unexpected connections. Thus, information is a necessary medium or material for eliciting and constructing knowledge. Information affects knowledge by adding something to it or restructuring it. Nonaka and Takeuchi (1995) further point out that information is a flow of messages, while knowledge is created by that very flow of information, anchored in the beliefs and commitment of its holder.

THE NATURE OF STRATEGIC INTELLIGENCE AND CHALLENGES

Strategically significant information is not a piece of static information that is readily available from certain sources. It is often derived from a sense making process that requires managerial knowledge and judgement. Strategically significant information can be viewed from different perspectives.

Internal vs. External Orientation

Strategic information has an internal or external orientation. Aguilar (1967) suggests two types of strategic information: *External strategic information* is information about events or relationships in a company's external environment that may change the company's current direction and strategy. *Internal strategic information* is information about a company's capacity and performance that significantly affect a company's strategic implementation. Because strategic decision is primarily concerned with external problems of a firm, the external orientation of strategic information has been emphasized by many researchers. Mintzberg (1973) reports that managers demonstrate a thirst for external information. This is supported by Macdonald (1995), who argues that change in an organization is seen as a process in which the acquisition of external information is critical. Yet, empirical research supporting this notion is limited. In contrast, Daft, Sormunen, and Parks (1988), reveals that senior managers rely as much on internal discussions and internal reports as they did on external media or personal contacts, senior mangers use internal and external source about equally. This view is reinforced by D'Aveni and MacMillan (1990) who found that managers of successful companies pay equal attention to both internal and external environments of their companies, but only during times of crisis, these managers focus more heavily on the external environment, which suggests that there may be a linkage between external information needs and the extent of environmental stability.

We anchor the view on internal-external orientation of strategic information (Xu & Kaye, 1995) by drawing an analogy between a manager navigating his company and driving a car, that is, managers cope with external changes by adjustments to the internal controls. Internal information is vital for controlling the operation, but cannot determine the direction of navigation. External information is of strategic importance, since strategic decisions are primarily long term with a balance towards external focus, whereas operational decisions are primarily short term and have an internal focus. External information is more dynamic and uncertain than internal information, and appears more difficult and costly to obtain than internal information. This poses a challenge of obtaining strategic intelligence from external environment.

Historical vs. Current, Future Orientation

Strategic information is also associated with its historical and future dimension. Information needed for performing routine tasks of daily operation and for short-range decisions will be different from information needed for long-range analysis and planning. Long term planning requires information about the past as well as projections of future conditions. Research (McNichol, 1993) suggests that senior managers demand more future and current information than historical information. This confirms Mintzberg's (1973) argument that managers indicate strong preferences for current information, much of which is necessarily unsubstantiated, and for information on events rather than on trends. Historical, aggregated information from the traditional formal information system provides little help in the performance of manager's monitoring role. Mintzberg's (1973)

summarize the information that executives received into five categories:

- **Internal operations:** Information on the process of operations in an organization, and on events that take place related to these operations, comes from regular reports, ad-hoc input from subordinates, observations from touring the organization.
- **External events:** Information concerning clients, personal contacts, competitors, associates, and suppliers, as well as information on market changes, political moves, and developments in technology.
- **Analysis:** Executives receive analytical reports of various issues, solicited and unsolicited, come from various sources.
- **Ideas and trends:** Chief executives develop a better understanding of the trends in the environment, and to learn about new ideas by using a number of means such as attending conferences, glancing at trade organization's reports, contacting with subordinates, paying attention to unsolicited letters from clients.
- **Presses:** In addition to the usual types of information, chief executives receive information in the form of presses of various kinds, that is, from subordinates, clients, directors or the public, with which the chief executives must allocate their time and efforts to deal with.

The issue concerned here is the right balance between receiving historical, current and future oriented information by executives.

Raw Data vs. Filtered, Refined Information

Contradictory views exist towards if executives prefer analyzed information over factual raw data.

Bernhardt (1994) argues that managers prefer analyzed information to detailed raw data, as analyzed information adds meaning and makes sense of the data. He believes that managers do not need lorry loads of facts or information; they need an analytical intelligence product, delivered on time, and in a format that can be easily and quickly assimilated. The analytical intelligence product shall be factual, meaningful, and actionable information. It has been revealed (Taylor, 1996) that current information systems produce sheer volume of data but little meaningful information to senior managers. Increasingly providing senior managers direct access to operational data and leaving them to their own devices is a disservice to the organization, as it creates the problem of "data deluge" and the frustrations that arise from time wasted in trying to assemble meaningful information from raw data. Data deluge and information meaningless runs the risk of compromising the advances of colourful, graphic design of an EIS. Even with graphic-interface, high-speed communications, and data-warehousing technology, it is extremely difficult for a decision maker to review thousands of products, hundreds of categories. When adding the task of looking outside, at the world of the competitors, suppliers, customers, and the environment, identifying critical changes becomes a daunting task. Finding the problem becomes the real problem, that is, data can be too much for an executive to spot trends, patterns, and exceptions in detailed data. Thus data may need to be refined in order to be useful. Wright, Pickton, and Callow (2002) reveals that the most common problems in disseminating intelligence is making the information and structure relevant to the audience while being brief yet useful. Wyllie (1993) defines information refining as a social-technological process that enables intelligent human beings to extract and organize systematically the key items of knowledge kept in any given choice of information sources. The purpose of the process is to enable people from executives downwards to be better

and more widely informed, while at the same time, reducing the amount of time they have to spend to keep up with headlines on media. The result of the refining process should be to bring about better, more informed decisions.

However, managers' demand for refined information has been questioned. Edwards and Peppard (1993) argue that refined information that reaches the top management team is likely to be distorted. The distortion may not be conscious, but due to the assumptions and knowledge used in handling the information, bring to bear on it. This suspicion is in line with the notion (Daft et al., 1988) that as strategic uncertainty increase, senior managers will want to form their own impression through direct contact with key environmental sources to ensure that data is undiluted and does not suffer from the loss of meaning associated with passing information through intermediaries. Mintzberg (1980) observed that managers clearly prefer to have information in the form of concrete stimuli or triggers, not general aggregations, and wish to hear specific events, ideas and the problems.

The issue concerned is whether strategic intelligence is more likely to be derived from refined data other than from data in its raw fashion. However, the debate is continuing but inconclusive.

Formal vs. Informal Systems

Strategic intelligence may be gathered from formal or informal systems. A formal system for information acquisition is defined as one with a set of procedure to follow, and is systematically used in regular basis, for example, the competitive intelligence cycle. An informal system is in contrast to the formal system that managers do not trace a map route from beginning to the end, and is intuitively used in ad hoc basis. Research suggests that managers often ignore formal systems, and in favour of informal systems for strategic significant information. Mintzberg (1980) argues that as a result of the distinct characteristics in information acquisition, managers often ignore the formal information system, as it takes time to process information. Managers therefore develop their own contacts and establish special communication channels to obtain information. Managers spend most of their time gathering information through less formal systems.

Empirical studies support the speculation that CEOs obtain most information through informal, irregular, human systems. In a study of executives of British Airways, Cottrell and Rapley (1991) found that the majority of executives spend their time in face-to-face or verbal contact (telephone or intercom) with peers and subordinates both inside and outside the organization. Most of the information is received in an unstructured way. Executives spend little of their time in reading or looking at highly structured information in reports or on computer screen.

The tendency towards using informal system by executives for intelligence poses a challenge to developing computer-based intelligence system that has often been regarded as a formal system.

Solicited vs. Unsolicited Intelligence

The terms "solicited searching" and "unsolicited searching" are rooted in social cognition theory regarding whether information scanning is directed by managers' intention or not (Kiesler & Sproull, 1982). In directed search, managers have intentions or objectives, exert efforts to scan information; in undirected search, managers follow perceptual process, which is relatively unaffected by intention and efforts. Aguilar (1967) used the term to appraise the effectiveness of managers' information scanning process, and managers' behavior in information acquisition: that is, whether the scanning is active or passive. If managers obtain most of their information on a solicited basis, their performance could be questioned on the grounds that they are not sensitive enough to valuable information other than what they actively seeking. In other words, solicited information may

limited a manager's vision as the manager only knows what the manager wants to know, but not what is needed to know.

Managers appear obtaining more unsolicited information than solicited information. Information from outside sources tends to be largely unsolicited, whereas information from inside sources is largely solicited. This tends to suggest that unexpected information is more likely to be regarded as strategic intelligence than solicited information. If this speculation is substantiated, there shall be a system to proactively feed managers with unexpected intelligence.

Information Specialist Support vs. Managers' Own Scanning

Senior managers may need specialist to support them in information acquisition and processing, because managers' information acquisition pattern tends to be informal and in ad-hoc basis. Schmitz, Armstrong, and Little (1992) revealed that senior managers often lack time which will not allow them the luxury to sit at a terminal and deal with their information needs. They argue that it is still remains primarily the work of staff members to access and decipher the necessary information for senior managers. Langley (1996) cited a managing director, saying "technology on its own could not add value without the input of people who understood the business problems and the meaning of the data." As more information is collected from external environment, information processing becomes more complex, this necessitates the selection of personnel with analytical skills to work with such complex information (Ramaswami, Nilakanta, & Flynn, 1992). Frolick (1994) has taken this view forward and argues that executives need information specialists to support them using EIS. He describes that EIS is no longer for executive use only, rather, many other organizational non-executive personnel use it. For example, the middle level managers who spend a great deal of their time preparing report for executive consumption. The support-staff members include such individuals as the executive's secretaries. Information system does not require hands-on use by executives themselves. The executives would delegate the use of EIS to these individuals and have them bring back printed reports or conveying the message to them by daily summaries, presentations, exception reports, and so forth. EIS increasingly designed to be used by most, if not all, knowledge workers. This raises a critical question as to whether strategic intelligence should be processed by intelligence specialists or solely by executives' themselves?

EMPIRICAL STUDIES ON COMPETITIVE INTELLIGENCE IN PRACTICE

Many empirical studies related to strategic intelligence concentrate on competitive intelligence. Wright, et al (2002) conducted a study to examine how UK companies conduct competitive intelligence through questionnaire and interviews. The study examined the attitude of gathering competitive intelligence, strategies for intelligence gathering, use of intelligence and organizational locations of the intelligence function. Two types of intelligence gathering are identified: (a) easy gathering—firms use general publications and or specific industry periodicals and consider these constitute exhaustive information, and (b) hunter gathering—in additional to easy gathering, companies conduct own primary research on competitors. CI function within an organization are either in ad-hoc location—no dedicated CI unit within the organizational structure, and intelligence activities are undertook on ad hoc basis, typically, by the marketing or sales department, or in designated locations—specific CI function established within the organization with staff working full-time on monitoring competitors and competitive environments. Pelsmacker, et al. (2005) report through a comparative study of

CI practice between South Africa and Belgium that companies in both countries are not well equipped with and not active to conduct effective CI, especially in the areas of planning, process and structure, data collection, data analysis, and skills development. CI-activities are not organized in a separate department, and if they are, are mostly done in the marketing and sales department. Sugasawa (2004) adds further evidence by showing that there is a strong interest in CI in Japan, but Japanese companies do not apply any specific analytical methodology to analyze intelligence. Dissemination of intelligence was primarily in written form rather than by electronic means. Computer-based systems are mainly used for intelligence storing and extracting.

In addition to ethic, lawful intelligence gathering by organizations, Crane (2004) suggests that many tactics are currently being used to gather industry espionage. The tactics take forms from clearly illegal, such as installing tapping device, stealing information, to rather more grey areas, this includes searching through a competitor's rubbish, hiring private detectives to track competitor's staff, infiltrating competitor organization with industrial spies, covert surveillance through spy camera, contacting competitors in a fake guise such as a potential customer or supplier, interviewing competitors' employees for a bogus job vacancy, and pressing the customers or suppliers of competitors to reveal sensitive information about their operations. Other means include conventional market research and competitor benchmarking through market scanning, industry profiling, debriefing of managers recruited from competitors.

An earlier study on competitive intelligence systems in the UK was conducted and reported by Brittin's (1991), which shed light on how companies gather and use competitive intelligence. As the findings tend to be comprehensive in terms of the CI cycle, the results are revisited and presented in Table 1.

Table 1. Competitor intelligence systems (Source: Brittin, 1991)

	Competitors monitored / Kind of Information	Information sources used	CI Systems	Data analysis	Output / dissemination
Case 1 **A large financial institution**	25 ~ 30 competitors ❶ Financial performance, ❷ specific competitive activities.	Companies house, Stock Exchange, Broker's report, Press Cutting Services, Electronic sources, Consultant, Meetings, Dinner party circuit.	Personnel in the Research Department (manual-based)	Manual-based data analysis and evaluation by the Data Analysts. Hypertext system in Apple Mac is used to store data.	Information disseminating project is to be developed in the form of briefing papers.
Case 2 **A distribution company**	10 competitors 90% ~ 50% external information	Trade and Business Press, Online services (e.g., Dialog, data-Star), Sales force monthly report, Competitor's trade literature, Consult and employees.	Manual-based system by the Marketing Intelligence Manager and one assistant	Use SWOT analysis, but a lot digging and guess work. No computerized database, Data stored in filing cabinet.	❶ Monthly bulletin to managers with analysis. ❷ A spin-off publication for public consumption. ❸ Twice yearly report for managing director. ❹ Ad hoc reports
Case 3 **An engineering company**	About 300 competitors ❶ All aspect of competitor activity ❷ Market information	Published information, Trade journals, statutory company accounts, customers, employees.	Computer-based system in Business information unit	PC-based European competitor database, Mainframe MIS, Computerized data summarizing, and manual-based qualitative data analysis	Newsletters (including solicited and unsolicited information of competitors)
Case 4 **A chemicals company**	500 on a regular basis ❶ Competitors and ❷ Competitive products ❸ Environment	Newspapers, journals, on-line databases (e.g. Dialog) business associations, FT Business Resource Centre Imp/exp. statistics, products literature	Computer aided system in Corporate Information Department	Abstracts have been put into full-text database. Others in filing cabinet. Data is not analysed	❶ Daily press scanning report ❷ Specific information bulletins ❸ Commercial business news bulletin for senior management ❹ Ad hoc inquiry reports in various format.
Case 5 **An automotive company**	About 10 competitors ❶ Competitor's strategic intention, ❷ 90% ~95% external information	News-type databases covering the industry, company reports, press releases, promotional materials, trade show	Manual-oriented system in Business Planning Department	Data is analysed, interpreted A lot of intelligent guesswork, but limited data modelling and statistics	Presentations (90%) -computer slides, and hard copies.

Brittin's (1991) study reveals that competitor intelligence systems were primarily manual-based in practice. Intelligence gathering relies on managers, data analysts, and sales force. Most intelligence is collected from sources both inside and outside the organization. In terms of processing intelligence, very little sophisticated data analysis techniques are used; much of the data analysis is based on intelligent guesswork. Collected data was frequently sent to managers without any degree of analysis and interpretation. Sugasawa (2004) who reported intelligence practice in Japan confirmed a lack of sophisticated intelligence analysis.

Case Study: An Insurance PLC

Bata Insurance Group Plc[1] is a worldwide insurance group operating in many countries with over 100 subsidiaries. In the UK the operating companies are divided by product and includes Beta General Insurance UK Ltd., Beta Life Insurance UK Ltd., Beta Insurance International Ltd., Beta Investment Ltd. The Group Holding Company comprises of several functional departments for example, Legal & Secretarial, Financial Control & Planning, Corporate Relations, International Division, and Strategic Research. The data were collected through action research by the author who participated in a CRM "Client Relationship Management" project in one of the operating companies. The Information Manager of the Group Holdings Company revealed the group's information searching systems for strategic intelligence. Table 2 presents the intelligence searching systems used by the group companies.

The major sources used to scan intelligence include:

- Use the city Business Library and the British Library Business Reference for research projects, and directories and handbooks such as Evandale's London Insurance Market Directory.

- **Subscription for newspapers and industry publications for manager's general information and background reading:** These include daily, weekly and monthly publica-

Table 2. Strategic intelligence systems

The Companies	The Intelligence Searching and Coverage
Beta Insurance Holding Plc	<ul><li>Comparison of main UK competitors from financial results, share price tracking, and press releases</li><li>Financial analysis of reinsurance companies from company reports and accounts</li><li>Monitoring UK composite insurers from city analyst's reports and a press cutting service</li></ul>
Beta General Insurance UK Ltd.	<ul><li>Press cutting services</li><li>PC-based marketing intelligence system, searching extracts from publications (ESMERK)</li><li>Data monitor reports on financial services</li><li>Networking with competitors</li></ul>
Beta Life Insurance UK Ltd.	<ul><li>Press cuttings</li><li>Use of published surveys</li><li>Market research association (external)</li></ul>
Beta Insurance International Ltd.	<ul><li>AM Best's on CD ROM</li><li>On-line news information services</li><li>Competitors financial data</li><li>"Soft" information database</li></ul>
Bata Investment Ltd.	<ul><li>Datastream online services</li><li>Bloombergs</li><li>Contact with external analysts</li><li>Track statistics on competitors</li></ul>

tions such as The FT, The Economist, DYP Newsletters-Europe, DYP Newsletters-Reinsurance, Best's Review—Property/Casualty, Best's Review - Life/Health, Insurance Times, FT World Insurance Report, and so forth.

- **Subscription for CD-ROM and on-line business database:** For example, Datastream
- **Company reports and accounts** collected from city library, Insurance association
- **Economic reports** from banks, stockbrokers, and reports by analysts on the insurance industry
- **Other free publications received by directors and executive staff:** For example, "Insurance Today" (where the advertisements are paying for the copy), giving details of the UK market products and developments. "European Insurance Bulletin" which can keep top management abreast of happenings.
- **The Association of British Insurers (ABI) and the Chartered Insurance Institute (CII) that provide services on insurance statistics, references, and articles on specific topic**
- **Ad hoc intelligence collection by company managers and staff members:** One department of the company also analyzes the financial results of reinsurance companies, periodically reminds the users of the service throughout the group that any "market intelligence" news on reinsurance company being vetted be passed to them. Overseas managers on their UK visits are also asked to set up meetings with them to discuss the local market situation.
- **Computer-based market intelligence system:** Staff throughout the regions is asked to pass on any piece of news they hear about competitors or brokers to central co-ordinators. The database in the UK head office containing news items on competitors, ar-

ticles from trade magazines, advertisements, and inter-company meetings is being made available over the network to the different areas.

It is reported that most members of the staff do not have the time to read and absorb all the information that is available. Therefore the information service workers look through most publications, mark up the articles of interest for cutting out, and file the data for any enquiry. This service is centralized to serve the whole group. On the other hand, some group executives (e.g., executives for overseas life operations) have made very little use of the research material available to them, as they had good personal contacts with a large number of people in other parts of the group. They naturally adapt at personnel networks for information gathering.

DISCUSSION

The empirical evidence suggests that external intelligence—primarily competitive intelligence and market/industry intelligence as reviewed above, has been addressed by many companies engaged in CI activities. A manager from Bata Group comments that "In today's rapidly changing business world the need for timely and accurate market intelligence will increase. We need to know what our competitors are doing almost before they do." The sources used for intelligence gathering are heterogeneous, but most intelligence tends to be gathered from public domain. Managers' intelligence needs are often fulfilled by using a broad range of approaches, which are characterized as manual-based and unsystematic tendencies. The current intelligence practice exhibits the following deficiencies:

- **Manual based:** Competitive intelligence is collected mainly by managers and information workers from various publications and general information sources. The current method of press cutting and searching is labour intensive. Computer-based intelligence systems are limited to data storage, retrieval, and CD-ROM/online database searching.

- **Intelligence scanning is ad hoc and the process is functionally divided:** Most organizations scanned intelligence irregularly. Scanning is commonly conducted by sales force, and relies on managers' own personal networks. Cobb (2003) argues established organizational CI processes often suffer from holes in data or data integrity causing errors in the interpretation of that data for intelligence purpose, and suggests that scanning activity will be accomplished by a separate, distinct department, unit, or individual that reports directly to the executives in the organization.

- **Lack of Filtering, Refining and Sense Making of Intelligence:** As revealed from the empirical studies, data scanned is not often filtered, processed, and interpreted into meaningful intelligence in required form before reaching the managers, and there is a lack of sophisticated intelligence analysis tools. This affirms Maier et al.'s (1997) assertion that the most common problem in the dissemination phase is making the information and structure relevant to the audience while being brief yet useful. Without data refining, providing increased data access and search facilities to senior managers can exacerbate the problem of data overload. However, filter and interpret intelligence through a systematic system faces great challenges, on the one hand, recognizing which data is of strategic importance needs management knowledge and judgement. Human cognition and intuition process often dominate interpreting, reasoning, and learning that are subtle. On the other hand, technology in semantic data searching, machine learning is limited to structured

data analysis, but not to dynamic strategic intelligence. Even with intelligent system and knowledge based expert system, letting computers represent a great deal of human knowledge for data interpretation is still a challenge, since knowledge may not exist in a visible, explicit form for acquisition.

THE SOLUTIONS

Organization-Wide Intelligence Scanning

The way to avoid ad hoc intelligence scanning is to have systematic and organization-wide scanning systems. It is believed that systematic scanning of business environment for strategic information can improve the completeness and quality of strategic intelligence. Huber (1990) assert that the use of computer-assisted information processing and communication technologies will lead to more rapid and more accurate identification of problems and opportunities; and the use of computer-assisted information storage and acquisition technologies will lead to organizational intelligence that is more accurate, comprehensive, timely, and available. Environmental scanning: as defined by Maier, Rainer, and Snyder (1997) is a basic process of any organization, acquires data from the external environment to be used in problem definition and decision-making. The environment consists of all those events, happenings, or factors with a present or future influence on the organization that, at the same time, lies outside the organization's immediate control. The primary purpose of environment scanning is to provide a comprehensive view or understanding of the current and future condition of the five environmental constituents: social, economic, political regulatory, and technological. Scanning invokes a process of externalization, causing the company to expand the focus of decision-making to include the perspectives of outsiders, for example, present and prospective competitors, customers, regulators, stakeholders, and the perspectives of economic condition, political climate, technology development, social and cultural changes. An information scanning mechanism could ensure systematically collection of relevant, important information from various sources available both inside and outside a company.

The current practice of intelligence gathering significantly relies on managers and sales forces. This runs the risk of missing significant intelligence being noticed due to time constraints and limited capabilities of individual managers, and the narrow focus of sales and marketing staff. To maximize the effectiveness and efficiency of environmental scanning, organization-wide intelligence scanning is desirable and possible. Because organization members have wide contacts with a variety of external entities, also they work closely in the front-line to interface with company's customers, hence, a variety of intelligence can be gathered for the attention of senior managers. Organization-wide intelligence scanning should focus on scanning external environment for intelligence. The scanning function can be performed through formal, informal intelligence collecting/reporting systems or third party agency, which are suggested as below:

Intelligence Scanning Through Informal Systems

The informal systems for organization-wide intelligence scanning can include, for example:

- **Sales force report:** Companies can ask their field sales forces to gather up intelligence about competitors, suppliers, and customers, as well as market intelligence.
- **Business trip report:** Business trip report by managers who visited foreign markets. The managers are briefed before the trip by a member of the corporate business intelligence unit, and on their return report back with findings related to the issues and questions raised at the briefing.
- **Intelligence gathering box and online intelligence forum:** Every employee may have something to contribute in terms of competitive intelligence. A company should encourage its staff to contribute information on market, competitors, ideas and suggestions or even rumour, gossip and office grapevines by using an intelligence box or an online forum where valuable intelligence can be collected and rewarded.
- **Friday round tables:** A company can organize a series of round-table meetings in various locations, where a particular topic related to intelligence gathering is discussed. With the aid of a knowledge team facilitator, knowledge for intelligence scanning/processing is articulated, captured.

Structured Intelligence Scanning: A Corporate Radar System

Formal methods are needed to systematically collect external information. A company's intelligence centre, and intelligence workers have the responsibilities to fulfil intelligence scanning and analyzing tasks. In addition, computer assisted system shall be considered to enhance intelligence scanning. Business organizations could develop a radar-type system (or function) to continuously but selectively detect significant signals from environment sectors. A corporate radar system for strategic information scanning is depicted in Figure 1.

The radar scanning system works according to two main criteria: the clarity of the signals detected from the environment and the level of strategic significance of the signals. Center to the scanning is the sensor that continually detects all signals emerged from the business environment. Each signal detected will be handled by four distinctive and related processors according to the nature of the signal, i.e.

Figure 1. A corporate radar system for environment scanning

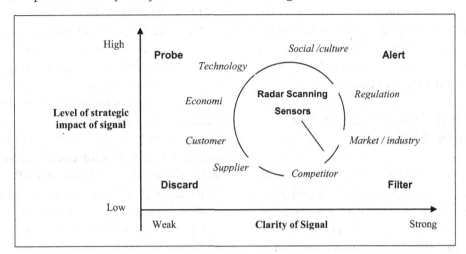

- **An alert:** If the signal detected is strategically important, and the signal is with strong clarity, that is, message is clearly stated and from reliable sources, the signal will be alerted immediately as hot intelligence to executives.

- **A filter:** If many signals being detected but not all of them are of strategic importance, for example, information regularly received by the company from its environment, the signals have to be selected from a potentially large mass of data, and filtered for relevance. Because most of the signals are less important to derive strategic information, the filter function thus is vital to screen out irrelevant information and to eliminate information overload.

- **A probe:** The radar system may detect a weak signal but it may have potential strategic impact on the organization, the signal thus must be probed and amplified. Information as such is often less structured and not easily to obtain. Much of this type of signal may fall into the "soft" information category, that is, opinions, predictions, hearsay, ideas, rumours, and gossips. The vague signal needs to be verified, and amplified in order

to assess its potential impact on the strategic direction of the organization.

- **A discard mechanism:** This is needed to handle large amount of weak signals that are not strategically important or relevant to the organization.

The aforementioned radar sensor, alert, filter, probe, and discard functions can be a computerized or a manual based system. Whatever it is, knowledge needs to be embedded within the system to underpin the operation of the radar system.

It is worthy to note that the environmental sectors for radar scanning may vary from one industry to another. We examined this in a previous study (Xu, Kaye, & Duan, 2003) that the significance of environmental sectors for scanning is industry specific. For example, in the computer industry, customer, competitor, market/industry, and technology sectors are more strategically important than other variables, showing that these sectors have high strategic impact signals. Thus the focus of radar scanning may need to be adjusted to target these environmental sectors. Stoffels (1994) addresses that "the strength of signals is related to the uncertainty of environment, that is, weaker signals are associated the remote environment, and strong signals with the task environment. The environment scanning effort is much required in the remote environment as the visibility of the future diminishes with increasing turbulence, and predictability deteriorates accordingly."

Using Third Parties to Carry Out Intelligence Gathering

A company may choose to use third parties to conduct intelligence scanning. External intelligence firms can be helpful in gathering and analyzing certain information. They can assist in synthesizing monthly intelligence, performing difficult information gathering tasks, and training employees. The third-party status also helps break down any political barriers that may exist within an organization. In this way the third party serves as a catalyst in the process. Tan, Teo, Tan, and Wei (1998) support this notion by asserting that use of external consultants results in effectiveness of environmental scanning. They explained that besides providing and interpreting information, external consultants have helped to equip organization with the knowledge and skills for doing environmental scanning on the Internet. These services include conducting courses on the use of Internet tools and compiling links to potentially useful information sources.

Organization-wide intelligence scanning is envisaged to enhance external intelligence scanning. However, systematically scanning the entire environment is both costly and inappropriate. A manager is interested in the environment that influences his decisions, hence, environmental scanning needs to be selective, yet ensure that sufficient variety is maintained to avoid missing important signals. Auster and Choo (1995) suggest that selecting which environment for scanning is effected by a variety of influential factors, for example, the turbulence of the environment, the difference of industry sectors, or the company's competition strategy. It can be argued from this study that for effective organization-wide intelligence scanning, making knowledge about which environment to scan explicit is vital.

Knowledge-Enriched Intelligence Filtering and Refining

In order to produce analytical intelligence product—meaningful and digestible information, it is vital to filter out irrelevant data and to refine data into meaningful intelligence. The current process of intelligence analysis is a human cen-

Figure 2. Intelligence process with scanning, refining, and supporting function

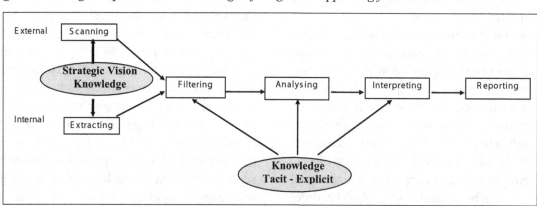

tred, knowledge intensive process, that is, relies on managers themselves and their knowledge and judgement. Thus the solution to refine intelligence must incorporate managerial knowledge used for intelligence scanning and analysis. Figure 2 shows the intelligence process by highlighting the knowledge enriched filtering and refining function.

As highlighted in the diagram, the intelligence scanning and refining (filtering-analyzing-interpreting) process should embed strategic vision and human knowledge. This can be achieved by:

- **Using intelligent agent-based system that uses knowledge base, case based reasoning, machine learning, or user feedback and interaction to semantic scanning and analysing intelligence according to user profile:** For example, intelligent agents could base on past information search activities and predefined information needs in "*user profiles*", which is generated by a learning agent, or defined by the user. The user profile can consist of executive's personal profile, executive's information needs and interests, executive roles, and organizational environment profile, which enable software agents to perform domain-specific acquisition, synthesis and interpretation of information. As a result, information processing becomes more personalized to the executive.
- **Creating a knowledge creation and sharing field/culture to turn tacit knowledge into explicit form so that employees,** particularly intelligence staff can be guided to detect and make sense of strategic significant information.

It is envisaged that computer based knowledge enriched intelligence scanning, refining can selectively and systematically scan and categorize, prioritize, and analyze large amounts of data on a continuous basis. Analyzed intelligence will report to, or alert managers to enlarge managers'

vision on strategic issues by providing consistent, routine surveillance of a wide range and a variety of data that would not be possible with current management reporting techniques.

Knowledge Workers/Intelligence Specialist Support

Although computer-based intelligence system (scanning, refining) may be developed, it is evident that many senior managers may not wish to use such systems to acquire strategic intelligence due to the nature of managerial work. The advanced systems may be better used by intelligence specialists/knowledge workers, so that analyzed intelligence can be delivered to the senior managers by the specialists. If managers' information requirements can be predefined, the specialist will search necessary databases and the external environment to locate the information as required. If however, managers do not solicit information, the intelligence specialist can continually scan the external environment and proactively report significant intelligence (most of them probably are unexpected) to the senior managers via written or verbal communication channels. Less important information is consolidated, synthesized, and digested to a brief level that managers receive on regular basis. With the support of intelligence specialists, both internal and external data can be systematically scanned, filtered, synthesized, and reported in both regular and ad hoc basis through formal and informal systems.

The challenge however is that intelligence specialists need to possess managerial knowledge and similar judgement that managers use to acquire information. This relies on knowledge sharing. In addition, intelligence specialists need to have rich knowledge of information sources and skills in exploiting, evaluating, and interpreting information.

IMPLEMENTATION

Implementation of the above solution will inevitably require a change of vision, intelligence process, organizational structure and culture. Managers need to develop a strategic vision in order to give a company's intelligence activity a sense of direction. The purpose is to give corporate members a mental map of the world they live in and to provide a general direction as to what kind of intelligence they ought to seek and report. A strategic vision created by senior management helps foster a high degree of personal commitment from middle managers and front-line workers.

A common problem in establishing intelligence functions might be that most companies prefer not to devote resources to such a function until it can prove that the function is necessary and will succeed. Therefore, a visionary leadership is needed, who can perceive the benefits of strategic intelligence and provides support for developing the intelligence function.

What remains critical is how managerial knowledge can be elicited to underpin the radar scanning system, and the refining system. The knowledge spiral model (Nonaka & Takeuchi 1995)—sharing knowledge through socialization could facilitate the process of sharing experiences and turning tacit knowledge to explicit knowledge, for example, in the form of an intelligence gathering event, briefing, club, online discussion forum.

There is probably no one structure that can fit a variety of different organizations. The variety very much depends on the size of the firm, the type of the business, the degree of centralization or decentralization of its activities and decision-making. It is perfectly possible that a centralized intelligence function is established to coordinate organizational-wide intelligence activities and to operate the corporate radar system. This can overcome the data integrity problem that often resulted from functionally divided organizational CI processes.

In accordance with structural change, a knowledge creating and intelligence gathering culture need to be created. Organization-wide intelligence gathering relies on every member's commitment to intelligence activity. Environmental scanning is an essential behavior attribute of culture because scanning provides the first step in a chain that culminates in organizational actions (Saxby, 2002). The briefing on intelligence gathering, incentives, the informal networks form an intelligence culture. Senior managers must continually reinforce the desired culture traits through their own behavior.

CONCLUSION

This chapter reviewed the nature of strategic intelligence and highlighted the challenges of systematically managing strategic intelligence. Strategic intelligence is not a static piece of information that can be easily obtained. What constitutes strategic intelligence is subject to managerial judgement and sense making that requires managerial knowledge. The current process of intelligence activity is either divided by organizational function, or is ad hoc relying on individual manager. Intelligence gather is primarily concentrated on competitive intelligence. Computerized system has played limited role in intelligence scanning and analysis. There is a lack of systematic intelligence scanning, analyzing and intelligence support, and culture.

The solution proposed to improve strategic intelligence activity addresses three significant intelligence functions that constitute a systematic intelligence process. The organization-wide scanning and the corporate radar system will ensure continuous monitoring and scanning of all signals from the market, competitors, and customers, and the far environment. The refining function is enriched with managerial knowledge so as to filter out irrelevant information and ensure meaningful intelligence is reached executives. Intelligence specialists as an organization's knowledge workers will provide complementary support for executives who are not inclined to use formal intelligence systems.

Managing strategic intelligence cannot be subject to sole technical solutions. Enabling technology to assist managers in their intelligence scanning and analysis activities is a challenging task. Therefore, effective managing strategic intelligence will rely much on an organizational approach including illustration of organizational vision, sharing tacit knowledge, establishing an intelligence culture and redesigning the process of intelligence gathering, analysis, and dissemination.

REFERENCES

Aguilar, F. (1967). *Scanning the business environment*. New York: The Macmillan Company.

Auster, E., & Choo, C. (1994). How senior managers acquire and use information in environment scanning. *Information Processing & Management*, *30*(5), 607-618.

Baatz, E. (1994, September). The quest for corporate smarts. *CIO,* pp. 48-51.

Bernhardt, D. (1994). I want it fast, factual, actionable: Tailoring competitive intelligence to executive's needs. *Long Range Planning*, *27*(1), 12-24.

Brittin, M. (1991). *Business research guide: How to develop your competitor intelligence system: Five case studies*. Cleveland, UK: Headland Press.

Chen, H., Chau, M., & Zeng, D. (2002). CI spider: A tool for competitive intelligence on the Web. *Decision Support Systems*, *34*, 1-17.

Cobb, P. (2003). Competitive intelligence through data mining. *Journal of Competitive Intelligence and Management*, *1*(3), 80-89.

Cottrell, N. & Rapley, K. (1991). Factors critical to the success of executive information systems in British airways. *European Journal of Information Systems, 1*(1), 65-71.

Crane, A. (2004). In the company of spies: When competitive intelligence gathering becomes industrial espionage. *Business Horizons*, *48*(3), 233-240.

D'Aveni, R., & MacMillan, I. (1990). Crisis and the content of managerial communications: A study of the focus of attention of top managers in surviving and failing firms. *Administrative Science Quarterly*, *35*, 634-657.

Daft, R., Sormunen, J., & Parks, D. (1988). Chief executive scanning, environmental characteristics, and company performance: An empirical study. *Strategic Management Journal*, *9*(2), 123-139.

Desouza, K. C. (2001). Intelligent agent for competitive intelligence: Survey of applications. *Competitive Intelligence Review*, *12*(4), 57-63.

Edwards, C., & Peppard, J. (1993). A taxonomy of executive information systems: Let the 4 Cs penetrate the fog. *Information Management & Computer Security, 1*(2), 4-10.

Frolick, M. (1994). Management support systems and their evolution from executive information systems *Information Strategy: The Executive's Journal,* pp. 31-38

Huber, G. (1990). A theory of the effects of advanced information technologies on organisational design, intelligence, and decision making. *Academy of Management Review, 15*(1), 47-71.

Kiesler, S., & Sproull, L. (1982). Managerial response to changing environments: Perspectives on problem sensing from social cognition. *Administrative Science Quarterly, 27,* 548-570.

Langley, N. (1996). Data excavation. *Computing,* p. 22.

Macdonald, S. (1995). Learning to change: An information perspective on learning in the organisation. *Organisation Science, 6*(5), 557-568.

Maier, J. L., Rainer, R. K., Jr., & Snyder, C. A. (1997). Environmental scanning for information technology: An empirical investigation. *Journal of Management Informaiton Systems, 14*(2), 177.

McNichol, J. (1993). What senior management wants from marketing research. *Medical Marketing & Media, 28*(5), 14-20.

Mintzberg, H. (1973). *The nature of managerial work.* New York: Harper and Row.

Mintzberg, H. (1980). *The nature of managerial work.* Englewood Cliffs, NJ: Prentice Hall.

Nonaka, I., & Takeuchi, H. (1995). *The knowledge-creating company: How Japanese companies create the dynamics of innovation.* Oxford: University Press, Inc.

Patton, K. M., & McKenna, T. M. (2005). Scanning for competitive intelligence. *Competitive Intelligence Magazine, 8*(2), 24-29.

Pelsmacker, P. D., Muller, M., Viviers, W., Saayman, A., Cuyvers, L., & Jegers, M. (2005). Competitive intelligence practices of South African and Belgian exporters. *Marketing Intelligence & Planning, 23*(6), 606-620.

Ramaswami, S., Nilakanta, S., & Flynn, E. (1992). Supporting strategic information needs: An empirical assessment of some organisational factors. *Journal of Strategic Information Systems, 1*(3), 152-162.

Sauter, V. L. (2005). Competitive intelligence systems: Qualitative DSS for strategic decision-making. *Buisness Information Review, 23*(1), 35-42.

Saxby, C. L., Parker, K. R., Nitse, P. S., & Dishman, P. L. (2002). Environemntal scanning and organisational culture. *Marketing Intelligence & Planning, 20*(1), 28-34.

Schmitz, J., Armstrong, G., & Little, J. (1992). CoverStory—Automated news finding in marketing. In C. Holtham (Eds.), *Executive information systems and decision support* (pp. 227-238). London: Chapman & Hall.

Simon, H. (1965). *The shape of automation for men and management.* New York: Harper & Row.

Stoffels, J. (1994). *Strategic issues management: A comprehensive guide to environment scanning.* OH: The Planning Forum.

Sugasawa, Y. (2004). The current state of competitive intelligence activities and competitive awareness in Japanese business. *Journal of competitive intelligence and management, 2*(4), 7-31.

Tan, S. L., Teo, H. H., Tan, B. C. Y., & Wei, K. K. (1998, December). Environmental scanning on the Internet. In *Proceedings of the International Conference on Information Systems* (pp.79-87), Helsinki, Finland.

Taylor, P. (1996, March). Information technology: Help is on hand from intelligent agents. *Financial Times* Review, p. 6.

Tyson, K. (1990). *Competitor intelligence manual and guide: Gathering, analysing, and using business intelligence.* Englewood Cliffs, NJ: Prentice Hall.

Wright, S. Pickton, D. W., & Callow, J. (2002). Competitive intelligence in UK firms: A typology. *Marketing Intelligence & Planning, 20*(6), 349-360.

Wyllie, J. (1993). The need for business information refineries. *Aslib Proceedings, 45*(4), 97-102.

Xu, X. M. & Kaye, G. R. (1995). Building market intelligence systems for environment scanning. *Logistics Information Management* (renamed as *Journal of Enterprise Information Management*), *8*(2), 22–29.

Xu, X., Kaye, G. R., & Duan, Y. (2003). UK executives' vision on business environment for information scanning: A cross industry study. *Information & Management, The International Journal of Information Systems Applications, 40*(5), 381-389.

ENDNOTE

[1]   The names of the Plc and the operating companies are fictitious to ensure confidentiality.

Chapter II
Developing and Analysing Core Compentencies for Alignment with Strategy

Keith Sawyer
Alpha Omega International, UK

John Gammack
Griffith University, Australia

ABSTRACT

Although it is widely accepted that alignment of knowledge with corporate strategy is necessary, to date there have been few clear statements on what a knowledge strategy looks like and how it may be practically implemented. We argue that current methods and techniques to accomplish this alignment are severely limited, showing no clear description on how the alignment can be achieved. Core competencies, embodying an organisation's practical know-how, are also rarely linked explicitly to actionable knowledge strategy. Viewing knowledge embedded in core competencies as a strategic asset, the paper uses a case study to show how a company's core competencies were articulated and verified for either inclusion or exclusion in the strategy. The study is representative of similar studies carried out across a range of organisations using a novel and practically proven method. This method, StratAchieve, was used here in a client situation to show how the core competencies were identified and tested for incorporation or not in the strategy. The paper concludes by considering the value of the approach for managing knowledge.

INTRODUCTION

Many companies have developed or adopted various knowledge management (KM) initiatives to try to surface and differentiate what they do know from what they need to know and also to identify the location of their knowledge gaps. Processes and tools that support efforts to capture knowledge are well known and widely used, such as expertise directories, intranets, communities of practice, knowledge audits, discussion forums, knowledge maps, building and documenting knowledge based and expert systems, storytelling, benchmarking, and the like. These efforts serve the strategy functions of organisations, aligning capability and know-how with strategic objectives.

Although the importance of strategic alignment is recognised, what is less understood is the practical means to determine what knowledge is strategically important and how this knowledge can be incorporated into the corporate strategy. Zack (1999) for example suggests that companies may have unique ways of doing this, (itself a competitive advantage) using techniques such as SWOT analysis. Zack's work, while providing a framework and some high-level questions, is light on actionable detail, and is silent on how the output of such efforts can be strategically assessed with sufficient reach to be implemented. The available literature on knowledge strategy alignment is generally very limited: although many documents refer to these issues, few go beyond noting the desirability of alignment, and even fewer provide any detailed methodological guidance. Few empirical studies appear to exist, and whilst academic comparison across unique cases is not always appropriate, the study reported in this paper describes a generic method that has also been used in several other organisations. The approach described here addresses *what* organisations know, and how it aligns with their wider strategy.

All organisations need to "know what they know" (and know what they don't know) to make strategic decisions on (for example) sourcing, customer satisfaction, recruitment and training, investment, and in identifying areas for process re-engineering, market development, or innovation. The familiar saying, "If only we knew what we know" is, however, flawed because it presumes that what exists as knowledge in organisations is always useful and needs to be formalised and

actioned. More appropriate is to say "If only we knew what we need to know". This means that organisations must also know what they no longer need to know because it no longer has a sufficient impact on the corporate objectives. Similarly, organisations must know what knowledge is most important and determine whether they already have this knowledge or need to acquire it. Apart from the rather limited SWOT analysis, or proprietary methods (e.g., AMERIN, n.d.) that may or may not include tools that help identify knowledge gaps, there are few clear statements on how, in practice, strategy may be structured in actionable alignment with organisational knowledge.

Organisations must structure their strategy so that strategic decisions and actions can be made on a variety of fronts, such as retaining and growing profitable customers, selling the right products to the right market, and recruiting and developing staff. To achieve this, organisations must manage their knowledge effectively to ensure it is directly translatable into strategic actions. Without knowing how to effectively manage their own stock of intellectual capital, such decisions cannot be actioned nor can the company be properly valued[1].

When turnover or loss of key staff is potentially a consequential threat, failure to manage the implicit knowledge assets underpinning this value may be seen as negligent. Intellectual capital is the main source of value creation (Edvinsson & Malone, 1997) and thus strategically linked directly to the organisation's future. In larger organisations especially, formalisation of this activity is required, not only for internal purposes, but also externally, such as shareholder value creation and outperformance of competitors. Identifying, securing and managing the various forms of intellectual capital (human and structural) within an organisation has thus become a central theme for knowledge management research as well as for knowledge valuing and reporting.

KM initiatives typically centre on the personnel who embody and can apply their knowledge in project or other business activity settings, and often entail recording or abstracting from the traces of their contextualised activities. Such KM initiatives implicitly recognise the centrality of the competencies of individuals and groups in transacting the strategic aims of the organisation at operational levels, and in potentially identifying the specific knowledge and abilities that give comparative advantages. Rarely, however, are such initiatives directly linked to corporate strategy and are (often inappropriately) typically designed and implemented through the organisation's IT support function (Berkman, 2001). A focus on the competencies related to strategic objectives and alignment with operational competencies is vital and is addressed in the following case study.

If organisations are centrally reliant on their knowledge for their survival, value and prosperity, their knowledge management strategies must be fully congruent with wider corporate strategy. Hackney, Burn, and Dhillon (2000) note, however, that comments on implementing such congruence have been few, and there remains a "prevalent disconnect between (business) and IT strategies". Their analysis of contemporary business strategy implies a reappraisal of the conventional and rational assumptions implicit in strategic IS planning (SISP) and where installing an IT "solution" is insufficient without coherent linkage to business strategy.

Hackney, Burn, and Dhillon (2000) cite research suggesting a necessary relationship between innovation and organisational *competence* and see assessing organisational competencies as a critically relevant challenge for SISP. The terms *competences* and *competencies* are both used in the literature to refer to such organisational abilities: we prefer to use *competencies* in this paper. The knowledge embedded in organisational competencies can be a key strategic asset, and conversely, strategy emerging from inherent capabilities and competencies provides flexibility and responsiveness. Identifying such competencies is prerequisite to their assessment, valuation, and

incorporation into strategy. These competencies, which are typically knowledge based, can form the essence of a knowledge strategy embedded within a wider corporate strategy that is not simply cast in terms of KM technologies over some planning period.

A company's core competencies (Prahalad & Hamel, 1990) are the areas in which it has competitive strength and thus form a platform for its strategic thrusts. Not knowing or appreciating these means its strategies may fail and compromise proper valuation of a company's knowledge assets underlying the support, adaptation, and maintenance of its activities. Core competencies are the "cognitive characteristics of an organisation, its know-how..." (Hatten & Rosenthal, 2001, p. 50), that is, an organisation's collective (functional) expertise. Built on the skills and experience of individuals and teams, they are housed in characteristic business functions: examples Hatten and Rosenthal (2001) cite include McDonald's HR competency in recruiting, hiring, training, and retaining part time labour and Intel's technology competency in state of the art design of microprocessor chip families. Although such functions are not necessarily unique to an organisation, the know-how and processes involved in them may well be, thus conferring advantage.

Core competencies are necessarily part of a knowledge strategy which itself is part of the overall strategy. A focus on competencies (which implies active and generative abilities) rather than the knowledge traces itself is preferable, since in times of change, accumulated knowledge may be a hindrance to new thinking: what Leonard-Barton (1995) has called "core rigidities". To give a sustainable strategic advantage, competencies should be valuable, rare, hard to imitate or substitute, and ideally will confer a dominating ability in their area. Bollinger and Smith (2001) view the knowledge resource as a strategic asset, with the "collective organisational knowledge, (rather than that) of mobile individuals", that is the essential asset. This suggests a focal shift towards organisationally understood activity and process, not merely data and record storage requiring leverage by particular individuals for effectiveness.

In the knowledge based view, nicely contrasted with the conventional rational view of strategy by Carlisle (1999) the strategic focus is on value *creation* arising from uniquely effective internal capabilities and competencies, rather than value *appropriation*, which emphasises "optimisation" activity in imperfect markets. Although over time advantages may be eroded, organisations with developed "capabilities for managing knowledge creation and exploiting (its value) are better able to adapt by developing new sustainable core competencies for the future" (Carlisle, 1999, p. 24). Dawson (2000, p. 323) also notes "It is far more useful to think (about developing) dynamic knowledge capabilities than about knowledge as a static asset …to be managed".

The theoretical literature on core competencies does not however generally relate their development to concepts of knowledge management operation, nor to strategy implementation. Nor, although recognising that some competencies are more important than others, does it distinguish strategic from operational core competencies. Although the literature does not imply that strategic competencies arise from operational ones, we find it useful in practice to differentiate these since the only way strategy can be realised is at the operational level, by competent people performing activities that achieve strategic goals. For this to occur, an explicit linkage between strategic goals and operational activity, between strategic core competencies and their implementation (and reciprocally between operational competencies and strategic objectives) must be articulated. This theoretical claim is demonstrated in the present case study.

Since contemporary thinking on strategy emphasises ability to respond to environmental changes quickly at all levels rather than planning in a controlled environment, an embedded knowledge strategy will act as the medium through which these levels can be brought into alignment and allow for emergent strategy to be developed across the organisation.

Klein (1998) asks the question "But how does a firm decide what set of operating-level initiatives would best meet its strategic goals?" and goes on to identify the "challenge of linking strategy with execution at the knowledge level" (p. 3) by a focus on various activities around intellectual capital. As an open research question however, specific implementation guidance is not offered, and associated literature (e.g., Graham & Pizzo, 1996) often notes only generic steps (identify strategic business drivers, determine business critical knowledge characteristics and locations, construct knowledge value chains, and find competency gaps).

Apart from private ownership tools, which may lack academic evaluation or an underlying original research base, there are few existing public domain management tools that offer help in modelling the different aspects a comprehensive knowledge-centric strategy development entails. These candidates include the "enterprise model" (Hatten & Rosenthal, 1999), later renamed the "action alignment (AA) model" and extended in Hatten and Rosenthal (2001); and more recently strategy maps (Kaplan & Norton, 2004). These generally provide broad areas for consideration, but give little or no guidance on strategy development or implementation beyond a flimsy structural outline. For knowledge strategy evaluation in financial terms, the KM valuation methodology of Clare and Detore (2000) applies, but this starts from a developed business strategy or KM project proposal.

The AA (Action Alignment) model is essentially a grid showing classical business functions (e.g., HRM, IT, and so on) crossed with business processes (e.g., order fulfilment) allowing visualisation of core junctures or problem (misaligned) areas, with supplementary tools to assess the fit or otherwise between customers and organisational capabilities and competencies. This appears to be essentially reactionary to the need for cross-functional alignment occasioned by new economy realities, but problematises the issue within an assumed industrial-era organisational structure of functionally defined silos, and without highlighting the knowledge activities required. The AA model has various other serious limitations in a knowledge-based view, in which traditional "Balkanised" organisational structures are considered obsolescent, and not conducive to the strategic planning and development of intangible assets and associated capabilities (Chatzkel, 2000).

The Balanced Scorecard (Kaplan & Norton, 1996) is a widely used performance measurement tool and has evolved since its origination in the early 1990s to more explicitly focus on strategy. Originally it aimed to address aspects of a company's performance not covered in simpler measures oriented primarily to financial performance. A customer perspective, an internal business perspective, an innovation and learning perspective, and a financial perspective provide a set of measures indicating aspects of performance relevant to various stakeholders. The strategy maps and supporting theory outlined in Kaplan and Norton (2004) are however very sketchy and conventional in relation to the knowledge based view — competency is effectively equated with job description (p. 225 et seq), and the references to the concepts of knowledge and KM are very shallowly treated. Furthermore, although the strategy maps show some linkages, the map's theoretical formulation is silent about the detailed linkages between these giving no guidance as to how the knowledge embodied in them can be identified, related to strategic competencies and leveraged with respect to achieving financially quantifiable targets such as market share, net profit or shareholder value, or other non-financial performance measures. Tools such as Kaplan and Norton's strategy map thus do not explicitly address knowledge-centric strategy development

and indeed a series of google searches in mid 2004 yielded few hits relevant to this aspect.

Yet an organisation's ability (or otherwise) to knowledgeably enact and leverage corporate processes and technologies is the essence of strategic competency. In a view of strategy that is not purely top down, but is essentially enacted dynamically by the knowledgeable activity of people in the "middle", it is crucial to reify these competencies in relation to strategy formulation. Current tools do not go far enough in guiding this, nor do they provide explicit methods for systematic engagement at this level.

THE CASE STUDY

Overview

We offer an approach addressing this by using a case study embodying action research techniques, beginning with a brief description of the organisation, its strategic position and the context of the fieldwork. A case study approach has been chosen since contemporary phenomena are being investigated in their real life context, with multiple variables of interest and converging sources of data; where the boundaries between the phenomena and the context are unclear and where the researcher has little control over behavioural events (Yin, 2002). The case study approach allows depth of understanding across many variables to occur. In this research an interpretivist position is adopted in which the organisation's own meanings and their negotiation are prioritised.

The case study reported here is of a UK accountancy company, and entailed the elicitation and reification of its hitherto poorly understood core competencies. The knowledge strategy was developed within a comprehensive corporate strategy overhaul and was built around the knowledge audit of its core competencies embodied in people and processes, supported by relevant technology.

The paper proceeds as follows. Having identified the need to provide detailed guidance on reifying an organisation's core competencies and to relate those effectively to knowledge strategy, we outline processes that address this weakness and show how they can be implemented within more generic strategic planning processes.

We illustrate these in the case study context to show how the organisation systematically identified its core competencies, as well as determining the core competencies that are no longer of strategic importance. In the process, learning that the company not only did not have the strategic competencies it thought it had, but that it had knowledge assets which it had not realised, provided the capability to explicitly incorporate the competencies into the strategy.

The result was an articulation of what the company "knew" as well as what it did not know but needed to know, both strategically and operationally. This enabled the company to consciously leverage its strengths but also identify areas in which it was deficient and therefore strategically vulnerable. The case study concludes by showing how the company had achieved a strong competitive position from which to strategically value its knowledge and other intangible assets in an informed manner for forward planning and reporting to shareholders and others. The detailing of this valuation is part of our ongoing research.

The Organisation

The UK accountancy company featured in this case study is involved in a broad range of financial services to a wide variety of customers, both large and small. For purposes of this paper, the company shall be called Target Accountancy. The company has 56 employees and has been existence since 1987. Staff turnover is low as a result of high loyalty and good conditions of employment.

Target Accountancy had never produced a formal strategy plan but realised it could not achieve the success it wanted without one. The saying "if you don't plan your company's future, it won't have one" was very pertinent in their case. The company possessed a rich abundance of talent but this was tacitly held in the minds of individuals; it wanted to be the formal owner of its capital knowledge. One of the aims of Target Accountancy was to verify whether the competencies it thought it possessed were being successfully engineered to generate the required competitive differentiators. There was thus a strong need to strategically specify and test the impact of its core competencies, to determine which were the most productive and identify gaps where new competencies were required.

The StratAchieve Method

One of us (Sawyer) was the external facilitator. The StratAchieve method[2] was chosen because of its proven capability in over 400 organisations to create and achieve strategies. Other tools currently on the market are geared either for helping to produce a strategy plan or to conduct project management, but not both. StratAchieve produces and combines the two, enabling iteration between the plan and implementation to take place.

The method is supported by software produced by Alpha Omega, which is used throughout the change programme. During a workshop session, a map is projected onto a screen and interactively developed through discussions, suggestions and learning from workshop delegates. An important aspect of the approach is its ability to integrate the various types of organisational strategies, such as customers, financial, HR, marketing, product, IS, and (crucially) knowledge, into a single, coherent corporate strategy.

The method enables organisations to determine, construct, legitimise, and achieve their strategy and conduct monitoring and controlling during implementation and provides the structure for all organisational strategic actions to be integrated. Thus, marketing, HR, finance, IT, and knowledge strategies are all holistically

Figure 1. The Knowledge Positioning Matrix showing examples from the workshop

	Do Know	Don't Know
Need to Know	Contact all our profitable customers monthly	Provide online accountancy services Provide hospitality packages
Don't Need	Provide doctoring services to ailing	✕

integrated into one coherent and comprehensive strategy. This will become apparent in the examples that follow.

The Strategy Tree provides the theoretical framework of the method (Sawyer, 1990) consisting of four or five layers of verb-fronted activities, logically related through *Why* and *How* connections. These Why and How relations provide a path that simultaneously justifies a given action at a higher level, whilst specifying an operational activity that achieves higher level aims. In discussions any given statement can be explored in either direction. For example rationale for the expressed operational competency "*Keep in regular contact with all clients*" was explored. The next higher-level activity was determined by asking, "why should we *Keep in regular contact with all clients*"? which elicited the response, because we want to "*Maintain excellent personal relationships with our clients*". A further Why interrogation on this activity produced the parent, "*Retain our current clients*" and a further Why activity resulted in the parent "*Increase our revenues*". A final Why activity generated the high-level statement

"*Increase our gross margin*" linked directly to strategic mission. In this example, a set of Why interrogations produced the higher-level activities which linked to the pre-set vision (increase our gross margin). Conversely, How statements can be elicited by starting with a high-level aim, and identifying child activities that follow from it, as reversing the previous example shows. Turning a competence into verb-fronted form emphasises a capability focus for knowledge, and leads eventually to activity based costing and specific required operational actions. The software tracking the map thus developed shows what must be done, when, how, why and by whom through specific supporting functions, and aids dynamic strategy construction.

Workshop Preparation

The process was initiated through a one-day workshop, attended by all senior members of Target Accountancy together with a range of staff from a variety of departments.

The Knowledge Positioning Matrix (KPM)

The KPM was developed to accommodate the core competency dimensions, as shown in Figure 1. The four quadrants provide a means for noting the knowledge that is strategically needed, and is already known; the knowledge that is required, but is not known; knowledge that is known, but not strategically required; and gaps in knowledge that do not bear on strategy anyway. Target Accountancy wanted to know whether its current set of core competencies were sufficiently robust to maximise their competitive performance. The company thus wanted to know what it *needed* to know (i.e., if only we knew what we needed to know) as opposed to the familiar saying "if only we knew what we know", to identify gaps in required knowledge, and to identify areas of knowledge that were no longer required. In other words, the company wanted to know which core competencies should be modified, deleted and created.

The StratAchieve Structure

The method naturally provides the structure and operations for the Knowledge Positioning Matrix. Figure 2 shows a four-level map. The *vision* is the prime focus of the organisation's strategy. Each successive level below the vision provides increased detail about the vision — what it is, what it means and how it can be achieved. The mechanism that does this is through top-down *How* and bottom-up *Why* explorations and checking.

The top-most activity of the tree represents the vision in the case of a company-wide strategy or the key objective of a department, division, or sub-strategy such as a marketing or a finance strategy. The levels below the top-most activity increase in specificity so that the day-to-day actions can be specified and actioned. There is thus full alignment between the vision and the day-to-day operations.

The second level of the StratAchieve Map is occupied by the Critical Success Factors (CSFs). CSFs are the vital factors that must be successfully actioned if the vision is to be fully achieved. The third level has the core competencies which in turn must successfully produce the CSFs. Traditionally, the number of organisational core competencies is suggested as five or six (Robson, 1994) at the maximum.

The top-down *How* and bottom-up *Why* structuring also provides the all-important alignment from the vision to the operational competencies on the lowest level of the StratAchieve Map. Only through this logical connectivity can alignment be achieved. This also provides a clear understanding to the fourth-level operational competencies. This also provides a clear understanding of what operational competencies must be actioned to achieve the core competencies, the CSFs and the vision. The process then provides for detailed operational specification of the requirement.

Knowing What We Need to Know

As mentioned, organisations need to "know what they need to know" (and know what they don't know) to make strategic decisions on various fronts. The first task in actioning the Knowledge Positioning Matrix is thus to establish "what needs to be known". From this capture, what is known and not known can then be determined.

To establish "what needs to be known", a set of core competencies was logically produced from the CSFs (top-down Hows) and verified through the operational competencies (bottom-up Whys). A fourth level of operational competencies were initially produced through logical How unpackings from the core competencies. Figure 2 shows two of the core competencies identified at the workshop, namely Customer Relationships and Requirements Satisfaction.

Although it would have been competitively desirable for Target Accountancy to action every operational competency, in practice this was not

Figure 2. A four-level StratAchieve Map showing all four company CSFs and two of the core competencies

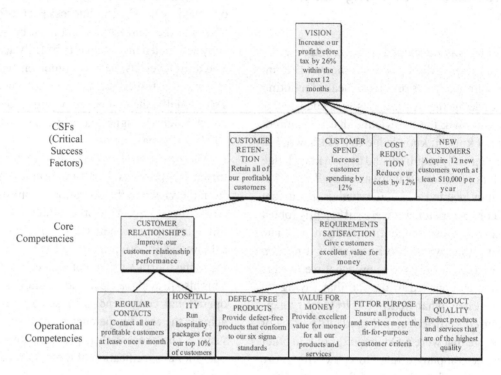

feasible through resource and time constraints.

In the course of establishing "what we need to know", it was found that two of the competencies were not distinct but instead were linked in a parent-child relationship. Figure 3 shows that two core competencies, namely Value for Money and Product Quality, share two child operational competencies. The more children that share the same two parents indicate the amount of overlapping of the parent activities. As a consequence of producing the StratAchieve Map, it was found that Product Quality should be a sub-set of Value for Money. Figure 4 shows how this competency structure was re-configured to account for the family resemblance.

Figure 5 shows two core competencies, Customer Satisfaction and Product Quality. Each has a set of identical sub-activities. This duplication of sub-activities indicates that the two seemingly different core competencies are actually the same because they share exactly the same competency children. The degree of similarity between competencies is thus verifiable through the amount of shared sub-activities. Where there are no shared sub-activities, the core competencies are distinctly separate. The workshop delegates wanted to Product Quality to be featured on the StratAchieve Map and therefore showed it as a sub-activity. Alternatively, they could have eliminated the activity, and shown its two sub-activities under Customer Satisfaction.

Need to Know and Do Know

Once the set of core competencies were identified (need to know), the next stage was to identify

Figure 3. Product Quality shares child competencies fully with Value for Money which means Product Quality is a sub-competency

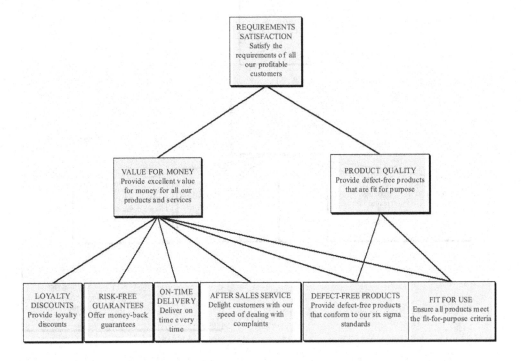

which core competencies were known (available expertise) and those that were unknown (unavailable expertise). Figure 2 shows how the CSF, *Customer Retention* was unpacked, first into the respective core competencies, and then into operational competencies.

At the workshop, delegates were asked to produce a knowledge map showing their key actions. A comparison was then made between the logically derived core competencies using StratAchieve and those competencies actually held by the individuals. Several competencies were matched while others were unmatched. Examples are shown in Figure 1.

Need to Know and Don't Know

The StratAchieve Why and How creations and connections produced the activity "use the In-

ternet to increase sales". It was agreed that this activity was important enough to be regarded as a potential core competency, where new skills would be needed. The exercise thus identified a knowledge gap, identifying what should be possessed as expertise and what was lacking.

The logical operational competency "operate hospitality packages" was created from the core competency "improve our customer relationship performance". The workshop delegates agreed that this activity (operate hospitality packages) was an important competency that needed to be included in the strategy as part of the core competency "improve our customer relationship performance".

A further action the company took after the workshop was to determine which competencies they lacked and needed to purchase through recruitment and consultancy. The core competencies

Figure 4. The revised structure showing Product Quality is a sub-set of Value for Money

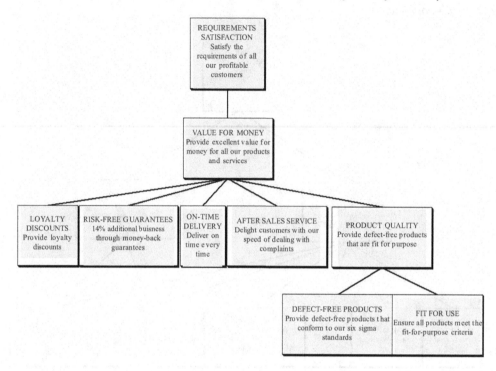

Figure 5. Product Quality and Customer Satisfaction are semantic duplications

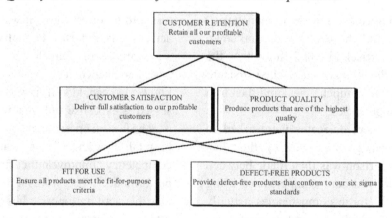

were also prioritised, based on agreed criteria such as contribution impact on the CSFs, resource demands (cost implications) and risk quantification. Through this process, it was possible to weight the core competencies and produce a ranked order of importance. Although supported within the method, this is not detailed further here.

Don't Need to Know and Know

The Knowledge Positioning Matrix shows "provide doctoring services to ailing companies" as a known competency, but one that does not have any impact on the current company-wide CSFs. Thus is because there is no logical Why connection into the newly formed CSFs. For example, there is no *Why* connect to Customer Retention since once the customer's company has been restored it will cease to be a customer. With no logical connection for this in the developed map, it was thus excluded.

Don't Need to Know and Don't Know

It follows that not knowing what we do not need to know is a null set and therefore is left blank in the Knowledge Positioning Matrix.

CONCLUSION

This paper described the importance of core competencies and demonstrated the utility of the StratAchieve method for testing the validity of knowledge-laden core competencies for strategic goals. It has shown how to test core competencies for logical compatibility with the strategy plan as well as to identify core competencies that are essential for strategic success. The software support links these logically, and through separate functionality relates them to timescales, costing, human resources, and progress indicators for subsequent monitoring. In doing this, we needed to unpack the meaning of the word "know". For example, in the phrase *do we know what we need to know,* two uses of the term can be discerned, namely know-what and know-how respectively. Both relate to awareness, not necessarily the skills available.

The case study has demonstrated the formulation of a corporate strategy from a consideration of the core operational activities and associated knowledge competencies forming the organisation's intellectual capital resource. Meanings of the operational and other activities that produce the emergence of achieved strategic objectives have been systematically elicited, negotiated, and agreed within a multi-stakeholder framework, which explicitly links the strategic requirement to the necessary activities and identifies the knowledge requirements for each strategic objective.

Although simplified and indicative examples only have been shown here, linked and cohesive *Strategy Trees* for major business functions have been produced in a form that translates directly into actionable specifications, with a motivated logic chain of abstraction upwards towards, or implementation downwards from, strategic activities and competencies. Core strategic competencies, such as "contact all our profitable customers monthly" have been illustrated to show the alignment of activities, and how a competency at one level can provide an advantage at another. Equally less advantageous competencies, without strategic import, are highlighted by the method. An emphasis on the terminology and meanings understood within the company, and its reporting norms, helps strategy ownership and implementation. A sort of "mediated objectivity" applies, which explicitly links the strategic requirement to the necessary activities and identifies the knowledge requirements for each one.

By expressing the required activities in the structure the focus is shifted towards dynamic strategy achievement through knowledge capability, rather than merely managing the organisational resources and by-products of business activity. Evaluation of the strategy is provided for within the method, though beyond the scope of this paper to describe. Monitoring, activity based costing, resource allocation, and progress and performance indicators are all linked explicitly to the strategy model developed. During the case study, each core competency was analysed to determine its value and hence impact contribution on the company's goals and vision. This core competency valuation and ranking method has been the subject of ongoing research.

The case study reported in this paper is one of several conducted over a 15-year period with organisations large and small, public and private and whilst the case is unique, the methods involved are considered generic and stable. Individual studies such as this one lie within a "declared intellectual framework of systemic ideas, ultimately allowing general lessons to be extracted and discussed" as recommended by Checkland (1991, p. 401).

Although a case study does not aim at generalisation rich, contextual understanding and utility value are indicated. Apart from the direct pragmatic value to the organisation, the "story told" in reporting the notion of mediated objectivity may help convey insights that transfer to the understanding of similar situations. Results from action research studies can provide rich and useful descriptions, enhancing learning and understanding which may itself be abstractly transferable to other organisations, or provide an underpinning to future inductive theory development. This potentially allows further contextualisation of the work in the more nomothetic terms implicit in multiple case study research designs.

This case study has shown the development of strategy: further action research with the company will evaluate its impact and value. In general through work with this, and with other organisations we aim to develop a competency valuation method so that the value of operational competencies in relation to strategy may be assessed.

ACKNOWLEDGMENT

We thank the participants at Target Accountancy, three anonymous reviewers and the associate editors for constructive comments on earlier versions

REFERENCES

AMERIN Products. (n.d). *Creating value from intangible assets and human capital.* Retrieved July 12, 2005, from http://www.amerin.com.au/products.htm

Berkman, E. (2001). *When bad things happen to good ideas.* Retrieved July 20, 2004, from http://www.darwinmag.com/read/040101/badthingscontent.html

Bollinger, A. S. & Smith, R. D. (2001). Managing knowledge as a strategic asset. *Journal of Knowledge Management, 5*(1), 8-18.

Carlisle, Y. (1999). Strategic thinking and knowledge management. In *OU MBA Managing Knowledge Readings Part 1* (pp. 19-29). Milton Keynes: Open University Business School.

Chatzkel, J. (2000). A conversation with Hubert Saint-Onge. *Journal of Intellectual Capital, 1*(1), 101-115.

Checkland, P. B. (1991). From framework through experience to learning: the essential nature of action research. In H. E. Nissen, H. K. Klein, & R. Hirschheim (Eds.), *Information systems research: Contemporary approaches and emergent traditions.* Amsterdam: International Federation for Information Processing (IFIP).

Clare, M. & DeTore, A. W. (2000). *Knowledge assets.* San Diego: Harcourt.

Dawson, R. (2000). Knowledge capabilities as the focus of organisational development. *Journal of*

Knowledge Management, 4(4), 320-327.

Edvinsson, L. & Malone, M. S. (1997). *Intellectual capital.* New York: Harper Collins.

Graham, A. B. & Pizzo V. G. (1996). A question of balance: Case studies in strategic knowledge management. *European Management Journal, 14*(4), 338-346. Reprinted in Klein DA (q.v.).

Hackney, R., Burn, J., & Dhillon, G. (2000). Challenging assumptions for strategic information systems planning. Theoretical perspectives. *Communications of the AIS, 3*(9).

Hatten, K. J. & Rosenthal, S. R. (1999). Managing the process centred enterprise. *Long Range Planning, 32*(3), 293-310.

Hatten, K. J. & Rosenthal, S. R. (2001). *Reaching for the knowledge edge.* New York: AMACOM.

Kaplan, R. S. & Norton, D. P. (1996). *The balanced scorecard.* Boston: Harvard Business School Press.

Kaplan, R. S. & Norton, D. P. (2004). *Strategy maps.* Boston: Harvard Business School Press.

Klein, D. A. (Ed.). (1998). *The strategic management of intellectual capital.* Boston: Butterworth-Heinemann.

Leonard-Barton, D. (1995). *Wellsprings of knowledge.* Boston: Harvard Business School Press.

Prahalad, C. K. & Hamel, G. (1990). The core competence of the corporation. *Harvard Business Review, 68*(3), 79-91.

Robson, R. (1994). *Strategic management and information systems.* London: Pitman.

Sawyer, K. (1990). *Dealing with complex organisational problems.* PhD Consortium, International Conference on Information Systems (ICIS), Copenhagen.

Sawyer, K. (1990). Goals, purposes and the strategy tree. *Systemist, 12*(4), 76-82.

Yin, R. K. (2002). *Case study research: Design and methods* (3rd ed.). Newbury Park: Sage.

Zack, M. H. (1999). Developing a knowledge strategy. *Californian Management Review, 41*(3), 125-145.

ENDNOTES

[1]   The valuation of intellectual capital is significant: the most authoritative estimates typically suggest that around 75% of a company's value lies in its intangible assets (Handy [cited in Edvinsson & Malone, 1997; Kaplan & Norton, 2004, p. 4]).

[2]   StratAchieve™ is a registered mark of Keith Sawyer.

This work was previously published in International Journal of Knowledge Management, Vol. 2, Issue 1, edited by M. E. Jennex, pp. 58-71, copyright 2006 by IGI Publishing, formerly known as Idea Group Publishing (an imprint of IGI Global).

Chapter III
Implementing Supply Chain Management in the New Era:
A Replenishment Framework for the Supply Chain Operations Reference Model

William Y. C. Wang
University of South Australia, Australia

Michael S. H. Heng
Universitas 21 Global, Singapore

Patrick Y. K. Chau
The University of Hong Kong, Hong Kong

ABSTRACT

Combining with the collaborations between business customers and suppliers, traditional purchasing and logistics functions have evolved into a broader concept of materials and distribution management, namely, supply chain management (SCM) (Tan, 2001). This chapter reviews the literature of SCM from several paths that can be the basis of a proposed framework for SCM within academic and managerial contexts. In addition, it includes the approaches of supply chain operations reference (SCOR) model, which was developed by the Supply Chain Council and is recognised as a diagnostic tool for SCM worldwide. This chapter also summarises the literature of performance control and risk issues in SCM and the SCOR Model and discusses a proposed framework for the future research.

INTRODUCTION

A supply chain is established when there is an integration of operations across its constituent entities, namely, the suppliers, partners, and business customers (Narasimhan & Mahapatra, 2004). It is an observation that individual firms compete as integral parts of supply chains in the global markets. Moreover, the evolution of information technology (IT) has particularly generated growing attention on searching for ways to improve product quality, customer services, and operation efficiency and remaining competitive by supply chain collaboration. As noted by Strader, Lin, and Shaw (1999), ". . .there has been a general movement towards organizing as partnerships between more specialised firms or business units as IT enables the costs of coordination decrease" (p. 361), implying the impact of IT and potential advances of supply chain management (SCM). A number of researchers and practitioners have, therefore, devoted their efforts to various approaches to manage the constituents and activities of a supply chain since the early 1980s. Yet conceptually, the management of supply chains has not been well organised or understood. Academia has continuously highlighted the necessity for clear definitional constructs and frameworks on SCM (Croom, Romano, & Giannakis, 2000; New & Mitropoulos, 1995; Saunders, 1997).

However, SCM research, which draws on industrial economics, information systems, marketing, financing, logistics and interorganisational behaviour, has a fragmented nature and lacks a universal model. Hence, what we set out to construct in this chapter are the general theoretical and managerial domains of SCM, thereby, attempting to contribute to the development of such discipline. The literature is surveyed to identify the cognitive components of the current subject, as it is a key question for any applied social research that concerns the strategic approach taken to its mapping (Tranfield & Starkey, 1998).

Theoretical models are needed in order to inform the understanding of the supply chain phenomena. An illustration of industrial dynamics in Forrester's (1958) model in fact instantiates the possibility of such applications that aid the comprehension of material flows along the supply chain. Further, it has remarkably laid the foundation for subsequent advancement of supply chain analyses and understandings (e.g., Min & Zhou, 2002; New & Payne, 1995; Sterman, 1989; Towill, Naim, & Wilker, 1992). SCM is not only concerned with the extraction of raw materials to their end of useful life, it also focuses on how firms utilise their suppliers' processes, technology, and capability to enhance sustainable competitive advantage (Farley, 1997). When all organisational entities along the supply chain act coherently, operation effectiveness is achieved throughout the systems of suppliers. Cooper, Ellram, Gardner, and Hawk (1997) advocate such a concept, and further indicate that much of SCM literature is predicated on the adoption and extension of extant theoretical concepts.

Our chapter is not so much a critical review of the literature as a taxonomy with which to map the subsequent research. In this context, it is our intention to try to provide a framework for conducting a project of supply chain management.

This chapter is organised into five sections corresponding to the initial idea of the book layout. In the first section, the supply chain operations reference (SCOR) model is introduced (SCC, 2001), underlying the common aspects and approaches, as it has gradually become a widely accepted standard of supply chain management in industry from its initial launch in 1996. One of the goals in this chapter is to identify the limitations of the SCOR Model and, therefore, to suggest a framework and supply chain implementation. Aligning with the SCOR model, we map the possible research areas by proposing a framework as a domain of research in supply chain design and for the managerial concerns in a project of supply chain management. The next section considers the bodies of literature associated with the stakeholder theory and network theory in organisational studies, which are applied to the interorganizational context (e.g., Premukumar, 2000; Rogers, 2004; Windsor, 1998). Then, we focus on the how to bridge the gaps towards the integration of the supply chain. We further explain the elements for facilitating transformation of the supply chain associated with business processes, organisation structure, and performance control in the following section. The chapter concludes with a summary with some conclusions that can be drawn from the content in terms of moving towards a coherent approach to supply chain management.

FINDING THE SUPPLY CHAIN CHALLENGES WITH THE SCOR MODEL

There is a profusion of literature related to the landscape of supply chain management. Various aspects can be found as the constituents of this subject, which leads to a confusion of meaning (New & Payne, 1995), thus causing difficulty in laying out the scope and content of supply chain design. The term *supply chain management* has not only been associated with logistics activities in the literature but also with the planning and control of materials and information flows of an enterprise, both internally and externally. Additionally, strategic issues, resources, interorganizational relationships, and even governmental intervention have been addressed in extant studies (e.g., Thorelli, 1986; Wang & Heng, 2004), and others discuss the effects of network externality (e.g., Gulati, 1999). These research domains are indeed relevant to the understanding of supply chain context; however, in this chapter, we consider the direct challenges that an enterprise may encounter in order to implement supply chain management. Therefore, the issues in the subsequent discussion follow the logical sequences of SCOR that have been widely adopted by industries such as AT&T, Boeing, and ACER for supply chain diagnosis and design.

The Supply Chain Operations Reference Model

Developed in 1996, SCOR is a standard model of supply chain processes and is used similarly to International Organization for Standardization (ISO) documents for intra-enterprise processes. The SCOR model also builds on the concepts of business process reengineering (BPR), performance measurement, and logistics management by integrating these techniques into a configurable, cross-functional framework. It is a model that links business processes, performance indicators (metrics), and suggested actions (best practice and the features). It was developed to be configurable and aggregates a series of hierarchical process components that can be used as a common language for enterprises to describe the supply chains and communicate with each other (Huang, Scheoran, & Keskar, 2005; SCC, 2001).

The SCOR model follows a set of "top-down" procedures, commencing from the corporate-level strategy that the procedures can help to identify thousands of business activities inside an organisation and spanning across the boundaries of the supply chain entities. The document of the SCOR model includes the following elements as a communicative platform among enterprise owners, project leaders, and corporate consultants of the supply chain planning activities:

- Standard descriptions of each business process along the supply chain that are categorised as "Plan," "Source," "Make," and "Delivery." There are also other two categories defining the product return as "Return"[1] and the supportive activities as "Enabler."
- Key performance indicators (KPI) are defined and classified by the attributes accompanying with each of the business processes; for example, "Total Source Cycle Time to Completion" is a KPI in the attribute of

"Supply Chain Responsiveness" of Source activities.

- Best practices are brought up in the SCOR model as recommendations if the diagnosis of certain processes by KPI shows the necessity for improvement.
- Identification of the associative software functionalities that can enable the best practices for business processes reengineering.

This SCOR model consists of four levels as the analytical stages leading to the implementation of an effective SCM strategy. The five distinct business processes, Plan, Source, Make, Deliver, and Return, are within the Level 1 stage and should be further decomposed into processes categories pending on the activities involved. Hence, Level 2 defines the core process categories that can be found in an actual and idealised supply chain around an enterprise. For example, the "source" category includes "source stocked products," "source made-to-order (MTO) products," and "source engineered-to-order (ETO) products" (Table 1). These different types of channel activities derive from the three major customer demands. Making stocked products corresponds to the situation of unknown demand quantities and

expects easily procurement of the raw materials, while making MTO and ETO products requires the accuracy of demand forecasting and transparent market estimation.

Because of the customer-oriented nature, the delivery processes actually affects the associated Make and Source activities, and hence the SCOR model spans at least the interactions of information and material flows from the understanding of aggregate demand to the fulfillment of each order. To portrait the business processes by recording down the Level 1 and Level 2 activities of current supply chain is also called "As-Is" stage, which requires the project team to canvas the business environment of an enterprise that should normally include two ties from the core firm (the centre of a supply chain, definition can be seen in Banerji & Sambharya, 1998, and Wang & Heng, 2002), that is, "the customer's customer" and the "supplier's supplier."

To begin with, it suggests an analysis to prepare the Level 1 document as to geographical context so as to reveal the transportation costs and trading relationships between the legal entities. Then, the diagram at Level 2 can be developed to describe the information flows of forecasts/orders and the material flow with the types of goods produced and delivered by connecting the business processes

Table 1. Supply chain activities based on SCOR level 1 & 2 (Adapted from SCC, 2001)

Plan		Source		Make		Deliver	
P1	Plan Supply Chain	S1	Source Stocked Product	M1	Make-to-Stock	D1	Deliver Stocked Product
P2	Plan Source	S2	Source MTO Product	M2	Make-to-Order	D2	Deliver MTO Product
P3	Plan Make						
P4	Plan Deliver	S3	Source ETO Product	M3	Engineering-to-Order	D3	Deliver ETO Product
Source Return				**Deliver Return**			
SR1	SR2	SR3		DR1	DR2		DR3
R1: Return Defective Product			R2: Return MRO Product			R3: Return Excess Product	

involved. Software has recently been developed to computerise the SCOR elements in enacting the interrelations of the processes, for example, ScorWizard, IBS Business Intelligence (BI), and i2 Enterprise Resource Planning (ERP) solutions. These are relatively helpful in simulating different scenarios based on the business strategies.

The SCOR model at Level 1 and Level 2 reveals the supply chain in a simplified way, thus enhancing its overall flexibility (Huang et al., 2005). Level 3 represents the decomposition of Level 2 processes in an interrelated way. For instance, there are four Level 3 components

decomposed from P1 (Plan Supply Chain), as shown in Figure 1:

- P1.1 – identify, prioritize, and aggregate production requirements
- P1.2 – identify, assess, and aggregate supply chain resources
- P1.3 – balance supply chain resources with supply chain requirements
- P1.4 – establish and communicate supply chain plans

To accomplish the Level 3 activities, the "To-Be" (future) processes model is developed to sup-

Figure 1. The "top-down" approach in implementing the SCOR model (Adapted from SCC, 2001)

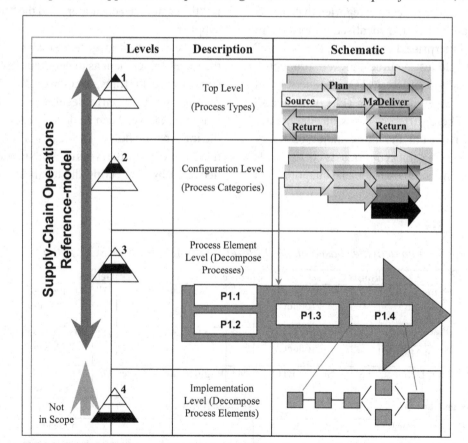

Notes: P1.1—Identify, prioritize, and aggregate supply-chain requirements; P1.2—Identify, assess, and aggregate supply-chain requirements; P1.3—Balance production resources with supply-chain requirements; P1.4—Establish and communicate supply-chain plans

port strategic objectives that should work within the new supply chain configuration at Level 2. At this level, all SCOR processes are interconnectively designed and running as an operation cycle of planning, execution, and enabling by certain frequency. The supply chain components at Level 4 are acting as the work statement that is expected to be set up by the project team without standardised documents. Eventually, the completed four levels become the guidelines for implementing supply chain management.

The SCOR model has become a topical issue, attracting not only the interest of enterprises themselves, but of industrial associations and government. Contrary to the industrial emphasis, there is a scarcity of academic literature regarding the application, adoption, benefits, and limitations of SCOR model, except for very few reports such as Huang et al. (2005) and Wang, Ho, and Chau (2005). The aspects of the framework that are of interests for further study in the literature are discussed in the subsequent sections.

THE PARTICIPANTS' ROLE IN SUPPLY CHAIN MANAGEMENT

When configuring a supply chain, it is necessary to identify who the stakeholders within the channel context are. However, an inclusion of all potential partners might complicate the analysis of the complete supply chain, since it may explode the number of partners added from one tier to another (Cooper et al., 1997; Min & Zhou, 2002). The key is to target the supply chain entities that are critical to the value-added processes and are manageable by the core firm, that is, the centre of a supply chain targeted and is influential and powerful to its affiliate firms (Banerji & Sambharya, 1998; Wang & Heng, 2002).

As noted by Lambert, Cooper, and Pagh (1998), marketing research has contributed to identifying the members in a supply chain context, describing the needs for channel coordination, and drawing a marketing network. There are also studies with similar aspects from the area of strategic alliances and business network (e.g., Liu & Brookfield 2000) that are concerned about the germination of channel structure and participants. Lambert et al. (1998) further claim that the extant literature has not built on early contributions to put an emphasis on the complete supply chain from suppliers, manufacturers, distributors, and product brand owners. Indeed, one of the major weaknesses of SCM literature is the assumption that everyone knows the participants within the scope of SCM.

In a complete supply chain, there are primary stakeholders of SCM who actually perform operational and managerial activities in the channel processes and secondary stakeholders playing the roles of supporting entities such as the banks and freighters (Lambert et al., 1998). Although such classification may not be clear in all cases, it helps to identify the key customers who trigger the supply chain flows from demands and the major suppliers for value-added activities. From this starting point, the current SCOR model that only spans two tiers of the core firm becomes insufficient for analytical purpose, since the channel structure is quite often not a linear type and the supporting participants are not included in the analysing scope of the SCOR model.

Understanding the structural dimension of supply chains is a prerequisite for analysing and configuring the process links among channel members (Min & Zhou, 2002). The supply chain is derived from the interrelationships of its stakeholders that actually cause a multidimensional structure. Lambert et al.'s (1998) supply chain network indicates that there are two structural dimensions: horizontal and vertical, as shown in Figure 2. The horizontal structure represents the numbers of tiers along the analytical scope of a supply chain, and the vertical structure represents the number of partners within each tier.

Based on such aspect, a change of channel partners will alter the dimension of the supply

Figure 2. Supply chain network structure

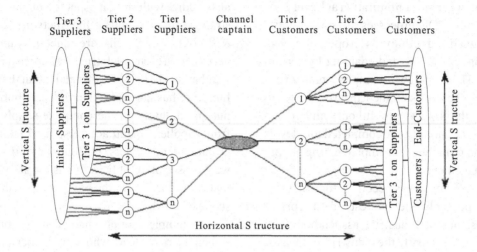

chain. For example, the horizontal spectrum may become narrower when some entities merge with others. Outsourcing decisions may further change the scope and structure of supply network. In fact, some outsourcing firms can form various network formations other than the tier structure, such as rings, stars, or fans (Liu & Brookfield, 2000; Wang & Heng, 2002). The shifting of the supply chain scope (or, in some literature, the boundaries of the business network), which is normally caused by the strategic moves toward channel partners, eventually affects existing design and current managerial performance of SCM. A recent example is the case of the ACER Group which is associated with the shifting of channel structure that is reported by Wang and Ho (2005).

Despite a delicate design and implementation of global SCM and ERP systems, the ACER Group has suffered from a low retention rate of IT professionals of ERP systems and a lack of patterns for business processes reallocation in new manufacturing bases. These challenges are actually due to insufficient ante-consideration of potential business reallocation. When a sudden rundown occurred at several subordinates with reduced production volume in The Philippines and operation scale in Canada, it was somehow too late to adjust the plans of SCM. Therefore, it is necessary to identify the proper scope for a SCM project with the entities involved and then determine which aspects (e.g., geographical ranges and time period) of the supply chain network should be configured (Min & Zhou, 2002). Comparing the SCOR model, there are at least three limitations that can be found; they are:

- SCOR can only present business flow in between legal or geographical entities, not any matrix organisational structure or the concept of "virtual enterprise".
- SCOR is limited to the presentation of one single supply chain, while most enterprises may be associated with multiple channels of markets and products.
- The activities of collaborative design and customer relationships management are not defined in SCOR.

In brief, modeling a supply chain requires the analysis of relationships among channel participants and the structures formed. Thus, a clear picture for defining the scope of a SCM project can be presented. Moreover, these processes may connect multitiered supply chains as the core firm is actively involved in tier one and a number of other links beyond it. The direct involvement of a core firm may not only allocate physical resources but also interorganizational powers, technology, and knowhow to its trading partners. There is also indirect involvement from non-integral parts of the supply chain structure, but it can influence the operations of channel participants. Those different characteristics of trading relationships affect the firms' decisions regarding resource allocation that lead to the concerns in supply chain configuration.

IMPLEMENTATION OF CHANNEL INTEGRATION

The Transformation toward the "To-Be" Stage

Subsequent to the right analysis and design of supply chain management, this section discusses issues in the implementation of SCM. Using the terminology of the SCOR model, it is the "To-Be" stage. Figure 3 shows the most common goals and components of the transformation that involves human factors, business processes, and the technology, so as to build up a unified order desk, purchasing channels, delivery tracking, and so on, for the support of supply chain decision. Although the SCOR model is a widely adopted industrial standard and possibly the only one it

Figure 3. The components of implementing SCM projects from As-Is to To-Be

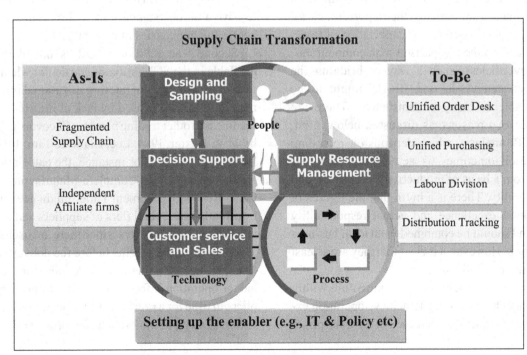

has not successfully addressed a transforming framework from the stages of "As-Is" to "To-Be" for SCM projects. In particular, it merely handles the components of business processes and technology without tackling any social factors or human issues.

The previous section has portrayed the "top-down" approaches by utilising SCOR model as a standard. That approach requires the team of a SCM project to lay out existing business processes and use the suggested SCOR metrics to diagnose current problems for the implementation of ideal SCM. At least the Level 1 and Level 2 business processes should be confirmed so that hundreds of metrics can be then applied to measure the current operation excellence along the specific supply chain, such as "day of inventory" (Level 2) in the category of cash-to-cash cycle time (Level 1) and "supplier on time and in full delivery" (Level 2) in the category of delivery performance (Level 1). The step of measuring KPI of the supply chain activities belongs to the second stage of SCOR, namely "gap analysis," which underpins the design of "To-Be" processes. In other words, the differences between current status and ideal performance are actually the opportunities for improvement based on the expectation of target firms and on the comparison with competitors.

Nevertheless, such a way of bridging the gap between "As-Is" and "To-Be" might not be applicable to many circumstances. There are at least two reasons, as discussed below. First, the KPI analysis, which depends on recording operation outcomes, is actually a measuring tool from a basis of productivity, efficiency, and profitability. There is a myth that the figures of operation excellence and actual responsibility can and should be combined in an ideal business situation. However, it is clear that they are at least partially contradictory.

First, on the one hand, the business units within a supply chain must try to achieve operation excellence for survival, and each of the enterprises

has the pressure and duty to earn a higher return on its shareholders' equity than occurred before the SCM project. The KPI figures that are made create trust on the part of investors and are usually reflected in short-term operation efficiency, making it easier to project to an image of corporate success. These indicators are not only a sort of management result, but also a source of enterprise competitive health and wealth at a supply chain context.

On the other hand, supply chain participants are networks of parties that work together by trading relationships toward both a shared goal and individual interests without being merely economic machines. Although an SCM initiator (mostly the core firms) represents a major role of the value of channel participants, it does not necessarily have enough power to force its partners to follow the integration contents. Likewise, it is also important for trust to develop between the SCM initiator and its external partners and other interest groups. Such trust can only be built up from ensuring that the perceived value of all entities and stakeholders along the supply chain are taken into account. However, it may be difficult to have a unique standard of KPI measurement across the boundaries of enterprises.

Second, the KPI of SCOR is not always available in the SCM initiator, particular when it involves the sharing of interorganizational information. It may be caused by lack of information readiness in other trading partners (Iacovou, Benbasat, & Dexter, 1995; Lee, Clark, & Tam, 1999; Wang et al., 2005). For instance, the calculation for the indicator of "Complete Manufacture to Order Ready for Shipment Time" might need the information of several tiers of suppliers and collaborative manufacturers, since there are usually several working segments before the delivery of final products. As such, the SCM initiator must gather operation information from various suppliers in time for a precise estimation of this KPI. Unfortunately, in the brick-and-mortar world, it is not easy to ensure equal systems readiness between an SCM initiator and its trading partners, albeit even the headquarter may find it difficult to obtain confidential information from its subordinators because their interests are potentially contradictory.

Last but not the least, KPI analysis has a limitation in corresponding to the strategic choices. For example, a SCM initiator may consider "Perfect Order Fulfil Rate" to be the most important target in the very beginning, when the distributors have equal or much more power than it does. This occurs in the supply chain of the Taiwanese IT industry (e.g., Wistron, Accton, and Asus); many of them initiate their projects of global logistics management with the major players such as Dell and IBM. They have to give in to the benefits of reducing inventory level for channel competency. Only when they ensure the higher bargain power with their customers would they adjust the ratio of some KPI evaluations along the supply chain.

Major Approaches of the Transformation

In a matrix of two-dimensional content analysis, Croom et al. (2000) highlight four major categories of supply chain elements for trading exchanges by summarising the extant literature. These categories are assets, information, knowledge, and relationships. In Croom et al.'s (2000) framework, SCM elements are further divided into three levels of dyadic, chain, and network forms. These elements are much richer than those defined in the SCOR model, which are very limited in the categories of assets and information and still less than the two-dimensional framework just mentioned. For example, SCOR does not include the analysis of total cost ownership (asset), business network redesign (information), human resource planning (knowledge), or trust/power/commitment (relationship). However, there is, in particular, a scarcity of research on knowledge elements for SCM that lead to their unclear and inconsistent

presence in the literature. The few examples are the subjects of knowledge with time-based capabilities in production activities (Handfield & Nichols, 1999) and configure-to-order for customised sales (Ton & Liao, 2002). The last category of Croom et al.'s (2000) framework is associated with "soft" elements, since relationship is a social tie existing among the supply chain entities. Although there have not been any widely accepted methods in industry (nor in SCOR) for managing the supply chain relationships, some scholars have considered it to be the most important figure in SCM. For example, Handfield and Nichols (1999) indicate that the efforts of other elements for implementing SCM in managing the flows of information and materials are likely to be unsuccessful if there is not a solid foundation of effective relationships in the channel context.

In order to mark up the insufficiency of the SCOR model and to map the Croom et al.'s (2000) elements, we propose a method in bridging current gaps for the SCM transformation processes. As shown in Figure 4, there are four major approaches, namely, KPI analysis, problem/opportunities analysis, expectation/constraints, and the experts' opinions, which can be amended to the SCOR model as explained next.

- **KPI analysis:** This approach follows the typical "top-down" SCOR analytical processes and is relevant when most operation figures are recorded and updated regularly. Since it requires information across the boundaries of firms, the SCM adopters may often encounter difficulties by merely using such an approach. It is even true in the situation in which most channel participants are subordinates or in joint ventures of a particular adopter because of unequal readiness of IT infrastructure or conflictions of management interests.

- **Problem/opportunity analysis:** When identifying the processes "gaps" by KPI information becomes less achievable, it is

Figure 4. Bridging the gap of the supply chain transformation

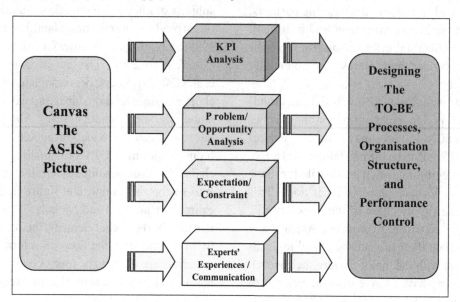

possible to find out the existing problems and difficulties by interviewing the employees from both upstream and downstream of the supply chain. Contrary to the KPI analysis that starts by enacting the supply chain strategy and comparing existing performance and the targets, problem/opportunity analysis is rather a "bottom-up" approach. It is suggested that the SCM project participants record various feedback and then map them into the different levels of SCOR processes. For instance, the KPI of "day sales receivable outstanding" in the Delivery element of SCOR Level 2 is related to the processes performance of the sales department. The same goal of identifying the SCM gaps can thus be achieved by directly finding problem/opportunity through individual interviewing and observation.

- **Expectation/constraint:** One of the successful key factors in implementing an SCM project is the participants' attitude with commitment to collaborative improvements. It

will affect the information gathering for KPI and problem analyses and the subsequent actions for supply chain modification that is sometimes accompanied by the adjustment of existing benefits among channel members. For example, the delivery routes, supply chain policies of pricing and return of goods, and requirements of forecasting between buyers-suppliers may be altered after the SCM implementation. It is, therefore, necessary to find out the expectations/constraints of channel participants so as to avoid the potential conflictions among supply chain entities.

Another example is that examining the demand management processes of the SCM initiator might lead to a tentative solution of implementing collaborative planning, forecasting and replenishment (CPFR) systems as suggested by SCOR model. However, doing so might require the adoption of new IT infrastructures and cause changes to the existing demand management processes in some of the suppliers. It is inevitable that compromises will have to be made in order for the transformation to happen in upstream and downstream of a supply chain. There are a few points should be considered when identifying the expectations and constraints of the supply chain stakeholders:

- Enterprise as a participant in a business ecosystem and supply network
- Cluster of firms that gradually evolves as a group—the coevolution effects
- Gradual development of shared vision—centred around a product or product group
- Further, the role of clusters in competitiveness

The experts' experiences/communication: The last approach for the supply chain transformation is to adopt an expert opinion from a third party. A SCM project covers the areas of channel collaboration in material management, production planning, sales/distribution, quality control, assets management, and cost controlling, and requires the knowledge of a business processes enabler, such as the adoption of information systems. Acquiring expert opinions is vital to the successfulness of any SCM project, not only because of the need for the above expertise, but also in the pre-selection adoption methods, business processes design, training, and customised IT systems. That means, most likely, that firms have to get the help of consulting companies to enact the proper adoption methods and learn from others' successful experiences. Nevertheless, the SCM project owners have to interact with outside consultants who are not always familiar with the "know-how" of a particular industrial context.

Quanta Computer Inc., one of the major players in the IT industry of global market, has a sales volume of USD 10 billion in 2004. Its implementation of SCM has become a legendary story in the Taiwanese IT industry, as Quanta Computer Inc. accomplished the supply chain processes redesign with its trading partners and established its ERP

systems (a modified version of SAP) in only half a year. It is a monumental SCM implementation project, not only because of such a short period of time, but also because of the success of building up the global supply network to dramatically achieve the target of cost cutting through low-level inventories. An interesting thing was, although the consultants for the SCM project of Quanta Computer Inc. had a strong background in SAP systems, only the project manager was initially conversant with the production line of IT products. Communication and exchange of ideas thus played a significant role before the commencement of SCM adoption. In addition, Quanta Computer Inc. and its trading partners have cooperated with consultants from various global regions throughout the adoption period.

In short, the transformation of existing supply chain processes and structure relies on identifying the gaps and opportunities for improvement. Both "top-down" and "bottom-up" approaches are keys to the success of supply chain configuration now and in the future. Moreover, it is necessary to discreetly survey the stakeholders' expectations from the standpoint of various supply chain entities in order to ensure substantial benefits and learn from the anatomy of successful/failed cases via the experiences of the experts from the third party.

Combining the Performance Control into SCOR Analysis

The important leverage gained from the supply chain integration is the mitigation of risk by certain control (Min & Zhou, 2002). It is generally believed that the implementation of an SCM project consumes considerable resources of human labour, materials, and time. It will definitely have an impact on the enterprise and its trading partners. Therefore, a part of reasonable performance control is to ensure that the supply chain operates right on track.

For such consideration, there are hundreds of KPI (metrics) mapping the levels of business processes defined in the SCOR model. Whether the KPI information of the supply chain entities is available for calculation or not, it is possible to find out the existing problems and difficulties of supply chain configuration, as suggested in previous section. The recorded "As-Is" process, as illustrated in Figure 5, can be labelled in the format of normal flowchart.

Then, each of the codified processes should be analysed by a set of SIPOC diagrams (Pyzdek, 2003), which were originally used as quality control tools and can detail the information deliver (supplier), data sent (input), data generated (output), and information receiver (customer) for the purpose of systems development. This instrument allows us to see the opportunities for improving current communication interfaces among departments and trading partners. The previously identified "gaps" should be then codified, grouped, and prioritised, since some of them may cause similar

problems, affect related business processes and supply chain entities, or be overcome by integrated solutions. The grouped and prioritised "gaps" thus become the basis for creating "To-Be" scenarios that are associated with the adjustment of corporate policies, organisation structures, business flows, and information systems.

As previously discussed, most of the KPI items are naturally related to existing business processes because of their formulas for calculation. For instance, the KPI "day sales receivable outstanding" in the D element of SCOR Level 2 is related to the processes performance of sales department. As most of the SCOR metrics are related to the business processes of a single organisation, we recommend an extended table to map the cross-functional channel activities for performance monitoring encompassing the supply chain entities within the scope of an SCM project.

Formulated in another way, the business processes can be divided into two types the planing and coordinating activities owned by the supply

Figure 5. Example of current processses coding in the flowchart

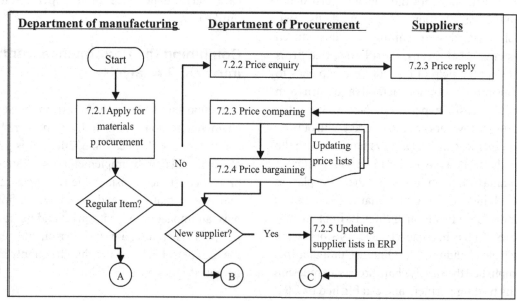

Table 2. The control panel of planning and decision-making activities

Collaborative activities			Individual Supply Chain Entities				
Business Processes	SCOR Code	'To-Be' SCOR KPI	Core firm (SCM initiator)	Distributor	Supplier 1	Supplier 2	Current Business Processes Code
Supply Chain Planing	P1 V	Provided by SCOR documents (should be further selected based on the top managers' opinion).					Recorded in 'As-Is' analysis and should be mapped into the planning processes.
Plan Sourcing	P2 V		V				
Plan Making	P3 V				V	V	
Plan Delivering	P4		V	V			

Notes: The level 3 SCOR code and the related departments of each supply chain entities should be shown on a real control panel. They are omitted in this table because of consideration of simplicity.

chain group and the operational activities of individual firms. Staff in the department of procurement in one firm might often play the role of directly and indirectly taking care of the purchasing decisions of other collaborative participants in the supply chain structure. The supply chain coordinating team may also negotiate with the customers' team to manage the suppliers' inventory level (Lambert & Pohlen, 2001). Ideally, it means that they should be evaluated both by the KPI of their original firms and the KPI of the suppliers and customers, based on certain percentages in order to monitor the two types of business processes. A control panel is thus generated in Table 2 for designing the KPI measurement and monitoring the supply chain performance.

Table 2 is an example of the control panel for planning and decision-making activities that maps the existing processes and "To-Be" processes in a project with four companies. It entails the information of how to control the supply chain functions across the boundaries of firms based on the selected KPI that are predefined by the SCOR standard. More importantly, this table contains the implications that the "gaps" between the current and future infrastructures of information exchange might be overcome by combining the current business processes codes that are embedded with SIPOC analyses and the responsible supply chain entities. One of the benefits is, for example, this joint process-metrics analysis of customer, supplier, and distributor will capture how the repositioning of inventory control improves total supply chain performance, whereas the information of inventory turns does not reflect any of the trade-offs that occurred in the channel links (Lambert & Pohlen, 2001). Consequently, it amends the insufficiency of using current SCOR metrics in the dyad and network supply chain structure.

CONCLUSION

We have stated in the foregoing sections that SCM plays a role in influencing the economic behaviour by the way business processes are managed. This, in itself, is certainly a very significant point, as it influences the costs of inventory holding, goods delivery, and manufacturing processes. In particular, it affects performance in customer fulfillment and cash-to-cash cycling, which are vital to enterprise survival (Garrison & Noreen, 2003). Achieving effectiveness of SCM does not only rely on process tuning, but also just-in-time communication and decision making through the enablers as performance measurement and information systems. Despite its importance, however, there is not much literature on the implementing framework, and most of the existing reports are individual case studies (Croom et al., 2000).

The SCOR model has been the most widely adopted standard and may be the only one for the analysis of SCM implementation. It has been modified several times since its first announcement by the Supply Chain Council in 1996. There is yet another point deserving the attention of academia and practitioners, namely, it is not a complete framework for implementation of an SCM project, but merely a referential tool for assigning business processes and associated factors of performance measures. It may actually be dysfunctional without considering the stakeholders' value/expectation and embedding the mutually owned processes into performance measurement. Therefore, we have amended its weakness by discussing the supply chain configuration and transformation and the implementation procedures.

Future research is required to test the proposed framework in actual business settings, including

Figure 5. The sequence of SCM implementation

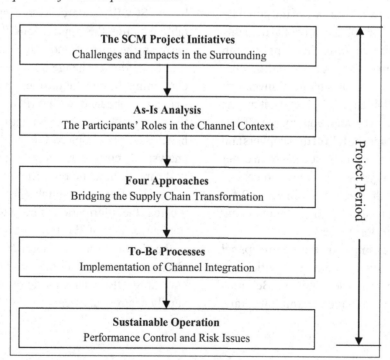

different industries and regions. Other barriers and limitations to SCM implementation and how they shall be overcome need to be further identified. These may consist of the demand up-size and down-size from order changes, for example, emergent orders or order cancelling, and the calculation of KPI for nonfinancial figures from the operation activities. To the extent that similar difficulties and solutions are identified in various supply chain context, it is possible that a refined framework can be developed for practitioners. Finally, progress should be tracked over time to prove the long-term benefits derived from implementing SCM based on such a framework.

REFERENCES

Banerji, K. ,& Sambharya, R. B. (1998). Effect of network organization on alliance formation: A study of the Japanese automobile ancillary industry. *Journal of International Management, 4*(1), 41-57.

Cooper, M. C., Ellram, L. M., Gardner, J. T., & Hank, A. M. (1997). Meshing multiple alliances. *Journal of Business Logistics, 18*(1), 67-89.

Croom, S., Romano, P., & Giannakis, M. (2000). Supply chain management: An analytical framework for critical literature review. *European Journal of Purchasing & Supply Management, 6*, 67-83.

Farley, G. A. (1997). Discovering supply chain management: A roundtable discussion. *APICS the Performance Advantage, 7*(1), 38-39.

Forrester, J. W. (1958). Industrial dynamics: A major breakthrough for decision makers. *Harvard Business Review, 36*(4), 37-66.

Garrison, R. H., & Noreen, E. W. (2003). *Managerial accounting* (10th ed.). Boston: McGraw-Hill Irwin.

Gulati, R. (1999). Network location and learning: The influence of network resources and firm capacities on alliance formation. *Strategic Management Journal, 20*(5), 397-402.

Handfield, R.B., & Nichols, E.L. (1999). *Introduction to supply chain management.* Upper Saddle River, NJ: Prentice-Hall International Editions.

Huang, S. H., Sheoran, S. K., & Keskar, H. (2005). Computer-assisted supply chain configuration based on supply chain operations reference (SCOR) model. *Computers & Industrial Engineering, 48*, 377-394.

Iacovou, C. L., Benbasat, I., & Dexter, A. S. (1995). Electronic data interchange and small organizations: Adoption and impact of technology. *MIS Quarterly, 19*(4), 465-85.

Lambert, D. M., Cooper, M. C., & Pagh, J. D. (1998). Supply chain management: Implementation issues and research opportunities. *International Journal of Logistics Management, 9*(2), 1-19.

Lambert, D. M. & Pohlen, T. L. (2001). Supply chain metrics. *International Journal of Logistics Management, 12*(1), 1-19.

Lee, H. G.., Clark, T., & Tam, K. Y. (1999). Research report: Can EDI benefit adopters? *Information System Research, 10*(2), 186-195.

Liu, R. J., & Brookfield J. (2000). Stars, rings and tiers: Organisational networks and their dynamics in Taiwan's machine tool industry. *Long Range Planning, 33*, 322-348.

Min, H., & Zhou, G. (2002). Supply chain modeling: Past, present, and future. *Computer and Industrial Engineering, 43*, 231-249.

Narasimhan, R., & Mahapatra, S. (2004). Decision models in global supply chain management. *Industrial Marketing Management, 33*, 21-27.

New, S., & Mitropoulos, I. (1995). Strategic networks: Morphology, epistemology, and praxis. *International Journal of Operations and Production Management, 16*(4), 19-34.

New, S. J., & Payne, P. (1995). Research frameworks in logistics: Three models, seven diners and a survey. *International Journal of Physical Distribution and Logistics Management, 25*(10), 60-77.

Premukumar, G. P. (2000). Interorganization systems and supply chain management: An information processing perspective. *Information Systems Management, 17*(3), 56-69.

Pyzdek, T. (2003). *The six sigma handbook, revised and expanded: The complete guide for greenbelts, blackbelts, and managers at all levels* (2nd ed.). New York: McGraw-Hill.

Rogers, S. (2004). Supply management: 6 elements of superior design. *Supply Chain Management Review, 8*(3), 48-54.

Saunders, M. J. (1997). *Strategic purchasing and supply chain management.* London: Pitman.

SCC. (2001). *Supply chain operations reference model: Overview of SCOR Version 6.2.* Pittsburgh, PA: Supply-Chain Council, Inc.

Sterman, J. D. (1989). Modeling managerial behavior: Misperceptions of feedback in a dynamic decision making experiment. *Management Science, 35*(3), 321-329.

Strader, T. J., Lin, F. R., & Shaw, M. (1999). Business-to-business electronic commerce and convergent assembly supply chain management. *Journal of Information Technology, 14*, 361-373.

Tan, K. C. (2001). A framework of supply chain management literature. *European Journal of Purchasing & Supply Management, 7*, 39-48.

Thorelli, H. B. (1986). Networks: Between markets and hierarchies. *Strategic Management Journal, 17*, 37-51.

Ton, L. L., & Liao, M. H. (2002). Optimized simulation of SCM: Cases on NB and PCB industries. In *Proceedings of the PCB Conferences on Production and Management.* (In Chinese)

Towill, D. R., Naim, M. M., & Wikner, J. (1992). Industrial dynamics simulation models in the design of supply chains. *International Journal of Physical Distribution and Logistics Management, 22*(5), 3-13.

Tranfield, D. & Starkey, K. (1998). The nature, social organization and promotion of management research: Towards policy. *British Journal of Management, 9*, 341-353.

Wang, W. Y. C., & Heng, M. S. H. (2002). Boundaries of business network in supply chain: Overcoming SMEs barriers in implementing business-to-business integration. In *Proceedings of the 4th International Conference on Electronic Commerce*, Hong Kong.

Wang, W. Y. C., & Heng, M. S. H. (2004). Bridging B2B e-commerce gaps for Taiwanese SMEs: Issues of government support and policies. In B. J. Corbitt & N. Al-Qirim (Eds.), *E-business, e-government & small to medium-sized enterprises: Opportunities and challenges* (pp. 244-268). Hershey, PA: Idea Group Publishing.

Wang, W. Y. C., & Ho, Michael, S. C. (2005). Information systems dispatching in the global environment: ACER, a case of horizontal integration. *Journal of Cases on Information Technology, 8*(2), 45-61.

Wang, W. Y. C., Ho, M. S. C., & Chau, P.Y. K. (2005). A process-oriented methodology for the supply chain analysis of implementing global logistics information systems. In *Proceedings of the 2nd International conference on Innovations in Information Technology*, Dubai, UAE.

Windsor, D. (1998). *The definition of stakeholder status.* Presented at the International Association for Business and Society (IABS) Annual Conference, Kona-Kailua, HI.

ENDNOTE

[1]   Addition to the processes introduced in this chapter, the Supply Chain Council has recently announced DCOR and CCOR models to define the design and customer service activities to amend SCOR model. Some professionals have considered them to be part of the enablers of existing SCOR processors.

This work was previously published in Supply Chain Management: Issues in the New Era of Collaboration and Competition, edited by W. Y. C. Wang, M. S. H. Heng, and P. Y. K. Chau, pp. 1-22, copyright 2007 by IGI Publishing, formerly known as Idea Group Publishing (an imprint of IGI Global).

Chapter IV
Behavioral Factors and Information Technology Infrastructure Considerations in Strategic Alliance Development

Purnendu Mandal
Lamar University, USA

ABSTRACT

Since behavioral and cultural factors play a major role in strategic alliances between partners, IT managers must understand the intricacies involved in the development of resultant IT infrastructure in satisfying both business requirements and cultural fit of the aligned partnering units. This paper first highlights the IT-related issues and cultural issues which are important in the process of developing a strategic alliance between partners. Then, a case study involving a major telecommunications organization and several retail electricity organizations is presented to illustrate the IT requirements and human-related considerations. The analysis focuses on the requirements of pre-strategic alliance phase of the negotiation process.

INTRODUCTION

Information technologies (IT) such as the Internet, WWW, EDI, and so forth, have already changed, and are still changing, the way organizations do business today (Housel & Skopec, 2001; Mandal & Gunasekaran, 2003). Significant movement that has occurred relatively recently is the push toward worldwide and national integration of information systems (Dutta, Lanvin, & Paua, 2003; Kumar & van Hillegersberg, 2000; Laughlin, 1999; Palaniswamy & Tyler, 2000; Shore 1996) for organizations to achieve competitive advantages. Since it has become critical for businesses to be able to get to relevant data and information quickly and easily, large information systems such as enterprise resource planning (ERP) systems, supply chain management (SCM), enterprise resource/relationship management (ERM), enterprise application integration (EAI), Web services, and customer relationship management (CRM), have recently grown in importance.

Large information systems are helping organizations to deal with increasing competition. Many organizations can no longer compete effectively by themselves; so, they must consider having partners to cope with the competition. The number of strategic alliances formed between organizations has increased dramatically and are projected to continue to increase in the future. Strategic alliances are a mutual agreement between two or more independent firms to serve a common strategic (business) objective (Bronder & Pritzel, 1992). Alliances have had a growth rate of 25% and are projected to have a value of $40 trillion by the year 2004 (Parise & Sasson, 2002). The "make versus buy" decision is becoming the "make versus buy versus partner decision". Through empirical analysis, Yasuda (2005) shows that the primary motivation of strategic alliances is the access to resources, followed by the shortening of time required for development or marketing.

A successful alliance should not imply an imposition of one organization's culture over another. Rather, it should create a new culture that brings together the best elements of each. Unfortunately, "creation of a new culture" is rarely practiced as alliances are often viewed solely from a financial perspective, leaving the human resource issues as something to be dealt with later and without a great deal of effort. The creation of a new culture involves operations, sales, human resources management, technology, and structure among other issues. It is undoubtedly expensive and time consuming to create a new culture, but, in the end, employees become contented and productive.

For an organization to exploit the benefits of alliances, human factors and information technology (IT) factors must be among the basic components for any analyses and plans. Yet, the literature is poor in this regard. Evidences of failure in the implementation of IT systems due to the lack of considerations of human factors have come to light in recent years, but a comprehensive consideration of human factors in strategic alliance, which is prompted by the possibility of major IT systems alignment, is still rare in IT literature. The main objective of this paper is to highlight the human-related issues in IT-centered strategic alliances. We focus specifically to human-related considerations before the actual negotiations for an alliance and its implementation.

To facilitate the discussion, we have used the case of a telecommunication (TEL) company. TEL identified a new market opportunity as a result of changed market conditions. The company is in the traditional business of telecommunications and information services, but identified a new market opportunity in the retail electricity distribution business that became apparent as a result of market deregulation in the electricity industry. The deregulation of the electricity industry presented TEL with a diversification opportunity. Should TEL enter into an electricity retailing business, or concentrate on its existing communications business, which is increasingly becoming more competitive? TEL's own strength in IT areas, its strong market position, and the opportunities in forming alliances with other business partners in the electricity industry are the main considerations for this strategic move.

The paper is organized in several sections: starting with a brief review of IT and strategic alliance. Cultural aspects in alliances and IT issues in alliances are discussed in the next two sections. The research methodology is presented next. This is followed by a short description of the case study. The cultural issues raised in this case study are discussed before the discussion section.

ISSUES IN STRATEGIC ALLIANCE

Strategic alliance focuses on combining resources of various organizations through acquisition, joint venture, or contracts. The main purpose of an alliance is to create one or more advantages such as product integration, product distribution, or product extension (Pearlson, 2001). Strategic alliances also help in utilization of resources even in small organizations (Gunasekaran & Ngai, 2003). In alliances, information resources of different organizations require coordination over extended periods of time.

Bronder and Pritzl (1992) suggest a strategic alliance exists when the value chain between at least two organizations (with compatible goals) are combined for the purpose of sustaining and/or achieving significant competitive advantage. Four critical phases of strategic alliance are: strategic decision for an alliance, alliance configuration, partner selection, and alliance management. These four phases provide basis for a continuous development and review of the strategic alliance, which increases the likelihood of the venture's success.

Typically, the first phase of a strategic alliance is the strategic decision. Phase I answers the question: Is this strategic alliance justified? Phase II (Configuration of a Strategic Alliance) focuses on setting-up the alliance's structure. Phase III (Partner Selection) is one of the most important success factors of the strategic alliance. Considerations such as fundamental fit (do the company's activities and expertise complement each other in a way that increases value potential?), strategic fit (do strategic goal structures match?), and cultural fit (is there a readiness to accept the geographically and internally grown culture of the partners?) are some of the concerns in this phase. The final phase, Phase IV, is concerned with managing a strategic alliance; how do partners continually manage, evaluate, and negotiate within the alliance to increase the odds of continued success?

According to Currie (2000), there are three major forces that are influencing the formation of alliances between organizations: globalization, deregulation, and consolidation. But, before organizations commit to strategic alliance, they should have a management plan on how to deal with human behavior aspects of the new organizational unit. Once a strategic alliance is a "done deal", the organizations must manage the alliance. Parise and Sasson (2002) discuss the knowledge management practices organizations should follow when dealing with a strategic alliance. They break the creation of a strategic alliance down in to three major phases:

- *Find* — making alliance strategy decisions and screening and selecting potential partners.
- *Design* — structuring and negotiating an agreement with the partners.
- *Manage* — organizations should develop an effective working environment with the partner to facilitate the completion of the actual work. This phase includes collecting data relating to performance and feedback from both partners on how they think the alliance might is progressing. Managing relationships and maintaining trust are particularly critical during the Manage Phase.

Knowledge management techniques are especially important for a successful alliance (Parise & Sasson, 2002). They discuss the need to develop a systematic approach for capturing, codifying, and sharing information and knowledge, a focus on building social capital to enable collaboration among people and communities, an emphasis on learning and training, and a priority on leveraging knowledge and expertise in work practices. They also state their study indicates easy access to information and knowledge is a recurring theme in successful alliances.

Parise and Sasson (2002) provide a list of the building blocks of alliance management. Four of their building blocks relating specifically to human behavior factors are:

- *Social capital.* Building trust and effective communication with the partner are necessary ingredients for an effective relationship.
- *Communities.* Communities of practice allow for the sharing of personal and experiences and tacit knowledge based on a common interest or practice. Communities can be realized using electronic meeting rooms and forums or more formal alliance committees.
- *Training.* Companies that rely heavily on strategic alliances should have formal training for managers and team members.
- *Formal processes and programs.* Alliance know-how should be institutionalized. An example of this is Eli Lilly, a leading pharmaceutical firm, created a dedicated organization, called the Office of Alliance Management, responsible for alliance management.

Company's that use alliance management techniques that stress knowledge management are more successful than those who do not. Leveraging knowledge management across a company's strategic alliance is a critical success factor for partnering companies. Strategic alliance is a management issue. Both cultural and information technology aspects play a significant role in strategic alliance, which is the topic of discussion in the next two sections.

CULTURAL ASPECTS IN ALLIANCES

As discussed in the preceding sections, alliance among firms naturally would result in many or-

ganizational changes. Leavitt (1965) concluded there are four types of interacting variables to consider when dealing with organizational change, especially in large industrial organizations: task variables, structural variables, technological variables, and human variables. He proposed structural, technological, and people approaches to organizational changes, which derive from interactions among the four types of variables mentioned earlier.

The earlier-mentioned four variables are highly interdependent so that a change in any one variable usually results in compensatory changes in other variables. The introduction of new technological tools — computers, for example — may cause changes in structure (communication system), changes in people (their skills and attitudes), and changes in performance and tasks. Therefore, it is imperative to consider all areas that might be affected when a company plans to introduce change to an organization.

Pre-existing, people-related problems at a target company often cause many alliances to fail to reach their full financial and strategic potential. Numerous case studies report failure of alliances due to lack of consideration for the potential impact of behavioral and structural aspects (Brower, 2001; Numerof & Abrams, 2000). To build an effective alliance, institutions must pay particularly close attention to cultural, personality, and structural incompatibilities. Leaders from alliance institutions need to recognize the personality differences in their managers as well as the demands required by the life cycle stage of their organizations (Segil, 2000). It has also been demonstrated that successful alliance partners share many strong similarities regarding performance and relationships (e.g., people skills) (Whipple & Frankel, 2000). Understanding potential incompatibilities gives institutions contemplating alliances a solid foundation on which to explore the feasibility of joint projects. It also increases the likelihood that the alliance will operate successfully (Whipple & Frankel, 2000).

Successful alliances are impeded when the culture of one or both associations highly differ in value. "High control value" is inconsistent with the toleration for ambiguity and the "willingness to compromise" often required for strategic alliances. Maron and VanBremen (1999) suggests the use of William Bridges' Organizational Character Index (OCI), which can be a useful tool for analyzing the cultural differences between two associations to determine how well they might work together. It promotes better understanding between two associations; fosters an appreciation for what both partners could bring to an alliance; and identifies underdeveloped qualities in both associations that could inhibit the success of an alliance.

IT ISSUES IN ALLIANCES

Long-term IT considerations, such as IT architecture, is a major consideration. A strategic consideration, such as new alliances, would require visioning of a different IT architecture. Applegate, McFarlan, and McKenney (1999) view IT architecture as an overall picture of the range of technical options as well as business options.

Just as the blueprint of a building's architecture indicates not only the structure's design but how everything—from plumbing and heating systems, to the flow of traffic within the building — fits and works together, the blueprint of a firm's IT architecture defines the technical computing,

Figure 1. Forces affecting overall IT architecture

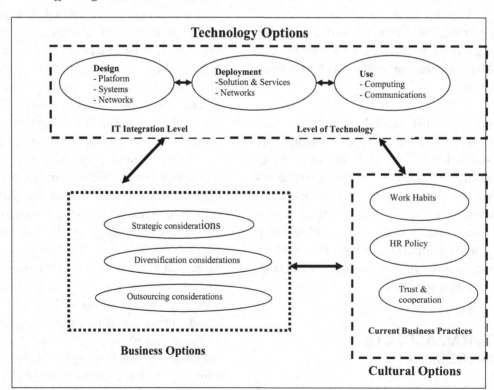

information management, and communications platform. (p. 209)

Figure 1 brings out the dynamic nature of the IT architecture development process. The technology part, shown by dotted oval, is concerned with design, deployment, and how it is used. This part is the core of IT architecture and a huge proportion of IT professionals' time is devoted to these activities. Consideration of business options, which feed to various technology options, are higher level activities in the IT architecture development process. Business options, such as strategic alliances, mergers and acquisitions, outsourcing, diversification, and so forth, are influenced by major internal as well as external factors, such as current business practices, business opportunities, and organizational strategy. There is a direct link between technology and organizational strategy. The technology (with its operational and technical settings) exerts a strong influence on the organization's future strategic direction. Thus, one can observe (as shown in Figure 1 through connecting lines), a close link between technical and other business factors, and, like ever-changing business, the IT architecture is a dynamically evolving phenomena.

An alliance can exist between any types of organization. For example, a telecommunication organization could form an alliance for international joint ventures, or an alliance can be established between a banking organization and an IT supplier. The notion of developing a strategic alliance suggests an organization's performance can be significantly improved through joint, mutually dependent action. For a strategic alliance to be successful, business partners must follow a structured approach to developing their alliances and should include as part of this process, strategic planning, communication, efficient and effective decision-making, performance evaluation, relationship structure, and education and training.

Strategists have often suggested that organizations should consider entering into similar or somewhat-related markets sectors to broaden their product/service portfolios (Henderson & Clark, 1990; Markides & Williamson, 1997). Both the dimensions of market (customer and product) in a related market can easily be identified and strategies formulated for deployment. The main advantage of adopting such a strategy is that an organization can easily use its competencies and strategic assets in generating a strategic competitive advantage (Markides & Williamson, 1997). Determining the design and the requirements of a new information system (IS) is a relatively simple task. In contrast, diversification into a significantly different market for an IT/IS organization is a very challenging task, which needs considerable evaluation of IT infrastructure and human relations.

RESEARCH METHODOLOGY

The focus of this research has been to understand the complexities that may arise in an alliance, particularly when an ICT organization *moves away from its traditional business activity arena.* From practitioners' point of view, this research aims to provide guidance in four avenues while an organization is negotiating various terms and conditions of strategic alliance with partners:

1. to define the new environment for the organization and its partners;
2. to highlight the complexity and complementarities in the alliance;
3. to provide details of technical strengths and limitations for the new situation; and
4. to provide an assessment of human-related strengths and limitations for the new situation.

There has been limited published research that has examined the pre-strategic alliance structures, particularly in the telecommunications industry. Thus, a case study approach was used to gain an in-depth understanding about the way in which the organizations went about examining the strategic alliance structure. A case study is basically a "methodology based on interviews, which are used to investigate technical aspects of a contemporary phenomenon with its real life context; when the boundaries between phenomenon and context are not clearly evident; and in which multiple sources of evidence are used" (Yin, 1994). Thus, a case study approach may lead to a more informed basis for theory development. It can provide analytical rather than pure statistical generalizations. Thus, "theory" can be defined as a set concepts and generalizations. A theory can provide a perspective and a way of seeing an interpretation, which ultimately leads to understanding some phenomenon (Benbasat, Goldstein, & Mead, 1987). In this case, the technical and human factors that need to be considered when forming a strategic alliance.

Interviews were conducted with CEOs of electricity operating agencies and market regulating organizations. IT managers in some of these organizations were also contacted to get an appreciation of how transactions and information flows take place within the electricity industry. The duration of each interview was approximately 40 minutes, where every interview was conducted on a one-to-one basis, so as to stimulate conversation and breakdown any barriers that may have existed between the interviewer and interviewee.

Information for this research was also collected from various sources such as government publications, industry reports, trade publications and informal/formal discussions with industry experts. WWW and the Internet were also a good source of information.

THE CASE STUDY

The telecommunication organization (TEL) provides services to its customers through its own telecommunications network and would like to improve its customer base by forming a strategic alliance with the retail electricity distribution organizations. TEL is a Fortune 500 company with annual revenue over $14.5 billion. TEL provides a full range of services in telecommunication markets to more than 10 million fixed line and 6 million mobile subscribers. Many experts believe that a handful of global power companies will soon provide the majority of the world's energy needs (Brower, 2001), and TEL aspires to be one among them. As large telecommunication organizations exhibit structural inertia, generating a competitive advantage in a new market poses an enormous challenge (Henderson & Clark, 1990). An organization must make a distinction between a new product and the means to achieve that new product. The recent merger between America Online and Warner Publishing clearly demonstrates that it is not too difficult for an IT organization to offer new products in an existing market. Considering this point, strategic alliances and partnership could be a way out for an IT organization to enter into a completely new product market. From a systems development perspective, alliances may result in the development of new interfaces to the existing ISs or alternatively a new integrated IS.

As per the deregulation rules, a retail distributor must make financial settlement with other suppliers of the electricity industry supply chain. This needs to cover the cost of electricity from the wholesale electricity market, tariffs for distribution of the same by the transmission and distribution service providers, and meter data collection from meter providers (MPs) and meter data agents (MDAs). The processes and systems therein must be able to interface with retail en-

Figure 2. Relationships between TEL and third parties

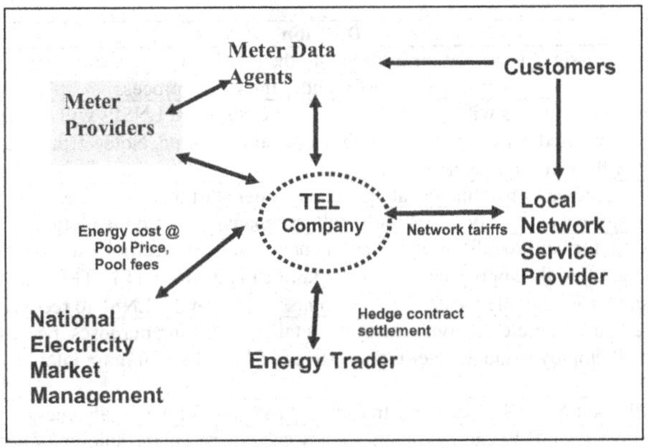

Table 1. Electricity retailers and third party relationships

Retailers	Relationships
Electricity sourcing	TEL will need to contract energy traders to purchase electricity in the national electricity market. TEL will be required to settle periodically with these organizations for services rendered.
NEMMCO	Tel will be required to settle periodically with National Electricity Market Management Company (NEMMCO) for wholesale electricity purchases. NEMMCO will provide billing reconciliation data.
MDA	TEL will contract with NEMMCO accredited MDAs for the collection and provision of customer electricity usage data for billing purposes. TEL will be required to settle periodically with MDAs for services rendered
MP	TEL, as an RP, will have a relationship with MPs in the provision and maintenance of meter installations, and TEL will be required to settle periodically for services rendered
LNSP	TEL will enter into service agreements with each local network service provider (LNSP) for the use of their distribution network and for the connection and supply of electricity. TEL will be required to settle periodically with LNSPs in terms of distribution fees for network use.
NEMMCO and State Regulators	TEL will pay fees to NEMMCO and state regulators for operating licences and other regulatory charges
Generators	TEL may contract with generators (outside of the spot market) for long-term energy requirements.
TEL Partner sales commissions	TEL could potentially enter into sales partnerships and pay appropriate commissions.

ergy distributors accounting and billing, service activation, and service assurance processes and systems.

To conduct business as a market participant TEL must purchase wholesale electricity and services for the physical delivery and metering to the customer. There are two clear options available to TEL to purchase electricity:

- By *direct participation* and trading in the national electricity market (NEM). This means that TEL would perform all electricity trader functions, including the act to bid and settle wholesale purchases in the national electricity market from its own resources and carry all market and prudential risks and responsibilities.

Table 2. Major business decisions TEL must make

Decision
TEL will require a customer-signed application form before the retail transfer process can commence.
TEL will not enter into and conduct a customer transfer under the BETS process.
The company will negotiate contracts with a LNSP, which will ensure that LNSPs will connect customers to their network at a customer-nominated date and time or within a reasonable time. Noteworthy each LNSP will perform service location work for the electricity connection.
TEL will appoint only registered to read meters at agreed customer start date and times.
An MP will install and remove electricity meters only with company's written instructions.
Each LNSP is responsible for fault rectification and maintenance of their electricity distribution network in their local area. TEL will hand off to the appropriate LNSP for fault calls made to TEL. TEL will pay the relevant service fee, but if the customer is culpable for the fault, the onus will be on the LNSP to recover costs.
MDAs are to provide all customer electricity usage to the retailer for billing purposes, typically daily overnight for smart meters. MDAs will employ manual meter readers to read SIMs at a minimum interval of monthly regardless of the billing cycle.
TEL will settle with MDAs, LNSPs, MPs, energy traders and the pool for electricity energy cost of goods sold.
TEL must provide energy forecasts to energy traders so they can determine the amount of energy to hedge.

Table 3. Structural and behavioral differences

Factors	TEL	Partners
Company organizational structure/size	Very complex and large in sales volume (Annual revenue $14.5 billion, Assets $24.9 billion)	Small to medium size, relatively simple structure (revenue in the order of million $)
Employee work habit	Flexible work hours	Relatively rigid work hours
Customer relations	Good relations with existing customers — excellent customer services	Indifferent to customer complaints
Employee training	Good opportunity for skill upgrading (formal training department)	Reasonable opportunity to technical skill development
IT system compatibility	Highly developed IT system	Manual or primitive IT systems
Employee satisfaction	Highly motivated, well paid work force.	Competent, but low paid work force.
Employee turn over	High turn over	Relatively low employee turnover.

- By *engaging an existing specialist energy trader*. This means that TEL would form a close and long-term relationship with one (or more) existing trader(s) who would operate all market trader functions and processes on TEL's behalf. This would be an outsourced supply arrangement. The sharing of risk and responsibilities is a matter for specific agreement with the trader.

The management of TEL must first realize the complexity and limitations of the IT infrastructure before they venture into the new business. TEL follows a standard procedure called PDOM (product development operational model) for any IT product development and this procedure was also applied in developing its IT architecture design. PDOM is very similar to standard SDLC (systems development life cycle).

Figure 2 shows the relationship between TEL and third parties that it must reconcile.

Reconciliation with these third parties is critical to ensure that the following items are accurate for customers: charges, dates (i.e., customer's start and end dates), rates, services received, usage, and loss factors. Reconciliation is also necessary to ensure that payments are settled for the correct dollar amount and are on time. The third parties with whom TEL will be required to settle with are NEMMCO (National Electricity Market

Management Company), LNSPs (local network service provider), MDAs, MPs, energy traders, and other retailers.

For the proposed alliance to become effective, TEL will be required to develop a number of third party relations with electricity retailers. These relationships are shown in Table 1.

To forge a meaningful alliance TEL would be required to make a number of major business decisions, which would influence the overall IT architecture. These decisions would form the core of the IT system and partnership relations and are presented in Table 2.

If these alliances are to eventuate, the existing processes and systems will be used to generate reports to partner sales and commissions. TEL would be required to provide a lot of technical support to potential strategic partners, since partners in the electricity retail business in general do not have well-developed information systems. In fact, most electricity retailers had manual settlement systems. This would be a serious limitation to full-scale system integration.

CULTURAL FIT BETWEEN TEL AND ITS PARTNERS

Table 3 shows that there are significant differences between TEL and the other partners. A strategic alliance in this situation would require a careful evaluation of the strengths and weaknesses of each firm, and detailed planning of what the reorganized alliance would look like. The IT architectural planning would not only present the overview of future challenges, but would also provide the chief information officers (CIOs) a summary of the nature of human-related activities they would be faced with once the alliance became a reality.

Before companies agree to participate in the strategic alliance, they should first determine if their organizations can work together harmoniously. To determine whether they can work well together, each company should attempt to determine what type of organization it is, that is, does an organization have a certain personality or culture? As shown in Table 3, both TEL and its partners exhibit a different cultural setting, this suggests the need for further investigation to make the proposed alliance effective.

The cultural differences between TEL and potential industry partners are so high, as evident from Table 3, that one might suggest the proposed alliance is a recipe for disaster. Unless there is a higher authority to ensure compliance, this alliance is likely to head for a failure. The perception of relational risks plays a dominant role in strategic alliance. As uncertainty regarding partner's future behavior and the presence/absence of a higher authority to ensure compliance dominate strategic alliance considerations, it seems to be that the relational risks are very high in this case. Delerue (2004) suggests that informal contextual factors have more influence on relational risks than the formal contextual factors.

There are three important reasons related to human behavior factors that might lead to partnership failure in this situation. The reasons are (as per Dixon & Marks, 1999): *inattention to the human resources issues; failure to plan for other human resources issues such as benefits, loyalty, identity, etc.; and poor communication.* In addition, it would be necessary to build a new culture and learning environment.

DISCUSSION AND FUTURE SCOPE

In today's competitive business environment, new methods of evolution from independence to interdependence are continuing to unfold; strategic alliance is one of those methods that can be used to achieve competitive advantage. In the process of developing a strategic alliance, IT infrastructure and human factors play important roles. In addition to considering the projected information systems the organization will require, information officers should focus on the human factors of its organization to increase the odds that an alliance will be successful. IT planning highlights major weaknesses and incompatibilities with information systems of various parties within an organization. Those incompatibilities, however, can intensify further due to operational and work practices in partner organizations. The development of an IT system and the serious consideration of human issues would lead to practical improvements in the way most organizations approach strategic alliance development planning.

As further enhancement in analysis of human-related issues, the author advocates the deployment of organizational character index (OCI) tool (Bridges, 1992), mentioned earlier in the paper. To determine whether partners should work together on possible strategic alliances, the American Society of Clinical Pathologists (ASCP) and the College of American Pathologists (CAP) suggest the use of the OCI tool (Maron & VanBremen, 1999). Bridges (1992) explains how OCI can be used to categorize organizations, similar to the way the Myers-Briggs Type Indicator describes the characteristics of the individual. OCI, a public domain tool, consists of a written questionnaire that takes 10 to 15 minutes to complete. Bridges stresses that there are not right or wrong types of organizations; it merely brings out organizational personalities. OCI categorizes organizations for the following types (Maron & VanBremen, 1999):

- Its orientation or source of energy (extroverted or introverted).
- How it gathers information or what it pays attention to (sensing or intuitive).
- Its way of processing information, how it judges situations, and how it makes decisions (thinking or feeling).
- How it deals with the external world (judging or perceiving).

The OCI tool was most useful in its ability to stimulate constructive discussions about the two company's cultural differences. Using the OCI tool, ASCP and CAP accomplished the following objectives:

- It promoted better understanding between the two associations.
- Fostered an appreciation for what both partners could bring to an alliance.
- Identified "underdeveloped" qualities in both associations that could inhibit the success of an alliance.

The OCI provides valuable insights into difficulties organizations with certain characteristics might face in a joint venture such as a strategic alliance. It also highlights the underdeveloped qualities of an organization. These qualities might then be improved. Improving on the qualities can increase the likelihood that a joint venture will be successful.

Maron and VanBremen (1999) stress that the "OCI is not a definitive diagnostic tool. It is best used as a way to stimulate discussion, largely because it helps potential partners better understand and articulate their own, and each other's values and expectations." To use the OCI tool, the following set of simple steps could be followed:

- Administer the OCI questionnaire.
- Tabulate the responses.
- Use the results as the basis for discussion by volunteer leadership and staff.

The OCI could assist the organizations in determining whether their organizational cultures might work well together, but there are other human factors to consider. Burrows (2000) stresses the importance of understanding the "people situation at the target company," if a successful long-term relationship is to result. Burrows (2000) argues that most companies misunderstand or ignore "pre-existing people problems", and once the joint ventures are created, man problems reveal themselves, which undermine value-creation opportunities, jeopardize relationships with customers, and reduce productivity.

REFERENCES

Applegate, L. M., McFarlan, F. W., & McKenney, J. L. (1999). *Corporate information systems management: Text and cases.* Boston: Irwin McGraw-Hill.

Benbasat, I., Goldstein, D. K., & Mead, M. (1987). The case research strategy in studies of information systems. *MIS Quarterly, 11*(3), 369-386.

Bridges, W. (1992). *The character of organizations: Using Jungian type in organizational development.* Palo Alto, CA: Davies-Black Publishing.

Bronder, C., & Pritzl, R. (1992). Developing strategic alliances: A successful framework for co-operation. *European Management Journal, 10*(4), 412-420.

Brower, D. (2001, October). Sizing up the power sector. *Petroleum Economist, 68*(10), 26-28.

Burrows, D. M. (2000). How people problems can sap value from a deal. *Merger and Acquisitions, 35*(9), 36-39.

Currie, W. (2000). *Global information society.* Chichester: John Wiley & Sons.

Delerue, H. (2004). Relational risks perception in European bio-technology alliances: The effects of contextual factors. *European Management Journal, 22*(5), 546.

Dixon, D., & Marks, M. (1999). Making mergers, acquisitions & alliances work. *Health Forum Journal*, November/December, 30-33.

Dutta, S., Lanvin, B., & Paua, F. (2003). *The global information technology report 2002-2003: Readiness for the networked world.* New York: Oxford University Press.

Gunasekaran, A., & Ngai, E. W. T. (2003). The successful management of a small logistics company. *International Journal of Physical Distribution & Logistics Management, 33*(9/10), 825.

Henderson, R., & Clark, K. (1990). Architectural innovation: The reconfiguration of existing product technologies and the failure of established firms. *Administrative Science Quarterly*, 35, 9-30.

Housel, T. J., & Skopec, E. W. (2001). *Global telecommunications revolution: The business perspective.* Boston, MA: McGraw-Hill/Irwin.

Kumar, K., & Van Hillegersberg, J. (2000, April). ERP experiences and evolution. *Communications of the ACM, 43*(4), 23-26.

Laughlin, S. (1999, January/February). An ERP game plan. *Journal of Business Strategy, 20*(1), 32-37.

Leavitt, H. J. (1965). Applied organizational change in industry: Structural, technological and humanistic approaches. In J. March (Ed.), *Handbook of organizations* (pp. 1144-1170). Randy, McNally & Company.

Mandal, P., & Gunasekaran, A. (2003). Issues in implementing ERP: A case study. *European Journal of Operational Research*, 146, 274-283.

Markides, C. C., & Williamson, P. J. (1997). Related diversification, core competencies and corporate performance. In A. Cambell, & K. Sommer Luchs (Eds.), *Core competency-based strategy* (pp. 96-122). London: International Thomson Business Press.

Maron, R. M., & VanBremen, L. (1999). The influence of organizational culture on strategic alliances. *Association Management, 51*(4), 86-92.

Numerof, R. E., & Abrams, M. N. (2000). Subtle conflicts that wreck merger visions. *Mergers and Acquisitions, 35*(3), 28-30.

Palaniswamy, R., & Tyler, F. (2000, Summer). Enhancing manufacturing performance with ERP systems. *Information Systems Management, 17*(3), 43-55.

Parise, S., & Sasson, L. (2002). Leveraging knowledge management across strategic alliances. *Ivey Business Journal*, March/April, 41-47.

Pearlson, K. E. (2001). *Managing and using information systems*. New York: John Wiley & Sons.

Segil, L. (2000). Understanding life cycle differences. *Association Management, 52*(8), 32-33.

Shore, B. (1996). Using information technology to achieve a competitive advantage: A study of current and further trends. *Journal of Computer Information Systems, 36*(4), 54-59.

Whipple, J., & Frankel, R. (2000). Strategic alliance success factors. *The Journal of Supply Chain Management: A Global Review of Purchasing and Supply*, Summer, 21-28.

Yasuda, H. (2005). Formation of strategic alliances in high-technology industries: Comparative study of the resource-based theory and the transaction-cost theory. *Technovation, 25*(7), 763.

Yin, R. K. (1994). *Case study research, design and methods* (2nd ed.). California: Sage Publications.

This work was previously published in International Journal of Enterprise Information Systems, Vol. 2, Issue 4, edited by A. Gunasekaran, pp. 77-88, copyright 2006 by IGI Publishing, formerly known as Idea Group Publishing (an imprint of IGI Global).

Section II
Development and Design Methodologies

Chapter V
A Methodology for Developing an Integrated Supply Chain Management System

Yi-chen Lan
University of Western Sydney, Australia

Bhuvan Unhelkar
University of Western Sydney, Australia

ABSTRACT

Integrated Supply Chain Management (ISCM) involves the linking of suppliers and customers with the internal business processes of an organization. ISCM solutions allow organizations to automate workflows concerning the execution and analysis of planning, sourcing, making, delivering, returns handling, and maintenance, to name but a few. Many of today's ISCM systems use primarily Web technology as the supporting infrastructure. Undoubtedly, the electronic (Internet-based) ISCM systems deliver the enterprises with a competitive advantage by opening up opportunities to streamline processes, reduce costs, increase customer patronage, and enable thorough planning abilities. However, there has been significant customer backlash concerning the inability of software vendors to deliver easy integration and promised functionality. Although various researchers have suggested strategies to overcome some of the failures in operating ISCM systems, there appears to be a lacunae in terms of architectural investigations in the analysis stage. The methodology proposed in this chapter seeks to resolve these gaps and provides a fundamental framework for analyzing ISCM systems.

INTRODUCTION

This is the age of communication based on Internet technologies. As a result, enterprises are able to conduct inter- and intra-organizational activities efficiently and effectively. This efficiency of communication has percolated in all arenas of organizational activities, including customer relationships, resource planning, and, in the context of this discussion, supply chains. Given the cost of logistics and their importance in order fulfillment process, organizations may want to capitalize on this opportunity to communicate in order to reengineer their supply chain operations that would sustain them in the globally competitive and challenging world of electronic business. With this invigorated growth of e-business, software vendors and consultants have been promising businesses the utopian Internet-based supply chain systems that would provide them with the capability to respond in real-time to changing product demand and supply and offer an easy integration functionality with backend information systems (PeopleSoft, 2002; Turner, 1993).

Although a number of Internet-based supply chain systems (or integrated supply chain management systems—ISCM systems) are available for adoption, enterprises do not guarantee to implement the systems in conjunction with their existing information systems. Furthermore, the ISCM systems may not fulfill the connection and implementation requirements among participants in the supply chain.

After the e-commerce hype had dissipated, surveys undertaken in 2001 tend to paint a different picture as to the success of these implementations. Smith (2002) concludes that at least 15% of supply chain system implementations during 2001 and 2002 were abandoned in the US alone. Although several reasons can be identified as the cause of implementation failure, the main problem rests with the fundamental analysis of ISCM operations and requirements.

The purpose of this chapter is to debunk some myths proposed by vendors with regard to the implementation of Integrated Supply Chain Environments (ISCE) and propose an analysis methodology for Integrated Supply Chain Management systems.

First, the chapter will examine some of the available literature regarding ISCE. The fundamentals of ISCE—technologies and processes—will be investigated in some detail. Vendors were quick to promote the benefits of ISCE yet were not so forthcoming as to possible barriers and other issues to watch for. Both of these also will

be discussed in this chapter.

Second, an analysis methodology is proposed, which intends to address some of the issues identified previously and construct a theoretical model for enterprises to adopt in the analysis phase of developing ISCM systems. This chapter concludes with a future research direction in investigating technological issues of ISCM systems operation.

INTEGRATED SUPPLY CHAIN MANAGEMENT OVERVIEW

ISCM involves the linking of suppliers and customers with the internal supply processes of an organization. Internal processes would include both vertically integrated functional areas, such as materials, sales and marketing, manufacturing, inventory and warehousing, distribution, and, perhaps, other independent companies involved in the supply chain (i.e., channel integration). Customers at one end of the process can potentially be a supplier downstream in the next process, ultimately supplying to the end user (Handfield et al., 1999; Turner, 1993).

ISCM Solutions

While, in many cases, ISCM systems are still in their infancy, the concept of establishing information flows between points in the supply chain has been around since the 1980s. Through Electronic Data Interchange (EDI), customers and suppliers have communicated supply data through direct dial-up interfaces and other mediums (Zieger, 2001). However, the ability for the Internet to create a common communication infrastructure has made integration much more cost-effective. ISCM has promised to deliver the right product to the right place at the right time and at the right price (Comptroller, 2002).

From the supply chain software development perspective, there are generally four large vendors identified; namely, Oracle, SAP, PeopleSoft, and

Ariba, and a multitude of medium-sized vendors in the ISCM solution space (Armstrong, 2002). All claim that ISCM will enable the enterprise to respond in real time to changes in demand and supply.

For instance, current ISCM solutions allow organizations to automate workflows concerning the execution and analysis of the following business activities (Comptroller, 2002; Gledhill, 2002; Peoplesoft, 2002):

1. **Planning:** Demand and supply planning, manage planning infrastructure.
2. **Sourcing (buy-side):** Strategic sourcing, eprocurement, services procurement, catalog management, collaborative contract/supply management, e-settlements/vendor payments.
3. **Making (in-side):** Product life cycle management, demand planning, production management, production planning, flow production, event management.
4. **Delivering (sell-side):** Inventory, order management, promotions management,

warehouse management, transportation management, delivery infrastructure management, e-bill payment, scm portal.
5. **Returns handling (from customers)**
6. **Maintenance**

ISCM Systems Architecture

Turner (1993) stated that information systems would be the enabler of integrated logistics. Armstrong (2002) affirms that Turner's view has come to fruition. Many of today's ISCM systems primarily use Web technology as the supporting infrastructure (Dalton et al., 1998). It is not uncommon in these instances to develop a three-tier or n-tier network architecture in order to provide robust support for ISCM systems.

For example, Advanced Software Design Inc. (2002) illustrated the three-tier ISCM integration architecture (Figure 1) in use by the US Department of Defense (DoD). Suppliers and customers access the DoD ISCM through the use of Web portals (the first tier of the ISCM). Web portals provide the necessary Web services to establish

Figure 1. ISCM integration architecture

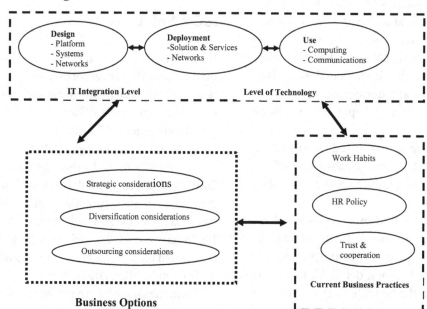

a common graphical interface for the DoD's stakeholders in accessing supply chain data. Customers, suppliers, distributors, and delivery agents can access custom information and services supplied by the ISCM. Supplier services could include access to business-to-business (B2B) marketplaces, support, and other push/pull supplier functionality. Alternately, customers can customize the site in order to access catalogs from the organization and external suppliers; customer transaction details; and other product, customer, and technical support.

The portals are supported by a messaging infrastructure (second tier), which provides the link to the underlying applications layer (third tier). The applications layer is independent of any particular interface (e.g., portals) and contains the necessary business logic and data access in order to perform operations. This includes access to SCM functionality, ERP systems, and decision support systems. Data and business logic also are stored independently.

The software architecture is constructed mostly in a Web-based environment that involves HTTP, server-side Java, and XML. ISCM systems are generally no different than other business applications but still require some interfacing with old technologies, such as aging ERPs and legacy systems (Zieger, 2001).

Benefits of ISCM Systems

ISCM delivers the enterprise with a competitive advantage by opening up opportunities to streamline processes, reduce costs, increase customer patronage, and utilize more thorough planning abilities (Turner, 1993). The benefits of ISCM systems are categorized into a number groups, including financial, customer, planning, production, and implementation. Each of these groups is further discussed in the following subsections.

1. Financial
    Cost Reduction: In some manufacturing organizations, the cost of the supply chain

can represent 60-80% of their total cost base (Cottrill, 1997). One of the core benefits of driving efficiency through the supply chain is cost reduction. ISCM allows the organization to maximize profitability through reduced customer service, administration, and inventory costs. Less staff is required to maintain the supply chain, and order/inventory details can be made available to customers directly without human intervention (Comptroller, 2002; Cottrill, 1997; Gledhill, 2002). Some organizations have quoted 25% cost reductions per transaction, despite a 20% increase in orders (Turner, 1993).

Quality Financial Information: Another benefit is the improvement and reliability of financial information. ISCM systems maintain centralized databases that are linked to other enterprise systems (e.g., ERP, CRM) providing integrity, consistency, and real-time data access to managers so that they can manage the supply chain with an organizational perspective (Comptroller, 2002; Turner, 1993).

2. Customer
    Retention: Supply chain systems, through customer portals, provide customers with an instantaneous and holistic view of the progress of their transactions within the organization. This level of service (coupled with benefits derived from production) result in higher customer satisfaction levels and, in turn, improve the firm's ability to attract new customers and, more importantly, retain them. Organizations have achieved customer service levels of 97% following the introduction of ISCM systems. This retention translates into greater revenue (Bergert, 2001; Comptroller, 2002; Cottrill, 1997; Gledhill, 2002; Turner, 1993).

    Behavior: The ability to capture customer transactions and preferences online provides the organization with the facility to track their behavior and, in turn, customize products and services to cater to them (Bragg, 2002).

Promise: Because of the level of work-flow automation and inventory statistics, organizations are able to provide accurate estimates of when orders will be filled at the time of ordering. This is known as capable-to-promise (CTP) capability. This capability allows the organization's customers to plan more effectively (Gledhill, 2002).

3. Planning

    Companies with ISCM systems have the ability to mathematically and graphically observe the performance of the supply chain, giving the manager the power to plan and make things happen (Turner, 1993). ISCM systems provide the organization with the capabilities to derive more accurate demand planning with improved precision, create shorter planning and production cycles, establish one central data repository for the entire organization, and facilitate enhanced communications through rapid information dissemination (Bragg, 2002; Comptroller, 2002; Gledhill, 2002).

4. Production

    ISCM provides the ability to holistically manage the supply chain, allowing managers to respond dynamically to any situation that may arise so as to minimize its impact on production.

    Inventory Management: By measuring the level of inventory and analyzing turnover, supply chain systems can improve turnover by reducing the need for safety stocks and the risk of retailer out-of-stocks. Inventory items need to be numbered consistently in order to facilitate measurement and tracking. These benefits reduce the overhead required to store high inventory levels (Cottrill, 1997; Gledhill, 2002). Turner's (1993) research claimed a 37% reduction in inventory levels as a result of ISCM implementation.

    Efficiency: ISCM systems measure the

performance of the supply chain through the generation of supply chain metrics. This allows process quality issues to be tracked and rectified, isolates bottlenecks in the process, and measures lead times so they can be aligned with available capacity in order to maximize plant utilization. All of this ensures quicker time-to-market for the firm's products (Bragg, 2002; Comptroller, 2002; Gledhill, 2002).

Other efficiency benefits include no data rekeying through simplified automated order placement, order status inquiries, delivery shipment, and invoicing (Bragg, 2002; Gledhill, 2002). ISCM implementations have resulted in a 50% overtime reduction for some organizations (Turner, 1993).

5. Implementation

    Consultants promise responsiveness and Plug & Play integrations. However, documented examples of supply chain failures by organizations such as Siemens AG, Nike, OPP Quimica, and Shell are evidence that the implementation of ISCM systems is not as easy as vendors claim. Claims of rapid integration and seamless linking seem to significantly underestimate the effort required to integrate ISCM with the rest of the enterprise (Oakton, 2003).

    For Nike, i2 ISCM software required a significant degree of customization in order to integrate the software to the rest of the organization. Customization to enterprise software comes with great risk and significant cost for ongoing maintenance. Nike's summation of the software was that it just didn't work. OPP Quimica (a Brazilian chemicals company) required the use of third-party integration software in order to assimilate i2 to the rest of the enterprise architecture. Shell's implementation proved problematic with the need to tie 85 ERP sites to a single SCM platform (Smith, 2002).

Issues and Barriers in ISCM Analysis

Similar to the hype attached to Enterprise Resource Planning (ERP) applications, there has been significant customer backlash concerning the inability of software vendors to deliver easy integration and promised functionality (Smith, 2002). Turner (1993) believes that "few companies claim to have fully implemented SCM and have sustained the benefits proposed ISCM would create" (p. 52). In fact, Fontanella (2001) indicates that only 25% of ISCM users are utilizing the full suite of supply chain applications and that only 12% of users are receiving data from inbound suppliers and customers—far from an integrated supply chain.

Many of these issues stem from a failure to undertake thorough analysis in the following key areas.

- **Focus on transaction systems over strategic systems to manage supply chains:** Organizations are not taking a strategic view of ISCM systems. More so, they tend only to focus on transactions systems (e.g., inventory control, order processing, etc.), which provide little visibility of the enterprise (Fontanella, 2001; Turner, 1993).

- **Failure to preempt change to business processes:** In a majority of implementations, analysis has focused on the technical aspects of integrating ISCM systems with the remaining architecture. One area that has been neglected is the effect on business processes. Organizations expect staff either to just accept change or to customize the software. Both of these options are generally flawed. In order to reap the cost savings from ISCM systems, significant analysis must be conducted regarding process reengineering in order to ensure collaboration and to continue to sustain benefits (Fontanella, 2001; Mol et al., 1997; Turner, 1993).

- **Failure to appreciate geographical, relational, and environmental considerations between buyer and supplier:** The nature of ISCM (especially with multinational corporations) involves transacting across the world—24 hours a day, seven days a week, 360°. Analysts fail to appreciate the geographical, relational, and environmental inhibitors for ISCM implementations of this scope (Mol et al., 1997). Cross-borders logistics, culture, language and economics, and regulatory climate are just some considerations that can affect the integration of business processes between regional offices and external organizations, creating communication issues throughout the supply chain. One ill-performing participant in the supply chain will affect the performance of the entire supply chain (Strausl, 2001).

- **Failure to accurately identify the costs and benefits of ISCM implementation:** Many implementations have been classified as failures because of ISCM system's perceived inability to reap benefits and produce cost savings, as expected. However, in many cases, it is the initial analysis of cost and benefits that has been flawed. Because of the nature and scope of ISCM implementations, it is difficult to accurately quantify attributable cost reductions from ISCM, because they could be derived throughout the supply chain and be complicated to calculate. In the same light, determining benefits share similar traits, with some having the additional complication of being intangible (e.g., benefits of a central database) and, therefore, difficult to quantify (New, 1994).

- **Insufficient capability:** The implementation and support of ISCM systems can be rather complex and, therefore, demands sophisticated resources and incremental implementations. Unfortunately, during the planning and analysis phases of implementation projects, organizations have failed to properly appreciate the level of complexity involved, resulting in significant under-resourcing. As a result, many organizations have suffered material cost overruns and delayed go-live times (Fontanella, 2001).

PROPOSED METHODOLOGY FOR ISCM SYSTEMS ANALYSIS

Due to the extent of failed ISCM system implementations, it is imperative to construct an appropriate analysis and development methodology that can be adopted as the roadmap for enterprises flourishing in ISCM systems development and operations. The proposed methodology demonstrates an overall picture for constructing an ISCM system from recognizing problems and analyzing requirements to the implementation and operation. It embraces eight phases:

1. Identifying information management structure
2. Identifying connecting components
3. Ensuring appropriate business processes
4. Establishing and developing interfaces
5. Developing new business processes
6. Confirming strategic alignment
7. Implementing ISCM systems
8. Testing efficacy of implementation

Following is a discussion and culmination of those eight phases within the proposed iterative framework.

Identifying Information Management Structure

Given the global nature of supply chain systems and their level of required integration, a common ICT (information and communication technology) infrastructure must be able to extend around the globe, to support open and rapid communication, and to integrate easily with the architecture of not just the organization but also the architecture of customers and suppliers. This will be conducive to information sharing (Comptroller, 2002).

The enterprise's information systems architecture must be properly analyzed to ensure that it satisfies the needs of ISCM systems and can support security boundaries, largely distributed database operations, and event-driven applications. The architecture needs to be durable, flexible, and embedded with the appropriate middleware in order to integrate as easily as possible (Zieger, 2001). It also must be sufficiently robust in order to cater to firewalls and other security measures and have 24/7 global access and redundant systems and processes in order to handle events when ISCM systems need to be off-line for maintenance, emergency, and recovery purposes.

In accordance with these criteria, the Internet-based structure can be considered the most appropriate platform to satisfy these requirements. Nevertheless, participants in the supply chain have various capability and maturity levels in information management structure. Hence, prior to adopting the Internet technology for integration, the existing information management structure of each participant must be determined.

Identifying Connecting Components

One of the most critical functions of supply chain management is to ensure the effective integration of information and material flows through the system. This includes understanding the value added to products and its related information flows (inputs and outputs) as it progresses through the supply chain (Michael-Donovan, 2002). This embraces analysis of the supply chain's real costs and cost and performance drivers (Seirlis, 2001).

Turner (1993) identifies some of the key components that need to be functionally integrated. These components also are considered the connecting components (or connecting business functions) among participants in the supply chain. These components include order management, customer service, invoicing, forecasting, distribution requirements planning (DRP), warehouse and inventory management, manufacturing planning, production control (MRPII), and integrated logistics.

Ensuring Appropriate Business Processes

In order to enhance the supply chain processes, it is important to understand what happens currently. Generally, supply chain processes may include the procurement, production, ordering, delivery, and inventory paths, both within the company and external parties.

First, analysts should analyze the supply chain processes and be able to appreciate the company's mix of products, end configurations, volumes, life cycles, channels, customer segments, and delivery outlets (Tyndall et al., 2002).

Each process then should be prioritized and broken down into its subprocesses, identifying each of its sources, outputs, transformations, timings, resources utilized, and requirements. This also would be an opportune time to gather metrics concerning each of the processes in order to establish a baseline for identifying problems and to measure future process improvement.

Additionally, any opportunities to benefit from quick-wins should be taken advantage of at this point (Michael-Donovan, 2002).

Establishing and Developing Interfaces

Once architectural issues have been resolved and data requirements have been determined, a structure needs to be established to enable common linkages between data providers and data recipients of the ISCM (i.e., customers and suppliers) and linkages within ISCM processes. This will require the need to ascertain whether there are any missing links and to determine how the data required will be sourced or provided and in which format.

The emerging technology for interface communications is XML (eXtensible Markup Language). XML uses HTML tags to enable the definition, transmission, validation, and interpretation of data. However, effort for this task should not be underestimated (Zieger, 2001). Significant resources may be required in analyzing sources from ERP and antiquated EDI systems. It has been suggested that third-party interface tools (e.g., Informatica & Brio) can be used to ease the transition for these types of systems (Zieger, 2001).

Developing New Business Processes

After conducting a detailed analysis of existing supply chain processes and identifying any inefficiencies and/or gaps in the process, a proposal should be created for the design of new processes. Not only should new processes cater to anticipated ISCM processing, but they also should be sufficiently visionary in order to accommodate other strategic initiatives (i.e., CRM, Supplier Management, Knowledge Management).

The new supply chain should be modeled in a manner so that supply chain blueprints can be generated (Comptroller, 2002; Zieger, 2001). Tyndall et al. (2002) suggest an iterative approach to process design, whereby a process is broken down into stages and then defined, analyzed, executed, assessed, and then redefined. This cycle continues until the appropriate performance expectations have been achieved. This process can become quite complex and convoluted, once organizations begin to incorporate backend systems and the processes of other organizations.

Based on metrics determined during the initial business process review, goals should be set for process improvement.

Confirm Strategic Alignment

At the completion of most of the analytical work, it is important to revisit some of the groundwork that would have been completed during the planning phase activity in the traditional SDLC.

It has been included in this framework to highlight the importance of ensuring an alignment between business strategy and expectations with the outcomes of the ISCM implementation—supply chain strategy is interdependent on the business strategic direction.

Analysts need to confirm that value is being delivered through ISCM by conducting a critical analysis on proposed benefits and costs in order to ensure that they are still realistic (Tyndall et al., 2002). In order to prevent misalignment of resources and skillsets, analysts also need to confirm that the business problem still can be solved with its current complement of staff.

Implementing ISCM Systems

This phase involves determining what activities will need to be undertaken to facilitate implementation of ISCM system—creating an action plan.

There are a number of factors that should be considered in this final phase of the methodology, such as setting up communication standards, developing business operation procedures, and establishing training programs.

Furthermore, this phase should be expanded to incorporate activities that can assist in the detailed analysis of implementation risks of the system. Conducting analyses in areas such as change management is one example. Inability to manage the implementation of change has been a key factor in project failure. Any enterprise system places great strain on the organization to adapt in order to reap the benefits. Change management involves more than simply conducting user-training programs but involves a continuing consultative relationship with end users to secure buy-in.

CONCLUSION AND FUTURE CHALLENGE

This chapter endeavors to propose an analysis and development methodology for ISCM systems. The discussion started with review and investigation of the current ISCM solutions and architectures, and identified a number of benefits, issues, and problems regarding the implementation of ISCM systems. Based on the examination of existing ISCM status, the proposed methodology for ISCM systems analysis is constructed by an eight-phase development framework. The methodology tends to illustrate a systematic roadmap for enterprises in developing ISCM systems.

The future challenge for enterprises in operating and maintaining ISCM systems stressed the overall maturity of technological availability and the flexibility of business processes aligning with the ISCM architecture.

REFERENCES

Advanced Software Design Inc. (2002). ASD supply chain solution. ASD Global. Retrieved July 21, 2003, from *http://www.asdglobal.com/products/dod.html*

Armstrong, E. (2002). The evolution of supply chain management software. *Logistics Management, 41*(9), 66-70.

Bergert, S, & Kazimer-Shockley, K. (2001). The customer rules. *Intelligent Enterprise, 4*(11), 31.

Bragg, S. (2002). 10 symptoms of poor supply chain performance. ARC Advisory Group. Retrieved July 21, 2003, from *http://www.idii.com/wp/arc_sc_perf.pdf*

Cottrill, K. (1997). Reforging the supply chain. *Journal of Business Strategy, 18*(6), 35-39.

Dalton, G., & Wilder, C. (1998). eBusiness—Global links—Companies are turning to the Internet for tighter integration with suppliers overseas. *Information Week, 674*, 18-20.

Fontanella, J. (2001). The overselling of supply chain suites. AMR Research. Retrieved July 21, 2003, from *http://www.amrresearch.com/Content/view.asp?pmillid=662&docid=8027*

Gledhill, J. (2002). Create values with IT investment: How to generate a healthy ROI across the enterprise. *Food Processing, 63*(9), 76-80.

Handfield, R., & Nichols Jr., E. (1999). *An introduction to supply chain management.* Prentice Hall.

Lan, Y., & Unhelkar, B. (2005). *Global enterprise transitions: Managing the process.* Hershey, PA: IRM Press.

Michael-Donovan, R. (2002). e-Supply chain management: Pre-requisites to success. Performance Improvement. Retrieved July 21, 2003, from *http://www.idii.com/wp/donovan_sc_part1.pdf*

Mol, M., & Koppius, O. (2002). Information technology and the internationalisation of the firm. *Journal of Global Information Management, 10*(4), 44-60.

New, S. (1994). A framework for analysing supply chain improvement. Manchester School of Management. Retrieved July 21, 2003, from *http://www.unf.edu/~ybolumol/tra_4202_011/Artiicles/sc_improvement.pdf*

Oakton. (2003). Manufacturing and supply chain solutions. Oakton Consulting. Retrieved July 21, 2003, from *http://www.infact.com.au/clients/manufacturing.htm*

OSD Comptroller iCenter. (2002). Integrated supply chain management: Optimising logistics support. Office of the Under Secretary of Defence. Retrieved July 21, 2003, from *http://www.dod.mil/comptroller/icenter/learn/iscmconcept.pdf*

Parkes, C. (2002). Supply chain management. Peoplesoft Inc. Retrieved July 21, 2003, from *http://peoplesoft.ittoolbox.com/documents/document.asp?i=836*

Seirlis, A. (2001). Integrated supply chain analysis. TLB Consulting. Retrieved July 21, 2003, from *http://www.tlb.co.za/library/comentary/integrated.html*

Smith, T. (2002). Sharing the risk: How to avoid a supply-chain nightmare. Internet Week.com. Retrieved July 21, 2003, from *http://www.internetweek.com/supplyChain/INW20020725S0007*

Strausl, D. (2001). Four stages to building an effective supply chain network. *EBN, (1251), 43.*

Turner, R. (1993). Integrated supply chain management: What's wrong with this picture? *Industrial Engineering, 25*(12), 52-55.

Tyndall, G., et al. (2002). Making it happen: The value producing supply chain. Centre for Business Innovation—Ernst & Young. Retrieved July 21, 2003, from *http://www.cbi.cgey.com/journal/issue3/features/makin/makin.pdf*

Zieger, A. (2001). Preparing for supply chain architectures. PeerToPeerCentral.com. Retrieved July 21, 2003, from http://www-106.ibm.com/developerworks/web/library/wa-supch.html?dwzone=web

Chapter VI
Challenges in Developing a Knowledge Management Strategy:
A Case Study of the Air Force Materiel Command[1]

Summer E. Bartczak
University of Central Arkansas, USA

Jason M. Turner
Air Force Institute of Technology, USA

Ellen C. England
ISN Software Corporation and Kaplan University, USA

ABSTRACT

It is widely acknowledged that knowledge management (KM) strategy is a desired precursor to developing specific KM initiatives. Strategy development is often difficult due a variety of influences and constraints. Using KM influences as a foundation, this case study describes issues involved in developing a KM strategy for the Air Force Material Command, including issues to be considered for future strategy development such as leadership support and understanding, conflicts with IT organizations, funding, technology usage and configuration, and outsourcing.

INTRODUCTION

Enablers, barriers, and influences of KM have been grouped into three broad categories: internal managerial influences, internal resource influences, and external environmental influences (Holsapple & Joshi, 2000, 2002). Managerial influences "emanate from the organizational participants responsible for administering the management of knowledge" (Holsapple & Joshi, 2000, p. 239); resource influences include human, financial, knowledge, and material resources that make KM a reality (p. 241); and environmental influences affect what "knowledge resources should or can be acquired in the course of KM, as well as what knowledge manipulation skills (e.g., human or technical) are available" (p. 242).

KM strategy is also generally regarded as essential to implementation and should be guided by organizational strategy (Zack, 1999). Earl (2001) provides a taxonomy of strategic starting points, seven "schools of knowledge management" and key attributes of each. Yet despite such insight, little is known about KM strategy within the military (Bower, 2001; Plant, 2000). Difficulties stem from the unique context in which KM must be implemented including culture, organization, and operating environment. Because of these unique attributes, an investigation of military KM may prove telling theoretically and practically.

CASE BACKGROUND

Headquartered in Dayton, Ohio, Air Force Material Command (AFMC) employs 85,000 military and civilian employees worldwide. AFMC has "cradle-to-grave" oversight for all aircraft, missiles, and munitions. The Directorate of Requirements (DR) is home to AFMC's Knowledge Management program.

In the early 1990s, AFMC/DR developed a repository of acquisitions regulations, process descriptions, and other miscellaneous information. The repository soon expanded into the Defense Acquisition Deskbook program and was managed by an interservice Joint Program Office. AFMC/DR continued updating Air Force (AF) documents within Deskbook; however, this did not require DR's entire budget. As a result, it was decided the excess funding was to be used for the development of an additional KM application that helped to document and disseminate overarching AF lessons learned.

AFMC/DR was also developing Web-based training for acquisitions personnel due to impending talent drains as more civilian personnel retired. To improve AFMC's preparedness, Deputy Director Robert Mulcahy became a KM champion. He consolidated deskbook, lessons learned, and web-based training into one KM system in order to provide better capture and dissemination of critical workforce knowledge.

Mulcahy assigned Randy Adkins to lead the consolidated AF knowledge management (AFKM) program. Initially, the AFKM program centered on the use of commercial KM processes and technologies for solving specific customer problems. Soon, however, the now-consolidated KM system grew beyond its original three components; by 2000, two new modules were added: the AFMC Help Center and Community of Practice (CoP) workspaces." The Help Center provided search capabilities for information across AFMC web sites; the CoP workspaces fostered information exchange, collaboration, and problem solving. The AFKM Hub/home page was a portal-like entrance into the entire system.

RESEARCH METHOD

AFMC was one of the first AF organizations to embrace KM; the AFKM team also faced significant challenges determining future directions for their efforts. It was therefore likely key issues impacting KM strategy development might be identified in this context. Additional case research was also needed to bridge the gap between KM theory and practical advice (Jennix, 2005, p. vii). Given these factors, an exploratory case study methodology was used.

Holsapple and Joshi's (2000, 2002) KM influences framework provided three foundational constructs for "analytic generalization" (Yin, 1994, p. 31); these factors—managerial, resource, and environmental—could be examined as potential barriers to KM strategy development. Considerations for design quality were made in accordance with Kidder and Judd (1986) and Yin (1994); however, internal validity was not addressed due to the study's exploratory nature.

Data included interviews, field notes, and physical traces. Open-ended interviews were taped and transcribed, then reviewed and approved by respondents. Twelve individuals were interviewed providing a cross-section of organizational leadership, the AFKM team, and AFKM customers. Transcripts were first searched and categorized according to a priori KM influence (and emergent) categories and themes. Resultant data was combined with field notes (capturing impressions about the interviews and observations of individual/organization dynamics) and physical traces (e.g., documents, Web sites, organizational charts, budget records, advertising media, etc.) to form a robust understanding of the case.

FINDINGS

The AFKM effort exhibited many of Holsapple and Joshi's (2000, 2002) influence factors; however, the military environment provided some unique constraints that further exacerbated the negative influences. On the whole, this study revealed a variety of latent and emergent issues that should be considered for any KM strategy development; key issues are discussed below.

Leadership Support and Understanding

Mulcahy had been a staunch supporter for KM efforts. David Franke replaced Mulcahy in 2000, and a new Director of Requirements was also appointed. Both were open to KM concepts and the AFKM program, but neither was as educated or enthused about KM as Mulcahy. Adkins indicated that Franke didn't see KM as needing emphasis above other AFMC programs, thereby increasing the difficulty of securing exposure and backing necessary to compete for scarce resources. Furthermore, few other individuals had much of an idea of what KM was about. Although it was easy to communicate the importance of individual

applications (e.g., lessons learned, document repositories, corporate yellow pages), it was more difficult to explain comprehensive KM concepts. Adkins realized "learning about KM" took time, but the ignorance of those upon whom he relied for support threatened the program's survival before it had a chance to prove itself on a large scale.

Conflict with the IT Organization

Dealing with AFMC's information technology (IT) organization was a continual challenge because it perceived its role as providing technology solutions for the customer, as did AFMC/DR. Additionally, a conflict arose when the IT organization mandated LiveLink® as AFMC's only authorized collaboration tool. LiveLink® directly conflicted with CoP development and was generally more sophisticated than was needed by the average customer. While Adkins' team had a wealth of KM knowledge and system development expertise, the IT organization was the authorized policy maker, and continued conflicts risked AFKM being changed, dismantled, or absorbed.

Funding

A $600,00 budget cut loomed that would eliminate six personnel impacting AFKM systems development workload distribution. Furthermore, many AFKM customer-specific applications had been developed without charge. Without such assistance, some customers would never get their KM efforts off the ground and AFKM's support practices would have to be re-evaluated

System Usage Concerns

Despite rave customer reviews about AFKM systems, Adkins was disturbed by low usage rates. Access metrics showed usage generally rising, and yet it was a small portion of what it could be. Publicity capmpaigns did little overall; it was clear the AFKM system tools were still in their infancy and the low usage statistics didn't help the team adequately justify the benefits or budget.

Technological Challenges

The AFKM team became so efficient at developing technology solutions that they could develop a "CoP in a box" with a few minor customizations in only a few days. Instead of providing content (i.e., deskbook, lessons learned), the team now provided software frameworks, in which customers added information and knowledge. However, a new AF portal was decreed the de-facto access point for all AF information and knowledge. This raised the question of how to design future applications. Adkins' team was heavily involved in the technology of CoPs, but the community-based capabilities of the AF portal might change everything.

Outsourcing KM

With so many issues impacting AFKM; Adkins needed a strategic vision and implementation roadmap to guide future development. Adkins' foremost concern was the development of a strategic vision and plan. He needed documents that would provide starting points for decision-making and describe how to proceed to the envisioned business environment.

Unfortunately, AeroCorp's recommendations captured the complexities of AFMC's environment, and yet were so broad and involved it was difficult to determine a starting point. AeroCorp also had difficulty developing concise methodologies or "blueprints" that addressed the enormity of what AFMC needed to do to evolve into a true knowledge-sharing organization. In particular, AeroCorp applied integrated definition (IDEF) modeling to KM. IDEF modeling was developed for systems engineering and often depicts "as-is" enterprise processes and information

requirements; it did not serve as a user-friendly methodology for fully explaining or depicting strategic KM needs.

After seeing the initial draft of the IDEF model, it was clear the process was "over-engineered." After a year of waiting, the promised roadmap was too unfamiliar and complicated for Adkins and others to practically implement. Faced with an impending budget cut, AeroCorp would likely not have an opportunity to make necessary changes. At this point, Adkins had no good answers.

LESSONS LEARNED

Adkins understood he needed a strategic vision to guide AFKM's direction and decision-making. When outsourcing KM strategy met with limited success, he rescoped and refocused the team on a few key areas under their immediate control. From 2002 forward, the AFKM team:

1. promoted CoPs as a key technique for KM across the AF,
2. provided enterprise Web search capabilities across AFMC and selected AF sites,
3. used a process approach for delivering CoP capability.

The team's strategy became one of building momentum by providing rapid KM services ("CoPs in a box") and following up with training and implementation support; leadership could observe successes at the grassroots level. Since the change in strategy, AFKM has enjoyed remarkable success. The AFKM Web site, now called AF Knowledge Now, continues to expand its capabilities and customer base. In 2004, Adkins secured key support from the AF Chief Information Officer; Adkins' team was dubbed the AF Center of Excellence for Knowledge Management, and AF Knowledge Now was integrated into the AF portal.

IMPLICATIONS AND CONCLUSION

This study highlighted some real-world examples of such barriers and several issues to be considered for strategy development: many of the same factors that act as barriers to implementation may also impede KM strategy development. This study highlighted some real-world examples, such as barriers and several issues to be considered for strategy development:

- KM is hard to define and communicate to others.
- KM initiatives must be championed and supported at the highest levels of any organization.
- KM strategy development is not easy, yet it is critical to the success of any KM initiative.
- Outsourcing KM can be very risky.
- Focusing on specific KM efforts is important for countering negative KM influences.

Despite rising awareness of KM and its benefits, we are reminded that such issues may well play out in any organization, military or otherwise, and should be accounted for preemptively during KM strategy development to improve the chances of improving long-term organizational performance.

REFERENCES

Bower, W. (2001). *Development of a decision framework for knowledge management projects.* Unpublished doctoral dissertation, Air Force Institute of Technology, Wright-Patterson AFB, Dayton, OH.

Earl, M. (2001). Knowledge management strategies: Toward a taxonomy. *Journal of Management Information Systems,18*(1), 215-233.

Holsapple, C., & Joshi, K. D. (2000). An investigation of factors that influence the management of knowledge in organizations. *Journal of Strategic Information Systems,9*, 235-261.

Holsapple, C., & Joshi, K. D. (2002). Knowledge management: A three-fold framework. *The Information Society, 18,* 47-64.

Jennix, E. (2005). *Case studies in knowledge management.* Hershey, PA: Idea Group Publishing.

Kidder, L., & Judd, C. M. (1986). *Research methods in social relations* (5th ed.). New York: Holt, Rhinehardt, and Winston.

Plant, T. (2000). *Introducing knowledge management into complex organizations* (unpublished manuscript). Australian Defense Force Academy, School of Computer Science, University College, University of New South Wales.

Yin, R. K. (1994). *Case study research: Design and methods* (2nd ed., Vol. 5). Thousand Oaks, CA: Sage Publications.

Zack, M. H. (1999). *Knowledge and strategy.* Boston: Butterworth-Heinemann.

ENDNOTE

[1] The views expressed in this case study are those of the authors and do not necessarily reflect the official policy or position of the Air Force, the Department of Defense, or the US Government.

This work was previously published in International Journal of Knowledge Management, Vol. 4, Issue 1, edited by M. E. Jennex, pp. 46-50, copyright 2008 by IGI Publishing, formerly known as Idea Group Publishing (an imprint of IGI Global).

Chapter VII
Developing a Global CRM Strategy

Michael Shumanov
Monash University, Australia

Michael Ewing
Monash University, Australia

ABSTRACT

While the managerial rationale for adopting customer relationship management (CRM) has been fairly well articulated in the literature, research on strategy development is scant. Moreover, reports of "CRM failures" in the popular business press have done little to inspire confidence. To date, what little research has been conducted in the area of CRM strategy development has been confined to a single country (often the U.S.). Global CRM strategy development issues have yet to be specifically addressed, particularly which elements of CRM strategy should be centralised/decentralised. The present study examines the complexities of global CRM strategy using the case of a leading financial services company. Interviews are conducted in 20 countries. Global Head Office and external IT consultant perspectives are also considered. Our findings confirm that a hybrid approach has wide practical appeal and that subsidiary orientation towards centralisation/decentralisation is moderated by firm/market size and sophistication.

INTRODUCTION

Recent advances in information technology (IT) have enhanced the possibilities for collecting customer data and generating information to support marketing decision making. CRM has been heralded by some as being the key to delivering superior business performance by focusing organisational efforts towards becoming more customer-centric and responsive (Davenport, Harris, & Kohli, 2001; Puschman & Rainer, 2001). However, others have cautioned that increasing information may actually *increase* the complexity of the decision-making process thereby adversely affecting decision-making performance (Van Bruggen, Smidts, & Wierenga, 2001).

Much of the extant academic literature on CRM has focused on identifying antecedents and consequences (e.g., Bull, 2003; Day & Van den Bulte 2002; Kotorov, 2003; Ryals & Knox, 2001). CRM has been variously conceptualised as (1) a process (e.g., Day & Van den Bulte, 2002; Galbreath & Rogers, 1999; Srivastava, Shervani, & Fahey, 1998); (2) a strategy (e.g., Croteau & Li, 2003; Verhoef & Donkers, 2001); (3) a philosophy (e.g., Fairhurst, 2001; Reichheld, 1996); (4) a capability (e.g., Peppers, Rogers, & Dorf, 1999) and (5) a technology (e.g., Shoemaker, 2001). Although there is clearly more to CRM than technology (Day & Van den Bulte, 2002; Reinartz, Krafft, & Hoyer, 2004), it is important to recognise that technology does play a central role in supporting the seamless integration of multiple customer touch points. IT also enables organisations to collect, store, develop, and disseminate knowledge throughout the organisation (Bose 2002; Crosby & Johnson, 2001). Customer knowledge is critical for successful customer relationship management (Crosby & Johnson, 2000; Davenport et al., 2001; Hirschowitz, 2001).

CRM Defined

The importance of technology in enabling CRM is exemplified by the attempts at defining the concept. CRM has been defined as the alignment of business strategies and processes to create customer loyalty and ultimately corporate profitability enabled by technology (Rigby, Reichheld, & Schefter, 2002). In a similar vain,

Ryals (2002) defines it as the lifetime management of customer relationships using IT. E-CRM is defined as the application of customer relationship management processes utlising IT and relies on technology such as relational databases, data warehouses, data mining, computer telephony integration, Internet, and multi-channel communication platforms in order to get closer to customers (Chen & Chen, 2004; Fjermestad & Romano, 2003). In many respects e-CRM is a tautology in that without "e," or technology, there would be no CRM. We therefore standardise on the term CRM throughout the paper.

As a business philosophy, CRM is inextricably linked to the marketing concept (Kotler, 1967) and market orientation, which stresses that firms must organise around, and be responsive to, the needs of customers (Kohli & Jaworski, 1990; Narver & Slater, 1990). From a capability perspective, CRM needs to be able to gather intelligence about current and prospective customers (Campbell, 2003; Crosby & Johnson, 2000; Davenport et al., 2001; Zablah, Bellenger, & Johnston, 2004) and apply that intelligence to shape its subsequent customer interactions. Furthermore, CRM processes need to acknowledge that relationships develop over time, have distinct phases, and are dynamic (Dwyer, Schurr, & Oh, 1987). Adopting this view highlights that CRM processes are best thought of as longitudinal phenomena. The interesting feature for firms is that they should interact and manage relationships with customers differently at each stage (Srivastava et al., 1998). Essentially, CRM involves the systematic and proactive management of relationships from initiation to termination across all channels (Reinartz et al., 2004). Another aspect of the relationship continuum is that not all relationships provide equivalent value to the firm. CRM requires firms to allocate resources to customer segments based on the value of the customer segment to the firm (Zablah et al., 2004; Zeithaml, Rust, & Lemon, 2001).

CRM Strategy

A high degree of CRM process implementation is characterised as where firms are able to adjust their customer interactions based on the life-cycle stages of their customers and their capacity to influence or shape the stages (i.e., extending relationships, Reinartz et al., 2004). Standardising CRM processes enables consistent execution to customers across all delivery channels. Successful CRM also requires organisational alignment (employee reward systems, organisational structure, training procedures) and investments in CRM technology. Interestingly, the level of technological sophistication of CRM technology makes no contribution to economic performance and supports the view that CRM is more than just software (Reinartz et al., 2004).

CRM can be conceptualised at three levels: (1) company wide, (2) functional, and (3) customer facing (Buttle, 2004). This study adopts the company-wide definition of CRM which views CRM as a core customer-centric business strategy focused on acquiring and retaining profitable customers (Buttle, 2004). This requires a customer-centric business culture, formal reward and recognition systems that promote employee behaviours that enhance customer satisfaction and the sharing of customer information and its conversion into useful knowledge.

Unfortunately, CRM's potential has, in many instances, failed to be realised. Successful implementation requires the adoption of a customer-centric business strategy and a redesign of functional activities, workflows, and processes (Galami, 2000; Nelson & Berg, 2000). Some organisations have begun focusing their business strategy around their customers and capturing, sharing, and applying customer knowledge to deliver superior service and customisation (Mitchell, 1998).

However, despite the rhetoric, empirical research on CRM strategy development is scarce. In particular, work on the vexing standardisation/localisation issue is lacking. In this increasingly globalised economy, it is surprising that researchers have overlooked cross-national differences and global CRM strategy issues. To address these gaps, the present study will seek to explore in depth the issues surrounding standardisation versus localisation of CRM strategy development. A case study of a leading financial services company is used to explore these issues. The paper reviews the localisation/centralisation literature, describes the study to be undertaken, and based on the findings draws a number of conclusions regarding global CRM strategy development and highlights areas worthy of future research.

GLOBAL CRM STRATEGY

In an increasingly competitive and complex market environment, multi-national enterprises (MNE's) are under constant pressure to re-assess the degree of autonomy they grant to their local subsidiaries. While headquarters are likely to have more expertise on strategic matters, local subsidiaries are likely to have more information on operational issues and be more responsive to dynamics impacting their specific market. Within a specific MNE context, centralisation refers to where decision making is vested largely with the global parent company (Cray, 1984). By contrast, decentralised organisations are defined as those where each subsidiary has a high degree of autonomy in making decisions on processes and products relevant to the needs of the local market (Edwards, Ahmad, & Moss, 2002).

There is some empirical evidence to suggest that although subsidiaries of global parent organisations may be given some autonomy in making operating decisions, strategic decision making is invariably controlled by the parent organisation (Bowman, Farley, & Schmittlein, 2000), which can be manifested through IT (Roche, 1996). Moreover, IT provides an efficient and effective decision support system to transfer information from the local subsidiary into the parent company's reporting models, increasing the capacity of headquarter management to engage in local company decision making (Clemmons & Simon, 2001; McDonald, 1996). Using a case study approach, Ciborra and Failla (2000) found that IBM failed in its vision for global CRM because of their fixation for standardisation and centralisation and the use of IT to enforce behaviours. Furthermore, they concluded that this variation in CRM adoption at the country level and unique regulatory requirements made the concept of "global CRM" tenuous at best, although they acknowledge that CRM is a "powerful weapon for centralisation" (Ciborra & Failla, 2000, p. 122).

This desire for greater parent company control is a function of perceived risk. That is, the greater the perceived level of risk, the greater the desire for active decision making (Garnier, 1982). The types of decisions likely to require parent company decision making include capital expenditure; acquisitions and divestments; and funding. A criticism of centralised decision making is that it is expensive and that local subsidiaries are unable to react quickly to changes in local market dynamics (Harris, 1992). There is some empirical evidence to suggest that organisations with decentralised decision making performed better than those organisations characterised as having centralised decision making with respect to marketing (Ozsomer & Prussia, 2000). Moreover, highly centralised organisations make less contribution to their host country in terms of investment, knowledge transfer, and management expertise than their decentralised counterparts (Fina & Rugman, 1996).

We have adopted a typology developed by Barlett and Ghoshal (1989) to classify the predisposition of organisations for a globalised/localised orientation. They describe organisations as: global, international, multi-national, and transnational. A global organisation is characterised as driven by the need for global efficiency, while having structures that are more centralised in their strategic and operational decisions. An international organisation is characterised as transferring and adapting the parent company's knowledge or expertise to foreign subsidiaries. The parent retains influence and control, but to a lesser extent than a classic global structure. A multi-national organisation manages its subsidiaries as though they were components of a portfolio of multi-national entities with headquarters exercising low control and low coordination. Finally, a transnational organisation seeks a balance between global integration and local responsiveness. This type of organisation has structures considered to be both centralised and decentralised simultaneously. Transnational firms have higher degrees of coordination with low control dispersed throughout the organisation. Using this typology, our focal firm can be characterised as a global organisation. That is, they employ structures that are more centralised in their strategic and operational decisions, and their products are homogenous throughout the world. Given a centralised structure, most of the decisions are made at headquarter level and imposed on subsidiaries.

Agency Theory

We use agency theory (Ross, 1973) as the theoretical foundation for describing the relationship between headquarters and country subsidiaries. Agency theory refers to the basic agency structure of a principal and agent who are engaged in cooperative behaviour, but having differing goals and attitudes to risk (Ross, 1973). In our research, the principal is headquarters and the agent is the subsidiary organisation. Goal differences, risk tolerance differences, and information asymmetry can create problems in agency relations (Eisenhardt, 1985). The first general problem is differences in the goals of principal and agents. Agents may act in their own self-interest at the expense of the principal. Secondly, principals and agents may have different tolerances towards risk.

In the context of CRM strategy development, the principal is likely to have a lower risk tolerance than the agent. The third problem, asymmetric information arises when one party has more information than the other, or when one party prefers to keep some information private.

There are two types of agent behaviour that could be detrimental to the principal. The first, adverse selection might refer to a subsidiary's misrepresentation of its ability to undertake/implement CRM. The second moral hazard refers to the fact that the agent may not act as diligently as anticipated in carrying out the will of the principal. However, agency theory proposes that better information management systems can reduce the agency problem and provide the principal with greater control and is consistent with our earlier discussion on global CRM strategy development. Control may take the form of behaviour-based or outcome-based strategies. Both rely on the principal's ability to evaluate the performance of the agent, either on a behaviour-by-behaviour basis or at the end of the project based on its outcome (Eisenhardt, 1985).

From the principal's perspective, adopting an outcome-based control strategy is likely to be difficult given that the principal would need to wait until the long-term outcomes became known. Consequently, a behaviour-based control strategy may be preferred by the principal in CRM strategy development. The degree of knowledge that the principal (headquarters) has about the agent (wholly owned subsidiary) in terms of market characteristics, customer profile, and processes, enables headquarters to more effectively monitor and control a subsidiary's behaviour (Kirsch, 1996). This is likely to mitigate the risk of subsidiaries acting in their own self-interest at the expense of the entire organisation. Agency theory (Ross, 1973) is therefore useful in addressing our research questions: what aspects of CRM strategy should be centralised/localised? and what are some of the complexities of cross-national CRM strategy development? Another fundamental concept is the level of involvement between the principal and agent in implementation. For instance, if the agent is able to customise the CRM implementation to reflect their country's requirements, then the principal has less ability to control the behaviour of local country CRM managers compared to where the local subsidiary is required to implement a standardised CRM solution. However, the control dichotomy needs to be balanced to avoid implementation failure particularly where headquarters does not have an in-depth understanding of local market conditions. Furthermore, where a standardised implementation is imposed, it is important to consider the level of knowledge and dynamic learning mechanisms that will need to be created in the local subsidiary to address system failures.

We also examined the channel coordination literature (i.e., Frazier, 1999; Frazier & Rody, 1991; Hunt & Nevin. 1974), which describes the relationship between buyer and seller involving a distribution channel. However, given that this research seeks to examine the relationship between headquarters and its subsidiaries, agency theory offers a more robust theoretical foundation with respect to CRM strategy development. The channel coordination literature relates more to relationships characterised as involving a distribution channel, rather than describing the parent-subsidiary relationship.

METHOD

Data Collection

Understanding both substantive and methodological context permits the reader to put the research into context and thus derive deeper meaning from the findings (Johns, 2001). Data were derived using the case study method and utilising a multi-sample longitudinal research design (Yin, 1994). Case studies enable the development of deep insights into respondent beliefs and assist in theory development (Beverland, 2001). Bonoma (1985), Hirschman (1986), and Deshpande (1983) have all advocated for greater application of qualitative research methods in marketing. In order to avoid cueing subjects into a desired response, respondents were asked fairly general questions on the topic in order to elicit themes (Strauss & Corbin, 1992). Specifically, two "grand tour" questions (McCracken, 1988) were asked. The first related to issues surrounding local subsidiary decision-making empowerment in relation to CRM strategy. The second, on what CRM processes and systems should be centralisation versus decentralisation. Each participant was also sent a copy of the final transcript for comment. Any comments were noted and the results adjusted accordingly (Johnston, Leach, & Liu, 1999). The research questions were then e-mailed to sample 1 respondents with a statement thanking them for participating in the initial depth interviews and reiterating the purpose of the research. This was broadly described as seeking to gain an understanding of global CRM strategy development complexities with the aim of sharing the eventual findings across the whole group. In order to cross validate the results using a different group of respondents, we e-mailed the same two research questions to a second sample of respondents coupled with a statement describing the research. The objective was to assess the robustness of the initial sample findings with a separate sample of respondents (Deshpande, Farley, & Webster, 1993).

Two rounds of interviews were conducted with managers having a functional responsibility for CRM in their respective national subsidiary. Whether CRM respondents were responsible for CRM strategy or implementation was dependent on the level of the respondent within the organisation. Invariably, more senior respondents were responsible for strategy formulation. We had a mix of both strategic and operational CRM respondents (see Tables 1 and 2). The first sample consisted of CRM representatives from the following subsidiaries: Australia, Belgium, Germany,

Italy, Netherlands, Spain, Switzerland, United Kingdom, and United States. To improve construct validity, interviews were also conducted with the internal strategy department at headquarters and with external consultants assisting in CRM strategy formulation. This provided a strategic level view of the vision for CRM from a Group/ HQ perspective (Deshpande, 1983; Johnston et al., 1999). Details of first round respondents are presented in Table 1.

The first round of interviews was conducted by one of the authors over the telephone (Holbrook, Green, & Krosnick, 2003) and recorded/transcribed in order to assist in thematic analysis. The transcribed data was then edited and any additional data was integrated to develop a case summary. Details of second-round respondents are presented in Table 2. Australia, Germany, Netherlands, Spain, and Switzerland were represented in both samples, although in this case an alternative respondent, having responsibility for CRM, was interviewed.

FINDINGS

In reporting our results, we quote actual statements made by respondents in order to improve the validity of the findings for the reader (Eisenhardt, 1989; Yin, 1994).

Perceived Complexities of Global CRM Strategy Development

The general consensus of both samples suggested that they are limited in their ability to make strategic decisions. *"[Subsidiaries] get a very strong framework from headquarters."* Most respondents also anticipate that strategic decision-making is unlikely to become more devolved. Some respondents noted a distinction between strategic decision-making in terms of IT and operations: *"I must say that the CRM project on the IT side is very much directed by the project group at head office. On the other hand, nobody asks us if CRM processes are in place and actively managed"* and *"CRM initiatives particularly system related are being governed on a global or regional basis [and the subsidiary] probably does not have an overriding influence on it."* An exception to this is country X, where the different stage of CRM development in that market has meant that *"[head office] kind of gave us the ability to operate outside of their purview."*

Respondents in both samples noted cultural differences and maturity of markets as contributing to the complexity of global CRM strategy development. For instance, *"local cultural differences make it difficult to offer standardised CRM tools."* Another respondent noted *"no one central system can accommodate all of the differences that exist."* And another: *"what works great in one country may not work at all in another country."* Another perceived complexity was the capacity to meet all the different subsidiary requirements. *"The number of countries and the differences in market size and maturity creates another layer of complexity."* And *"you have to deal with a lot of market specifics—market-specific business processes and market-specific system adaptations."* Process concerns were also articulated, *"...existing local IT systems and related business processes cause issues when trying to overlay a global IT system."* Interestingly, hardly any respondents considered software-related issues as potential barriers to CRM strategy development, which may reflect their view that CRM is more than just software. However, one respondent noted, *"fractured information flows between head office and local subsidiaries results in misinformation regarding CRM developments."* And another respondent (in the second sample) raised the issue of cross functionality: *"CRM can't be implemented easily because it is cross functional."* Some respondents also noted that *"country-specific legislation also needs to be considered."*

Standardised Across Markets or Tailored to Local Market Requirements?

On the question of whether CRM processes and systems should be centralised, or decentralised, a "hybrid" approach has practical merit. That is, embracing a centralised CRM IT system which can then be configured by subsidiaries to meet local market requirements. The perceived benefits of this approach are that it is cost and resource efficient. Nearly all agreed that there were considerable advantages to centralisation. For example, *"If you just let every country do what they wanted, it would be chaos. Everybody would come up with unique solutions, there would be double investments and duplication of effort, there would no cooperation and I think the organization would suffer."* And *"centralise as much as possible and localise as little as possible."* A small market perspective was that *"we feel that some sort of centralisation in one country can very much benefit smaller countries due to budget constraints impeding their ability to develop their own systems."* The general consensus was that decentralisation would be inefficient in terms of resource utilisation, costs, and duplication of effort. On the other hand, they did recognise that complete centralisation would lead to a situation of inflexibility. *"If you do everything on a central basis, one size fits all, then you are going to end up with inertia of the organization—think global act local."* There was some dissension on whether centralisation was more cost efficient than localisation. *"From a high level perspective [centralisation] might be cheaper, but down the road, one country will have a couple of hundred requirements, another country will also have another couple of hundred and the question is whether it is going to be worth it. The money that you and everyone is going to spend for changes will be [the] same as having a local solution."* The answer seems to be somewhere in the middle. *"In my opinion, I think it makes sense to develop them centrally and to adapt to local requirements. Each market is different and has different cultures, has different issues and so to develop things centrally makes sense because of development costs. But each market has to adapt them locally."* And, *"You may need to develop some tools that are able to have some consistency at its core, but which can then be configured to meet local needs, because its in the local market where you have got to survive."* And *"a centralised CRM tool is cost efficient and easy to update if you want to further develop the tool. If it is decentralised, then each country may spend a lot of financial resources doing that. The negative thing is that it doesn't take into account the local needs of the market."*

Another perspective viewed lack of market-specific information as a potential barrier to centralisation. *"My perspective is that markets know more what they need than the central department. I think the processes are not that different from country to country, but the key integration points are different for each market and are not well understood by headquarters. I think that when you try and bring a group approach to a specific problem its not going to work."* Another respondent noted the possibility for resistance, *"...what I can see, there is high resistance [to a centralised tool] from the markets because they want a lot of customisation which is not allowed and that causes a lot of problems."* Similarly, *"I think that CRM processes should be decentralised because of the respective market idiosyncrasies and it is important to set common objectives and standards and pursue them. In my opinion, centralisation is much more expensive [compared to localisation] because of the customisation costs."* One respondent noted that performance measurement also needs to be standardised in order to enable comparability. *"Success measurement KPIs need to be defined so that the performance of one market can be objectively compared against another market."*

One respondent suggested a set of guiding principles or framework could be utilised to assist in providing some direction, but ultimately subsidiaries would be responsible for decision making given their more intimate understanding of the market. *"I think there needs to be a strategic framework which is applicable for all subsidiaries all over the world and you can act within this framework to bring in your own experience, bring in your market-specific issues."* Another respondent noted that an alternative to the centralisation-decentralisation dichotomy is clustering markets based on similar characteristics and then applying a common approach. *"It might be a European solution for say all European countries, 'an Americas solution' for North and South America and so forth."*

Global Strategy

Local subsidiaries are often not empowered to make strategic decisions with respect to CRM. This may be a function of the perceived risk (Garnier, 1982). This finding is consistent with Bowman et al. (2000) who found that strategic decision making was controlled by the parent company. There also appears to be some dissension on whether the organisation has achieved a global strategy for CRM. *"Is there one [a global strategy]? To my mind we have only managed to derive some more or less binding rules for the subsidiaries, which tell them the 'do's', and 'don'ts' in treating their customers. A concise strategy focused on retention and acquisition to my mind does not yet exist."* In summing up, one respondent noted that, *"CRM is really about the business first and the business processes. The system should be designed to support this, not the other way round."* A number of large market respondents noted that there should be a global platform for knowledge management. *"We need to capture the key learnings from each market and leverage off these for the next country."* And *"lets stay connected and learn from each other."*

Cross-National Differences

In comparing differences between countries a clear pattern begins to emerge: two countries are demonstrably more advanced in terms of CRM implementation than the other 18, who are largely still in a passive "data collection" phase, not yet using customer data in their marketing strategies to anywhere near its full potential. The two advanced countries, by contrast, are well ahead of the curve—using advanced customer analytics for segmentation purposes to proactively manage customer relationships. The other interesting dynamic within this context is the fact that Head Office has largely allowed the advanced country "to get on with it" and granted them a high degree of autonomy. Among the other 18, there is another fairly obvious partition, between more advanced and less advanced. We say obvious because the split is fairly predictable and is driven by country size, stage of economic/social development, and market size. Basically, mature versus developing economies.

There also appears to be a feeling that the group strategy favours large markets and the needs of smaller subsidiaries in emerging markets are subordinated. *"There needs to be more attention paid to the smaller [market] solution and strengthening central support."* And *"from the point of view of small markets, you might think that decisions are sometimes based on the big market."*

DISCUSSION

Most respondents recognised the many advantages of standardisation. They could see the merit in having a universal strategic framework to guide the CRM process. They acknowledged that IT systems should be standardised to avoid resource duplication and any possible re-inventing of the wheel. This was particularly evident in smaller and/or less developed markets. However, a number of problems with standardisation were also acknowledged. These included inability to factor into account cultural differences/idiosyncrasies, country-specific legislation, and complexities arising from the inherently cross-functional nature of CRM. Thus, somewhat predictably, calls for a hybrid approach can de deduced from the data. However, based on the strength of arguments and also drawing on the literature, we conclude that local adaptation needs to be well justified and should be viewed more as the exception rather than the norm.

Theory-Building and Managerial Implications

This paper makes at least two significant contributions to the extant CRM literature. First, given the lack of empirical research in the area, it extends on earlier work on the complexities of global CRM strategy development (Ciborra & Failla, 2000; Massey, Montoya-Weiss, et al. 2001). Findings confirm that there is a lack of clarity regarding what the important antecedents are to global CRM success. The more mature markets in this study seem to have a better developed understanding of the importance of these dimensions and invest resources in enhancing their competencies in these areas. Second, we have shed some light on the perennial standardisation/adaptation question and have provide a preliminary framework of what elements may be amenable to centralisation and which to localisation. For global CRM managers and strategists, the findings suggest that a centralised approach has merit. Indeed, the majority of CRM functionality could well be centrally located, with the more customer-centric elements driven at the subsidiary level. The benefit of this approach is that it improves control and coordination while reducing transaction costs (Clemmons & Simon, 2001).

Limitations and Future Research

A number of limitations of this research are noted. First, the non-random selection of respondents introduced an element of judgement into the sampling process. Furthermore, for the majority of subsidiaries, a single informant may not accurately represent the entire view of the organisation. However, it was felt that the manager identified as responsible for CRM activities was the most qualified to respond to in-depth interview questions. Another limitation of this study is that it only involves a single organisation in a single industry and therefore the results may not be generalisable to other organisations or industries. The researchers attempted to mitigate the limitations of the sample by utilising two respondent samples (Deshpande et al., 1993). A problem also arises in attempting to find a suitable second informant in small subsidiaries, and some initial respondents may object to having a cross-validation process. Finally, stringent university "Ethics in Research Involving Humans" guidelines prevented us from identifying verbatim quotes with individual respondents because that would compromise respondent anonymity.

A number of directions for future research have emerged from this exploratory study. First, a study examining global CRM strategy development across industries would be useful to test the generalisability of these findings. In addition, further research is required to examine the relative importance of those global CRM factors we have identified and test whether there are some other factors which contribute to global CRM complexity, which have been overlooked in the current study. Also further work is required to quantify the cost-benefit of localisation versus centralisation. It is not clear whether the inflexibility that a centralised CRM tool mandates compensates for the anticipated cost benefits. It may be that the costs of local market customisation

erode these cost benefits. An interesting stream for future research would be to attempt to develop a framework that provides organisations with some insights into the required sequencing of CRM activities consistent with stage of implementation in order to build a solid foundation for the development of further CRM capabilities. Finally, from a cross-cultural perspective, the applicability of a stage model to global CRM implementation is worth considering.

REFERENCES

Barlett, C., & Ghoshal, S. (1989). *Managing across borders. The Transnational Solution.* Boston: Harvard Business School Press.

Beverland, M. (2001). Contextual influences and the adoption and practice of relationship selling in a business to business setting: An exploratory study. *Journal of Personal Selling & Sales Management, 21*(3), 207-215.

Bonoma, T. (1985). Case research in marketing: Opportunities, problems, and a process, *Journal of Marketing Research, 22,* 199-208.

Bose, R. (2002). Customer relationship management: Key components for IT success. *Industrial Management and Data Systems, 102*(½), 89-97.

Bowman, D., Farley, J., & Schmittlein, D. (2000). Cross national empirical generalisation in business services buying behaviour. *Journal of International Business Studies, 31*(4), 667.

Bull, C. (2003). Strategic issues in customer relationship management (CRM) implementation. *Business Process Management Journal, 9*(5), 592-602.

Buttle, F. (2004). *Customer relationship management.* Oxford, UK: Elsevier Butterworth-Heinemann.

Campbell, A. (2003). Creating customer knowledge competence: Managing customer relationship management programs strategically. *Industrial Marketing Management, 32*(5), 375.

Chen, Q., & Chen, H. (2004). Exploring the success factors of eCRM strategies in practice. *Database Marketing & Customer Strategy Management, 11*(4), 333-343.

Ciborra, C., & Failla, A. (2000). Infrastructure as a process: The case of CRM in IBM. In C. Ciborra (Ed.), *From control to drift: The dynamics of corporate information infrastructures* (pp. 105-124). Oxford University Press.

Clemmons, S., & Simon, S. (2001). Control and coordination in global ERP configuration. *Business Process Management Journal, 7*(3), 205-215.

Cray, D. (1984). Control and coordination in multinational corporations. *Journal of International Business Studies, 15*(2) 85-98.

Crosby, L. and Johnson, S. (2001). Technology: friend or foe to customer relationships. *Marketing Management, 10* (4), 10-11.

Croteau, A. M., & Li, P. (2003). Critical success factors of CRM technological initiatives. *Canadian Journal of Administrative Sciences, 20*(1), 21-34.

Davenport, T. H., Harris, J. G., & Kohli. (2001). How do they know their customers so well? *Sloan Management Review, 42*(2), 63-73.

Day, G., & Van den Bulte, C. (2002). *Superiority in customer relationship management consequences for competitive advantage and performance.* Marketing Science Institute.

Deshpande, R. (1983). Paradigms lost: On theory and method in research in marketing. *Journal of Marketing, 47*(4), 101-111.

Deshpande, R., Farley, J., & Webster, F. (1993). Corporate culture, customer orientation and innovativeness. *Journal of Marketing, 57*(1), 23-38.

Dwyer, R., Schurr, P., & Oh, S. (1987). Developing buyer-seller relationships. *Journal of Marketing, 51*(2), 11-28.

Edwards, R., Ahmad, A., & Moss, S. (2002). Subsidiary autonomy: The case of multinational subsidiaries in Malaysia. *Journal of Internal Business Studies, 33*(1), 183.

Eisenhardt, K. (1985). Agency theory: An assessment and review. *Academy of Management Review, 14*(1), 57-74.

Eisenhardt, K. (1989). Building theories from case study research. *Academy of Management Review, 14*(4), 532-550.

Fairhurst, G. (2001). Values at work: Employee participation meets market pressure at mondragon. *Communication Theory, 11*(2), 242.

Fina, E., & Rugman, A. (1996). A test of internalization theory and internationalization theory: The Upjohn company. *Management International Review, 36*(3), 199-214.

Fjermestad, J., & Romano, N. (2003). Electronic customer relationship management: Revisiting the general principles of usability and resistance An integrative implementation framework. *Business Process Management Journal, 9*(5), 572-591.

Frazier, G. (1999). Organizing and managing channels of distribution. *Journal of the Academy of Marketing Science, 27*(2), 226-240.

Frazier, G., & Rody, R. (1991, January). The use of influence strategies in interfirm relationships in industrial product channels. *Journal of Marketing, 55,* 52-69.

Galami, J. (2000). *Strategic analysis report: CRM IT requirements and strategies for payer prganisations.* Gartner Group.

Galbreath, J., & Rogers, T. (1999), Customer Relationship Leadership: A Leadership and Motivation Model for the Twenty-First Century Business, *The TQM Magazine, 11* (3), 161-171

Garnier, G. (1982). Context and decision making autonomy in the foreign affiliates of US multinational corporations. *Academy of Management Journal, 25*(4), 893-909.

Harris, G. (1992). International marketing centralisation. *European Business Journal, 4*(3), 50-55.

Hirschman, E. (1986). Humanistic inquiry in marketing research: Philosophy, method and criteria. *Journal of Marketing Research, 23,* 237-249.

Hirschowitz, A. (2001). Closing the CRM loop: The 21st century marketer's challenge: Transforming customer insight into customer value. *Journal of Targeting, Measurement and Analysis for Marketing, 10*(2), 168-179.

Holbrook, A., Green, M., & Krosnick, J. (2003). Telephone versus face-to-face interviewing of national probability samples with long questionnaires. *Public Opinion Quarterly, 67*(1), 79-125.

Hunt, S., & Nevin, J. (1974). Power in a channel of distribution: Sources and consequences. *Journal of Marketing Research, 11*(1), 186-193.

Johns, G. (2001). In praise of context. *Journal of Organizational Behavior, 22*(1), 31-40.

Johnston, W., Leach, M., & Liu, A. (1999). Theory testing using case studies in business to business research. *Industrial Marketing Management, 28,* 201-213.

Kirsch, L. (1996). The management of complex tasks in organizations: Controlling the systems development process. *Organization Science, 7*(1), 1-22.

Kohli, A., & Jaworski, B. (1990). Market orientation: The construct, research propositions, and managerial implications. *Journal of Marketing, 62*(4), 20-35.

Kotler, P. (1967). *Marketing management: Application, planning, implementation and control.* Upper Saddle River, NJ: Prentice Hall.

Kotorov, R. (2003). Customer relationship management: Strategic lessons and future directions. *Business Process Management Journal, 9*(5), 566-571.

Massey, A. P., Montoya-Weiss, M. M., et al. (2001). Re-engineering the customer relationship: Leveraging knowledge assets at IBM. *Decision Support Systems, 32*(2), 155-170.

McCracken, G. (1988). *The long interview, qualitative research methods.* Newbury Park, CA: Sage.

McDonald, W. (1996). Influences on the adoption of global marketing decision support systems: A management perspective. *International Marketing Review, 13*(1), 33-46.

Mitchell, P. J. (1998). Aligning customer call center for 2001. *Telemarketing and Call Center Solutions, 16*(10), 64-69.

Narver, J., & Slater, S. (1990). The effect of a market orientation on business profitability. *Journal of Marketing, 54*(4), 20-36.

Nelson, S., & Berg, T. (2000). *Customer relationship management: An overview.* Gartner Group.

Ozsomer, A., & Prussia, G. (2000). Competing perspectives in international marketing strategy: Contingency and process models. *Journal of International Marketing, 8*(1), 27-51.

Peppers, D., Rogers, M., & Dorf, B. (1999). Is your company ready for one-to-one marketing? *Harvard Business Review, 77*(1), 151-161.

Puschmann, T., & Rainer, A. (2001). Customer relationship management in the pharmaceutical industry. In *Proceedings of the 34th Hawaii International Conference on System Sciences.*

Reichheld, F. (1996). Learning from customer defections. *Harvard Business Review, 74*(2), 56-68.

Reinartz, W., Krafft, M., & Hoyer, W. (2004). The customer relationship management process: Its measurement and impact on performance. *Journal of Marketing Research, 61*(1), 293-305.

Rigby, D., Reichheld, F., & Schefter, P. (2002, February). Avoid the four perils of CRM. *Harvard Business Review, 80*(2), 101.

Roche, E. (1996). Strategic alliances—An entrepreneurial approach to globalisation. *Journal of Global Information Management, 4*(1), 34.

Ross, S. (1973). The economic theory of agency: The principal's dilemma. *The American Economic Review Proceedings, 63,* 134-139.

Ryals, L. (2002). Measuring risk and returns in the customer portfolio. *Journal of Database Marketing, 9*(3), 219-227.

Ryals, L., & Knox, S. (2001). Cross functional issues in the implementation of relationship marketing through customer relationship management. *European Management Journal, 19*(5), 534.

Shoemaker, M. (2001). A framework for examining IT enabled market relationships. *Journal of Personal Selling & Sales Management, 21*(2), 177-186.

Srivastava, R., Shervani, T., & Fahey, L. (1998). Market based assets and shareholder value: A framework for analysis. *Journal of Marketing, 62*(1), 2-18.

Strauss, A., & Corbin, J. (1992). *Basics of qualitative research: Grounded theory procedures and techniques.* Newbury Park, CA: Sage.

Van Bruggen, G., Smidts, A., & Wierenga, B. (2001). The powerful triangle of marketing data, managerial judgement, and marketing management support systems. *European Journal of Marketing, 25*(7/8), 796-814.

Verhoef, P., & Donkers, B. (2001). Predicting customer potential value: An application in the insurance industry. *Decision Support Systems, 32*(2), 189.

Yin, R. (1994). *Case study research: Design and methods.* Thousand Oaks, CA: Sage.

Zablah, A. R., Bellenger, D. N., & Johnston, W. J. (2004). An evaluation of divergent perspectives on customer relationship management: Towards a common understanding of an emerging phenomenon. *Industrial Marketing Management, 33*(6), 475-489.

Zeithaml, V., Rust, R., & Lemon, K. (2001). The customer pyramid: Creating and serving profitable customers. *California Management Review, 43*(4), 118-146.

This work was previously published in International Journal of E-Business Research, Vol. 3, Issue 2, edited by I. Lee, pp. 70-82, copyright 2007 by IGI Publishing, formerly known as Idea Group Publishing (an imprint of IGI Global).

Chapter VIII
Improving IT–Enabled Sense and Respond Capabilities:
An Application of Business Activity Monitoring at Southern International Airlines

Richard Welke
Georgia State University, USA

Gabriel Cavalheiro
Ernst & Young, NL

Ajantha Dahanayake
Georgia College & State University, USA

EXECUTIVE SUMMARY

Commercial airlines face an extremely challenging operating and competitive environment. To remain in business they must comply with ever-changing regulatory requirements while, at the same time, minimizing their operational costs without sacrificing customer expectations of service levels. Increasingly, airlines are realizing that a "plan-execute" mode of operation must give way to a "sense-respond" mode of operation; in other words they must become a real-time (agile) organization, capable of sensing the occurrence of unforeseen events such as the placement of a last-minute shipping order, flight delays, and cancellations, and respond effectively in real-time to such events. To enable enterprises in general, and the airline industry in particular, to improve their sense-and-respond capabilities and ensure better resource utilization, a number of software vendors are offering event stream processing and Business Activity Monitoring (BAM) solutions. This case examines a longitudinal set of real-world implementation projects using such a solution at a major US airline (referred to as Southern International Airlines) and the results and lessons gained from this deployment.

ORGANIZATIONAL BACKGROUND

This case involves the interactions between two organizations—a solutions provider (Quantive, LLC) and a client for Quantive's products and services: Southern International Airlines (not their real name).

Quantive, LLC (www.quantive.com) is a small product and services company, founded in 2000 by Dwight Jones, and based in Alpharetta, Georgia. It employs several people as well as having contractual relationships with additional personnel when needed to staff projects for clients. As its Web site indicates, it uses a combination of software tools and services to: capture critical business events in real-time without touching existing application systems, and translates these events into actionable business information (called "BAM-alerts"). It does this without the need to engage IT staff at the client organization, save to make a one-time network connection to a router on the client organization's network. To do this, it uses a stack of software to capture transactional packets of data moving over the network (Packeterm), translating these captured packets into logical transactional events (Inquisitor), and then examining these resulting events to identify exception or alert situations, and sending messages to a manager or an application to take action regarding the BAM-alert (Medusa). Finally, Quantive Factory provides additional ways to evaluate and present event alert information from Medusa. For a more complete picture of their offering, see Appendix A.

Southern International Airlines (SIA) provides both domestic and international air travel and shipping from its primary base in the Southwest as well as other hubs located throughout the world. It was founded through an incorporation of several airline companies in 1930. It operates approximately 1,000 aircraft that fly ca. 420 million seat-miles per day with 3,900 flights per day to 250+ locations. Although SIA is better known for its passenger service, its cargo division flies roughly 5 million pounds of cargo each day, with services to 250 cities in 40 countries, providing one of most extensive cargo networks in the airline industry.

SETTING THE STAGE

Initial Problem

Southern International Airlines' original motivation to adopt a (Quantive) BAM solution was to improve compliance with federal regulations issued by the US Federal Aviation Administration (FAA) and thereby reduce (or avoid) the high cost of non-compliance. In the context of this implementation project, the relevant regulation is FAA AC 43.13-1B: *Acceptable Methods, Techniques, and Practices—Aircraft Inspection and Repair*, which came into force on September 8, 1998 (FAA, 2002). More specifically, chapter 10 of this regulation sets requirements for both the calculation of take-off parameters for commercial aircrafts and the disclosure of corresponding compliance figures.

The primary reason for issuing this regulation is to improve flight safety. It is to ensure that if a significant weight variation takes place after the initial flight parameters are loaded that new parameters are re-loaded. If no action is taken to recalculate these parameters, the aircraft is likely to take-off with inadequate stabilizer settings and thus decrease flight safety. In this scenario, depending on the significance of the shift in the center of gravity resulting from the non-computed weight variations, these changes could cause the aircraft to exhibit dangerous flight characteristics (FAA, 1999). To prevent this scenario from happening, Southern International Airlines must have a proper weight and balance control system to enable the cockpit crew to know the actual values of the take-off parameters in order to set the stabilizer trim properly, prior to take-off. This involves monitoring factors influencing the weight and balance condition of an aircraft, such as total weight and position of load as well as the amount and distribution of fuel. Typically, significant weight variations can result from the loading of heavy freight, an exceptionally high fuel use during ground operations due to, say, airport congestion and/or flight cancellations causing many new last-minute passengers on the flight. Under such circumstances, the take-off configuration of the aircraft must be recalculated, taking into account the new weight and balance condition.

In addition, this particular FAA regulation emphasizes the need to improve accuracy on the disclosure of information when non-compliance occurs. Non-compliance conditions are those situations where this FAA regulation is violated and an aircraft takes off with inappropriate trim settings. To gather data about this type of non-compliance, the FAA relies on data submitted by SIA on a self-disclosure basis. On the face of it, the FAA is only able to enforce compliance by auditing the control systems of SIA in order to assess their capabilities of complying with the regulation and reporting requirements.

Beyond risks for flight safety, repeated violations of the noted FAA regulation can lead to large fines, loss of reputation, and SIA managers can be held legally liable for any resulting consequences of inappropriate weight and balance settings. Compliance with this and other FAA regulations became a primary concern and SIA must be able to demonstrate to the FAA, via audits, that their weight and balance control systems are capable of:

- Detecting significant shifts in the center of gravity of aircrafts as they occur and warning those responsible for the calculation of the take-off configurations
- Recording weight and balance non-compliance cases for FAA disclosure purposes

Assessing the Business Needs

Despite the fact that the AC 43.13-1B regulation of the FAA has been in place for some time, compliance with the mentioned requirements remained an issue for SIA. Although the information about the weight and balance condition of any given SIA aircraft could, in principle, be evaluated across several transactions generated by SIA for all its flights, detecting significant weight variations in time to take compensating action (i.e., real-time) was not feasible for several reasons. First, the application systems creating these transactions did not converse with one another. And second, the detection of an out-of-balance condition was not programmed into the current systems and the reporting of the underlying transactions could not be done in real-time.

Typically, the full content of the transactions relevant to detecting an out-of-balance condition are written directly to a "flight log". Because SIA operates approximately 3,900 flights per day, the resulting flight log is very large. To gather data about a certain flight, the personnel of SIA must search through the time-ordered sequence of messages associated with a particular flight and print out several of its sections to analyze the situation for any particular flight. This was a labor-intensive and time-consuming process that could only be justified in the most serious cases. And, in its current, manual state, the analysis process could take from hours to days and thus could only be used for off-line, retrospective analyses where situations had to be reconstructed.

The end result was that, even though the basic information on different aspects of aircraft weight distribution and changes were available in the flight log, SIA did not have the capability for detecting significant weight variations in real-time, as required by the FAA, and SIA's managers knew they were unable to respond to these variations and avoid penalties or worse.

Technical Constraints to Implementing a Solution

There were important technical constraints to be taken into account when implementing a solution for the preceding FAA compliance problem. These constraints stem from the dependence of Southern International Airlines on their transactional systems and the need to keep them running and available 24x7. The characteristics of the transactional systems of Southern International Airlines will be briefly explained below.

Most load and balance procedures are carried out by the flight operations system. This is a legacy system that has been used by SIA for nearly 40 years. Though this old system is stable and reliable, it is not easily modified, nor is it capable of providing real-time visibility into take-off parameters. The system was originally designed to carry out transactions rapidly and reliably, rather than to provide adequate control mechanisms to monitor specific transaction information. Despite the fact that the transactions processed by this system contain all the information involving the weight and balance condition of aircrafts, it was not possible to directly access this information during the execution interval of the relevant transactions; only well after the fact via the resulting flight log.

Modifying the flight operations system to directly satisfy regulatory requirements was viewed as infeasible because it would involve a long project with a high degree of implementation risk and, due to the dependency of SIA on this system, any potential risk of adversely affecting the existing flight operations system was deemed unacceptable. While there are plans to replace the old system with a new system that will be fully operational in a few years, SIA remains dependent on the current system for the immediate future.

To conclude, the time and accessibility gap between information available from the existing flight operations system and that needed to assure load balancing requirements in real-time, cannot be remedied by patching the existing flight operations system due to the SIA's high dependency on this system, it's age, and the risk to ongoing operations inherent in making any change to the system. Instead, SIA had to look for a different way to solve the problem that did not in any way impact the existing flight operations system. This led them to explore the use of an event capture and reporting system (Business Activity Monitoring or "BAM") and to Quantive as a prospective solution provider.

Understanding Business Activity Monitoring (BAM)

BAM is a relatively new way of conceptualizing and solving business-related problems, Chandy and McGoveran (2004) describe BAM solutions as real-time control systems that capture events in real-time from multiple, heterogeneous sources and selectively raise alerts within time-limited windows of opportunity. These quick (low latency) alerts are aimed at providing their recipients (often operational managers) with sufficient operational insights to enable effective response to critical events (DeFee & Harmon, 2004). As such, BAM solutions are particularly well suited to managers who need to respond to exceptional combinations of events, in real time. This approach can be distinguished from seemingly similar approaches such as real-time data warehousing in that the source of the information is the accumulated events themselves (event log) rather than an ETL (extract-transfer-load) from a transaction processing system's database into a specifically designed data warehouse (Golfarelli et al., 2004).

Another important aspect of a BAM approach is that it does not affect the performance of the underlying transactional systems. Rather, BAM solutions provide a transparent platform in which events are detected by separately examining individual, pre-existing transactions and defining patterns of events over an event stream that, should they occur, warrant managerial intervention. To support the development of event-driven applications, BAM solutions are likely to include event-modelling functions that define and validate event patterns (Gassman, 2004). This makes BAM solutions highly adaptable, as new event-driven applications can be rapidly developed to address new or changing business problems.

To represent BAM solutions, Gartner, Inc. proposed a BAM model in 2002 that distinguishes three basic layers: the "Event Absorption Layer," the "Event Processing and Filtering Layer," and the "Event Delivery and Display Layer." In this model, the border of a BAM solution is the "Event Delivery and Display Layer", which is the interface of the BAM solution with the recipients of BAM alerts (Govekar et al., 2002). A simple representation of the basic three-tiered BAM model can be found in Figure 1. A more sophisticated model can be found in Schiefer and McGregor (2004).

The Event Absorption Layer detects and acquires events that arrive from multiple and heterogeneous data sources (Gassman, 2004). The source of event messages will most often be business or process-related. However, technical events, such as the occurrence of technical fail-

ures during the execution of business processes might also be collected (Gassman, 2004). These sources can include both internal sources, such as (legacy) transaction processing systems, ERP systems, and RFID applications, as well as external sources such as those made available via the Internet (e.g., weather events), thus enabling a broader and richer view of business operations and its environment (McCoy et al., 2001).

These "raw" events, regardless of source, are first fed into the Event Absorption Layer. The Event Absorption Layer is most easily achieved by tapping into the stream of transaction events moving across a network via a middleware layer (i.e., data message transport layer) that carries transactional data messages across a network from transaction origination to the transaction application systems that process and store them. As these transactions move across the network, they can be defined, captured, and collected as events of potential interest and kept in an of event log, without disrupting their normal flow and usage.

At the next stage, Event Processing and Filtering software correlates this independent event stream data (McCoy, 2004). This layer sifts

Figure 1. Conceptual Model for BAM. Adapted from Govekar et al. (2002)

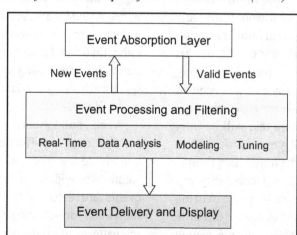

through and inter-relates the captured events, looking for combinations of events that occur, or should occur and does not, that in turn warrant managerial attention and intervention. More specifically, a set of event-based business rules are pre-defined and used by this layer to identify situations that are exceptions and create the conditions for an alert.

In the final layer (Event Delivery and Display) alerts created by the preceding layer are sent to those parties who are able to understand the nature of the exception and, as appropriate, take the necessary action to circumvent or avoid an emerging problem that is identified by the event rules. The alerts can populate a display and/or trigger an action (Gassman, 2004). Alerts that are used to populate a display are often delivered via graphical displays in the form of BAM "dashboards" containing real-time values of critical business performance indicators. These corporate dashboards are normally customized for use in different parts of the enterprise and for different audiences (McCoy et al., 2001). Alternatively, or in addition to, the alerts can be sent as messages to specific recipients who are empowered to act, via existing channels such as e-mails, instant messages, pagers, and so forth (McCoy, 2003).

Table 1. Application characteristics of weight and balance

	Application Characteristics
Performance-Indicators	Position center-of-gravity, total weight
BAM recipient	Operational Managers in the Weight and Balance Department
Tolerance for Latency	Seconds-minutes

Figure 2. Release IWBT filter: screenshot provided by quantive

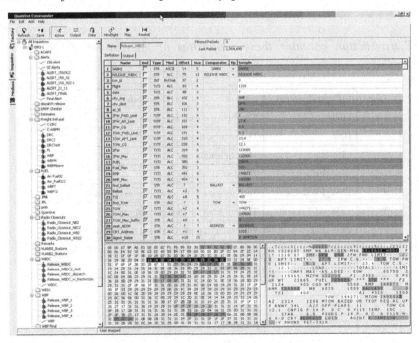

CASE DESCRIPTION

Initial Case: The Weight and Balance Solution

The Quantive BAM solution was first used by Southern International Airlines to design and deploy an event-driven application to improve compliance with FAA regulations. This section highlights this event-driven application by describing the event filtering conditions. In order to characterize the real-time decision support needs of the recipient for these "out-of-balance" BAM alerts, the performance-indicator monitored by the event-driven application and the tolerance for latency are taken into account. Table 1, summarizes the focus of this application.

For this case, SIA's BAM event-driven application raises alerts whenever significant weight changes occur after the initial flight parameters are set. These alerts, in turn, makes it possible for an operational manager in the weight and balance department to take corrective actions to ensure that the center of gravity is re-positioned within acceptable limits according to the aircraft flight manual before the aircraft takes off, as well as informing the cockpit crew about the actual take-off condition so that they can reset the stabilizer trim prior to take-off.

The primary event source is the Initial Weight and Balance Transaction (IWBT) used by the Flight Operations System, which contains the needed event properties that affect the weight and c.g. of an aircraft. This transaction is first captured at the absorption layer, then processed and filtered to create BAM alerts. The resulting application notifies appropriate BAM recipients (operational managers in the weight and balance department) of significant weight changes occurring that can affect the position of the aircraft's c.g.

Figure 2 provides a screenshot of all event properties captured using Quantive's event definition and absorption software, and contained in the IWBT transaction.

Table 2 shows the particular fields of the IWBT transaction that are captured in order to build the event to be logged and subsequently processed.

Table 2. IWBT transaction contains these properties of interest for real-time weight-balance monitoring

Line	Event Property	Description
4	Flight	The flight number, as seen by the traveling public
5	Date	The numeric day of the month
6	City_org	The origination city
7	City_dest	The destination city
9	ZFW_FWD_Limit	The "forward limit" of the center of gravity
10	ZFW_AFT_Limit	The "aft limit" of the center of gravity
11	ZFW_CG	The center of gravity value at the time of transaction
19	RMP	Aircraft weight before it leaves the gate (Ramp weight)
20	RMP_Max	Max allowed Ramp weight
22	Ballast	Ballast weight the aircraft is carrying
25	TOW	Expected Take-Off weight
26	TOW_Max	Max. allowable Take-Off weight

Event processing consists of using the resulting ZFW_CG, RMP, and TOW_WT values. Whenever one of those values comes within 2% of the forward and aft limit of the aircraft, an alert is raised and, at the third layer of BAM, a dashboard is updated to provide real-time visibility into this critical performance indicator.

Alerts raised by the weight and balance BAM application are also stored in a database. This makes it possible for SIA to disclose these alerts when reporting to the FAA about the occurrence of significant weight variations along with the corrective actions taken by SIA. In addition, the database is used to improve SIA's knowledge on patterns of balance event occurrences and, as a result, to provide this additional information to the FAA as well.

Follow-On BAM Applications

Although Southern International Airlines' decision to adopt Quantive's BAM solution was initially driven by the need to improve regulatory compliance without disturbing existing transactional systems, once managers began to see the power of re-thinking operational problems and potential solutions in terms of business events and event exceptions, other event-driven applications were identified and subsequently pursued. An additional attraction of the adopted BAM approach was that these applications could be implemented by the operations personnel directly. There was no need to have the IT unit involved in developing these solutions; operation's own people could easily master the identification of transactions moving across the organization's WAN (wide-are network) and create event definitions, filters, alerts, analysis, and display capabilities. This pattern of assimilation and adoption tended to follow the widely studied "diffusion of innovation" patterns documented in the marketing and information systems literature (Rogers, 1995).

At the time of this case (2005), ten event-driven applications, employing event 60 filters, had been implemented by Southern International Airlines. According to Quantive, these 10 applications raise an average of 30 to 40 alerts per day, each indicating a potential exception condition requiring intervention. At that level, the alert recipients are able to respond to all BAM alerts. However, it should be noted that as the number of event-driven applications increases, the risk increases of overloading the alert recipients with too many alerts (McCoy & Govekar, 2002). In such cases, BAM recipients are likely to start ignoring some of the alerts due to a lack of time to interpret and react upon the information contained in the alert (Klein & Besson, 2003). This situation is often referred to as cognitive overload (of the BAM recipient).

Three of these follow-on applications are given. Each highlights a problem identified by specific business unit managers following the installation and presentation on the original (weight-balance) application. Of these, the first two were successful. A third, while technically feasible and economically attractive, was nevertheless abandoned due to inadequate attention to social constraints.

Freight Refusal Application

Freight refusal presents an interesting problem to SIA, with significant negative financial implications. It involves scenarios in which sufficient cargo space is available on an aircraft but some of the freight booked for that flight is not loaded. This condition is referred to as freight refusal. For the sake of maximizing SIA's resources and revenues, it is obviously important to ensure that the maximum amount of freight booked for a flight is loaded onto the aircraft prior to take-off, especially for perishable goods that quickly deteriorate if they are not loaded and shipped as originally planned (e.g., flowers). In this case, SIA would have to reimburse customers for their resulting loss in addition to the loss of SIA shipping revenue. Since urgency and perishability are two of the primary reasons for using air cargo

Table 3. Application characteristics of Freight Refusal

Application Characteristics	
Performance-Indicators	Shipping status
BAM recipient	Supervisors of Ramp Crew
Tolerance for Latency	Hours-Days

over other logistical choices, nearly all freight refusal conditions have significant economic and quality of service impacts. Table 3 summarizes the characteristics of this application.

In examining the freight refusal scenario, SIA managers determined that there are both legitimate and non-legitimate reasons for freight refusals. The list of legitimate reasons include lack of space in the aircraft, insufficient time to load all booked freight before the scheduled departure time due to late arrival of the aircraft, the freight itself was not delivered to the airport in time, loading equipment damage, and so forth. In general, non-legitimate reasons result directly from failure of the ramp crew to load awaiting freight.

Southern International Airlines needed to identify the occurrence of non-legitimate freight refusal so that corrective measures could be taken with the associated ramp crew. However, the effort required investigating the reason for the occurrence of freight refusal and also required a time-consuming search of the flight log. Again, given the large volumes of data stored there, such an analysis was rarely undertaken and disciplinary measures seldom initiated, while non-legitimate freight refusal continued to occur.

The basic pattern for freight loading was then examined for the existence of signal events that could aid in identifying cases of freight refusal. For every flight of Southern International Airlines, there is a ramp controller who is in charge of registering the status of booked freight in a manifest document (transaction) provided by the flight

operations system. In the case of freight refusal, the ramp controller is supposed to register the reason for not loading the booked freight.

The event-driven application designed to tackle the non-legitimate occurrences of freight refusals work was based on monitoring the execution of transactions containing cargo information. Basically, after the first IWBT is executed, a system transaction (the Cargo Transaction) containing event properties pertaining to cargo, is also executed. These two transactions, in turn, provide the basis to develop a set of event rules and BAM application that would provide real-time notification of the occurrence of non-legitimate freight refusals.

While the actual set of transaction events and associated properties used is complex, to provide a sense of this application, a few simplifications are made. First, the Cargo Transaction contains an event property that identifies each product to be shipped, which is called PIC (Product Identification Code). Second, there is an event property to indicate the status of all products that are booked for shipment on a specific flight, called SPBS (Status of Products Booked for Shipment). SPBS can assume the values:

- *Confirmed*, meaning that product is ready for shipment
- *Cancelled*, meaning that a legitimate reason exists for not shipping the product according to shipment book
- *Shipped*, meaning that product was loaded into the aircraft

The event logic then becomes that of comparing the change of SPBS values during the loading process. Specifically, alerts are generated indicating non-legitimate freight refusals by searching for *confirmed products* that do not change their status to *shipped* in the course of the loading process. By this logic, it is possible to identify a possible failure of the assigned ramp controller for this flight to load that particular product shipment.

Monitoring Flight Planners

The allocation of passenger-sensitive resources to a particular flight is the responsibility of SIA's flight planners. Such resources can range from the number of meals carried to the fuel to be loaded on the plane. SIA management sought a way to develop an event-driven application to monitor the individual performance of flight planners with respect to optimal resource allocation. It is important to mention that flight planners' work in a non-unionized department, otherwise such monitoring would likely be opposed by their representation union officials. Table 4 highlights the properties of this application.

The event-analysis approach taken here relied upon two transactional events occurring within the flight operations system: the IWBT transaction and a Passenger Destination Transaction (PDT). After the IWBT is executed, the flight operations system executes a PDT transaction that contains properties indicating passenger destinations. The analysis showed that the Passenger Destination Transaction is executed automatically for the first time between 150 and 92 minutes prior to departure.

By aggregating the PDT's at a particular time point, one can compare the number of passengers at a particular point in time with the passengers indicated from a preceding point in time. This, in turn, can be compared to the flight planner's resource allocation for the flight (from a different transaction). In principle, the passenger configu-ration of a flight should not vary significantly, especially as the time of departure approaches. Variations beyond a pre-determined, SIA-speci-fied level, can signify that the flight planner is not keeping up with the changing status of the flight in a proper way.

Using this application it becomes possible for SIA management to analyze the performance of individual flight planners with respect to their allocating resources to their assigned flights and identify those flight planners who may need additional training and/or mentoring.

And, while this application was a post-mortem analysis, the same logic could be used to provide event alerts to the flight planner and/or his/her supervisor in real-time.

Monitoring Dispatchers

Not all event-based applications that were considered by SIA were successfully deployed. At the beginning it was acknowledged by the Quantive-provided trainers and developers that organizational resistance could be an obstacle to the deployment of some event-based applications. This proposed application is one such example.

The way of event-thinking that resulted in the preceding flight planner monitoring application led SIA management to consider extending the concept into an application to monitor the dispatchers that provide information support to the cockpit crew. The idea was to monitor whether dispatchers were paying sufficient attention to

Table 4. Application characteristics of monitoring flight planners

Application Characteristics	
Performance-Indicators	Variation in number of passengers near flight departure
BAM recipient	Supervisor of Flight Planners
Tolerance for Latency	Minutes-Hours

Table 5. Application characteristics of monitoring dispatchers

Application Characteristics	
Performance-Indicators	Time length of communication between cockpit crew and dispatcher
BAM recipient	Supervisors of Dispatchers
Tolerance for Latency	Minutes-Hours

all flights by examining a combination of transactional events drawn from the flight operations system to assess the frequency and duration of message interactions between the cockpit crew and the dispatcher, as suggested in Table 5. However, this prospective application did not proceed beyond the conceptualization phase.

In contrast to flight planners, the dispatchers work in a unionized department. For this reason, the proposed development of an event-driven application to monitor individual performance of dispatchers triggered fierce resistance from their union. To avoid possible conflicts with the union, the decision was taken to cancel any further development and deployment of this application. The experience gained with this attempted application demonstrates that an application that is technically and economically feasible can be socially infeasible. As such, the organizational setting becomes a very important aspect to be taken into account when considering event-driven monitoring applications.

CURRENT CHALLENGES FACING THE ORGANIZATION

A first challenge arises from the fact that many of Southern International Airlines business processes are highly regulated. As new regulations are added, these in turn require SIA to implement new, real-time control systems to monitor for compliance. However, in order for SIA to comply, they must continue to rely on their legacy transac-

tional systems, which were not designed to comply with such regulations. The challenge, then, is to overlay the existing systems with a new layer of processing that is transparent to the functioning of the existing systems while providing the needed regulatory compliance. While SIA was able to do this for the weight balancing regulation, there are many other regulations requiring compliance that must also be met in a cost-effective fashion. For example, the arrival of Sarbanes-Oxley (SarbOx) requires, among other things, the monitoring and control of various financial transactions and the early reporting of material events affecting financial disclosures "Section 409 is also important because material changes affecting financial disclosures must be reported on a rapid and current basis. This means systems must be able to provide timely information within days, not weeks, of an event." (Kaarst-Brown & Kelly, 2005, p. 2). Can an approach similar to the FAA compliance problem be taken to this set of regulations? If so, how does one expand the other areas of the organization, base of knowledge gained by the SIA flight operations managers in ways of event-thinking?

Another challenge (or more correctly, opportunity) faced by Southern International Airlines, once they had their initial BAM capability in place, was to re-think non-compliance-related problem-solution scenarios in event-based terms. As this case points out, there is a type of "ah-ha" moment that seems to occur when (some) managers begin to re-interpret other problems they are having in a manner that fits an event-stream,

BAM-like solution. While SIA could continue to rely on random awakenings to form the strategy for their next applications, is there a better way to identify opportunities and determine which of these are most applicable for solving using a BAM approach? Conversely, how should one avoid over-use of such a capability—the all-too-familiar problem of a solution looking for problems?

A third challenge that is associated a broader application of BAM-style application, particularly into areas with higher exception frequencies, is the already mentioned "alert overload" problem. Even though the number of alerts per day has been relatively small for the applications implemented to date, an increase in the number of event-driven applications could easily overload BAM recipients with too many alerts in much the same way that e-mails have done. While the volume of alerts can obviously be throttled back by more aggressive event filtering, this gives rise to the well know statistical problem of Type I and Type II errors, for example, rejecting events that should be seen versus accepting events as alerts that are not important. Can risk analyses similar to deciding Type I vs. Type II error levels be applied here? Or, are there other, better ways to accomplish this, drawn from (say) the area of Decision Support Systems?

A fourth and final challenge is how organizations in general, and SIA in particular, should anticipate and overcome organizational issues and constraints that often accompany real-time monitoring situations. As with any system change, technical and economic feasibility are not the only pre-conditions for a successful system implementation and change. It is widely known that "social failures" (i.e., the rejection of the system by the users themselves) are a major, if not primary cause of IT implementation failures. The last case discussed illustrates that unionized departments strongly tend to oppose the implementation of applications designed to monitor individual performance of employees. But more employees in general (unionized or not) are averse to having

their work monitored in real-time, particularly when the monitoring results in disciplinary action. And, while they may not be able to prevent its implementation, as the unionized employees were in this case, there are many other ways they can cause the resulting system to fail.

It should be noted, however, that BAM-style monitoring solutions are not inherently punitive; they can be used proactively as well as reactively. For example, in the case of dispatcher monitoring, the alerts could instead be sent to the dispatchers themselves as a stimulus to them to increase their engagement with the specific flight crew. Rather, from the applications presented (both implemented and withdrawn) it appears that SIA management is of the "Theory X" style and some of the BAM solutions implemented allow them to become even more so. How, then could the developers of these solutions approach their design so that the result to monitoring is more proactive/supportive rather than reactive/punitive? Should they? More generally, could/should BAM development adopt a socio-technical approach (Bostrom & Heinen, 1977; Mumford & Weir, 1979) to development so as to enhance implementation success, rather than the more mechanistic development approaches taken from real-time mechanical control system design, where the objects being monitored are machines rather than humans?

CONCLUSION

The implementation of a BAM solution at Southern International Airlines resulted in significant improvement of the event-response capabilities of the airline without having to modify or add to existing transactional systems and in time frames measured in days and weeks rather than months or years. The benefits produced by the projects described include: better regulatory compliance, reduction of operational costs, improved flight safety, greater management visibility into on-going operations, and improved customer service.

As with any new set of concepts and tools, the standard pattern of innovation diffusion can be observed as potential users of the system slowly begin to re-cast problems they may have in terms of events, real-time event monitoring and alerts. This diffusion is made particularly difficult in that the development of event-driven applications requires a combination of knowledge about business processes, regulations, transactional systems, and the BAM solution itself. A final consideration of the cases presented suggests the need for a broader framework and methodology base that addresses and integrates all the many aspects involved in an event-driven BAM implementation project and its subsequent implementation success.

REFERENCES

Bostrom, Robert P., & Heinen, Stephen J. (1977). MIS Problems and Failures: A Socio-Technical Perspective. Part I: The Causes. *MIS Quarterly, 1*(3), 17-32.

Chandy, M., & McGoveran, D. (2004). The Role of BAM. *Business Integration Journal*. Retrieved April 12, 2005, from http://www.bijonline.com/PDF/chandy%20role %20of%20bam%20april.pdf

Defee, J. M. & Harmon, P. (2004). *Business Activity Monitoring and Simulation*. Business Process Trends, White paper.

FAA (1999). *Aircraft Weight and Balance Handbook*. Retrieved December 08, 2005, from http://av-info.faa.gov/data/training book/faa-s-8083-1.pdf

FAA (2002) *Acceptable Methods, Techniques, and Practices- Aircraft Inspection and Repair* (AC 43.13-1B). Retrieved December 08, 2005, from http://www.faa.gov/certification/aircraft/av-info/dst/43-13/default.htm

Fowler, M., & Scott, K. (2001). *UML Distilled; A Brief Guide to the Standard Object Modeling Language*, (2nd ed.). New York: Addison Wesley Longman.

Gassman, B. (2004). How the Pieces of a BAM Architecture Work (TU-22-3754). Gartner.

Golfarelli, M., Rizzi, S., & Cella, I. (2004). Beyond data warehousing: what's next in business intelligence? *Proceedings of the 7th ACM international Workshop on Data Warehousing and OLAP*. (pp. 1-6). New York: ACM Press..

Govekar, M., McCoy, D., Dresner, H., & Correia, J. (2002). *Turning the Theory of BAM into a Working Reality* (COM-14-9785). Gartner

Kaarst-Brown, Michelle & Kelly, Shirley (2005). IT Governance and Sarbanes-Oxley: The Latest Sales Pitch or Real Challenges for the IT Function? *Proceedings of the 38th Hawaii International Conference on System Sciences*. Track 8. 236a. New York: IEEE Computer Society.

Klein, M., & Besson, F. (2003). Business Activity Monitoring; The End-Game of the Real-Time Enterprise. *Business Integration Journal*. Retrieved May 05, 2005, from http://www.bijonline.com/PDF/BIJ%20Dec%20-%20Klein%20%20Besson.pdf

McCoy, D. (2003). *Blending Business Process Management and Business Activity Monitoring*. Gartner-Strategic Planning, RU.

McCoy, D. (2002). *Business Activity Monitoring; Calm Before the Storm* (LE-IS-9724). Gartner,

McCoy, D. (2004). *The Convergence of BPM and BAM* (SPA-20-6074). Gartner

McCoy, D., & Govekar, M. (2002). *Evolving Interaction Styles in Business Activity Monitoring* (COM-17-8576). Gartner,

McCoy, D., Schulte, R., Buytendijk, F., Rayner, N., & Tiedrich, A. (2001). *Business Activity Monitoring; The Promise and Reality* (COM-13-9992). Gartner,

Mumford, E., & Weir, M. (1979). *Computer Systems in Work Design—The ETHICS Method.* London: Associated Business Press.

Rogers, Everett (1995). *Diffusion of Innovation* (4th ed.). New York: The Free Press.

Schiefer, J., & McGregor, C. (2004). Correlating Events for Monitoring Business Processes. In E. Seruca et al. (Eds.), *Proceedings of the Sixth International Conference on Enterprise Information Systems* (pp. 320-327). Porto Portugal: INSTICC.

APPENDIX A. TECHNICAL NOTE ON BAM SOLUTIONS

Business Activity Monitoring is a comparatively new concept, first introduced ca. 2002 in the professional literature (McCoy, 2002) and appearing in the academic literature ca. 2004; primarily in conference proceedings (cf. Golfarelli, et al, 2004). In order provide additional insight into SIA's implementation project, additional details regarding the Quantive BAM solution are provided below.

Figure A-1 places the Quantive BAM solution within the SIA flight operations "event cloud" of generated transactions and adopts the nomenclature of the previously presented Gartner conceptual model for BAM. At each level, the Quantive BAM solution provides products or built components that represent their approach to the functional need associated with the generic BAM model level.

Event Execution

For the initial SIA weight-and-balance application, the primary event of interest is considered a "complex event," for example, one that is defined as the occurrence of several basic transactional events that occur in a predefined sequence. For this application, the initial weight and balance transaction (IWBT) is the initiating transaction (triggering event) indicating the existence of a flight. The IWBT contains the basic flight information and the first execution of this transaction confirms that a flight is

Figure A-1. Functional components of the quantive BAM solution

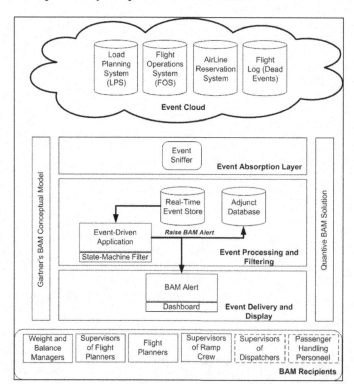

Figure A-2. Set of events of interest monitored by Southern International Airlines

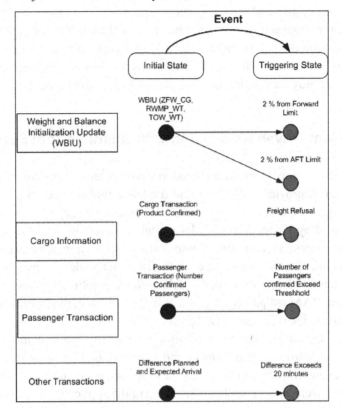

scheduled for departure within about 4 hours. There is a timing relationship between the IWBT and the other transactions carrying information about a certain flight. After IWBT's detection, a transaction sequence containing transactions about basic flight information regarding passengers, freight, fuel, and other elements of the flight occurs. Figure A-2 illustrates the associated events of interest that are then monitored by event-driven applications that were deployed by Southern International Airlines. When a pre-specified set of transactions and their associated events occur with specific values, a complex event of interest to the weight-and-balance application is then said to occur.

Event Sourcing

The primary source of events for this implementation project is the flight operations system. This is a widely distributed, message-based transactional system that is responsible for managing resources of all flights of Southern International Airlines throughout the world. The flight operations system supports transaction-based applications used by SIA's personnel to carry out business processes related to flights. Alongside the flight operations system, Quantive's BAM solution also monitors event streams output by other systems that interact with the flight operations system, such as the Loading Planning System (LPS) and Southern International Airlines' reservation system. The LPS is a subsystem of the flight operations system, which was designed to automate the load planning processes. The LPS sits on the top of the flight operations system, but executes underlying transactions that require data from both the flight operations system and the reservation system.

To acquire all the raw transactional events, Quantive's solution literally taps into SIA's switched LAN and, using transaction definition filters created by SIA's operations personnel, it reconstructs the packets of data moving into complete images of the various transactions moving across SIA's corporate network. More generally, any transaction moving over the LAN can be defined, captured and logged in this manner.

Developing an Event-Driven Application with Quantive Tool Set

Quantive's BAM solution includes an application development environment called the Quantive Factory. This environment provides business event modeling tools to specify event selectors used by applications to detect both single and complex events of interest. The application development environment, which is illustrated by Figure A-3, includes modeling functions that can be used to specify the performance indicators to monitor, logic formulas to characterize a complex event pattern corresponding to an exceptional situation of interest, and the characteristics of the alert to be issued when the defined, complex event is detected. Alerts are normally delivered by graphic displays "dashboards" that are customized for different BAM recipients, although as in the SIA case, they were also sent as (real-time) messages to appropriate devices (pagers, PDA's).

The interface of the Quantive Factory was designed for use by business managers, rather than IT developers. As such, complete applications can be and were developed without the need for IT-specialist knowledge. For this reason, the development cycle of event-driven applications was much shorter then would be the case for conventional IT applications. Each of the applications discussed in this case took days or several weeks to develop and implement and in some cases, less than a day. It also provides a much higher degree of "ownership" by the business unit itself, as well as providing a tool for subsequent adaptation and experimentation.

Figure A-3. Graphical user interface of quantive's event-driven application development environment. source: quantive

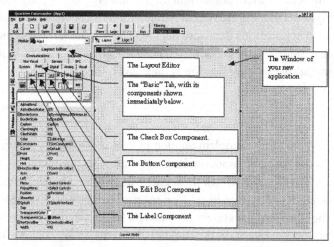

Section III
Tools and Technologies

Chapter IX
Intelligent Design Advisor:
A Knowledge–Based Information System Approach for Product Development and Design

Quangang Yang
University of South Wales, Australia

Carl Reidsema
University of South Wales, Australia

ABSTRACT

The rapid development of computing technology has facilitated its use in engineering design and manufacturing at an increasing rate. To deliver high quality, low cost products with reduced lead times, companies are focusing their efforts on leveraging this technology through the development of knowledge-based systems such as an IDA. An IDA, which can also be referred to as a design information system, is a part of the overall enterprise information system framework, and plays an important role in improving competitiveness in product development oriented companies. Not only must such a system utilize human expertise and address CE issues in decision making, it must also lead to the preservation and transfer of technical knowledge to minimize the knowledge loss from organizational moves such as personnel retirements and company relocation. The emphasis in CE is to consider downstream aspects of different phases in the product life cycle as early as possible in the design stage. These aspects include production process planning and realization, manufacturing and assembly resources, maintainability, costing and other factors. Both human expertise and downstream aspects predominantly consist of information that is descriptive. This paper discusses the structure and development of a knowledge-based design information system that can convert this descriptive information into forms that are suitable for embedding within decision-making algorithms. Information in such a system is sorted in terms of its nature into three groups: input data information, constraint information, and objective information, all having different representations. Information is also mapped to the relevant design objectives and ranked in importance to facilitate the trade-off analysis.

INTRODUCTION

Concurrent Engineering (CE) has become a very attractive and enthusiastically discussed product development approach in recent times. To realize the concurrent design process, a key demand is to find an appropriate way to present life cycle information to the design stage. On the other hand, designs are normally required to achieve a set of objectives. Generally, these objectives are correlated to each other with either positive or negative dependencies. Therefore, solving a design problem always involves numerous trade-off decisions. It is a big challenge even for an expert to find an optimal compromising point and almost an impossible task for a less experienced designer. Thus, designers need a computer system to support the design course by providing them with the right advice at the right time (Reidsema, 2001). The rapid development in computer science and information technology has given birth to many new software tools for product development. Computer-Aided Design (CAD), Computer-Aided Manufacturing (CAM), Computer-Aided Engineering (CAE), Computer-Aided Process Planning (CAPP), Design for Manufacturing (DFM), and Design for Assembly (DFA) are quite commonly-used tools in today's product development practice. To a large or less extent, these tools adopt some aspects of the concurrent approach through the inclusion of product data management and collaborative work tool functionalities. Quality Function Deployment (QFD) is another successful product development technique which is also compatible with the idea of CE as it provides a systematic methodology for ensuring that constraints and objectives identified in the client specification phase are maintained through the entire development phase. Although

these systems may provide the designer with very good support at specific points, they lack the ability to observe the design problem from an overall point of view.

Knowledge Based Engineering (KBE) represents potentially the most significant product development technique to date. It provides a new strategic approach for realizing the concurrent product development process to improve effectiveness in design and manufacturing. It also facilitates the preservation and transfer of knowledge in companies that operate in a physically-distributed environment. Not only does it utilize traditional elements in the design process such as geometric models, it also captures other underlying attributes of design such as experience and expertise. In our research, an Intelligent Design Advisor (IDA) is proposed based on this approach in an integrated, concurrent engineering environment. On the one hand, it addresses the "life cycle" design challenges by incorporating multi-disciplinary knowledge resources into the system to achieve design and manufacturing intent, and other subsequent requirements generated through the product's distribution, use, and disposal. On the other hand, it utilizes an expert's knowledge in the course of product development to guide less experienced designers. The system can also suggest design alternatives in terms of cost, time, equipment availability, or other critical requirements to enable the creation of a fully-engineered design by acquiring, representing, planning, reasoning and then communicating the intent of the design process. Thus, it can provide the necessary degree of intelligent interaction that enhances the designers own inherent skills and creativity (Cooper, Fan, & Li, 2001).

To implement the IDA, all related product information, including raw numerical input data, physical design and manufacturing constraints, design objectives and various other life cycle requirements, as well as human expertise, must be stored in a design information system. The information must be attained and saved in a structured and reusable manner to emulate expert-like problem-solving styles (Yang & Reidsema, 2004), which can improve overall efficiency and solution accuracy, and reduce development costs. With such an information system, the generation and evaluation of new design alternatives can occur quickly and easily by changing and analyzing only the relevant parts of the system within the IDA. This frees the engineer from time-intensive, detailed engineering tasks such as repetitive and unnecessary calculations and allows more time for creative design work. An IDA also provides a proprietary intellectual base to avoid the loss of knowledge within a company, and can guide new designers towards a solution which represents "best practice" according to company requirements.

As a part of the whole Enterprise Information System (EIS), an IDA plays an important role in a product-development-oriented company. Unlike other earlier information systems such as Material Requirement Planning (MRP) and Manufacturing Resource Planning (MRPII), which focus on manufacturing aspects, an IDA is concerned with the product development and the design function of an organization. It may also interact with other information systems, such as Computer-Aided Design (CAD) and Computer-Aided Manufacturing (CAM), to increase functional integration within a company and to perform information verification, characterization, development and distribution in the overall perspective of the company.

In this paper, a brief literature review is first carried out, and the basic requirements for a KBE system are summarized. Then, a matrix-based approach to represent design information within a concurrent product development environment is explained including its configuration, working principle and failure recovery mechanism.

LITERATURE REVIEW

KBE has found a large number of applications in product and process design. Chau and Albermani

(2002) have developed a system prototype to assist in the preliminary design of liquid retaining structures by providing expert advice to the designer in selection of design criteria, design parameters and optimum structural section based on the minimum cost. Kwong, Smith, and Lau (1997) presented a blackboard-based system for concurrent process design of injection molding to obtain process solutions quickly and easily. Both systems are focused on the particular products. They are difficult to extend to the other applications because they do not have a general implementation frame. Reidsema and Szczerbicki (2001) discussed the development of a general knowledge-based system for the design planning process in concurrent engineering by utilizing the Blackboard Database Architecture (BBDA). However, this system is mainly concerned with process planning rather than specific design parameter selection. There are also some commercial KBE systems; among them, ICAD is one of the first developed and most commercially successful system. It consists of two interfaces: the CAD interface handles the geometric model and the knowledge interface deals with the programming of rules (KTI, ICAD). Although ICAD provides a connection between the actual geometry and the associated knowledge, the design process is still a repetitive loop, and thus efficiency is compromised. Moreover, knowledge preservation in ICAD is not emphasized. Studer, Benjamins, and Fensel (1998) pointed out that reuse of knowledge is advantageous in reducing development costs of knowledge-based systems because such a system can be constructed from ready-made modules instead of being developed from scratch. Recent research on KBE has concentrated on the knowledge preservation and utilization within companies and institutions. A useful approach is the case-based reasoning approach (Pokojski, Okapiec, & Witkowski, 2002; Pokojski, Strzelecki, & Sledziona, 2002) which involves solving new design problems on the basis of similar solutions from previous problems. The stored cases are previously solved problems that include not only the final solutions but also the project evolution history. Gardan and Gardan (2003) proposed to record knowledge from experts that can be invoked within CAD software in the form of scripts. The purpose of using such design scripts is to separate the knowledge from the implementation, and then to bridge the gap between design and knowledge management. Though knowledge storage is achieved more or less in these methods, it is not easy to maintain, structure, and re-process the preserved knowledge.

In summary, a KBE system must be easy to access, maintain and be documented, and most importantly, is able to solve a design problem correctly and efficiently. Some basic requirements include:

- Correctness and efficiency: It must ensure that a design problem can be solved efficiently and accurately.
- Maintainability: The model must be flexible so that it is easy to add/remove or modify knowledge.
- Compatibility: The model must be easily associated with other commercial software tools to improve its accuracy and efficiency, and broaden its use.
- Communicability: It should be easy for a designer to access and communicate with the model, and monitor and intervene in its progress.
- Reusability: It must be structured in a re-usable manner so that it can be retained as generic design knowledge.

Our proposed IDA can be referred to as a matrix-based design information system since information in this system is presented as a matrix pattern and involves activities of acquisition, structuring, and processing. It has the ability to take comprehensive consideration of all design objectives and also utilizes an objective-oriented approach by mapping design parameters to the relevant design objectives. The IDA can also be used as a product development frame. It can generate, or at least suggest, a new design automatically based on a previous example and new design objectives through structuring and characterizing the design information

The matrix-based design information system meets most of these requirements. Organizing all information in a matrix promotes maintainability as any information can be included in the matrix, and it is easy to add/remove and modify information. Matrices are a simple, straightforward yet powerful representation pattern. It is easy for people to accept, understand and handle, and therefore improves communicability. The matrix is also able to record a large amount of knowledge and leads to the preservation of technical knowledge to minimize the loss from organizational moves such as personnel retirements and company relocation. Once a design project is finished, the information matrices, including characterized sub-matrices and the detailed problem-solving process, can be saved in design history storage for future use. In this system, information processing is finished before making decisions in the selection of design parameters. The information processing results can also be stored for future re-use. Thus, solving a new design problem becomes relatively easy, and the time and cost can be saved because of reduced and simplified computations.

CONFIGURATION OF THE INTELLIGENT DESIGN ADVISOR

The configuration of our proposed matrix-based IDA can be shown in Figure 1. Within such a system, we assume that a project library has been established in a company. The library contains all existing products that a company has developed, and is saved in an information model that contains such attributes as geometry, decomposition scheme, information matrices, characterization results, and decision tables. For a new design, a

Figure 1. Configuration of the IDA

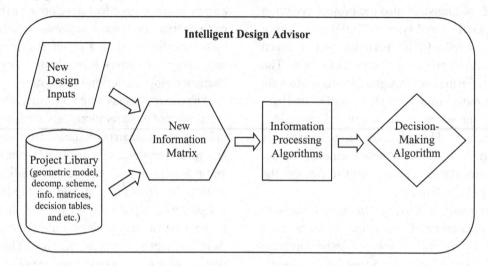

Figure 2. Information handling in IDA

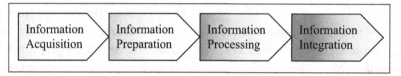

new information matrix can be established based on previous similar design examples and new design inputs, then after a series of processing stages, a decision-making algorithm will provide solutions or present suggestions to the new design objectives.

The configuration of the IDA also indicates that such an information system can be summarized into four typical stages from the sequential point of view. As described in Figure 2, after the first step of information acquisition, the information is prepared for introduction to the processing stage. Then, processed information is integrated to facilitate the decision-making process.

Information Acquisition

In the information acquisition stage, all information that is relevant to the design problem, such as attributes, requirements, constraints, and objectives, is collected. This is a particularly difficult

stage as it requires manual inputs from designers. This stage also involves searching for previous similar examples from the design project library in order to develop a new or adapted design based on the previous product. The design project library can be thought as part of the information system used as long-term memory (Yang & Reidsema, 2004). It should be well-organized and indexed to enable efficient searching.

When a finished design is saved into the project library, it will be allocated to an appropriate family domain from a list of existing domains under which it can be saved. Alternatively, a new family domain can be created. Once a new family domain is created, it will then appear in the option list in future saving and searching processes. The name of the family domain must be meaningful and descriptive to describe the nature of the model clearly. After choosing the appropriate family domain, critical factors must be selected from a list, and their relevant values

Figure 3. An actuator arm and its name code

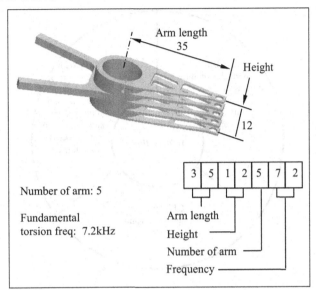

entered to be saved together. Newly identified critical factors, which are associated with this family domain, can be added to the list. In general, the designer will be given information such as key design specifications and design targets at the beginning of the design process. Therefore, to facilitate the searching process, these key design specifications and targets are normally chosen as the critical factors. For example, in the design of an actuator arm for a hard disk drive as shown in Figure 3, the height, arm length, and the number of arms can be thought as the critical factors, as well as the fundamental torsion frequency which is a key design target for actuator arms in general. These critical factors can serve as a searching index. During searching, the process is quite similar to that describe earlier. First, the designer is asked to choose a family domain, and then must provide preferred target critical factors and their desired values. Based on these values, it would be relatively easy to obtain one (or even more) close design example upon which the new design can be developed.

Alternatively, instead of setting critical factors, we may develop a name code system to label the critical parameters and their respective values (or value ranges) for a particular product. As shown in the actuator arm, its name can be coded as 3112572 in which the first two digits indicate the length, the third and fourth indicates the height, the fifth suggests how many arms it has, and the last two indicate the fundamental frequency. However, this method may not be as flexible as the first method since it prevents the designer from freely adding new codes.

Information Preparation

The second phase of information preparation includes elimination of duplicated or unnecessary items and the sorting of these items. This must be done manually by the designer. The aim of doing this is to cross-check the gathered information so that it is suitable to be introduced into the next processing stage. Normally, the gathered initial

Figure 4. Information wheel

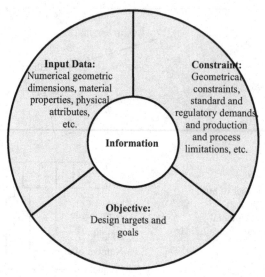

information is unstructured and needs to be cleared up. The designer can answer questions regarding the redundancy or necessity of the information in order to discard all unnecessary information. This sorting is also very important in order to classify the information in terms of its nature. All information items can be sorted in terms of their nature into three groups: input data information, constraint information and objective information, as shown in the information wheel in Figure 4. Input data are in numerical form and include geometric dimensions, material properties, physical attributes and characteristics, as well as production and process data. Constraint information includes geometrical constraints, standard and regulatory demands, and production and process limitations. There are two types of geometrical constraints: numerical constraints such as distance and angle, and symbolic constraints such as coincidence and parallel (Wang, 2003). For instance, in the design of a slot, it is required that its width should not be less than a certain value, and its two edges must be parallel. Hence, the width requirement is a numerical constraint while the parallel condition is a symbolic

constraint. Constraints are normally expressed either in declarative forms, "if-then" rules, or as mathematical equations. Constraint information is extremely important in a knowledge-based system as constitutes a critical component of the knowledge and can allow for constraint relaxation methods to be employed when possible solutions become overly constrained. Objective information includes certain targets and goals that the design is expected to achieve. These should be clearly stated and uncomplicated. An ambiguous or ill-defined design objective can easily result in either a failure to arrive at a solution or an excellent but incorrect recommendation. Some objectives may be uncertain, such as minimum cost and mass for a design. In such a case, certain levels can be set for them based on the previous example.

It should be pointed out that it may not draw a clear line to distinguish the objective and the constraint information. Constraints are something that must be followed in the design process and are used to guide parameter selection. The objectives can be thought of as indications that a design has been finished successfully. Objectives can also be used to evaluate the performance of a design.

In the previous example of an actuator arm, an engineer may be asked to design an arm for which the fundamental torsion frequency is not lower than 7 kHz and the length of the arm is between 33 mm and 37 mm. The first requirement is a design objective and the latter is a constraint.

The preparation stage may also involve the preliminary analysis of information. First, the previous similar design example(s) need to be modified based on the new design requirements, in order to remove any conflicting elements. For instance, the overall length of the selected design case may be a little less than required. Thus, it can be identified as a parameter that must be modified to form the new design. In other cases, analyses such as FEA might be carried out on the initial model to obtain preliminary physical and structural characteristics. These preliminary analytical results are introduced into the information processing model as well to give a measure of the initial performance of the design based on the new design objectives.

Information Processing and Integration

The third phase of information processing is a core part in an IDA. The main processing activities in a matrix-based IDA system involve the following steps:

- Identification of relationships between information items,
- Problem decomposition by grouping input information items into families towards objectives,
- Quantification of relationship strength, and
- Measurement of factor priorities.

The design problem may be decomposed into smaller more tractable sub-problems in the information processing stage. However, each sub-problem may involve only specific points, and

therefore, all sub-problems need to be integrated again after the information processing phase in order to solve the overall design problem. Based on the integrated information processing results and the constraint information, a decision table can be established, and the decision-making algorithm in the IDA can then provide design solutions in terms of new design requirements.

Suitability of the IDA System

In solving a design problem, the four main phases involved are (Dixon & Poli, 1995):

- Engineering conceptual design,
- Configuration design,
- Parametric design, and
- Detail design.

The first two phases of this process are to establish the function structures and define the geometric features. This requires a significant amount of creative work for the designer and is very difficult to enable through the use of a computer-based system. The parametric and detail design phases mainly focus on identifying and classifying the specific design parameters. A computer system may provide help in the selection of suitable parameters to meet certain design goals. The IDA will focus on these two phases, aiming to guide the less-experienced designers to achieve multiple-design goals that satisfy both company objectives and general design requirements such as performance and manufacturability.

The computer-based generation of original or unique design concepts is a problem that has yet to be solved. The approach that is taken in this research is a case-based approach where the inputs to an information matrix are based on previous design cases. In industry, about 75% of design work is of either the adaptive or variant type (Singh, 1996). In adaptive or variant design, a new design is derived from an existing design case that has a high degree of similarity. Hence, the implementation of an IDA in this research will be based on proposing solutions based on variants to a designer.

WORKING PRINCIPLE OF MATRIX-BASED IDA INFORMATION SYSTEM

The working principle of this system can be described by the information processing tower in Figure 5. Climbing up to the top of the tower, the information processing is completed. All information items are listed in a matrix through which the information relationships can be identified, and then the problem can be decomposed by grouping interrelated information into families. Following that the characterization is carried out for each sub-problem to obtain the quantitative information matrix, and all input data information items are rated to show their effectiveness towards the objective information. Finally, all the sub-problems are integrated again to arrive at an overall solution.

Figure 5. Information processing tower

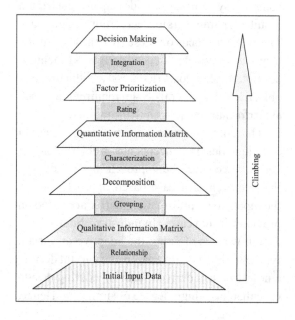

Problem Decomposition

In the first matrix, all collected initial information items are listed both across the top and down the left of the matrix. Their interdependencies are then qualitatively identified. This may be performed automatically by the system and then reviewed by the human designers. To illustrate this, consider a hypothetical design scenario involving eight input data information items, four constraint items and three objectives. The information matrix for this situation is shown in Figure 6. A star indicates that the two information items are interrelated to each other.

For a large and complex design problem, the divide-and-conquer strategy is often used. The problem is decomposed into smaller tractable sub-problems which can be solved separately and in parallel. A matrix-based method called a Design Structure Matrix (DSM) has been used to determine the process sequence of interrelated known subtasks of product development and manufacturing (Chen & Lin, 2003; Yassine, 2004). However, instead of focusing on the process sequence, the decomposition we discuss here aims to divide the design problem into subtasks by grouping the information to form sub-systems based on the qualitative matrix. It results in another matrix as shown in Figure 7. Different algorithms, such as the Similarity Coefficient Method (Kusiak & Cho, 1992), Branch and Bound algorithm (Kusiak & Wang, 1993), and Genetic Algorithm grouping technology (Falkenauer, 1998) may be employed in order to obtain appropriate decomposition schemes depending on the type of problem under consideration, The decomposition shown in Figure 7 is an ideal case in which all sub-systems are independent of each other (that is there is zero interaction density). Practically this may not be achieved. However, as it is pointed out by Yang and Reidsema (2004), independence can be achieved by allowing an information item to appear in different sub-problems if a link is introduced to maintain the equality. Figure 8 shows

Figure 6. Information matrix with qualitative relationship

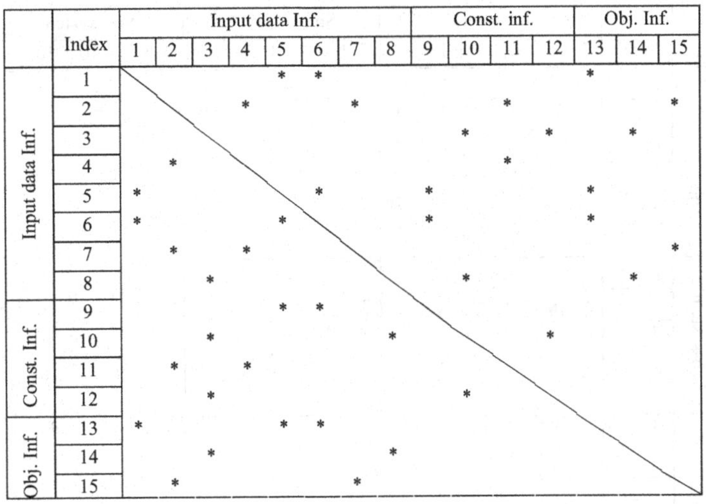

		Input data Inf.								Const. inf.				Obj. Inf.		
	Index	1	2	3	4	5	6	7	8	9	10	11	12	13	14	15
Input data Inf.	1					*	*							*		
	2			*			*				*					*
	3										*		*		*	
	4		*								*					
	5	*				*				*				*		
	6	*			*					*				*		
	7		*		*											*
	8			*							*				*	
Const. Inf.	9				*	*										
	10			*				*				*				
	11		*		*											
	12			*							*					
Obj. Inf.	13	*			*	*										
	14			*				*								
	15		*				*									

Figure 7. Information matrix after grouping

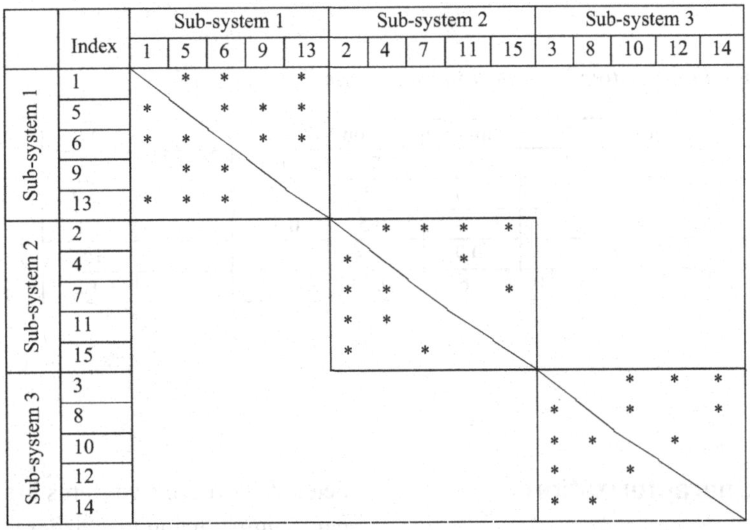

		Sub-system 1					Sub-system 2					Sub-system 3				
	Index	1	5	6	9	13	2	4	7	11	15	3	8	10	12	14
Sub-system 1	1		*	*		*										
	5	*		*	*	*										
	6	*	*		*	*										
	9		*	*												
	13	*	*	*												
Sub-system 2	2							*	*	*	*					
	4						*		*							
	7						*	*		*						
	11						*	*								
	15						*		*							
Sub-system 3	3												*	*		*
	8											*		*		*
	10											*	*		*	
	12											*		*		
	14											*	*			

a decomposed matrix with shared items in which item 3 is included in both Sub-system 1 and 3, indicating they are related to each other.

An expected decomposition is that each sub-system has no more than one objective. Thus, all the information can be mapped to respective objectives after decomposition. In the case where a sub-system doesn't have objective information, it is still acceptable if it has shared items with other sub-systems which include objective information. In such a case a shared item can be treated as an objective. Otherwise, such an independent sub-system without an objective can be deleted since it does not affect any objectives.

Figure 8. Decomposed information matrix with shared item

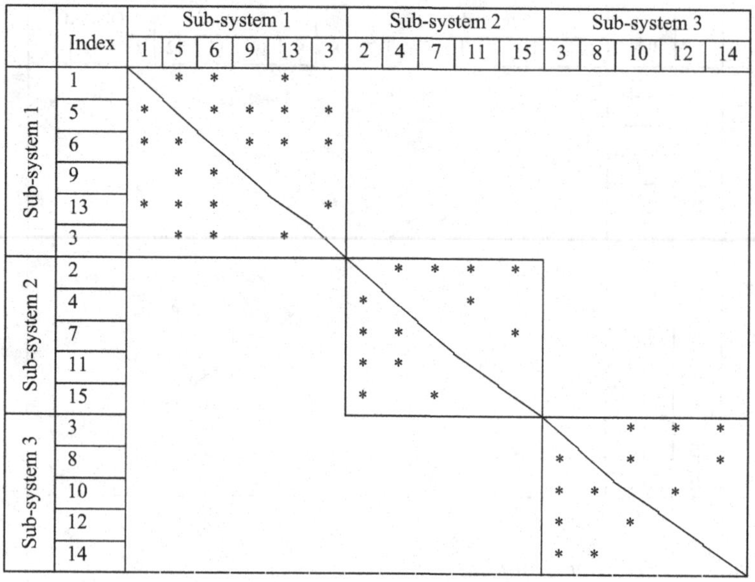

	Index	Sub-system 1						Sub-system 2					Sub-system 3				
		1	5	6	9	13	3	2	4	7	11	15	3	8	10	12	14
Sub-system 1	1		*	*		*											
	5	*		*	*	*	*										
	6	*	*		*	*	*										
	9		*	*													
	13	*	*	*			*										
	3		*	*		*											
Sub-system 2	2								*	*	*	*					
	4							*			*						
	7							*	*			*					
	11							*	*								
	15							*		*							
Sub-system 3	3														*	*	*
	8												*		*		*
	10												*	*		*	
	12												*		*		
	14												*	*			

Figure 9. Rearranged qualitative information matrix for Sub-system 1

Index	Input Information				C. I.	O. I
	1	3	5	6	9	13
1	1	0	.3 -	0.45		-0.9
3 1		-	0.5	0.75		1.1
5	1.2	-0.9 1	-	1.5	*	1.8
6	-0.8 0	.6 -	0.67 1	*	-	1.2

Relationship Characterization

After decomposition, problem solving can then be carried out on each sub-system separately. A particular concern is to determine the strength of relationships. That is, how much it affects the others, especially the objective information, when one information item is varied. For a hypothetical case with continuous linear relationships, a rearranged quantitative information matrix of Sub-system 1 can be shown in Figure 9. It must be noted that two rows, (Constraint Information item 9 and Objective Information item 13) are deleted, as these two items are defined as fixed parameters during the earlier stage of characterization. It can be seen that constraint information item 9 is related to input data information items 5 and 6, meaning it defines the physical relationship between these two items.

In order to compare the effect among different items, a normalized number is used in the matrix. The sign indicates a positive or negative effect. For example, if the value of item 1 is increased by 10%, this results in the value of item 5 increasing 3%, item 6 decreasing 4.5%, and objective information item 13 decreasing 9%. Therefore, the information

Figure 10. A fixed-length rod with two complementing segments

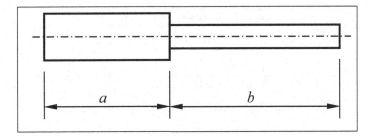

Figure 11. An illustrative multi-range qualitative information matrix of Sub-system 1

Index	Input Data Information								C. I.	O. I.		Range key:
	1		3		5		6		9	13		
1	1	1			0	0.25	-0.1	-0.2		-1.1	-1.0	1 2
	1	1			0.4	0.5	-0.3	-0.3		-0.8	-0.6	3 4
3			1	1	-0.6	-0.6	0.8	0.6		0.5	0.5	
			1	1	-0.6	-0.8	0.4	0.2		0.5	0.5	
5	1.1	1.1	-0.6	-0.6	1	1	1.5	1.5		1.2	1.2	
	1.3	1.5	-0.6	-0.8	1	1	1.5	1.5	*	1.5	1.5	
6	-0.8	-0.8	0.4	0.4	-0.7	-0.7	1	1		-0.3	-0.5	
	-0.9	-1.0	0.4	0.5	-0.7	-0.7	1	1	*	-0.5	-0.7	

matrix can be represented by $I_{1\text{-}5} = 3/10 = 0.3$, $I_{1\text{-}6} = -4.5/10 = -0.45$, and $I_{1\text{-}13} = -9/10 = -0.9$ (in which I denotes the information matrix). In this case, the row suggests the influence *on* the other items while the column indicates the influence *from* the other items. It is worth noting that the alterable range of an item can also be identified in the characterization.

Characterization also provides a chance to cross-check the information matrix. If two items have both the same row and column characterization results, they can be regarded as two identical items, and either one can be deleted from the matrix. On the other hand, extra attention must be payed to any two items with opposite results, such as item 5 and 6 in Figure 9. This may result from two different situations. First, there may be two conflicting items that have negative correlations. Normally, this conflict is of concern as it

represents the condition in which trade-offs might occur. Second, there may be two complementary elements and one of them can be deleted. For example, in the design of a part such as a rod with varied diameter but fixed overall length, as shown in Figure 10, the length of two segments, *a* and *b*, are two complementary items since the increase of one means the decrease of another. From the characterization results, it can also be determined whether two items with negative correlations are complementary. As shown in this example, a 1% increase of item 5 will cause a 1.5% decrease of item 6. Moreover, in both row and column, all results of item 5 are *-1.5* times of item 6. Thus, they are two complementary items, and either one can be deleted.

The earlier discussion is focused on the case with continuous linear relationships. However, for non-linear cases the characterization becomes

Figure 12. Prioritization of input data information

Index	Input Information			O. I.	P_i
	1	3	5	13	
1	1	0	.3 -	0.9	3.0
3	1	-	0.5	1.1	3.4
5	1.2	-0.9 1	1	.8 2	.1
Weight 2	3	2	4		

much more complicated. For relatively simple cases, the characterization can be implemented by focusing on a smaller range. The correlations of items within the range can then be treated as approximately linear. This can be illustratively shown in Figure 11. For further complex problems, two methods can be used to measure the interdependencies of relationships. First, using the order notation (Big O) method can be used to characterize the algorithm efficiency of a program, where an order family can be established to indicate the strength of relationships. Second, the dependencies of relationships can be more accurately expressed by approximate polynomials. The coefficients and the order of power suggest the strength of influence. This is compatible with the concept of Principal Component Analysis (Matthews, Blessing, & Wallace, 2002).

In an IDA, the characterization may be associated with other software tools such as FEM packages. Characterization is a stage with heavy computations. It is necessary to select the most suitable algorithm for a certain sub-system. This selection is mainly based on the type of objective information within the sub-system, because the objective information is normally related to the domain concerned, such as engineering functional objectives and financial objectives. The motivation of characterization is to reduce repetitive computations to increase the computational efficiency. Since the strength of a relationship is characterized in advance, any subsequent changes of an event are very easy to compute by utilizing the quantitative relationships.

Factor Prioritization

The characterized information system provides a basis for calculating subsequent variations of an event. However, we may often need to select a parameter to work on among a number of candidates so that there is a greater probability of achieving an objective with the least compromise on other design requirements. It is, therefore, necessary to refine the matrix by prioritizing the input data information. All information items are first ranked in terms of their importance, and weight numbers are assigned to them; the priority index P_i can then be calculated for each input data information item using the formula:

$$P_i = \sum W_o \left| I_o \right| - \sum_{j \neq i} W_j \left| I_j \right|$$

in which W_o and W_i are the weight numbers, I_o and I_j are the normalized values of objective and input data information respectively. For instance, for the sub-system shown in Figure 9 (where item 6 is deleted because it is a complement element of item 5), P_i of item 5 can be computed by 4*1.8-3*0.9-2*1.2 = 2.1, as shown in Figure 12. The formula is established based on the criterion of "most contributions and least side-effects" because its first term represents the contributions toward the objective information, and the second term suggests its side effects on other input data information. The priority index offers another quantitative measure to the input data information to facilitate the trade-off analysis.

Problem Integration and Decision Making

After characterization, the design problem can then be solved. In order to achieve the overall solution, all of the sub-problems must be considered as a whole since they are normally related to each other. Thus, they need to be integrated again. An initial plan must be first generated based on the analysis of the directional relationship among all sub-problems. The analysis should focus on the shared items to distinguish the input and output parameters of sub-problems to establish a sequential order. Sub-problems that are independent of each other can be implemented concurrently, while sub-problems with unidirectional dependency have to be executed sequentially. For those interdependent sub-problems, an iteration plan needs to be developed. This plan would consist of determining the sub-problems to start the iteration process based on an initial guess or estimate of a missing piece of information and then revise the estimation after iteration (Yassine, 2004). The decision-making process will be performed by the IDA based on an appropriate framework, such as the Blackboard Database Architecture (BBDA) or Expert System (ES) (Corkill, 1991; Nii, 1986; Reidsema, 2001). A decision table can be established to facilitate this process. Constraint information plays a key role here as it controls and guides the decision making. The factor priority index offers a reasonable quantitative sense in the selection of appropriate design features and parameters to avoid a blind "trial and error" process. A more in-depth discussion of this aspect of decision making however is beyond the scope of this paper.

FAILURE RECOVERY

In cases where the desired solutions cannot be achieved, or where conflicts occur in the process preventing the problem-solving from continu-ing, the system is considered to have failed in its efforts to solve the problem. This necessitates consideration of a failure recovery strategy. Failure recovery can concentrate on the following four aspects in accordance with the information processing flow:

- Check where the failure occurs and then examine whether the corresponding sub-problems are correctly characterized.
- Verify the decomposition scheme to see if it is suitable. If necessary, try to decompose the problem using other algorithms.
- Inspect the initial information matrix to see if any relationships are not included. For those relationships which are unsure or unessential, they must be included in the matrix. Although this may complicate the decomposition and characterization stages, it can avoid failure occurring. In fact, the characterization can cross-check whether a pre-defined relationship exists or not. For example, a zero value may indicate no relationship exists between two pieces of information.
- Review the information gathering and preparation processes to see if any information is overlooked and whether constraint and objective information is adequately defined.

DISCUSSION AND CONCLUSION

In this research, we propose a matrix-based IDA system. As a part of the overall enterprise information system framework, an IDA is a knowledge-based design information system. It can utilise human expertise and address CE issues in decision making. It also leads to the preservation and transfer of technical knowledge to minimize the knowledge loss from organizational moves. It is easy to access, maintain, able to solve a design problem correctly and efficiently, and has the ability to take comprehensive consideration of all design objectives. This paper has discussed its configuration and working principle in detail based on the information handling process in such a system. The information is sorted in terms of its nature into three groups: input data, constraint and objective information, all having different representation strategies. After decomposing the problem into sub-problems, information is then mapped to the relevant design objectives and processed separately and in parallel to quantitatively characterize the strength of relationships. Following that, all information items are rated, according to their importance, with weight numbers assigned in order to measure their priorities towards the design objectives. Finally, all sub-systems are integrated again to achieve the final solutions through trade-offs between interdependent sub-systems.

At the problem level, our proposed IDA information system can be summarized as Generation, Decomposition, Distribution and Integration (GDDI) (Reidsema, 2001) where:

- Generation refers to defining the problem including collecting and classifying information to present to the information system.
- Decomposition entails applying the "divide and conquer" method to split the overall problem into smaller, more tractable sub-problems in terms of the interrelationships between gathered information pieces.
- Distribution involves handling sub-problems separately through characterizing them according to the nature or objective of the sub-problems.
- Integration requires all characterized sub-problems to be brought together and then solved in an integrated and collaborated environment.

The success of an IDA is determined by the accuracy of the identification of dependent relationships, and the characterization of relationship strength. In our proposed matrix-based informa-

tion system, relationships are stressed because all the relationships are important elements of knowledge. This has been pointed out by Compton and Jansen (1990), where they state that knowledge only has meaning in relation to other knowledge and can be explored in terms of relationships. This system is also an objective-oriented model. By sorting all information, the design objectives are clarified. By decomposing the problem, related information is mapped to respective objectives. By characterizing the strength relationships, the priorities of input data information toward the objectives are quantitatively measured.

REFERENCES

Chau, K. W., & Albermani, F. (2002). Expert system application on preliminary design of water retaining structures. *Expert Systems with Applications*, 22, 169-178.

Chen, S. J., & Lin, L. (2003). Decomposition of interdependent task group for concurrent engineering. *Computer and Industrial Engineering*, 44, 435-459.

Compton, P. J., & Jansen, R. (1990). A philosophical basis for knowledge acquisition. *Knowledge Acquisition*, 2, 241-257.

Cooper, S., Fan, I.-S., & Li, G. (2001). Achieving competitive advantage through knowledge based engineering - A best practice guide. Department of Trade and Industry U.K. Retrieved from http://www.ktiworld.com/pdf/kti_dti.pdf

Corkill, D. D. (1991). Blackboard systems. *AI Expert, 6*(9), 40-47.

Dixon, J. R., & Poli, C. (1995). *Engineering design and design for manufacturing*. MA: Field Stone Publisher.

Falkenauer, E. (1998). *Genetic Algorithms for Grouping Problems*. New York: Wiley.

Gardan, N., & Gardan, Y. (2003). An application of knowledge based modelling using scripts. *Expert Systems with Applications*, 25, 555-568.

KTI, ICAD. Knowledege Technologies International. Retrieved August 24, 2005, from http://www.ktiworld.com/our_products/icad.shtml

Kusiak, A., & Cho, M. (1992). Similarity coefficient algorithm for solving the group technology problem. *International Journal of Production Research, 30*(11), 2633-2646.

Kusiak, A., & Wang, J. (1993). Decomposition of the design process. *Journal of Mechanical Design*, 115, 687-695.

Kwong, C. K., Smith, G. F., & Lau, W. S. (1997). A blackboard-based approach to concurrent process design of injection moulding. *Journal of Materials Processing Technology*, 70, 258-263.

Matthews, P. C., Blessing, L. T. M., & Wallace, K. M. (2002). The introduction of a design heuristics extraction method. *Advanced Engineering Informatics*, 16, 3-19.

Nii, H. P. (1986). Blackboard system: The blackboard model of problem-solving and evolution of blackboard architectures, part I. *AI Magazine, 7*(2), 38-53.

Pokojski, J., Okapiec, M., & Witkowski, G. (2002, November 13-15). Knowledge-based engineering, design history storage, and cased-based reasoning on the basis of car gear box design. In *Artificial Intelligence Methods,* Gliwice, Poland.

Pokojski, J., Strzelecki, P., & Sledziona, L. (2002, November 13-15). Modelling with features, design history storage, cased-based reasoning on the basis of machine shaft design. In *Artificial Intelligence Methods,* Gliwice, Poland.

Reidsema, C. (2001). *A conceptual blackboard database model for design process planning in concurrent engineering.* Doctoral dissertation, The University of Newcastle.

Reidsema, C., & Szczerbicki, E. (2001). A blackboard database model of the design planning process in concurrent engineering. *Cybernetics and Systems: An International Journal, 32*(7), 755-774.

Singh, K. (1996). *Mechanical design principles.* Melbourne: Nantel Publications.

Studer, R., Benjamins, V. R., & Fensel, D. (1998). Knowledge engineering: Principles and methods. *Data & Knowledge Engineering*, 25, 161-197.

Wang, Y. (2003). Constrain-enabled design information representation for mechanical products over the Internet. Doctoral dissertation, University of Pittsburgh.

Yang, Q., & Reidsema, C. (2004). Consideration of human problem-solving style in the conceptual design of a blackboard-based design system. *Portland International Center for Management of Engineering and Technology (PICMET)*, Seoul, South Korea.

Yassine, A. (2004). An introduction to modeling and analyzing complex product development processes using the design structure matrix (DSM) method. *Italian Management Review*, 9, 72-88. Retrieved from http://www.quaderni-di-management.it

This work was previously published in International Journal of Enterprise Information Systems, Vol. 2, Issue 1, edited by E. Szczerbicki, pp. 1-16, copyright 2006 by IGI Publishing, formerly known as Idea Group Publishing (an imprint of IGI Global).

Chapter X
Data Quality–Based Requirements Elicitation for Decision Support Systems

Alejandro Vaisman
Universidad de Buenos Aires, Argentina

ABSTRACT

Today, information and timely decisions are crucial for an organization's success. A decision support system (DSS) is a software tool that provides information allowing its users to make decisions timely and cost effectively. This is highly conditioned by the quality of the data involved, usually stored in a data warehouse, and by a sound and complete requirements analysis. In this chapter we show that conventional techniques for requirements elicitation cannot be used in DSS, and present a methodology denoted DSS-METRIQ, aimed at providing a single data quality-based procedure for complete and consistent elicitation of functional (queries) and nonfunctional (data quality) requirements. The outcomes of the process are a set of requirement documents and a specification of the operational data sources that can satisfy such requirements. We review the state-of-the-art in the field, and show that in spite of the tools and methodologies already proposed for the modeling and design of decision support systems, DSS-METRIQ is the first one that supports the whole process by means of an integral technique.

INTRODUCTION

It is a well-known fact that, among the phases of the software development process, analysis and specification of functional and nonfunctional requirements is a crucial one. The lack of good requirements specification is a major cause of failure in software development (Thayer, 2002). The software engineering community has developed many useful tools for requirements analysis in transactional systems. These kinds of systems deal with the day-to-day operation of an organization. Decision support systems (DSS) are of a completely different kind: they are focused on integrating data and models in order to improve the decision-making process. The data that feed a DSS generally reside in a data warehouse. The software development cycle of DSS has particularities that require applying methodologies different than the ones used for operational systems. The reason for this is twofold: on the one hand, traditional methodologies have been thought and designed with transactional systems in mind; on the other hand, specific methodologies applicable to DSS arose as ad-hoc answers to practical needs, and most of them are just mere enumerations of activities that must take place in order to implement the system, focusing on populating the data repository while ignoring important issues like the impact of changes in the operational data sources, or worse, if these data sources satisfy the users' information requirements. New sources of failure are present in DSS: correctness and trustworthiness of the information are the basis of the decision-making process. We do not only need to understand the user's information needs, but also account for keeping the data repository up-to-date according to user specifications. Also, update processes and their frequency must be considered, as well as the analysis of the quality and completeness of the data sources.

It follows that there is a need for techniques that, besides accounting for the software process cycle and functional requirements, also consider the quality of the information the system will deliver. There are several reasons for this. For instance, most of the time, people developing information systems do not consider the impact of low quality data (Kimball, Reeves, Ross, & Thornthwaite, 1998). Low data quality is more a rule than an exception. Just to give an example, it has been detected in the U.S., that approximately 50 to 80% of the computerized criminal records are inaccurate, incomplete, or ambiguous (Strong, Yang, & Wang, 1997). So far, the contribution of software engineering for addressing the problems stated has been limited, although many techniques have been proposed in order to analyze and measure a data quality requirement. Some examples of these techniques are GQM (goal question metric)

(Basili, Caldiera, & Rombach, 1992) and QFD (quality function deployment) (Akao, 1997).

In summary, traditional software development methodologies do not apply to DSS, and focus on software correctness, paying little attention to the problem of data quality and completeness, given that, in general, this is not considered an issue in the requirement analysis phase of the software development cycle for operational systems. Based on these points, we propose a methodology called DSS-METRIQ that integrates concepts of requirements engineering and data quality, in order to provide a comprehensive solution to the requirements elicitation process specifically oriented to DSS.

Case Study

Throughout the chapter we will discuss the following case study. We must collect requirements for a DSS for a wholesale chain called "Los Andes" (specialized in food products). The chain has three branches in the Argentina countryside. The project involves the development of a data warehouse and a DSS for supporting the daily tasks of decision makers. The company has many different sources of operational data. We must carry out the requirements elicitation process, with the following goals in mind: discovery and documentation of user queries, addressing the information quality required by our customer (*that we must also help to define*). It will also be our task to analyze data quality in each one of the data sources, indicating for each piece of data, the data source from which we will obtain it and the data quality we can expect. Thus, we must specify the queries (functional requirements) that could be addressed by the system (given the available data sources) satisfying the data quality levels imposed by our customer (nonfunctional requirements). There will be a requirements engineering team, composed of a project leader, a training team, a team for carrying out the interviews, a data processing team, and a dictionary manager (more on dictionaries in the following sections). Our customer provided a list containing the contact information of the employees (belonging to different areas), who will cooperate in the process.

Contributions and Chapter Organization

We introduce a methodology (denoted DSS-METRIQ) for requirements elicitation in DSS, aimed at providing an integrated process specification for the complete and consistent analysis of functional (queries) and nonfunctional (data quality) requirements in DSS. We provide detailed mechanisms for collecting functional and nonfunctional requirements as a whole, addressing data quality and completeness of the operational data sources. We give tools allowing answering the following questions: (a) *can we answer the set of queries required by the user with the data currently available in the data sources?* (b) *what is the quality of the answers we will obtain?* (c) *does this quality satisfy users' requirements?* This is a subject often ignored in other proposals. The outcomes of the process are a set of documents and a ranking of the operational data sources that can satisfy the users' quality and information requirements, based on two parameters denoted *local* and *global data source performance*. As far as we are aware of, no other proposal has addressed the problem in this way. Of course, the analysis may also trigger corrective actions over data that do not reach the required level of quality. Finally, each phase of this methodology needs a technical solution from the software engineering or data warehousing communities. For instance, for requirements elicitation we adapt the GQM (goal question metric) methodology. For data source selection we introduce a technique based on QFD (quality function deployment).

In this chapter we first review related work and study the differences between DSS and operational systems with respect to requirements

elicitation. After presenting basic data quality concepts we introduce DSS-METRIQ and explain each phase of the methodology in detail. We conclude with a discussion on possible research directions.

RELATED WORK

The software development cycle involves different stages or phases, each one of them composed of a set of activities. The final goal is obtaining a software product reflecting user requirements in the best possible way. *Waterfall* and *Baseline Management* are popular models for software development. There are five phases in these models: requirements analysis, design, coding, testing, and system integration, in sequential form. Modeling through *prototypes* consists in quickly developing a system for helping to determine software requirements. Another popular technique, the *Spiral model* emphasizes the idea that requirements cannot be determined in a precise way from the start, leading to the idea of a "spiral" which includes a complete cycle that must be revised iteratively until the final system satisfies the expected functionality. In all of these models, the requirements analysis phase is divided into four main activities: requirement elicitation, analysis and modeling, specification, and validation. During *requirements elicitation*, requirement engineers gain understanding of the user needs. A requirements engineer carries out interviews, classifies and integrates the information obtained. Techniques like IBIS (issue-based information system) (Christel & Kang, 1992), or JAD (joint application development), are widely used. The *analysis and modeling* outcome is the definition of user requirements. The most popular methods for these tasks are enterprise modeling, data modeling (through entity-relationship modeling), object-oriented techniques, and structured methodologies like SADT (structured analysis and design techniques) (Ross & Schoman, 1979).

Specification is the process of generating the requirements documentation. CORE (*controlled requirements expression*) (Mullery, 1979) can be used in this step. The purpose of *requirements validation* is to certify that requirements are an acceptable description of the system to be implemented. Inputs for the process are the requirements document, organizational standards, and organizational knowledge. The output is a list that contains the reported problems and the actions necessary to cope with them. Requirements reviews and requirements testing are common techniques used for this activity.

Decision support systems extract information from a database and use it to support the decision making process. A DSS usually requires processing great volumes of data for generating valuable information. Gill and Rao (1996) classify these kinds of systems as (a) data-driven, which emphasizes access and manipulation of large structured databases; (b) model driven, which emphasizes the access and manipulation of a model; (c) knowledge driven, which recommends actions to the managers, often customized for a certain domain; and (d) document driven, integrating a variety of storage and processing technologies. A DSS is made up of: (a) database (typically a data warehouse); (b) components for data extraction and filtering, used to extract and validate the data taken from the operational databases; (c) query tools; and (d) presentation tools. A *data warehouse* gathers data coming from different sources of an organization (Chaudhuri & Dayal, 1997). *Data warehousing* involves a series of processes that turn raw data into data suitable to be queried. A set of data transformation processes denoted ETL (Extraction, Transformation, Loading) exports data from the operational databases (generally in heterogeneous formats), and after some depuration and consolidation, load them into the data warehouse. OLAP (online analytical processing) tools are used for querying the warehouse.

System development involves three clearly defined phases: design, implementation, and maintenance. However, in the development cycle of traditional software system, activities are carried out sequentially, while in a DSS they follow a heuristic process (Cippico, 1997). Thus, methodologies for developing operational and DSS systems are different. For instance, in *operational systems* (a) the development cycle is *process driven*, based on a stable data model; (b) data must be normalized in order to support transaction processing; (c) hardware is defined in the planning phase, remaining quite stable; and (d) there is no periodic data loading. In DSS, we have (a) the development cycle is *data driven*; (b) data is generally denormalized; (c) hardware changes dynamically; and (d) periodical data loading is a typical process.

In spite of the popularity gained by DSS in the last decade, a methodology for software development has not been agreed upon. Thus, it is not surprising that most contributions on requirements analysis for DSS came from consulting companies and software vendors. The *NCR methodology* is aimed at developing and maintaining the data warehouse infrastructure, assuring data quality, and improving performance encouraging the use of traditional database design techniques. The *SAS Institute Rapid Development methodology* is based on the argument that the two great sources of failure of data warehouse projects are the lack of experience and the development of very large projects. Thus, this methodology tries to handle such risk dividing the project into units called "builds." Each cycle of these builds consists of the following stages: valuation, requirements, design, implementation, final testing, and distribution. *Microsoft methodology* proposes eight activities: four devoted to creating the data warehouse and four to reviewing and maintaining it, with feedback from the processes. Kimball et al. (1998) propose a "federated" architecture, with data marts based on star schemas. All the methods are focused on the development of the infrastructure for decision support systems, but none of them handles data quality in a comprehensive fashion.

There are several proposals addressing the design of data warehouses and data marts. Many of them use some of the techniques we propose in this chapter. *However, these works do not compare with ours because the goals are different*: we are interested in the requirement elicitation process itself, and not in the design process, which belongs to a later stage. For example, the work by Moody and Kortink (2000) proposes the use of the entity-relationship model for data warehouse design. With a different approach, Bonifati, Cattaneo, Ceri, Fuggetta, and Paraboschi (2001) introduced an interesting requirements-driven design methodology for data marts. However, they focus on the design stage, and only address functional requirements in the requirements elicitation phase (they use GQM for this task). Vassiliadis, Bouzeghoub, and Quix (1999) also use GQM, but in this case for identifying metrics that allow evaluating the quality of a data warehouse once it has been developed. Closer to our proposal, Winter and Strauch (2003, 2004) introduced a demand-driven methodology (i.e., a methodology where end users define the business goals) for data warehousing requirement analysis. They define four steps where they identify users and application type, assign priorities, and match information requirements with actual information supply (i.e., data in the data sources). There are several differences with the methodology we present here. The main one resides in that our approach is based on data quality, which is not considered in the mentioned paper. Moreover, although the authors mention the problem of matching required and supplied information, they do not provide a way of *quantifying* the difference between them. On the contrary, we give a method for determining the data sources that best match the information needs for each query defined by the user. Paim and Castro (2003) introduced DWARF, a methodology that, like DSS-METRIQ, deals with functional and nonfunctional requirements. They adapt requirements engineering techniques and propose a methodology for requirements definition for data

warehouses. For nonfunctional requirements, they use the extended-data warehousing NFR Framework (Paim & Castro, 2002). Although DWARF and this framework are close to the rationale of DSS-METRIQ, the main differences are (a) we give a more detailed and concrete set of tools for nonfunctional requirements elicitation; (b) we provide a QFD-based method for data source ranking on a quantifiable basis; and (c) we give a comprehensive detail of all the processes and documents involved. Prakash and Gosain (2003) also emphasize the need for a requirements engineering phase in data warehousing development. This phase precedes the logical, conceptual, and physical design phases they propose as components of the data warehouse development process. They propose the GDI (goal decision information) model. However, the authors do not provide a level of detail that may allow a more in-depth analysis.

In summary, although our proposal intersects many other similar ones, it integrates the most popular techniques, resulting in a comprehensive and self-contained methodology where each phase has clearly defined steps, as we will see in the following sections. Most of all, DSS-METRIQ addresses the overlooked problem of data source qualification and selection.

QUALITY CONCEPTS

When speaking about quality, people do not always refer to the same concept (Bobrowski, Marré & Yankelevich, 1999). Many techniques have been developed for measuring quality. In what follows, we survey the ones we are going to use in the remainder of this chapter.

Goal Question Metric (GQM)

GQM is a framework for metric definition (Basili et al., 1992). It defines a top-down procedure allowing for specifying what is going to be measured, and to trace how measuring must be performed, providing a framework for result interpretation. The outcome of the process is the specification of a system of measurements that consists of a set of results and a set of rules for the interpretation of the collected data. The model defines three levels of analysis: (a) conceptual (Goal), where a goal for a product, process, or resource is defined; (b) operational (Question): at this level, a set of questions is used for describing the way a specific goal will be reached; and (c) quantitative (Metric): the metric associated with each question. The model is a hierarchical structure that starts from a goal, follows with a set of questions refining the goal, and ends with the metrics that will help answer the questions. For example, if our goal consists in measuring the legibility of a certain text, the question would be "what is the level of readers' comprehension?" The metric will be the number of readers who understood the text.

Quality Function Deployment (QFD)

Quality function deployment (QFD) (Akao, 1997) is a method proposed in the 1960s by Yoji Akao in Japan. It was first conceived as a method for the development of new products under the framework of total quality control. QFD aims at assuring design quality while the product is still in its design stage. The central instrument of the methodology is a matrix called "House of Quality." This matrix is composed of information blocks, and it is filled out in a sequence of steps: first, interviews are used to model customer needs. Here, requirements are expressed in a vague or ambiguous way, and must be refined. Then, technical solutions for solving user needs are proposed. The process iterates until it finds all the solutions. With the results obtained in the previous steps, the matrix of interrelationships is completed. After identifying the relationships between technical factors, the roof of the *House of Quality* is completed and possible conflicts

between technical solutions are detected. Two tables are completed: customer's valuations and the valuations of the technical solutions. The last two steps involve prioritizing user requirements and prioritizing technical requirements.

Data Quality

Organizations are conscious of data quality problems. Nevertheless, efforts generally focus on data accuracy, ignoring many other attributes and important quality dimensions (Wang & Strong, 1996). Thus, quality validation and verification techniques are still required. Usually, these techniques concentrate only on software and assume that external agents provide the data (Bobrowski et al., 1999). Poor information quality is due to several causes: (1) Problems in the processes: to understand the processes that generate, use, and store the data, it is essential to understand data quality. In an organization, the owners of the processes must be responsible for the quality of the data they produce or use. (2) Problems in the information systems: often related to poor system development (incomplete documentation or systems that have been extended beyond their original intention). (3) Problems of policies and procedures: a policy about data must cover security, privacy, inventory of the information that is controlled, or data availability. (4) Problems in data design: more often than not, data are used for tasks they were not defined for.

Data Quality Dimensions

There are basically two ways of defining data quality: the first one uses a *scientific approach* and defines data quality dimensions rigorously, classifying them as dimensions that are or are not *intrinsic* to an information system (Wang, Storey, & Firth, 1995). The second one is a *pragmatic approach* aimed at defining data quality in an operational fashion (Wand & Wang, 1996). Wang

& Strong (1996) identified four data quality categories after evaluating 118 variables (Wang & Strong, 1996): (1) *intrinsic* data quality; (2) *contextual* data quality (defines the quality of the information within the context of the task); (3) *data quality for data representation*: determines if the system presents the information in a concise, consistent, understandable way; and (4) data quality regarding *data access* (defines quality in terms of the role of the information system in the provision of the data). Table 1 summarizes the results of academic research on the multiple dimensions applicable to information quality, comparing results from Delone and McLean (1992), Hoxmeier (2000), Jarke and Vassiliou (1997), Lee, Strong, Kahn, and Wang (2002), Wand and Wang (1996), and Zmud (1978).

DSS-METRIQ OVERVIEW

In this section we introduce DSS-METRIQ. The methodology is composed of five phases: *scenario, information gathering, requirements integration, data source selection,* and *document generation,* and from any phase it is possible to go back to any former one. The whole process can be summarized as follows: on the one hand, the data consumer's functional requirements are analyzed, unified, and documented. On the other hand, the quality of data in the data sources is collected from the data producer users. This information is then analyzed as a whole, and a collection of documents is produced. These documents will allow matching the requirements with the available data. In the remainder of this section we introduce the

Table 1. Quality dimensions

Proposal	Intrinsic	Contextual	Representation	Accessibility
Lee et al.	Accuracy Credibility Reputation Objectivity	Understandable data Concise representation Interpretability Consistency	Added value Relevance Completeness Timeliness	Accessibility Security Easy operation
Zmud	Accuracy	Reliability Timeliness	Order Legibility	
Jarke and Vassiliou	Accuracy Consistency Completeness Credibility	Relevance Timeliness Usefulness Up-to-date Volatility	Interpretability Syntax Semantics Alias Source	Accessibility Availability Privileges
Delone and McLean	Reliability Accuracy Precision	Relevance Timeliness Usefulness Content Completeness Opportunity	Understanding Legibility Clarity Format "Look and feel" Conciseness Uniqueness Comparability	Usefulness Accessibility Convenience
Wand and Wang	Correctness Ambiguity	Completeness	Meaning	

general framework of the methodology, and the conceptual basis over which it is built. Each phase of the methodology will be described in detail later in this chapter.

Framework

We first define the participants, concepts, techniques, and tools that will be used in the requirement analysis process.

- **Team:** The methodology defines the following roles and participants in the team that will carry out the project: (a) project leader: manages the working team and interacts with the customer; (b) training leader: carries out the training of the users on the concepts, methodologies, or technologies associated with the project; (c) requirements engineer: performs requirements elicitation, working jointly with the users (must be an experienced professional); (d) query and data manager: analyzes the queries; and (e) information administrator: deals with changes in the information that supports the methodology (dictionaries, forms, etc.).
- **Users:** Any person participating in the project is considered a *user*. Users to be interviewed are (a) *data producers*, who will participate in interviews aimed at understanding data; (b) *data consumers*, who will be interviewed for defining the queries that will be posed to the system; (c) *referent users* are users with a higher hierarchy in the organization than the ones defined in (a) and (b); referent users participate in interviews where the scope of the system and priorities are defined. She also solves conflicts between requirements of different users. Priorities are defined for users, ranging from 1 to 5. Users are associated to *domains* (sales, acquisitions). Each domain has a priority, also ranging between 1 and 5.

- **Data sources:** DSS-METRIQ defines two kinds of data sources: *physical* and *logical*. The former are sources where data are actually stored. The latter are sets of data sources producing a data element (i.e., set of physical data sources producing a view).

Example 1: The attribute daily_sales is stored in the table Daily_Sales_Summary, belonging to the operational database Sales-Central. This database is a physical data source. The attribute buy_sell_daily_balance is computed as the difference of two attributes representing daily buys and sales, that are located in two different tables, in two different databases: the "BuysCentral" database and the "SalesCentral" database. Thus, buy_sell_daily_balance is a logical data source. We will give this data source a name, say LDS_1 (standing for Logical Data Source 1).

- **Interviews:** DSS-METRIQ considers two kinds of interviews: (a) group interviews: in the requirements phase, JAD is used (Christel & Kang, 1992); and (b) individual interviews: the user requirements, mainly from the data consumers, can be obtained through traditional structured or unstructured interviews.

Supporting Elements

DSS-METRIQ provides elements for supporting the management of the information collected throughout the process. These elements are *forms, matrices, a data dictionary,* and *an aggregations dictionary.* Forms are elements that register the collected information. As usual, forms are divided in two main sections: the *heading* and the *body.* The heading contains name of form, phase of the methodology, step within the phase, version, and revision number. In the body of the form, the collected or generated information is written. Of course, forms can be updated during the process. Thus, requirements evolution is supported in this way (meaning that any change that occurs during the process can be reflected and documented in the forms). Matrices are equipped with a certain intelligence that allows weighting the information contained in the forms, in order to qualify and prioritize requirements. A data dictionary is a catalogue of data that contains names, aliases, and detailed descriptions of the atomic elements that compose the user queries, data sources, and the data warehouse. Its purpose is the definition of a common meaning for each one of these elements, allowing expression of user requirements on the basis of a common terminology. It can be updated throughout the process. The aggregations dictionary is a catalogue containing information on dimensions, dimension levels, and aggregations (Chaudhuri & Dayal, 1997).

Data Quality Requirements

DSS-METRIQ is a quality-based and quality-led methodology. Its main goal is to integrate functional requirements and data quality. As such, the data quality dimensions to be used must be defined. We adapted and integrated the main existing proposals commented previously, considering not only the relevance of each quality dimension, but also the possibility of quantifying it. Based on this, we will work with the following quality dimensions: *accuracy, consistency, completeness, timeliness, query frequency, source availability,* and *accepted response time.* Associated with *timeliness,* we also add *currency* and *volatility.*

- **Accuracy:** Measures how close to the value in the real world the data under consideration are. Another vision, from the ontological point of view, defines *inaccuracy* as the probability that an information system represents an incorrect state of the real world (Wand & Wang, 1996). The accuracy of a

data warehouse is influenced by two main factors: (a) accuracy of the data sources and (b) the error factor that the ETL process can introduce.

- **Consistency:** We adopt the ontological point of view, which describes consistency as the "logical consistency" of information. The underlying idea is that given two instances of representation for the same data, the value of the data must be the same. For example, if it is known that the sales of a company exceed a certain monthly value *v*, we expect the database to reflect this fact.

- **Completeness:** Is the information system able to represent every significant state of the real world. The methodology presented here emphasizes representation instead of structure. For instance, if there are 250 employees in the organization, we expect at least one record for each one of them to be in the database.

- **Timeliness:** It measures the delay between a change in the state of the real world and the corresponding data warehouse update. This dimension is tightly associated with other two: currency and volatility. Timeliness is affected by three main factors: (a) speed at which the state of the information system is updated after the changes occur in the real world; (b) frequency of change of the state of the real world; and (c) the instant when the data are actually used. The first aspect depends on the design of the system, while aspects (b) and (c) are design-independent.

- **Currency:** Measures the age of the data. It is computed as follows (Wang & Reddy, 1992)"

Currency(d) = $t_c - t_0$

Where d is the data element under consideration, t_c is the present time, and t_0 is the instant in the real world when the data element was created. An alternative definition is:

Currency(d)= t_f + (t_l + t_e + t_q)

t_f = time in the data source: the time elapsed between the instant when the data were "born" in the real world and stored in the data source, and the moment when they are transferred to the data warehouse.

t_l = the duration of the loading process.

t_e = time elapsed between the moment when data are available for querying in the data warehouse, and the moment when the query is posed.

t_q = the query response time.

- **Volatility:** It represents the length of the interval during which data are valid in the real world (Wang & Reddy, 1992). Pipino, Lee, and Wang (2002) define *Timeliness* as a function of currency and volatility:

Timeliness (d)=MAX [1−currency (d)/ volatility (d), 0]^s, where s > 0

The coefficient *s* (not considered in our methodology) is denoted *sensitivity*; it reflects the criteria of the analyst, and depends on the task being performed. Timeliness ranges between 0 (worst case) and 1 (desirable value).

- **Data source availability:** It is the time during which the data source is available (Jarke, Lenzerini, Vassiliou, & Vassiliadis, 2003).
- **Expected query response time:** It is the maximum accepted time for getting the answer to a query.
- **Query frequency:** It is the minimum time between two successive queries.

Measuring Quality

There are many different ways of analyzing and measuring the required data quality parameters. Thus, it is necessary to define a common way of specifying user needs and measuring whether the DSS or the data warehouse will be able to fulfill the minimum levels of quality required. To this end, we propose to apply GQM to each one of the dimensions defined previously. This technique is used for specifying user requirements and measuring the actual values for data quality in the available data sources. Due to space constraints, next we only show how the technique is applied to the *accuracy, consistency,* and *completeness* dimensions. For *accuracy* we have the following:

a. Specifying user requirements (*data consumer users*).
- **Goal:** Specify the level of accuracy required for each data element in a query.
- **Question:** What is the maximum acceptable difference between the answers obtained and the actual value of the data element in the real world?
- **Metric:** The user must specify the accepted difference (in %) between the value of a data element in the data warehouse and its value in the real world (Quix, Jarke, Jeusfeld, Vassiliadis, Lenzerini, Calvanese, & Bouzeghoub, 2002).
b. Measuring accuracy in the data sources (*data producer users*).
- **Goal:** Determine the accuracy of the data in each source.
- **Question:** What is the divergence between the value of the data in the source and in the real world?

- **Metric:** Accuracy of the data source for a certain attribute.
- **Measuring methodology:** Given a representative sample of the data in the real world, we define the accuracy of the data source empirically as:

$$\text{Accuracy} = [\text{ MAX } \sqrt{((X - Xreal)^2/Xreal)}] * 100$$

where X and Xreal are the data in the sample and in the real world, respectively.

Regarding *consistency,* if the condition is mandatory for the data element under consideration, we require a 100% level of fulfillment. Consistency in the data sources is measured obtaining samples from each source and measuring the number of inconsistent records with respect to a user query. This means that the user knows in advance the answer to this query over the sample. Analogously, *completeness* is specified as in the previous case and measured from a data sample, posing a set of queries over this sample and applying the following formula:

(# of queries with incomplete answers / # of queries) * 100

where an incomplete answer is one such that a record (or a part of it) is missing (remember that we know in advance all the records from the sample that satisfy the query). We proceed analogously for the other quality dimensions. This allows determining which data sources can be considered apt for developing the DSS, meaning that if a data source does not fulfill the minimum bound for a quality dimension, either data cleaning methods are applied or the data source must be discarded.

Integrated Requirement Analysis

After finishing the interview phase, and when all functional and quality requirements have been obtained, information is consolidated, yielding a single requirements document that will be input for the later phases of design. In this process we need to establish priorities and solve conflicting requirements. Thus, we define a set of *priorities* for each functional and nonfunctional requirement. Conceptually, this priority indicates the level of importance of the requirement. Priorities are assigned a number between 1 and 5 as follows: optional requirement = 1; low importance requirement = 2; intermediate importance requirement = 3; high importance requirement = 4; mandatory requirement = 5. When two conflicting requirements have the same priority, a high-level user must decide which one will be considered. Once conflicts are solved, *requirements validation* is performed.

- **Data source selection and document generation:** With the information collected in the previous phases, interviews are carried out with data producer users in order to determine the quality of data in the data sources, with the goal of matching user requirements and available data. As this is the cornerstone of our methodology, we will explain it in detail in the next section.

DSS-METRIQ in Detail

In this section we describe the phases of the methodology, giving details of the processes within each phase. DSS-METRIQ can be adapted to the most used software development models, like waterfall, spiral, or prototyping. As we explained in the previous section, the methodology has five phases, each one grouping together tasks that are conceptually related: scenario, information gathering, requirements integration, data source selection, and document generation. Each phase consists of a set of atomic steps. In the following sections we describe each phase in terms of a set of *initial requirements*, a sequence of *steps,* a set of *forms,* and the *output* of the phase (the information obtained). During the process, several documents and forms will be manipulated, namely (a) master files, to be denoted with the prefix MAS; (b) hierarchy documents (e.g., dimension hierarchies, user hierarchies), with prefix HIE; (c) dictionaries (data and aggregation); (d) query forms, with prefix QRY, containing the most common queries that the user will pose to the system; (e) requirements forms, with prefix REQ; and (f) matrices for processing the information obtained (with prefix MAT). Due to space limitations we will not show all of these documents, but we will describe their content and give examples from our case study.

Phase I: Scenario

The goal of this phase is to introduce the project to the different levels of the company, building a consensus about the scope and boundaries of the project (e.g., users, domains), priorities, and the initial configuration of the information.

The *input* of this phase consists of (1) details of the project; (2) initial list of domains involved; and (3) scope and list of participants of the introductory meetings. The *output* of the phase is a set of documents containing (1) domains and domain hierarchy (MAS_DOM); (2) users and user hierarchy (MAS_USR); (3) quality dimensions (MAS_QTY); and (4) data dictionary (DIC_DATA); aggregation dictionary (DIC_AGGR). The steps of this phase are *skills acquisition* and *interviews with referent people.*

During *skills acquisition,* lectures are given to the project team in order to unify concepts to be addressed in the process. In the *project presenta-* tion step, the project is presented to the company's decision levels, explaining goals, potential benefits, impact, and the working methodology. In the *global definitions* step, JAD meetings are carried out, aimed at obtaining consensus on:

a. **Domains:** Sectors that will use the data warehouse (e.g., Sales Department). The form MAS_DOM is produced, with fields domain name, domain responsible, contact information, and relevance (a number between 1 and 5) of the domain within the organization. For example, in our case study, the MAS_DOM form contains the line *<D1, Sales, Jose Hernandez, ext. 2162, 5>,* stating that *Jose Hernandez* is responsible for the *Sales* domain (with domain id *D1*), can be contacted on phone *extension 2162,* and the domain has the highest importance (5).

b. **Quality dimensions:** The final set of quality dimensions to be considered, taking into account organizational policies, goals, scope, development time, and preferences. This may imply pruning the initial set of requirements. The form MAS_QTY is produced. In our running example, four quality dimensions were chosen: *Accuracy, Timeliness, Consistency,* and *Completeness.*

c. **Initial data dictionary:** An initial collection of terms that will become the common vocabulary to be used throughout the software development cycle. The form DIC_DATA is produced. A sample record in the data dictionary for the "Los Andes" project is *<D5, customer, customer name, account>,* stating that there is a data element with id = *D5,* denoted *customer,* representing a *customer's name,* and referred also with the alias *account.*

d. **Initial aggregations dictionary:** The goal of this dictionary is to record information regarding facts and dimensions to be used in later phases of the project, in order to produce the preliminary star schema. The form DIC_AGGR is produced. In our project, a record in the aggregations dictionary looks like *<D13, customerId, no, sale|purchase, Accounts, customer, 10, days>*. This record states that there is a data element with id = D13, with name *customerId*, that does *not* represent a fact; the data element is a level in the *Accounts* dimension, denoted *customer*, having a volatility of *10 days*.

In the *referent people interviews* step, the users that will participate in the project are defined, and information about them is registered. The file MAS_USR is produced. In our project, a record in this file is *<U1, Jose Hernandez, D1, referent, 5>*, meaning that user *U1* named *Jose Hernandez* belongs to the domain *D1* and is a *referent user* with hierarchy level *5* (the highest one). For another user type we have *<U2, Maria Lopez, D1, data consumer, 1>*.

Phase II: Information Gathering

The phase's goal is capturing and documenting functional (queries) and nonfunctional (quality) requirements, taking into account the scope defined in Phase I. The *output* of the phase includes (1) a list of the queries expected to be posed to the system; (2) data quality requirements forms; and (3) a quality dimensions hierarchy. Next we describe the steps of this phase.

- **Interviews with users and referent people:** Aimed at documenting queries and the associated quality parameters. Each user provides a list of queries (expressed as questions in English) the user needs for a daily task. Initially, the vocabulary is *unrestricted*. However, certain terms may have different meanings for different users, or team participants. For example, "the best customer" or "the largest source of buying orders." These expressions are disambiguated and converted to, for example, "best

customer is the one averaging buying orders for more than $1000 monthly." The analyst must identify these kinds of ambiguous expressions and translate them as explained. The form QRY_USR is produced. This form contains, for each user and query, (1) *user ID*; (2) a *query ID* (a unique value of the form "Q" plus a sequential number); (3) the query expressed in English; (4) a *priority* for the query: the requirements engineer must guide the user in this task, avoiding overestimating the query hierarchy; (5) a *query frequency* (the minimum elapsed time between two instances of the same query); (6) the *accepted response time* (maximum time required for getting the query answer); and (7) a *global priority* for the query. The *global priority* is left blank and will be defined in a later phase. As an example, user U2 (Maria Lopez) has declared that a query she will be posing regularly is *"Number of monthly contracts per sales representative."* The entry in QRY_USR, for user U2 will be *<Q1, Number of monthly...,5, 24hs,50sec>*.

- **Query analysis:** Here we perform data recollection and validation against the data dictionary. The goal of the former is the discovery of atomic data required for satisfying each query defined in the previous step. However, initially the QRY_USR form may contain queries with redundant, ambiguous, or even incorrect terms. Thus, analysts and users review the queries and agree on a (possibly) new set of queries, using the information obtained from the data and aggregations dictionaries. For example, in query Q1 from user U2, the word *contracts* will be replaced by the word *sales*, according to the information in the data dictionary. These queries must be validated against the data dictionary, and all terms not present in this dictionary must be added, using the form DIC_DATA. This is a cyclic process, which results in a final QRY_USR form where data referred in the queries are absolutely consistent with data in the dictionaries.

- **Preliminary identification of facts, dimensions, and aggregations:** The analyst tries to identify the underlying facts and dimensions from the queries. This is a manual or semiautomatic process (for example, this process can make use of one of the many algorithms that use an entity-relationship diagram for obtaining the star schema for the data warehouse), which includes the validation against the aggregations dictionary DIC_AGGR (updating this dictionary, if necessary).

- **Quality survey interviews:** After the queries are validated, a list of data elements will be extracted from the query definitions collected in the former step. These are the data elements that will be required for answering the queries. Recall that for each data element there is an entry in the data dictionary. The quality requirements for these data elements is then defined and registered in three forms: QRY_QTY I, QRY_QTY II, and QRY_QTY III. The first one contains, for each query, the following information: (1) Query ID and (2) Data ID: one for each data element in the query. This is the identifier of the element in the data dictionary. All data elements *directly or indirectly* related to the query must be included. For example, if a query asks for the *"Average monthly sales,"* although it does not *directly* include the dollar value of each sale, this value is involved in the computation of the average, so we need to specify its quality requirement; (3) description of the element; (4) aggregation: indicates if the data expresses a dimension level; (5) range (valid range for the data element); (6) timeliness; and (7) accuracy. (Timeliness and accuracy apply to our case study, other cases may require different quality dimensions). The other two forms, QRY_QTY II

and QRY_QTY III, specify consistency and completeness requirements respectively.

Example 2: In our case study, in the form QRY_USR, the entry for query Q2, informed by user U5 (George Martinez) reads: "Top 50 customers, among the customers with monthly average sales higher than $1500." This query includes the following data elements: D1 (sales), D4 (month), D5 (customer name), D7 (year), and D13 (customerId). For each of these elements, there is an entry in form QRY_QTY1. For instance, <Q2, D1, sales, NO, -, high, 10>, meaning that in query Q2, data element D1, representing sales, will not be used to aggregate, requires a "high" value for timeliness, and a minimum accuracy of 10% (i.e., maximum accepted divergence between data and real world value). Analogously, form QRY_QTYII contains the consistency conditions for data D5 in query Q2. The condition ID is Q2C, and the description is "the best customers must be the ones classified as 'international.'" For D5, consistency is mandatory. The form QRY_QTYIII records completeness conditions for data element D5 in query Q2. The condition states that "all customers registered since 2001 must be in the database," and it is also mandatory.

- **Prioritizing quality factors:** The user assigns a priority to quality dimensions. For instance, some departments may be more interested in the *accuracy* of the reported data than in *timeliness*. This criteria is determined for each user and applied to each query posed. The form HIE_QTY is filled out, containing, for each quality dimension, the dimension's name and a priority (a number between 1 and 5).

Example 3: In our running case study, we have four quality dimensions, denoted F1 to F4: accuracy, timeliness, consistency, and completeness. User U2, from the Sales Department (domain D1) has defined the following priorities: 5,5,4,3, respectively. User U3, from domain D2 (Purchasing Department) defined these other set of priorities: 4,3,5,1, respectively.

Phase III: Requirements Integration

In this phase, requirements from all users and domains are unified, using a criteria based on QFD (Akao, 1997). In the *input* of the phase we have (1) a query list; (b) a hierarchy of quality dimensions; (3) a data quality requirements form; (4) data and aggregation dictionaries; (5) a hierarchy of domains; and (6) a hierarchy of users. The *output* of the phase is a set of documents containing the unified data model, the query priorities, and the data requirements matrix. The steps of the phase are *analysis of query redundancy, unified query prioritizing,* and construction of the *data requirements matrix.*

- **Analysis of query redundancy:** Equivalent requirements are identified, that is, requirements such that queries and associated data quality are the same. Its goal is to reduce the number of requirements to the data sources. We do not have this situation in our case study.
- **Unified query prioritizing:** During the initial phases we worked with different domains. We now need to unify all requirements from these domains, and define priorities between them. DSS-METRIQ proposes the following order of priorities: *Priorities between domains -> Priorities between users -> Priorities between queries of the same user:* Intuitively, the idea is that the requirement with the least priority in a domain prevails over the requirement with the highest priority in the domain

immediately following (in importance) the previous one. The following formula defines the global priority computation for a query "Q" denoted PriorityG(Q). This empirical expression is intends to capture the order of priorities defined previously:

PriorityG $(Q) = \text{PriorityD} (D) * X^2 + \text{PriorityU} (U) * X + \text{PriorityQ} (Q)$

where PriorityD (D), PriorityU (U), and PriorityQ (Q) are the domain, users, and query priorities. As a result of this step we obtain a set of queries ordered by priority. The form QRY_USR is updated in order to complete the *Global priority* field. These priorities are a tool for solving conflicting requirements. For example, in our case study, query *Q1* has priority 5 for user *U2* (with priority 1), who belongs to domain *D1* (with priority 5). Thus, the global priority for query *Q1* is *135.*

- **Data requirements matrix:** This is the integrated requirements form. This form is used for exchanging information with data producer users. The form MAT_REQ_DATA is filled out.

Example 4: Figure 1 shows a portion of the form MAT_REQ_DATA for our case study. Each triple domain-user-query has associated with it a set of data quality dimensions and values for these dimensions. Note that this form summarizes information obtained during the previous phases.

Phase IV: Data Source Selection

In this phase, data sources are studied in order to determine if they fulfill the information requirements collected in phases I to III. The *outputs* of the phase are (1) a query evaluation report and (2) a data source selection order for each data element.

Figure 1. Data requirements matrix

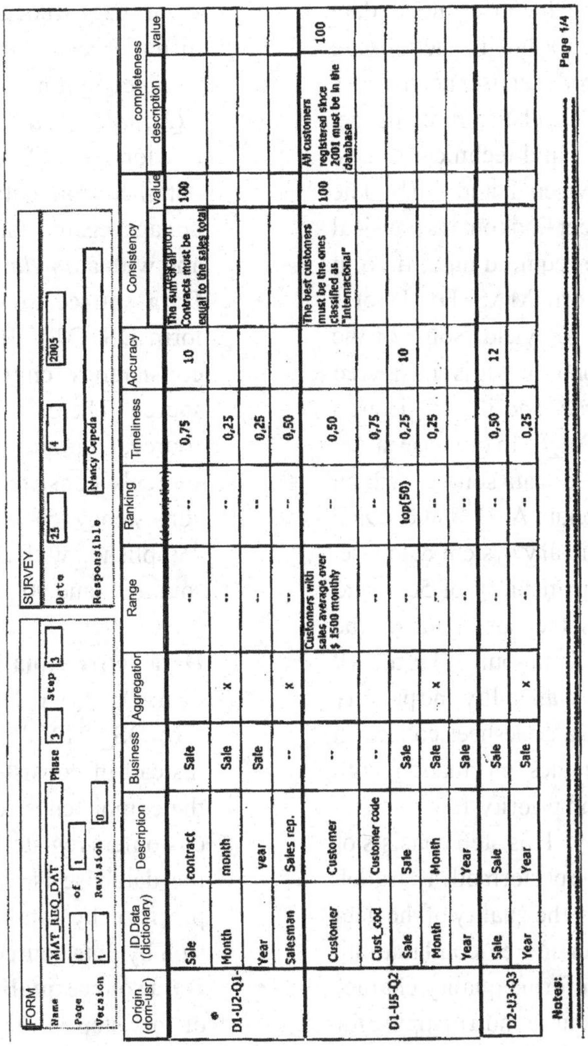

Origin (dom-usr)	ID Data (dictionary)	Description	Business	Aggregation	Range	Ranking	Timeliness	Accuracy	Consistency description	Consistency value	Completeness description	Completeness value
	Sale	contract	Sale		--	--	0,75	10	The survey option Contracts must be equal to the sales total	100		
D1-U2-Q1	Month	month	Sale	x	--	--	0,25					
	Year	year	Sale		--	--	0,25					
	Salesman	Sales rep.	--	x	--	--	0,50					
	Customer	Customer	--		Customers with sales average over $ 1500 monthly	--	0,50		The best customers must be classified as "internacional"	100	All customers registered since 2001 must be in the database	100
D1-U5-Q2	Cust_cod	Customer code	--		--	--	0,75					
	Sale	Sale	Sale	x	--	top(50)	0,25	10				
	Month	Month	Sale		--	--	0,25					
	Year	Year	Sale	x	--	--						
D2-U3-Q3	Sale	Sale	Sale		--	--	0,50	12				
	Year	Year	Sale	x	--	--	0,25					

FORM — Name: MAT_REQ_DAT — Phase 3 — step 3 — page __ of __ — Version __ Revision __ — SURVEY — Date 25 — 4 — 2005 — Responsible Nancy Cepeda

Notes:

Page 1/4

This process is central to our methodology. As far as we are aware of, this is the first proposal addressing this topic in a quantitative fashion. Now we describe the steps of the phase.

- **Analysis of data sources:** Meetings with data producers are carried out (with the help of the documents produced so far), where the set of data sources and the quality of their data are documented. Also, information on source availability is collected. Two forms, MAS_DS_P and MAS_DS_L, are used for *physical* and *logical* data sources, respectively. Each form contains a data source identifier, values for data source availability, and a source priority defined by the data producer user. In the case of logical data sources, for each data element the corresponding expression for obtaining the data must be specified. The following actions are taken: (a) the data producer user determines the priority criteria for data source usage, based on experience and technical issues. Priority ranges between 1 and 5. (b) The requirements engineer finds out if a physical source contains the required data; if so, it is registered in the form MAS_DS_P. (c) If a combination of fields yields some of the required data, this combination is considered a *logical data source*, and it is registered in the form MAS_DS_L. In our case study we have three physical data sources, which for simplicity we denote A, B, and C. Data source A is a proprietary system database, with transactional availability of 50% and priority 5 (contains the core data of the business processes). Data source B is a SAP repository with 50% availability and priority 4. Data source C is a stylesheet collection (containing monthly sales information) with availability 100% and priority 1.

- **Data source quality:** This step consists of three tasks that can be performed in parallel. The goal is obtaining the quality of the data source for each data-source combination. The data provider informs quality characteristics of the data source and a mapping for the required fields (i.e., where is the required data located, and under which name?).

- **Data source quality (data):** The form DS_QTY_I is completed. This form contains, for each query, for each data element in the query, and for each data source, the following information: (a) *mapping:* field in the data source containing the data element, or field to which a function must be applied. For instance, the month of a sale could be obtained as month(date). (b) *Aggregation:* tells if the aggregated data is or is not present in the source, or can be computed from

the data in the source. (c) *Accuracy.* (d) *Timeliness.* The last two dimensions apply to our case study, but can be replaced by a different set of dimensions if the problem at hand requires it. In our case study, the record *<Q2, sales, B, amount, NO, 70, 5min>* tells that for query *Q2*, data element *sales* can be obtained from data source *B* (where it is in nonaggregated form), with 70% *accuracy* and with a *timeliness of* 5 minutes.

- **Data source quality (consistency):** The form DS_QTY_II is completed, with the consistency characteristics of the data source. There is one entry for each data source, containing an evaluation of the source's consistency. In our case study, consistency condition Q2C above is accomplished with a 100% precision by data source A, and 90% precision by data source B.

- **Data source quality (completeness):** The form DS_QTY_III is filled analogously to form DS_QTY_II, addressing completeness instead of consistency. In our case study, the completeness condition stating that all customers registered since 2001 must be in the database is accomplished with 100% precision by data source A, and 99% precision by data source B.

- **Data source quality assessment:** The goal of this step is the integration, in a single data source assessment matrix, of the three essential components of the methodology: (a) data requirements; (b) quality requirements; and (c) data sources. The output of the process is, for each data element, the best data source for obtaining it, and a range with the qualification for each data source. The *Global Data Source Performance* is computed, using a procedure that adapts the QFD methodology.

Example 5: The data source quality assessment matrix for our running case study

Figure 2. Quality assessment matrix

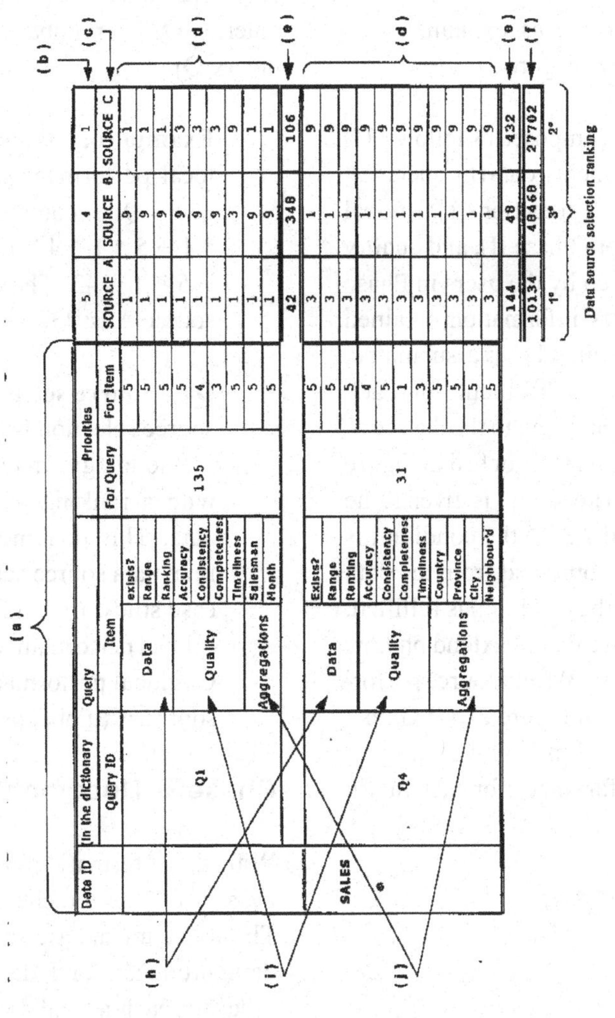

is depicted in Figure 2. We only show the data element "sales" and two queries: Q1 (from user U2) and Q4 (from user U3). The information gathered so far is:

a. Query Q1
    Priorities of quality dimensions: accuracy: 5, consistency: 4, completeness: 3, timeliness: 5.
    Global priority of the query: 135 (as explained in Phase III).
    Aggregations required: month and salesman.

b. Query Q4
    Priorities of quality dimensions: accuracy: 4, consistency: 5, completeness: 1, timeliness: 3.
    Global priority of the query: 31
    Aggregations required: Country, province, city, neighborhood.
    Finally, the data producer user provided the following information:

Available data sources: A, B, and C (c in Figure 2), with priorities 5,4,1 respectively, as explained previously (b in Figure 2).

Each matrix block is composed as follows: (1) Consumer users' requirements: data (h), query ID, quality dimensions (i), aggregations (j), global priority of the query (from Phase II), and quality dimension priorities given by the users in Phase III; (2) Data producer users' information, obtained in the previous step of this phase: a submatrix indicating requirements fulfillment for each available data source. According to the degree of fulfillment, a value is given (1, 3, or 9, d in Figure 2), using the following criteria: "1" is given if the condition is not fulfilled; "3" if the condition is not fulfilled, but can be computed from the data in the source; and "9" if the condition is fulfilled. For the sake of brevity we do not extend on how to determine these values. (3) Data source performance for each query (e in Figure 2); (4) Global data source performance (f in Figure 2).

The data source performance for each query is computed as:

PerfLocal(S,Q,D) = $\sum$ (pri$_i$ * rel$_i$),

where

PerfLocal (S,Q,D): *Data source performance of source S for data D in query Q*

Pri$_i$: *Data, quality, and aggregations priorities, for data D in query Q*

Rel$_i$: *Degree of fulfillment of data source S for query Q and data element D*

The global data source performance is computed as:

PerfGlobal(F,Q) = $\sum$ HierGlobal(Qj) * PerfLocal(S,Q,D)

For all queries Qj involving data element D, and given a set **F** of a data source and a set of queries **Q**. HierGlobal (Qj): Global priority of query Qj.

Example 6: For the table in Example 5, the local performance for data source A and query Q1 is computed as 5 * 1 + 5 * 1 + 5 * 1 + 5 * 1 + 4 * 1 + 3 * 1 + 5 * 1 + 5 * 1 + 5 * 1 = 42. The global performance for source A is: 135 * 42 + 31 * 144 = 10134.

- **Data source selection:** Although the *final* source selection is beyond the scope of the methodology, a document is generated, with a ranking of data sources for each data. This document will be used in the final data source selection process. For our case study, the ranking is 1: data source B (global performance 48,468), 2: data source C (global performance 27,702), and 3: data source A (global performance 10,134).

Phase V: Document Generation

With the information collected on Phases I to IV, a set of requirements documents is produced. These documents are reviewed by the referent, data producer, and data consumer users, in order to reach a final agreement for closing the requirements elicitation phase. We describe these documents next.

- **Query requirements document:** Contains all the queries obtained in phases I to IV, ordered by global priority. Each query is qualified as follows: a value of "1" means that the query can be answered with the information contained in the data sources; "2" means that the query involves values not in the data sources, thus, it cannot be answered; "3" means that a query "close" to the original one can be answered with the data available in the sources (e.g., modifying the required granularity or the required accuracy). In the "Los Andes" project, queries Q1 to Q3 were rated "1."

- **DSS requirements document:** Summarizes all the requirements collected during the process. Contains, for each query: the query identifier, the name of the user who specified the requirement, the query expressed in English, the same query after disambiguation, the query frequency, the query's global priority, and the expected response time. For each data attribute associated to each query, the form includes the identifier in the data dictionary, description, name to be displayed when showing the data, and all the quality conditions required. *Data warehouse requirements documents:* There are two documents: a metrics document and a quality document. The *metrics* document specifies, for each quality dimension, the range of values that are acceptable for each attribute involved in a requirement, and the metrics to be used in the data warehouse design. The *quality* document specifies the range of values acceptable for each requirement. For each required attribute, the document defines (1) maximum time for data loading; (2) minimum value for data currency (i.e., the age of the data); and (3) acceptable values for consistency and completeness. For each dimension, the report includes the formula for obtaining maximum or minimum values.

- **Preliminary data model:** With the collected information building a preliminary version of the star schema model for the data warehouse is straightforward.

- **Data source requirements document:** With the information obtained in Phase IV a document containing the data sources is produced. This document contains for each data source an identifier, a description, and the data source availability.

- **ETL process requirements document:** A complete listing of the required data and a mapping from the required data to the data source fields from which these data are obtained is provided, possibly including formulas involving more than one data field. This information will be used for the design and implementation of the ETL process.

Summary and Research Directions

In this chapter we showed that methodologies for software development in operational systems do not apply in the DSS setting. Based on this conclusion, we presented a methodology for requirements elicitation with focus on data quality dimensions and data source selection. The methodology aims at finding out if the data currently available in the operational data sources allow answering a set of queries (functional requirements) satisfying certain data quality conditions (nonfunctional requirements). In order to quantify the answer to such question, we adapted the quality function deployment (QFD) technique. Finally, DSS-METRIQ specifies the set of forms needed to support the requirements elicitation process.

Future research directions include a Web-based implementation of the framework, currently in progress, and developing a data source selection engine that can deliver different combinations of data sources fulfilling the requirements with different levels of quality. Data quality evolution, and how it affects data source selection, allowing dynamically changing the data source being selected, must also be accounted for in future work.

REFERENCES

Akao, Y. (1997). *QFD, past, present and future.* Presented at the Third International QFD Symposium (QFD'97), Linköpin, Sweden.

Basili, V., Caldiera, G., & Rombach, H. (1992). *The goal question metric approach* (Computer Science Technical Report Series CS-TR-2956). College Park: University of Maryland.

Bobrowski, M., Marré, M., &Yankelevich, D. (1999). An homogeneous framework to measure data quality. In Y. W. Lee & G. K. Tayi (Eds.), *Proceedings of IQ'99* (pp. 115-124). Cambridge, MA: MIT Press.

Bonifati, A., Cattaneo, F., Ceri, S., Fuggetta, A., & Paraboschi, S. (2001). Designing data marts for data warehouses. *ACM Transactions on Software Engineering and Methodology, 10*(4), 452-483.

Chaudhuri, S., & Dayal, U. (1997). An overview of data warehousing and OLAP technology. *SIGMOD Record, 26*(1), 65-74.

Christel, M. G., & Kang, K. C. (1992). *Issues in requirements elicitation* (Tech. Rep. No. CMU/SEI-92-TR-12). Carnegie Mellon University.

Cippico, V. (1997). Comparison of the decision support systems and transaction support system development methodologies. In *Advances in database and information systems* (pp. 416-426). St. Petersburg, FL: Nevsky Dialect.

Delone, W. H., & Mclean, E. R. (1992). Information systems success: The quest for the dependent variable. *Information Systems Research, 3*(1), 60-95.

Gill, H., & Rao, P. (1996). *Data warehousing.* Indianapolis, IN: Prentice Hall.

Hoxmeier, J. A. (2000). Database quality dimensions. *Journal of Business and Management, 7*(1).

Jarke, M., Lenzerini, M., Vassiliou, Y., & Vassiliadis, P. (2003). *Fundamentals of data warehouse.* Berlin, Germany: Springer-Verlag.

Jarke, M., & Vassiliou, Y. (1997). Data warehouse quality: A review of the DWQ project. In D. Strong & B. Kahn (Eds.), *Proceedings of the 1997 Conference on Information Quality* (pp. 299-313). Cambridge, MA: MIT Press.

Kimball, R., Reeves, L., Ross, M., & Thornthwaite, W. (1998). *The data warehouse lifecycle toolkit.* New York: John Wiley & Sons.

Lee, Y. W., Strong, D., Kahn, B., & Wang, R. (2002). AIMQ: A methodology for information quality assessment. *Information & Management, 40*(2), 133-146.

Moody, D., & Kortink, M. (2000, June 5-6). From enterprise models to dimensional models: A methodology for data warehouse and data mart design. In *Proceedings of the International Workshop on Design and Management of Data Warehouses (DMDW2000)* (pp. 5:1-5:12). Stockholm, Sweden.

Mullery, G. P. (1979, September). CORE: A method for controlled requirement specification. In *Proceedings of the 4th international conference on Software engineering*, Munich, Germany (pp. 126-135).

Paim, F., & Castro, J. (2002). Enhancing data warehouse design with the NFR framework. In *Proceedings of the 5th Workshop on Requirements Engineering (WER2002)* (pp. 40-57).

Paim, F., & Castro, J. (2003, September 8-12). DWARF: An approach for requirements definition and management of data warehouse systems. In *Proceedings of the 11th IEEE International Conference on Requirements Engineering* (pp. 75-84).

Pipino, L., Lee, Y. W., & Wang, R. (2002). Data quality assessment. *Communications of the ACM, 45*(4), 211-218.

Prakash, N., & Gosain, A. (2003, June 16-20). Requirements driven data warehouse development. In *Proceedings of the 15th Conference on Advanced Information Systems Engineering*, Klagenfurt / Velden, Austria.

Quix, C., Jarke, M., Jeusfeld, M., Vassiliadis, P., Lenzerini, M., Calvanese, D., & Bouzeghoub, M. (2002). *Data warehouse architecture and quality model* (Tech. Rep. No. DWQ-RWTH-002). LuFg Theoretical Computer Science, RWTH Aachen.

Ross, D., & Schoman, K. (1979). Structured analysis for requirements definition. *IEEE Transactions on Software Engineering, 3*(1), 6-15.

Strong, D., Yang, W., & Wang, R. (1997). Data quality in context. *Communications of the ACM, 40*(5), 103-110.

Thayer, R. (2002). Software requirements engineering: A tutorial. *IEEE Computer, 35*(4), 68-73.

Vassiliadis, P., Bouzeghoub, M., & Quix, C. (1999). Towards quality-oriented data warehouse usage and evolution. In *Proceedings of the International Conference on Advanced Information Systems Engineering* (pp. 164-179).

Wand, Y., & Wang, R. Y. (1996). Anchoring data quality dimensions in ontological foundations. *Communications of the ACM, 39*(11), 86-95.

Wang, R. Y., & Reddy, M. P. (1992). *Quality data objects.* (Total Data Quality Management Research Program, TDQM-92-06). MIT Sloan School of Management.

Wang, R., Storey, Y., & Firth, C. (1995). A framework for analysis of data quality research. *IEEE Transactions on Data and Knowledge Engineering, 7*(4), 623-640.

Wang, R. Y., & Strong, D. M. (1996). Beyond accuracy: What data quality means to data consumers. *Journal of Management Information Systems, 12*(4), 5-34.

Winter, R., & Strauch, B. (2003). A method for demand-driven information requirements analysis in data warehousing projects. In *HICSS-36,* Hawaii (pp. 231-231). IEEE Press.

Winter, R., & Strauch, B. (2004). Information requirements engineering for data warehouse systems. In H. Haddad, A. Omicini, R. L. Wainwright, & L. M. Liebrock (Eds.), *Proceedings of SAC'04,* Nicosia, Cyprus (pp. 1359-1365). ACM Press.

Zmud, R. (1978). Concepts, theories and techniques: An empirical investigation of the dimensionality of the concept of information. *Decision Sciences, 9*(2), 187-195.

Chapter XI
A Knowledge Integration Approach for Organizational Decision Support

Kee-Young Kwahk
Kookmin University, Korea

Hee-Woong Kim
National University of Singapore, Singapore

Hock Chuan Chan
National University of Singapore, Singapore

ABSTRACT

This study proposes a new methodology that facilitates organizational decision support through knowledge integration across organizational units. For this purpose, this study develops a decision support loop and explains how to organize individual knowledge related to a specific business problem and formulate and test the organized knowledge using cognitive modeling techniques for decision support. This study discusses the proposed approach in the context of an application case involving a beverage company. The application case shows the validity and usefulness of the proposed approach.

INTRODUCTION

Knowledge management (KM) can be defined as the uncovering and managing of various levels of knowledge within individuals and teams and within an organization. The aim of KM is to improve organizational performance. One of the prerequisites for successful KM is an appreciation of what Nonaka (1994) described as "tacit" knowledge. Effective KM requires such "tacit" knowledge to be transformed into "explicit" knowledge and then organized accordingly (Brown & Dugid, 1998). Integrating individual knowledge from diverse areas into organizational knowledge leads not only to new knowledge but also to new understanding (Cai, 2006; Huber, 1991; Siau 2000). This in turn helps decision makers choose the appropriate action to achieve organizational goals (Brown & Dugid, 1998; King, 2006; Stein, 1995).

However, competitive advantage results from applying knowledge, rather than knowledge itself (Alavi & Leidner, 2001). However, most KM research (Davenport, De Long, & Beers, 1998; Grover & Davenport, 2001; Kankanhalli, Tan, & Wei, 2005; Lee & Kim, 2001; Sambamurthy & Subramanu, 2005; Xu, Tan, & Yang, 2006) has focused on identifying, storing and sharing knowledge for efficient and effective transaction processing. There has been little research into the application of organizational knowledge or KM in the core business management tasks of decision making and strategy development. Yet the scope of knowledge application in these top-level tasks is organization wide. Knowledge application at this level, therefore, would influence organizational performance even more than knowledge management in transactions processing, where the scope is more localized. The research gap shows the need to shift the focus away from obtaining and storing knowledge to using it appropriately for business decision making.

Based on the research needs outlined above, this study aims to propose a new methodology for organizational decision support through knowledge integration across organizational units. Bridging the gap between having knowledge and using it is a very valuable endeavour, both for theorists from the descriptive perspective and for practitioners from the normative perspective. For this purpose, this study develops a decision support loop. The developed decision support loop explains (1) how to organize individual knowledge related to a specific business problem using cognitive modeling, and (2) formulate and test the problem reflected in the organized knowledge using cognitive matrix and causal path identification for decision support. We apply the proposed approach to a decision support case of a beverage company. The application case shows the validity and usefulness of the proposed approach.

This paper is organized as follows. First, we propose a decision support loop formed by integrating individual knowledge as it resides in mental models into an organizational model. Next, we compare the approach of this study with other approaches. We then discuss the proposed model based on its application to a real-world managerial problem.

Figure 1. Decision support loop

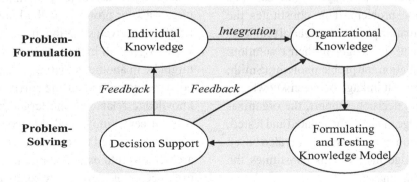

Table 1. An overview of a cognitive modeling methodology for the decision support loop

Step	Objective	Task	Details
Individual knowledge	Lower-level cognitive model generation	Specify goals Identify causal factors Identify causal connections	Use brainstorming, interview, document analysis, and survey
Organizational knowledge	Higher-level cognitive model generation	Integrate lower-level cognitive models	Link maps based on common causal factors Resolve discrepancies through meetings
		Assign causal values	Use an eigenvector assignment algorithm
Formulating/testing knowledge model	Identification of significant causal paths	Identify causal impact paths and compute the causal values	Use a causal path computation algorithm
Decision support	Identification of core factors	Identify the most positive/negative impact factor for the organizational goal	Compute the most positive/negative impact value for the goal factor
	Identification of core business activities	Identify the path that makes the most positive impact factor stronger	Compute the largest path value for the most positive impact factor
		Identify the path that makes the most negative impact factor weaker	Compute the smallest path value for the most negative impact factor

DECISION SUPPORT THROUGH KNOWLEDGE INTEGRATION

This study proposes a decision support loop through knowledge integration across multiple knowledge sources, as illustrated in Figure 1. Based on an identified managerial problem, individual knowledge is gathered and then integrated into organizational knowledge, which captures and defines the problem. This constitutes the problem formulation phase. Managerial problems commonly entail two stages in their resolution: problem formulation and problem solving (Smith, 1989). To provide a linkage between knowledge integration and decision support, the organizational knowledge model is formulated and tested, and then decision guidelines are generated based on the knowledge model. This constitutes the problem-solving phase.

To facilitate this decision support loop, we propose a cognitive modeling methodology. Table 1 illustrates an overview of the proposed methodology. We will discuss the goal, tasks, and details of each step in the following sections.

Individual Knowledge

Knowledge is useful only when it is related to a target task or problem. If the knowledge is not helpful in a given situation, it can be deemed not knowledge at all in that situation, even though it might be in another situation. Individual knowledge means individual and partial mental model knowledge related to the target problem. As a way for capturing knowledge, cognitive modeling has been used to represent relationships that are perceived to exist among the attributes and/or concepts of a given environment or problem

(Eden, 1988; Fiol & Huff, 1992). The cognitive modeling method thus can be applied to capture individual (departmental) or partial knowledge (Lenz & Engledow, 1986).

As one of the tools for cognitive modeling, the cognitive map has been widely used in previous research (e.g., Axelrod, 1976; Siau & Tan, 2005, 2006; Zhang, Wang, & King, 1994). Cognitive mapping techniques are known as effective tools to elicit and represent human cognition (Siau & Tan, 2005). In this study, the cognitive map is represented in matrix as well as diagram forms. Diagram representation is used for capturing cause-effect relationships in an organization because it is relatively easy to see how each of the causal factors relates to each other. Matrix representation is used for identifying the most effective causal path because it is convenient to apply a mathematical algorithm.

A prior cognitive model or belief structure shapes each department's interpretation of information, and affects its decision making or task processing (Huber, 1991). These cognitive models vary across organizational units, depending on their different responsibilities and viewpoints. For example, the marketing team might have knowledge regarding the way in which delays in delivery affect sales volume, but not know how such a delivery delay could be minimized. In contrast, the delivery team might know little about increasing sales but a lot about minimizing delivery delay. In this way, each team has a partial mental model or individual team knowledge about the target issue.

In this study, the cognitive model is generated through three tasks. The first task, specifying the goal, facilitates the generation of a robust cognitive map from the rest of the tasks because goals serve as guides to action (Simon, 1964). Clarifying the goal of each functional unit, therefore, helps to capture the cause-effect relationships among cognitive elements. A number of techniques can be used to generate and validate the cognitive maps

of the organization: brainstorming, interview, document analysis, and survey.

Organizational Knowledge

In real-world situations, not only human employees but also each functional department tends towards a silo viewpoint and understanding. Before knowledge is integrated across functional areas, each department may diagnose a business problem from its own viewpoint. Thus, each department may identify a core issue and suggest a solution without first adopting a cross-functional viewpoint. For this reason, cross-domain knowledge integration and sharing have been suggested as an important issue for KM (e.g., Hanse, 2002; Nadkarni & Nah, 2003; Nilakanta, Miller, & Zhu, 2006) and for enhancing organizational performance (e.g., Cai, 2006; Nambisan & Wilemon, 2000).

For organizational knowledge modeling, we generate an integrated global (higher-level) cognitive model by combining local (lower-level) cognitive models, which leads to a combined view for the problems. The integrated cognitive model represents the cognitive model of the group, which consists of individual departments. Local reasoning is done at each functional (operating or product) unit to form its own local cognitive model. However, global reasoning is necessary to combine local cognitive models into an integrated cognitive model. Because cognitive maps tend to impose structure on a vague situation, group members can gain a clearer understanding of problems and opportunities (Weick & Bougon, 1986).

In order to combine the local cognitive maps, we first identify the common causal factors between any two local cognitive maps, and link the maps based on these factors. Each common causal factor plays the role of a coupling device. In turn, the next local cognitive map is joined with the previous result. In this way, the combination process continues until all local cognitive maps are exhausted. While the local cognitive maps are being combined into a global cognitive map, various discrepancies between the maps might arise. In that case, these discrepancies should be detected and resolved through the meeting in which the related functional units participate in order to create a complete global cognitive map.

Integrating the different bodies of individual knowledge constitutes organizational knowledge in that a network of knowledge is produced across different areas in the organization. Organizational knowledge is a specific knowledge model related to a target concern or problem. It can also be modeled on a cognitive model. For example, for the purpose of revenue enhancement, individual knowledge from the sales, production, and delivery teams can be integrated as in Figure 2. This integrated organizational knowledge can explain many issues to the various teams. The teams can then collaborate and know how sales are affected by delivery delay and how they can shorten delivery delay. That is, the organizational knowledge model regarding the target issue shows all the relationships among elements across all areas, and it helps decision makers understand the problem clearly and choose appropriate actions to achieve organizational goals. As such,

organizational knowledge constitutes the core competency of management.

Although teams and individuals create their respective knowledge models, work that is shared among teams calls into use separate bodies of individual knowledge and generates an organizational knowledge model as well. The organizational knowledge model becomes a basis for understanding the dynamic complexity of the target situation. It enables decision makers and subunits to understand the entire structure of the target business problem (e.g., how to increase revenue). It also helps them assess the behavioural mechanism involved, thus facilitating the choice of appropriate actions to achieve organizational goals.

Formulating and Testing Knowledge Model

For the purpose of decision support, the most important thing is to identify several decision options and validate the best option for solving the problem at hand. For this purpose, the organizational knowledge model must be translated into an analyzable form. Although cognitive maps improve communication and comprehension among

Figure 2. Representation of organizational knowledge using cognitive maps

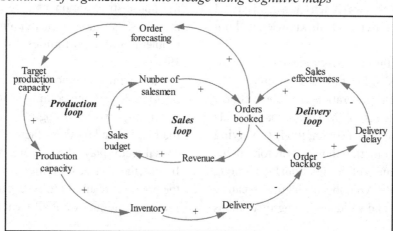

their users, they may not render an organizational knowledge model adequately analyzable.

There are various ways to analyse a cognitive model. One alternative is to investigate causal paths. This aims to identify the paths leading to either causes or effects for each causal factor. For this purpose, the organizational cognitive model should be analysed in terms of the strength of the impact between causal factors. The cognitive model includes the indirect causal paths as well as the direct causal paths. Direct causal paths easily can be identified from the cognitive map, but it is difficult to do so with indirect causal paths. In addition, there are usually multiple indirect causal paths. In this context, the aim is to identify the causal paths that have the maximum causal impact among all causal paths, regardless of whether the impact is direct or indirect. To capture those causal paths, some studies have proposed methods that combine heuristic algorithms with the cognitive model (Kwahk & Kim, 1999; Zhang et al., 1994).

Table 2 illustrates how to create and analyse a knowledge model. This method is helpful in analysing the organizational knowledge model because it takes into consideration both the qualitative and quantitative aspects of the cognitive model.

A cognitive map is composed of three components: causal factor, causal value, and causal connection. The main difficulty lies in determining the causal value component. Specification of the causal value is the most challenging problem in generating a cognitive map because it has a qualitative property reflecting people's cognitive status, which cannot be directly measured. Besides, human perception is often inconsistent. Direct scale values have been used by most of the methods for cognitive modeling (Eden & Ackermann, 1989; Zhang et al., 1994). However, this direct assignment approach has limitations in that the procedure is not systematic and the result heavily depends on the analysts' or participants' subjective judgment.

For this method, an eigenvector approach through pairwise comparison was chosen for more systematic determination of causal values.

Table 2. Creating and formulating a knowledge model

Objective	Task	Output	Tools
Cognitive model generation	Specify goals	Goal statement	Brainstorming Interview Document analysis Survey Eigenvector algorithm
	Identify causal factors - List all causal factors - Cluster the causal factors	Causal factor list	
	Identify causal connections - Identify the relationships between clusters - Identify the relationships between causal concepts	Cluster relationship diagram Causal factor relationship diagram	
	Assign causal values - Conduct pair-wise comparison - Compute eigenvectors	Pairwise comparison matrix Causal values	
Causal path identification	Initialize cognitive matrix	Cognitive matrix	Matrix operation Causal path computation algorithm
	Compute causal impact paths and values	Causal impact paths and values matrix	

This approach is based on the analytic hierarchy process (AHP) method developed in the 1970s (Saaty, 1980). Strength of the AHP method lies in its ability to structure a complex problem hierarchically and to evaluate the relationships between entities systematically. In the application of AHP method, the eigenvector assignment approach is conducted through pairwise comparison and eigenvector computation.

Pairwise comparison technique starts from the idea that the measurements based on experience and understanding are obtainable only from relative comparisons and not in an absolute way (Saaty, 1980). The intensity of our feelings serves as a scale adjustment device to put the measurement of some objects on a scale commensurate with that of other objects. The results of pairwise comparisons are represented in a form of matrix, called pairwise comparison matrix. A pairwise comparison matrix has cell entries as a scale indicating the relative strength with which elements in one cluster influences other elements in other clusters. This scaling process can then be translated into impact weights. The eigenvalue method is the most preferred approach for the estimation (Saaty, 1980). When a pairwise comparison matrix has a maximum eigenvalue and the corresponding eigenvector whose components are all positive, this eigenvector becomes a ratio scale that are the estimates of relative impact values of elements under comparison. Eliciting causal values in a cognitive map can be viewed as a process that transforms qualitative mental status into quantitative numerical scale. The eigenvector approach provides a way for calibrating a numerical scale, particularly in areas where measurements and quantitative comparisons do not exist.

The completed global cognitive map is analyzed in terms of the strength of the impact between causal factors. Our concern is to identify the causal paths with the maximum causal impact among all causal paths regardless of the direct or indirect impact. These causal paths take negative or positive path values, depending on their causal values. In order to identify the causal path(s) with the maximum causal impact, we adopted the algorithm proposed by Zhang et al. (1994) and extended it to find the paths and values simultaneously. The algorithm produces an $n \times n$ matrix called the causal impact path and a value matrix consisting of X_{ij}, where X_{ij} is the set of $\{+p_{ij}, -p_{ij}, +v_{ij}, -v_{ij}\}$: $+p_{ij}$ is a positive causal impact path from element i to j, $-p_{ij}$ is a negative causal path, $+v_{ij}$ is a maximum positive causal impact value corresponding to $+p_{ij}$, and $-v_{ij}$ and is a maximum negative causal impact value corresponding to $-p_{ij}$. The algorithm is applied iteratively, while either maximum positive value ($+v_{ij}$) or maximum negative value ($-v_{ij}$) can be improved; in other words, until new dominant values cannot be identified (refer to Appendix 1 for the simplified algorithm).

Decision Support

The analyzed knowledge model should suggest guidelines for decisions on managerial problems. A decision guideline can be generated in view of the organizational goal, based on the organizational knowledge model (or cognitive model) and the causal path analysis. An organizational goal is a desired future state of affairs that the organization attempts to realize (Etzioni, 1964). A goal pertains to the future, but it influences current activities. Because organizations are goal-attainment entities, goals play a role in setting directions for its members' activities, leading their thoughts and actions to a specific result (Hamner, Ross, & Staw, 1983). Decision guidelines thus can be identified by analyzing people's thoughts and actions with respect to their organizational goals.

To facilitate decision support, we propose analyzing the organizational knowledge represented in cognitive maps in terms of the causal paths and strengths among the causal factors. The causal impact paths and values among the causal factors can be computed based on the proposed methodology, as mentioned in the previous section. The derived matrix includes the negative path and value as well as the positive path and value for each relationship among the causal factors.

Regardless of the polarity of the impact, it is first necessary to focus on the most effective causal factor in achieving the goal. This factor can be an opportunity, if it has a positive impact, but it can be a problem, if it has a negative impact. It is then necessary to identify the relevant feedback loop paths that strengthen the positive impact and weaken the negative one. For a causal factor with a positive impact, this involves making its positive loop more positive and making its negative loop less negative. For a causal factor with a negative impact, this involves making its positive loop less positive and making its negative loop more negative.

The output from such a process enables a decision to be made on a managerial problem. There are many reasons that update individual and organizational knowledge and upon which the selection of an appropriate option can be made. That is, there is a feedback process from integrated knowledge and decision support to individual knowledge and mental models. This is a kind of organizational learning process. Although decision makers cannot apply the same option and the same knowledge to similar problems in the future, they can now understand the dynamic complexity of the target problem, the structure among the elements, and the behavioural patterns. Decision making via understanding dynamic complexity, based on a cognitive model, enables the acquisition of real leverage in managerial problems (Fiol & Huff, 1992; Senge, 1990; Sterman, 2001).

COMPARISON WITH OTHER APPROACHES

The proposed approach can be compared with other KM methods. Our research focuses on enterprise wide improvement by enhancing managerial decision support by means of organizational knowledge, whereas other KM methods (Davenport, 1998; Davenport et al., 1998; Kankanhalli et al., 2005) aim to obtain better efficiency and effectiveness in task processing by knowledge attainment and knowledge repository management. Due to this difference in approach, other KM methods are more concerned with individual or departmental tasks at the operational level. They highlight declarative knowledge (which is related to each employee's cognitive model) and procedural knowledge (which is stored as document- or database-type knowledge). In contrast, the proposed method that we have presented emphasizes integrating the partial knowledge of different departments and employees into organizational knowledge. By doing so, our method facilitates effective business decision making and strategic planning.

The proposed approach can be compared with other cognitive modeling methods. Several cognitive modeling methods and tools using the cognitive map have been developed in various domains, including business policy establishment, organizational learning, and strategic option development (Eden & Ackermann, 1989; Hall, 1984; Lee, Courtney, & O'Keefe, 1992). However, most cognitive modeling methods emphasize map representation as a knowledge representation scheme rather than as a problem-solving tool (Kwahk & Kim, 1999). The proposed approach provides a representation scheme as well as some guidelines for problem solving, by further investigating the knowledge represented in the cognitive map, based on the analysis of the most effective paths.

The proposed matrix approach also can be compared with system dynamics (Sterman, 2001). System dynamics is a methodology aimed at designing better behaved system, by understanding the target system, especially with feedback loops among system components and behaviour patterns over time. System dynamics attempts to conceptualize any business problem with a causal loop diagram, and formulate and test it after transforming the causal loop diagram into a stock-flow diagram. The standard application of system dynamics includes identifying the core loop and core factors as part of policy development. However, identifying the core loop and core factors relies on either the intuition of the modeler or user, or the somewhat cumbersome simulation testing of several alternatives. While the identification of the core loop and core factors is very critical to the application of system dynamics and effective policy development, little research has been done in the area. By proposing a new method for identifying the core loop and core factors, this study has contributed to system dynamics literature.

APPLICATION CASE

We applied the proposed decision support loop to a beverage company with an annual sales volume of about $600 million. The company was about to start a business process redesign implementation project, and before that, the management wanted to know the main target of the process redesign, especially across the marketing and production departments. Accordingly, we applied the proposed approach in finding the leverage points in decision making for increasing profit by identifying core factors and core activities.

The application of the proposed method was carried out by two researchers who had knowledge about the proposed method and cognitive map, along with the company's project team, which mainly consisted of members of related departments. Two researchers educated the project team about the procedure and the use of cognitive map, particularly, focusing on the knowledge elicitation of individual department. This study lasted for a month until the business process redesign implementation project started.

Individual Knowledge

Individual knowledge was gathered from the marketing and production departments. To generate a cognitive map for each department, a brainstorming session and interviews with participants from each department were held. Following the discussion and interviews, the participants established the goals for their respective departments. The marketing department set increasing sales as its goal, while the production department decided on improving productivity. Next, we attempted to extract all the causal factors for each department, including business-related activity concepts. The brainstorming technique again was used. When all the causal factors had been listed, they were clustered according to their functional similarity and behavioral homogeneity. Based on these clusters, the relationships between clusters were identified, along with their directions and polarities. A cognitive map was derived from the list of causal factor clusters and the cluster relationships; this was done by replacing clusters with their corresponding causal factors and making appropriate connections among causal factors. Then cognitive maps were generated from the two departments along with the relevant goals, as illustrated in Figure 3.

Organizational Knowledge

Knowledge related to organizational goals is dispersed across a company, and it is kept by the top management, departmental managers, and departmental staff members of the firm. This knowledge is identified and organized through "externalization" and "combination." Although some information or knowledge can be obtained from documents or databases, large portions of knowledge reside in mental models. In our case application, we conducted interviews with the top managers and the middle managers of the two departments to identify partial knowledge. By having these interviews, we could detect and resolve discrepancies between the cognitive maps of the two departments.

Combining the individual knowledge models of the two departments generated the organizational knowledge model as depicted in Figure 4. The synthesizing process revealed organizational knowledge that was not known explicitly to the departments. The two departments became aware of how elements in one department could affect the other department. For example, efforts to increase market share by the marketing department could lead to increasing ordering time and delivery time, thus resulting in diminished productivity, which is of interest to the production department.

Formulating and Testing the Knowledge Model

The organizational knowledge represented in the cognitive map was analyzed in terms of the

Figure 3. Individual knowledge models of two departments

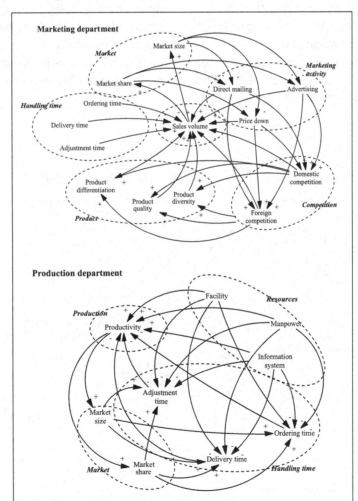

causal paths and strengths among the elements to identify the leverage points in decision making. The causal impact paths among the causal factors as well as their values were computed. In this application case, core business activities were identified from the causal impact paths and values matrix, as illustrated in Table 3 (and also in Figure 5).

When increasing profit was considered as a target goal, the two most effective causal factors were identified from the causal impact paths and values matrix (refer to Table 4). One was productivity, which was the most positive causal factor. It represented an opportunity to accomplish the organizational goal because productivity enhancement contributes most to increasing corporate profit. The other one was ordering time, which was the most negative causal factor. It represented a problem for the attainment of the goal because an increase in ordering time undermines profit increases through a decrease in sales volume. The objective was, therefore, to strengthen the positive

causal factor ("productivity") and weaken the negative casual factor ("ordering time").

As can be seen in Table 3 and Figure 5, the causal factors—productivity and ordering time—possessed *positive* feedback loops of {Productivity–Profit–Information system–Productivity} and {Ordering time–Productivity–Profit–Information system–Ordering time}, respectively. In addition, the two factors possessed *negative* feedback loops of {Productivity–Market share–Ordering time–Productivity} and {Ordering time–Sales–Market share–Ordering time}, respectively. It seems clear that the paths, {Productivity–Profit–Information system} and {Ordering time–Productivity}, were the main drivers that could accelerate an improvement in productivity and a decrease in ordering time. Thus, by designating the above two paths of related activities as core business activities, it would be possible to focus on how to use information technologies in redesigning the processes related to productivity and ordering time.

Figure 4. The organizational knowledge model between the two departments

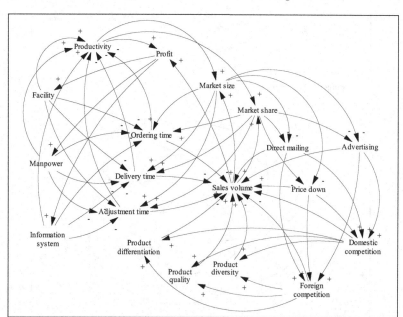

Decision Support

Based on the above organizational knowledge and consensus, the ordering process was identified as a candidate target process for possible redesign. The existing ordering process depended heavily on manual handling and required the intervention of the sales branches. This resulted in long ordering time and inefficiency in production and delivery. Including a new client-server system in the redesign of the ordering process could significantly reduce total ordering time.

In the redesigned ordering process, every agency could send its orders directly to the factory through the network without the intervention of the sales branches. Reducing the branches' role in order taking was expected to result in shorter ordering time, which in turn was likely to increase efficiency in production and delivery and, in the long run, contribute to profit. In addition to discovering the best decision option, the top management and managers at other levels came to understand the elements involved in the business process, the relationships among them, and

the behavioural mechanism of the target business problem.

At the end of the application of the proposed method, the results and insights were presented to the top management of the firm and the two departments. The top management came to understand what factors affected organizational profit and how the factors were related across the two departments. In addition, the management could now perceive why the proposed decision guidelines would be effective. The two departments and the individual employees also could expand their department-constrained knowledge into cross-department knowledge. Thus, the proposed method facilitated understanding of the behavioural mechanism regarding the target managerial problem by linking knowledge integration to decision support.

In summary, the goal in the application case was to identify the decision options to increase profit. For company-level decision making, such as in the application case, knowledge integration (regarding how to increase profit and what factors affect profit) across functional areas is essential.

Table 3. Analysis of core business activities

Causal factor		Feedback loops
The most positive impact factor: Productivity	Positive	Path = {Productivity - Profit – Information system - Productivity} Value = +0.52*
	Negative	Path = {Productivity - Market share - Ordering time - Productivity} Value = -0.19*
The most negative impact factor: Ordering time	Positive	Path = {Ordering time - Productivity - Profit - Information system - Ordering time} Value = +0.36*
	Negative	Path = {Ordering time - Sales - Market share - Ordering time} Value = -0.32*

* Values can be calculated based on the path of feedback loops and the corresponding causal values as follows: $+0.52=(+0.67)*(+1.0)*$ $(+0.77)$; $-0.19= (+0.33)*(+0.83)*(-0.70)$; $+0.36= (-0.70)*(+0.67)*(+1.0)*(-0.77)$; $-0.32=(-0.57)*(+0.67)*(+0.83)$ (refer to Appendix 2).

As part of knowledge management, the proposed approach facilitates the identification and integration of partial knowledge (as in Figure 3) into organized knowledge (as in Figure 4). In decision making, there could be several decision options. Identifying the best option or core factors is one of the main goals in decision support (as in Figure 5). Thus, the matrix method enabled us to identify the core factors regarding the goal of decision making based on the combined knowledge model. In the case study, the management and the two departments gained newly identified knowledge through our proposed process.

DISCUSSION

Any problem is characterized by its complexity type: detail complexity and dynamic complexity (Senge, 1990; Sterman, 2000). Detail complexity arises when it focuses on the static aspect of a structured problem by highlighting the correctness of selected variables. Dynamic complexity arises when it focuses on the dynamic aspect of an unstructured problem by highlighting the interactions among the variables. Any problem characterized by detail complexity tends to entail mathematical modeling approach to find an optimal solution. In contrast, any problem characterized by dynamic complexity tends to entail the cognitive modeling approach to design a better behaved system by understanding the behavior mechanism. Organizational problems (or business management problems) are characterized by dynamic complexity, tacit knowledge factors, feedback effects over time, and unstructuredness (Sterman, 2001).Organizational problems especially require (tacit and explicit) knowledge gathering and integration across employees and organization units (Argote, McEvily, & Reagans,

Figure 5. Feedback loops related to the target goal

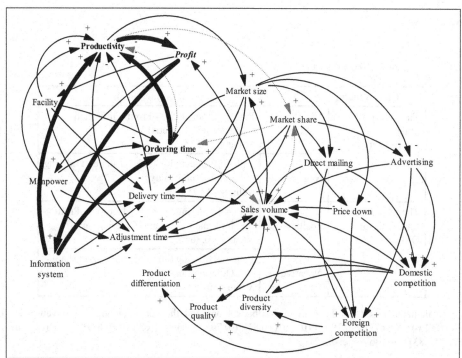

Table 4. Part of causal impact paths and values matrix (causal factor "profit" column)

Cell (*i, j*)	Positive		Negative	
	Value	Path	Value	Path
(01, 01)	+0.516	1- 14- 11- 1	-0.114	1- 14- 15- 2- 19- 15- 11- 1
(02, 01)	+0.330	2- 1	-0.261	2- 19- 15- 11- 1
(03, 01)	+0.026	3- 2- 1	-0.021	3- 2- 19- 15- 11- 1
(04, 01)	+0.198	4- 2- 1	-0.156	4- 2- 19- 15- 11- 1
(05, 01)	+0.160	5- 7- 9- 2- 1	-0.159	5- 6- 2- 1
(06, 01)	+0.175	6- 2- 19- 15- 11- 1	-0.221	6- 2- 1
(07, 01)	+0.211	7- 9- 2- 1	-0.167	7- 9- 2- 19- 15- 11- 1
(08, 01)	+0.056	8- 2- 1	-0.044	8- 2- 19- 15- 11- 1
(09, 01)	+0.254	9- 2- 1	-0.201	9- 2- 19- 15- 11- 1
(10, 01)	+0.020	10- 2- 1	-0.016	10- 2- 19- 15- 11- 1
(11, 01)	+0.670	11- 1	-0.128	11- 19- 15- 11- 1
(12, 01)	+0.114	12- 11- 1	-0.022	12- 11- 19- 15- 11- 1
(13, 01)	+0.080	13- 15- 11- 1	-0.025	13- 15- 2- 19- 15- 11- 1
(14, 01)	+0.516	14- 11- 1	-0.114	14- 15- 2- 19- 15- 11- 1
(15, 01)	+0.149	15- 2- 19- 15- 11- 1	-0.469	15- 11- 1
(16, 01)	+0.026	16- 2- 19- 15- 11- 1	-0.040	16- 11- 1
(17, 01)	+0.086	17- 2- 19- 15- 11- 1	-0.161	17- 11- 1
(18, 01)	+0.025	18- 15- 2- 19- 15- 11- 1	-0.080	18- 15- 11- 1
(19, 01)	+0.138	19- 5- 6- 2- 1	-0.389	19- 15- 11- 1

Note: 1 represents-profit; 2 represents sales amount; 3 represents DM; 4 represents advertising; 5 represents price down; 6 represents domestic competition; 7 represents foreign competition; 8 represents product differentiation; 9 represents product quality; 10 represents product diversity; 11 represents productivity; 12 represents facility; 13 represents manpower; 14 represents information system; 15 represents ordering time; 16 represents delivery time; 17 represents adjustment time; 18 represents market size; and 19 represents market share.

2003; King, 2006). In addition, a systematic approach is needed to identify and capture knowledge within the organization (Cai, 2006; Nah, Siau, & Tian, 2005). Based on these needs, this study proposed a knowledge integration approach for organizational decision support by developing a cognitive modeling methodology together with the decision support loop. We believe the developed decision support loop and the methodology (including tasks and relevant methods in each step over the two common stages) is unique compared to other decision support approaches.

The case described in the previous section may be best discussed as an exercise in knowledge conceptualization. During the conceptualization process, the knowledge related to the target problem was identified and structured from the causal relationship perspective using cognitive maps. The analysis enabled decision makers to: (1) trace the basic causes of unexpected outcomes;

(2) understand which decision factors had more significant impacts on performance; and (3) make trade-offs between decision alternatives. The reasoning process had effects on both the value of decision factors and the causal relationships.

Our proposed approach is characterized by its learning process and organizational memory. Learning allows individuals to obtain knowledge and insight from the results of experiences, and facilitates the application of this knowledge to future circumstances (Fiol & Lyles, 1985). Organizational learning aims to obtain knowledge, store it in the organizational memory, and revise it by experience; the accumulated organizational knowledge is thus diffused (Huber, 1991; Senge, 1990). Organizational memory refers to "the means by which knowledge from the past [is] brought to bear on present activities, thus resulting in higher or lower levels of organizational effectiveness" (Stein, 1995 p. 22). Ramesh (1999) suggested the development of organizational memory through the identification of information that should be provided as part of cognitive feedback, together with the interdependencies within this information. Organizations update their respective organizational memories that consist of knowledge through learning. Our proposed approach enables an organization to obtain of previous knowledge from individuals or organizational knowledge models, allows for the creation of new organizational knowledge, and allows for its revision by reasoning and new experiences. The management and teams of an organization can share the collective tacit/explicit knowledge to improve their understanding of the target situation, which will enable them to be more cooperative in their dealings with each other. The organizational knowledge model, thus, plays a role in organizational memory.

Compared to other general decision support approaches, our approach would be more appropriate to the decision-making context with highly constrained tasks involving resource allocation. Highly constrained tasks can be classified as mixed-motive negotiation tasks in which participants have mixed motives to compete and cooperate (McGrath, 1984; Rees & Barkhi, 2001). It is, therefore, important to understand the overview of the system, and this should be shared among participants with respect to how one part of a decision can affect other parts. Decision-making support should aid individuals or subunits in an organization in exchanging information and making coordinated decisions (Barkhi, 2001–2002). The proposed approach enables individuals or subunits in an organization to make decisions consistent with the organizational goals, leading them to collaborate with each other by linking organizational knowledge to decision support.

As part of the proposed approach, the matrix method seeks to provide problem-solving guidelines in a systematic way that is lacking in most cognitive map methods. The merit of our approach is that it quantifies the knowledge represented in the map and identifies core factors and the relationships among them. The identified factors and relationships are new knowledge that comes with the application of our method. Their importance is reflected in the fact that they are the main target for decision making. Therefore, our matrix method plays an important role in the proposed organizational decision support through knowledge integration across organizational units.

Our proposed matrix approach is more appropriate for testing linear problems, but many real-world problems (or systems) are characterized by nonlinearity. The main focus of system dynamics is to conceptualize and test the effect of nonlinearity over time. While our proposed approach captures nonlinearity in structuring a problem, the matrix method has its limitations in testing nonlinearity effects over time. Nevertheless, the limitation can be eased by combining the proposed matrix approach with the typical system dynamics approach. Based on the identified core loop and factors from the matrix approach, we can further test the model (or business problem) with the format of the stock-flow diagram of the system dynamics approach. In the testing, we could consider nonlinearity in the system; and we could validate whether the identified core loop and factors produce real leverage effect in the nonlinear system.

CONCLUSION

The core contribution of our study lies in proposing a methodology for organizational decision support based on knowledge gathering and integration across organization units and people. While most previous research on knowledge management has focused on identifying and sharing knowledge mainly for transaction processing in an organization, this study explains how organizations can apply knowledge management (i.e., knowledge gathering and integration across multiple individuals and organizational units) for organizational decision support. For this, we have developed and proposed the decision support loop. The decision support loop facilitates integrating individual knowledge into organizational knowledge, then formulating and testing it for decision support. For the knowledge representation, formulation, and testing, we used the cognitive modeling method, which enables decision makers to estimate the strength of the impact between causal factors. The generation of alternatives and the testing of those alternatives enable decision makers to appreciate the behavioural mechanism and the inherent structure of the target business problem. The application case showed the validity and usefulness of the proposed method.

ACKNOWLEDGMENT

The authors are grateful to the editor-in-chief and the anonymous reviewers for their excellent suggestions. This work was supported by the 2006 new faculty research program of Kookmin University in Korea.

REFERENCES

Alavi, M., & Leidner, D. E. (2001). Knowledge management and knowledge management systems: Conceptual foundations and research issues. *MIS Quarterly, 25*(1), 107-136.

Argote, L. B., McEvily, B., & Reagans, R. (2003). Introduction of the special issue on managing knowledge in organizations: Creating, retaining, and transferring knowledge. *Management Science, 49*(4), v-viii.

Axelrod, R. (1976). *Structure of decision: The cognitive maps of political elites*. NJ: Princeton University Press.

Barkhi, R. (2001-2002). The effects of decision guidance and problem modelling on group decision-making. *Journal of Management Information Systems, 18*(3), 259-282.

Brown, J. S., & Dugid, P. (1998). Organizing knowledge. *California Management Review, 40*(3), 90-111.

Cai, J., (2006). Knowledge management within collaboration processes: A perspective modeling and analyzing methodology. *Journal of Database Management, 17*(1), 33-48.

Davenport, T. H. (1998). *Working knowledge*. MA: Harvard Business School Press.

Davenport., T. H., De Long, D. W., & Beers, M. C. (1998). Successful knowledge management projects. *Sloan Management Review,* 43-57.

Eden, C., & Ackermann, F. (1989). Strategic options development and analysis (SODA)-using a computer to help with the management of strategic vision. (198-207) In G. Doukidis, F. Land, & G. Miller (Eds.), *Knowledge-based management support systems*. UK: Ellis Horwood.

Eden, C. (1988). Cognitive mapping. *European Journal of Operational Research, 36,* 1-13.

Etzioni, A. (1964). *Modern organizations*. NJ: Prentice-Hall.

Fiol, C. M., & Huff, A. S. (1992). Maps for managers: Where are we? Where do we go from here? *Journal of Management Studies, 29*(3), 267-285.

Fiol, C. M., & Lyles, M. A. (1985). Organizational learning. *Academy of Management Review, 10*(4), 803-813.

Grover, V., & Davenport, T. (2001). General perspectives on knowledge management: Fostering a research agenda. *Journal of Management Information Systems, 18*(1), 5-21.

Hall, R. (1984). The natural logic of management policy making: Its implications for the survival of an organization. *Management Science, 30*(8), 905-927.

Hamner, W. C., Ross, J. & Staw, B. M. (1983). Motivation in organizations: the need for a new direction. In R. M. Steers & L. W. Porter (Eds.), *Motivation & work behaviour* (pp. 52-72). NY: McGraw-Hill.

Hanse, M. T. (2002). Knowledge networks: Explaining effective knowledge sharing in multiunit companies. *Organization Science, 13*(3), 232-248.

Huber, G.. P. (1991). Organizational learning: The contributing process and the literature. *Organization Science, 2*(1), 88-115.

Kankanhalli, A., Tan, B., & Wei, K. K. (2005). Contributing knowledge to electronic knowledge repositories: An empirical investigation. *MIS Quarterly, 29*(1), 113-143.

King, W. R. (2006). The critical role of information processing in creating and effective knowledge organization. *Journal of Database Management, 17*(1), 1-15.

Kwahk, K. Y., & Kim. Y. G. (1999). Supporting business process redesign using cognitive maps. *Decision Support Systems, 25,* 155-178.

Lee, S., Courtney, J. F., & O'Keefe, R. M. (1992). A system for organizational learning using cognitive maps. *Omega, 20*(1), 23-36

Lee, J. H., & Kim, Y. G. (2001). A stage model of organizational knowledge management: A latent content analysis. *Expert Systems with Application, 20*(4), 299-311.

Lenz, R. T., & Engledow, J. L. (1986). Environmental analysis: The applicability of current theory. *Strategic Management Journal, 17*(4), 329-346.

McGrath, J. E. (1984). *Groups: Interaction and performance*. NJ: Prentice Hall.

Nadkarni, S., & Nah, F. F. (2003). Aggregated causal maps: An approach to elicit and aggregate the knowledge of multiple experts. *Communications of the Association for Information Systems, 12,* 406-436.

Nah, F., Siau, K., & Tian, Y. (2005). Knowledge management mechanisms of financial service sites. *Communications of the ACM, 48*(6), 117-123.

Nambisan, S., & Wilemon, D. (2000). Software development and new product development: Potentials for cross-domain knowledge sharing. *IEEE Transactions on Engineering Management, 47*(2), 211-220.

Nilakanta, S., Miller, L. L., & Zhu, D. (2006). Organizational memory management: Technological and research issues. *Journal of Database Management, 17*(1), 85-94.

Nonaka, I. (1994). A dynamic theory of organizational knowledge creation. *Organization Science, 5*(1), 14-37.

Ramesh, B. (1999). Towards a meta-model for representing organizational memory. *Proceedings of Hawaii International Conference on Systems Science* (pp. 320-329).

Rees, J., & Barkhi, R. (2001). The problem of highly constrained tasks in group decision support systems. *European Journal of Operational Research, 135,* 220-229.

Saaty, T. L. (1980). *The analytic hierarchy process.* NY: McGraw-Hill.

Sambamurthy, V., & Subramanu, M. (2005). Special issue on information technologies and knowledge management. *MIS Quarterly, 29*(2), 193-195.

Senge, P. (1990). *The fifth discipline: The art and practice of the learning organization.* NY: Currency Doubleday.

Siau, K. (2000). Knowledge discovery and an aid to organizational creativity. *Journal of Creative Behaviour, 34*(4), 248-158.

Siau, K., & Tan, X. (2005). Improving the quality of conceptual modelling using cognitive mapping techniques. *Data and Knowledge Engineering, 55*(3), 343-365.

Siau, K., & Tan, X. (2006). Cognitive mapping techniques for user-database interaction. *IEEE Transactions on Professional Communication, 49*(2), 96-108.

Simon, H. (1964). On the concept of organizational goals. *Administrative Science Quarterly, 9,* 1-22.

Smith, G. F. (1989). Defining managerial problems: a framework for prescriptive theorizing. *Management Science, 35*(8), 963-981.

Stein, E.W . (1995). Organizational memory: Review of concepts and recommendations for management. *International Journal of Information Management, 15*(2), 17-32.

Sterman, J. (2000). *Business dynamics: Systems thinking and modelling for a complex world.* NY: McGraw Hill.

Sterman, J. (2001). System dynamics modelling: Tools for learning in a complex world. *California Management Review, 43*(4), 8-25.

Weick, K. E., & Bougon, M. G. (1986). Organizations as cognitive maps. In H. P. Sims & D. A. Gioia (Eds.), *The thinking organization: Dynamics of organizational social cognition* (pp. 103-135). CA: Jossey-Bass.

Xu, Y., Tan, B., & Yang, L. (2006). Who will you ask? An empirical study of interpersonal task information seeking. *Journal of the American Society for Information Science and Technology, 57(12),* pp. 1666-1677.

Zhang, W. R., Wang, W., & King, R. S. (1994). A-pool: An agent-oriented open system shell for distributed decision process modeling. *Journal of Organizational Computing, 4*(2), 127-154.

APPENDIX

1. Simplified algorithm for computing causal impact paths and values

Initialization

Set X$_{ij}$ such as

$+p_{ij} = \{i, j\}$, $-p_{ij} = \{\phi\}$, $\quad +v_{ij} = u_{ij}$, $\quad -v_{ij} = 0$, $\quad$ If $u_{ij} > 0$

$+p_{ij} = \{\phi\}$, $\quad -p_{ij} = \{i, j\}$, $\quad +v_{ij} = 0$, $\quad -v_{ij} = u_{ij}$, $\quad$ If $u_{ij} < 0$

$+p_{ij} = \{\phi\}$, $\quad -p_{ij} = \{\phi\}$, $\quad +v_{ij} = 0$, $\quad -v_{ij} = 0$, $\quad$ If $u_{ij} = 0$

Main procedure

Do while being improvement

  For $i = 1$ **To** n

    For $j = 1$ **To** n

      For $k = 1$ **To** n

        Read $-v_{ij}$, $+v_{ij}$, $-v_{ik}$, $+v_{ik}$, $-v_{kj}$, $+v_{kj}$

        If $-v_{ij} > (-v_{ik}) * (+v_{kj})$

          Set $-v_{ij} = (-v_{ik}) * (+v_{kj})$

          Set $-p_{ij} = (-p_{ik}) \cup (+p_{kj})$

        End If

        If $-v_{ij} > (+v_{ik}) * (-v_{kj})$

          Set $-v_{ij} = (+v_{ik}) * (-v_{kj})$

          Set $-p_{ij} = (+p_{ik}) \cup (-p_{kj})$

        End If

        If $+v_{ij} < (+v_{ik}) * (+v_{kj})$

          Set $+v_{ij} = (+v_{ik}) * (+v_{kj})$

          Set $+p_{ij} = (+p_{ik}) \cup (+p_{kj})$

        End If

        If $+v_{ij} < (-v_{ik}) * (-v_{kj})$

          Set $+v_{ij} = (-v_{ik}) * (-v_{kj})$

          Set $+p_{ij} = (-p_{ik}) \cup (-p_{kj})$

        End If

      Next k

    Next j

  Next i

Loop

2. Organizational knowledge model with causal values

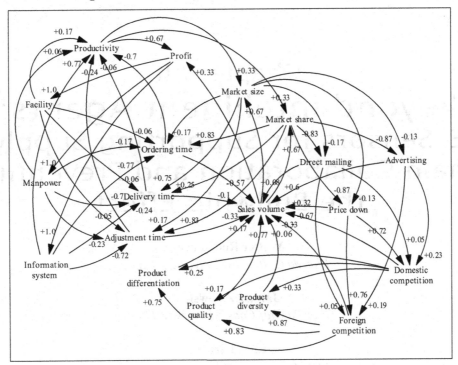

Chapter XII
Beyond Intelligent Agents:
E–Sensors for Supporting Supply Chain Collaboration and Preventing the Bullwhip Effect

Walter Rodriguez
Florida Gulf Coast University, USA

Janusz Zalewski
Florida Gulf Coast University, USA

Elias Kirche
Florida Gulf Coast University, USA

ABSTRACT

This article presents a new concept for supporting electronic collaboration, operations, and relationships among trading partners in the value chain without hindering human autonomy. Although autonomous intelligent agents, or electronic robots (e-bots), can be used to inform this endeavor, the article advocates the development of e-sensors, i.e., software based units with capabilities beyond intelligent agent's functionality. E-sensors are hardware-software capable of perceiving, reacting and learning from its interactive experience through the supply chain, rather than just searching for data and information through the network and reacting to it. E-sensors can help avoid the "bull-whip" effect. The article briefly reviews the related intelligent agent and supply chain literature and the technological gap between fields. It articulates a demand-driven, sense-and-response system for sustaining e-collaboration and e-business operations as well as monitoring products and processes. As a proof of concept, this research aimed a test solution at a single supply chain partner within one stage of the process.

INTRODUCTION: FROM E-BOTS TO E-SENSORS

As e-business and e-commerce has grown, so has the need to focus attention on the: (1) Electronic communications between e-partners; (2) operational transactions (e.g., sales, purchasing, communications, inventory, customer service, ordering, submitting, checking-status, and sourcing, among others); and (3) monitoring improvements in the supply (supply, demand, value) chain of products, systems, and services (Gaither & Fraizer, 2002).

Integrating continuous communication protocols and operational and supply chain management (SCM) considerations, early on in the enterprise design process, would greatly improve the successful implementation of the e-collaboration technologies in the enterprise. It is particularly important to examine the resources and systems that support the electronic communications, and relationships among partners, in the supply chain.

In addition, there is a need for obtaining (sensing) real time data for managing (anticipating, responding) throughout the supply chain. Typically companies need to synchronize orders considering type, quantity, location, and timing of the delivery in order to reduce waste in the production and delivery process. The data collection and availability provided by the e-sensing infrastructure/architecture discussed later in this article will allow for a collaborative environment, improve forecast accuracy, and increase cross-enterprise integration among partners in the supply chain.

Current supply chain information technologies (IT) allow managers to track and gather intelligence about the customers purchasing habits. In addition to point-of-sale Universal Product Code (UPC) barcode devices, the current IT infrastructure may include retail radio frequency identification (RFID) devices and electronic tagging to identify and track product flow. These technologies aid mainly in the marketing and resupply efforts. But, how about tracking partners' behaviors throughout the chain in real time?

Artificial intelligent agents (or e-bots) can be deployed throughout the supply chain to seek data and information about competitive pricing, for instance, e-bots can search for the cheapest supplier for a given product and even compare characteristics and functionality. For this reason, the concept of an *agent* is important in both the Artificial Intelligence (AI) and the e-operations fields.

The term "intelligent agent" or "e-bot" denotes a software system that enjoys at least one of the following properties: (1) Autonomy; (2) "Social" ability; and (3) Reactivity (Wooldridge & Jennings, 1995). Normally, agents are thought to be autonomous because they are capable to operate without direct intervention of people and have some level of control over their own actions (Castelfranchi, 1995). In addition, agents may have the functionality to interact with other agents and automated systems via an agent-communication language (Genesereth & Ketchpel, 1994). This agent attribute is termed here *e-sociability* for its ability to interact with either people, or systems (software).

The next evolution of the intelligent agent concept is the development of integrated hardware/software systems that may be specifically designed to sense (perceive) and respond (act) within certain pre-defined operational constrains and factors, and respond in a real time fashion to changes (not a just-in-time fashion) occurring throughout the supply chain. These integrated hardware-software systems are termed *e-sensors*, in this article. Indeed, there is a real opportunity for process innovation and most likely organizations will need to create new business applications to put e-sensors at the centre of a process if they want to be competitive in this new supply chain environment. Aside from asset tracking, each industry will have specialized applications of e-sensors that cannot be generalized. Before getting into the e-sensors details, let us review some key supply chain management (SCM) issues relevant to this discussion.

SUPPLY CHAIN MANAGEMENT IN THE E-COLLABORATION CONTEXT

SCM is the art and science of creating and accentuating synergistic relationships among the trading partners in supply and distribution channels with the common shared objective of delivering products and services to the 'right customer' at the 'right time.' (Vakharia, 2002)

In the e-collaboration/e-business context, supply chain management (SCM) is the operations management discipline concerned with these synergistic communications, relationships, activities and operations in the competitive Internet enterprise. SCM involves studying the movement of physical materials and electronic information and communications—including transportation, logistics and information-flow management to improve operational efficiencies, effectiveness and profitability. SCM consists in the strategies and technologies for developing and integrating the operations, communications and relationships among the e-trading partners (producers,

manufacturers, services providers, suppliers, sellers, wholesalers, distributors, purchasing agents, logisticians, consultants, shipping agents, deliverers, retailers, traders and customers) as well as improving their operations throughout the products' or services' chain.

Integrated e-business SCM can enhance decision making by collecting real time information as well as assessing and analyzing data and information that facilitate collaboration among trading partners in the supply chain.

To achieve joint optimization of key SCM decisions, it is preferable that there be a free flow of all relevant information across the entire chain leading to a comprehensive analysis. (Vakharia, 2002)

As shown in Figure 1, IT systems, such as, enterprise resource planning (ERP), point of sale (POS), and vendor managed inventory (VMI) systems permit and, to some extend, automate information sharing.

The advent of reliable communication technologies has forced business partners throughout

Figure 1. Information flow using electronic information technologies in the supply chain (after Burke & Vakharia, 2002; Vakharia, 2002)

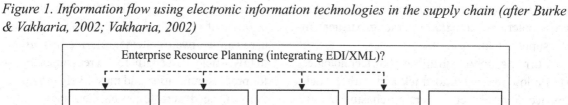

the supply chain to rethink their strategies as well as change the nature of the relationships with suppliers and customers. Companies that have made the shift have benefited from: "Reduced operating expenses, increased revenue growth, and improved customer levels," according to IBM ERP/Supply Management Division (Cross, 2000). According to the same source, the companies that have implemented supply chain improvement projects have been able to increase forecast accuracy and inventory reduction (up to 50% in overall improvement!). Some of the newer activities being implemented include: Supply-and-demand auctions, integrated collaborative product design (CAD/CAM), cross-enterprise workflow processes, demand management collaboration. In addition, some companies are even deploying SCM as an offensive tactic to gain a competitive edge (Cross, 2000).

Meixell's "Collaborative Manufacturing for Mass Customization" (2006)site, at http://www. som.gmu.edu/faculty/profiles/mmeixell/collabor ative%20Planning%20&%20Mass%20Customiz ation.pdf, provides extensive information about the use of collaborative technologies in the supply chain. The same author recently compiled a literature review; particularly, on decision support models used for the design of global supply chains (Meixell & Gargeya, 2005). This, however, does not mean that there are no strategic and technological gaps in the supply chain.

PARADIGM SHIFT: FROM 'PUSH' (SCM) TO 'PULL' (SRS)

We are not smart enough to predict the future, so we have to get better at reacting to it more quickly. (GE saying quoted by Haeckel, 1999)

E-business forces have shifted both the enterprise landscape and the competitive power from the providers of goods and information (makers, suppliers, distributors and retailers) to the purchasers of goods and information (customers). For this reason, e-businesses must collaborate electronically and sense-and-respond very quickly to the individual customer's needs and wants. So, rather than considering SCM analysis from the "supply" perspective, some researchers and practitioners advocate analyzing the market operations from the "demand" perspective: Sensing-and-responding to the consumer changing needs and wants by quickly collaborating and communicating in real-time throughout the chain. Researchers argue that e-businesses should measure and track customers' demands for products and services, rather than relying solely on demand forecasting models.

Fisher (1997) studied the root cause of poor performance in supply chain management and the need to understand the demand for products in designing a supply chain. Functional products with stable, predictable demand and long lifecycle require a supply chain with a focus almost exclusively on minimizing physical costs—a crucial goal given the price sensitivity of most functional products. In this environment, firms employ enterprise resource planning systems (ERP) to coordinate production, scheduling, and delivery of products to enable the entire supply chain to minimize costs and maximize production efficiency. The crucial flow of information is internal within the supply chain. However, the uncertain market reaction to innovation increases the risk of shortages or excess supplies for innovative products. Furthermore, high profit margins and the importance of early sales in establishing market share for new products, the short product lifecycles increasing the risk of obsolescence, and the cost of excess supplies require that innovative products have a responsive supply chain that focuses on flexibility and speed of response of the supplier. The critical decision to be made about inventory and capacity is not about minimizing costs, but where in the chain to position inventory and available production capacity in order to hedge against uncertain demand. The crucial flow of information occurs not only within the chain, but also from the market place to the chain.

While Selen and Soliman (2002) advocate a demand-driven model, Vakharia (2002) argues that push (supply) and pull (demand) concepts apply in different settings. That is, since businesses offering mature products have developed accurate demand forecasts for products with predictable lifecycles, they may rely more heavily on forecasting models. While businesses offering new products, with unpredictable short cycles, are better off operating their chains as a pull (demand) system, because it's harder to develop accurate demand forecasts for these new (or fluctuating demand) products.

The difficulty in synchronizing a supply chain to deliver the right product at the right time is caused by the distortion of information traveling upstream the supply chain. One of the most discussed phenomena in the e-operations field is called the Forrester (1958) or "bullwhip" effect which portrays the supply chain's tendency to amplify or delay product demand information throughout the chain (Sahin & Robinson, 2002). For instance, a particular supplier may receive a large order for their product and then decide to replenish the products sold. This action provides the quantity to restock the depleted products, plus some additional inventory to compensate for potential variability in demand. The overstated order and adjustments are passed throughout the supply chain causing demand amplification. At some point, the supply chain partners loose track of the actual customer demand.

Lee et al., (1997) proved that demand variability can be amplified in the supply chain as orders are passed from retailers to distributors and producers. Because most retailers do not know their demand with certainty, they have to make their decisions based on demand forecast. When it is not very accurate, the errors in the retailers forecast are passed to the supplier in the form of distorted order. They found that sharing information alone would provide cost savings and

inventory reduction. Other factors that contribute to the distortion of information is over reliance on price promotion, use of outdated inventory models, lack of sharing information with partners, and inadequate forecasting methods.

An important question in supply chain research is whether the bullwhip effect can be preventable. Chen et al., (2000) quantified the bullwhip effect for a multi-stage system and found that the bullwhip effect could be reduced but not completely eliminated, by sharing demand among all parties in the supply chain. Zhao et al., (2002) also studied the impact of the bullwhip effect and concluded that sharing information increases the economical efficiency of the supply chain. In a later study, Chen (2005) found that through forecast sharing the bullwhip effect can be further reduced by eliminating the need for the supplier to guess the retailer's underlying ordering policy.

The causes of uncertainty and variability of information leading to inefficiency and waste in the supply chain can be traced to demand forecasting methods, lead-time, batch ordering processes, price fluctuation, and inflated orders. One of the most common ways to increase synchronization among partners is to provide at each stage of the supply chain with complete information on the actual customer demand. Although this sharing of information will reduce the bullwhip effect, it will not completely eliminate it (Simchi-Levy et al., 2003). Lee et al., (1997a, 2004) suggests a framework for supply chain coordination initiatives which included using electronic data interchange (EDI), internet, computer assisted ordering (CAO), and sharing capacity and inventory data among other initiatives. Another important way to achieve this objective is to automate collection of Point of Sale data (POS) in a central database and share with all partners in a real time e-business environment. Therefore, efficient information acquisition and sharing is the key to creating value and reducing waste in many operations. A specially designed adaptive or sense-and-response system may help provide the correct information throughout the supply chain. The proposed system would have two important system functions—maintaining timely information sharing across the supply chain and facilitating the synchronization of the entire chain.

Haeckel (1999) indicates that "unpredictable, discontinuous change is an unavoidable consequence of doing business in the information age." And, since this "intense turbulence demands fast—even instantaneous—response," businesses must manage their operations as adaptive systems. Adaptive (sense-and-response) models may help companies systematically deal with the unexpected circumtances, particularly, e-businesses need to be able to anticipate and preempt sensed problems.

SENSE-AND-RESPONSE SYSTEM (SRS) MODEL AND FRAMEWORK

Figure 2 shows the proposed SRS model and framework for integrating real-time electronic communications, information sharing, and materials flow updating as well as monitoring the e-supply/demand/value chain—towards a new e-collaboration paradigm.

The "e-sensors" in the diagram are computer programs (software code) and its associated data and information collection devices (hardware), and communication interfaces. These sensors are designed for e-collaboration, data capturing (sensing), and information sharing, monitoring

Figure 2. SRS framework for integrating communication, information and materials flow and monitoring the e-business supply/demand chain

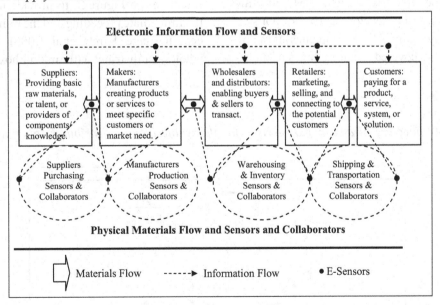

and evaluating data (input) throughout the value chain. Ultimately, this approach would result in semi-automated analysis and action (response) when a set of inputs are determined (sensed) without hindering human autonomy. That is, the sensors will gather the data, monitor, and evaluate the exchange in information between designated servers in the e-partners (suppliers and distribution channel) networks. Sensors will adjust plans and re-allocate resources and distribution routes when changes within established parameters are indicated. In addition, sensors will signal human monitors (operations or supply chain managers) when changes are outside the established parameters. The main advantage of this approach is that sensors will be capable of assessing huge amounts of data and information quickly to respond to changes in the chain environment (supply and demand) without hindering human autonomy. Particularly, e-sensors can provide the real-time information needed to prevent the bullwhip effect.

Companies like Cisco, Dell, IBM and Wal-Mart have led the development of responsive global supply chains. These companies and a few others have discovered the advantages of moni-

toring changes in near real-time. By doing so, they have been able to maintain low inventories, implement lean production and manufacturing operations, and even defer building and assembly resulting in lower costs and increase responsiveness to variable customer demands. This practice can be extended to incorporate e-sensors and human collaborators throughout the value chain and perceive and react to the demands.

SYSTEM ARCHITECTURE AND IMPLEMENTATION

To develop the implementation of the entire framework outlined in Figure 2 one faces involvement of multiple supply chain partners and months, if not years, of work just to develop a reliable communication infrastructure. In order to provide an immediate viable solution to test the concepts, in this research, the authors aimed at a single supply chain partner/company at only one stage illustrated in Figure 2, to provide interfaces to the immediate preceding and the immediate succeeding stage (Kirche et al., 2005). Choosing a wholesaler/distributor (the middle box in Figure 2)

Figure 3. Architecture of distributed services for the wholesaler or distributor (after Kirche et al, 2005)

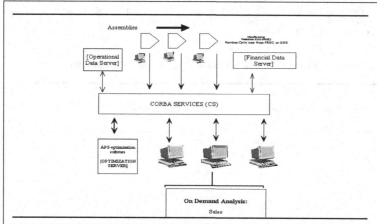

as the company to automate its information flows and material flows with e-sensors and e-controls interfacing to the manufacturers and retailers, as well as to internal storage and distribution centers, we developed the overall design architecture as illustrated in Figure 3.

The selected communication architecture is based on CORBA (Common Object Request Broker Architecture), a standard solution available from multiple vendors (Bolton, 2002). CORBA is an open system middleware with high scalability and potentially can serve an unlimited number of players and virtually any number of business processes and partners in the supply chain environment. As a communication infrastructure, it enables an integrated view of the production and distribution processes for an efficient demand management. Other benefits include continuous

availability, business integration, resources availability on demand, and worldwide accessibility. The architecture presented in Figure 3 gives the wholesaler/distributor direct access to the assembly lines of the manufacturers and their shipping/transportation data via the operational data server. Full communication with the retailers is available. The wholesaler/distributor company does have itself full control over their financial data server and optimization server. The detailed functions of this architecture are described in (Kirche et al., 2005).

The goal of the real time system based on this architecture is to dynamically integrate end-to-end processes across the organization (key partners, manufacturers and retailers) to respond with speed to customer changes and market requirements. The real time CORBA framework enables

Figure 4. Context diagram of the system being implemented (DAQ stands for data acquisition and control, 802.11 stands for an IEEE Std 802.11 for wireless networks, SQL stands for standard query language)

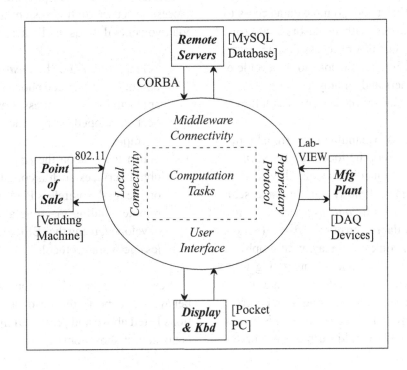

Figure 5. PDA client connectivity/performance test

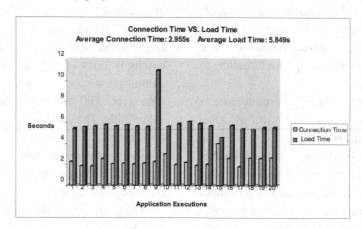

employees to view current process capability and load on the system and provide immediate information to customers, by enabling tuning of resources and balancing workloads to maximize production efficiency and adapt to dynamically changing environment.

A sample implementation of the system architecture from Figure 3 is presented in the form of a context diagram in Figure 4. To achieve the project's objective, that is, remote data access to enterprise networks with e-sensors/e-controls, we provide the capability of accessing enterprise-wide systems from a remote location or a vehicle, for both customers and employees.

The overall view of the system is as follows:

- When access to manufacturers from Figure 2 is considered, the focus can be on *plant access* for immediate availability of data and functions of the system; in that case, a remote *e-sensor/e-control* application using LabVIEW data acquisition software (Sokoloff, 2004) comes into play, with graphical user interface capable of interacting with remote users connected via the Internet.
- When access to warehousing from Figure 2 is considered, the focus can be on *business integration* via a multi-purpose enterprise-

wide network; in that case, a CORBA based framework is employed for a remote access to data objects identified as *e-sensors*, that can be stored on typical SQL database servers (Kirche et al., 2005).

From the network operation and connectivity perspective, e-sensors and e-controls provide business services, so they play the role of servers. Access to servers in this system is implemented via two general kinds of clients:

- When focus is on the *customer access* to obtain services, a cell phone location-aware application for business transactions has been developed, using order services as an example
- When focus is on the *employee access* to obtain services, such as conducting business on the road, a wireless PDA application for remote vending machine access has been developed, using the IEEE Std 802.11 wireless network protocol.

Several tests have been conducted to check behavior and performance of all four applications listed above and presented in Figure 4. For concision, it shows only a sample behavior of a

PDA client via connectivity/performance test, in Figure 5. The graph shows how long it takes for the server to receive the connection request from the client application after the application was started. It is marked "Connection time." Another bar on the same chart shows how long the program itself took to load completely after being started (marked "Load time"). The connection graph was created to give an indication of how long, on average, one can expect for requests to be acknowledged and accepted by the server. Since all requests are handled the same way as the initial connection, this average connection time reflects sending and receiving of data to and from the client application. The load time is just a measure of performance for the application on the PDA itself. The data collected that way show the feasibility of all applications built within the SRS framework, as presented in Figure 2, for the architecture outlined in Figure 3.

CONCLUSION

This article briefly reviewed the current intelligent agent and supply chain paradigm and presented a conceptual framework for integrating e-collaboration tools in the operation and monitoring of products and services across value chain networks without hindering human autonomy. The demand-driven, sense-and-response framework model incorporates e-sensors and e-collaborators (humans using communication tools, computer software programs and its associated data-capturing hardware devices) throughout the supply chain. In practice, these e-sensors would be designed for data-capturing (sensing), monitoring and evaluating data (input) throughout the value chain, while humans collaborate and communicate in real-time, as tested in the above solution.

The implications of this new framework are that it contributes to the enhancement of the current SCM/DCM systems (such as Manugistics' demand planning system) that analyzes manufac-

turing, distribution and sales data against forecasted data. The addition of SRS sensors would signal human monitors (operations or supply chain managers) when changes are outside the established parameters. The main advantage of this approach is that sensors would be capable of assessing huge amounts of data and information quickly to respond to changes in the chain environment (supply and demand) without hindering human autonomy.

Ultimately, this approach would result in the semi-automated analysis and action (response) when a set of inputs are determined (sensed) without hindering human autonomy. That is, the e-sensors would gather the data and monitor and evaluate the exchange in information between designated servers in the e-partners (suppliers and distribution channel) networks. E-sensors would adjust plans and re-allocate resources and distribution routes when changes within established parameters are indicated. Particularly, the new approach will aid managers in the prevention of the bullwhip effect.

Having real time data is critical in managing supply chain efficiently. Typically companies need to synchronize orders considering type, quantity, location and timing of the delivery in order to reduce waste in the production and delivery process. The data collection and availability provided by the e-sensing infrastructure/architecture will allow for a collaborative environment, improve forecast accuracy and increase cross-enterprise integration among partners in the supply chain. E-sensors will also offer a more proactive solution to current ERP systems by giving them the ability to process in real time relevant constraints and simultaneously order the necessary material type and quantities from multiple sources.

This e-sensor concept opens additional research opportunities within the boundaries of the operations management and information technology fields, particularly in the development of new software-hardware interfaces, real-time data capturing devices and other associated technologies. Finally, it leads to future 'automated decision-making' where IT/operations managers can "embed decision-making capabilities in the normal flow of work" (Davenport and Harris, 2005).

REFERENCES

Burke, G., & Vakharia, A. (2002). Supply chain management. In H. Bidgoli (Ed.), *Internet Encyclopedia*, New York: John Wiley.

Bresnahan, J. (1998). Supply chain anatomy: The incredible journey. *CIO Enterprise Magazine*, August 15. Retrievedon March 12, 2006 from http://www.cio.com site

Bolton, F. (2002). Pure CORBA: A code intensive premium reference. Indianapolis: Sams Publishing.

Castelfranchi, C. (1995). Guarantees for autonomy in cognitive agent architecture. In Wooldrige, M. and Jennings, N. R. (Eds.), *Intelligent Agents: Theories, Architectures, andLanguages*, 890, pp. 56-70. Heidelberg, Germany: Springer-Verlag.

Chen, L. (2005). *Optimal information acquisition, inventory control, and forecast sharing in operations management*. Dissertation thesis. Stanford, CA: Stanford University.

Cheng, F., Ryan, J.K., & Simchi-Levy, D. (2000). Quantifying the 'bullwhip effect' in a supply chain: The impact of forecasting, lead times, and information. *Management Science, 46*(3), 436–444.

Cross, Gary J. (2000). How e-business is transforming supply chain management. *Journal of Business Strategy, 21*(2), 36-39.

Davenport, T.H., & Harris, J.G., (2005). Automated decision making comes of age. *MIT Sloan Management Review, 46*(4), 83-89.

Fisher, M. (1997). What is the right supply chain for you? *Harvard Business Review,* March-April, 105-117.

Forrester, J. W. (1958). Industrial dynamics. *Harvard Business Review,* July-August, 37-66.

Frohlich, M.T. (2002). E-integration in the supply chain: Barriers and performance, *Decision Sciences, 33*(4), 537-556.

Gaither, N. & Frazier, G. (2002). *Operations Management*, 6th Edition, Cincinnati: Southwest.

Genesereth, M. R. & Ketchpel, S.P. (1994). Software agents. *Communications of the ACM, 37*(7), 48-53.

Haeckel, S.H. (1999). *Adaptive enterprise: Creating and leading sense-and-response organizations*. Boston: Harvard Business School Press.

Kirche, E., Zalewski, J., & Tharp, T. (2005). Real-time sales and operations planning with CORBA: Linking demand management and production Planning. In C.S. Chen, J. Filipe, I. Seruca, J. Cordeiro (Eds.), *Proceedings of the 7th International Conference on Enterprise Information Systems* (pp. 122-129). Washington, DC: ICEIS, Setubal, Portugal.

Lee, H., Padmanabhan, V., & Whang, S. (1997). The bullwhip effect. *Sloan Management Review, 38*(3), 93-103.

Lee, H., Padmanabhan, V., & Whang, S. (1997a). Information distortion in a supply chain: The bullwhip effect. *Management Science,43*, 546 – 548.

Lee, H., Padmanabhan, V., & Whang, S. (2004). Information distortion in a supply chain: The bullwhip effect/comments on "information distortion in a supply chain: The bullwhip effect." *Management Science, 50*(12), 1875 – 1894.

Meixell, M.J. (2006). *Collaborative manufacturing for mass customization*. George Manson University. Retrieved February 15,2006 http://

www.som.gmu.edu/faculty/profiles/mmeixell/collaborative%20Planning%20&%20Mass%20Customization.pdf

Meixell, M.J. & Gargeya, V.B. (2005). Global supply chain design: A literature review and critique. *Transportation Research, 41*(6), 531- 550 Science Direct. Retrieved February 15, 2006 http://top25.sciencedirect.com/index.php?subject_area_id=4 .]

Sahin, F. & Powell Robinson, E.P. (2002). Flow coordination and information sharing in supply chains: Review, implications, and directions for future research. *Decision Sciences, 33*(4), 505-536.

Selen, W., & Soliman, F. (2002). Operations in today's demand chain management framework. *Journal of Operations Management, 20*(6), 667-673.

Schneider, G.P., & Perry, J.T. (2000). *Electronic Commerce.* Cambridge, MA: Course Technology.

Simch-Levy, D., Kaminsky, P., & Simchi-Levy, E. (2003). *Designing and managing the supply chain— concepts, strategies and case studies, Second Edition.* New York: McGraw-Hill.

Sokoloff, L. (2004). *Applications in LabVIEW.* New Jersey: Prentice Hall.

Vakharia, A.J. (2002). E-business and supply chain management. *Decision Sciences, 33*(4), 495-504.

Wooldridge., M. & Jennings, N.R. (1995). Intelligent agents: Theory and practice. GRACO. Retrieved on February 15, 2006 at http://www.graco.unb.br/alvares/DOUTORADO/disciplinas/feature/agente_definicao.pdf .]

This work was previously published in International Journal of e-Collaboration, Vol. 3, Issue 2, edited by N. Kock, pp. 1-15, copyright 2007 by IGI Publishing, formerly known as Idea Group Publishing (an imprint of IGI Global).

Section IV
Utilization and Application

Chapter XIII
Making Decisions with Data:
Using Computational Intelligence within a Business Environment

Kevin Swingler
University of Stirling, Scotland

David Cairns
University of Stirling, Scotland

ABSTRACT

This chapter identifies important barriers to the successful application of Computational Intelligence (CI) techniques in a commercial environment and suggests a number of ways in which they may be overcome. It identifies key conceptual, cultural and technical barriers and describes the different ways in which they affect both the business user and the CI practitioner. The chapter does not provide technical detail on how to implement any given technique, rather it discusses the practical consequences for the business user of issues such as non-linearity and extrapolation. For the CI practitioner, we discuss several cultural issues that need to be addressed when seeking to find a commercial application for CI techniques. The authors aim to highlight to technical and business readers how their different expectations can affect the successful outcome of a CI project. The authors hope that by enabling both parties to understand each other's perspective, the true potential of CI can be realized.

INTRODUCTION

Computational Intelligence (CI) appears to offer new opportunities to a business that wishes to improve the efficiency of their operations. It appears to provide a view into the future, answering questions such as, "What will my customers buy?", "Who is most likely to file a claim on an insurance policy?", and "What increase in demand will follow an advertising campaign?" It can filter good prospects from bad, the fraudulent from the genuine and the profitable from the loss-making.

These abilities should bring many benefits to a business, yet the adoption of these techniques has been slow. Despite the early promise of expert systems and neural networks, the application of computational intelligence has not become mainstream. This might seem all the more odd when one considers the explosion in data warehousing, loyalty card data collection and online data driven commerce that has accompanied the development of CI techniques (Hoss, 2000).

In this chapter, we discuss some of the reasons why CI has not had the impact on commerce that one might expect, and we offer some recommendations for the reader who is planning to embark on a project that utilizes CI. For the CI practitioner, this chapter should highlight cultural and conceptual business obstacles that they may not have considered. For the business user, this chapter should provide an overview of what a CI system can and cannot do, and in particular the dependence of CI systems on the availability of relevant data.

Given the right environment the technology has been shown to work effectively in a number of fields. These include financial prediction (Kim & Lee, 2004; Trippi & DeSieno, 1992; Tsaih, Hsu, & Lai, 1998), process control (Bhat & McAvoy, 1990; Jazayeri-Rad, 2004; Yu & Gomm, 2002) and bio-informatics (Blazewicz & Kasprzak, 2003). This path to successful application has a number of pitfalls and it is our aim to highlight some of the more common difficulties that occur during the process of applying CI and suggest methods for avoiding them.

BACKGROUND

Computational Intelligence is primarily concerned with using an analytical approach to making decisions based on prior data. It normally involves applying one or more computationally intensive techniques to a data set in such a way that meta-information can be extracted from these data. This meta-information is then used to predict or classify the outcome of new situations that were not present in the original data. Effectively, the power of the CI system derives from its ability to generalize from what it has seen in the past to make sensible judgements about new situations.

A typical example of this scenario would be the use of a computational intelligence technique such as a neural network (Bishop, 1995; Hecht-Neilsen, 1990; Hertz, Krogh, & Palmer, 1991) to predict who might buy a product based on prior sales of the product. A neural network application would process the historical data set containing past purchasing behaviour and build up a set of weighted values which correlate observed input patterns with consequent output patterns. If there was a predictable consistency between a buyer's profile (e.g., age, gender, income) and the products they bought, the neural network would extract the salient aspects of this consistency and store it in the meta-information represented by its internal weights. A prospective customer could then be presented to the neural network which would use these weights to calculate an expected outcome as to whether the prospect is likely to become a customer or not (Law, 1999).

Although neural networks are mentioned above, this process is similar when used with a number of different computational intelligence approaches. Even within the neural network field, there are a large number of different approaches that could be used (Haykin, 1994). The common element in this process is the extraction and use of information from a prior data set. This information extraction process is completely dependent upon the quality and quantity of the available data. Indeed it is not always clear that the available data are actually relevant to the task at hand—a difficult issue within a business environment when a contract has already been signed that promises to deliver a specific result.

BEING COMMERCIAL

This chapter makes two assumptions. The first is that the reader is interested in applying CI techniques to commercial problems. The second is that the reader has not yet succeeded in doing so to any great extent. The reader may therefore be a CI practitioner who thoroughly understands the computational aspects and is having difficulties with the business aspects of selling CI, or a business manager who would like to use CI but would like to be more informed about the requirements for applying it. In this chapter we offer some observations we have made when commercializing CI techniques, in the hope that the reader will find a smoother route to market than they might otherwise have taken.

If you are hoping to find commercial application for your expertise in CI, then it is probably for one or more of the following reasons:

- You want to see your work commercially applied.
- Commercialization is stipulated in a grant you have won.
- You want to earn more money.

Many technologists with an entrepreneurial eye will have heard the phrase, "When you have invented a hammer, everything looks like a nail." Perhaps the most common mistake made by any technologist looking to commercialize their ideas for the first time is to concentrate too much on the technology and insufficiently on the needs of their customers (Moore, 1999). The more tied you are to a specific technique, the easier this mistake is to make. It is easy to concentrate on the technological aspects of an applied project, particularly if that is where your expertise lies.

CONCEPTUAL, CULTURAL, AND TECHNICAL BARRIERS

We believe that Computational Intelligence has a number of barriers that impede its general use in business. We have broken these down into three key areas: conceptual, cultural and technical barriers. On the surface, it may appear that technical barriers would present the greatest difficulties, however, it is frequently the conceptual and cultural barriers that stop a project dead in its tracks. The following sections discuss each of these concepts in turn. We first discuss some of the main foundations of CI under the heading of "Conceptual Barriers," this is followed by a discussion of the business issues relating to CI under the topic of "Cultural Barriers" and we finish off by covering the "nuts and bolts" of a CI project in a section on "Technical Barriers."

Conceptual Barriers

CI offers a set of methods for making decisions based on calculations made from data. These calculations are normally probabilities of possible outcomes. This is not a concept that many people are familiar with. People are used to the idea of a computer giving definitive answers—the value of sales for last year, for example. They are less comfortable with the idea that a computer can make a judgement that may turn out to be wrong.

The end user of a CI system must understand what it means to make a prediction based on data, the effect of errors and non-linearity and the requirements for the right kind of data if a project is to be successful. Analysts will understand these points intuitively, but if managers and end users do not understand them, problems will often arise.

Core Concepts

In this section, we will define and explain some of the mathematical concepts that everybody involved in a CI project will need to understand. If you are reading this as a CI practitioner, it may seem trivial and somewhat obvious. This unfortunately is one of the first traps of applying CI—there will be people who do not understand these concepts or perhaps have an incomplete understanding, which may lead them to expect different outcomes. These differences in understanding must be resolved in order for a project to succeed. We highlight these mathematical concepts because they are what makes CI different from the type of computing many people find familiar. They are conceptual barriers because their consequences have a material impact on the operation of a CI-based system.

Systems, Models, and The Real World

First, let us define some terms in order to simplify the text and enhance clarity. A system is any part of the real world that we can measure or observe. Generally, we will want to predict its future behaviour or categorize its current state. The system will have inputs: values we can observe and often control, that lead to outputs that we cannot directly control. Normally the only method available to us if we want to change the values of the outputs is to modify the inputs. Our goal is usually to do this in a controlled and predictable manner.

In the purchasing example used above, our inputs would be the profile of the buyer (their age, gender, income, etc.) and the outputs would be products that people with a given profile have bought before. We could then run a set of possible customers through the model of the system and record those that are predicted to have the greatest likelihood of buying the product we are trying to sell.

Given that a CI system is generally derived from data collected from a real-world system, it is important to determine what factors or variables affect the system and what can safely be ignored. It is often quite difficult to estimate in advance all the factors or variables that may affect a system and even if it were, it is not always possible to gather data about those factors.

The usual approach, forced on CI modelers through pragmatism, is to use all the variables that are available and then exclude variables that are subsequently found to be irrelevant. Time constraints frequently do not allow for data on further variables to be collected. It is important to acknowledge that this compromise is present since a model with reduced functionality will almost certainly be produced. From a business point of view, it is essential that a client is made aware that the limitations of the model are attributable to the limitations of their data rather than the CI technique that has been used. This can often be a point of conflict and therefore needs to be clarified at the very outset of any work.

Related to this issue of collecting data for all the variables that could affect a system is the collection of sufficient data that span the range of all the values a variable might take with respect to all the other variables in the system. The goal here is to develop a model that accurately links the patterns in the input data to corresponding output patterns and ideally this model would be an exact match to the real-world system. Unfortunately, this is rarely the case since it is usually not possible to gather sufficient data to cover all the possible intricacies of the real-world system.

The client will frequently have collected the data before engaging the CI expert. They will have done this without a proper knowledge of what is likely to be required. A significant part of the CI practitioner's expertise is concerned with the correct collection of the right data. This is a complex issue and is discussed in detail in Baum and Haussler (1989).

A simple example of this might be the collection of temperature readings for a chemical process. Within the normal operation of this process, the temperature may remain inside a very stable range, barely moving by a few degrees. If regular recordings of the system state are being made every 5 seconds then the majority of the data that are collected will record this temperature measurement as being within its stable range. An analyst may however be interested in what happens to the system when it is perturbed outside its normal behaviour or perhaps what can be done to make the system optimal. This may involve temperature variations that are relatively high or low compared to the norm. Unless the client is willing to perturb their system such that a large number of measurements of high and low temperatures can be obtained then it will not be possible to make queries about how the system will react to novel situations.

This lack of relevant data over all the "space" that a system might cover will lead to a model that is only an approximation to the real world. The model has regions where it maps very well to the real world and produces accurate predictions, but it will also have regions where data were sparse or noisy and its approximations are consequently very poor.

Inputs and Outputs

Input and output values are characterized by variables—a variable describes a single input or output, for example "temperature" or "gender." Variables take values— temperature might take values from 0 to 100 and gender would take the values "male" or "female." Values for a given variable can be numeric like those for a temperature range or symbolic like those of "gender." It is rare that a variable will have values that are in part numeric and in part symbolic. The general approach in this case is to force the variable to be regarded as symbolic if any of its values are symbolic. Fuzzy systems can impose an order on symbolic data, for example we can say that "cold" is less than "warm" which is less than "hot." This enables us to combine the two concepts.

Numbers have an order and allow distances to be calculated between them, symbolic variables do not, although they may have an implied scale such as "small," "medium" or "large." Ignoring the idea of creating an artificial distance metric for symbolic variables, a Computational Intelligence system cannot know, for example, that blue and purple are closer than blue and yellow. This information may be present in the knowledge of a user, but it is not obvious from just looking at the symbolic values "blue" and "yellow."

Coincidence and Causation

If two things reliably coincide, it does not necessarily follow that one caused the other. Causation cannot be established from data alone. We can observe that A always occurs when B occurs, but we cannot say for sure that A causes B (or indeed, that B causes A). If we observe that B always follows A, then we can rule out B causing A, but we still can't conclude that A causes B from the data alone. If A is "rain" and B is "wet streets" then we can infer that there is a causal effect, but if A is "people sending Christmas cards" and B is "snow falling" then we know that A does not cause B nor B cause A, yet the two factors are associated. Generally, however, if A always occurs when B occurs, then we can use that fact to predict that B will occur if we have seen A. Spotting such co-occurrences and making proper use of them is at the heart of many CI techniques.

Non-Linearity

Consider any system in which altering an input leads to a change in an output. Take the relationship between the price of a product and the demand for that product. If an increase in price of \$1 always leads to a decrease in demand of 50 units regardless of the current price then the relationship is said to be linear. If, however, the change in demand following a \$1 increase varies depending on the current price, then the system is non-linear. This is the standard demand curve and is an example of non-linearity for a single input variable.

Adding further input variables can introduce non-linearity, even when each individual variable produces a linear effect if it alone is changed. This occurs when two or more input variables interact within the system such that the effect of one is dependent upon the value of the other (and vice versa). An example of such a situation would be the connection between advertising spend, price of the product and the effect these two input variables might have on the demand for the product. For example, adding $1 to the price of the product during an expensive advertising campaign may cause less of a drop in demand compared with the same increase when little has been spent on advertising.

Non-linearity has a number of major consequences for trying to predict a future outcome from data. Indeed, it is these non-linear effects that drove much of the research into the development of the more sophisticated neural networks. It is also this aspect of computational intelligence that can cause significant problems in understanding how the system works. A client will frequently request a simplified explanation of how a CI system is deriving its answer. If the CI model requires a large number of parameters (e.g., the weights of a neural network) to capture the non-linear effects, then it is usually not possible to provide a simplified explanation of that model. The very act of simplifying it removes the crucial elements that encode the non-linear effects.

This directly relates to one of the more frequently requested requirements of a CI system—the decision-making process should be traceable such that a client can look at a suggested course of action and then examine the rationale behind it. This can frequently lead to simple, linear CI techniques being selected over more complex and effective non-linear approaches because linear processes can be queried and understood more easily.

A further consequence of non-linearity is that it makes it impossible to answer a question such as "How does x affect y?" with a general all encompassing answer. The answer would have to become either, "It depends on the current value of x" in the case of x having a simple non-linear relationship with y, and "It depends on z" in cases where the presence of one or more other variables introduce non-linearity.

Here is an example based on a CI system that calculates the risk of a person making a claim on a motor insurance policy. Let us say we notice that as people grow older, their risk increases, but that it grows more steeply once people are over 60 years of age. That is a non-linearity as growing older by one year will have a varying effect on risk depending on the current age.

Now let us assume that the effect of age is linear, but that for males risk gets lower as they grow older and for females the risk gets higher with age. Now, we cannot know the effect of age without knowing the gender of the person in question. There is a non-linear effect produced by the interaction of the variables "age" and "gender." It is possible for several inputs to combine to affect an output in a linear fashion. Therefore, the presence of several inputs is not a sufficient condition for non-linearity.

Classification

A classification system takes the description of an object and assigns it to one class among several alternatives. For example, a classifier of fruit would see the description "yellow, long, hard peel" and classify the fruit as a banana. The output variable is "class of fruit," the value is "banana." It is tempting to see classification as a type of prediction. Based on a description of an object, you predict that the object will be a banana. Under normal circumstances, that makes sense but there are situations where that does not make sense, and they are common in business applications of CI.

A CI classification system is built by presenting many examples of the descriptions of the objects to be classified to the classifier-building algorithm. Some algorithms require the user to specify the classes and their members in this data. Other algorithms (referred to as clustering algorithms) work out suitable classes based on groups of objects that are similar enough to each other but different enough from other things to qualify for a class of their own.

A common application of CI techniques in marketing is the use of an existing customer database to build a CI system capable of classifying new prospects as belonging to either the class "customer" or "non-customer." Classifying a prospect as somebody who resembles a customer is not the same as predicting that the person will become a customer. Such systems are built by presenting examples of customers and non-customers. When they are being used, they will be presented with prospective customers (i.e., those who do not fall into the class of customer at the moment since they have not bought anything). Those prospects that are classified by the CI system as "customer" are treated as good prospects as they share sufficient characteristics with the existing customers.

It must be remembered, however, that they currently fall into the non-customer category, so the use of the classification to predict that they would become customers if approached is erroneous. What the system will have highlighted is that they have a greater similarity to existing customers than those classified as "non-customer." It does not indicate that they definitely will become a "customer."

For example, if such a system were used to generate a mailing list for a direct-mail campaign, you would choose all the current non-customers who were classified as potential customers by the CI system and target them with a mail shot. If a random mailing produced a 1% response rate and you doubled that to 2% with your CI approach, the client should be more than satisfied. However, if you treated your classification of customers as

a prediction that those people would respond to the mailing, you would still have been wrong on 98% of your predictions.

Prospect list management is increasingly seen as an important part of Customer Relationship Management (CRM) and it is in that aspect that CI can offer real advantages. Producing a list of 5,000 prospects and predicting that they will all become customers is a sure way of producing scepticism in the client at best, and at worst of failing to deliver.

Dealing with Errors and Uncertainty

Individual predictions from a CI system have a level of error associated with them. The level of error may depend on the values of the inputs for the current situation, with some situations being more predictable than others. This lack of certainty can be caused by noise in the data, inconsistencies in the behaviour of the system under consideration or by the effects of other variables that are not available to the analysis. Dealing with this uncertainty is an important part of any CI project. It is important both in technical terms—measuring and acting on different levels of certainty—and conceptual levels—ensuring that the client understands that the uncertainty is present. (See Jepson, Collins, & Evans, 1993; Srivastava & Weigend, 1994 for different methods for measuring errors.)

We have stated that a classification can be seen as a label of a class that a new object most closely resembles, as opposed to being a prediction of a class of behaviour. A consequence of this is that a CI system can make a prediction or a classification that turns out to be wrong. In the broadest sense, this would be defined as an error but could also be seen as a consequence of the probabilistic nature of CI systems. For example, if a CI system predicts that an event will occur with a probability of 0.8 and that event does not occur for a given prediction, then the prediction and its associated probability could still be seen as being correct. It is just that in this instance the most probable outcome did not occur. In order to validate the system, you must look at all the results for the all the predictions. If a CI model assigns a probability of 0.8 to an event, it should occur 8 times out of 10 for the system to be valid but you should still expect it to misclassify 2 out of 10 events.

For example, if a given insurance claim is assigned a probability of being fraudulent of 0.8 then one would expect 8 out of 10 identical claims to be fraudulent. If this turned out not to be the case, for example only 6 out 10 turned out to be fraudulent, then the CI system would be considered to be wrong.

Returning to the customer-prospecting example, it is clear that the individual cost of a wrong classification in large campaigns is small. If we have made it clear that the prospects were chosen for looking most like previous customers and that no predictions are made about a prospect actually converting, the job of the CI system becomes to increase the response rate to a campaign.

There are many cases where it is necessary to introduce the concept of the CI system being able to produce an "I don't know" answer. Such cases are defined as any prediction or classification with a confidence score below a certain threshold. By refusing to make a judgement on such cases, it is possible to reduce the number of errors made in all other cases.

The authors have found that neural network based systems are very useful for the detection of fraudulent insurance claims. A system was developed that could detect fraudulent claims with reasonable accuracy. However, the client did not want to investigate customers whose claims looked fraudulent but were not. By introducing the ability of the system to indicate when it was uncertain about a given case, we were able to significantly reduce the number of valid claims that were investigated.

The two aspects that had to be considered when looking at the pattern of errors within the above example were the cost of a false positive and the cost of a false negative. An example of a false positive would be a situation where an insurance fraud detection system classified a claim as "positive" for fraud (i.e., fraudulent) but subsequent investigation indicated the claim to be valid. In the case of a false negative, the insurance fraud system might indicate that a claim is "negative" for fraud when in fact it was actually fraudulent. In the latter case you would not know that you had paid out on a fraudulent claim unless you explicitly investigated every claim while validating the fraud detection system.

False positives and false negatives have a cost associated with them in any specific application. The key to dealing with these errors lies in the cost-benefit ratio for each type of error. A false positive in the above case may cost two days work for an investigator. A false negative (i.e., paying out on a missed fraudulent claim) may cost many thousands of dollars.

Interpolation vs. Extrapolation

Many users want a model that they can use to make predictions about uncharted territory. This involves either interpolation within the current model or extrapolation into regions outside the data set from which the model was built. This might happen in a case where the user asks the system to make a prediction for the outcome of a chemical process when one of the input variables, such as temperature, is higher than any example provided in the recorded data set.

Without a measure of the non-linearity in the system, it can be difficult to estimate how accurate such predictions are likely to be. For example, interpolation within a data-rich area of the variable space is likely to produce accurate results unless the system is highly non-linear. Conversely, interpolation within a data-poor area is likely to produce almost random answers unless the system is very linear in the region of the interpolation. The problem with many computational systems is that it is often not obvious when the model has strayed outside its "domain knowledge."

A good example comes from a current application being developed by the authors. We are using a neural network to predict sales levels of newly released products to allow distributors and retailers to choose the right stocking levels. The effect on sales of the factors that we can measure is non-linear, which means that we do not know how those factors would lead to sales levels that were any higher than those we have seen already. The system is constrained to predicting sales levels up to the maximum that it has already seen. If a new product is released in the future, and sells more than the best selling product that we have currently seen, we will fall short in our prediction.

In the case of interpolation, the simplest method for ensuring that non-linearity is accurately modelled is to gather as much data as possible.

This is because the more data we have, the more likely it is that areas of non-linearity within the system will have sample data points indicating the shape of the parameter space. If there were insufficient data in a non-linear part of the system, then a CI method would tend to model the area as though it were linear.

In the extreme, you only need two data points to model a linear relationship. As soon as a line becomes a curve then we need a multitude of data points along the curve to map out its correct shape. Figure 1 (a) shows a simple case of identifying a linear relationship in a system with two variables. With only two points available, the most obvious conclusion to draw would be that the system is linear. Figure 1 (b) highlights what would happen if we were to obtain more data points. Our initial assumptions would be shown to be potentially invalid. We would now have a case for suspecting that the system is non-linear or perhaps very

Figure 1 (a) A simple linear system derived from 2 points. (b) The addition of further data reveals non-linearity. (c) A CI system fits a curve to the available data. (d) The shape of the estimated curve showing how further data produces a new shape—extrapolation would fail in these regions.

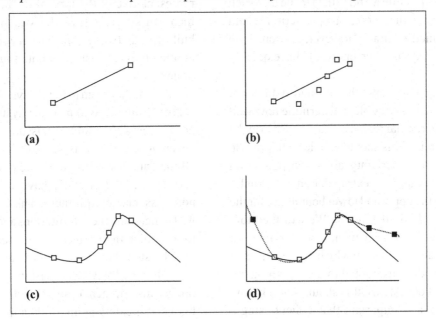

noisy. A CI model would adapt to take account of the new data points and produce an estimate of the likely shape of the curve that would account for the shape of the points (Figure 1 (c)).

It can be seen from Figure 1 (c) that if we had interpolated between the original two points shown in Figure 1 (a) then we would have made an incorrect prediction. By ensuring that we had adequate data, the non-linearity of the system would be revealed and the CI technique would adapt its model accordingly.

Related to this concept is the possibility of extrapolating from our current known position in order to make predictions about areas outside the original data set used to build the model. Extrapolation of the linear system in Figure 1 (a) would be perfectly acceptable if we knew the system was actually linear. However, if we know the system is non-linear, this approach becomes very error prone. An example of the possible shape of the curve is shown in Figure 1 (c), however, we have no guarantee that this is actually where the curve goes. Further data collection in the extremes of the system (shown by black squares) might reveal that the boundaries of the curve are actually quite a different shape to the one we have extrapolated (Figure 1 (d)). While we remained in the data-rich central area of the curve, our prediction would have remained accurate. However, as soon as we went to the extremes, errors would have quickly crept in.

Given that we have the original data set at our disposal, it is possible to determine how well sampled a particular region is that we wish to make a prediction in. This should enable us to provide a measure of uncertainty about the prediction itself. With regards to extrapolation, we usually know what the upper and lower bounds are for the data used to build the model. We will therefore know that we have set a given input variable to a value outside the range on which the data used to build the model was limited to. For anything but the simplest of systems, this should start ringing alarm bells. It is important that a client using a

CI system understands the implications of what they are asking for under each of these situations and where possible, steer away from trying to use such information.

Generalization

This leads us to the concept of generalization—an important issue in the development of an actual CI system. Generalization is concerned with avoiding the construction of a CI system that is very accurate when tested with data that has been used to build it, but performs very poorly when presented with novel data. With regard to the previous section, generalization deals with the ability of a non-linear system to accurately interpolate between points from the data used to construct it.

An idealized goal for a CI system is that it should aim to produce accurate predictions for data that it has not seen before. With a poorly constructed CI system that may have been built with unrepresentative data, the system is likely to perform well when making predictions in the region of this unrepresentative data and very poorly when tested with novel data that is more representative of the typical operating environment. In simple terms, the system attempts to build a predictive system that very closely follows all the observed historical data to the detriment of new data.

If all the data used to build a system completely captured the behaviour of the system then generalization would not be an issue. This is almost never the case, as it is very difficult to capture all the data describing the state of a system and furthermore data usually have some degree of noise associated with them. The CI practitioner will understand these limitations and will attempt to minimize their effects on the performance of the CI system. For the business manager interested in applying CI with the assistance of the practitioner, this will generally present itself as a need for a significant amount of data in an attempt to overcome the noise within it and ensure that a representative sample of the real-world system has been captured.

Cultural Barriers

CI's apparent power lies in its ability to address issues at the heart of a business: choosing prospects, pricing insurance, or warning that a machine needs servicing. These are high-level decisions that a business trusts experts to perform. Can you go into a business and challenge the expertise of their marketing team, their underwriters, or their engineers in the same way that production line robots have replaced car assembly workers? We look at these cultural barriers and the ways in which they have been successfully overcome. Whether you are an external consultant selling to a client or an internal manager selling an idea to the board, you will need to understand how to win acceptance for this new and challenging approach if your project is to succeed.

People who are experts at their job do not like to think that a computer can do it better. In general, computers are regarded as dumb tools—there to help the human experts with the tedious aspects of their work. Robots and simple machines have successfully replaced a lot of manual labor. There have been barriers to this replacement—protests from unions and doubts about quality for example—but automation of manual labor is now an integral aspect of the industrialized world.

Computational Intelligence might be vaunted as offering a modern computational revolution where machines are able to replace human decision-making processes. This replacement process should free up people to focus on special cases that require thought and knowledge of context that the computer may be lacking. Given these positive aspects, there are still many reasons why this shift might not come about. In the first instance, there is the position of power held by the people to be replaced. The people who make the decisions are less than happy with the idea that

they might be replaceable and that they might be called upon to help build the systems that might replace them. Manual workers have little say in the running of an organization. However, marketing executives and underwriters are higher up a company's decision-making chain—replacing them with a computer is consequently a more difficult prospect.

Next there is the issue of trust. I might not believe that a machine can build a car, but show me one that does and I have to believe you. If I do not believe that a computer can understand my customers better than me, you can show me an improved response to a mail campaign for a competing company, but I will still believe that my business is different and it will require a lot of evidence before I will change my mind.

Related to the issue of trust is that of understanding. This is a problem on two levels—first people do not always understand how they themselves do something. For example, we interviewed experts in spotting insurance fraud, who said things like, "You can just tell when a claim is dodgy—it doesn't look right." You can call it intuition or experience, but it is hard to persuade somebody that it is the result of a set of non-linear equations served up by their subconscious. The brain is a mysterious thing and people find the idea that in some areas it can be improved upon by a computer very hard to swallow.

The second problem is that people have difficulty believing that a computer can learn. If a person does not understand the concepts of computer learning and how it is possible to use data to make a computer learn, then it is hard for them to make the conceptual leap required to believe that a computer could be good at something that they see as a very human ability.

Here is an example to illustrate the point. A printing company might upgrade from an old optical system to a complete state-of-the-art digital system. In the process they would replace the very core of their business with a new technology, perhaps with the result that their old skills become obsolete. A graphic designer, however, would not want to buy a system that could automatically produce logos from a written brief, no matter how clever the technology.

Our experience has shown that many of these problems can be overcome if the right kind of simplification is applied to the sales pitch. That is not to say that technical details should be avoided or that buyers should be considered stupid. It means choosing the right level of technical description and, more importantly, setting the strength of claims being made about the technology on offer.

We shall use the task of building a CI system for use in motor insurance as an example. We developed a system that could calculate the risk associated with a new policy better than most underwriters. It could spot fraud more effectively than most claims handlers and it could choose prospective customers for direct marketing better than the marketing department. Insurance could be revolutionized by the use of CI (Viaene, Derrig, Baesens, & Dedene, 2003), but the industry has so far resisted.

An insurance company would never replace its underwriters, so if we are to help them with a CI system, it must be clearly positioned as a tool—something that helps them do their job better without doing it for them. Even though you could train a neural network to predict the probability associated with a new policy leading to a claim better than the underwriter can, it would do too much of his or her job to be acceptable.

Our experience has shown us that approximately 90% of motor insurance policies carry a similar, low probability of leading to a claim. There are 5% that have a high risk associated with them and 5% that have a very low risk. A system for spotting people who fall into the interesting 10% in order to avoid the high risks and increase the low risk policies would leave the underwriters still doing their job on the majority of policies and give them an extra tool to help avoid very high risks. The CI system becomes the basis

of a portfolio management system and the sale is then about better portfolio management and not about intelligent computing—a much easier prospect to sell.

Within the context of the insurance fraud example, investigators spent a considerable amount of their time looking at routine cases. Each case took a brief amount of time to review but, due to the large number of them, this took up the majority of their time. If you put forward the argument that the investigators would be better spending their time on the more complex cases where their skills could truly be used, then you can make a case for installing a CI system that does a lot of the routine work for them and only presents the cases that it regards as suspicious.

Another barrier to the successful commercialization of CI techniques is, to put it bluntly, a lack of demand. It is easy to put this lack of demand down to a lack of awareness, but it should be stated with more strength than that: CI is not in the commercial consciousness. Perhaps if prospective customers understood the power of CI techniques, then they would be easily sold on the idea. To an extent, of course, that is true. But to find the true reason behind a lack of demand, we must look at things from a customer's point of view. Will CI be on the customer's shopping list? Will there be a budget allocated? Are there pressing reasons for a CI system to be implemented? If the answer to these questions is no, then there is no demand. There is only, at best, the chance to persuade a forward-thinking visionary in the company who has the time, resources and security to risk a CI approach.

To use our e-commerce example again, a company building an online shop will need to worry about secure servers, an e-commerce system, order processing, delivery and promotion of the site. Those things will naturally be on their shopping list. An intelligent shop assistant to help the customer choose what to buy might be the only thing that would make a new e-commerce site stand out. It might be a perfect technical application of CI, and it might double sales, but it will not be planned, nor budgeted for. That makes the difference between you having to sell and the customer wanting to buy.

Technical Barriers

It has been our experience that the most common and fundamental technical barrier to most CI applications concerns access to source data of the correct type and quality. Obviously, if there is no data available relating to a given application, then no data-driven CI technique will be of use. A number of more common problems arise, however, when a client initially claims to have adequate data.

Is the client able to extract the data in electronic form? Some database systems actually do not have a facility for dumping entire table contents, compelling the user to make selections one-at-a-time. Some companies still maintain paper-only storage systems and some companies have a policy against data leaving their premises. It is also well worth remembering that the appropriate data will not only need to be available at the time of CI system development, but at run time, too. A typical use of CI in marketing is to make predictions about the buying behaviour of customers. It is easy to append lifestyle data to a customer database off-line ready for analysis, but will that same data be available online when a prediction is required for any given member of the population as a whole?

Does the data reflect the task you intend to perform and does it contain the information required to do so? Ultimately, finding the answer to this question is the job of the CI expert, but this is only true when the data appears to reflect the application well. It can be worth establishing early on that the data at least appears useful.

There are also technical aspects of a CI project that will have an impact on the contractual arrangements between you and the client. These are consequences of the fact that it is not always possible to guarantee the success of a CI project since the outcome depends on the quality of the data.

If the client does not have suitable data but is willing to collect some, it is important to be clear about what is to be collected and when that data will be delivered. If your contract with the client sets out a time table, be sure that delays in the data collection (which are not uncommon) allow your own milestones to be moved. Be clear that your work cannot start until the data are delivered. You may also want to be clear that the data must meet a certain set of criteria.

You also need to make it very clear what the client is buying. Most clients will be used to the idea that if they have a contract with (say) a software company to develop a bespoke solution, then that solution will be delivered, working as agreed upon in the specification. If it is not, then the contract will usually allow for payment to be reduced or withheld. It should be made clear to the client that their data, and whether or not it contains the information required to allow the CI approach to work, will be the major contributing factor to the success or otherwise of the project. The client must understand that success cannot be guaranteed. It has been our experience that the client often does not see it this way—the failure of the CI model to accurately predict who their customers are is seen as a failure of CI, not their carefully collected data.

Another consequence of the lack of available data at the start of a project is the difficulty it presents if you plan to demonstrate your approach to a prospective client. You can generate mock data that carries the information you hope to find in your client's database, but this proves little to the client as it is clearly invented by you. You can talk about (and possibly even demonstrate) what you have done for similar, anonymous clients, but each company's situation is usually different and CI models are very specific to each customer. The difficulty of needing data therefore remains.

There are many specific technical problems including choosing the right CI technique and using it to produce the best results. Each CI technique has its own particular requirements and issues. It is beyond the scope of this chapter to cover such topics—we have focussed on the elements that occur generally across the diverse set of CI approaches. Further chapters in this book address technique specific issues.

FUTURE TRENDS

We believe that CI technology is currently at a stage of development where weaknesses in the techniques are not the major barriers to immediate commercial exploitation. We have identified what we consider to be the main cultural, conceptual and technical barriers to commercialization of CI and the reader may have noticed that the technical barriers did not include any shortcomings of the CI methods themselves.

There is a large gap between the power of the techniques available and the problems that are currently being solved by those techniques. Unusually, however, it is the technology that is ahead. One can easily imagine impressive applications of CI techniques that are yet to be perfected—Web agents that can write you an original essay on any topic you choose, robot cars capable of negotiating the worst rush hour traffic at high speeds, and intelligent CCTV cameras that can recognize that a crime is taking place and alert the police. None of these applications are possible today and they are likely to remain difficult for a long time to come. The small improvements to the techniques that are possible in commercially viable time scales will not bring about a step change in the types of applications to which the techniques may be applied.

Our view of the near future of the commercial exploitation of CI, therefore, is concentrated on the methods of delivery of existing techniques and not the development or improvement of those techniques. Of course, the development of CI techniques is important, but it is the commercialization that must catch up with the technology, and not the converse. The consequence of this observation is, we believe, that the near future of the commercial exploitation of CI techniques requires little further technical research. The current techniques can do far more than they are being asked to do.

We expect to see a shift away from selling the idea of the techniques themselves and towards selling a product or service improved by the techniques without reference to those techniques. The search engine Google is a good example. People do not care about the clever methods behind it. They just know it works as a very good search engine. Another good example of underplayed technology comes from the world of industrial control. Most industrial control is done using a technique known as PID. Many university engineering departments have produced improvements to the PID controller and very few of them have found their way into an industrial process. One reason for this is that everybody in the industry understands and trusts PID controllers. Nobody wants to open the Pandora's box of new and challenging techniques that might fragment the industry and its expertise.

One company developed an improvement to the PID controller and did not even admit to its existence. They simply embedded it in a new product and sold it as a standard PID controller. It worked just that bit better than all the others. Nobody really knew why it was better, but it was. The controller sold very well, nobody was threatened by the new technique, and there was no technical concept to sell. It just worked better.

An alternative and related example is the use of CI systems to spot fraudulent credit card behaviour. It is simply not practical for investigators to analyze every single credit card transaction. A CI system can be used to monitor activity for each user and determine when it has become unusual. At this point an investigator is alerted who can contact the owner of the card to verify their spending behaviour. People are generally not aware that CI systems are behind such applications, and for all practical purposes, this does not matter. The important issue is the benefits they bring rather than their technical sophistication.

The authors have put this approach into practice. Having spent several years selling CI technology to direct marketing agencies with little success, they have recently launched a Web-based direct marketing system that is driven by CI techniques. The service allows clients to upload their current customer database to a Web server. It then appends lifestyle data to the names in the database, which is then used to generate a new list of prospects for the client to download.

The primary selling point of the service is that it is easy to use and inexpensive (the techniques are automated). These are far easier concepts to sell because they are clearly demonstrable—the client can see our prices and visit our Web site to see how easy the process is to use. Having got a foot in the door of the mailing list market, our system quietly uses some very straightforward CI techniques to produce prospect lists that yield response rates up to four times better than the industry standard.

Our approach is proving successful and it is based on the following points:

- We selected a market where there was clearly money to be made from delivering an improvement to the existing, inefficient norm.
- The main selling point of the product is not technical, thus all problems associated with explaining and selling the CI concept are avoided.
- We deliver a service that the customer needs, already has budgeted for, and understands perfectly.
- The data we receive are always in the same format (names and addresses) and we provide all the additional data required.

Consequently, we never have a problem with data quality.

This approach has a number of advantages. It removes the need for the client to worry that they are taking a risk by using a new technology. It removes the need for us to try and sell the idea of the technology, and it allows us to sell to a mature market.

SUMMARY

We have seen that there are a number of barriers to the successful commercialization of CI techniques. There is a lack of awareness and understanding from potential customers. Their mathematical nature and the fact that the success of a project depends on the quality of the data it uses can make the concept hard to sell. The lack of awareness also means that companies are not actively looking for CI solutions and are consequently unlikely to have budgets in place with which to buy them.

CI techniques face cultural barriers to their adoption as they could potentially replace existing human expertise. The existing human experts are often in a powerful position to prevent even the risk of this replacement and their unwillingness to change should not be underestimated. We have also touched upon technical barriers, such as accessing the correct data both at design and run-time, and the problems of specifying, demonstrating and prototyping a system based on data.

We have suggested a number of approaches designed to overcome the barriers discussed in this chapter. These approaches can be summarized by the notion of putting yourself in your prospective customer's position. Ask yourself what the customer needs, not what you can offer. Think about how much change a customer is likely to accept and whether or not they could cope with that change. Ask yourself whether you are making more work for the customer or making their life easier. Think about whether the customer is likely to have a budget for what you offer. If not, can you present it as something they do have budget for? Find out what level of technical risk the customer is likely to be comfortable with. Are they early adopters or conservative followers?

We believe that the future success of CI will rely on keeping your customer on board and giving them what they want, not impressing them with all the clever tricks that you can perform. The key element is for both you and the client to maintain the same point of view of the problem you are both trying to solve. This will primarily mean that if you are the provider of the CI solution, you will need to adapt your perspective to fit that of the client. It is, however, important that the client understands the conceptual limits of CI as discussed in the early parts of this chapter. In order to maintain a positive working relationship with a client, it is important that they understand both the benefits and limitations of Computational Intelligence and therefore know, at least in principle, what can and cannot be done.

REFERENCES

Baum, E. B., & Haussler, D. (1989). What net size gives valid generalisation? *Neural Computation, 1*(1), 151-160.

Bhat, N., & McAvoy, T. J. (1990). Use of neural nets for dynamic modelling and control of chemical process systems. *Computer Chemical Engineering, 14*(4/5), 573-583.

Bishop, C. M. (1995). *Neural networks for pattern recognition*. Oxford, UK: Oxford University.

Blazewicz, J., & Kasprzak, M. (2003). Determining genome sequences from experimental data using evolutionary computation. In G. G. Fogel & D. W. Corne (Eds.), *Evolutionary computation in bioinformatics* (pp. 41-58). San Francisco: Morgan Kaufmann.

Haykin, S. (1994). *Neural networks, a comprehensive foundation*. New York: Macmillan.

Hecht-Nielsen, R. (1990). *Neurocomputing*. Reading, MA: Addison Wesley.

Hertz, J., Krogh, A., & Palmer, R. G. (1991). *Introduction to the theory of neural computation*. Redwood City, CA: Addison Wesley

Hoss, D. (2000). The e-business explosion: Strategic data solutions for e-business success. *DM Review, 10*(8), 24-28.

Jazayeri-Rad, H. (2004). The nonlinear model-predictive control of a chemical plant using multiple neural networks. *Neural Computing and Applications, 13*(1), 2-15.

Jepson, B., Collins, A., & Evans, A. (1993). Post-neural network procedure to determine expected prediction values and their confidence limits. *Neural Computing and Applications, 1*(3), 224-228.

Kim, K., & Lee, W. B. (2004). Stock market prediction using artificial neural networks with optimal feature transformation. *Neural Computing and Applications, 13*(3), 255-260.

Law, R. (1999). Demand for hotel spending by visitors to Hong Kong: A study of various forecasting techniques. *Journal of Hospitality and Leisure Marketing, 6*(4), 17-29.

Moore, G. (1999). *Crossing the chasm: Marketing and selling high-tech products to mainstream customers*. Oxford, UK: Capstone.

Srivastava, A. N., & Weigend, A. S. (1994). Computing the probability density in connectionist regression. In M. Marinara & G. Morasso (Eds.), *Proceedings ICANN, 1* (pp. 685-688). Berlin: Springer-Verlag.

Trippi, R. R., & DeSieno, D. (1992). Trading equity index futures with a neural-network. *Journal of Portfolio Management, 19,* 27-33.

Tsaih, R., Hsu, Y., & Lai, C. C. (1998). Forecasting S & P 500 stock index futures with a hybrid AI system. *Decision Support Systems*, *23*(2), 161-174.

Viaene, S., Derrig, R. A., Baesens, B., & Dedene, G. (2003). A comparison of state-of-the-art classification techniques for expert automobile insurance claim fraud detection. *Journal of Risk and Insurance*, *69*(3), 373-421.

Yu, D. L., & Gomm, J. B. (2002). Enhanced neural network modelling for a real multivariable chemical process. *Neural Computing and Applications*, 10(4), 289-299.

This work was previously published in Business Applications and Computational Intelligence, edited by K. E. Voges and N. K. L. Pope, pp. 19-37, copyright 2006 by IGI Publishing, formerly known as Idea Group Publishing (an imprint of IGI Global).

Chapter XIV
EBBSC:
A Balanced Scorecard–Based Framework for Strategic E–Business Management

Fen Wang
University of Maryland, Baltimore County, USA

Guisseppi Forgionne
University of Maryland, Baltimore County, USA

ABSTRACT

E-business is far more about strategy than technology, and the strategy of e-business is very important in today's dynamic and competitive environment. In this article, we describe a balanced scorecard-based framework in detail and discuss its potential e-business uses. This framework enables e-business managers to plan and allocate resources more effectively and align strategic objectives with performance results. It also provides a stable point of reference for e-businesses to understand and manage the fundamental changes introduced by e-business initiatives.

INTRODUCTION

The Link of Objectives to Strategies

E-business has rapidly developed from being a vision of the future world of business to being "the" way of doing business (Whelan & Maxelon, 2001). This business opened new channels for communication and selling, a new source of data on customers and competitors, and changed the face of competition tremendously (Koutsoukis, Dominguez-Ballesteros, Lucas, & Mitra, 2000; Porter, 2001). Clearly, business processes of the 21st century must be more efficient and dynamic to build and sustain value across the organization, though having a dot-com presence does not necessarily point to success. As Raisinghani and Schkade (2001) pointed out "perhaps, one of the best ways to succeed in the world of e-business is to start off with a dynamic and new e-business strategy" (p. 601).

E-business is far more about strategy than technology. An effective e-business strategy is an elaborate and systematic plan of action that incorporates different organizational levels, different parties, different elements, and growth pattern features (Bakry & Bakry, 2001). Unlike traditional business strategy, e-business strategy considers a company's business management architecture and how it can be improved, integrated and automated by instant and global Internet communication. Indeed, the Internet has spawned new e-business strategy and radically transformed existing models (Basu & Muylle, 2002; Pant & Ravichandran, 2001). These new models incorporate Internet technology, universal connectivity, and Web browser capabilities to integrate business processes within and beyond an enterprise. As a result, old business models should be adapted to the new conditions, and companies worldwide should develop an effective e-business strategy to fit the new conditions (Whelan et al., 2001).

What distinguishes many of the dot-coms from traditional organizations is not their new technical power, but their innovative and imaginative new business models (Hamel, 2000). This study proposes a balanced scorecard based e-business framework for the development and assessment of e-business strategy in this new age. Aided by this innovative and comprehensive e-business framework, managers can identify the major decision factors involved in their e-business strategies, specify the direct and indirect relationships among the factors, and generate strategies that would improve overall business performance.

BACKGROUND REVIEW

The Evolution of E-Business Models

A commonly cited reason for e-business failure has been the lack of a workable and concrete strategic business model to guide e-business efforts (Paper, Pedersen, & Mulbery, 2003). While a comprehensive framework for strategic e-business management seems desirable, there are few studies that offer complete and integrated views of e-business strategy (Dubosson-Torbay, Osterwalder, & Pigneur, 2001). In the business model literature, many academic studies have provided a theoretical basis for, and some empirical testing of, the models (Horsti, Tuunainen, & Tolonen, 2005). These studies fall into two broad categories. The first group develops subsystem models in support of a specific aspect of e-business applications, while the second group involves generic frameworks to reflect e-business reality.

Table 1 provides a brief overview of the existing subsystem model studies. As this table demonstrates, although each of the subsystem models involves operationalized views of a particular aspect of e-business, none offer a complete and integrated view of e-business strategy as a whole.

Among the generic e-business strategy models, Whelan et al. (2001) proposed a five element e-business architecture. The five elements are product, channel, customer management, resource management, and information. Afuah and Tucci (2001) presented a more detailed list of model components including scope, customer value, revenue sources, connected activities. Like Whelan et al. (2001), these researchers did not specify the interrelationships and causality between these components. Hamel (2000) offered a more complete model than the others. This researcher used a four part framework that describes links

Table 1. The first group sub-system e-business model studies

Model Focus/Purpose	Model Components/Factors involved	Sample Studies
A generalized pricing model	Order Unit; Territory; Customer; Price Type; Interval; Contract; Currency	Kelkar, Leukel & Schmitz Price, 2002
A demand model for variety	Utility structure: good variety; price	Kim, Allenby & Rossi, 2002
A model to support supply chain activities	A cooperative virtual network structure; A supply chain infrastructure; Change management; Organizational adaptation	Cheng, Li, Love & Irani, 2001
A statistical model e-business capacity	Utilization of capacity; Cost of capacity; Revenue benefits; Service quality; Operations risk	Goldszmit, Palma & Sabata, 2001
A mental cognitive model for e-customer profile	e-customer behavior; Web site semantics; e-services; internet marketing	Kwan, 2002
A five-stage model for explaining and predictin Net-based customer service (NCSS)	NCSS Interaction Value; NCSS usefulness; Experience Quality; Cost of NCSS Use	Piccoli, Brohman, Watson & Parasuraman, 2004
A model decribing the values exchanged in an e-business process	Base actor (organization & customer), order of value transfer (business order), order of communicative acts (process order)	Jayaweera, Johannesson & Wohed, 2001
A shared process model for e-business transactions	Process speed/credibility, task independence, task synchronization, e-business autonomy	Park, 2002
Macro-level matching algorithms to compose a Web-based business process	Service capabilities and properties, activities in a process request, business requirments and objectives	Lee & Park, 2003
Hayes and Wheelwright four-stage model of	Operation negative impact, best-practice operation, stategy-support operation competitive-advantage operation	Banes, Hinton & Mieczkowska, 2004
A methodology for design, implementation and continuous improvement of e-business processes	Process vision, process specification, process realization, process improvement	Kirdmer, 2004
e-knowledge networks for collaborative e-business	Supply chain management networks, Adserver networks, Content syndication networks, B2B exchange networks	Warkentin, Sugumaran & Bapna, 2001
Knowledge management in e-business and CRM	Customer relationships, knowledge on customers, customer needs	Plessis & Boon, 2004
A virtual community activity framework from an e-business perspective	Community knowledge sharing activity, virtual community outcomes, loyalty to the service provide	Koh & Kim, 2004

between model components (e.g., "Configuration" to connect the "Core strategy" and "Strategic resources"). Similarly, Dubosson-Torbay et al. (2001) used a framework to analyze e-business with four principal components: product innovation, customer relationship, infrastructure management, and financial aspects. Damanpour (2001) also identified four elements of e-business from a systematic perspective: business/financial models, relationships, commerce, and

responsiveness. Still another e-business model is composed of a value cluster, marketing offering, resource system, and financial model (Rayport & Jaworski, 2001). Going beyond the segment frameworks, De, Mathew, and Abraham (2001) developed a pragmatic framework that offers a series of different perspectives for the analysis of e-business: transaction costs, switching costs, infrastructure investment, revenue models, and other elements.

Table 2 summarizes the scope and model components of the generic e-business frameworks. As this table illustrates, no operational generic models have been offered, or implemented, by the proponents. The generic frameworks, instead, provide theoretical guidance on components that could be included in a comprehensive and integrated e-business strategy model.

One exception is the high level e-business framework, with preliminary empirical evidence, proposed by Hasan and Tibbits (2000). These researchers developed a BSC-based case study for e-business management in an Australian state-government utility. The researchers, however, did not identify and formulate the goals, measures, and targets in each scorecard perspective.

As Tables 1 and 2 indicate, the literature has not offered a comprehensive and concrete model of e-business strategy. The electronic business balanced scorecard (EBBSC) model proposed in this study attempts to close that research gap by linking business strategies to a broad range of measures, examining important business issues facing e-business managers, and providing a complete and integrated view of e-business management.

Table 2. 2ⁿᵈ group generic e-business framework studies

Afuah & Tucci (2001)	Damanpour (2001)	De et al. (2001)	Dubosson et al. (2001)	Hamel (2000)	Hasan & Tibbits (2000)	Rayport & Jaworski (2001)	Whelan & Maxelon (2001)
price, revenue sources, sustainibility (what is difficult to initiate of the business model)	business financial models (business model and opportunities)	Revenue models (Advertising, retail, banking & information harvesting)	Product innovation (market segment, value proposition), Financial Aspects (cost & revenue structures)	Core Strategy (business mission, product/ market scope, differentiation basis), Pricing structure	Finance/ Business value	Financial model	Product
Customer value (distinctive offering or low cost), Scope (customer & products/services)	Relationships (relationships & collaboration management)	Transaction and Switching costs, User Experience, Models, Versioned products/ niche marketing	Customer Relationship, Infastructure Management I (partner network)	Customer Interface (support. info & insight, re la ti os hip dynamics); Customer benefits	Customer User perspectives	Marketing offering	Customer management
connected activities (interdependency between different activities)	Responsiveness (efficiency & timing of transactions) Commerce (e-buying & selling mechanism)	Network externalities, Infastructure investment	Infastructure Management II (activities & processes)	Strategic resources (core processes); Configuration; Value network, company boundaries	Internal business/ Process	Value cluster	Channel
Implementation (resources needed); Capabilities (skills needed)	--	--	Infastructure Management III (resources/ assets)	Strategic resources (core competencies, strategic assets)	Innovation/ Learning future readiness	Resource system	Resource management; Information

EBBSC FRAMEWORK SPECIFICATION

The proposed EBBSC framework identifies four essential perspectives. These perspectives include the financial, customer, internal processes, and learning and growth views. First introduced in the early 1990s as the balanced scorecard (BSC), these views provide a balanced picture of current operating performance as well as the drivers of future performance in traditional businesses (Kaplan & Norton, 1992, 1996). The underlying motivation for this vision and strategy has been explored repeatedly (Dutta & Manzoni, 1999; Lee & Ko, 2000; Lohman, Fortuin, & Wouters, 2004; Marr & Schiuma, 2003; Soliman & Youssef, 2001; Sandstrom & Toivanen, 2002) and is therefore not repeated here.

Because the methodology of the BSC explicitly focuses on links among business decisions and outcomes, it is intended to guide strategy development, implementation, and communication, and to provide reliable feedback for management control and performance evaluation (Malina & Selto, 2001). Although most implementations emphasize BSC success as a commercial product, the rationale behind the BSC does appeal to managers who face new challenges in the modern business environment (Hasan et al., 2000).

As indicated by Hasan et al. (2000), the real challenge is to determine how the BSC can be successfully applied in the context of e-business. E-business functions in a constantly changing environment of interdependencies, which has been perceived as highly uncertain, stemming from increased information visibility and dynamic market structures (Golicic, Davis, McCarthy, & Mentzer, 2002; Wang, 2001). In this environment, traditional success measures may be incomplete, and possibly misleading, and the original BSC framework may require radical modification.

Using literature findings and underlying theories, we adapted the original BSC into the comprehensive e-business management framework (EBBSC) shown in Figure 1. As this figure indicates, the EBBSC consists of four perspectives, including the business core, analytic e-CRM, process structure, and e-knowledge network.

Tables 3 and 4 compare this EBBSC concept with the subsystem and generic model studies. As this comparison indicates, the EBBSC framework is based on the e-business model literature but represents a more complete, explicit, and integrated view of e-business strategy. Such a framework can be utilized to translate e-business strategies into conceptual blueprints for strategic management control and performance evaluation. The EBBSC framework also provides a stable point

Figure 1. Adapted four perspectives for strategic e-business management (Adapted from Wang & Forgionne, 2005)

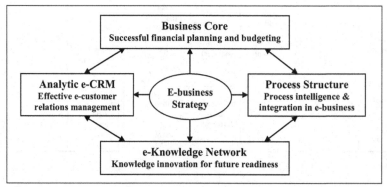

Table 3. The first group sub-system e-business model literature comparison

EBBSC Framework Perspectives	Comparative Model Components in Literature	Sample Representative Studies
Business Core Successful financial planning and budgeting	Profit maximization, Pricing mechanisms, Price structures, Revenue sources, Demand uncertainties, Budget mode, Financial performance, Market optimization, Internet marketing	Kelkar, Leuke; & SchmitzPrice, 2002: Kim, Allenby & Rossi, 2002; Valadares Tavares, Pereira & Coelho, 2002; Motiwalla & Riaz Khan, 2003; Liu, Wynter & Xia, 2003; Chen, Liu & Song, 2004
Analytic e-CRM Effective e-customer relations management	Customer value, Customer knowledge, E-customer profile, Customer efficiency, Consumer power, Customer needs, e-CRM essence, Customer perception, Mass customization model	Bielski, 2000; Rowley, 2002; Mei & Harker, 2002; Wan, 2002; Fletcher, 2003; Olsson & Karlson, 2003; Wang & Tang, 2003; Vrechopoulos, 2004; Piccoli, Brohman, Watson & Parasuraman, 2004
Process Structure Process intelligence & integration in e-business	Process patterns, E-logistics platform, Process (semi)-automation, Process independence & sychronization, Operation management, Value (e) -chain, Process networks	Jayaweera, Johannesson & Wohed, 2001; Par, 2002; Lee & Park, 2003; Oh, Hwang, & Lee, 2003, Barnes, Hinton & Mieczkowska, 2004; Kirchmer, 2004
E-Knowledge Network Knowledge innovation for future readiness	Knowledge Management, E-knowledge networks, E-knowledge decision model, Knowledge exchange, Customer knowledge, Knowledge chain model, Knowledge sharing	Malhotra, 2000; Warkentin, Sugumaran & Bapna, 2001; Raisinghani & Mead, 2002; Malhotra, 2002; Rowley, 2002; Allard & Holsapple, 2002; Plessis & Boon, 2004, Koh & Kim, 2004

Table 4. The second group generic e-business framework comparison

Framework commonality	Afuah & Tucci (2001)	Damanpour (2001)	De et al. (2001)	Dubosson et al. (2001)	Hamel (2000)	Hasan & Tibbits (2000)	Rayport & Jaworski (2001)	Whelan & Maxelon (2001)
Business Core Perspective	price, revenue sources, sustainibility (what is difficult to initiate of the business model)	business financial models (business model and opportunities)	Revenue models (Advertising, retail, banking & information harvesting)	Product innovation (market segment, value proposition), Financial Aspects (cost & revenue structures)	Core Strategy (business mission, product/market scope, differentiation basis), Pricing structure	Finance/ Business value	Financial model	Product
Analytic e-CRM Perspective	Customer value (distinctive offering or low cost), Scope (customer & products/services)	Relationships (relationships & collaboration management)	Transaction and Switching costs, User Experience, Models, Versioned products/niche marketing	Customer Relationship, Infastructure Management I (partner network)	Customer Interface (support. info & insight, re la ti os hip dynamics); Customer benefits	Customer User perspectives	Marketing offering	Customer management
Process Structure Perspective	connected activities (interdependency between different activities)	Responsiveness (efficiency & timing of transactions) Commerce (e-buying & selling mechanism)	Network externalities, Infastructure investment	Infastructure Management II (activities & processes)	Strategic resources (core processes); Configuration; Value network, company boundaries	Internal business/ Process	Value cluster	Channel
e-Knowledge Network Perspective	Implementation (resources needed); Capabilities (skills needed)	--	--	Infastructure Management III (resources/ assets)	Strategic resources (core competencies, strategic assets)	Innovation/ Learning future readiness	Resource system	Resource management; Information

of reference for e-businesses to understand and explore e-business initiatives effectively.

Business Core Perspective

Although e-business models differ somewhat from traditional brick and mortar models, the fundamental needs of consumers and businesses remain the same. Consumers want desirable products and services at competitive prices, while businesses want profitable marketing and production. The focus should be on long-term and short-term decision making in the dynamic, competitive, and compressed business cycles of the global e-era. Figure 2 depicts the business core perspective in the framework. As indicated in the figure, the primary objective is profit maximization.

Within the e-business value cycle, many intangible and tangible firm and industry-specific factors may affect profit through revenue and cost influences (Spanos, Zaralis, & Lioukas, 2004). Some factors involve Internet considerations, such as network performance (e.g., network security and e-capacity). Risk and uncertainty will be created by intangible organizational and environmental factors (Palmer & Wiseman, 1999). Representative decision factors in the business core perspective as a result of the Internet effect are highlighted in Figure 2.

Revenues increase from product and service expansions, new customers and markets, and higher value re-pricing. Price, capacity, supply chain management efficacy, and staff proficiency are the major determinants of the quantity supplied. Capacity is limited by the equipment and/or available personnel, but also by the limit associated with network technology (Goldszmidt et al., 2001). A stronger emphasis on supplier relationship management reduces uncertainty (Craighead et al., 2003; Golicic et al., 2002). Supply chain management efficacy can be used as an indicator of the bargaining power of suppliers (Porter, 2001).

On the demand side, there are traditional determinants, including customer retention and the marketing mix, and new e-business factors. Customer retention measures the company's customer loyalty (Smith, 2002) or stickiness (Ingsriswang et al., 2001). Since customers can now compare prices and services with a-click, it is more challenging to attract and retain customers in the virtual business world.

The marketing mix, coined by Borden (1965), consists of traditional price, product, promotion, and place (Borden, 1965; Brooksbank, 1999; Kotler & Armstrong, 1997; Smith & Saker, 1992), as well as enhancements unique to e-business. For example, pricing must be adjusted to the specific requirements of e-procurement (Kelkar et al., 2002). The original "Place" factor is decomposed into e-marketing presentation and distribution effort. Similar to the store design of a physical shopping mall, the Web presentation style and structure can attract online customers and build customer loyalty in e-business (Chittaro & Ranon, 2002). Distribution involves traditional and Internet (as called e-channel or virtual e-chain) management and innovation (Manthou et al., 2004; Mascarenhas et al., 2002).

Another way to maximize profit, besides increasing revenue, is to reduce fixed and variable cost (Lee & Brandyberry, 2003). Traditionally, fixed cost refers to invariable selling and administrative expenses. In the context of e-business, fixed cost can include e-business system development and maintenance expenses, as well as other utility and management overhead. Variable cost measures the materials, money, and labor expenses involved in producing/importing and selling the product. In the context of e-business, labor expenses should include the effort spent on knowledge management (transmission, sharing, and innovation), building relationships, and education in e-era technology (Ash & Burn, 2001; Cash et al., 2004).

Figure 2. Business model perspective of strategic e-business management

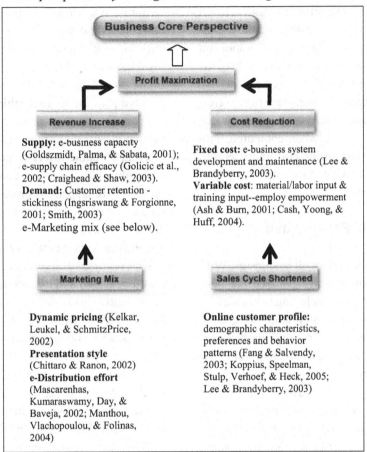

Figure 3. e-CRM perspective of strategic e-business management

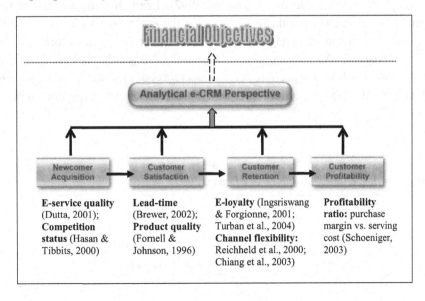

One indirect, but potentially effective, method to reduce cost is to shorten the sales cycle. In addition to product quality, price, and the e-marketing mix, the customer profile is an important determinant of the e-business sales cycle. This profile is a composite variable that reflects the customers' demographic characteristics, preferences, and behavior patterns. As noted by Lee and Brandyberry (2003), when compared with traditional customers, online customers tend to be less stable due to their "Logical," rather than "Physical," relationships.

Analytic e-CRM Perspective

Customers are at the core of all businesses. With the Internet, customers have realized the benefits of shopping online, including convenience, broader selection, competitive pricing, and greater access to critical business information (Chen et al., 2004). Relationships and collaborations are forged in e-business to enter new markets or enhance customer, supplier and business interactions (Damanpour, 2001). On the other hand, customers' involvement in online retailing is impeded by security and privacy concerns, download time, and other technology barriers, or unfamiliarity (Chen et al., 2004). Furthermore, customers can switch to other competitive URLs in seconds with minimal financial cost (Ingsriswang et al., 2001), which makes successful customer management especially vital in e-business (Ace, 2002).

Figure 3 depicts the e-CRM perspective. As indicated in the figure, the keys to achieve cus-tomer profitability are customer acquisition and customer retention, i.e., to continuously attract newcomers and retain loyal customers. Achieving customer satisfaction can turn newcomers into loyal customers. Representative decision factors in the e-CRM perspective, which have not been covered previously, are highlighted in Figure 4.

The success or failure of a customer acquisition campaign depends on precise, timely targeting that delivers valuable offers to prospects and keeps costs low. This targeting could involve finding previously untapped customers (for example, baby diapers for new parents) or competitors' customers (Berson, Smith, & Thearling, 1999). While acquisition costs vary widely among various businesses, optimized targeting with proper customer profile research and e-marketing mix strategy is consistently a top priority, as is e-service quality and competitive status. E-service quality involves network reliability and customer support (Dutta, 2001), while competition status represents the company's external relationship with the supplier, availability of other distribution channels, entry barriers, rivalry, and product substitutes (Kaplan et al., 1992; Hasan et al., 2000).

The next step is to ensure customer satisfaction with lead time, product quality, service quality, and competitive pricing (Kaplan et al., 1992). Lead time measures the time required for the company to meet its customers' needs, sometime referred to as "order-to-delivery cycle time" (Brewer, 2002). Quality measures the defect level of products as perceived and measured by the customer. A product with high quality

Figure 4. A generic value chain (Adapted from Lewis, 2001)

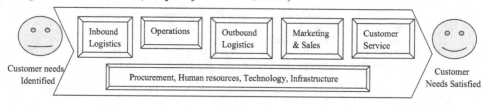

and a high level of customization may increase the degree of customers' satisfaction (Fornell & Johnson, 1996). E-service quality and price also will greatly impact satisfaction.

However, satisfied customers are not necessarily loyal customers (Gale, 1997). Loyal customers, who repeat their purchases or visits persistently, are valuable business assets (Turban et al., 2004). According to Reichheld and Schefter (2000), e-loyalty is an economic necessity in the e-era. The idea is to develop and maintain long-term relationships with customers by creating superior customer value and satisfaction (Ingsriswang et al., 2001).

Goodwill, the favor or prestige that a business has acquired beyond the mere value of what it sells (Merriam-Webster online, 2005), reflects the cumulative impact of marketing and customer satisfaction (Anderson & Fornell, 1994; Jennings & Robinson, 1996). Companies should determine their and use their core competencies to target the market (Smith, 2002). Channel flexibility refers to the convenience and availability of distribu-tion channels besides the Internet. According to Reichheld et al (2000), the seamless integration of different channels can prove to be valuable. This finding has been verified by Chiang et al. (2003)'s, who determined that the e-channels could increase the e-business companies' profit indirectly through retail channels.

All customers are not created equal. If the company could properly measure the profitability of its customers, it can implement corresponding margin strategies to achieve higher customer and corporate profitability. Profitability can be measured at either the individual or segment level by identifying the customers' purchase to cost margin. Costs uniquely traceable to customers include customer transactional cost, customer service and support cost, packaging, delivery, and post sales costs. The ratios of the mix of customer purchase margin to the customer serving cost are thereby revealing when compared on an individual customers basis, as well as by segment or channel (Schoeniger, 2003).

Figure 5. Process structure perspective for e-business strategy

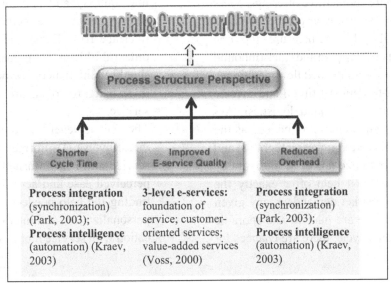

Process Structure Perspective

E-business should feature speed, flexibility and fluidity, sometimes described as agility (Introna, 2001; Metes, Gundry, & Bradish, 1998). Existing business processes must be seamlessly integrated with the new, electronic form of interaction with suppliers and customers. A generic value chain is illustrated in Figure 4, which offers an abstract description of the processes within any type of business (including e-business). To be feasible in e-business, the internal process view should consider the flexibility and intelligence of the process structure (Hasan et al., 2000).

For e-businesses to operate successfully there must be flexibility and scalability to accommodate continuous process changes, readiness to provide an up-to-the-minute and integrated view of the product, process and equipment, and capability to collect and store the results of historical and proactive analysis for future process innovation. Such process improvements can be achieved through intelligence and integration of business models and data with the Internet and with the systems of the company's trading partners. As summarized in Figure 5, improved effectiveness and efficiency in these core business processes will lead to faster cycle times, enhanced service quality, reduced overhead, and more competitive offerings.

Different from the customer-perspective sales cycle, the general cycle time measures the time needed by the business to plan and stock (inbound logistics), inventory and schedule (operations), lead time (order-to-delivery time), and invoice a particular product (outbound logistics). Accordingly, incremental costs are induced as the cycle lengthens. Effective process integration and intelligence can optimize this cycle, measurably reduce inventories and help offer exactly the products that the market demands at any given time. Wherever there are manual and sporadic tasks in the product cycle, there are chances for

overhead costs, delays, and errors, all of which can all contribute to longer cycle times.

In the EBBSC framework, process integration is a composite variable that reflects the degree of problem critical data, information and knowledge sharing, and transmission across different departments and groups (from downstream to upstream and inbound to outbound). Process integration also incorporates the effectiveness of two or more identical (horizontal) or successive (vertical) stages in producing or distributing a particular product. Process intelligence represents the ability of the business processes to perceive and act in the surrounding environments, to respond appropriately to the prevailing circumstances in a dynamic business situation, to learn and to improve the process with prior experiences.

As emphasized in the e-CRM perspective, e-service is the glue that holds the e-business process together (Tschohl, 2001). According to Voss (2000), customer service generally involves three levels of service and overall e-service quality can be estimated by incorporating the quality indicators of the three levels of e-services.

- The first level, foundation of service in e-business, includes minimum necessary services, such as site responsiveness (e.g., how quickly and accurately the service is provided), site effectiveness (e.g., site interface friendliness and freshness), and order fulfillment. The e-business companies should monitor network performance and infrastructure to ensure basic customer service.
- The second level, customer-oriented services, involve: (1) informational capabilities: service and help information availability, perceived ease and actual convenience of finding the help needed, customer profile personalization, and interactive communication with service representatives, and (2)

transactional capabilities: site security and privacy, order configuration, customization and tracking, complete support during the ordering process and after the purchase period.

- The last level, value-added services are extra services, such as location sensitive selling and billing or online training and education that add value to overall service quality. Some value-added services may stand alone from an operational perspective, while others add value to existing services. Overall, value-added services provide operational and administrative synergy between or among other levels of services.

Being agile and flexible, the virtual process of e-business replaces the traditional product inquiry and physical clearinghouse process and provides greater operating advantages that may lead to reduced overhead. As the cycle time is shortened through process integration and intelligence, overhead will be reduced accordingly. Process integration and intelligence is a significant advantage in achieving e-business focus and flexibility because, in many instances, these capabilities can replace the need for a well-defined organizational structure and often whole layers of staff.

E-Knowledge Network Perspective

Targets for success keep changing so that the company must make continual improvements to survive and succeed in the intensive global competition (Kaplan et al., 2001). Organizations operating in the new business environment should be adept at creation and application of new knowledge as well as ongoing renewal of existing knowledge archived in company databases (Malhotra, 2000; Soliman et al., 2001).

E-business knowledge (or "e-knowledge"), including knowledge about internal functions and processes, about customers and markets, and about strategic partners, can be created, shared, and managed more effectively by a combination of new organizational designs and the adoption of new technologies, such as data mining and intelligent agents. Organizations are now creating knowledge networks to facilitate improved communication of data, information, and knowledge, while improving coordination, decision making, and planning based on the Internet-driven "new economy" technologies that were unavailable until recently (Warkentin, Sugumaran, & Bapna, 2001).

Figure 6 highlights some of the characteristics of e-knowledge networks.

Figure 6. E-knowledge networks characteristics (Adapted from Warkentin et al. 2001)

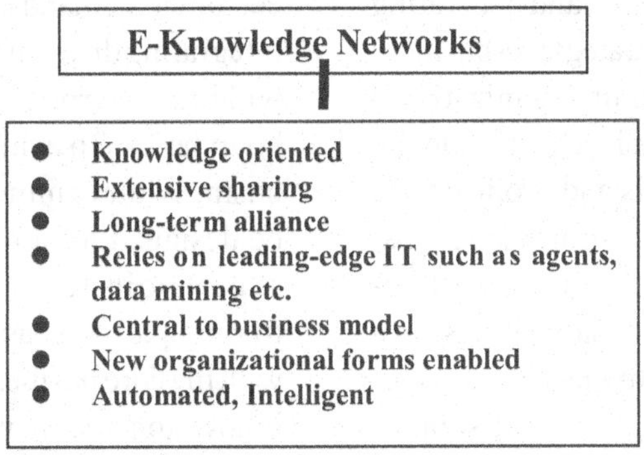

E-Knowledge Networks

- Knowledge oriented
- Extensive sharing
- Long-term alliance
- Relies on leading-edge IT such as agents, data mining etc.
- Central to business model
- New organizational forms enabled
- Automated, Intelligent

Figure 7. E-knowledge network perspective of strategic e-business management

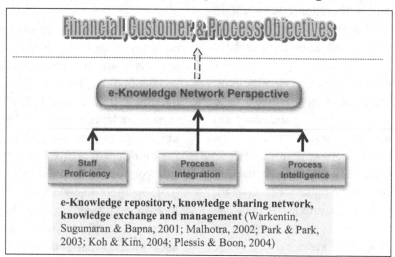

This enhanced e-knowledge innovation and management will lead to greater back-office efficiency, flexible adaptation to market changes, greater customer intimacy, improved strategic planning, improved decision making, rapid and flexible relationship management processes, and other organizational benefits. There are additional implications of staff proficiency, process integration, and process intelligence, as summarized in Figure 7.

Specific manager proficiency and employee skills are required to operate in the new competitive e-business environment. E-business managers are responsible for identifying the major factors involved in their business strategy, specifying the relationships between the factors, and generating long-term and short-term strategic e-business plans that will improve overall organizational performance. Similarly, employees should be provided with particular skills and proficiencies across different departments. For instance, customer service team is capable of assisting customers throughout their online purchase process in a timely and friendly manner to ensure customer satisfaction and retention. A technical support team is in charge of ensuring that the site runs properly and securely under all circumstances.

The e-knowledge network offers a repository where new knowledge is created and collected, while existing knowledge, archived in data warehouses, is renewed and updated. Management and operational judgment, knowledge, and experiences are shared and managed to facilitate improved communication, coordination, decision making, and planning. Staff training can be utilized to improve employee skills and maintain currency with the technology shift.

Process integration enables a company to unify every aspect of its back-end infrastructure and increase responsiveness to inventory levels, customer demands, and delivery schedules by integrating disparate business processes, not only within an enterprise, but also across organizational boundaries. To achieve process integration in e-business, the communication infrastructure must be designed for a mission-critical environment, scalable to increasing numbers of transactions and trading partners, and robust enough to integrate with the core business applications. E-knowledge innovation and management facilitates the integration process by creating e-knowledge networks that are characterized by automated exchange of rich knowledge by unattended computer systems, programmed to capture and evaluate knowledge with data mining algorithms, share it with strategic allies, and direct the operation of key interactive processes. Through e-knowledge networking, internal business data can be retrieved and shared across different departments and groups, and problem critical information and knowledge can be transmitted, integrated and processed from downstream to upstream as well as inbound to outbound.

Table 5. Description of the measures & factors in the EBBSC framework

Factor (symbol)	Explanation	Factor (symbol)	Explanation
Profit (Profit)	The difference between the revenue and cost	Marketing-mix (M)	The company's effort on commercial processes involved in promoting/selling
Revenue (R)	Total income in a given period	Customer Acquisition (CA)	The number of new customers acquired in a given period
Cost (C)	The total expense (e.g. money, time, and labor) incurred in a given period	Customer Satisfaction (CS)	Measure of determination that a product meets a customer's expectations and needs
Price (P)	The amount of money needed to purchase the product	Customer Retention (CR)	Measure of customers revisit to the site and repeat purchases over a period of time
Purchases (PU)	The total quantity of product actually sold to customers	Customer Profitability (CP)	The ratio of the customer serving costs to the mix of customer purchase margin
Quantity Demanded (QD)	The total quantity customers are willing and able to purchase	Staff Proficiency (SP)	The efficiency of the company staff in providing the product and service
Quantity Supplied (QS)	The total quantity the company offers for a sale	E-service quality (EQ)	Measure of the company's e-service quality
Variable Cost (VC)	The portion of cost that varies in relation to the level of production activity	Process Integration (PIG)	The degree of the company's business process integration
Sales Cycle (SC)	The time between the point the product is listed and the point the product is sold	Process Intelligence (PIL)	The ability of the company's business process to respond to and improve its position in the business environment
Cycle Time (CT)	Time that elapses in conducting inbound operations, and outbound logistics	Knowledge Network Efficacy (KNE)	The company's investment in knowledge transmission, sharing, and innovation
Unit Cost (UC)	The cost per product	Capacity (CT)	The equipment, personnel, and technology capacity of the company
Fixed Cost (FC)	The portion of cost that is independent of the number of products produced/sold	Goodwill (G)	The company's accumulative prestige and perceived value in the market
Product (PD)	Measure of the product quality, positioning, and Internet branding etc.	Competition (CO)	Measure of the rivalry between the company and other businesses in the market
Presentation	The selection of product presentation and distribution formats	Channel Flexibility (CF)	The convenience and availability of distribution channels besides the Internet
Promotion (PM)	The company's expenditures on product promotion	Supply Chain Efficacy (SCE)	The effectiveness of the company in managing relationships with its suppliers
Profile (PF)	The target customers' average disposable income, needs or preferences index	Staff Qualification (SQ)	General rating of the company's staff skill level
Distribution Effort (DE)	The company's effort on distribution channel	Staff Training (ST)	The company's investment in staff training

Figure 8. An overview of the EBBSC framework

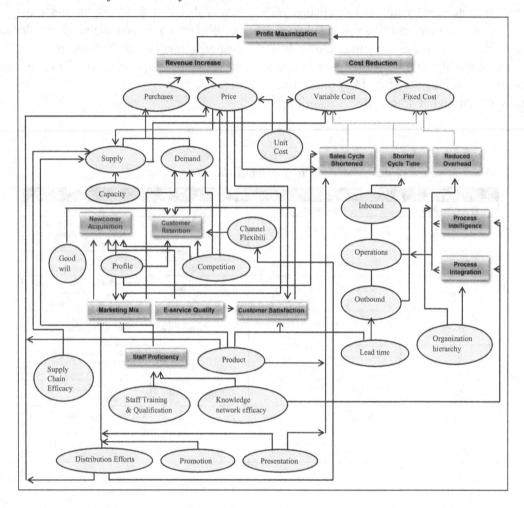

The flattening of the organizational hierarchy also contributes to process integration, which leads to higher process efficiency, visibility and transparency. In contrast, traditional organization structures are hierarchical and functionally oriented (Chen & Ching, 2002). As a result, information is filtered and modified as it makes its way through different levels of management. Enabled by e-business capabilities, companies with a flattened organizational hierarchy have the built-in flexibility to move swiftly toward capturing new opportunities, react quickly to shifts in the environment, and respond promptly to the customers needs.

Process intelligence facilitates matches between the company's offering and target customers, competitors, and the current business by automating the decision and action processes and initiating real time analytics of sales and e-services as well as business notification and alerting (Park & Park, 2003). Such effort requires a wide range of process steps to be understood and represented, not only within an organization, but communicated to trading partners.

Figure 9. EBBSC strategy evaluation model

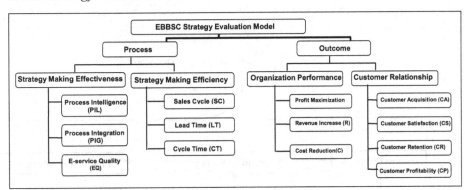

An e-knowledge network generates and stores immediate (real-time) knowledge about internal functions and processes, about customers and markets, about strategic partners, and about supply chain partners (suppliers, vendors, dealers, and distributors). Using the knowledge repository, the company can create new internal and external structures and relationships, which leads to further knowledge and continuous strategy improvements. Intelligent technology, which enables communication with trading partners across different platforms, can help represent, implement and track external business processes (contact agents of other companies, request information on merchandise/suppliers, and negotiate with them about purchase conditions) in a dynamic and flexible way (Park et al., 2003).

EBBSC SUMMARY AND ILLUSTRATION

Using the EBBSC components, we can develop the major measures and factors involved in the EBBSC framework. These measures and factors, which have been identified in each EBBSC perspective, are summarized in Table 5.

The major measures (Square) and the corresponding decision factors (Oval) and relationships

(Arrow Lines) specified in the EBBSC framework are illustrated in Figure 8. This framework also forms the basis for specifying a precise and explicit functional model for strategic e-business management. At the conceptual level, it offers the e-business manager a big-picture perspective that is critical in generating effective e-business strategies. Aided by this framework, e-business companies can identify the major factors regarding the four e-business perspectives and specify the direct and indirect relationships among the various factors.

As an illustration, consider an e-business that seeks to acquire more customers in the next planning period. The manager first will locate the strategic measure of new customer acquisition in the framework and identify the relevant decision factors. As the EBBSC framework indicates, these factors include the customer profile, competition, the marketing mix, and e-service quality. Next, the manager can formulate a tentative strategy plan. In this case, the framework suggests that the company needs critical data and information regarding the prospective customer population and the competitors. Based on the collected information, management must decide on a specific marketing mix and e-service solution. Starting from the market mix or e-service quality components, the EBBSC framework suggests the steps

Figure 10. EBBSC mediated decision support architecture for e-business strategy

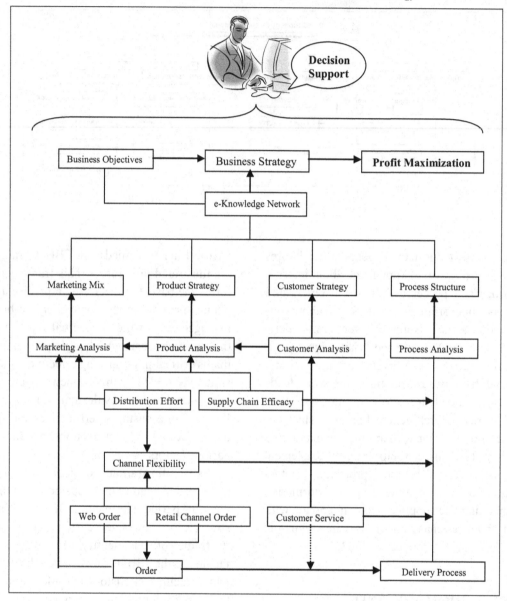

to create the mix and quality plan. Having the priority of the strategic objective at each stage, the manager can plan and allocate the available budgets and resources more effectively to achieve these objectives.

DISCUSSION AND CONCLUSION

In this study, we have developed a balanced score-card-based framework for strategic e-business management, which contributes to both theory and practice. From a theoretical standpoint, the balanced scorecard adaptation offers an innovative methodology to formulate and evaluate e-business strategy. The EBBSC framework also indicates that e-business strategy making will involve multiple decision criteria. Using this framework, the decision maker can establish an evaluation model for strategic e-business decision support. Figure 9, for example, shows such a multi-criteria e-business strategy evaluation model utilizing the strategic measures specified in the EBBSC framework. Based on the Analytic Hierarchy Process (AHP) concept (Forgionne, 1999), this EBBSC strategy evaluation model associates a hierarchy of evaluation measures relevant to the context of e-business strategy in an integrated fashion.

Using the hierarchy in Figure 9, the decision maker can make pairwise comparisons of decision criteria across the multiple dimensions. The AHP methodology then will convert the multiple measures into an overall scorecard value for each considered strategy. This AHP-based EBBSC evaluation model, then, will identify, in rank order, the most promising e-business strategies.

In practice, the EBBSC provides a means of identifying business opportunities and threats in both the internal and external environment, analyzing current business capabilities and resources to address the opportunities and threats, and generating effective e-business strategies that would improve the company's overall business performance and profitability. As illustrated in Figure 10, proper decision technology can deliver the EBBSC model, provide intelligent decision support to practitioners in overcoming analytical and technical barriers, and guide e-business managers towards an effective e-business strategy. The EBBSC also provides a stable point of reference for e-business companies to understand and manage e-business initiatives, enables e-business managers to plan and allocate resources (including tangible and intangible strategic assets) more

effectively, and align strategic objectives with performance results.

As an innovative and exploratory framework for strategic e-business management, the EBBSC offers several opportunities for future endeavor. First, empirical research is needed to specify the measures, decision factors, and corresponding functional relationships in each e-business perspective. Another possible extension is to apply the EBBSC methodology to both profit driven and non-profit e-businesses.

To illustrate a potential non-profit application, consider an academic surgical organization. Under the business model perspective, instead of profit or revenue oriented indicators, specific measures would include management expenses, research grants, billings or collections, and days in receivables for outstanding invoices. Comparatively, the e-CRM perspective can be measured by patient satisfaction, number of outside referrals, invited lectures given or articles published in peer-reviewed journals. The process structure could include measures of operating room cases, consultations performed, clinic cancellations or length of stay. Finally, e-knowledge learning and growth could include measures of internal and external clinical program development or research development and faculty promotion. The specifications of the conceptual model will be determined by the specific application settings and the data sources selected to operationalize the model. Such empirical issues could possibly result in different versions of the operationalized model in practice, but the conceptual EBBSC framework remains feasible and applicable across different practice fields.

ACKNOWLEDGMENT

The authors are grateful to Dr. Jeet Gupta and the anonymous reviewers for providing insightful comments on earlier versions of the chapter.

REFERENCES

Ace, C. (2002). *Effective promotional planning for e-business.* Oxford: Butterworth- Heinemann (BH).

Afuah, A., & Tucci, C. L. (2001). *Internet business models and strategies: Text and cases.* Boston: McGraw-Hill.

Allard, S., & Holsapple, C. W. (2002). Knowledge management as a key for e-business competitiveness: From the knowledge chain to KM audits. *Journal of Computer Information Systems, 42*(5), 19-25.

Anderson, E. W., & Fornell, C. (1994). Customer satisfaction, market share, and profitability: *Findings from Sweden. Journal of Marketing, 58*(3), 53-66.

Ash, C., & Burn, J. (2001). m-powering personnel for e-business change. Proceedings of the 2001 ACM SIGCPR Conference on Computer Personnel Research.

Bakry, S. H., & Bakry, F. H. (2001). A strategic view for the development of e-business. *International Journal of Network Management, 11*(2), 103-112.

Barnes, D., Hinton, M., & Mieczkowska, S. (2004). The strategic management of operations in e-business. *Production Planning & Control, 15*(5), 484-494.

Basu, A., & Muylle, S. (2002). Online support for commerce processes by Web retailers. *Decision Support Systems, 34*, 379-395.

Berson, A., Smith, S., & Thearling, K. (1999). *Building data mining applications for CRM.* McGraw-Hill Osborne Media.

Bielski, L. (2000). E-business models stress putting the customer first. *ABA Banking Journal, 92*(7), 67-71.

Borden, N. H. (1965). *The concept of the marketing mix. Science in Marketing.*Chichester, Wiley, 386-97.

Brewer, P. (2002). Putting strategy into the balanced scorecard. *Strategic Finance,* 44-52, January 2002.

Brooksbank, R. (1999). The theory and practice of marketing planning in the smaller business. *Marketing Intelligence & Planning, 17*(2), 78-90.

Cash, E., Yoong, P., & Huff, S. (2004). The impact of e-commerce on the role of IS professionals. *ACM SIGMIS Database, 35*(3), 50-63.

Chen, J., & Ching, R. K. H. (2002). A proposed framework for transitioning to an e-business model. *Quarterly Journal of Electronic Commerce, 3*(4), 375-389.

Chen, J., Liu, Y., & Song, X. (2004). Comparison of group-buying online auction and posted pricing mechanism in an uncertain market. *Journal of Electronic Science and Technology of China, 2*(3), 1-5.

Chen, L., Gillenson, M. L., & Sherrell, D. L. (2004). Consumer acceptance of virtual stores: A theoretical model and critical success factors for virtual stores. *ACM SIGMIS Database, 35*(2).

Cheng, E. W. L., Li, H., Love, P. E. D. & Irani, Z. (2001). An e-business model to support supply chain activities in construction. *Logistics Information Management, 14*(1/2), 68-77.

Chiang, W. K., Chhajed, D., & Hess, J. D. (2003). Direct marketing, indirect profits: A strategic analysis of dual-channel supply chain design. *Management Science, 49*(1), 1-20.

Chittaro, L., & Ranon, R. (2002). Dynamic generation of personalized VRML content: A general approach and its application to 3D e-commerce. *Proceeding of the 7th International Conference on 3D Web Technology.*

Craighead, C. W., & Shaw, N. G. (2003). E-commerce value creation and destruction: A resource-based, supply chain perspective. *ACM SIGMIS Database, 34*(2), 39-49.

Damanpour, F. (2001). E-business e-commerce evolution: Perspective and strategy. *Managerial Finance, 27*(7), 16-33.

De, R., Mathew, B., Abraham, D. M. (2001). Critical constructs for analyzing eBusinesses: Investment, user experience, and revenue models. *Logistics Information Management, 14*(1/2), 137-148.

Dubosson-Torbay, M., Osterwalder, A., & Pigneur, Y. (2001). eBusiness model design, classification, and measurements. *Thunderbird International Business Review, 44*(1), 5-23.

Dutta, A. (2001). Business planning for network services: A systems thinking approach. *Information Systems Research, 12*(3), 260-285.

Dutta, S., & Manzoni, J. F. (1999), *Process re-engineering, organisational change, and performance measurement.* McGraw-Hill, Maidenhead.

Fang, X., & Salvendy, G. (2003). Customer-centered rules for design of e-commerce Web sites. *Communications of the ACM, 46*(12), 332-336.

Fletcher, K. (2003). Consumer power and privacy: The changing nature of CRM. *International Journal of Advertising, 22*(2), 249-272.

Forgionne, G. A. (1999). An AHP model of DSS effectiveness. *European Journal of Information Systems, 8,* 95-106.

Fornell, C., & Johnson, M. D. (1996). The American customer satisfaction index: Nature, purpose, and findings. *Journal of Marketing, 60*(4), 7-18.

Gale, B. (1997). Satisfaction is not enough. *Marketing News*, Oct. 27, p.18.

Goldszmidt, M., Palma, D., & Sabata, B. (2001). On the quantification of e-business capacity. *Proceedings of the 3rd ACM conference on Electronic Commerce.*

Golicic, S. L., Davis, D. F., McCarthy, T. M., & Mentzer, J. T. (2002). The impact of e-commerce on supply chain relationships. *International Journal of Physical Distribution & Logistics Management, 32*(10), 851-871.

Hamel, G. (2000). Leading the revolution. Boston: Harvard Business Press.

Hasan, H., & Tibbits, H. (2000). Strategic management of electronic commerce: An adaptation of the balanced scorecard. *Internet Research, 10*(5), 439-450.

Horsti, A., Tuunainen, V. K., & Tolonen, J. (2005). Evaluation of electronic business model success: Survey among leading Finnish companies. In *Proceedings of the 38th Hawaii International Conference on System Sciences.*

Ingsriswang, S., & Forgionne, G.A. (2001). Stickiness: Implications for Web-based customer loyalty efforts. *Proceedings of IRM'01 Conference*, Canada, May 21-23.

Introna, L. (2001). Defining the virtual organization. In S. Barnes & B. Hunt (Eds.), *E-commerce & v-business: Business models for global success* (pp.143-152). Oxford: Butterworth-Heinemann.

Jayaweera, P., Johannesson, P., & Wohed, P. (2001). Collaborative process patterns for e-Business. *ACM SIGGROUP Bulletin, 22*(2), 21-28.

Jennings, R., & Robinson, J. (1996). The relation between accounting goodwill numbers and equity values. *Journal of Business Finance & Accounting, 23*(4), 513-533.

Kaplan, R. & Norton, D. P. (1992). The balanced scorecard: Measures that drive performance. *Harvard Business Review, 70*(1), 71-9.

Kaplan, R. & Norton, D. P. (1996). Linking the balanced scorecard to strategy. *California Management Review, 39*(1), 53-79.

Kaplan, R. S., & Norton, D. P. (2001). Transforming the balanced scorecard from performance measurement to strategic management: Part II. *Accounting Horizons, 15*(2), 147-161.

Kelkar, O., Leukel, J., & SchmitzPrice, V. (2002). Modeling in standards for electronic product catalogs based on XML. *WWW2002*, May 7-11, Honolulu, Hawaii, USA.

Kim, J., Allenby, G. M., & Rossi, P. E. (2002). Modeling consumer demand for variety. *Marketing Science, 21*(3), 229-250.

Kirchmer, M. (2004). E-business process networks--successful value chains through standards. *Journal of Enterprise Information Management, 17*(1), 20-30.

Koh, J., & Kim, Y. G. (2004). Knowledge sharing in virtual communities: An e-business perspective. *Expert Systems with Applications, 26*(2), 155-66.

Koppius, O., Speelman, W., Stulp, O., Verhoef, B., & Heck, E. (2005). Why are customers coming back to buy their airline tickets online? Theoretical explanations and empirical evidence. Proceedings of the *7th International Conference on Electronic Commerce ICEC'05*.

Kotler, P., & Armstrong, G. (1997). *Marketing: An introduction 4th edition*. Upper Saddle River, NJ: Prentice Hall.

Koutsoukis, N. S., Dominguez-Ballesteros, B., Lucas, C. A., & Mitra, G. (2000). A prototype decision support system for strategic planning under uncertainty. *International Journal of Physical Distribution & Logistics Management, 30*(7/8), 640-660.

Kwan, I. S. Y. (2002). A mental cognitive model of Web semantic for e-customer profile. In Proceedings of *13th International Workshop on Database and Expert Systems Applications, DEXA'02*. IEEE Comput. Soc (pp. 116-20).

Lee, J., & Park, M. S. (2003). E-logistics platform with business process automating component. *Journal of Computer Information Systems, 44*(1), 82-92.

Lee, S. C., & Brandyberry, A. A. (2003). The e-tailer's dilemma. *ACM SIGMIS Database, 34*(2), 10-22.

Lee, S. F., & Ko, A. S. (2000). Building balanced scorecard with SWOT analysis, and implementing "Sun Tzu's The Art of Business Management Strategies" on QFD methodology. *Managerial Auditing Journal, 15*(1), 68-76.

Lewis, W. J. (2001). *Data warehousing and e-commerce*. Upper Saddle River, NJ: Prentice Hall PTR.

Liu, Z., Wynter, L., & Xia, C. (2003). Usage-based versus flat pricing for e-business services with differentiated QoS. In *Proceedings of IEEE International Conference on E-Commerce, CEC'03* (pp. 355-62).

Lohman, C., Fortuin, L., & Wouters, M. (2004). Designing a performance measurement system: A case study. *European Journal of Operational Research, 156*(2), 267-286.

Malhotra, Y. (2000). Knowledge management for e-business performance: Advancing information strategy to "internet time." *Information Strategy: The Executives Journal, 16*(4), 5-16.

Malhotra, Y. (2002). Enabling knowledge exchanges for e-business communities. *Information Strategy: The Executive's Journal, 18*(3), 26-31.

Malina, M. A., & Selto, F. H. (2001). Communicating and controlling strategy: An empirical study of the effectiveness of the balanced scorecard. *Journal of Management Accounting Research, 13*, 47-90.

Manthou, V., Vlachopoulou, M., & Folinas, D. (2004). Virtual e-Chain (VeC) model for supply chain collaboration. *International Journal of Production Economics, 87*(3), 241-250.

Marr, B., & Schiuma, G. (2003). Business performance measurement--past, present, and future. *Management Decision, 41*(8), 680-687.

Mascarenhas, B., Kumaraswamy, A., Day, D., & Baveja, A. (2002). Five strategies for rapid firm growth and how to implement them. *Managerial and Decision Economics, 23*(4-5), 223-241.

Mei, X., & Harker, P. T. (2002). Customer efficiency: Concept and its impact on e-business management. *Journal of Service Research, 4*(4), 253-267.

Metes, G., Gundry, J., & Bradish, P. (1998). *Agile networking: Competing through the internet and intranets.* Upper Saddle River, NJ: Prentice Hall PTR.

Motiwalla, L. F., & Riaz Khan, M. (2003). financial impact of e-business initiatives in the retail industry. *Journal of Electronic Commerce in Organizations, 1*(1), 55-73.

Oh, S., Hwang, J., & Lee, Y. (2003). E-logistics platform with business process automating component. *Journal of Computer Information Systems, 44*(1), 158-61.

Olsson, A., & Karlsson, S. (2003). The integration of customer needs in the establishment of an e-business system for internal service. *International Journal of Logistics: Research & Applications, 6*(4), 305-317.

Palmer, T., & Wiseman, R. (1999). Decoupling risk taking from income stream uncertainty: A holistic model of risk. *Strategic Management Journal, 20*, 1037-1062.

Pant, S., & Ravichandran, T. (2001). A framework for information systems planning for ebusiness. *Logistics Information Management, 14*(1/2), 85-98.

Paper, D., Pedersen, E., & Mulbery, K. (2003). An e-commerce process model: Perspectives from e-commerce entrepreneurs. *Journal of Electronic Commerce in Organizations, 1*(3), 28-47.

Park, J. H., & Park, S. C. (2003). Agent-based merchandise management in business-to-business electronic commerce. *Decision Support Systems, 35*, 311-333.

Park, N. (2002). A shared process model for independent and synchronized e-business transactions. *Journal of Intelligent Manufacturing, 13*(6), 499-510.

Piccoli, G., Brohman, M. K., Watson, R. T., & Parasuraman, A. (2004). Net-based customer service systems: Evolution and revolution in Web site functionalities. *Decision Sciences, 35*(3), 423-455.

Plessis, M. du, & Boon, J. A. (2004). Knowledge management in eBusiness and customer relationship management: South African case study findings. *International Journal of Information Management, 24*(1), 73-86.

Porter, M. E. (2001). Strategy and the Internet. *Harvard Business Review, 79*(3), 63-78.

Raisinghani, M. S., & Meade, L. M. (2002). Strategic decisions in e-knowledge: An analytic network process. In *Proceedings of IRMA 2002 Conference.*

Raisinghani, M. S., & Schkade, L. L. (2001). E-business strategy: key perspectives and trends. In *Proceedings of IRMA 2001 Conference.*

Rayport, J., & Jaworski, B. (2001). Introduction to e-commerce. Boston: McGraw-Hill/Irwin.

Reichheld, F., & Schefter, P. (2000). E-loyalty: Your secret weapon on the Web. Harvard Business Review, 78(4), 105-113.

Reichheld, F. F., Markey, R. G., Jr., & Hopton, C. (2000). E-customer loyalty—applying the traditional rules of business for online success. *European Business Journal, 12*(4), 173-179.

Rowley, F. E. (2002). Reflections on customer knowledge management in e-business. *Qualitative Market Research: An International Journal, 5*(4), 268-280.

Sandstrom, J., & Toivanen, J. (2002). The problem of managing product development engineers: Can the balanced scorecard be an answer? *International Journal of Production Economics, 78*(1), 79-90.

Schoeniger, E. (2003). Customer profitability: Is the customer King or Cost? *CEO Insights: A Supplement to Chief Executive Magazine*, 1-4, April, 2003.

Smith, A. D. (2002). Loyalty and e-marketing issues. *Quarterly Journal of Electronic Commerce, 3*(2), 149-161.

Smith, G., & Saker, J. (1992). Developing marketing strategy in the not-for-profit sector. *Library Management, 13*(4), 6-21.

Soliman, F., & Youssef, M. (2001). The impact of some recent developments in e-business on the management of next generation manufacturing. *International Journal of Operations & Production Management, 21*(5/6), 538-564.

Spanos, Y. E., Zaralis, G., & Lioukas, S. (2004). Strategy and industry effects on profitability: Evidence from Greece. *Strategic Management Journal, 25*(2), 139-165.

Tschohl, J. (2001). *e-Service: Speed, technology, and price built around service*. Minneapolis, MN: Best Sellers Publishing.

Turban, E., King, D., Lee, J., & Viehland, D. (2004). *Electronic commerce: A managerial perspective*. Upper Saddle River, NJ: Prentice Hall PTR.

Valadares Tavares, L., Pereira, M. J., & Coelho, J. S. (2002). A multidimensional dynamic regulation model for e-marketplaces: DYNEX. *Towards the Knowledge Society eCommerce, eBusiness and eGovernment—Second IFIP Conference on E-Commerce, E-Business, E-Government* (13E 2002) (pp. 67-81).

Voss, C. (2000). Developing an eService strategy. *Business Strategy Review, 11*(11).

Vrechopoulos, A. P. (2004). Mass customisation challenges in Internet retailing through information management. *International Journal of Information Management, 24*(1), 59-71.

Wan, I. S. Y. (2002). A mental cognitive model of Web semantic for e-customer profile. In Proceedings of *13th International Workshop on Database and Expert Systems Applications, DEXA'02*. IEEE Comput. Soc (pp. 116-20).

Wang, F., & Forgionne, G. (2005). BSC-based framework for e-business strategy. In M. Khosrow-Pour (Ed.),*Encyclopedia of e-commerce, e-government, and mobile commerce*. Hershey, PA: Idea Group Reference.

Wang, S. (2001). Designing information systems for electronic commerce. *Industrial Management & Data Systems, 101*(6), 304-314.

Wang, Y., & Tang, T. (2003). Assessing customer perceptions of Web site service quality in digital marketing environments. *Journal of End User Computing, 15*(3), 14-31.

Warkentin, M., Sugumaran, V., & Bapna, R. (2001). E-knowledge networks for inter-organizational collaborative e-business. *Logistics Information Management, 14*(1/2), 149-162.

Whelan, J., & Maxelon, K. (2001). *e-business matters: A guide for small and medium-sized enterprises*. Great Britain, London: Pearson Education Limited.

This work was previously published in International Journal of E-Business Research, Vol. 3, Issue 1, edited by I. Lee, pp. 18-40, copyright 2007 by IGI Publishing, formerly known as Idea Group Publishing (an imprint of IGI Global).

Chapter XV
An Application of Multi-Criteria Decision-Making Model to Strategic Outsourcing for Effective Supply-Chain Linkages

N. K. Kwak
Saint Louis University, USA

Chang Won Lee
Jinju National University, Korea

ABSTRACT

An appropriate outsourcing and supply-chain planning strategy needs to be based on compromise and more objective decision-making procedures. Although factors affecting business performance in manufacturing firms have been explored in the past, focuses are on financial performance and measurement, neglecting intangible and nonfinancial factors in the decision-making planning process. This study presents development of an integrated multi-criteria decision-making (MCDM) model. This model aids in allocating outsourcing and supply-chain resources pertinent to strategic planning by providing a satisfying solution. The model was developed based on the data obtained from a business firm producing intelligent home system devices. This developed model will reinforce a firm's ongoing outsourcing strategies to meet defined requirements while positioning the supply-chain system to respond to a new growth and innovation.

INTRODUCTION

In today's global age, business firms are no longer able to manage all supply-chain processes from new product development to retailing. In order to obtain a successful business performance, appropriate outsourcing and supply-chain practices should be identified, established, and implemented within the firm. The growth of business scale and scope forces business decision-makers to resolve many of the challenges confronting business firms. These tasks and activities are often not well-defined and ill-structured. This new paradigm in business practices can deliver unprecedented opportunities to establish the strategic outsourcing and supply-chain planning in business firms (Heikkila, 2002; Li & O'Brien, 2001). Due to the technology and market paradigm shift, strategic outsourcing and supply-chain planning process in business firms may become more tightly coupled with new product research and development, capacity and financial planning, product launching, project management, strategic business alliances, and revenue planning.

Successful linkages of these complicated processes play a critical role affecting business performance in manufacturing settings (Cohen & Lee, 1988; Fisher, 1997; Min & Zhou, 2002; Quinn & Hilmer, 1994). Strategic outsourcing and supply-chain planning is a growing requirement for improving productivity and profitability. Many outsourcing studies have been conducted with supply-chain linkages directly and indirectly as follows: capacity planning (Lee & Hsu, 2004), downsizing (Schniederjans & Hoffman, 1999), dual sourcing (Klotz & Chatterjee, 1995), information system decision (Ngwenyama & Bryson, 1999), line balancing (Liu & Chen, 2002), service selection (Bertolini, Bevilacqua, Braglia, & Frosolini, 2004), transportation mode choice (Vannieuwenhuyse, Gelders, & Pintelon, 2003), and vendor selection (Karpak, Kumcu & Kasuganti, 1999).

In spite of a plethora of outsourcing studies in the existing literature, multi-criteria decision making (MCDM) applications are scarce and seldom identified as the best practice in business areas. Especially, an integrated MCDM model comprising goal programming (GP) and analytic hierarchy process (AHP) is rarely applied to manage an emerging outsourcing and supply-chain concern. This chapter has dual purposes: (1) to develop a decision-making model that aims at

designing a strategic outsourcing and supply-chain plan, and (2) to provide the decision-makers with an implication for effectively managing strategic outsourcing and supply-chain planning in business firms and other similar settings.

The chapter is organized in the following manner. The "Introduction" section presents current research issues in both strategic outsourcing and supply-chain planning and MCDM in a business setting. The next section "Multicriteria Decision Making" provides a review of MCDM models. After that, a problem statement of the case study along with description of data collection is described. The model development to a real-world setting and the model results and a sensitivity analysis are provided, followed by concluding remarks.

MULTI-CRITERIA DECISION MAKING

Multi-criteria decision making (especially integrated MCDM) is defined as an applied linear programming model for a decision process that allows the decision-maker to evaluate various competing alternatives to achieve certain goals. Relative importance is assigned to the goal with respect to a set of chosen criteria. MCDM is appropriate for situations in which the decision-maker needs to consider multiple criteria in arriving at the best overall decisions. In MCDM, a decision-makers select the best strategy among a number of alternatives that they evaluate on the basis of two or more criteria. The alternatives can involve risks and uncertainties; they may require sequential actions at different times; and a set of alternatives might be either finite or infinite. A decision-maker acts to maximize a value or utility function that depends on the chosen criteria. Since MCDM assumes that a decision-maker is to select among a set of alternatives, its objective function values are known with certainty. Many

MCDM problems are formulated as multiple objective linear, integer, nonlinear, and/or interactive mathematical programming problems.

One of the most widely used MCDM models is goal programming (GP). Charnes and Cooper (1961) conceptualized the GP technique and applied to an analytical process that solves multiple, conflicting, and noncommensurate problems. There are many different methods and models used to generate solutions for GP models. The natural decision-making heuristic is to concentrate initially on improving what appears to be the most critical problem area (criterion), until it has been improved to some satisfactory level of performance.

Classical GP assumes that there are some absolute target levels that can be specified. This means that any solution cannot always satisfy all the goals. Thus, the objective of GP is to find a solution which comes as close as possible to the target.

The formulation of a GP model assumes that all problem constraints become goals from which to determine the best possible solution. There are two types of constraints in GP: goal constraints and systems constraints. Goal constraints are called the goal equations or soft constraints. Systems constraints are called the ordinary linear programming constraints or hard constraints which cannot be violated.

One major limitation of GP is that the decision-makers must subjectively prioritize goals in advance. The concept of nondominated (noninferior) solutions for noncommensurable goals cannot make an improvement of one goal without degrading other conflicting goals. Regardless of the weighting structures and the goals, GP can lead to inefficient and suboptimal solutions. These solutions are not necessarily optimal for the decision-maker to acquire so that a satisfying solution is provided.

Among the MCDM models, the analytical hierarchy process (AHP) is another popular decision-making tool for multi-criteria decision-making problems. AHP provides a method to assess goals and objectives by decomposing the problem into measurable pieces for evaluation using a hierarchical structure. The procedure requires the decision-maker to provide judgments about the relative importance of each criterion and then specify a preference on each criterion for decision alternatives. The output of AHP is a prioritized ranking indicating the overall preference for each of the decision alternatives. An advantage of AHP is that it enables the decision-maker to handle problems in which the subjective judgment of an individual decision-maker constitutes an important role of the decision-making process (see Saaty, 1980 for a detailed analysis).

PROBLEM BACKGROUND

Problem Statement

A consortium of seven different firms developing and manufacturing the related products of the smart home system for home security was established in Korea. The consortium firm has recently released the smart home system to the general public.

The consortium firm secured $20 million for new product development in the 5-year period (2004-2008). It currently possesses a world-class frontier for developing a smart home system. Each member company has its own unique, special knowledge and human resources to carry on required manufacturing. There are five primary systems for making a smart home system: (1) multifunction home server with an Internet gateway function, (2) intelligent context awareness-based agent system, (3) digital video recorder for home security and applications, (4) biokey system with fingerprint access control solution, and (5) wireless digital home controller functions. It is intended to support a further growth and innovation in home security, home automation, remote controlling, and mobile multimedia functions. The infusion of additional information technology must be consistent with the business mission, strategic direction, business plans, and priorities of the consortium firm.

This special project for an integrated intelligent information technology is intended to address the dramatic growth in information technology use, to foster continued innovation and adoption of new technologies, and to expand information technology foundation for the next-generation smart home system. Thus, the consortium's information technology investment strategies throughout the next five years have been developed.

Data Collection

The data utilized to formulate this MCDM model was collected from the consortium of business firms developing and manufacturing the smart home system for home security. All the necessary data on budget, technical services, and personnel resources was gathered through the consortium's strategic business units. Additional data for establishing the consortium's resource allocation model was collected through the consortium's

international business development directors who are in charge of outsourcing and supply-chain management. Project managers participated in the strategic planning process and identified the necessary goals and criteria derived from the proposal for strategic outsourcing and supply-chain planning.

The data was validated by the consortium decision-makers in the outsourcing and supply-chain planning process. The validation of the consortium's resource allocation model is critical to accept the model solutions and to implement the result. The validation process provides the management with a meaningful source to ensure the input, decision-making process, and the outcomes.

The success of the model is based on the accurate measurement of the established goals and criteria. Decision-makers involved in the current outsourcing and supply-chain planning process to complete the validation reviewed the results of both prioritization of the goals, as well as the related projects/alternatives. Figure 1 presents a framework for strategic goals and related criteria.

Figure 1. Strategic goals and criteria

Vision	Strategic Outsourcing Goals	Criteria
Becoming the industry leader in smart home systems →	Quality Improvement (G_1) Cost Effectiveness (G_2) Customer Satisfaction (G_3) Customizing Services (G_4) Manpower Quality (G_5) Supplier Competency (G_6) Strategic Partnership (G_7) →	Financial Criteria (C_1) Customer Criteria (C_2) Internal Business Criteria (C_3) Innovation and Learning Criteria (C_4)

MODEL DEVELOPMENT

Goal Decomposition and Prioritization

In the MCDM model development of outsourcing and supply-chain planning process, the AHP has been utilized for establishing goal decomposition and prioritization. In order to obtain the overall relative importance of the seven goals, a synthesized priority is calculated for each goal. The proposed model requires the evaluation of goals with respect to how much these goals affect the overall effectiveness of strategic outsourcing and supply-chain planning for resource allocation in the consortium firm. Since no prior quantitative data exists for each goal combination, the decision-maker will make pairwise comparisons of

Table 1. AHP results for goal prioritization

Criteria		Goal Decomposition							GEV	CEV	CR
		G_1	G_2	G_3	G_4	G_5	G_6	G_7			
C_1										.165	.083
	G_1		4	3	4	6	8	8	.352		
	G_2			2	2	4	6	7	.218		
	G_3				3	3	5	6	.144		
	G_4					3	4	5	.139		
	G_5						2	3	.070		
	G_6							2	.044		
	G_7								.032		
C_2										.620	.046
	G_1		4	3	4	6	8	8	.404		
	G_2			2	2	4	6	7	.200		
	G_3				3	3	5	6	.168		
	G_4					3	4	5	.110		
	G_5						2	3	.056		
	G_6							2	.035		
	G_7								.026		
C_3										.142	.086
	G_1		4	3	4	6	8	8	.342		
	G_2			2	2	4	6	7	.238		
	G_3				3	3	5	6	.158		
	G_4					3	4	5	.116		
	G_5						2	3	.078		
	G_6							2	.034		
	G_7								.034		
C_4										.073	.059
	G_1		4	3	4	6	8	8	.334		
	G_2			2	2	4	6	7	.258		
	G_3				3	3	5	6	.174		
	G_4					3	4	5	.099		
	G_5						2	3	.067		
	G_6							2	.041		
	G_7								.026		
Goal Priority		.347	.244	.168	.106	.068	.040	.028			

Table 2. Estimated price ($) per system component in each supplier group

System Component	Outsourcing Supplier Group					Monthly Demand Level (00 units)
	1	2	3	4	5	
Home server	80	75	90	90	85	144
Awareness agent	90	85	75	80	90	360
Recorder database	75	90	80	90	75	380
Biokey	85	80	90	75	90	420
Controller box	90	85	75	80	90	320
Monthly Supply Level (00 units)	300	300	300	300	300	

Table 3. Project categories and available budgets for three stages

Project Category	Product Development			Available Project Budget ($000)
	Stage 1	Stage 2	Stage 3	
Security	150	100	130	380
Automation	120	200	130	450
Remote control	100	60	70	230
Mobile multimedia	150	110	100	360
Total	520	470	430	1,420

each goal with all others, using the AHP judgment scale.

The AHP values for goal prioritization provide their eigenvalue and consistency ratio. There are four derived criteria, such as financial (C_1), customer (C_2), internal business (C_3), and innovation and learning criteria (C_4).

Strategic outsourcing and supply-chain management is prioritized with AHP weights as follows: quality improvement (G_1), cost effectiveness (G_2), customer satisfaction (G_3), customizing services (G_4), manpower quality (G_5), supplier competency (G_6), and strategic partnership (G_7).

Decision Variables

The integrated GP problem consists of two types of decision variables in this study. The consortium firm wants to contract for the supply of five different smart home system components. Five outsourcing suppliers are being considered for contracting on the system components. Tables 2 and 3 present the necessary information for decision variables and constraints. The decision variables are:

X^s_{ij} = decision variables for demand levels assigned to different types of component i (i =1,2,..,5) to be selected with various suppliers j (j =1,2,..,5) in demand capacity

where $X^s_i \geq 0$

X^p_{ij} = decision variables for project i (1, 2, 3, and 4) to which available amounts can be allocated over three-stage period j (1,2 and 3)

where:

$$X^P_{ij} = \begin{cases} 1 & \text{if ith project is selected} \\ \\ 0 & \text{otherwise} \end{cases}$$

Constraints

The MCDM model has 37 constraints: 14 systems constraints and 23 goal constraints. Systems constraints for this consortium firm's outsourcing and supply-chain planning are (1) demand-supply constraints for each system component, and (2) supply-chain linkages on the number of certain projects development.

Systems constraint 1: Set the demand-supply constraints for five components. 14,400 units [displayed as 144(00)].

$$X^s_{11} + X^s_{12} + X^s_{13} + X^s_{14} + X^s_{15} \leq 144(00) \quad (1)$$

$$X^s_{21} + X^s_{22} + X^s_{23} + X^s_{24} + X^s_{25} \leq 360 \quad (2)$$

$$X^s_{31} + X^s_{32} + X^s_{33} + X^s_{34} + X^s_{35} \leq 380 \quad (3)$$

$$X^s_{41} + X^s_{42} + X^s_{43} + X^s_{44} + X^s_{45} \leq 420 \quad (4)$$

$$X^s_{51} + X^s_{52} + X^s_{53} + X^s_{54} + X^s_{55} \leq 320 \quad (5)$$

$$X^s_{11} + X^s_{21} + X^s_{31} + X^s_{41} + X^s_{51} = 300 \quad (6)$$

$$X^s_{12} + X^s_{22} + X^s_{32} + X^s_{42} + X^s_{52} = 300 \quad (7)$$

$$X^s_{13} + X^s_{23} + X^s_{33} + X^s_{43} + X^s_{53} = 300 \quad (8)$$

$$X^s_{14} + X^s_{24} + X^s_{34} + X^s_{44} + X^s_{54} = 300 \quad (9)$$

$$X^s_{15} + X^s_{25} + X^s_{35} + X^s_{45} + X^s_{55} = 300 \quad (10)$$

Systems constraint 2: Select one project for supply-chain management perspectives in each development stage.

$$X^P_{11} + X^P_{12} + X^P_{13} = 1 \quad (11)$$

$$X^P_{21} + X^P_{22} + X^P_{23} = 1 \quad (12)$$

$$X^P_{31} + X^P_{32} + X^P_{33} = 1 \quad (13)$$

$$X^P_{41} + X^P_{42} + X^P_{43} = 1 \quad (14)$$

There are seven goals to achieve in this study. Necessary goal priorities are presented next.

Priority 1 (P_1): Avoid overachievement of the financial resource level by providing appropriate system resources in terms of a continuous quality improvement goal (G_1), (See Table 3).

$$150X^P_{11} + 120X^P_{21} + 100X^P_{31} + 150X^P_{41} + 100X^P_{12} + 200X^P_{22} + 60X^P_{32} + 110X^P_{42} + 130X^P_{13} + 130X^P_{23} + 70X^P_{33} + 100X^P_{43} - d^+_1 = 1,420$$
$$(15)$$

Priority 2 (P_2): Avoid underachievement of the budget level meeting to all outsourcing suppliers of \$138(00,000) in terms of cost effectiveness goal (G_2), (See Table 2).

$$80X^s_{11} + 75X^s_{12} + 90X^s_{13} + 90X^s_{14} + 85X^s_{15} + 90X^s_{21} + 85X^s_{22} + 75X^s_{23} + 80X^s_{24} + 90X^s_{25} + 75X^s_{31} + 90X^s_{32} + 80X^s_{33} + 90X^s_{34} + 75X^s_{35} + 85X^s_{41} + 80X^s_{42} + 90X^s_{43} + 75X^s_{44} + 90X^s_{45} + 90X^s_{51} + 85X^s_{52} + 75X^s_{53} + 80X^s_{54} + 90X^s_{55} + d^-_2 = 138$$
$$(16)$$

Priority 3 (P_3): Do not overutilize the available market resource level for each product development stage in terms of customer satisfaction goal (G_3), (See Table 3).

$$150X^P_{11} + 120X^P_{21} + 100X^P_{31} + 150X^P_{41} - d^+_3 = 520$$
$$(17)$$

$$100X^P_{12} + 200X^P_{22} + 60X^P_{32} + 110X^P_{42} - d^+_4 = 470$$
$$(18)$$

$$130X^p_{13} + 130X^p_{23} + 70X^p_{33} + 100X^p_{43} - d^+_5 = 430 \quad (19)$$

Priority 4 (P_4): In terms of customizing services goal (G_4), avoid underachievement of resources to select an outsourcing supplier by using a total budget amount ($000) for (1) a home server outsourcing of $1,200; (2) an awareness agent component outsourcing of $3,060; (3) a digital recorder database component outsourcing of $3,200; (4) a biokey component outsourcing of $3,500; and (5) a controller box component outsourcing of $2,700 (see Table 2).

$$80X^s_{11} + 90X^s_{21} + 75X^s_{31} + 85X^s_{41} + 90X^s_{51} + d^-_6 = 1,200 \quad (20)$$

$$75X^s_{12} + 85X^s_{22} + 90X^s_{32} + 80X^s_{42} + 85X^s_{52} + d^-_7 = 3,060 \quad (21)$$

$$90X^s_{13} + 75X^s_{23} + 80X^s_{33} + 90X^s_{43} + 75X^s_{53} + d^-_8 = 3,200 \quad (22)$$

$$90X^s_{14} + 80X^s_{24} + 90X^s_{34} + 75X^s_{44} + 80X^s_{54} + d^-_9 = 3,500 \quad (23)$$

$$85X^s_{15} + 90X^s_{25} + 75X^s_{35} + 90X^s_{45} + 90X^s_{55} + d^-_{10} = 2,700 \quad (24)$$

Priority 5 (P_5): Implement projects in the three product development stages in terms of manpower balancing goal (G_5).

$$X^p_{11} + X^p_{12} + X^p_{13} + X^p_{14} + d^-_{11} - d^+_{11} = 1 \quad (25)$$

$$X^p_{21} + X^p_{22} + X^p_{23} + X^p_{24} + d^-_{12} - d^+_{12} = 1 \quad (26)$$

$$X^p_{31} + X^p_{32} + X^p_{33} + X^p_{34} + d^-_{13} - d^+_{13} = 1 \quad (27)$$

Priority 6 (P_6): Determine the demand capacity in each supplier to assign an appropriate outsourcing supplier group in terms of supplier competency goal (G_6).

$$X^s_{11} + X^s_{12} + X^s_{13} + X^s_{14} + X^s_{15} + d^-_{14} - d^+_{14} = 1 \quad (28)$$

$$X^s_{21} + X^s_{22} + X^s_{23} + X^s_{24} + X^s_{25} + d^-_{15} - d^+_{15} = 1 \quad (29)$$

$$X^s_{31} + X^s_{32} + X^s_{33} + X^s_{34} + X^s_{35} + d^-_{16} - d^+_{16} = 1 \quad (30)$$

$$X^s_{41} + X^s_{42} + X^s_{43} + X^s_{44} + X^s_{45} + d^-_{17} - d^+_{17} = 1 \quad (31)$$

$$X^s_{51} + X^s_{52} + X^s_{53} + X^s_{54} + X^s_{55} + d^-_{18} - d^+_{18} = 1 \quad (32)$$

Priority 7 (P_7): In terms of strategic supplier partnership goal (G_7), decision-makers in the consortium firm decide that all suppliers are assigned to supply a certain component.

$$X^s_{11} + X^s_{21} + X^s_{31} + X^s_{41} + X^s_{51} + d^-_{19} - d^+_{19} = 1 \quad (33)$$

$$X^s_{12} + X^s_{22} + X^s_{32} + X^s_{42} + X^s_{52} + d^-_{20} - d^+_{20} = 1 \quad (34)$$

$$X^s_{13} + X^s_{23} + X^s_{33} + X^s_{43} + X^s_{53} + d^-_{21} - d^+_{21} = 1 \quad (35)$$

$$X^s_{14} + X^s_{24} + X^s_{34} + X^s_{44} + X^s_{54} + d^-_{22} - d^+_{22} = 1 \quad (36)$$

$$X^s_{15} + X^s_{25} + X^s_{35} + X^s_{45} + X^s_{55} + d^-_{23} - d^+_{23} = 1 \quad (37)$$

Objective Function

The objective of this MCDM problem is to minimize the sum of the deviational variable values subject to constraints (1)-(37), satisfying the preemptive priority rules. The objective function depends on the preemptive priority sequence of the goals that have seven priorities.

$$\text{Minimize: } Z = P_1 d^+_1 + P_2 d^-_2 + P_3 \sum_{i=3}^{5} d^+_i + P_4 \sum_{i=6}^{10} d^-_i +$$

$$P_5 \sum_{i=11}^{13} (d^+_i + d^-_i) + P_6 \sum_{i=14}^{18} (d^+_i + d^-_i) + P_7 \sum_{i=19}^{23} (d^+_i + d^-_i)$$

MODEL ANALYSIS

Model Solution and Discussion

In this MCDM model, decision-makers seek a solution that satisfies as close as possible a set of goals. Thus, GP requires the concept of measuring discrepancy from the goals. The concept of nondominated solutions for noncommensurable goals cannot make an improvement of one goal without a trade-off of other conflicting goals. In the GP problem, a nondominated solution is examined. A nondominated solution is defined in the following manner: a feasible solution to an MCDM problem which is efficient, if no other feasible solutions yield an improvement in one goal, without sacrificing another goal. This MCDM model was solved using AB: QM system software (Lee, 1996). Table 4 presents an analysis of the objective function. Table 5 exhibits the results of both decision and deviational variables.

Priority 1 (P_1) is to avoid overachievement of the financial resource level for continuous quality improvement (i.e., G_1). Priority 1 is fully satisfied ($P_1 = 0$). The related deviational variable (d^+_1) is zero.

Priority 2 (P_2) is to avoid underutilization of the budget level for cost effectiveness. Priority 2 is fully satisfied ($P_2 = 0$). The related deviational variable (d^-_2) is zero.

Priority 3 (P_3) is to not overutilize the available market resource level in each product development period for customer satisfaction. The management desires that their market resource of outsourcing should not be overutilized in each development stage 1 (d^+_3), stage 2 (d^+_4), and stage 3 (d^+_5). This third priority goal is fully satisfied ($P_3 = 0$), and its related deviational variables (d^+_3, d^+_4, and d^+_5) are zero.

Priority 4 (P_4) is to avoid underachievement of resources to select outsourcing suppliers who have the industrial leading knowledge in five different smart home system components, since the management considers that all five technology resources are highly unattainable. This priority goal is fully satisfied ($P_4 = 0$). Its related deviational variables are all zero: underachievement in home server technology outsourcing resources ($d^-_6 = 0$); underachievement in awareness agent technology outsourcing resources ($d^-_7 = 0$); underachievement in recorder database technology outsourcing

Table 4. Analysis of the objective function

Priority	Goal Achievement	Values
P_1	Satisfied	0
P_2	Satisfied	0
P_3	Satisfied	0
P_4	Satisfied	0
P_5	Partially satisfied	1
P_6	Partially satisfied	1,495
P_7	Partially satisfied	1,495

Table 5. Analysis of decision and deviational variables

Decision Variable (supplier)	Solution Value	Decision Variable (project)	Solution Value	Deviational Variable*
X^s_{11}	0	X^P_{11}	0	$d^-_1 = 1{,}030$
X^s_{12}	0	X^P_{12}	0	$d^+_2 = 125{,}102$
X^s_{13}	0	X^P_{13}	1	$d^-_3 = 420$
X^s_{14}	144	X^P_{21}	0	$d^-_4 = 310$
X^s_{15}	0	X^P_{22}	1	$d^-_5 = 300$
X^s_{21}	0	X^P_{23}	0	$d^+_6 = 24{,}300$
X^s_{22}	0	X^P_{31}	1	$d^+_7 = 23{,}840$
X^s_{23}	0	X^P_{32}	0	$d^+_8 = 19{,}300$
X^s_{24}	36	X^P_{33}	0	$d^+_9 = 21{,}340$
X^s_{25}	200	X^s_{41}	1	$d^+_{10} = 22{,}800$
X^s_{31}	0	X^s_{42}	0	$d^+_{11} = 1$
X^s_{32}	280	X^s_{43}	0	$d^+_{14} = 143$
X^s_{33}	0	X^s_{44}		$d^+_{15} = 235$
X^s_{34}	0			$d^+_{16} = 379$
X^s_{35}	100			$d^+_{17} = 419$
X^s_{41}	300			$d^+_{18} = 319$
X^s_{42}	0			$d^+_{19} = 299$
X^s_{43}	0			$d^+_{20} = 299$
X^s_{44}	120			$d^+_{21} = 299$
X^s_{45}	0			$d^+_{22} = 299$
X^s_{51}	0			$d^+_{23} = 299$
X^s_{52}	20			
X^s_{53}	300			* All other
X^s_{54}	0			deviational
X^s_{55}	0			variables are zero.

resources ($d^-_8 = 0$); underachievement in biokey technology outsourcing resources ($d^-_9 = 0$); and underachievement in controller box technology outsourcing resources ($d^-_{10} = 0$).

Priority 5 (P_5) is to implement appropriately four projects in the three product development periods for securing outsourcing manpower balancing. This priority goal is partially satisfied ($P_5 = 1$). Its related deviational variables are not all zero ($d^+_{11} = 1$, $d^+_{12} = 0$, $d^+_{13} = 0$, $d^-_{11} = 0$, $d^-_{12} = 0$, $d^-_{13} = 0$). There is one project with overachievement. However, this does not mean that the goal is not achieved because four projects should be assigned

in any product development stage.

Priority 6 (P_6) is to meet the demand-supply level to select an appropriate outsourcing supplier group for a supplier competency goal. This priority goal is partially satisfied ($P_6 = 1{,}495$). Its related deviational variables are not all zero ($d^+_{14} = 143$, $d^+_{15} = 235$, $d^+_{16} = 379$, $d^+_{17} = 419$, $d^+_{18} = 319$, $d^-_{14} = 0$, $d^-_{15} = 0$, $d^-_{16} = 0$, $d^-_{17} = 0$, $d^-_{18} = 0$). Table 6 indicates demand levels that are assigned to supplier groups for each system component. Supplier 1 is assigned to a demand level of 300 biokey components. Likewise, supplier 2 has demand levels of 280 recorder database and 20 control box

Table 6. Demand level assigned supplier groups to system components

System Component	Outsourcing Supplier Group				
	1	2	3	4	5
Home server				144	
Awareness agent				36	200
Recorder database		280			100
Biokey	300			120	
Controller box		20	300		

Table 7. Assigned projects in each development stage

Project Category	Product Development		
	Stage 1	Stage 2	Stage 3
Security			X
Automation		X	
Remote control	X		
Mobile multimedia	X		

components; supplier 3 for a demand level of 300 control box components; supplier 4 for demand levels of 144 home server, 36 awareness, and 120 biokey components; and supplier 5 for demand levels of 200 awareness agent and 100 recorder database components.

Priority 7 (P_7) is to assign certain contracts to supplier groups to achieve a strategic partnership goal. This priority goal is partially satisfied (P_6 = 1,495). Its related deviational variables are not all zero (d^+_{19} = 299, d^+_{20} = 299, d^+_{21} = 299, d^+_{22} = 299, d^+_{23} = 299, d^-_{19} = 0, d^-_{20} = 0, d^-_{21} = 0, d^-_{22} = 0, d^-_{23} = 0). Table 7 presents the selected projects assigned to each development stage. In stage 1, remote control function and mobile multimedia function will be recommended to develop. Home automation function will be developed in stage 2 and home security function in stage 3.

Outsourcing and supply-chain planning in supply-chain management perspective has become a significant and integral activity of strategic planning in a firm. The goals surrounding outsourcing and supply-chain planning decisions are complex and conflicting. Like other business decision making problems, outsourcing problems cannot derive a single optimal solution. Most top decision-makers agree that this planning process ultimately depends on a firm's business strategies, competitiveness roadmap, and business value and mission. In order to improve the system's overall effectiveness, decision-makers should recognize the ways to improve product quality, to enhance the internal and external customer satisfaction, to provide more strong commitment to manpower management, and to establish a sound alliance and collaboration with other business partners.

Sensitivity Analysis

Sensitivity analysis is an evaluation tool that is used once a satisfying solution has been found. It provides an insight into how satisfying solutions are affected by changes in the input data. Sensitivity analysis is performed with two scenarios. The management considers three goals (G_1, G_6, and G_7) to be evaluated. Quality improvement goal (G_1)

Table 8. Sensitivity analysis with two scenarios

Original Option		Revised Scenario 1		Revised Scenario 2	
Decision Variables	Solution Value	Decision Variables	Solution Value	Decision Variables	Solution Value
X^s_{11}	0	X^s_{11}	144	X^s_{11}	0
X^s_{12}	0	X^s_{12}	0	X^s_{12}	64
X^s_{13}	0	X^s_{13}	0	X^s_{13}	0
X^s_{14}	144	X^s_{14}	0	X^s_{14}	0
X^s_{15}	0	X^s_{15}	0	X^s_{15}	80
X^s_{21}	0	X^s_{21}	0	X^s_{21}	0
X^s_{22}	0	X^s_{22}	256	X^s_{22}	236
X^s_{23}	0	X^s_{23}	0	X^s_{23}	0
X^s_{24}	36	X^s_{24}	0	X^s_{24}	0
X^s_{25}	200	X^s_{25}	0	X^s_{25}	0
X^s_{31}	0	X^s_{31}	80	X^s_{31}	0
X^s_{32}	280	X^s_{32}	0	X^s_{32}	0
X^s_{33}	0	X^s_{33}	0	X^s_{33}	0
X^s_{34}	0	X^s_{34}	0	X^s_{34}	180
X^s_{35}	100	X^s_{35}	300	X^s_{35}	200
X^s_{41}	300	X^s_{41}	76	X^s_{41}	300
X^s_{42}	0	X^s_{42}	44	X^s_{42}	0
X^s_{43}	0	X^s_{43}	0	X^s_{43}	0
X^s_{44}	120	X^s_{44}	300	X^s_{44}	120
X^s_{45}	0	X^s_{45}	0	X^s_{45}	0
X^s_{51}	0	X^s_{51}	0	X^s_{51}	0
X^s_{52}	20	X^s_{52}	0	X^s_{52}	0
X^s_{53}	300	X^s_{53}	300	X^s_{53}	300
X^s_{54}	0	X^s_{54}	0	X^s_{54}	0
X^s_{55}	0	X^s_{55}	0	X^s_{55}	0
X^p_{11}	0	X^p_{11}	0	X^p_{11}	0
X^p_{12}	0	X^p_{12}	0	X^p_{12}	0
X^p_{13}	1	X^p_{13}	1	X^p_{13}	1
X^p_{21}	0	X^p_{21}	0	X^p_{21}	0
X^p_{22}	1	X^p_{22}	1	X^p_{22}	1
X^p_{23}	0	X^p_{23}	0	X^p_{23}	0
X^p_{31}	1	X^p_{31}	1	X^p_{31}	1
X^p_{32}	0	X^p_{32}	0	X^p_{32}	0
X^p_{33}	0	X^p_{33}	0	X^p_{33}	0
X^s_{41}	1	X^s_{41}	1	X^s_{41}	1
X^s_{42}	0	X^s_{42}	0	X^s_{42}	0
X^s_{43}	0	X^s_{43}	0	X^s_{43}	0

and supplier competency goal (G_6) are changed (i.e., $P_{6 \rightarrow} P_1$ and $P_{1 \rightarrow} P_6$); and quality improvement goal (G_1) and strategic partnership goal (G_7) are changed (i.e., $P_{7 \rightarrow} P_1$ and $P_{1 \rightarrow} P_7$).

With sensitivity analysis available for the management, various scenarios can be evaluated more easily at less cost. Table 8 presents the results of two scenarios. It shows an important implication for strategic planning considering effective outsourcing and supplier management. Solution values of supplier decision variables in the original option and the revised scenarios indicate the new demand levels that are assigned to the supplier groups.

The top decision-makers in the consortium firm have accepted the final results as valid and feasible for implementing the outsourcing planning in their real business setting. The consortium firm has started its strategic outsourcing and supplier-customer management planning with ongoing base. The effects from these model outputs will be evaluated in the next fiscal year or two. The future outsourcing and supplier management planning agenda will be identified to compare with this proposed MCDM model for the strategic outsourcing planning. The strategic outsourcing planning based on the proposed MCDM model will provide the management with a significant insight to set an appropriate outsourcing strategy, while enhancing customer satisfaction and relationship management, and improving the firm's global competitiveness. Thus, the consortium firm currently reviews all these alternatives as possible outsourcing strategies.

CONCLUSION

This study presents an MCDM model for outsourcing and supply-chain planning in a smart home system components manufacturing industry in Korea. The proposed MCDM model will provide the management with better understanding of outsourcing and supply-chain planning. This

proposed model would give a practical decision-making way for analyzing the outsourcing resource planning. This study indicates that the effective decision-making process in outsourcing and supply-chain planning can enforce the firm's competitive advantages and improve the firm's business performance. It is necessary to be able to assess the relative contribution of the individual member organizations within the supply chain. This requires a performance measurement system that can not only operate at several different levels but also link or integrate the efforts of these different levels to meeting the objectives of the supply chain.

When management considers several conflicting goals to achieve, subject to a set of constraints, MCDM models can provide effective decision-making results for strategic outsourcing and supply-chain planning in business operational environments. Subjective decision-making processes can make the multiple and complicated business problems into the worst situation of both business performance and business partnership due to the potential irrational decision-making. Thus, an appropriate use of MCDM models for effective decision-making is essential to create a long-term strategic plan for a competitive advantage and survival of any business organization in challenging environments.

ACKNOWLEDGMENT

This work was supported by the Korea Research Foundation Grant (KRF 2003-041-B20171).

REFERENCES

Bertolini, M., Bevilacqua, M., Braglia, M., & Frosolini, M. (2004). An analytical method for maintenance outsourcing service selection. *International Journal of Quality & Reliability Management, 21*(7), 772-788.

Charnes, A., & Cooper, W. W. (1961). *Management models and the industrial applications of linear programming.* New York: Wiley.

Cohen, M., & Lee, H. (1988). Strategic analysis of integrated production-distribution systems: Models and methods. *Operations Research, 36*(2), 216-228.

Fisher, M. L. (1997). What is right supply chain for your product? *Harvard Business Review, 75*(2), 105-116.

Heikkila, J. (2002). From supply to demand chain management: Efficiency and customer satisfaction. *Journal of Operations Management, 20*(6), 747-767.

Karpak, B., Kumcu, E., & Kasuganti, R. (1999). An application of visual interactive goal programming: A case in vendor selection decisions. *Journal of Multi-Criteria Decision Analysis, 8*(2), 93-105.

Klotz, D., & Chatterjee, K. (1995). Dual sourcing in repeated procurement competition. *Management Science, 41*(8), 1317-1327.

Lee, C.-E., & Hsu, S.-C. (2004). Outsourcing capacity planning for an IC design house. *The International Journal of Advanced Manufacturing Technology, 24*(3-4), 306-320.

Lee, S. M. (1996). *AB:QM system software.* Englewood Cliffs, NJ: Prentice Hall.

Li, D., & O'Brien, C. (2001). A quantitative analysis of relationships between product types and supply chain strategies. *International Journal of Production Economics, 73*(1), 29-39.

Liu, C.-M., & Chen, C.-H. (2002). Multi-section electronic assembly line balancing problems: A case study. *Production Planning & Control, 13*(5), 451-461.

Min, H., & Zhou, G. (2002). Supply chain modeling: Past, present, and future. *Computers and Industrial Engineering, 4*, 231-249.

Ngwenyama, O. K., & Bryson, N. (1999). Making the information systems outsourcing decision: A transaction cost approach to analyzing outsourcing decision problems. *European Journal of Operational Research, 115*, 351-367.

Quinn, J. B., & Hilmer, F. G. (1994). Strategic outsourcing. *Sloan Management Review, 35*(4), 43-55.

Saaty, T. L. (1980). *The analytic hierarchy process.* New York: McGraw-Hill.

Schniederjans, M. J., & Hoffman, J. J. (1999). Downsizing production/operations with multi-objective programming. *International Journal of Operations & Production Management, 19*(1), 79-91.

Vannieuwenhuyse, B., Gelders, G., & Pintelon, L. (2003). An online decision support system for transportation mode choice. *Journal of Enterprise Information Management, 16*(2), 125-133.

Chapter XVI
The Cognitive Process of Decision Making

Yingxu Wang
University of Calgary, Canada

Guenther Ruhe
University of Calgary, Canada

ABSTRACT

Decision making is one of the basic cognitive processes of human behaviors by which a preferred option or a course of actions is chosen from among a set of alternatives based on certain criteria. Decision theories are widely applied in many disciplines encompassing cognitive informatics, computer science, management science, economics, sociology, psychology, political science, and statistics. A number of decision strategies have been proposed from different angles and application domains such as the maximum expected utility and Bayesian method. However, there is still a lack of a fundamental and mathematical decision model and a rigorous cognitive process for decision making. This article presents a fundamental cognitive decision making process and its mathematical model, which is described as a sequence of Cartesian-product based selections. A rigorous description of the decision process in real-time process algebra (RTPA) is provided. Real-world decisions are perceived as a repetitive application of the fundamental cognitive process. The result shows that all categories of decision strategies fit in the formally described decision process. The cognitive process of decision making may be applied in a wide range of decision-based systems such as cognitive informatics, software agent systems, expert systems, and decision support systems.

INTRODUCTION

Decision making is a process that chooses a preferred option or a course of actions from among a set of alternatives on the basis of given criteria or strategies (Wang, Wang, Patel, & Patel, 2004; Wilson & Keil, 2001). Decision making is one of the 37 fundamental cognitive processes modeled in the layered reference model of the brain (LRMB)

(Wang et al., 2004; Wang, 2007b). The study on decision making is interested in multiple disciplines such as cognitive informatics, cognitive science, computer science, psychology, management science, decision science, economics, sociology, political science, and statistics (Berger, 1990; Edwards & Fasolo, 2001; Hastie, 2001; Matlin, 1998; Payne & Wenger, 1998; Pinel, 1997; Wald, 1950; Wang et al., 2004; Wilson et al., 2001). Each of those disciplines has emphasized on a special aspect of decision making. It is recognized that there is a need to seek an axiomatic and rigorous model of the cognitive decision-making process in the brain, which may be served as the foundation of various decision making theories.

Decision theories can be categorized into two paradigms: the *descriptive* and *normative* theories. The former is based on empirical observation and on experimental studies of choice behaviors; and the latter assumes a rational decision-maker who follows well-defined preferences that obey certain axioms of rational behaviors. Typical normative theories are the expected utility paradigm (Osborne & Rubinstein, 1994) and the Bayesian theory (Berger, 1990; Wald, 1950). Edwards developed a 19-step decision-making process (Edwards et al., 2001) by integrating Bayesian and multi-attribute utility theories. Zachary, Wherry, Glenn, and Hopson (1982) perceived that there are three constituents in decision making known as the *decision situation*, the *decision maker*, and the *decision process*. Although the cognitive capacities of decision makers may be greatly varying, the core cognitive processes of the human brain share similar and recursive characteristics and mechanisms (Wang, 2003a; Wang & Gafurov, 2003; Wang & Wang, 2004; Wang et al., 2004).

This article adopts the philosophy of the *axiom of choice* (Lipschutz, 1967). The three essences for decision making recognized in this article are the *decision goals*, a set of *alternative choices*, and a set of *selection criteria* or strategies. According to this theory, decision makers are the engine or executive of a decision making process. If the three essences of decision making are defined, a decision making process may be rigorously carried out by either a human decision maker or by an intelligent system. This is a cognitive foundation for implementing expert systems and decision supporting systems (Ruhe, 2003; Ruhe & An, 2004; Wang et al., 2004; Wang, 2007a).

In this article, the cognitive foundations of decision theories and their mathematical models are explored. A rigorous description of decisions and decision making is presented. The cognitive process of decision making is explained, which is formally described by using real-time process algebra (RTPA). The complexity of decision making in real-world problems such as software release planning is studied, and the need for powerful decision support systems are discussed.

A MATHEMATICAL MODEL OF DECISIONS AND DECISION MAKING

Decision making is one of the fundamental cognitive processes of human beings (Wang et al., 2004; Wang, 2007a; Wang, 2007b) that is widely used in determining rational, heuristic, and intuitive selections in complex scientific, engineering, economical, and management situations, as well as in almost each procedure of daily life. Since decision making is a basic mental process, it occurs every few seconds in the thinking courses of human mind consciously or subconsciously.

This section explores the nature of selection, decision, and decision making, and their mathematical models. A rigorous description of decision making and its strategies is developed.

The Mathematical Model of Decision Making

The *axiom of selection* (or *choice*) (Lipschutz, 1967) states that there exists a selection function for any nonempty collection of nonempty disjoint sets of alternatives.

Definition 1. Let $\{A_i \mid i \in I\}$ be a collection of disjoint sets, $A_i \subseteq U$, and $A_i \neq \varnothing$, a function

$$c: \{A_i\} \to A_i, \ i \in I \qquad (1)$$

is a *choice function* if $c(A_i) = a_i$, $a_i \in A_i$. Or an element $a_i \in A_i$ may be chosen by c, where A_i is called the set of alternatives, U the universal set, and I a set of natural numbers.

On the basis of the choice function and the axiom of selection, a decision can be rigorously defined as follows.

Definition 2. A *decision, d,* is a selected alternative $a \in A$ from a nonempty set of alternatives A, $A \subseteq U$, based on a given set of criteria C, i.e.:

$$\begin{aligned} d &= f(A, C) \\ &= f: A \times C \to A, \ A \subseteq U, A \neq \varnothing \end{aligned} \qquad (2)$$

where $\times$ represents a Cartesian product.

It is noteworthy that the criteria in C can be a simple one or a complex one. The latter is the combination of a number of joint criteria depending on multiple factors.

Definition 3. *Decision making* is a process of decision selection from available alternatives against the chosen criteria for a given decision goal.

According to Definition 2, the *number of possible decisions, n,* can be determined by the sizes of A and C, for example:

$$n = \#A \bullet \#C \qquad (3)$$

where $\#$ is the cardinal calculus on sets, and $A \cap C = \varnothing$.

According to Eq.3, in case $\#A = 0$ and/or $\#C = 0$, no decision may be derived.

The previous definitions provide a generic and fundamental mathematical model of decision making, which reveal that the factors determining a decision are the alternatives A and criteria C for a given decision making goal. A unified theory on fundamental and cognitive decision making can be developed based on the axiomatic and recursive cognitive process elicited from the most fundamental decision-making categories as shown in Table 1.

Strategies and Criteria of Decision Making

According to Definition 2, the outcomes of a decision making process are determined by the decision-making strategies selected by decision makers when a set of alternative decisions has been identified. It is obvious that different decision making strategies require different decision selection criteria. There is a great variation of decision-making strategies developed in traditional decision and game theories, as well as cognitive science, system science, management science, and economics.

The taxonomy of strategies and corresponding criteria for decision making can be classified into four categories known as *intuitive, empirical, heuristic,* and *rational* as shown in Table 1. It is noteworthy in Table 1 that the existing decision theories provide a set of criteria (C) for evaluating alternative choices for a given problem.

As summarized in Table 1, the first two categories of decision-making, *intuitive* and *empirical*, are in line with human intuitive cognitive psychology and there is no specific rational model for explaining those decision criteria. The rational

Table 1. Taxonomy of strategies and criteria for decision-making

No.	Category	Strategy	Criterion (*C*)
1	**Intuitive**		
1.1		Arbitrary	Based on the most easy or familiar choice
1.2		Preference	Based on propensity, hobby, tendency, expectation
1.3		Common senses	Based on axioms and judgment
2	**Empirical**		
2.1		Trial and error	Based on exhaustive trial
2.2		Experiment	Based on experiment results
2.3		Experience	Based on existing knowledge
2.4		Consultant	Based on professional consultation
2.5		Estimation	Based on rough evaluation
3	**Heuristic**		
3.1		Principles	Based on scientific theories
3.2		Ethics	Based on philosophical judgment and belief
3.3		Representative	Based on common rules of thumb
3.4		Availability	Based on limited information or local maximum
3.5		Anchoring	Based on presumption or bias and their justification
4	**Rational**		
4.1	Static		
4.1.1		Minimum cost	Based on minimizing energy, time, money
4.1.2		Maximum benefit	Based on maximizing gain of usability, functionality, reliability, quality, dependability
4.1.3		Maximum utility	Based on cost-benefit ratio
4.1.3.1		- Certainty	Based on maximum probability, statistic data
4.1.3.2		- Risks	Based on minimum loss or regret
		- Uncertainty	
4.1.3.3		- Pessimist	Based on maximin
4.1.3.4		- Optimist	Based on maximax
4.1.3.5		- Regretist	Based on minimax of regrets
4.2	Dynamic		
4.2.1		Interactive events	Based on automata
4.2.2		Games	Based on conflict
4.2.2.1		- Zero sum	Based on $\sum (\text{gain} + \text{loss}) = 0$
4.2.2.2		- Non zero sum	Based on $\sum (\text{gain} + \text{loss}) \neq 0$
4.2.3		Decision grids	Based on a series of choices in a decision grid

decision-making strategies can be described by two subcategories: the *static* and *dynamic* strategies and criteria. The *heuristic* decision-making strategies are frequently used by human beings as a decision maker. Details of the heuristic decision-making strategies may be referred to cognitive psychology and AI (Hastie, 2001; Matlin, 1998; Payne et al., 1998; Wang, 2007a).

It is interesting to observe that the most simple decision making theory can be classified into the intuitive category such as arbitrary and preference choices based on personal propensity, hobby, tendency, expectation, and/or common senses. That is, a naïve may still be able to make important and perhaps wise decisions every day, even every few seconds. Therefore, the elicitation of the most fundamental and core process of decision making shared in human cognitive processes is yet to be sought in the following sections. Recursive applications of the core process of decision making will be helpful to solve complicated decision problems in the real world.

The Framework of Rational Decision Making

According to Table 1, rational and complex decision making strategies can be classified into the static and dynamic categories. Most existing decision-making strategies are static because the changes of environments of decision makers are independent of the decision makers' activities. Also, different decision strategies may be selected in the same situation or environment based on the decision makers' values and attitudes towards risk and their prediction on future outcomes. When the environment of a decision maker is interactive with his or her decisions or the environment changes according to the decision makers' activities and the decision strategies and rules are predetermined, this category of decision making needs are classified into the category of dynamic decisions such as games and decision

grids (Matlin, 1998; Payne et al., 1998; Pinel, 1997; Wang, 2005a,b).

Definition 4. The *dynamic strategies and criteria* of decision-making are those that all alternatives and criteria are dependent on both the environment and the effect of the historical decisions made by the decision maker.

Classic dynamic decision making methods are decision trees (Edwards et al., 2001). A new theory of decision grid is developed in Wang (2005a,b) for serial decision making. Decision making under interactive events and competition is modeled by games (Matlin, 1998; Payne et al., 1998; von Neumann & Morgenstern, 1980; Wang, 2005a). Wang (2005a) presents a formal model of games, which rigorously describes the architecture or layout of games and their dynamic behaviors.

An overview of the classification of decisions and related rational strategies is provided in Figure 1. It can be seen that games are used to deal with the most complicated decision problems, which are dynamic, interactive, and under uncontrollable competitions. Further discussion on game theories and its formal models may be referred to von Neumann et al. (1980), Berger (1990), and Wang (2005a,b). Decision models may also be classified among others point of views such as structures, constraints, degrees of uncertainty, clearness and scopes of objectives, difficulties of information processing, degrees of complexity, utilities and beliefs, ease of formalization, time constraints, and uniqueness or novelty.

Typical Theories of Decision Making

Decision making is the process of constructing the choice criteria (or functions) and strategies and use them to select a decision from a set of possible alternatives. In this view, existing decision theories are about how a choice function may be created for finding a good decision. Different decision

Figure 1. A framework of decisions and strategies

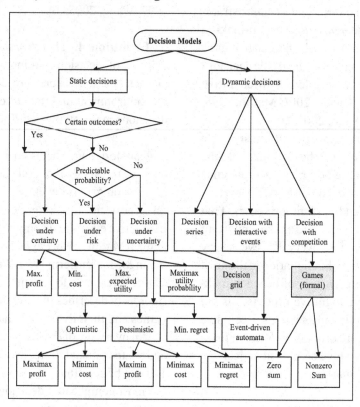

theories provide different choice functions. The following are examples from some of the typical decision paradigms as shown in Table 1.

(a) The Game Theory

In game theory (Osborne et al., 1994), a decision problem can be modeled as a triple, for example:

$$d = (\Omega, C, \mathcal{A}) \tag{4}$$

where Ω is a set of possible states of the nature, C is a set of consequences, and $\mathcal{A}$ is a set of actions, $\mathcal{A} \subset C^{\Omega}$.

If an action $a \in \mathcal{A}$ is chosen, and the prevailing state is $\omega \in \Omega$, then a certain consequence $\alpha(\omega) \in C$ can be obtained. Assuming a probability

estimation and a utility function be defined for a given action a as $p(a)$: $A \rightarrow \mathfrak{R}$ and u: $C \rightarrow \mathfrak{R}$, respectively, a choice function based on the utility theory can be expressed as follows:

$$d = \{ a \mid \sum_{\Omega} u[a(\omega)]p(a) = max (\sum_{\Omega} u[x(\omega)]p(x)) \wedge x \in \mathcal{A})\} \tag{5}$$

(b) The Bayesian Theory

In Bayesian theory (Wald, 1950; Berger, 1990) the choice function is called a decision rule. A loss function, L, is adopted to evaluate the consequence of an action as follows:

$$L: \Omega \times \mathcal{A} \rightarrow \mathfrak{R} \tag{6}$$

where Ω is a set of all possible states of nature, $\mathcal{A}$ is a set of actions, and $\Omega \times \mathcal{A}$ denotes a Cartesian product of choice.

Using the loss function for determining possible risks, a choice function for decision making can be derived as follows:

$$d = \{ \ a \ |p[L(\omega,\alpha)] = \min_{x \in A}(p[L(\omega,x)])\} \qquad (7)$$

where $p[L(\omega,\alpha)]$ is the expected probability of loss for action x on $\omega \in \Omega$.

Despite different representations in the utility theory and Bayesian theory, both of them provide alternative decision making criteria from different angles where loss in the latter is equivalent to the negative utility in the former. Therefore, it may be perceived that a decision maker who uses the utility theory is seeking optimistic decisions; and a decision maker who uses the loss or risk-based theory is seeking pessimistic or conservative decisions.

THE COGNITIVE PROCESS OF DECISION MAKING

The LRMB model has revealed that there are 37 interacting cognitive processes in the brain (Wang et al., 2004). Relationships between the decision-making process and other major ones in LRMB are shown in Figure 2. Figure 2 indicates that, according to UML semantics, the decision-making process inherits the *problem-solving* process. In other end, it functions by aggregations of or supported by the layer 6 processes *comprehension*, *qualification*, and *quantification*, as well as the layer 5 processes of *search*, *representation*, and *memorization*. Formal descriptions of these related cognitive processes in LRMB may be referred to in Wang (2003b), Wang et al., (2003), and Wang et al. (2003, 2004).

In contrary to the traditional *container* metaphor, the human memory mechanism can be described by a *relational* metaphor, which perceives that memory and knowledge are represented by the connections between neurons in the brain, rather than the neurons themselves as information containers. Therefore, the cognitive model of human memory, particularly the long-term memory (LTM) can be described by two fundamental artifacts (Wang et al., 2003): (a) *Objects*: The abstraction of external entities and internal concepts. There are also sub-objects known as *attributes*, which are used to denote detailed properties and characteristics of an object. (b) *Relations*: Connections and relationships between object-object, object–attributes, and attribute-attribute.

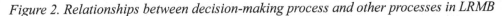

Figure 2. Relationships between decision-making process and other processes in LRMB

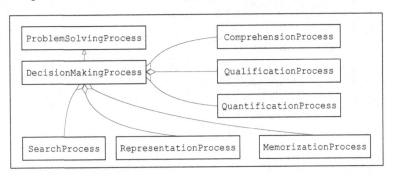

Based on the previous discussion, an object-attribute-relation (OAR) model of memory can be described as a triple (Wang & Wang, 2004; Wang et al., 2003), for example:

$$OAR = (O, A, R) \qquad (8)$$

where O is a given object identified by an abstract name, A is a set of attributes for characterizing the object, and R is a set of relations between the object and other objects or attributes of them.

On the basis of the LRMB and OAR models developed in cognitive informatics (Wang, 2003a,

2007b), the cognitive process of decision making may be informally described by the following courses:

1. To comprehend the decision making problem and to identify the decision goal in terms of Object (O) and its attributes (A).
2. To search in the abstract layer of LTM (Squire, Knowlton, & Musen et al. 1993; Wang & Wang, 2004) for alternative solutions ($\mathcal{A}$) and criteria for useful decision strategies (C).

Figure 3. The cognitive process of decision making

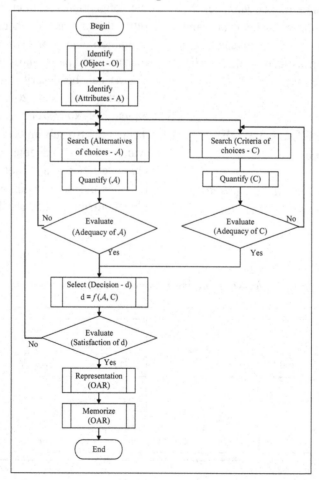

3. To quantify $\mathcal{A}$ and C and determine if the search should be go on.
4. To build a set of decisions by using $\mathcal{A}$ and C as obtained in previous searches.
5. To select the preferred decision(s) on the basis of satisfaction of decision makers.
6. To represent the decision(s) in a new sub-OAR model.
7. To memorize the sub-OAR model in LTM.

A detailed cognitive process model of decision making is shown in Figure 3 where a double-ended rectangle block represents a function call that involve a predefined process as provided in the LRMB model.

The first step in the cognitive process of decision making is to understand the given decision-making problem. According to the cognitive process of comprehension (Wang et al., 2003), the object (goal) of decision will be identified and an initial OAR model will be created. The object, its attributes, and known relations are retrieved and represented in the OAR model. Then, alternatives and strategies are searched, which result in two sets of $\mathcal{A}$ and C, respectively. The results of search will be quantified in order to form a decision as given in Eq. 2, for example: $d = f\colon \mathcal{A} \times C \to \mathcal{A}$, where $\mathcal{A} \subseteq U$ and $\mathcal{A} \neq \varnothing$.

When the decision d is derived, the previous OAR model will be updated with d and related information. Then, the decision maker may consider whether the decision is satisfied according to the current states of nature and personal judgment. If yes, the OAR model for the decision is memorized in the LTM. Otherwise, the decision-making process has to be repeated until a satisfied decision is found, or the decision maker chooses to quit without a final decision. During the decision making process, both the mind state of the decision maker and the global OAR model in the brain change from time to time. Although the state of nature will not be changed in a short period during decision making, the perception

towards it may be changed with the effect of the updated OAR model.

As described in the LRMB model (Wang et al., 2004), the process of decision making is a higher-layer cognitive process defined at Layer 6. The decision making process interacts with other processes underneath this layer such as search, representation, and memorization, as well as the processes at the same layer such as comprehension, qualification, quantification, and problem solving. Relationships between the decision-making process and other related processes have been described in Figure 1 and in Wang and Wang (2004) and Wang et al. (2004).

FORMAL DESCRIPTION OF THE COGNITIVE DECISION MAKING PROCESS

On the basis of the cognitive model of decision making as described in Figure 3, a rigorous cognitive process can be specified by using RTPA (Wang, 2002; Wang, 2003b). RTPA is designed for describing the architectures, static and dynamic behaviors of software systems (Wang, 2002), as well as human cognitive behaviors and sequences of actions (Wang, 2003b; Wang et al., 2003).

The formal model of the cognitive process of decision making in RTPA is presented in Figure 4. According to LRMB and the OAR model of internal knowledge representation in the brain, the result of a decision in the mind of the decision maker is a new sub-OAR model, or an updated version of the global OAR model of knowledge in the human brain.

As shown in Figure 4, a decision-making process (DMP) is started by defining the goal of decision in terms of the object attributes. Then, an exhaustive search of the alternative decisions ($\mathcal{A}$) and useful criteria (C) are carried out in parallel. The searches are conducted in both the brain of a decision maker internally, and through external resources based on the knowledge, experiences,

Figure 4. Formal description of the cognitive process of decision-making in RTPA

The Decision Making Process (DMP)

DMP_Process(I:: O$; O:: OAR(d$)ST) ≙
{ // **I. Form decision goal(s)**
↦ Identify (O)   // The decision making goal
↦ Identify (A)   // Sub decision making goals

→ { $\overset{I}{R}$ (↦ Search ($\mathcal{A}$)
      Satisfaction of As = **F**

                              ↦ Quantify ($\mathcal{A}$)

                              ↦ Evaluate ($\mathcal{A}$)
)

‖ $\overset{I}{R}$ (↦ Search (C)
      Satisfaction of C = **F**

                              ↦ Quantify (C)

                              ↦ Evaluate (C)
)
}

// **II. Select decisions**
→ d = f: $\mathcal{A} \times C \to \mathcal{A}$ // Refers to Eq. 2
↦ Evaluate (d)
→ (◆ s(d) ≥ k   // k: a satisfaction threshold
      ↦ Memorize (OAR**ST**)
      → ⊗
   | ◆ ~   // Otherwise
      → (◆ GiveUp**BL** = **F**
            ↦ DMP_Process(I:: O$; O:: OAR(d)**ST**)
         | ◆ ~
            →
)
)

// **III. Represent decisions**
   → R = <d, $\mathcal{A}$, C>   // Form new relation on d
   → OAR**ST** = <O, A, R>   // Form new OAR model for d
}

and goal expectation. The results of searches are quantitatively evaluated until the searching for both $\mathcal{A}$ and C are satisfied. If nonempty sets are obtained for both $\mathcal{A}$ and C, the n decisions in d have already existed as determinable by Eqs. 2 and 3.

It is noteworthy that learning results, experiences, and skills of the decision maker may dramatically reduce the exhaustive search process in DMP based on known heuristic strategies.

When one or more suitable decisions are selected from the set of d by decision makers via evaluating the satisfaction levels, satisfied decisions will be represented in a sub-OAR model, which will be added to the entire knowledge of the decision maker in LTM.

SOLVING COMPLEX PLANNING PROBLEMS BY DECISION SUPPORT SYSTEMS

The decision-making models and the formal description of the cognitive decision-making process as presented in the second through fourth sections, can be used to address the solution of wicked planning problems in software engineering. Wicked planning problems are not only difficult to solve but also difficult to be explicitly formulated. The notion of a wicked planning problem was introduced by Rittel and Webber (1984), where several characteristics were given to classify a problem as wicked. One of them states that there is no definite formulation of the problem. Another one states that wicked problems have no stopping rule. So, in these cases, does it make sense to look into a more systematic approach at all or shouldn't we just rely on human intuition and personnel experience to figure out a decision?

A systematic approach for solving the wicked planning problem of software release planning was given in Ngo-The and Ruhe (2006). Release planning is known to be cognitively and computationally difficult (Ruhe & Ngo-The 2004). Different kinds of uncertainties make it hard to be formulated and solved because real-world release planning problems may involve several hundred factors potentially affecting the decisions for the next release. Thus, a good release plan in decision-making is characterized as:

- It provides a maximum utility value from offering a best possible blend of features in the right sequence of releases.
- It is feasible to the existing hard constrains that have to be fulfilled.
- It satisfies some additional soft constraints sufficiently well. These soft constraints, for example, can be related to stakeholder satisfaction, consideration of the risk of implementing the suggested releases, balancing of resources or other aspects which are either hard to formalize or not known in advance.

It seems that uncertain software engineering decision problems are difficult to be explicitly modeled and completely formalized, since the constraints of organizations, people, technology, functionality, time, budget, and resources. Therefore, all spectrum of decision strategies as identified in Table 1 and Figure 1 need to be examined. This is a typical case where the idea of decision support arises when human decisions have to be made in complex, uncertain, and/or dynamic environments. Carlsson and Turban (2002) point out that the acceptance of theses systems is primarily limited by human related factors: (1) cognitive constraints, (2) understanding the support of such a model, (3) difficulty in handling large amounts of information and knowledge, and (4) frustration caused by complicated theories.

The solution approach presented in Ngo-The et al. (2006) address the inherent cognitive and computational complexity by (1) an evolutionary problem solving method combining rigorous solution methods to solve the actual formalization of the problem combined with the interactive involvement of the human experts in this process; (2) offering a portfolio of diversified and qualified solution at all iterations of the solution process; and (3) using the multi-criteria decision aid method ELECTRE (Roy, 1991) to assist the project manager in the selection of the final solution from the set of qualified solutions. Further research is ongoing to integrate these results with the framework of the decision-making models and the improved understanding of the cognitive process of decision-making as developed in this article.

CONCLUSION

Decision-making is one of the basic cognitive processes of human behaviors by which a preferred option or a course of actions is chosen from among a set of alternatives based on certain criteria. The interest in the study of decision-making has been widely shared in various disciplines because it is a fundamental process of the brain.

This article has developed an axiomatic and rigorous model for the cognitive decision-making process, which explains the nature and course in human and machine-based decision-making on the basis of recent research results in cognitive informatics. A rigorous description of the decision process in real-time process algebra (RTPA) has been presented. Various decision-making theories have been comparatively analyzed and a unified decision-making model has been obtained, which shows that existing theories and techniques on decision-making are well fit in the formally described decision process.

One of the interesting findings of this work is that the most fundamental decision that is recurrently used in any complex decision system and everyday life is a Cartesian product of a set of alternatives and a set of selection criteria. The larger both the sets, the more ideal the decisions generated. Another interesting finding of this work is that, although the cognitive complexities of new decision problems are always extremely high, they become dramatically simpler when a rational or formal solution is figured out. Therefore, the reducing of cognitive complexities of decision problems by heuristic feedbacks of known solutions in each of the categories of decision strategies will be further studied in intelligent decision support systems. According to case studies related to this work, the models and cognitive processes of decision-making provide in this article can be applied in a wide range of decision-support and expert systems.

ACKNOWLEDGMENT

This work is partially sponsored by Natural Sciences and Engineering Research Council of Canada (NSERC) and Information Circle of Research Excellence (iCORE) of Alberta. The authors would like to thank the anonymous reviewers for their valuable suggestions and comments on this work.

REFERENCES

Berger, J. (1990). *Statistical decision theory--Foundations, concepts, and methods*. Springer-Verlag.

Carlsson, C., & Turban, E. (2002). DSS: Directions for the next decade. *Decision Support Systems, 33*, 105-110.

Edwards, W., & Fasolo, B. (2001). Decision technology. *Annual Review of Psychology, 52*, 581-606.

Hastie, R. (2001). Problems for judgment and decision-making. *Annual Review of Psychology, 52*, 653-683.

Lipschutz, S. (1967). *Schaum's outline of set theory and related topics*. McGraw-Hill Inc.

Matlin, M. W. (1998). *Cognition* (4th ed.). Orlando, FL: Harcourt Brace College Publishers.

Ngo-The, A., & Ruhe, G. (2006). A systematic approach for solving the wicked problem of software release planning. Submitted to *Journal of Soft Computing*.

Osborne, M., & Rubinstein, A. (1994). *A course in game theory*. MIT Press.

Payne, D. G., & Wenger, M. J. (1998). *Cognitive psychology*. New York: Houghton Mifflin Co.

Pinel, J. P. J. (1997). *Biopsychology* (3rd ed.). Needham Heights, MA: Allyn and Bacon.

Rittel, H., & Webber, M. (1984). Planning problems are wicked problems. In N. Cross (Ed.), *Developments in design methodology* (pp 135-144), Chichester, UK: Wiley.

Roy, B. (1991). The outranking approach and the foundations of ELECTRE methods. *Theory and Decision, 31*, 49-73.

Ruhe, G. (2003). Software engineering decision support—Methodologies and applications. In

Tonfoni and Jain (Eds.), *Innovations in decision support systems*, *3*, 143-174.

Ruhe, G., & An, N. T. (2004). Hybrid intelligence in software release planning. *International Journal of Hybrid Intelligent Systems*, *1*(2), 99-110.

Squire, L. R., Knowlton, B., & Musen, G. (1993). The structure and organization of memory. *Annual Review of Psychology*, *44*, 453-459.

von Neumann, J., & Morgenstern, O. (1980). Theory of games and economic behavior. Princeton University Press.

Wald, A. (1950). Statistical decision functions. John Wiley & Sons.

Wang, Y. (2002). The real-time process algebra. *Annals of Software Engineering*, *14*, 235-274.

Wang, Y. (2003a). On cognitive informatics. *Brain and Mind: A Transdisciplinary Journal of Neuroscience and Neurophilosophy*, *4*(2), 151-167.

Wang, Y. (2003b). Using process algebra to describe human and software behavior, *Brain and Mind: A Transdisciplinary Journal of Neuroscience and Neurophilosophy*, *4*(2), 199-213.

Wang, Y. (2005a). Mathematical models and properties of games. In *Proceedings of the 4th IEEE International Conference on Cognitive Informatics* (ICCI'05) (pp. 294-300), IEEE CS Press, Irvin, California, USA, August.

Wang, Y. (2005b). A novel decision grid theory for dynamic decision-making. In *Proceedings of the 4th IEEE International Conference on Cognitive Informatics* (ICCI'05) (pp. 308-314), IEEE CS Press, Irvin, California, USA, August.

Wang, Y. (2007a). *Software engineering foundations: A software science perspective.* CRC Software Engineering Series, Vol. II/III, CRC Press, USA.

Wang, Y. (2007b). The theoretical framework of cognitive informatics. *The International Journal of Cognitive Informatics and Natural Intelligence* (IJCINI), *1*(1), 1-27.

Wang, Y., & Gafurov, D. (2003). The cognitive process of comprehension. In *Proceedings of the 2nd IEEE International Conference on Cognitive Informatics* (ICCI'03) (pp. 93-97), London, UK.

Wang, Y., & Wang, Y. (2004). Cognitive informatics models of the brain. *IEEE Transactions on Systems, Man, and Cybernetics (C)*, *36*(2), 203-207.

Wang, Y., Liu, D., & Wang, Y. (2003). Discovering the capacity of human memory. *Brain and Mind: A Transdisciplinary Journal of Neuroscience and Neurophilosophy*, *4*(2), 189-198.

Wang, Y., Wang, Y., Patel, S., & Patel, D. (2004). A layered reference model of the brain (LRMB). *IEEE Transactions on Systems, Man, and Cybernetics (C)*, *36*(2), 124-133.

Wilson, R. A., & Keil, F. C. (2001). *The MIT Encyclopedia of the Cognitive Sciences.* MIT Press.

Zachary, W., Wherry, R., Glenn, F., Hopson, J. (1982). Decision situations, decision processes, and decision functions: Towards a theory-based framework for decision-aid design. In *Proceedings of the 1982 Conference on Human Factors in Computing Systems*.

This work was previously published in International Journal of Cognitive Informatics and Natural Intelligence, Vol. 1, Issue 2, edited by Y. Wang, pp. 73-85, copyright 2007 by IGI Publishing, formerly known as Idea Group Publishing (an imprint of IGI Global).

Section V
Critical Issues

Chapter XVII
Information System Development Failure and Complexity:
A Case Study

Abou Bakar Nauman
COMSATS Institute of Information Technology, Pakistan

Romana Aziz
COMSATS Institute of Information Technology, Pakistan

A.F.M. Ishaq
COMSATS Institute of Information Technology, Pakistan

ABSTRACT

This chapter examines the causes of failure in a Web-based information system development project and finds out how complexity can lead a project towards failure. Learning from an Information System Development Project (ISDP) failure plays a key role in the long-term success of any organization desirous of continuous improvement via evaluation and monitoring of its information systems (IS) development efforts. This study reports on a seemingly simple (but only deceptively so) failed ISDP to inform the reader about the various complexities involved in ISDPs in general, and in developing countries in particular. An existing framework from contemporary research is adopted to map the complexities found in the project under study and the critical areas, which lead to the decreased reliability and failure in Web-based information system development, are highlighted.

INTRODUCTION

Information and Communication Technologies (ICTs) are globally recognized as an enabler of economic and social growth, and Information Systems (IS) can play a key role in accelerated growth and development if applied properly. In the developing countries, there is much talk of "development leapfrogging" by deployment of

Information and Communication Technologies (ICT). Developing countries are making direct deployment of the latest technologies, techniques, and methodologies for the use of information systems without the step-by-step use of previous technologies already abandoned in the Western-developed countries. In this scenario, most development efforts in the field of Information Systems are overshadowed by organizational dissatisfaction and schedule and cost overruns resulting in project abandonment and failure. The following quote from a UN report (Gilhooly, 2005, p. 25), mentioning Least Developed Countries (LDC), sums up the severity of the situation:

Failure to urgently and meaningfully exploit the available means to bridge the digital divide may consign many developing countries, particularly LDCs, to harmful and even permanent exclusion from the network revolution.

In this chapter, our focus is Information System Development Project (ISDP) failure from the perspective of a developing country. Learning from an ISDP failure plays a key role in the long-term success of any organization desirous of continuous improvement via evaluation and monitoring of its information systems development efforts. The "learning from failure" factor assumes a higher level of significance in the context of developing countries. In developing countries it is very important that the scarce resources are optimally utilized in such a way that the probability of failure is minimized. This study reports on a seemingly simple (but only deceptively so) failed ISDP to inform the reader about the various complexities involved in information systems development projects in general and in developing countries in particular.

This chapter is organized in five sections. In section two we describe the general information system development process and the associated rate of failure in this industry. Section three discusses the relationship between failure and

complexity. A case study is presented in section four, followed by conclusions in section five.

BACKGROUND

Most of the IS research reported in the literature falls in three main categories, that is, positivist, interpretive, and critical, and there is widespread consensus that interpretive style with a critical stance is most suited for researching the IS-related issues in developing countries. The research is interpretive in nature, and an interview approach is used for investigations. The research is of significance to a wide audience in the IS community who are interested in understanding the impact and influence of various factors on failure of an ISDP in the peculiar environment of a developing country.

An organization may have one or many business processes (work processes) producing products, services, or information. In order to run properly, these processes need support from:

- **External environment,** including regulatory policies, supplier, and competitor behavior; and
- **Internal environment,** in the form of resources and managerial and organizational commitment.

Information systems support or automate the business or work processes by processing the information which is usually limited to capturing, transmitting, storing, retrieving, manipulating, and displaying information. An innovative information system usually changes the existing business/work processes in order to make them more suitable for automation.

A typical organization is created, established, and eventually evolved through a mix of indigenous factors like social, cultural, technical, and political mechanisms and interventions. IS are tools that contribute to the effectiveness and efficiency of the certain processes of an organization; therefore, IS development efforts in the organizations of a developing country have to be oriented towards local innovation needs and prevalent professional techniques and methods. These techniques and methods bear a strong influence of the above-mentioned indigenous factors. In order to understand and analyze information systems in organizational context, it is useful to first review the issues that cast a strong influence on the implementation and success or failure of an IS. The theory of information systems has discussed these issues in different pedagogical forms. For example, Alter's theory (Alter, 1999) defines an information system as a particular type of work system that "processes information by performing various combinations of six types of operations: capturing, transmitting, storing, retrieving, manipulating, and displaying information". The fourteen statements characterizing a work system in general and an information system in particular, as described by Alter (Alter, 1999, p. 8) are given below:

1. **Definition of work system:** A work system is a system in which human participants and/or machines perform a business process using information, technology, and other resources to produce products and/or services for internal or external customers. Organizations typically contain multiple work systems and operate through them.

2. **Elements of a work system:** Understanding a work system requires at least cursory understanding of six elements: the business process, participants, information, technology, products, and customers.

3. **Environment of a work system:** Understanding a work system usually requires an understanding of its environment, including the external infrastructure that it relies upon in order to operate and the managerial, organizational, regulatory, and competitive context that affect its operation.

4. **Fit between elements of a work system:** The smooth and painless operation of a work system depends on the mutual balance and alignment between the various elements of the system plus adequate support from the external environment.

5. **Definition of an information system as a work system:** An information system is a work system whose internal functions are limited to processing information by performing six types of operations: capturing, transmitting, storing, retrieving, manipulating, and displaying information.

6. **Roles of information systems in work systems they serve:** An information system exists to produce information and/or to support or automate the work performed by other work systems.

7. **Degree of integration between an information system and a work system it serves:** The information system may serve as an external source of information; it may be an interactive tool; it may be an integral component of the work system; the information system and work system may overlap so much that they are virtually indistinguishable. The information system may also serve as shared infrastructure used in many diverse work systems.

8. **Content vs. plumbing in information systems:** An information system can be viewed as consisting of content and plumbing. Its content is the information it provides and the way that information affects the business process within the work system. Its plumbing is the details that concern information technology rather than the way information affects the business process.

9. **Impact of an information system:** An information system's direct impact on work system performance is determined primarily by how well it performs its role in the work systems it supports.

Table 1. Phases of information system development

Phase	Activities
Initiation	• Detection of performance gap • Formation of attitudes • Development of proposal • Strategic decision-making
Description: The efficiency of certain work/business processes and tasks can be improved with an information system. These candidate processes and tasks are identified in the initiation phase, and an analysis is carried out about the extent and nature of changes that are necessary for improved efficiency; also, the people likely to be affected by these changes are also considered. A cost benefit analysis is carried out to ensure that the benefits of the proposed information system outweigh its costs, and then necessary resources are allocated for the project.	
Development	• Development of abstract system • Development of concrete system • Establishment of project infrastructure
Description : In this phase, the information system and supporting documents are produced and the related procedures are defined.	
Implementation	Introduction of concrete system to operational and organizational context
Description: In this phase, the new system is introduced in the workplace and users are trained to use it.	
Operation	Operation, maintenance, and enhancement
Description: In this phase, the new system is accepted and is running smoothly in the work environment. In case a major change is required by the users, a new iteration of the four phases will start.	

10. **Definition of a project as a work system:** A project is a time-limited work system designed to produce a particular product and then go out of existence.

11. **Phases of a project that creates or significantly changes a work system:** A project that creates or significantly changes a work system goes through four idealized phases: initiation, development, implementation, and operation and maintenance.

12. **Impact of the balance of content and plumbing in a project:** For projects of any particular size, those in which both content and plumbing change significantly have more conceptual and managerial complexity than projects in which the changes are mostly about content or mostly about plumbing.

13. **Work system success:** The success of a work system depends on the relative strength of internal and external forces supporting the system versus internal and external forces and obstacles opposing the system.

14. **Inheritance of generalizations, truisms, and success factors:** Generalizations, truisms, and success factors related to work systems also apply to information systems and to projects (because these are work systems).

Information System Development Project

According to Alter, an Information System Development Project is also a work system, though a time-limited one. The development process of an information system incorporates a high level of innovation, and therefore inherently possesses uncertainty of results. Chris Sauer (1993) divides this process into four stages as shown in Table 1. These stages are identified by the objectives and problems they posses, and at each of the four stages there are some influences from supporters, users, and developers on this innovation process.

ISDP Failure, Definitions, and Classification

All human endeavors, scientific, technological, or other result in success or failure. This success or failure outcome is also related with technological and organizational efforts regarding development of information systems. Generally success is praised at every level, and itself defends its characteristics and long-term effects; however, it is considered better to disown a failure. In a particular project, both success and failure can be companions, that is, when the project is facing a status of partial failure. Richard Heeks (2000) describes these three statuses of an information system as:

- **Total failure:** In this type of failure, a system is either not implemented or it is discarded soon after the implementation.
- **Partial failure:** In some cases a system is implemented and used for some period of time; however, the system fails to meet some of its primary objectives. This type of failure can also result in producing some undesirable byproducts or features in that system. In other words, the system only covers a subset of its objectives. Partially-failed projects are also referred to as challenged projects in literature.
- **Success:** The success is straightforward, a status of project where all the objectives of all the stakeholders are fulfilled by the resulting system.

Many researchers have believed that the study of failed information system projects can enrich information systems' body of knowledge by making us aware of the dynamic and cross-cutting reasons that lead to partial or full failure. An information systems development project can fail due to any number of reasons and the possible list can easily stretch to triple figures. Therefore, in order to understand the reasons that lead to failure in information systems development it is important to first understand the different categories of failure. One classification of failures is proposed by Chris Sauer (1993) and it defines the following five categories of failure:

- **Correspondence failure:** When a particular ISDP is not able to achieve its predefined objectives, it is categorized as correspondence failure, for example, the selected project was not able to meet the objectives defined in the contract.
- **Process failure:** When a development process is not able to produce the desired system or could not meet the resource limitations, it is categorized as process failure.
- **Interaction failure:** Sometimes, it happens that the users are not satisfied with the delivered system or some portion of the delivered system, which leads the users to lose interest in that system, and hence the level of system use is decreased subsequently. This situation is referred to as interaction failure.
- **Expectation failure:** A project always starts with some tough and high expectations of its stakeholders; however, the resultant product may not be able to fulfill the expectations of any or all stakeholders, thus resulting in expectation failure.
- **Terminal failure:** This is the case when a project is abandoned or cancelled before the final delivery. Termination of a project is the last thing that can happen to a failing project, that is, when there are no hopes of

meeting any of the objectives of the project, it is terminated.

ISDP Failure Statistics

Many researchers have attempted to study the extent of failure in the IS industry. A milestone study in this area is the Chaos Report of 1994 by the Standish Group (1994). They surveyed 365 companies and conducted a number of focus groups and interviews in order to determine:

- The scope of software project failures
- The major factors that cause software projects to fail

The Chaos Report stated that 16.2% of projects were successful, that is, these projects completed on-time and on-budget, with all features and functions as initially specified. 52.7% of projects were partial failures, that is, these projects were completed and they became operational, but were over-budget, over the time estimate, and offered fewer features and functions than originally specified. 31.1% of projects failed, that is, they were canceled at some point during the development cycle. This research survey also tried to determine the most important success, partial failure, and failure criteria. Table 2 lists the three criteria in descending order of importance.

To emphasize the gravity of the prevailing problem of failure in IS projects, some more re-

Table 2. Criteria of success and failure

	Success	Partial Failure	Failure
1.	User Involvement	Lack of User Input	Incomplete Requirements and Specifications
2.	Executive Management Support	Incomplete Requirements and Specifications	Lack of User Involvement
3.	Clear Statement of Requirements	Changing Requirements and Specifications	Lack of Resources
4.	Proper Planning	Lack of Executive Support	Unrealistic Expectations
5.	Realistic Expectations	Technology Incompetence	Lack of Executive Support
6.	Smaller Project Milestones	Lack of Resources	Changing Requirements and Specifications
7.	Competent Staff	Unrealistic Expectations	Lack of Planning
8.	Ownership	Unclear Objectives	Did Not Need It Any Longer
9.	Clear Vision and Objectives	Unrealistic Time Frames	Lack of IT Management
10.	Hard-Working, Focused Staff	Use of New Technology	Technology Illiteracy

Table 3. Failure statistics

	The Robbins-Gioia Survey	The Conference Board Survey	The KPMG Canada Survey	The OASIG Survey
Year	2001	2001	1997	1995
Country	USA	USA	Canada	UK
Survey Size	232	117	176	45
Survey Method	Not Mentioned	Interview	Questionnaire	Interview
IS Type	ERP	ERP	Multiple	Multiple
Failure Rate	51%	40%	61%	70%

ports are examined and a summary of findings is presented in Table 3 (IT Cortex, 2005).

- The Robbins-Gioia Survey was primarily focused on studying the implementation of Enterprise Resource Planning Systems in 232 companies. Out of these 232 companies, only 36% had experience of ERP implementation. The success or failure of the ERP implementation was measured based on perception instead of some objective criteria. Fifty-one percent of the companies perceived their ERP implementation as unsuccessful.
- The Conference Board Survey also studied ERP implementation. The most important finding of this survey was that 40% of the projects failed to achieve the business case within one year of going live. Projects covered in this survey were 25% over budget.
- The KPMG Canada survey was focused on identifying the reasons that lead to failure of IT projects. The survey reported that 61% of the analyzed projects were judged as failure. In this survey, more than 75% of projects were late and more than 50% of projects were over budget.
- The OASIG Survey reported that 7 out of 10 IT projects fail in some respect.

These statistics show the edge of the iceberg in the ocean of information system developments. The above-mentioned reports are concluded in these statements:

- An IT project is more likely to be unsuccessful than successful;
- About one out of five IT projects is likely to bring full satisfaction; and
- The larger the project, the more likely the failure.

These surveys are from the developed economies of the world. The financial costs of these failed projects no doubt present a constant threat for the companies in these countries; however, these countries have a solid financial base. This solid financial base lets them absorb the losses incurred by the failed projects. Now let us see some of the statistics of developed countries where the financial base is not strong enough, and the impact of a single project failure can do a lot of damage.

ISDP Failure Statistics for Developing Countries

Information Technology (IT) innovation is now considered necessary for development; during the last two decades, an understanding has emerged

Table 4. Success and failure rates in developing countries

Classification	Literature	Poll	Survey
Success	15%-	20 %	15%
Partial Failure	60%+	30 %	50%
Total Failure	25%+	50 %	35%

that IT can effectively be used to narrow the gap between the industrialized and developing countries. Information systems are now an important part of the diffusion and implementation of IT. In developing countries, information system development efforts are most widespread in areas of governance, health care, education, finance, and poverty alleviation. The main thrust of these initiatives has been to apply technology appropriately in such a manner that its adoption brings the perceived socio-economic benefits. There have been cases where imported information system solutions have been used as a starting point for adaptation, but mostly developing countries and donors have focused on developing appropriate and sustainable local information systems. The emerging trend is that most of the information system initiatives have not been appropriately conceived or developed, and therefore they have failed to fulfill the desired outcomes. There is not much empirical evidence available on whether information systems failure rate is very similar or widely different in developing countries as compared with developed countries. Very little research has been conducted in general IS failure in developing countries, and in the particular area of information systems for e-government there are some statistics available.

In developing countries, e-government is a representative area of IS development as it involves sufficient financial and technical resources. Richard Heeks (2003) presents a generic situation in his report about success and failure rates of e-government projects in developing countries. This report presents findings of multiple surveys and studies which help to draw a wider picture. The estimates from past surveys present a situation that encourages Heeks to conclude that the failure rate in developing countries is higher than in the developed countries. The success and failure rates estimated in the Richard Heeks (2003) report from past surveys are in Table 4.

Results of some more existing studies from developing countries are summarized as:

- Braa and Hedberg (2000) have reported wide-spread partial failure of high-cost health information systems in South Africa;
- Kitiyadisai (2000) has concluded that in the public sector, IS initiatives failure cases seem to be the norm in Thailand;
- Baark and Heeks (1999) found that all donor-funded projects in China were partial failures; and
- Moussa and Schware (1992) concluded that almost all World Bank-funded projects in Africa were partial failures.

These findings tell us that at least one quarter of the projects in the developing countries tend to fail, and this rate may be as high as 50%. The success rate range is 15% to 20%. A majority of the projects tend to end in what is termed as partial failure where major goals of the project were not achieved or there were significant undesirable results. These statistics of success and failure in developing countries become even graver when other factors pertaining particularly to the under-developed world are also taken into consideration. For example, as a general rule the investments involved in big IS projects are always high from a developing country's perspective, and if the project fails, the resultant losses incur long-term negative effects on the progress of a developing country. Also, IS development companies in developing economies are small and do not have sufficiently deep pockets to survive the impact of a failed project. As a result, a high failure rate in the IS industry indirectly impedes the growth of the IS industry.

ISDP Failure and its Effects on Developing Countries

Information systems projects are initiated in developing countries typically in institutions like governance, management, healthcare, and education, and usually the general aims are to increase efficiency, introduce transparency in working, and improve accountability. The above-mentioned institutions in developing countries are very local in context and have deep historical roots. The evolution of these institutions has been different from that of the similar institutions in the developed countries. Information system projects in developing countries are usually perceived as pure technical initiatives aimed at making the functioning of an organization or institution more efficient and effective. The current prevalent IS strategies have matured in the developed countries and thus have a strong association with a particular way of management and administration style. It is difficult to embed these IS strategies in local institutions of developing countries without regarding social and organizational aspects.

The main objectives of an information system are to enhance capabilities of an organization and to help the organization save monetary resources by reducing workforce, travel, communication costs, and so forth (Mirani & Lederer, 1994). A good information system is expected to help an organization meet its information requirements at all levels and produce the appropriate information results. The information systems of e-government projects are meant to provide access to information at all levels of society with faster retrieval or delivery of information, with features like concise and better format, flexibility, and reliability. The aim is to improve the responsiveness of public organizations. These benefits are expected to fulfill the needs of a developing country, save its resources and provide better living standards to its society at minimum cost. This particular goal is an attempt to bridge the gaps of digital divide in the world and to compete in the race of progress. A typical IS project requires a high level of investment in terms of resources and efforts. Once a project is started, expected results are projected at all levels of society and stakeholders. Unfortunately, if a project fails, it generates much more relative damage in a developing country than in developed countries. With the failure, not only all the prestigious and scarce resources involved in that project are lost, but it is considered as a setback to the progress and development of the country. In the long run, this failure is considered as a bad example for future investments in that type of IS project. This scenario discourages further attempts to develop information systems projects in the developing country. Hence a developing economy takes a long time to fully recover from the effects of failure in a large-scale IS project.

Web-Based Information System and Reliability

The failure in Web-based information systems is an area which is being studied with great interest. The case study presented in this chapter provides us an in-depth analysis of the causes of deficiency in reliability of a Web-based application. This lack of reliability not only decreased the use of the application, but also made the higher management reluctant to enforce its use on a regular basis.

Web-based applications, like the academic records management portal in our case study, are a unique type of information systems which interconnect a large number of users with the organization and cater to variable access rates. As the pool of users is big, the variation of influences is also wide ranging, which makes the user preferences a significant factor in the development of such applications.

With the increasing use of Web interfaces across organizations, for example, corporate and supporting applications, comes a dramatic increase in the number of users of the resulting systems. Due to this trend of connecting more and more of an organization's staff and clients together via Web interfaces, the system design models are becoming more user-centric, and place user requirements higher on the priorities list. Moreover, user satisfaction is also a major performance and quality indicator. This trend is also evident in our case study. As we report, the development team tended to focus totally on the user satisfaction and kept on incorporating the new and changing user requirements in the project design even to the last stages of development. This factor brought the Web application closer to failure due to a decrease in reliability.

Learning Lessons from a Failure

The IS failure in developing countries carries more importance for learning and investigation of failure causes, as it not only wastes the scarce and precious allocated resources but also discourages further investment. The opportunity costs are certainly higher in developing countries because of the more limited availability of resources such as capital and skilled manpower. This situation is best described (Heeks, 2000, p. 4) in the following words:

The failures keep developing countries on the wrong side of the digital divide, turning ICTs into a technology of global inequality.

For these types of reasons, a failure in development of IS in developing country poses a significantly important area of study. In countries like Pakistan, where domestic market and domestic IS demand has traditionally been very low, ISDP failures discourage further demands and growth in IS industry. This scenario has established the need for studying ISDP in Pakistan, especially the failed ones. We believe that there are more opportunities and lessons for learning from failed IS projects, than there are from the successful IS projects. We are not aware of an existing study that has reported on the extent of failed IS projects in Pakistan. This chapter is a first step to fill this gap. We have chosen one small and simple IS project to study ISDP failure in Pakistan. We would also like to point out that a single case study can provide no basis for estimation of overall failure/success rates in Pakistan, and further work needs to done in this direction.

ISDP FAILURE AND COMPLEXITY

In this section we discuss the type of factors that can participate in an information system development failure and the associated role of project complexity in failure.

ISDP Factors and Dependencies

In this section we discuss what type of factors can participate in an information system development failure. During the four stages of the information system development process (initiation, development, implementation and operation), the development process is influenced by various factors; however, the degree of influence of these factors varies at different stages. There is no definite list of factors and no definite degree of influence which they make on the process. In order to understand the different possible factors, it is useful to discuss them from different perspectives. One

Figure 1. Triangle of dependencies

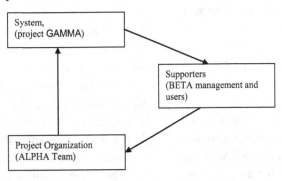

perspective is that of the user factors (Havelka, 2002); these include:

- Biasness of users towards system performance;
- Commitment of users towards providing support to project;
- Communication skills of the users: whether or not the users can elaborate the needs and shortcomings of delivered system;
- Computer literacy levels of the users: whether or not the users can understand barriers and bottlenecks of common systems;
- Extent of users' participation in requirement gathering phase to the training phase;
- Users' know-how about the organizational processes and work flows; and
- Users' understanding of the requirements of the new information system.

Ananth Srinivasan (1987) has discussed organizational factors and the type of effects that these make on the IS development process. These include:

- Available resources (both human and financial): The human resources affect the development process positively, but increased financial resources are related to team disagreement;

- External influences on the development process: The degree of external influence on the system development effort needs to be carefully monitored and controlled; and
- Project team's exposure to information systems: Systems exposure in the firm allows an increase in the degree of awareness among project group members about the different problems encountered by users and systems staff.

There are also some exogenous factors involved in influencing the development process as discussed by Chris Sauer (1993). These factors are cognitive limits, technical process environment, organizational politics, structure, and history. The environment is a collection of some other factors such as suppliers, technology, customers, competitors, interests, regulators, and culture.

All of these factors exist in their respective contexts and influence the information system development project. This is not a definite list; however, it helps to understand that there exist different factors when the system is studied with different perspectives. To examine the roles and dependencies of these factors in an integrated environment of information system development project, Chris Sauer presented Triangle of Dependencies (Sauer, 1993). The triangle of dependencies presents a cycle of interaction between supporters/users, the project development organization, and the system (under development) itself.

Model of IS Project: Triangle of Dependencies

The project organization (ALPHA in this case study) is defined as a group of people who, at a particular point in time, are occupied with the development, operation, or maintenance of a given information system (project GAMMA in this case). The information system must serve some organizational stakeholders and thereby function as a resource for the project organization in gathering support. Supporters (BETA and its employees in this case) provide support in terms of monetary resources, material resources, information, and so forth. This triangle is depicted in Figure 1, and it is not a closed triangle. Each relationship is subject to a variety of exogenous factors which influence how it will affect the rest of the triangle. It was obvious that some resources were given to ALPHA development team by BETA management and the development of project GAMMA started. ALPHA delivered documentations and presentations on the working and status of the project to BETA at different milestones, to win the support from them by satisfying their needs.

It is important to keep in mind that information systems are developed and exists to fulfill the needs of stakeholders, and it is important for stakeholders to support the system in return. As the project organization plays the creator role for the system development, it is not possible to do it without any support from the users. Thus this situation exists like a triangle where the user organization supports the developers so that they can develop a system which fulfills their needs. If the system satisfies the users, they support the developer's organization in the development process, which enhances the system for further needs.

Dependencies of the Factors

This triangle clearly presents three sides of the software development process. It starts with the flow of support from supporters to project organization, the second side is the relation of system to supporters and the third side is the relationship of project organization to the information system. In the next paragraphs, the sides and corners of this triangle are discussed in detail.

The project organization is the group of people who are involved in the development of the system. Different people play different roles in the complete information system process, for example, development, implementation, and maintenance. The team leader plays an important role; he guides the whole team towards a particular goal. The competency of the team in understanding the problem and scope of the problem, as well as the development model they follow, are two of the major factors beside many others which influence the project.

The supporters are the people who support the project organization by providing them with resources as well as problem scope and definition. The resources, including monetary resources, material resources, information, social legitimacy, and control of strategic contingencies, are provided by the supporters to the project development organization. The supporters can also be categorized as funders (because they provide financial resources), power brokers (because they exert influence on project organization), and fixers (because they provide information and control decisions) (Sauer, 1993). Users of the system are an important part of the supporters as they not only provide basic information and requirements but also provide feedback to the funders and power brokers to make long-term decisions. It is important to note that the factors like organizational politics, nature and sources of power, history, and environment of the organization are the factors which make direct influences on the triangle.

The relationships among the system, project organization, and supporters are also interesting to examine. Each relationship contains different types of characteristics and factors which also influence the whole system. For the supporters-project organization relationship, the most significant thing is the flow of support. If the system satisfies the supporters, then the support for the system is there; if the system does not meet the goals, as perceived by the supporters, then the flow of support becomes problematic. The supporters-project organization relationship is based on human cognitive behaviors and is directly affected by organizational structure and politics. The second relationship is the system-supporters relationship, which also depends on the organizational factors. The needs of the organization for the system may change with time, due to which the system may become unacceptable. There can be some political changes due to which the degree of satisfaction may diminish. Factors related to users (biasness, skills, commitment, and understanding of needs) as well as the technical process by which the system is being evaluated directly influence this relationship. The relationship between project organization and system has a technical orientation, as it mainly consists of a technical process of information system development. This process consists of designing, creating, implementing, and making changes as required by the supporters. In this relationship, factors like communication and cooperation among team members, tools for development, requirement specification, the team's exposure to information systems, development process, and skills have influences. There are also some factors which come from the other sides of triangle to affect this relationship, for example, structural changes in the user organization can cause changes in requirements, and the system may need to be modified accordingly. The project organization might be at a stage where it cannot afford any shortage of support from the supporters, and the system may also be at a stage where it needs major changes and as a result may overshoot schedule. These types of problems demand a great skill set from the team leader.

Flaw

As discussed in the previous section, there are many factors which influence an information system development project, and these factors have different dependencies among each other. Every factor influences the project, and its effect is important for the success or failure of the project. Thus one cannot say that a particular factor should be ignored or its influence should be negated. These influences create a state of balance between different stakeholders and can make a project successful. However, at some stage the effect of these influences makes some aspects of the process uncontrollable, but at the same time, helps other factors to render positive influences. These unbalanced influences create flaws in the process, and the result is a flawed system/project (Sauer, 1993). The factors which highly influence a system and then tend to create flaws and make hurdles in the success of an IS project are termed as risks (Ward, 1995).

Information systems development process is open to flaws, and every information system is flawed in some way. However flaws are different from failure. Flaws are a characteristic of the system itself and also of the innovation process. Flaws are never desired by any stakeholder, for example, project organization, users, or supporters. Flaws are corrected at a cost or are accepted at some other cost. One technical type of flaw is a bug, which either stops a running program or destroys the results. Another type of flaw is any system characteristic which the users find inconvenient or otherwise undesirable, for example, a particular data entry form. This kind of flaw can also be corrected or accepted at a cost. There may also be flaws in the development process that are introduced by a decision about how to proceed in a particular step in the process. A particular decision

Figure 2. Taxonomy of ISD projects complexity

	Structural	Dynamic
Organizational	Structural Organizational Complexity	Dynamic Organizational Complexity
vs.		
Technology	Structural IT Complexity	Dynamic IT Complexity

Structural vs. Dynamic

may give the desired result with perhaps a greater cost, or may produce some other flaws.

Thus flaws are problems which occur as a consequence of events in the development process. Unless there is support available to cope with them, they will have the effect of reducing the system's capacity to serve its supporters or of resulting in further flaws. As this capacity to serve the supporters decreases and cost of managing the flaws increases, the project becomes more prone to failure. No stakeholder can continue to support the costs of flaws forever. In the long run, they will start to take notice of rising costs and undesirable results and reduce their support. When the support dries up, the system lacks the necessary resources and tends towards failure.

Complexity

We have discussed flaws in information systems and their negative effects on information system development, and one may reach the logical argument that flaws of a system should be removed. However, as these flaws are caused by interconnected factors, removing a flaw can generate negative effects on other parts of system. This situation renders complexity into the information system development process, where removing one flaw can develop other flaws. The definition of complexity varies in different contexts. Baccarini (1996, p 202) defines complexity as:

The complexity can be defined as an interaction of several parts which can be made operational differently and in interdependent ways.

Suppose we have a particular system in which there are many components. All these components have some intra-component dependencies. Each component may be independent and may have a particular behavior and influence in the whole system. Every component is not only dependent on its internal dependencies but is also affected by other components. These inter-component dependencies help the components to make a complete system for a particular purpose. All these components interact with each other to fulfill requirements and dependencies of other components. As all the components are independent, and have their own intra-component structure, they can work and behave differently if some changes occur in their internal composition. When these components work in a system, they can operate in different ways, and can have different effects on the system at different times. One or more than one independent component can lead to a situation where it has different effects on the system, and these influences can create an imbalance in the system's working. Now the problem solving can produce a complex situation, that is, which factors of a component should be negated to let the system keep working?

A similar situation arises in an information system development project, where the project is a collection of many different sub-processes and components. Each sub-process is not only separate but also dependent on the other components of project. In this type of system, the complexity is a situation where we have to leave a negative effect of a component on the system to let the system not be destroyed due to negative effects of other components. Thus the complexity of most information systems means that:

Cost of leaving a flaw uncorrected may be significant because of consequential effects it might have on other parts of system. (Sauer, 1993, pp. 63-64).

Suppose in a particular project a new requirement is made by the user and the project is delayed because of this particular requirement. Now if the requirement is not provided in the system, the user is not willing to accept the project, and if the requirement is fulfilled the project is delayed. This is a complex situation where we need to leave one flaw to avoid consequential cascading effects on the project. The factors involved in creating imperfection lead toward increasing the complexity of an ISDP and subsequently decrease its probability of success.

Complexity and Failure Relationship

Although flaws are in every system, they are not the cause of every failure; however, flaws lead a system towards failure. The relationship between flaws and complexity has been discussed in the previous section, and we saw that complexity also leads an information system towards failure. The complexity which is caused by the flaws is one of the major risk factors involved in the failure of information system development projects. Presence of complexity is considered one of the biggest risk factors involved in project failure (Barki, Rivard, & Talbot, 1993). Level of complexity and time duration of project are directly related to failure. As the complexity of the project increases, the time duration needed to solve the

problems also increases, and on the other hand the sense of urgency also creeps up and wrong decisions are made. One way to reduce the level of project risk and failure is to reduce the level of complexity (Murray, 1993). British Computer Society (2003) found that the most common attribute underlying the failed projects was the high level of inherent complexity in the failed projects. Thus it is obvious that to improve ISDP success rate and the rate of return on IS investment, organizations must address the problem of complexity in ISDP and reduce it within manageable limits (Xia & Lee, 2004).

Virtually every IS project will increase in complexity once it has been initiated. Sense of urgency in announcing the end date and addition of post-initiation components/technology are two major causes of complexity for an IS system (Murray, 1993). Size is also a source of increasing complexity, because to solve a bigger problem the project is decomposed in smaller components, and thus complexity of interaction between the components increases (AlSharif, Walter, & Turky, 2004). This implies that complexity is one of the major causes of failure of information systems, thus studying the complexity of an information system can reveal the causes of failure. Dissecting a particular failure in the light of complexity will help us to understand the areas and flaws which should be provided more careful analysis in the development process.

Classification of Complexity

Complexity is one of the major reasons for information system development project failure, which encourages one to study an information system development project and analyze different complexities related to it. For this purpose we select a framework for ISDP complexity to classify different complexities. In this classification the ISDP complexity is divided into four different categories including technological and organizational factors. Xia and Lee (2004)

Table 5. Factors of ISDP complexity (Xia & Lee, 2004)

Complexity Factor
Structural Organizational Complexity - The project manager did not have direct control over project resources. - Users provided insufficient support. - The project had insufficient staffing. - Project personnel did not have required knowledge/skills. - Top management offered insufficient support.
Structural IT Complexity - The project involved multiple user units. - The project team was cross-functional. - The project involved multiple software environments. - The system involved real-time data processing. - The project involved multiple technology platforms. - The project involved significant integration with other systems. - The project involved multiple contractors and vendors.
Dynamic Organizational Complexity - The project caused changes in business processes. - Users' information needs changed rapidly. - Users' business processes changed rapidly. - The project caused changes in organizational structure. - Organizational structure changed rapidly.
Dynamic IT Complexity - IT infrastructure changed rapidly. - IT architecture changed rapidly. - Software development tools changed rapidly.

classifies complexity in two major dimensions, organizational and technological, and then plots it against a third dimension called uncertainty for both the organizational and technological dimensions. As a result, four classifications emerge which are depicted in Figure 2.

Structural Organizational Complexity

A project always gets maximum influences from the organizational environment for which the project is being developed. The current organizational environment and the business processes present their own influences and complexities. This category of complexity presents the nature and strength of the relationships among project elements in the organizational environment, including project resources, support from top management and users, project staffing, and skill proficiency levels of project personnel.

Structural IT Complexity

The technology is itself a factor which causes many complex situations in the development project. Information technology not only includes the hardware, but also represents the software engineering and project development factors. This category represents the complexity of the relationships among the IT elements, reflecting the diversity of user units, software environments, nature of data processing, variety of technology, need for integration, and diversity of external vendors and contractors.

Dynamic Organizational Complexity

As the time passes in the stages of development of an information system project, there come many changes in organizational environment and its business processes. The dynamic organizational complexity covers the pattern and rate of change in ISDP organizational environments, including changes in user information needs, business processes, and organizational structures; it also reflects the dynamic nature of the project's effect on the organizational environment.

Dynamic IT Complexity

Information technology is rapidly growing and changing. In the life span of an information system development project, there come many changes in the underlying information technology platform and tools for software engineering. This dimension of complexity measures the pattern and rate of changes in the ISDP's IT environment, including changes in IT infrastructure, architecture, and software development tools.

Now let us discuss some of the factors from each of the categories and understand their effect on increasing the complexities. In a particular project, the users may not provide the type of support needed by the project organization. In this situation, the requirements may not be provided correctly to the development team, which in turn may produce a faulty system which may not satisfy the needs of users or supporters. This situation can be worse if the top management does not give sufficient support, as the financial support is directly under the control of top management. The formation of the development team also plays a crucial role, as lack of team staffing or their skills can delay the time lines and lose further support. Then there are also some organizational factors from both of the users' and developers' organizations. As time progresses, there are some changes in the organizational environments and some new factors emerge from this situation. There may be some changes occurring in the organization itself, for example, the business processes of the organization are changed by the management. The management structure of the organization can also change; and this can cause changes in the organizational needs and rules. These changes can also be due to the new information system, and in this case the developer has to face an opposition from different sectors of the user organization.

Table 6. Structural complexity categories and their impact on GAMMA

Complexity Factor	Effect in this case	Level of Risk
Structural Organizational Complexity	Yes/ No	
- The project manager did not have direct control over project resources.	No	
- Users provided insufficient support.	Yes	High
- The project had insufficient staffing.	No	
- Project personnel did not have required knowledge/skills.	No	
- Top management offered insufficient support.	No	
Structural IT Complexity		
- The project involved multiple user units.	Yes	High
- The project team was cross-functional.	Yes	Medium
- The project involved multiple software environments.	No	
- The system involved real-time data processing.	No	
- The project involved multiple technology platforms.	No	
- The project involved significant integration with other systems.	Yes	Low
- The project involved multiple contractors and vendors.	No	

Table 7. Dynamic complexity categories and their impact on GAMMA

Complexity Factor	Effect in this case	Level of Risk
Dynamic Organizational Complexity		
- The project caused changes in business processes.	Yes	High
- Users' information needs changed rapidly.	Yes	High
- Users' business processes changed rapidly.	Yes	Medium
- The project caused changes in organizational structure.	No	
- Organizational structure changed rapidly.	Yes	Medium
Dynamic IT Complexity		
- IT infrastructure changed rapidly.	No	
- IT architecture changed rapidly.	Yes	Low
- Software development tools changed rapidly.	Yes	Low

Some organizations do not have a defined set of business processes or have flexibilities in them; due to adoption of information systems, these flexibilities are limited and this scenario can also cause opposition from the users.

The nature of the project also poses its own complexities, for example, if the project involves multiple user units or involves different vendors and contractors. This type of project is open to different stakeholders to impose their decisions, and prone to different influences and flaws in return. These factors are summarized in Table 5.

THE CASE STUDY

In our case study, the developer is referred to as ALPHA and the client is referred to as BETA. ALPHA was one of the leading software houses in Pakistan operating as an independent business unit of a large and reputed international company. BETA was a top bracket public sector university. The ISDP was a Web-based portal for academic records management referred to as project GAMMA in this case study.

Research Methodology

In order to understand the factors which led the project GAMMA to failure, we conducted several in-depth qualitative interviews. These interviews were flexible and exploratory in nature. In these interviews our later questions were adjusted according to the response of the interviewee in answering the earlier questions. Our aim was to clarify the earlier responses, to follow new lines of inquiry, and to probe for more detail. The overall interview style was unstructured and conversational, and the questions were open-ended and designed to elicit detailed, concrete information.

The persons interviewed included the ALPHA Project manager and the ALPHA technical team lead, and the BETA team lead, BETA coordinator, and a few users at BETA. The answers that warranted more clarification or were, to some extent, conflicting to the views expressed by the other side were further probed in the second round of discussions. ALPHA and BETA interviews were segregated from each other. Interview settings included individual and collective participation of the interviewees. The information collected was mapped on contemporary theoretical frameworks discussed in Sauer (1993) and Xia and Lee (2004) to analyze the responses and understand the role of different factors that led to the failure of our specific case under study. The information was then examined with the help of Taxonomy of ISDP complexities, and factors of each category were identified.

In the sections bellow, the process of different phases of information system development is discussed.

Figure 3. Crucial area in ISDP complexity with respect to case study

Organizational	Structural Organizational Complexity	Dynamic Organizational Complexity
vs.		
Technology	Structural IT Complexity	Dynamic IT Complexity

Structural vs. Dynamic

The Team from ALPHA

ALPHA had a team of skilled software engineers, and the average experience of team members was three-and-a-half years. The manager of the ALPHA team had software project management experience of six-and-a-half years. The ALPHA team comprised of a blend of analysts, designers, coders, and testers. ALPHA followed the incremental development approach for projects with a time period of more than eight weeks, and hence the same approach was followed in this case.

The Team from BETA

BETA made a focal team comprising of senior faculty members from different departments led by one Head of the Department. The focal team at BETA was mandated to collaborate with the ALPHA team. The responsibilities of the focal team were to help the ALPHA team to capture the information about policies and procedures of the academic and administrative departments and units of BETA. Its main role was also to help ALPHA understand the processes and verify the requirements against specific processes. The focal team acted as the client representative and in the later stages also tested the portal and gave feedback to ALPHA team.

The Complete Process

At the start of the project, a preliminary set of requirements was agreed upon between the BETA focal team and the ALPHA team. A total of eleven modules were identified, out of which eight modules were deemed to be more critical than others. The technological requirements were not rigid, and it was generally agreed to encourage the platform-independent technologies including Java and Linux. Regarding the choice of database, BETA preferred to use Oracle as it already had the license. Next the ALPHA team analyzed the preliminary requirements by collecting the data

and observing the business processes and procedures. Both of the teams visited different academic departments and held meetings with the heads of the departments and different other employees. The same was done in the administrative units to record the data and procedures of different business processes. After analyzing the collected information and additional requirements, a standard requirement specification document was developed and agreed upon.

In the meanwhile, some significant changes occurred at BETA. Due to some routine and policy decisions, some of the members of the focal team from BETA were transferred, and newly-appointed persons took their place. As the people changed, the mindset changed and the vision about the project also changed. Changes at the organizational level of BETA led to some new requirements emerging from nowhere and caused frequent changes in the old requirements.

Surprisingly, ALPHA team had to face many objections on the already-settled requirements, which were conveyed from the user departments and the end users themselves. The new members of the BETA focal team were not clear about the scope and objectives of the project GAMMA, and they also did not agree with the version of the requirements provided by the former members of the BETA focal team. Due to this kind of divisive environment, a huge time was lost in the advancement of the project. ALPHA team was willing to work according to the satisfaction of the client organization and hence wanted to listen to the client's focal team members. As there was no consensus on requirements within the client organization, ALPHA decided to conduct some presentations and meetings with the representatives of all departments and the focal team.

After some presentation and discussion sessions, the analysis of the requirements with a conclusive set of requirements was presented, and the software requirements specification document was once again finalized after incorporating the revised requirements.

At this stage, in order to minimize the impact of organizational changes on the project, the management of BETA appointed a software engineer to lead the BETA focal team with the mandate that the newly-appointed lead person will work continuously in the next phases until the completion of project GAMMA. The new lead person coordinated with the ALPHA team and helped them to complete the trial version of the project. ALPHA finalized the trial version of the project and deployed it at BETA. In April, 2004, the first version of the project was deployed at BETA, and testing was done by ALPHA's testers using real data.

At this stage, training sessions were held by the ALPHA team members to guide the key potential users at BETA, with the objective that these people will use this portal and identify errors, bugs, and changes. As per the evaluation and trial report of the project, the users complained about a number of deficiencies. They reported variances in the expected and actual implementation of different functionalities. There were errors in data processing which caused the potential users at BETA to lose their interest. They also complained that the training was of very basic level and was not properly designed and executed. The ALPHA team was of the opinion that people attending the training sessions were mostly used to using an older existing IS system and thus were reluctant to shift to the new system. Their association and familiarity with the older system created hesitancy and an attitude of disinterest which prevented them from appreciating and exploring the full functionality of the new portal.

It was observed that for some particular processes there were no standard operating procedures, and different departments followed different procedures. This situation demanded flexibility in different data structures and functionalities of the GAMMA system. As an example, the pattern of student registration numbers varied in different departments. Such anomalies caused some requirements changes, even at the later phases, and delayed the implementation.

At this stage, the person who was hired earlier and was leading the BETA focal team through the development phase left BETA for another job. This particular development compelled BETA to restore the old structure of the focal team of BETA. Now the Head of the Department of Computer Sciences was assigned the role of team lead by the client organization. The project at this stage required transferring the existing data from the old system to the new system, and new data entry as well as testing the real-time application behavior. The developers from ALPHA provided scripts to convert data from the old system based on SQL server to the new system. However, according to BETA, the scripts did not work as per requirements which had to be modified time and again. BETA formed another team referred to as "Testing Analysis Team", to test the portal, and the team members were provided training by ALPHA. Moreover a person was selected from each faculty as master trainer, who was entrusted the task to further train the end users within his faculty. This task took another six months of time and further delayed the successful implementation.

The project started in September, 2002, with the planned completion date of December, 2003. A formal audit was conducted by the external auditors, engaged by ALPHA, in December, 2003, who found that the delay was justified as the requirement engineering phase took a much longer time as discussed above. The project took off a little in September, 2004, when the Head of the Department of Computer Sciences started to lead the team to implement the project. However, the project implementation came to a standstill in December, 2004, when the client organization desired deputation of full-time experts by the ALPHA organization to supervise the implementation, which included training of the end users to use the system and subsequently adopt it. ALPHA expressed their inability to depute an expert without charging further expenditure to BETA.

At present the status of the new portal is that it is being used as a passive repository of data. The new system has not been adopted by the end users, and the system that earlier existed is in use at the organizational level. ALPHA has received part of the agreed payment amount and has an outstanding claim for the balance payment from BETA. Both organizations consider it a failed project. BETA considers it a failure as it has not been implemented and adopted at the organizational level. ALPHA considers it as a failed project because, besides the financial loss, the product is termed unsatisfactory by the end users and has not been successfully deployed and adopted at organizational level.

The main reasons for the failure of this simple IS project can be summarized as follows:

• Adaptation and modification of underlying organizational processes in such a way that they become conducive for automation is an issue deeply intertwined with project definition and has to be tackled in the very beginning. Once the processes have been reengineered, only then the scope of an automation project can be fully visualized by all the stakeholders. This factor was initially ignored in the project GAMMA when the first version of project requirements was specified. Halfway through the development process of project GAMMA, the inadequacy of the organizational processes of BETA, in terms of their capacity to lend themselves to automation, was realized.

• The existing organizational processes of BETA were not fully mature. Introduction of a new organization-wide IS system for records management and decision-making implied a number of changes in the way things were done at BETA. Alignment of organizational processes and the IS systems was very important for successful implementation of GAMMA. The end users at BETA were not ready to adopt the changed

organizational processes necessitated by the introduction of new technology.

The various complexity factors (Xia & Lee, 2004) and their impact on project GAMMA is summarized in Table 6 and Table 7.

CONCLUSION

The main aim of the GAMMA project was to implement a Web portal for the academic and administrative records management of BETA. Hence system GAMMA was required to capture, store, and process data for a number of departments within BETA. Each department had its own perspective regarding the policies and procedures of data and records management. Being in the same organization, these processes were interlinked and processed similar data.

The different departments of BETA created complexity for the requirement analysis team to decide on a particular set of requirement specifications. On the other hand, the users also did not provide sufficient support, and their behavior was critical. The users from the lower management just pointed out the flaws in the system, even if they were because of flaws in the organizational processes of BETA. They did not accept the changes in business/organizational processes which were caused by the new information system. On the other hand, the business processes kept on changing due to their own needs as the people were also changing in the BETA organization. The changes in business processes caused the rapid change in information needs. At the technological dimension, there were also some changes in IT architecture and software development tools, which caused more complexity in managing the project on target. The analysis shows that Dynamic Organizational Complexity, Figure 3, contributed most to the project failure in this case.

One of the important objectives of IS in developing countries is to bring about improvement in organizational and business processes. The information systems support the current processes to enhance the operations and improve information processing, which is helpful to the organization for making its business processes more efficient. These improvements are not without incurring any risk, as modifications or improvements are prone to introduce complexities (Heeks, 2000). However, this case study shows that the changes towards improvements in the processes caused by IS were not accepted by the supporters, which in turn increased the weight of various risk factors. On the other hand, the change in processes, due to the organization itself, caused delays and led the requirements to change significantly, which in the end proved fatal for the project. The inability of the development team to freeze the requirements and stick to the standard requirement specification is a major cause of the failure. However, the business scenarios, in developing countries like Pakistan, demand this type of flexibility in business agreements and job specifications.

With the help of this case study, we are able to identify a major problem area in the development of information systems in general and Web-based applications in particular. The lack of standard operating procedures in business processes and the evolution of new knowledge of business processes and technology encourage the managers of an organization to demand more features as well as the flexibility in them. The managers want to include many processes in the Web-based information system while these processes are either immature or are in phase of standardization; consequently, this demands extra flexibility from the developers and consumes more time. On the other hand, these immature processes are prone to changes as a result of political or structural changes. These business processes become the first target of new management to show that they are making changes in the organization. A weak legal environment in the developing countries like Pakistan does not allow the development team to challenge the client on the basis of service level

agreement. This leaves only one choice for the developer's organization to adjust the demands (which look small as they come in pieces at a time) of the client, so that the support can be won from the client in the shape of financial resources. After some time it is realized by the developers that the small changes have combined, and there is a big requirement change demanding huge amounts of extra effort and time. The developers try to make these efforts and invest time in the project; however, at a certain moment it is realized that the complexities have been increased beyond control, and the project is heading towards failure.

The dynamic organizational complexities demand that a project should cover the business processes which have been standardized, or the information system should be allowed to standardize these processes. It is also the responsibility of the organization to show respect to the agreements and demand minimum changes in the requirements. In case of political and structural changes, a project should be owned by the organization, and the changes should not affect the project scope.

The responsibility of the developers is also high, as they should be aware of these complexities and adopt a strategy to cope with them. They should be able to take strong business and technical decisions to restrict the changes in requirements to a minimum level. On the technical end, they should be able to provide maximum flexibility in a minimum time frame. It can be concluded that responsibility of these types of failures cannot be given to one stakeholder; rather it is the responsibility of both the developers as well as the client organization to facilitate a project towards success.

REFERENCES

Alter, S. (1999, March). A general, yet useful theory of information systems. *Communications of AIS, 1*(13), 1-70.

AlSharif, M., Walter, P. B., & Turky, A., (2004, April). Assessing the complexity of software architecture. In *Proceedings of the 42ⁿᵈ Annual Southeast Regional Conference* (pp. 98-103).

Baark, E., & Heeks, R. (1999). Donor-funded information technology transfer projects. *Information Technology for Development, 8*(4), 185-197.

Baccarini, D. (1996, August). The concept of project complexity: A review. *International Journal of Project Management, 14*(4), 201-204.

Barki, H., Rivard, S., & Talbot, J. (1993). Toward an assessment of software development risk. *Journal of Management Information Systems, 10*(2), 203-225.

Braa, J. & Hedberg, C. (2000). Developing district-based health care information systems. In *Proceedings of the IFIP WG9.4 Conference 2000, Cape Town, South Africa. Information flows, local improvisations, and work practices*(pp. 113-128).

British Computer Society (2003, April). *The challenges of complex IT projects* (Report). The Royal Academy of Engineering.

Gilhooly, D. (2005, April). Innovation and investment: Information and communication technologies and the millennium development goals. *United Nations Information and Communication Technologies Task Force Millennium Project.* Retrieved September 16, 2005, from http://www.unicttaskforce.org/perl/documents.pl?id=1519

Havelka, D. (2002). User personnel factors that influence information system development success. *Issues in Information Systems, 3,* 229-235.

Heeks, R. (2000). Failure, success, and improvisation of information systems projects in developing countries (Development Informatics Working Paper Series, Paper No. 11). *Institute for Development Policy and Management, University of Manchester, UK.* Retrieved April 1, 2005, from

http://www.sed.manchester.ac.uk/idpm/publications/wp/di/di_wp11.htm

Heeks, R. (2003). E-government for development success and failure rates of e-government in developing/transitional countries: Overview. *E-Government for Development Information Exchange IDPM, University of Manchester, UK.* Retrieved April 8, 2005, from http://www.egov4dev.org/sfoverview.htm

IT Cortex (2005). Failure rate, Statistics over IT projects failure rate. Retrieved April 10, 2005, from http://www.it-cortex.com/Stat_Failure_Rate.htm

Kitiyadisai, K. (2000). The implementation of IT in reengineering the Thai revenue department. In *Proceedings of the IFIP WG9.4 Conference 2000, Cape Town, South Africa. Information flows, local improvisations, and work practices.*

Mirani, R., & Lederer, A. L. (1994, April). Anticipated benefits of new jnformation systems: The role of the prosper. In *Proceedings of the 1994 Computer Personnel Research Conference on Reinventing IS. Managing information technology in changing organizations* (pp. 155-164).

Moussa, A., & Schware, R. (1992). Informatics in Africa. *World Development, 20*(12), 1737-1752.

Murray, J. (1993). Reducing IT project complexity. *Information Strategy, 16*(3) (Spring, 2000), 30-38.

Sauer, C. (1993). *Why information systems fail: A case study approach.* Oxfordshire, UK: Alfred Waller Ltd., Publishers.

Srinivasan, A., & Kaiser, K. M. (1987, June). Relationships between selected organizational factors and systems development. *Communications of the ACM, 30*(6) (June, 1987), 556-562.

The Standish Group (1994). The CHAOS report. Retrieved September 15, 2005, from http://www.

standishgroup.com/sample_research/chaos_1994_2.php

Ward, J. (1995). *Principles of information system management*. Routledge Publications.

Xia, W., & Lee, G. (2004, May). Grasping the complexity of IS development projects. *Communications of the ACM, 47*(5), 69-74.

This work was previously published in Architecture of Reliable Web Applications Software, edited by M. A. Radaideh and H. Al-Ameed, pp. 278-306, copyright 2007 by IGI Publishing, formerly known as Idea Group Publishing (an imprint of IGI Global).

Chapter XVIII
Empirical Assessment of Factors Influencing Success of Enterprise Resource Planning Implementations

Fiona Fui-Hoon Nah
University of Nebraska-Lincoln, USA

Zahidul Islam
Independent University, Bangladesh

Mathew Tan
Agilent Technologies, Malaysia

ABSTRACT

Enterprise resource planning (ERP) implementations in multinational manufacturing companies have experienced various degrees of success. This article investigates factors influencing the success of ERP implementations in multinational manufacturing companies in the Malaysian Free Trade Zone. The results indicate that enterprise-wide communication and a project management program are key factors influencing the success of ERP implementations, while other factors such as top management support as well as teamwork and composition are not as critical to the out-come. Organizational culture is a moderator of the relationships between enterprise-wide communication, a project management program, and the success of ERP implementations.

INTRODUCTION

Enterprise resource planning (ERP) refers to a seamlessly integrated family of software packages designed to integrate various financial, human resources, supply chain, and customer information functions. This system is a natural development and progression of Material Requirements Planning (MRP/MRP II) that was popular in the 1970's. Initially conceived to increase the efficiency of materials planning, the suite of software packages eventually evolved to cover a wide scope of organizational functions, including inventory control, finance, human resources, and manufacturing. Many companies experienced successes, but many more failed in their implementations. Some companies, such as FoxMeyer Corporation, experienced bankruptcy and resorted to suing the software company for failing to deliver the promises of the ERP system.

ERP implementation is a massive and costly affair (Davenport, 2000; Lee, Siau, & Hong, 2003; Siau, 2004). ERP implementations frequently consume a large portion of a company's time and resources (Siau & Messersmith, 2002, 2003). After more than twenty years of implementation and software development, much research has been gathered on the subject for developed nations (Bingi, Sharma, & Godla, 1999; Everdingen, Hilleegersberg, & Waarts, 2000; Kermers & van Dissel, 2000; Kumar, Maheshwari, & Kumar, 2003; Nadkarni & Nah, 2003; Scott & Vessey, 2002). However, the Southeast Asia region faced many challenges with ERP implementations (Davison, 2002; Soh, Sia, & Tay-Yap, 2000). The literature is scarce concerning ERP implementations and their success in this region (Tarafdar & Roy, 2003). The primary users of ERP systems are large multinational companies because local or regional small- to medium-sized companies have yet to fully embrace the benefits of ERP systems. In this research, we focus on investigating the factors contributing to the success of ERP implementations in multinational manufacturing companies in the Malaysian Free Trade Zone—a central zone in Southeast Asia.

LITERATURE REVIEW

ERP is a solution to fragmentation of information in large business organizations (Davenport,

1998). An ERP system typically comprises a central, state-of-the-art, comprehensive database that collects, stores, and disseminates data across all business functions and activities in an enterprise. By integrating all business functions, economies of scale are obtained and the business gains a significant operating cost reduction, in addition to improved capabilities and information transparency. The increased business trends of globalization, mergers, and acquisitions demand that companies must have the ability to control and coordinate increasingly remote operating units. An ERP system can help to achieve this by enabling the sharing of real-time information across departments, currencies, languages, and national borders.

The dream of creating an enterprise-wide system began in the 1970's, but was then unrealized due to the technological barriers at that time. Instead, most companies created what McKenney and McFarlan (1982) termed "islands of automation", which naturally evolved as new IT applications were introduced to fill the constantly-emerging business needs. This gave rise to a plethora of different systems that were loosely interfaced. As a result, information was scattered throughout an organization, and detailed analyses of an organization's performance across its business functions were not possible. Such information was impossible to obtain unless manual record-sifting or specialized programming requirements were carried out. In time, the organizational costs to maintain these "legacy" systems began to exceed the funds available for building new systems (Lientz & Swanson, 1980).

Enterprise systems provide a backbone of information, communication, and control for a company (Buckhout, Frey, & Nemec, 1999), and embody the current best business practices for organizational processes (Esteves & Pastor, 2000). Numerous benefits include improvements in:

- Cooperation between managers and employees.

- Consolidation of finance, marketing and sales, human resource, and manufacturing applications.
- Management information available—real-time information available anywhere, anytime.
- Informal systems for materials management/inventory/production control.
- Lead-times, manpower costs, overtime, safety stocks, work-in-progress.
- Delivery times.

An ERP system is a set of customizable and highly-integrative real-time business application software modules sharing a common database and supporting core business, production, and administrative functions such as logistics, manufacturing, sales, distribution, finance, and accounting. Companies that are structurally complex, geographically dispersed, and culturally vibrant tend to present unique challenges to ERP implementation (Markus, Tanis & Fenma., 2000). Unique issues of change management are particularly important for multinational companies where their parent sites are geographically separate. This complexity involves several dimensions including business strategy, software configuration, technical platform, and management execution. Of these four, management execution contributes toward ERP implementation success to the greatest degree (Nah, Zuckweiler, & Lau, 2003). Different managerial reporting lines, languages, and national cultures also make managing a multi-site ERP implementation project challenging (Markus et al., 2000). Local management must therefore be prepared to deal with the issues of enterprise-wide implementation on a site level. In particular, companies in Asia confront issues substantially different from those faced by companies in the developed world (Tarafdar & Roy, 2003) due to the differences in sophistication of IT use and cultural influences.

THEORETICAL BACKGROUND ON FACTORS CONTRIBUTING TO ERP IMPLEMENTATION SUCCESS

To investigate specific metrics for ERP implementation success, we reviewed the literature and identified three sets of taxonomy or classification. They are: (i) the unified critical success factors model (see Table 1) proposed by Esteves and Pastor (2000), (ii) 22 critical success factors (see Table 2) identified by Somers and Nelson (2001, 2004), and (iii) seven broad categories of critical success factors (see Table 3) developed by Nah and Delgado (2006) which were derived from the 11 critical success factors (see Table 4) identified by Nah, Lau, and Kuang (2001).

Esteves and Pastor (2000) classify critical success factors into Organizational and Technological, and then further sub-divide them into strategic and tactical factors. By cross-referencing each of the factors with its citations in the literature, Esteves and Pastor (2000) derived the ERP implementation success matrix (also termed unified critical success factors model) presented in Table 1.

Somers and Nelson (2001) identified 22 critical success factors presented in Table 2 and evaluated them across stages of ERP implementation. The top six factors across the stages are: (i) top management support, (ii) project team competence, (iii) inter-departmental cooperation, (iv) clear goals and objectives, (v) project management, and (vi) inter-departmental communication.

Another comprehensive examination of the critical success factors of ERP implementation was carried out by Nah and her colleagues (Nah, et al., 2001; Nah, et al., 2003; Nah & Delgado, 2006). These factors fall into seven broad categories (see Table 3) and can be further broken down into 11 critical success factors (see Table 4).

Among the 11 critical success factors presented in Table 4, the top six critical success factors iden-

Table 1. Unified critical success factors model

	Strategic	Tactical
Organizational	• Sustained management support • Effective organizational change management • Good project scope management • Adequate project team composition • Comprehensive business process reengineering • Adequate project champion role • User involvement and participation • Trust between partners	• Dedicated staff and consultants • Strong communication inwards and outwards • Formalized project plan/schedule • Adequate training program • Preventive troubleshooting • Appropriate usage of consultants • Empowered decision-makers
Technological	• Adequate ERP implementation strategy • Avoid customization • Adequate ERP version	• Adequate software configuration • Legacy systems knowledge

Table 2. Twenty-two critical success factors model

Critical Success Factors
1. Top management support
2. Project team competence
3. Interdepartmental cooperation
4. Clear goals and objectives
5. Project management
6. Interdepartmental communication
7. Management of expectations
8. Project champion
9. Vendor support
10. Careful package selection
11. Data analysis and conversion
12. Dedicated resources
13. Use of steering committee
14. User training on software
15. Education on new business processes
16. Business process reengineering
17. Minimal customization
18. Architecture choices
19. Change management
20. Partnership with vendor
21. Use of vendors' tools
22. Use of consultants

tified by Chief Information Officers of Fortune 1000 companies are: (i) top management support, (ii) project champion, (iii) ERP teamwork and composition, (iv) project management, (v) change management program and culture, and (vi) effective enterprise-wide communication (Nah et al., 2003).

Hence, top management support, project management, and enterprise-wide (or inter-departmental) communication are three common factors in Nah et al.'s (2003) and Somers and Nelson's (2001) "top factors" lists, whereas "ERP teamwork and composition" in Nah et al.'s (2003) list captures key aspects of project team competence and inter-departmental cooperation in Somers and Nelson's (2001) list. Therefore, we selected this set of four factors—top management support, project management, enterprise-wide communication, and ERP teamwork and composition—as independent variables for our study. These four factors are also ranked among the top five factors in Nah and Delgado's (2006) case study on ERP implementations in two organizations.

Figure 1 shows the research model, and the next section provides justifications for the hypotheses.

Hypotheses 1-4 specify the direct hypothesized effect of the independent variables—top manage-

Table 3. Seven broad categories of critical success factors

1. Business plan and vision 1.1 Business plan/vision 1.2 Project mission/goals 1.3 Justification for investment in ERP	**6. Top management support and championship** 6.1 Approval and support from top management 6.2 Top management publicly and explicitly identifies project as top priority 6.3 Allocate resources 6.4 Existence of project champion 6.5 High-level executive sponsor as champion 6.6 Project sponsor commitment
2. Change management 2.1 Recognizing the need for change 2.2 Enterprise-wide culture and structure management 2.3 Commitment to change—perseverance and determination 2.4 Business process reengineering 2.5 Analysis of user feedback 2.6 User education and training 2.7 User support organization and involvement 2.8 IT workforce re-skilling	**7. Systems analysis, selection, and technical implementation** 7.1 Legacy system 7.2 Minimum customization 7.3 Configuration of overall ERP architecture 7.4 Vigorous and sophisticated testing 7.5 Integration 7.6 Use of vendor's development tools and implementation methodologies 7.7 ERP package selection 7.8 Selection of ERP architecture 7.9 Selection of data to be converted 7.10 Data conversion 7.11 Appropriate modeling methods/techniques 7.12 Troubleshooting
3. Communication 3.1 Targeted and effective communication 3.2 Communication among stakeholders 3.3 Expectations communicated at all levels 3.4 Project progress communication	
4. ERP team composition, skills, and compensation 4.1 Best people on team 4.2 Balanced or cross-functional team 4.3 Full-time team member 4.4 Partnerships, trust, risk-sharing, and incentives 4.5 Empowered decision-makers 4.6 Performance tied to compensation 4.7 Business and technical knowledge of team members and consultants	

Table 4. Eleven key critical success factors

Critical Success Factors
1. ERP teamwork and composition
2. Change management program and culture
3. Top management support
4. Business plan and vision
5. Business process reengineering with minimum customization
6. Project management
7. Monitoring and evaluation of performance
8. Effective enterprise-wide communication
9. Software development, testing, and troubleshooting
10. Project champion
11. Appropriate business and IT legacy systems

5. Project management
5.1 Assign responsibility
5.2 Clearly establish project scope
5.3 Control project scope
5.4 Evaluate any proposed change
5.5 Control and assess scope expansion requests
5.6 Define project milestones
5.7 Set realistic milestones and end dates
5.8 Enforce project timeliness
5.9 Coordinate project activities across all affected parties
5.10 Track milestones and targets

Figure 1. Research model

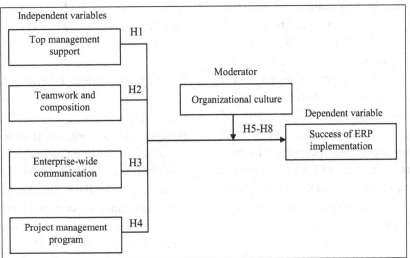

ment support, teamwork and composition, enterprise-wide communication, project management program—on the dependent variable—success of ERP implementation, whereas Hypotheses 5-8 state the moderating effect of organizational culture on these relationships.

ERP CRITICAL SUCCESS FACTORS

Rockart (1979) is one of the first researchers to study critical success factors of IT implementations. According to his account, these factors are the "areas in which results, if they are satisfactory, will ensure successful competitive performance for the organization" (p. 85).

Most of the literature in the MIS field list in excess of 20 critical success factors (Nielsen, 2002). Esteves and Pastor (2000) present a unified model of critical success factors, and further studied the effects of these factors in SAP's ASAP implementation methodology. To study key critical factors influencing ERP implementation success, we identified four "top" factors—top manage-

ment support, ERP teamwork and composition, enterprise-wide communication, and project management program—that we examine in this research. Technological factors such as system configuration, customization, and legacy data migration are outside the scope of this research and are excluded from this study.

Top Management Support

Not only is the criticality of top management support widely cited throughout the ERP literature (e.g., Dong, 2001; Somers & Nelson, 2004), several studies (Akkermans & van Helden, 2002; Esteves & Pastor, 2000; Nah et al., 2003; Somers & Nelson, 2001) have also identified top management support as the top and most crucial factor in ERP implementation. Similarly, Sarker and Lee (2003) identified strong and committed leadership as a necessary condition for success in ERP implementation. Willocks and Sykes (2000) noted that senior-level sponsorship, championship, support, and participation is one of the critical enabling factors for success in an ERP project. Public, explicit, and sincere support for the project must be present to emphasize the priority of the project. Accordingly, commitment of valuable resources to the implementation effort (Holland, Light, & Gibson, 1999; Roberts & Barrar, 1992) provides the practical support that is needed to ensure success in an ERP project. Top management commitment is the most widely-studied factor in successful IS implementations (Dong, 2001) and is also the most severe source of difficulty in IS implementations. Top management support is even more important in the case of ERP because of the scale of the project and the amount of resources needed for the enterprise-wide project. Hence, we hypothesize that:

H1: *Top management support increases the level of success of ERP implementation.*

Teamwork and Composition

The ERP team should comprise the best people in the organization to maximize the chances of success of the project (Buckhout et al., 1999; Bingi et al, 1999; Rosario, 2000). The team should be cross-functional and possess the necessary technical and functional skills for design, implementation, and assimilation. The team will have to integrate business functions with the capabilities of the software as well as possess the necessary credentials to influence business process changes where necessary. The effective use of consultants also improves the likelihood of success of the project (Haines & Goodhue, 2003). Compensation, incentives, and the mandate for successfully implementing the system on time and within budget should be given to the team to foster teamwork in the project (Buckhout et al., 1999). It is also helpful to ensure that the ERP team is colocated to facilitate teamwork and coordination among the members. We, therefore, hypothesize that:

H2: *The use of cross-functional teams that comprise people with the best business and technical knowledge increases the level of success of ERP implementation.*

Enterprise-Wide Communication

Communication across the different levels and functions of an organization is necessary for success in ERP implementation (Akkermans & van Helden, 2002; Falkowski, Pedigo, Smith, & Swanson, 1998; Parr, Shanks, & Darke, 1999). Communication is a complex factor that includes, but is not limited to, specifications of individual roles and responsibilities, clear definitions of the project milestones, pre-implementation training, and unambiguous definition of the time horizon (Petroni, 2002). Monthly bulletins, newsletters, weekly meetings, and frequent e-mail updates are among the tools that can be employed. This communication needs to be two-way to avoid design gaps that can occur if the exact business requirements or comments and approval from the ground up are ignored. Esteves and Pastor (2000) also noted that both "outward" communication to the whole organization and "inward" communication to the project team are very important.

Rosario (2000) advocates an early "proof of concept" to minimize skepticism and sustain excitement. This kind of demonstration should be public and well endorsed by key project champions and top management. Keeping the morale high and convincing the users that the new ERP system is of benefit while convincing them to abandon the old, comfortable systems requires persuasiveness and acts of showmanship on the part of management and the implementation team. Users need to know that the feedback they provide will be considered and acted upon (Rosario, 2000). Among the stakeholders of companies studied by Holland et al. (1999), it was found that communication is a critical success factor of ERP implementation. For example, Shanks, Parr, Hu, Corbitt, Thanasankit, and Seddon (2000) found that the likelihood of ERP implementation failure increased when dates were not properly communicated well in advance to stakeholders.

Based on the above discussion, we hypothesize that:

H3: *Enterprise-wide communication during the implementation increases the level of success of ERP implementation.*

Project Management Program

The proper and effective management of an ERP project is essential for its success (Nah et al., 2003). An ERP project management program requires well-defined task assignments, accounting for resource allocations, project control-keeping, and avoiding "creep" (Bagranoff & Brewer, 2003; Rosario, 2000) which is the tendency of the project to acquire additional software requirements and customization and to uncover hidden issues as time goes by. Jiang, Klein, and Balloun (1996) found that a competent project manager is the second most important factor in an IS implementation. The scope of the project should be clearly established, managed, and controlled (Shanks et al., 2000). Ross (1999) indicated that establishing program scope is the key to successful ERP implementation. Proposed changes should be evaluated against business benefits, and scope expansion requests should be assessed in terms of the additional time and cost of proposed changes (Sumner, 1999). In addition, approved changes need to be coordinated across all affected parties (Falkowski et al., 1998). Schniederjans and Kim (2003) proposed that ERP systems implementations can be supplemented by Total Quality Management (TQM) and Business Process Re-engineering (BPR) programs to prepare an organization to be more receptive to the new ERP system. They suggested that the actual ERP

implementation be preceded by BPR and followed up by a rigorous TQM program, to produce the effect of Lewin's (1951) recommended change criteria of unfreezing (BPR), change (ERP), and refreezing (TQM).

As discussed above, project management is essential to the success of ERP implementations. Thus, we hypothesize that:

H4: *A project management program increases the level of success of ERP implementation.*

ORGANIZATIONAL CULTURE

The organizational culture paradigm, as defined by Johnson and Scholes (2005), is a set of assumptions held relatively in common and taken for granted in an organization. It includes collective experience, values, beliefs, and behavioral norms. These assumptions exist at the organizational level, and they have worked well enough to be considered valid. An organizational culture that promotes learning and innovation can be especially influential to the success or failure of an organization's IT innovation or strategy (Johnson & Scholes, 2005; Sitkin, 1992). Scott and Vessey (2000) provide case study evidence to show that organizational culture can impact the success or failure of ERP implementation.

According to Sitkin (1992), the proximity of an organization towards a "learning" state would, in theory, greatly facilitate the process of change. An organizational culture that promotes learning encourages involvement/participation and adaptation. Edwards and Panagiotidis (2000) support the proposition that organizational culture is useful in understanding successful ERP implementations. They proposed a Business Systems Purpose Analysis (BSPA) methodology and recommended its integration into SAP's ASAP implementation methodology.

Skok and Legge (2002) highlight the importance of cultural as well as business process changes. According to them, ERP problems commonly lie in the employees feeling uncomfortable with the cultural changes, which follow from process changes in the ERP implementation. Thus, unless the organizational culture promotes openness in communication and facilitates learning, the employees may behave in a detrimental fashion towards the new ERP system, causing its failure.

Organizational Culture as a Moderator of ERP Implementation Success

A management team that readily accepts new concepts and is able to learn to accept and adapt to new tools as they become available is able to drive the implementation of a new enterprise-wide system more effectively, as opposed to a management team that prefers to maintain the "status quo" and is suspicious of progress (Dong, 2001). Since learning in an organization needs to be led from all levels of the organization, particularly from top-level management, a management team that is conducive to change (as in the case of an open and supportive organizational culture) is more likely to convince and persuade the rest of the organization to follow suit, which contributes toward the success of the ERP implementation.

H5: *Organizational culture moderates the relationship between top management support and the success of ERP implementation.*

ERP implementation teams are by necessity cross-functional, as the new system brings together and integrates the various functions within an organization. In order to derive the best benefits from the ERP system, the cross-functional teams working on the project should not only be able to work well together, but also understand and appreciate the different strengths and skills that each member brings to the teams.

Closed or non-learning organizations are more prone to encounter difficulties in facilitating teamwork and coordination among members of cross-functional teams.

H6: *Organizational culture moderates the relationship between ERP teamwork-and-composition and the success of ERP implementation.*

An organizational culture that promotes openness in communication facilitates the process of organizational learning, which contributes toward ERP implementation success. An open and supportive organizational culture encourages increased interaction and improved communication, which help to facilitate communication of new and complex concepts of ERP systems to the end-users. Since the sheer scale and complexity of an ERP system will require almost all company personnel to learn new tools and new ways of working, organizational culture can facilitate the learning process involved in such implementations that are necessary for successful implementation.

H7: *Organizational culture moderates the relationship between enterprise-wide communication and the success of ERP implementation.*

Team leaders faced with the challenge of managing a project this massive typically face tight deadlines and a near-impossible means of disseminating all the required training to end-users. Furthermore, the leaders of the project team need to clearly specify responsibilities, establish and control project scope, evaluate any proposed change, assess scope expansion requests, define and set project milestones, enforce timeliness of the project, and coordinate project activities across all affected parties. Thus, a learning culture benefits these processes and increases the success of the implementation.

H8: *Organizational culture moderates the relationship between a project management program and the success of ERP implementation.*

SUCCESS OF ERP IMPLEMENTATION

The dependent variable in this study is success of EPR implementation. "Success" can be defined in several ways. For project leaders, a successful implementation means that the project is completed on time and within budget and where there is minimal disruption to product shipment and customer service during the cutover period. However, from a strategic point of view, success does not only refer to meeting the "Go Live" date, but also to the increased value of the business from usage of the new ERP system.

Markus and Tanis (2000) also pointed out that success means different things depending on the perspectives that one is taking and the person defining it. For example, project managers often define success in terms of completing the project on time and within budget. The business, however, takes the view of a smooth transition to stable operations with the new system, achieving intended business improvements like inventory reductions,

and gaining improved decision-support capabilities (Markus & Tanis, 2000). Markus and Tanis define optimal success as the "best outcomes the organization could achieve with enterprise systems, given its business situation, measured against a portfolio of project, early operational, and longer-term business results metrics" (p. 186). Similarly, in this study, we will adopt the business value and performance perspective of success in ERP implementation. This perspective is also adopted by other researchers studying IS/IT success (Langdon, 2006; Mukhopadhyay, Kekre, & Kalathur, 1995; Tallon & Kraemer, 2006).

Petroni (2002) pointed out that simply asking users to rate their level of satisfaction would not be accurate or sufficient to assess success of an implementation. Neither would it be practical to ask a manager to define an implementation as anything less than successful, since no one is typically willing to shoulder the responsibility of failure. Petroni therefore suggests a set of criteria for judging the success of implementation (see Table 5) to help minimize respondent bias. We adapt Petroni's criteria, which include assessment of both performance and user satisfaction, to quantify optimal success from the business and strategic perspective. These criteria are also in line with Gable, Sedera, and Chan's (2003)

Table 5. Optimal success criteria

Improved ability	Ability to meet volume/product changes Capacity planning Cost estimation Inventory control Delivery dates Production scheduling
Improved efficiency and user satisfaction	Cooperation between managers and employees Coordination between finance, marketing, and sales
Reductions	Delivery or lead-times Informal systems for materials management Informal systems for inventory control Informal systems for production control Expediting of shipments Expediting of incoming materials Work in progress (WIP)

Table 6. Summary of reliability analysis

Variables	Number of items	Cronbach Alpha
Top Management Support	5	.82
Teamwork and Composition	5	.72
Effective Communication	5	.89
Project Management Program	5	.75
Organizational Culture	6	.83
Success of ERP Implementation	5	.83

measurement model for enterprise system success which covers organizational and individual impact as well as user satisfaction.

RESEARCH METHODOLOGY

The primary source of data collection was a survey, which was administered to both managerial and non-managerial staff from multinational companies in the Free Trade Zone of Malaysia. These companies had implemented ERP systems and were involved in distribution and manufacturing activities. The survey questionnaire was adapted from Nah et al. (2003) and Petroni (2002), and is presented in the Appendix. Pilot studies were conducted to validate these measures prior to finalizing the questionnaire. The primary means of distributing the survey questionnaire was via e-mail. The questionnaire was distributed after pre-contacting the recipients and informing them about the pending survey. Two hundred copies of the questionnaire were distributed, and the responses were collected electronically over a three-month period. A total of 110 questionnaires were returned. Hence, the response rate is 55%.

RESULTS

Respondents were asked to provide demographic information. Analysis of the demographic data indicates that 63% of the respondents were male and 37% were female. In terms of education, 66% reported holding a Master's degree and 14% have a Ph.D. Thirty-seven percent of the respondents reported holding managerial positions, while 54% were in non-managerial positions. A majority of the respondents (63%) have been with their companies for less than five years, and 18% of the respondents have been with their companies for 6 to 10 years. Eighty percent of the respondents were from companies that exceeded $4 million USD in annual revenue, and 64% have more than 3,000 employees in their organizations.

Table 6 shows the reliability assessments for both the independent and dependent variables. To assess the internal consistency and stability of data, Cronbach Alpha was used to establish the inter-item consistency. Since the Cronbach Alpha coefficients are all above 0.7 (Nunnally, 1978), it can be concluded that the measures are reliable.

Regression analysis was first carried out to assess H1-H4. Hierarchal regression was then used to test H5-H8, the moderating effect of organizational culture on the relationships between the independent variables and success of ERP implementation. We used a significance level of 0.05, or 5%, as the basis for accepting or rejecting the hypotheses.

As shown in the regression table in Table 7, the coefficient of R^2 is 0.389, indicating that the four independent variables explain 38.9% of the

Table 7. Summary of regression model output

R² = 0.389		Sig. = 0.00		
F-value = 15.80		Durbin Watson = 1.71		
Variables	**Beta**	**Sig. (p)**	**Tolerance**	**VIF**
MSUP	0.089	0.42	0.52	1.94
TEAM	0.099	0.42	0.41	2.45
COMM	0.334	**0.01***	0.35	2.83
PROJECT	0.294	**0.04***	0.32	3.11

*p<0.05

variance. Durbin Watson of 1.71 indicates that there is no auto-correlation problem. Tolerance and VIF values are also within the acceptable range indicating that there is no multi-collinearity problem.

The results presented in Table 7 prompted rejection of Hypotheses 1 and 2, and acceptance of Hypotheses 3 and 4. The results suggest that top management support ($p=0.42$) and teamwork and composition ($p=0.42$) did not influence success of ERP implementation. On the other hand, enterprise-wide communication ($p<0.05$) and project management ($p<0.05$) have significant impact on success of ERP implementation.

The results of hierarchical regression analysis for the moderating variable, organizational culture, are shown in Table 8. Recall that the R-square value is 0.389 when no moderating variable is taken into account. This value increases to 0.495 when culture is considered in the model and to 0.543 when culture is considered to moderate the interaction terms. The increased R-square suggests that organizational culture is a moderator in the proposed model.

The model with organizational culture as a moderator explains 54.3% of the variance of success of ERP implementation. Durbin-Watson of 1.70 falls within the accepted range (1.5—2.5), indicating no auto-correlation problem. Condition index, VIF, and tolerance are all within the ac-

Table 8. Summary of hierarchical regression models

Model	R²	Change in R²	Change in F	Change in Sig.	Durbin Watson
1 (OC ignored)	.389	.389	15.58	.00	
2 (OC as IV)	.495	.107	20.50	.00	
3 (OC as moderator)	.543	.048	2.42	.05	1.70

Variables	Beta	Sig. (p)
MSUP	0.089	0.42
TEAM	0.099	0.42
COMM	0.334	0.01*
PROJECT	0.294	0.04*
CULTURE	0.381	**0.00***
MSUP*CULTURE	0.209	0.82
TEAM*CULTURE	-0.409	0.68
COMM*CULTURE	2.501	**0.01***
PROJECT*CULTURE	2.850	**0.04***

*p<0.05

ceptable range (Condition Index < 40, Tolerance > 0.1 and VIF < 10), which means there is no multi-collinearity problem. Histograms for the regression model were plotted to validate that normality distribution is achieved and there is no heteroscedasticity problem.

The moderated relationship between enterprise-wide communication and success of ERP implementation is significant ($p<0.05$), which implies that organizational culture moderates the relationship between enterprise-wide communication and success of ERP implementation. We also tested the moderating effect of organizational culture on the relationship between project management and success of ERP implementation, and the result is significant ($p<0.05$), implying that organizational culture moderates the relationship between project management and success of ERP implementation. The results, however, indicate that organizational culture is not a moderator of the relationships between each of top management support ($p=0.82$) and teamwork-and-composition ($p=0.68$), and success of ERP implementation.

DISCUSSION OF RESULTS

The degree of enterprise-wide communication on the EPR implementation impacts positively on the success of the ERP implementation. This finding is also supported by the work of other researchers (e.g., Esteves & Pastor, 2000; Falkowski et al., 1998; Petroni, 2002; Rosario, 2000). Our research provides support for the importance of enterprise-wide communication and its purported benefits on ERP implementation in the context of multinational companies operating in Malaysia.

A project management program is also found to be important for ERP implementation success, which is consistent with the findings by Rosario (2000) and Bagranoff and Brewer (2003). A project management program is essential for success, as it establishes project scope and ensures that scope expansion requests are carefully assessed

before they are approved. An effective project management program defines and sets realistic milestones and enforces them. The success of ERP implementation also depends on coordination of project activities across the different parties involved, which is another important component of a project management program.

A surprising finding of this study is that top management support does not impact the success of ERP implementation. This contradicts findings of previous research (Dong, 2001; Esteves & Pastor, 2000; Nah et. al., 2003; Sarker & Lee, 2003) where top management support was cited as the top or a key factor influencing ERP implementation success. However, not all the previous studies run contradictory to this finding, as many studies have focused on different aspects of management involvement. For example, the unified critical success factors model by Esteves and Pastor (2000) examined *sustained* management support at all levels and phases of the implementation, which is conceptually different from top management support. Others, like Petroni (2002), found that top management support was a far more critical factor for small- and medium-sized firms than for large multinationals. Another possible explanation for this observed phenomenon lies in the nature of management style in multinational corporations operating in South-East Asia. Tarafdar and Roy (2003) indicated that management staff in developing nations confronted issues differently from management staff in developed countries. Hence, top management support may be more critical for ERP implementation in developed than developing countries. Power distance between top management and the employees could also account for the difference. In other words, with high power distance in Malaysia, the mandate for ERP implementation is strong across the different levels of an organization regardless of whether top management support is perceived to be present. Since the majority of the ERP literature has mainly focused on top management support in primarily developed nations, this new finding suggests that top management support may act more like an "enabling" rather than a "necessary" factor for the success of ERP implementation in developing nations. Another possible explanation is that top management support, when measured against optimal success from the business and strategic perspective, may not influence success. In other words, top management support may be necessary for the completion of an ERP project but may not directly affect the effectiveness of the system.

Another result of this study suggests that teamwork and composition of ERP implementation teams does not relate to ERP implementation success. This further contradicts previous findings (Bingi et al, 1999; Buckhout et al., 1999; Rosario, 2000). In the context of a multinational environment, it is likely that the selected teams might be too far removed from the actual implementation details and were focusing more on the system architecture rather than the change process, a phenomenon that is cautioned against by Davenport and Stoddard (1994). This is even more likely to happen if the company believes that the IS architecture is the most important aspect or if customization to suit existing business processes is given precedence (Brehm, Heinzl, & Markus, 2001) without due consideration of the pros and cons of customizing the software versus making changes to business processes to suit the new ERP system. It was established earlier that ERP systems are more about adaptation of business processes to the demands of the ERP system (Davenport, 2000) rather than the design of the ERP system to fit the demands of the business. It is also possible that the optimal teamwork and composition for ERP implementation is harder to achieve in developing nations due to limitations in human and technological resources.

The relationship between enterprise-wide communication and success of ERP implementation is positively moderated by the presence of a learning culture. A culture that is open to continuous learning and challenge, as evidenced in a "learning organization" (Senge, 1994), can help to facilitate effective communication across the enterprise, which is a key to success in ERP implementation. Similarly, an open and learning organizational culture also facilitates the execution of a project management program, which increases the chances of success in ERP implementation. These findings validate research by proponents of the learning culture theory (Edwards & Panagiotidis, 2000; Senge, 1994; Skok & Legge, 2002). In fact, the moderating influence of organizational culture was found to be so strong that it warrants cultural change programs as proposed by Schniederjans and Kim (2003) as the means to adjust the culture of an organization to one that is more receptive to changes.

CONCLUSION

From a comprehensive review of the literature on critical success factors of ERP implementation, Finney and Corbett (2007) identified a major gap in the literature, which is the lack of research to examine ERP critical success factors from the perspectives of key stakeholders. Our study is one of the few that examine success of ERP implementation from the perspectives of key stakeholders by assessing business value derived from ERP implementation. In addition, this is one of the few studies that examine ERP implementation in developing nations. Despite these strengths, our study also has limitations.

One of the limitations of this study is its generalizability. The findings of this study may be limited to multinational corporations operating in Malaysia. Follow-up work is needed to assess if the results are applicable to corporations in other developing nations. Another limitation is that a wider range of CSFs was not included due to practical constraints such as time and cost. The survey questionnaire spans several pages, and we were concerned that adding more factors would increase its length to the point where reliability of the responses would be affected (due to respondents' fatigue) or participation would be discouraged/avoided. Some key CSFs that were deemed important but were not included in this study are:

- Comprehensive business process re-engineering (BPR),
- Project championship,
- ERP customization, and
- Adequate training program.

ERP implementation is a challenging task due to its complexity and cost. This research provides further insights into the critical success factors of ERP implementation, and presents some guidelines for organizations to focus their attention and resources in carrying out such implementations. This study has highlighted the significance of enterprise-wide communication and project management programs on ERP implementation success. It also reveals the importance and crucial role of organizational culture for ERP implementation success.

The findings of this study also suggest that the traditional views of change management are insufficient to influence success of ERP implementation. Businesses have to realize that their top managers, while functioning as leaders of the organization, are insufficient on their own to guarantee success. While continuous management support is required, more effort and focus on communication across the different functions and levels of the organization, management of the project, and the capability of the organization to learn are key considerations. In addition, due to the critical role of project management, it is recommended that businesses form a separate and formal project management team that works closely with the rest of the organization to manage both the implementation and the changes associated with the implementation.

Several studies have examined critical success factors across stages of ERP implementation (Holland & Light, 2001; Nah & Delgado, 2006; Somers & Nelson, 2001; Somers & Nelson, 2004). This is an important research direction, as it provides more specific guidelines on the key factors across the different stages of the implementation. However, since ERP implementation in most multinational companies is moving into the various stages of maintenance, it is also important to study and understand the various factors, issues, and activities in ERP maintenance to better utilize existing ERP resources and to further improve efficiency and effectiveness in organizations (Kang, 2007; Nah, Faja, & Cata, 2001). For example, data warehousing interoperability for extended enterprises (Triantafillakis, Kanellis, & Martakos, 2004) and challenges in upgrading ERP systems (Nah & Delgado, 2006) are also issues that warrant further research.

This study provides a unique view of multinationals operating in Malaysia's Free Trade Zone. It cautions us against assuming that best practices and success factors in developed nations will necessarily apply for developing nations. This is especially important for multinational companies intending to implement major changes to their operations in Malaysia or developing nations in the Southeast Asia. Accordingly, adapting to the ERP system environment can help to establish a win-win scenario for multinational companies, but management of the implementation is critical to achieve this goal.

REFERENCES

Akkermans, H., & van Helden, K. (2002). Vicious and virtuous cycles in ERP implementation: A case study of interrelations between critical success factors. *European Journal of Information Systems, 11*, 35-46.

Bagranoff, N. A., & Brewer, P. C. (2003). PMB investments: An enterprise system implementation. *Journal of Information Systems, 17*(1), 85-106.

Bingi, P., Sharma, M. K., & Godla, J. (1999). Critical issues affecting an ERP implementation. *Information Systems Management, 16*(3), 7-14.

Buckhout, S., Frey, E., & Nemec, J., Jr. (1999). Making ERP succeed: Turning fear into promise. *IEEE Engineering Management Review, 19,* 116-123.

Brehm, L., Heinzl, A., & Markus, M. L. (2001). Tailoring ERP systems: A spectrum of choices and their implications. *Proceedings of the 34th Hawaii International Conference on System Sciences, Wailea Maui, Hawaii.*

Davenport, T. H. (1998). Putting the enterprise into the enterprise system. *Harvard Business Review, 76*(4), 121-131.

Davenport, T. H. (2000). *Mission critical: Realizing the promise of enterprise systems.* Harvard Business School Press.

Davenport, T. H., & Stoddard, D. B. (1994). Re-engineering: Business change or mythic propositions? *MIS Quarterly, 18*(2), 121-127.

Davison, R. (2002). Cultural complications of ERP. *Communications of the ACM, 45*(7), 109-111.

Dong, L. (2001). Modelling top management influence on ES implementation. *Business Process Management Journal, 7*(3), 243-250.

Edwards, J. S., & Panagiotidis, P. (2000). Organisational learning—A critical systems thinking discipline. *European Journal of Information Systems, 10*(3), 135-146.

Esteves, J., & Pastor, J. (2000). Towards the unification of critical success factors for ERP implementation. *Proceedings of 10th Annual BIT Conference, Manchester, UK* (pp. 60-69).

Everdingen, Y. V., Hillegersberg, J. V., & Waarts, E. (2000). ERP adoption by European midsize companies. *Communications of the ACM, 43*(4), 27-31.

Falkowski, G., Pedigo, P., Smith, B., & Swanson, D. (1998, September). A recipe for ERP success. *Beyond Computing,* 44-45.

Finney, S., & Corbett, M. (2007). ERP implementation: A compilation and analysis of critical success factors. *Business Process Management Journal, 13*(3), 329-347.

Gable, G. G., Sedera, D., & Chan, T. (2003). Enterprise systems success: A measurement model. *Proceedings of the International Conference on Information Systems, Seattle, WA* (pp. 576-591).

Haines, M. N., & Goodhue, D. L. (2003). Implementation partner involvement and knowledge transfer in the context of ERP implementations. *International Journal of Human-Computer Interaction, 16*(1), 23-38.

Holland, C. P., & Light, B. (2001). A stage maturity model for enterprise resource planning systems use. *Database for Advances in Information Systems, 32*(2), 34-45.

Holland, C. P., Light, B., & Gibson, N. (1999). A critical success factors model for enterprise resource planning implementation. *Proceedings of the 7th European Conference on Information Systems, Bled, Slovenia* (pp. 273-297).

Jiang, J. J., Klein, G., & Balloun, J. (1996). Ranking of system implementation success factors. *Project Management Journal, 27,* 49-53.

Johnson, G., & Scholes, K. (2005). *Exploring corporate strategy, 7th ed.* Prentice Hall.

Kermers, M., & van Dissel, H. (2000). ERP system migrations. *Communications of the ACM, 43*(4), 53-56.

Kang, D. (2007). Categorizing post-deployment IT changes: An empirical investigation. *Journal of Database Management, 18*(2), 1-24.

Kumar, V., Maheshwari, B., & Kumar, U. (2003). An investigation of critical management issues in ERP implementation: Empirical evidence from

Canadian organizations. Technovation. The International *Journal of Technological Innovation and Entrepreneurship, 23*(9), 793-807.

Landgon, C. S. (2006). Designing information systems capabilities to create business value: A theoretical conceptualization of the role of flexibility and integration. *Journal of Database Management, 17*(3), 1-18.

Lee, J., Siau, K., & Hong, S. (2003). Enterprise integration with ERP and EAI. *Communications of the ACM, 46*(2), 54-60.

Lewin, K. (1951). *Field theory in social science.* Harper & Row.

Lientz, B. P., & Swanson, E. B. (1980). Impact of development productivity aids on application system maintenance. *Data Base, 11*(3), 114-120.

Markus, M. L., Tanis, C., & Fenma, P. C. (2000). Multisite ERP implementations. *Communications of the ACM, 43*(4), 42-46.

Markus, M. L., & Tanis, C. (2000). The enterprise system experience: From adoption to success. In R. Zmud (Ed.), *Framing the domains of IT management: Projecting the future through the past* (pp. 173-207). Cincinnati, OH: Pinnaflex Educational Resources.

McKenney, J. L., & McFarlan, F. W. (1982). The information archipelago: Maps and bridges. *Harvard Business Review*, 109-119.

Mukhopadhyay, T., Kekre, S., & Kalathur, S. (1995). Business value of information technology: A study of electronic data interchange. *MIS Quarterly, 19*(2), 137-156.

Nadkarni, S., & Nah, F. (2003, October). Aggregated causal maps: An approach to elicit and aggregate the knowledge of multiple experts. *Communications of the Association for Information Systems, 12*(Article 25), 406-436.

Nah, F., & Delgado, S. (2006). Critical success factors for ERP implementation and upgrade. *Journal of Computer Information Systems, 46*(5), 99-113.

Nah, F., Faja, S., & Cata, T. (2001). Characteristics of ERP software maintenance: A multiple case study. *Journal of Software Maintenance and Evolution, 13*(6), 399-414.

Nah, F., Lau, J., & Kuang, J. (2001). Critical factors for successful implementation of enterprise systems. *Business Process Management Journal, 7*(3), 285-296.

Nah, F., Zuckweiler, K., & Lau, J. (2003). ERP implementation: Chief information officers' perceptions of critical success factors. *International Journal of Human-Computer Interaction, 16*(1), 5-22.

Nielsen, J. L. (2002). *Critical success factors for implementing an ERP system in a university environment: A case study from the Australian HES.* Unpublished thesis, Griffith University. Retrieved from http://ecommerce.cit.gu.edu.au/cit/docs/theses/JNielsen_Dissertation_ERP.pdf

Nunnally, J. C. (1978). *Psychometric theory, 2nd ed.* McGraw-Hill.

Parr, A., Shanks, G., & Darke, P. (1999). Identification of necessary factors for successful implementation of ERP systems. In *New information technologies in organizational proceses: Field studies and theoretical reflections on the future work* (pp. 99-119). Kluwer Academic Publishers.

Petroni, A. (2002). Critical factors of MRP implementation in small and medium sized firms. *International Journal of Operations & Production Management, 22*(3), 329-348.

Roberts, H. J., & Barrar, P. R. N. (1992). MRPII implementation: Key factors for success. *Computer Integrated Manufacturing Systems, 5*(1), 31-38.

Rockart, J. F. (1979). Chief executives define their own data needs. *Harvard Business Review, 57*(2), 81-93.

Rosario, J. G. (2000). On the leading edge: Critical success factors in ERP implementation projects. *Businessworld* (Philippines).

Ross, J. W. (1999). Surprising facts about implementing ERP. *IT Professional, 1*(4), 65-68.

Sarker, S., & Lee, A. S. (2003). Using a case study to test the role of three key social enablers in ERP implementation. *Information & Management, 30*, 813-829.

Schniederjans, M. J., & Kim, G. C. (2003). Implementing enterprise resource planning systems with total quality control and business process re-engineering. *International Journal of Operations & Production Management, 23*(4), 418-429.

Scott, J. E., & Vessey, I. (2000). Implementing enterprise resource planning systems: The role of learning from failure. *Information Systems Frontiers, 2*(2), 213-232.

Scott, J. E., & Vessey, I. (2002). Managing the risks of enterprise systems implementations. *Communications of the ACM, 45*(4), 74-81.

Senge, P. M. (1994). *The fifth discipline: The art and practice of the learning organization.* Doubleday.

Shanks, G., Parr, A., Hu, B., Corbitt, B., Thanasankit, T., & Seddon, P. (2000). Differences in critical success factors in ERP systems implementation in Australia and China: A cultural analysis. *Proceedings of the 8th European Conference on Information Systems, Vienna, Austria* (pp. 537-544).

Siau, K. (2004). Enterprise resource planning (ERP) implementation methodologies. *Journal of Database Management, 15*(1), i-vi.

Siau, K., & Messersmith, J. (2002). Enabling technologies for e-commerce and ERP integration. *Quarterly Journal of Electronic Commerce, 3*(1), 43-52.

Siau, K., & Messersmith, J. (2003). Analyzing ERP implementation at a public university using the innovation strategy model. *International Journal of Human-Computer Interaction, 16*(1), 57-80.

Sitkin, S. B. (1992). Learning through failure: The strategy of small losses. *Research in Organizational Behaviour, 14*, 231-266.

Skok, W., & Legge, M. (2002). Evaluating enterprise resource planning (ERP) systems using an interpretive approach. *Knowledge and Process Management, 9*(2), 72-82.

Soh, C., Sia, S. K., & Tay-Yap, J. (2000). Cultural fits and misfits: Is ERP a universal solution? *Communications of the ACM, 43*(4), 47-51.

Somers, T. M., & Nelson, K. (2001). The impact of critical success factors across the stages of enterprise resource planning implementations. *Proceedings of the 34th Hawaii International Conference on System Sciences, Wailea Maui, Hawaii.*

Somers, T. M., & Nelson, K. G. (2004). A taxonomy of players and activities across the ERP project life cycles. *Information & Management, 41*, 257-278.

Sumner, M. (1999). Critical success factors in enterprise wide information management systems projects. *Proceedings of the 5ᵗʰ Americas Conference on Information Systems, Milwaukee, WI* (pp. 232-234).

Tallon, P. P., & Kraemer, K. L. (2006). The development and application of a process-oriented "thermometer" of IT business value. *Communication of AIS, 17*, 2-51.

Tarafdar, M., & Roy, R. K. (2003). Analyzing the adoption of enterprise resource planning systems in Indian organizations: A process framework. *Journal of Global Information Technology Management, 6*(1), 31-51.

Triantafillakis, A., Kanellis, P., & Martakos, D. (2004). Data warehousing interoperability for the extended enterprise. *Journal of Database Management, 15*(3), 73-84.

Willocks, L., & Sykes, R. (2000). The role of the CIO and IT functions in ERP. *Communications of the ACM, 43*(4), 32-38.

APPENDIX

Questionnaire : Success of ERP Implementation

A. Top Management Support

Please indicate the extent to which you agree with the following statements by marking an "X" against the appropriate scale shown.	Strongly Disagree	Disagree	Neither agree nor disagree	Agree	Strongly agree
Sufficient incentive for ERP implementation was provided by top management.					
The ERP implementation is/was viewed as a strategic decision by (local) top management.					
There is/was sufficient top management commitment to this ERP implementation.					
The CEO, CIO, or COO is/was actively supporting this ERP implementation.					
The ERP implementation received explicit identification from (local) top management as a critical priority.					

B. Teamwork and Composition

Please indicate the extent to which you agree with the following statements by marking an "X" against the appropriate scale shown.	Strongly Disagree	Disagree	Neither agree nor disagree	Agree	Strongly agree
The people selected for ERP implementation teams had the best business and technical knowledge.					
A variety of cross-functional people were selected for the ERP implementation.					
Those selected for the ERP implementation were working on the project full-time as their only priority.					

Sufficient incentives or compensation were given to those selected for the ERP project.

Those selected for the ERP project were relocated together.

C. Enterprise-Wide Communication

Please indicate the extent to which you agree with the following statements by marking an "X" against the appropriate scale shown.

Strongly Disagree	Disagree	Neither agree nor disagree	Agree	Strongly agree

The project team or core design team was well-prepared to communicate effectively with the users.

Persons involved in the ERP project clearly understood the goals/objectives/purposes of the implementation.

There were enough communication channels to inform the users of the stage of the ERP project and help users resolve problems.

Enough reviews were conducted to ensure continued ERP end-user satisfaction.

There were enough evaluations to assess the workings of the ERP system.

D. Project Management Program

Please indicate the extent to which you agree with the following statements by marking an "X" against the appropriate scale shown.

Strongly Disagree	Disagree	Neither agree nor disagree	Agree	Strongly agree

During the ERP implementation, milestones were set with measurable results.

There was commitment to promote and manage the ERP implementation project.

Regular communication of expectation and challenges, education, training, and support were provided during the ERP implementation.

Task assignments were well-defined during the ERP implementation.

Customization of the ERP system was well-managed by the business team.

E. Organizational Culture

Please indicate the extent to which you agree with the following statements by marking an "X" against the appropriate scale shown.

Strongly Disagree	Disagree	Neither agree nor disagree	Agree	Strongly agree

In my organization . . .

Employees are supportive and helpful.

Adequate organizational resources are available to the employees.

There is willingness to collaborate across organizational units.

Employees are encouraged or rewarded by their superiors to express and exchange their opinions and ideas regarding work.

Opportunities are provided for individual development, other than formal training (e.g., work assignments and job rotation).

Employees are encouraged to analyze mistakes that have been made and learn from them.

F. ERP Implementation Success

Please compare the following statements to the situation before ERP/MRPII/MRP implementation and indicate the extent to which you agree with the statements by marking an "X" against the appropriate scale shown.

	Strongly Disagree	Disagree	Neither agree nor disagree	Agree	Strongly agree
There is a reduction in informal systems for either materials management, inventory, or production control.					
Capacity planning, cost estimation, and inventory control has improved.					
Cooperation between finance, marketing, production, engineering, and sales have improved.					
Employee job satisfaction and morale has improved.					
There is a reduced need for "expediting" business requirements such as customer orders.					

G. Demographics

Your job position in your company:

- Managerial
- Non-managerial
- Other. Please specify

How long have you been in your company:

- < 1 year
- 1-5 years
- 6-10 years
- > 10 years

Your education level:

- PhD
- Masters
- Bachelors
- Diploma
- Others. Please specify

Organizational annual revenue:

        < USD 1.0m

        USD 1.0-4.0m

        > USD 4.0m

Number of employees at your site:

        <100

        101-1000

        1001-3000

        3001-5000

        >5000

Gender:

        Male

        Female

Thank you very much for spending your time to participate in this questionnaire. Your inputs are of tremendous importance to my research. Any constructive feedback would be very much appreciated.

Chapter XIX
IT Training as a Strategy for Business Productivity in Developing Countries

Shirish C. Srivastava
National University of Singapore, Singapore

Thompson S. H. Teo
National University of Singapore, Singapore

ABSTRACT

Most existing studies on technology training address the operational issues of training process (e.g., training needs assessment, learning, delivery methods, etc.). The strategic concerns of IT training for enhancing business productivity largely are not addressed by the current literature. In this article, we explore the strategic concerns of IT training in hierarchical organizations, which are typically prevalent in developing countries. We synthesize various ideas in the literature on change management, training needs analysis, and IT adoption in order to evolve a strategic IT training framework for hierarchical organizations. The proposed framework recognizes the differences in IT training requirements for different levels of employees and suggests a differentiated training content for different segments of employees.

The training framework provides an actionable and comprehensive tool that can be used for systematically planning IT training for enhancing productivity of organizations.

INTRODUCTION

Most existing studies on technology training address the operational issues of training process in the context of the western world; for example, training needs assessment (Nelson, Whitener, & Philcox, 1995), learning styles (Bostrom, Olfman, & Sein, 1990), and delivery methods (Compeau & Higgins, 1995; Sein & Bostrom, 1989). The strategic issues related to IT training in developing countries (e.g., what kind of training is required for employees; should the training given to all employees be similar in content and delivery) remain relatively unexplored in past research. In this article, we explore these strategic concerns of IT training for hierarchical organizations, which are more prevalent in developing countries. We reiterate the strategic objectives of IT training that usually are lost sight of in the mundane and routine training activities in organizations.

Need for Systematic Training

IT training in many organizations is a matter of chance rather than a planned initiative. Training, in contrast, refers to a planned effort by a company to facilitate the learning of specific knowledge, skills, or behaviors that employees need in order to be successful in their current job (Goldstein, 1992). The pressure for better training is expanding due to the increasingly popular view that people, rather than technology, represent the primary source of enduring competitive advantage (Ford, 1997). Although the need for training is being realized by many organizations, in many cases in developing countries, the training for new technology is not in tandem with organizational requirements. Some employees do receive IT training, but it is mostly a result of the personal initiative of that particular employee in the field of his or her interest. This field may or may not be of direct consequence to his or her job. In some cases, it is the mere persuasion of the training provider that initiates the training nominations from these firms. Consequently, the content and context of IT training often is decided by the training provider and not by the firm. This results in incongruence between training outcomes and organizational requirements. Effective training has to be in consonance with existing organizational structures and practices. There is a need to consider the interface between the organizational system and training (Goldstein, 1992; London, 1989) in order for the outcome to be fruitful and effective.

In many cases, IT training is thought of as a necessary evil and not as a strategic tool for enhancing productivity. For example, Indian Railways, one of the biggest employers in the world with more than 1.6 million employees, does not have a systematic IT training program for its employees, though it is one of the biggest users of IT resources. Employees are imparted IT training on the basis of their emergent skill needs rather than as a part of a well-thought strategic plan. Some firms are proactive in realizing the importance of IT training but till are not able to plan their training modules systematically for want of critical knowledge about the who and what of IT training (i.e., which employees should be trained in what aspects for better leveraging of IT resources). An example in which the firm's success can be attributed to its well-thought-out and planned IT training is the Housing Development Board (HDB) in Singapore. HDB realized the importance of systematic IT training for its employees and was able to leverage training for its success. One of the major contributing factors was top management's proactive attitude toward IT adoption and training (Teo, 1999; Teo & Ranganathan, 2003).

There is no doubt about the fact that everyone in an enterprise does not require the same kind of training in IT for effective adoption and performance (Srivastava & Teo, 2004). In the context of developing countries, where most of the organizations are hierarchical in nature, these organizations have a well-defined chain of command, and the position of employees in the organizational hierarchy determines their responsibilities. The proposed framework seeks to identify the training requirements for different segments of employees so that customized IT training programs can be designed to facilitate speedy and fruitful IT adoption by these enterprises. Effective training requires a systematic approach to training needs assessment, which determines not only who to train but also what to train (McGhee & Thayer 1961). McGhee & Thayer (1961) also cite a lack of theoretical models for providing systematic training. Surprisingly, this gap in IT training literature still has not been addressed in a systematic and convincing way. This study seeks to present a comprehensive, conceptual, actionable strategic IT training framework for business enterprises, which will help in efficient and effective IT proliferation and usage.

Strategic IT Training Framework

Noe and Ford (1992) have stated the need for training practice to be used as a part of the strategic planning process of the firm. In contrast to this, most firms view IT training as an operational or functional necessity rather than as a strategic tool to gain competitive advantage. In line with the changing market conditions, the training systems in organizations also have to evolve continuously. Using training as a strategic tool is equally valid, not only for IT but for all other functions as well. IT training presents yet a more challenging endeavor, because it calls for a complete transformation of most of their existing systems. For example, the proliferation of ERP and CRM techniques often are based on the concept of business process re-engineering, which requires a major revamping of the existing systems. The rate of evolution for all new technology tools and methods, including IT, definitely has to be at a much faster pace. Tannenbaum and Yukl (1992) have stressed the need for training to be viewed as a system embedded in the organizational context. Training should be conceptualized as integral to the strategic goals of the organization (Schuler & Walker, 1990) and a component of the human resource planning process (Jackson & Schuler, 1990). The orientation of training typically has been micro in its orientation with a focus on individual learning development and change. This is true despite the fact that at the conceptual level, training needs assessment (McGhee & Thayer, 1961), evaluation (Kirkpatrick, 1967), and instructional design models (Goldstein, 1992) state that training should be aligned with the organizational goals. A key question to be addressed is "what is to be

learned?"(Campbell, 1988), and equally important is to know "by whom."

McGhee and Thayer (1961) and Goldstein (1992) argue that a thorough need analysis will include (a) organizational analysis, (b) task analysis, and (c) person analysis. At the organizational level, we are concentrating on typical organizations, which are hierarchical in structure. At the task analysis level, we are considering the job requirements of various levels of management, and at the person analysis level, we are generalizing the personnel at different levels. Ostroff and Ford (1989) applied a multilevel perspective to needs analysis and noted that the previous three facets may reside at different or even multiple levels of analysis. The training program of the organization needs to be linked to the organizational business strategy (Brown & Read, 1984), the changes in the strategic plan should be reflected in the revised training objectives (Hussey, 1985), and the needs assessment must incorporate a future orientation (Scheinder & Konz, 1989).

Levels in an Organization

All personnel in an organization can be classified in three distinct levels based on the kind of work that level performs. Anthony (1965) made the distinction between the three levels of management based on their decision-making functions (strategic, tactical, and operational). The three levels into which all the employees of an organization can be classified are top, middle, and frontline. The top level includes the CEO and various unit heads. They are the people who are responsible for spelling out the road map of the company. Their decisions have long-term implications not only for the company but also all for its employees. The role of this level in smaller organizations like SMEs is even more important, because not only are they aware of the key strategic problems of the company, but the smaller size of the company brings them closer to the actual workplace; hence, they also are able to monitor the effects of their decisions. The middle level includes the functional managers. They are largely responsible for the smooth functioning of the areas under them within the broad framework of policies and guidelines spelled out by top management. They are required to plan and source the various resources for production and marketing. This group of personnel requires having a thorough knowledge of working procedures of the industry. The frontline personnel include all the employees excluded from the upper two categories. They include supervisors, inspectors, and workers. They are the employees who actually are involved in the day-to-day business operations and are required to have well-developed skills in handling the various devices and systems that they operate.

Since different levels of employees have different kinds of functions to perform, it implies that these three levels have different informational needs in relation to their function. Hence, their training needs also are quite different from each other (Daft, Lengel, & Trevino, 1987; Srivastava & Teo, 2004). Further, the different levels require different kinds of knowledge, skills, and attitudes (KSAs). The different types of knowledge

acquisition require different types of training methodologies. Anderson (1982) made a distinction between declarative knowledge, which is fact knowledge (knowing what), and procedural knowledge, which is knowledge of procedures (knowing how). The frontline level may require more of the procedural knowledge, whereas as we go higher, the personnel may require more declarative knowledge related to IT.

Figure 1 presents a strategic IT training framework for organizations, which takes into consideration the hierarchical nature of most organizations in developing countries. The framework recognizes that the IT training needs for the different levels of employees in organizations are quite divergent in terms of content. The three broad contents of IT training are attitude toward IT, knowledge of IT, and on-the-job IT operational skills. The change in the breadth of the triangle and quadrilateral in Figure 1 indicates the change in requirement of the training content for different levels of hierarchy.

The proposed framework seeks to offer answers to questions regarding training component for different levels of the organization and serves as a practical tool for hierarchical organizations

Figure 1. Strategic IT training framework

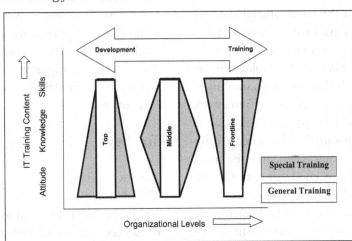

Table 1. Summary of training content

Training Content	Fundamental Question	Explanation With Example
Attitudes	***Why?*** The answers to such questions determine the strategic direction of the firm and are usually provided by top management	It seeks to explain the importance of IT and why it should be adopted by the organization, the kind of benefits (long-term as well as short-term) that can be derived from the use of IT. The emphasis is more on molding the views toward leveraging IT in order to improve business productivity and competitiveness. In the case of ERP, such training will inform the participants about the significant benefits that IT is capable of giving to the firms. It seeks to develop the enthusiasm and remove inhibitions by informing about the real business value of IT. The trainees are taught about the various technologies available as well as their potential impact so that they can better decide on the choice of technology for the company.
Knowledge	***What?*** These decisions determine the tactical course of action of the firm and are mostly in the domain of middle management of the firm	This seeks to inform about the details for a particular technology. It aims at empowering trainees with the requisite background in order to distinguish and decide which among the options available for a particular technology may be beneficial and suited for their business. Going further with the ERP example, the knowledge component of the training provides the ability to decide among various choices of ERP systems that are available to suit their needs.
Skills	***How?*** The frontline workers require this expertise to operate the various systems in an enterprise	This aspect of training provides the necessary ground tools to the workers to actually work on the chosen systems. It provides workers with the necessary expertise to operate the specific software and hardware chosen by the company. An example of skills may include the techniques for operating the different modules in SAP ERP system. This skills training logically comes after the two vital preceding decisions have been taken (1) to use ERP system in the company and (2) among available ERP systems to use SAP

in planning their IT training initiatives. The profound problem with IT training has been that, in most of the cases, the training is not directed to the informational needs of that level, and often there is a mismatch. This mismatch of the IT training content with the informational needs of the employee results in a twofold wastage. First, the money spent on training that employee is wasted, since it will not help the employee in his or her job. Second, the time spent on training is also a wasted resource. The proposed framework (Figure 1) explores IT training for different levels of organizational personnel with regard to training content. Training content expounds the broad parameters (in terms of knowledge, skills, and attitudes) on which the planners should organize the training for the different levels of employees. A summary of the training content is illustrated

with illustrative examples in Table 1 in the context of ERP implementation.

This differential hierarchical IT training of employees has been implemented successfully by the Housing and Development Board (HDB) in Singapore, which encompasses formal and structured IT training programs for different levels of staff from junior officers to the CEO (Teo, 1999). The IT training programs are designed according to the job and informational requirements of the level of personnel.

Top Level

Top-level managers are usually the perpetrators of underlying currents and culture in an organization. In most traditional organizations, the top managers often are viewed as trendsetters whom

Table 2. Training requirements for different levels of employees

Level/ Requirement	Attitudes	Knowledge	Skills
Top	· Positive belief toward IT relevance · Enthusiasm for IT proliferation · Creative, innovative, and risk-taking attitude · Ability to enthuse and motivate others for IT adoption	· The latest developments and trends in IT · In-depth business knowledge and emerging IT standards for their industry	· General office and communication software (e.g., e-mail, word processing, spreadsheet, etc.)
Middle	· Positive, proactive, and enthusiastic toward IT adoption · Attitude to learn and teach new things for better efficiency and productivity	· In-depth knowledge about the capabilities of the available hardware and software systems · Knowledge about the implementation impediments for various IT systems · Latest developments and trends about IT usage in similar industries	· General office and communication software (e.g., e-mail, word processing, spreadsheet, etc.) · Understanding of the operational requirements for the software and hardware systems being used by their department · Specific skills for the critical IT systems in their department
Frontline	· Positive and enthusiastic toward new learning and IT adoption	· Generic knowledge about the capabilities of IT for their industry and specific knowledge about the IT systems on which they have to work	· General office and communication software (e.g., e-mail, word processing, spreadsheet, etc.) · Understanding of the software and hardware systems being used by their department · Specific specialist operational skills for the software and hardware systems being used by them · General skills and ability to handle related IT systems in their organization

all employees in the organization try to emulate. Hence, it is very important for top management to have positive and favorable attitudes toward IT and new technology adoption. This has implications on the training content for these top-level managers. This group of people requires more attitudinal training toward IT (Table 2). They should be able to realize the importance of IT and the impact that it can have in transforming their enterprise. They require relatively little IT-specific knowledge or skills. These leaders should be trained in a way so that they understand the potential benefits of IT adoption as well as the potential costs of not adopting IT. Such understanding by top management would enable them to be better able to enthuse and motivate their employees for IT adoption. The tapering pyramid in the proposed framework expounds training mostly in understanding "whys" (i.e., attitudes). The requirement of training about "what" (i.e., knowledge) and "how" (i.e., skills) is comparatively less.

Their preparation should be aimed more toward the developmental dimension than toward the training dimension. They require having a broad understanding of the various ways in which IT can help their business. They should be aware of the various kinds of IT available in the market and the latest trends in the industry worldwide. They should have enough knowledge in order to decide about the kind of systems relevant for the business.

The objectives of employee development are not tied necessarily to a specific job or task. London (1989) defined development as courses, workshops, seminars, and assignments that influence personal and professional growth. Development is focused less on specific skills; instead, it focuses on the comprehensive knowledge and attitudes required for improving the long-term personal effectiveness of the employee, which results in an overall benefit to the firm. Top management in a firm is responsible for deciding the course of action for the enterprise; hence, their overall development in IT will result in empowering them with the right attitudes for executing this function effectively and efficiently.

Middle Level

The middle level is concerned mostly with the tactical decisions in an enterprise. Middle-level managers are required to make decisions on how to best utilize the existing systems in an enterprise per the directions of top management. Suppose top management has been imparted an attitudinal training in IT, and they decide that ERP system is suitable for their enterprise. They give necessary directions to middle-level management to implement ERP in their organization. Now, middle-level management should have the critical knowledge to appreciate the functionality of the ERP system. They should be able to spell out the relative benefits of using the ERP system and, consequently, help top-level management choose the required system, consultants, and so

forth. Thus, their training sequence is next in importance to the top level, and their training content is focused more on the knowledge aspect of training. They require a thorough knowledge and understanding of the various systems of the firm and the IT capabilities and, more importantly, how they can be integrated.

The training program planning procedures need to identify and consider the technical as well as the managerial skills needed for advanced technologies well in advance of its implementation (Kozlowski, 1987; Majchrzak, 1988). This requires knowledge of planning techniques that are not well-represented by the conventional needs assessment models (Kraut, Pedigo, McKenna, & Dunnette, 1989). The hexagon shown in the framework emphasizes the need to have a greater emphasis on knowledge-related aspects of IT in training rather than attitudes or skills. Once they are able to spell out what is to be adopted by the enterprise, then the frontline workers can be imparted the specialized training of skills set. Thus, the training programs for middle-level managers should be more knowledge-related so that they are able to comprehend the IT options available in the industry and are able to make informed decisions (Srivastava, 2001). Many German mid-size firms are adopting Linux as their cost-effective platform (Blau, 2003). Such a decision can come only from a well-informed middle management that has a thorough knowledge of the various options and has the capability to make a comparison.

Frontline Level

The frontline workers are the actual executors of the various tasks in an organization. Top-level management brings the idea (concept) into the enterprise, middle-level management gives form (methodology for operationalizing the concept) to that idea, and frontline workers actually execute (operationalize) this idea. Frontline workers should have rigorous training in the actual systems and IT modules related to their jobs. If we consider the

ERP implementation example again, then frontline workers require requisite skills for operating the selected modules of the IT systems chosen. Their training may be very specialized, depending on the skills set required for operating the particular systems. As shown in the proposed framework, they require maximum training in specialized skills and comparatively less in knowledge and attitude-related training. There is no doubt about the fact that they do require a positive attitude toward IT, and this attitude can be instilled in them through socialization and proliferation from top management. Their training need not be directed toward IT-related attitudes and knowledge but should be focused on the specific skills required by them for execution of the particular job. Their skill-acquiring activity can begin only after top management is prepared to embark upon the IT odyssey and middle management has chosen the ship for this journey; hence, logically, the sequence of their IT training in an enterprise is after top and middle management.

General and Special Training

IT training requirements of personnel in any organization also can be classified as general and special. General training (composed of attitudes, knowledge, and skills) is the common training component that has to be imparted to all employees for efficient functioning in the organization; whereas, special training is given according to the specific job requirements of the employee. Specialist training can be person-, group-, or level-specific. The strategic training framework in Figure 1 captures this in terms of general and special training for all levels of employees. From the framework, it is clear that all categories of employees require some basic grounding in IT-related attitudes, knowledge, and skills for efficient functioning. The only difference in the content in the specialist and general training is that top management may require negligible specialist training in IT skills, whereas frontline manage-

ment may require much less specialist training in attitudes. At this point, we also would like to emphasize that it is not possible to achieve IT success in an organization without imparting some general IT training in all three aspects (attitudes, knowledge, and skills) for all categories of employees. For example, in an organization, top management may require general IT skills such as checking e-mails and working on a word processor and a spreadsheet, but may require specialist training in attitudes (e.g., being more creative and proactive toward new technologies, risk-taking ability, perseverance, persistence, etc.). On the other end of the spectrum, the frontline staff may require specialist knowledge about the various IT-related systems that it is using for different operational requirements (e.g., specialized software packages) and functional knowledge of ERP modules. Their requirement of operational knowledge does not discount their basic attitudinal requirements of their enthusiasm for learning and using new technologies. The point about general and special training for different levels of organizational personnel also is highlighted in Table 2, which charts the requirements for different levels of employees.

Huang (2002) also has highlighted the importance of training employees in certain fundamentals of information technology, which will remain nearly constant even in a dynamic technological environment. The general training in the proposed framework (Figure 1) is similar to general technology education, and the special training has been captured in the business application training and just-in-time training (Huang, 2002)

Again considering the case of IT training in HDB, Singapore, the training categories are divided into four levels (basic, advanced, extended, and continuing), depending on the job requirement and computer literacy of the individual staff member (Teo, 1999). This is done with a view to provide a better fit between the actual training imparted and the job requirements (Brown & Read 1984; Kirkpatrick 1967). The attitudinal training in HDB also is brought about through seminars, conferences, and discussions as well as through the promotion of professionalism among IT users through formal certification (accredited by the Singapore Computer Society) of its staff (Teo, 1999; Teo & Ranganathan, 2003).

CONTRIBUTIONS AND CONCLUSION

The motivation for this article is to provide a theoretical basis for providing an IT training framework applicable to hierarchical business organizations, which is more common in developing countries. Through this study, we provide a comprehensive, actionable, conceptual strategic IT training framework, which is the first contribution of this study. As systematic training is an important input for IT adoption in enterprises, we hypothesize that the presented IT training framework will help to transform technological shyness to technological savviness, leading to enhanced business productivity and competitiveness. We have highlighted the applicability of the proposed framework by drawing some examples from HDB, Singapore, an organization recognized for its efficient and effective IT training programs (Teo, 1999; Teo & Ranganathan, 2003).

Second, we reiterate that training should be viewed not only as a means for serving operational needs but also as a strategic tool (Noe & Ford 1992; Schuler & Walker 1990). The proposed training framework segments organizations in the traditional hierarchical structure and identifies the broad content of IT training in the context of these levels of employees to facilitate IT adoption in a systematic way. Top management personnel of an enterprise who are supposed to provide a strategic direction to the enterprise are the ones who should have a positive attitude toward IT adoption and should understand the tangible and intangible benefits that IT offers them in the short as well as the long term. They

not only should be the first ones in an enterprise to be trained in IT, but their training also should focus on empowering them with the attributes that result in fruitful IT adoption by these enterprises. Once top management sets the ball rolling with their right attitudes, then middle management should be in a position to execute the IT plans in an enterprise. Hence, they must have the right knowledge in order to make the right decisions about the choice of platforms, software, and so forth. Their training, therefore, should infuse in them the knowledge to understand and to make decisions best suited for the firm. The role of the frontline workers is at the delivery stage of the IT plan, conceptualized by top management and operationalized by middle management. These frontline workers should be skilled in operating the chosen software and hardware systems so that right results are delivered to the firm by IT adoption. Hence, their training requirement is more on the skills aspect and actual performance at the delivery stage.

Third, enterprises are faced with the problem of dwindling resources and increasing competition. The proposed framework provides guidelines to practitioners and managers to efficiently deploy their resources on fruitful IT training. It gives a direction to managers for planning IT training of its personnel so that there are no wastages and so that the various levels of personnel get the IT knowledge that is functionally and strategically relevant for them.

Fourth, the proposed framework reiterates that not all employees in hierarchical organizations require similar kinds of IT training, which is especially applicable in the context of developing countries. The informational needs of top, middle, and frontline personnel are very different. Hence, IT training programs for these levels must be designed according to their roles and requirements in order to avoid wastage of scarce resources. Systematic IT training per the proposed framework will make these enterprises competitive in the global economy. Overall, the framework provides researchers and practitioners with a useful tool in order to better understand the different training requirements for different levels of the organization. Such understanding would pave the way for more effective usage of scare resources to ensure that personnel at various levels are adequately trained to leverage IT effectively in order to improve business productivity and enhance competitiveness.

There are three main limitations of this framework. First, in the present-day world, organizational structure is undergoing a major transformation. We are gradually moving toward flatter organizations in which the classification per the traditional structure may not hold good for many organizations. However, organizations (especially those in developing countries) tend to be slow in adopting newer organizational structure and tend to continue to have a hierarchical structure. Second, some organizations are relatively small, and top management at times also may be performing the operational and tactical role in addition to the strategic role. Hence, the framework has to be modified suitably for such enterprises. Third, we have assumed that IT adoption should be driven from the top. Sometimes, middle-level and frontline personnel are the ones who bring to management's attention what the competitors are doing with regard to the deployment of IT. Nevertheless, top management support for IT is an essential element for successful IT deployment. Such support will be difficult if top management does not have favorable attitudes toward IT adoption.

Future research can identify the detailed elements of KSAs required for the various levels of personnel for particular IT system implementation (e.g., ERP and CRM). Extensions of this article also can be done by studying some of the successful organizations and by analyzing their IT training strategy for its employees compared to the proposed strategic IT training framework.

REFERENCES

Anderson, J.R. (1982). Acquisition of cognitive skill. *Psychological Review, 89*, 369–406.

Anthony, R.N. (1965). *Planning and control systems: A framework for analysis.* Boston: Harvard University.

Blau, J. (2003). German midsize firms go for Linux. *IDG News Service.* Retrieved from http://www.infoworld.com.article/03/10/29/HNgermangoforlinux_1.html

Bostrom, R.P., Olfman, L., & Sein, M.K. (1990). The importance of learning style(s)? In end-user training. *MIS Quarterly, 14*(1), 101–119.

Brown, G.F., & Read, A.R. (1984). Personnel and training policies—Some lessons from western companies. *Long Range Planning, 17*(2), 48–57.

Campbell, J.P. (1988). Training design for performance improvement. In J.P. Campbell, R.J. Campbell, & Associates (Eds.), *Productivity in organizations* (pp. 177–216). San Francisco: Jossey-Bass.

Compeau, D.R., & Higgins, D.A. (1995). Computer self-efficacy: Development of a measure and initial test. *MIS Quarterly, 19*(2), 189–211.

Daft, R.L., Lengel, R.H., & Trevino, L.K. (1987). Message equivocality, media selection, and manager performance: Implications for information systems. *MIS Quarterly, 11*(3), 355–366.

Ford, J.K. (1997). Advances in training research and practice: An historical perspective. In J.K. Ford, & Associates (Eds.), *Improving training effectiveness in work organizations* (pp. 1–16). Hillsdale, NJ: Lawrence Erlbaum Associates.

Goldstein, I.L. (1992). *Training in organizations: Needs assessment, development, and evaluation* (3rd ed.). Pacific Grove, CA: Brooks/Cole.

Huang, A.H. (2002). A three-tier technology training strategy in a dynamic business environment. *Journal of End User Computing, 14*(2), 30–38.

Hussey, D.E. (1985). Implementing corporate strategy: Using management education and training. *Long Range Planning, 18*(5), 28–37.

Jackson, S.E., & Schuler, R.S. (1990). Human resource planning: Challenges for industrial/organizational psychologists. *American Psychologist, 45*, 223–239.

Kirkpatrick, D.L. (1967). Evaluation of training. In R.L. Craig, & L.R. Bittel (Eds.), *Training and development handbook* pp. 87–112). New York: McGraw-Hill.

Kozlowski, S.W.J. (1987). Technological innovation and strategic HRM: Facing the challenge of change. *Human Resource Planning, 10*, 69–79.

Kraut, A.I., Pedigo, P.R., McKenna, D.D., & Dunnette, M.D. (1989). The role of manager: What's really important in different managerial jobs. *Academy of Management Executive, 3*, 286–293.

London, M. (1989). *Managing the training enterprise.* San Francisco: Jossey-Bass.

Majchrzak, A. (1988). *The human side of factory automation.* San Francisco: Jossey-Bass.

McGhee, W., & Thayer, P.W. (1961). *Training in business and industry.* New York: Wiley.

Nelson, R.R., Whitener, E.M., & Philcox, H.H. (1995). The assessment of end-user training needs. *Communications of the ACM, 38*(7), 27–39.

Noe, R.A., & Ford, J.K. (1992). Emerging issues and new directions for training research. *Research in Personnel and Human Resource Management, 10*, 345–384.

Ostroff, C., & Ford, J.K. (1989). Assessing training needs: Critical levels of analysis. In I.L. Goldstein (Ed.), *Training and development in organizations* (pp. 25–62). San Francisco: Jossey-Bass.

Scheinder, B., & Konz, A. (1989). Strategic job analysis. *Human Resource Management, 28*, 51–63.

Schuler, R.S., & Walker, J.W. (1990). Human resources strategy: Focusing on issues and actions. *Organizational Dynamics, 19*(1), 5–19.

Sein, M.K., & Bostrom, R.P. (1989). Individual differences and conceptual models in training novice users. *Human Computer Interaction, 4*, 197–229

Srivastava, S.C. (2001). IT training needs for mechanical department over Indian railways. In *Proceedings of the Seminar on Training Needs for Indian Railway Officials, Indian Railways Institute of Mechanical & Electrical Engineering* (IRIMEE), Jamalpur (pp. 8–16).

Srivastava, S.C., & Teo, T.S.H. (2004). IT training as a strategy for business productivity: A framework for small and medium-sized enterprises in Asia. In *Proceedings of the Eighth Pacific Asia Conference on Information Systems, (PACIS 2004),* Shanghai, China.

Tannenbaum, S., & Yukl, G. (1992). Training and development in work organizations. *Annual Review of Psychology, 43*(1), 399–441.

Teo, T.S.H. (1999). Managing information technology at the housing and development board in Singapore: A holistic approach for the public sector. *Journal of Information Technology Cases and Applications (JITCA), 1*(3), 26–44.

Teo, T.S.H., & Ranganathan, C. (2003). Leveraging IT resources and capabilities at the housing and development board. *Journal of Strategic Information Systems, 12*, 229–249.

This work was previously published in International Journal of Information and Communication Technology Education, Vol. 2, Issue 4, edited by L. Tomei, pp. 51-63, copyright 2006 by IGI Publishing, formerly known as Idea Group Publishing (an imprint of IGI Global).

Chapter XX
Customer Relationship Management (CRM) Metrics:
What's the Holdup?

Timothy Shea
University of Massachusetts Dartmouth, USA

Ahern Brown
HDR Inc., USA

D. Steven White
University of Massachusetts Dartmouth, USA

Catharine Curran-Kelly
University of Massachusetts Dartmouth, USA

Michael Griffin
University of Massachusetts Dartmouth, USA

ABSTRACT

Adopting a focus on CRM has been an industry standard for nearly two decades. While evidence suggests that a majority of the attempts to implement CRM systems fail, no single reason for the failures has been identified. Assuming that CRM implementation is an extension of a customer-oriented business strategy and assuming successful integration with Enterprise Information Systems such as Enterprise Resource Planning (ERP) systems, the authors contend that the lack of valid and reliable CRM metrics leads to the perception of failed CRM implementation. Only through the development, application, and use of CRM metrics can organizations hope to achieve their CRM goals.

INTRODUCTION

For nearly two decades, businesses worldwide have sought a means to connect meaningfully with their customers. For many, the integration of information technology and marketing has provided a platform on which to build this connection. Thus, Customer Relationship Management (CRM) has emerged as the strategic bridge between information technology and marketing strategy (Wehmeyer, 2005). CRM is a customer-centric business strategy in which an organization seeks to increase customer satisfaction and loyalty by offering customer-specific services (Kristoffersen & Singh, 2004). CRM allows companies to collect and analyze data on customer patterns, interpret customer behavior, develop predictive models, respond with timely and effective customized communications, and deliver product and service value to individual customers (Chen & Popovich, 2003). Acquiring a better understanding of existing customers allows companies to interact, respond, and communicate more effectively with them in order to improve retention rates, among other things. The goal is to return to the feeling of yesteryear, when small business owners and customers knew each other intimately and shared a sense of community (Chen & Popovich, 2003).

Since CRM requires an integration of information technology and marketing, cross-functional cooperation becomes mandatory for success (Nairn, 2002). But this cooperation isn't the only prerequisite for success. Two other critical success factors have been identified: (1) a customer-centric business model (Chen & Popovich, 2003) and (2) appropriate business processes and integrated systems (Bull, 2003). In addition, resource constraints impact CRM implementation. It is estimated that the average investment in CRM applications per company is U.S.$2.2 million (Chen & Popovich, 2003). Estimates of 2004 global corporate expenditures on CRM range from U.S.$23.5 billion (Bull, 2003) to U.S. $125 billion (Adebanjo, 2003; Winer, 2001).

OVERLAP BETWEEN ENTERPRISE RESOURCE PLANNING (ERP) AND CUSTOMER RELATIONSHIP MANAGEMENT (CRM)

Many CRM packages were developed by legacy systems vendors (ERP) to be seamless additions or modules (Adebanjo, 2003). ERP systems are thought of as back-office systems, whereas CRM systems are thought of as front-office systems (Corner & Hinton, 2002). ERP systems address fragmented information systems, while CRM systems address fragmented customer data. The two systems work together interactively in order to produce data on which managers are able to increase competitiveness by reducing costs and increasing sales. The goal of CRM technology is to link front-office (i.e., sales, marketing, and customer service) and back-office (i.e., financial, operations, logistics, and human resource) functions with the company's customers (Chen & Popovich, 2003).

The importance of integrated corporate applications such as ERP and CRM is increasing despite reports of negative experiences and failed implementations (Huang, Yen, Chou & Xu, 2003). But prior to focusing on the pitfalls of CRM implementation, the following sections offer the potential benefits sought by businesses that pursue CRM as an active business strategy.

POTENTIAL BENEFITS OF CRM

There are many potential benefits of integrating ERP and CRM systems (Huang et al., 2003). Some of the possible outcomes of successful CRM implementation include increased competitiveness through higher revenues and lower operating costs; increased customer satisfaction and retention rates; increased customer value; potential to assess customer loyalty, profitability, and ability to measure repeat purchase; dollars spent;and customer longevity (Chen & Popovich, 2003; Ling & Yen, 2001).

Companywide, CRM systems provide each employee with a tool to manage contacts, activities, documents, and the information necessary for personalizing or customizing marketing efforts in order to meet individual consumer needs (Bygstad, 2003). The most frequently cited critical success factors for implementation include defining a CRM strategy that is consistent with corporate strategy and determining the scope and scale of the cross-departmental infrastructure changes needed (Kotorov, 2003). Finally, all businesses seeking to develop and implement a CRM system would be wise to realize that the goal of developing a perfect CRM system is unattainable (Corner & Rogers, 2005).

THE DARK SIDE OF CRM

CRM implementation is hard work (Bygstad, 2003). By some estimates, 75% to 85% of the CRM systems implementations either are outright failures (Bygstad, 2003; Earley, 2002; Tafti, 2002) or disappoint to the level that CRM frequently has come to mean "Can't Recover Money." In a recent study of Australian businesses that adopted CRM systems, 60% were less than satisfied with the results achieved to date (Ang & Buttle, 2005).

Therefore, it is safe to say that many of the companies who have implemented CRM systems have failed to realize the potential benefits sought (Kristoffersen & Singh, 2004). The question is why? Many companies underestimate the complexities of CRM, lack clear business objectives, and tend to invest inadequately in implementation (Bull, 2003). Others fail because they assume that the same methodologies used for implementing

ERP systems are suitable for implementing CRM systems (Corner & Rogers, 2005). Still others fail because they do not successfully integrate with ERP systems (Chan, 2005). To be fair, the failure rate is consistent with the implementation success rate of other Enterprise Information Systems such as ERP systems. How can we improve the situation? One interesting area to investigate is the use, or lack of use, of CRM metrics. Chan (2005) contends that the inability to align the correct metrics across business activities is a critical reason for CRM failure.

THE CURRENT STATUS OF CRM METRICS

In a sample drawn from Fortune 1000 companies, 39% had no CRM metrics, 48% had internal metrics, and only 12% had external goals and metrics (Rogers, 2003). The need for valid and reliable metrics is clear. In order to optimize CRM performance, metrics need to be enterprise-wide, customer-centric (Chan, 2005), and relevant (Rogers, 2003). Metrics from sales, marketing, customer service, and operations should be unified in order to drive measures of customer profitability, customer satisfaction, and market share (Chan, 2005). The disconnect between CRM and CRM metrics negatively impacts marketing effectiveness, customer retention, and loyalty (Chan, 2005). The problem with CRM metrics today is that they mostly are focused internally, measuring items such as increase in sales revenue, improved sales productivity, reduction in marketing waste, reduction in costs in call centers, reduction in sales cycle time, increase in campaign response, and decrease in cost of response. In order to be useful, metrics are needed that focus on the customer's experience, measuring items such as improvement in first contact resolution or improved speed of order fulfillment (Rogers, 2003).

BUILDING THE CASE FOR THE DEVELOPMENT OF CRM METRICS

The emergence of the quality movement in the 1980s in the United States, spurred on by Edward Demming's mantra "You can't manage what you can't measure," helped energize the push for performance management, benchmarking, metrics, and the like. While initially focused on financial and non-financial measures for manufacturing, performance measures have evolved to include the full range of activities within a company, including service activities and even strategic activities. The Metrus Group (2002) is one of many to document the effectiveness of performance management.

At the same time, as already addressed, there is also considerable evidence that CRM implementations today are not very good at measuring their impact or the benefit to the company, and the company often lacks an established approach to metrics or analytics. Granted, like other new technology waves, the CRM wave began with too many vendors promoting flash over substance. However, now that we are about 10 years into the wave and have the benefit of thousands of ERP and CRM implementations, what's the holdup? Why are we still fumbling with metrics?

It is true that metrics simply cannot be slapped on to the front bumper and be expected to provide value. A company needs to know what it is trying to accomplish with its CRM before developing metrics. That is, a company first needs to have an overall strategic plan as well as an enterprise-wide CRM strategy that integrates information needs, technology needs, and alignment with company processes and goals. The CRM should have organizational goals, technology goals, and goals for customer offerings (Sawhney, 2001). A company with many legacy systems that make it difficult to integrate across various information silos will have a slow start.

Others have suggested that people, culture, and processes also are factors that can inhibit a company from adding value across its customer value chain from the integrated information that a CRM can provide. Put a slightly different way, we suggest it is not the technology anymore, be it data communications issues or application maturity; it is people, culture, and change. A simple example is a new CRM system that identifies problem areas. Who wants to be the messenger to deliver the bad news in a corporate culture that does not support such activities?

Distance learning technology was at a similar point about five years ago. For a number of years, people had plenty of legitimate complaints about distance learning technology: it doesn't work, the server is down too often, the connection is too slow, the software is too frustrating and doesn't do what I need it to do, it takes too much time, and so forth. Over a few short years, connection speeds even to the home became fast and reliable, the learning management software matured, and adequate infrastructure such as servers was in place. Seemingly in a flash, the discussions moved from technology to pedagogy and assessment. Likewise, we believe the maturity of CRM applications available today and the experience of companies using CRM applications are now permitting companies to move from a technology focus to an application focus as well as the evaluation of CRM's performance and benefits.

We believe it is time to revisit and reinvigorate efforts to develop, implement, and research CRM metrics. Some CRM metrics, such as developing useful measures to support return on investment (ROI) or using the balanced scorecard technique, can take time to learn and implement. One such metric proposed is the Customer Value Scorecard (CVS). The CVS is a customer performance metric that looks at transition rates from stages and segments that affect the value of the customer base (Hansotia, 2002). However, many current CRM metrics exist today that can be applied quite readily to help demonstrate value and profitability. Metrics such as Relative Customer Satisfaction, Customer Retention, and Customer Lifetime

Table 1. Benefits of strategic performance management (© Metrus Group, 2002)

Measure of Success	Measurement-Managed Organizations	Non-Measurement-Managed Organizations
Industry leader over the past three years	74%	44%
Three-year return on investment (ROI)	80%	45%
Success in last major change effort	97%	55%
Clear agreement on strategy among senior management	93%	37%
Effective communication of strategy to organization	60%	8%

Value provide valuable benchmarks for managers (Rogers, 2003). The following suggested metrics assume a full CRM implementation, integration with ERP reporting, and data mining capabilities. CRM metrics include the following:

- **Changes in Conversion or Sales Rate.** An increase in the number of opportunities vs. the number of wins can show growth. Data-mining techniques can show conversion results in specific markets or within a range of customers.
- **Changes in Cross-Selling Rate for Existing Customers.** Silos often are built in organizations between diverse product offerings. The ability to show an increase in cross selling to existing customers provides many intrinsic returns in an organization's ability to maximize its share of customer wallets.
- **Evaluating Marketing Campaigns.** The ability to measure the productivity of a campaign with hard numbers and trend data is especially important to organizations in which larger individual investments in marketing are needed to produce a win.
- **Predicting Future Sales.** Over time, an integrated CRM system can provide more information about future sales and more accurate probabilities about potential wins.
- **Evaluating the CRM System.** The data documenting the effectiveness of the customer life cycle for customers, including order and supply process improvements, customer support, sales, sales and marketing expenses, and customer satisfaction, can document the value of the CRM system.
- **Bringing New Marketing and Sales Personnel up to Speed.** Staff transition is a fact of doing business, especially in today's dynamic environment. CRM systems metrics as well as the valuable history of past and present interactions with customers can significantly speed up a new employee's productivity learning curve.

The following do not require an integrated, full CRM implementation. They just some time and, for most of them, an Excel spreadsheet:

- **Cost Per Acquisition.** Customer acquisition costs are the costs associated with convincing a consumer to buy a product or service, including marketing, research, advertising costs, and Web content. It is calculated by dividing the costs by the number of acquisitions. Customer acquisition cost should be considered along with other data, especially the value of the customer to the company and the resulting return on investment (ROI) of acquisition.

- **Customer Lifetime Value.** Loyal customers mean future revenues. Customer Lifetime Value (CLV) is the present value of the future revenue generated from a customer for as long as you retain that customer. If CLV is an indication of the value of a relationship, companies must find ways to maximize CLV by utilizing strategies that maximize incremental sales and by launching effective customer loyalty programs. The formula for CLV is Customer Lifetime Value = Revenue from initial purchase + Present Value of Future Revenues over the Projected Lifetime—the Acquisition Cost of the Customer

- **Changes in Customer Satisfaction.** While satisfaction measures may not provide verifiable results as quickly as other metrics, they provide important overall, long-term trends as well as valuable feedback on the organization's most important customers.

- **E-mail Effectiveness.** E-mail effectiveness can be measured a number of ways. The Return on Investment (ROI) of a particular e-mail campaign can be calculated by dividing the total cost of the mailing into the net income produced. A monthly e-mail churn rate (number of undeliverable e-mail names plus the names deleted from the list during the month divided by the total number of e-mail names on your list at the end of the month) measures how much your customer base rolls over every month.

- **Web Traffic Analysis.** There are a number of Web traffic analysis packages available, many of which are very affordable (e.g., ClickTracks, Hitslink, FastCounter Pro). They can support Web marketing through

ROI analysis, detailed visitor analysis, content performance, and ad tracking.

SUMMARY

For some, the development and use of CRM metrics is a case of too little too late and can only confirm that the organization is already in trouble (Rogers, 2003). But this should not dissuade organizations from the pursuit of the development of well-defined CRM metrics. Metrics provide actionable data, either positive or negative, and have the ability to help to demonstrate the value and profit attributable to a CRM implementation. Our hope is to illustrate that an opportunity exists for developing customer-focused CRM metrics and that starting down the road of CRM metric development does not require either a Ph.D. in statistics or even a full CRM implementation.

It is clear that just as the implementation of a CRM system is a cross-functional endeavor, so is the development of the metrics needed to manage these systems. We are attempting to walk the walk: one author is a management information systems professor, two are marketing professors, one is an accounting and finance professor, and the final one is from the CRM industry. Our goal is to promote and reinvigorate the CRM metrics conversation. We issue a challenge to our colleagues in the academy to join us in our pursuit of the development of valid and reliable CRM metrics that have broad applications. Do you measure up?

REFERENCES

Adebanjo, D. (2003). Classifying and selecting e-CRM applications: An analysis-based proposal. *Management Decision, 41*(5/6), 570–577.

Ang, L., & Buttle, F. (2005). CRM software, applications and profitability. In *Proceedings of the*

2005 Academy of Marketing Annual Conference, Dublin, Ireland (pp. 1–11).

Bull, C. (2003). Strategic issues in customer relationship management (CRM) implementation. *Business Process Management Journal, 9*(5), 592–602.

Bygstad, B. (2003). The implementation puzzle of CRM systems in knowledge-based organizations. *Information Resources Management Journal, 16*(4), 33–45.

Chan, J.O. (2005). Toward a unified view of customer relationship management. *Journal of American Academy of Business, 6*(1), 32–38.

Chen, I.J., & Popovich, K. (2003). Understanding customer relationship management (CRM): People, process and technology. *Business Process Management Journal, 9*(5), 672–688.

Corner, I., & Hinton, M. (2002). Customer relationship management systems: Implementation risks and relationship dynamics. *Qualitative Market Research, 5*(4), 239–251.

Corner, I., & Rogers, B. (2005). Monitoring qualitative aspects of CRM implementation: The essential dimension of management responsibility for employee involvement and acceptance. *Journal of Targeting, Measurement and Analysis for Marketing, 13*(3), 267–274.

Earley, R. (2002). How to avoid the CRM graveyard. *Customer Interaction Solutions, 20*(12), 26–30.

Hansotia, B. (2002). Gearing up for CRM: Antecedents to successful implementation. *Journal of Database Management, 10*(2), 121–132.

Huang, A., Yen, D., Chou, D., & Xu, Y. (2003). Corporate applications integration: Challenges, opportunities, and implementation strategies. *Journal of Business and Management, 9*(2), 137–150.

Kotorov, R. (2003). Customer relationship management: Strategic lessons and future directions. *Business Process Management Journal, 9*(5), 566–571.

Kristoffersen, L., & Singh, S. (2004). Successful application of a customer relationship management program in a non-profit organization. *Journal of Marketing Theory and Practice, 12*(2), 28–42.

Ling, R., & Yen, D. (2001). Customer relationship management: An analysis framework and implementation strategies. *The Journal of Computer Information Systems, 41*(3), 82–97.

Metrus Group. (2002). Measurement-managed organizations. Retrieved from http://www.metrus.com

Nairn, A. (2002). CRM: Helpful or full of hype? *Journal of Database Marketing, 9*(4), 376–382.

Rogers, B. (2003). What gets measured gets better. *Journal of Targeting, Measurement and Analysis for Marketing, 12*(1), 20–26.

Sawhney, M. (2001). Don't homogenize, synchronize. *Harvard Business Review, 79*(7), 100–108.

Tafti, M.H.A. (2002). *Analysis of factors affecting implementation of customer relationship management systems.* In Proceedings of the IRMA 2002 Annual Conference, Hershey, PA.

Wehmeyer, K. (2005). Aligning IT and marketing—The impact of database marketing and CRM. *Journal of Database Marketing and Customer Strategy Management, 12*(3), 243–256.

Winer, R.S. (2001). A framework for customer relationship management. *California Management Review, 43*(4), 89–105.

This work was previously published in International Journal of Enterprise Information Systems, Vol. 2, Issue 3, edited by A. Gunasekaran, pp. 1-9, copyright 2006 by IGI Publishing, formerly known as Idea Group Publishing (an imprint of IGI Global).

Chapter XXI
Supply Chain
Risk Management:
A Game Theoretic Analysis

Thorsten Blecker
Hamburg University of Technology, Germany

Wolfgang Kersten
Hamburg University of Technology, Germany

Hagen Späth
Hamburg University of Technology, Germany

Birgit Koeppen
Hamburg University of Technology, Germany

ABSTRACT

This chapter introduces a game-theoretic approach to supply chain risk management. The focus of this study lies on the risk of a single supply chain member defecting from common supply chain agreements, thereby jeopardizing the overall supply chain performance. The chapter goes on to introduce a manual supply chain game, by which dynamic supply chain mechanisms can be simulated and further analyzed using a game-theoretic model. With the help of the game-theoretic model, externalities are identified that negatively impact supply chain efficiency. The conclusion drawn from this chapter is that incentives are necessary to overcome these externalities in order to align supply chain objectives. The authors show that the game-theoretic model, in connection with the supply chain game presented, provides an informative basis for the future development of incentives by which supply chains can be aligned in order to reduce supply chain risks.

INTRODUCTION

In recent years, supply chain management (SCM) has experienced considerable attention. Trends, such as lean management, have unleashed outsourcing with the aim of improving corporate efficiency, which, in turn, considerably reduced the vertical range of production. The result is that original equipment manufacturers (OEMs) have outsourced as much as 80% of their value chain. This resulted in an increasing dependency of companies on their suppliers. Intricate supply networks evolved, shifting competition from the single company level to the supply chain level. Thereby, supply chain management became an asset when it comes to guaranteeing efficiency and high service levels (Christopher, 2004).

As a consequence of the interorganizational dependencies, supply chain competition fosters risks. These dependencies and the rising complexity of supply chain networks have increased the importance of supply chain risk management. Although connectivity between the players and transparency across the supply chain are core aspects propagated by SCM in contemporary literature, reality shows that insufficient communication among supply chain participants still prevails. Therefore, interorganizational risks have the potential to become one of the core fields of supply chain risk management (SCRM) research in future.

As supply chain participants are always (potential) competitors, the intensity of collaborative efforts are always a matter of how high single organizations prioritize supply chain alignment. Incentives are a way to overcome the barriers keeping organizations from aligning their objectives. Finding the right incentives for SCRM can turn out to be an extremely hazardous and difficult task for supply chain risk managers. One option is to create mathematical models based on economic settings. However, whether all variables have been considered is only validated the moment the incentive is tested in a realistic setting for a certain period of time. This realistic setting can either be simulated by means of an electronic simulation model, a manual business game, or on a real supply chain. Since it is difficult to analyze

the influence of a particular change within a supply chain—particularly due to the vast amount of interactions and the fact that such a change can also negatively influence a chain—the last option can be aborted. The first option does not include the variable that human beings make organizational and interorganizational decisions, which we considered to be central to SCRM. Therefore, we opted for the manual business game. Supply chain risks are evaluated in the so-called supply chain game. The supply chain risks analyzed here are specifically inventory risks, caused by interorganizational drivers. Bringing supply chain networks in connection with strategy and competition addresses a matrix of risk drivers within the locus of this level: horizontal and vertical competition and cooperation. Interorganizational aspects include "co-opetition," a combination of cooperation and competition, as coined by Brandenburger and Nalebuff (1997). This chapter will focus on the vertical organizational and interorganizational risk drivers related to these aspects. To date, SCRM has largely focused on combating the impact of supply chain risks or improving the resilience of supply chains to be able to react to unfavorable changes taking place. Therefore, we can deduct that current SCRM is largely reactive.

Proactive SCRM would require that sources and drivers of supply chain risks are manipulated in a sense that they are, in the best case, avoided, reduced, or at least controlled. Incentives provide the opportunity to do so. However, although incentives have gained wider popularity since the birth of the balanced scorecard (Kaplan & Norton, 1996), they have not yet been implemented as proactive measures in SCRM, and the effects of specific incentives are unclear. In a first step to developing such a proactive incentive framework, it will be shown that the supply chain game enables an ideal test surrounding for testing implications of certain incentives on SCRM. It will be shown that the game correlates to supply chain and market conditions, which justifies it as a reference model.

Since natural advantages exist among the supply chain participants, an in-depth analysis can be conducted on their nature. Therefore, a game-theoretic model will be developed based on the findings in the game. The ultimate goal will be to use the model developed in this chapter, which provides the necessary informative basis to deduct incentives to align supply chain objectives.

BACKGROUND TO SUPPLY CHAIN RISK MANAGEMENT

The effective and efficient management of the supply chain can become a core competency of a company. By definition, SCM is: "the integration of key business processes from end user through original suppliers that provides products, services, and information that add value for customers and other stakeholders" (Stock & Lambert, 2001, p. 54). Simchi-Levi, Kaminsky, and Simchi-Levi (2003) specify the value added as "minimizing system wide costs while satisfying service-level requirements" (p. 2). Poor SCM, therefore, results in the inefficient allocation of resources, which poses a risk, both to the company itself and the entire supply chain. Not only does it pose a threat to the competitive situation of a single enterprise, the entire supply chain is only as strong as its weakest link. It should be comprehensive that in times of decreasing vertical ranges of production, competition no longer is limited to two directly competing enterprises. Competition is increasingly dependent on innovation of suppliers and the effective and efficient management of their processes, as stated above. Therefore, no supply chain would tolerate a weak link over a long period of time, which would pose an unnecessary source of risk to the entire supply chain. We define the term *supply chain risk* as:

an uncertainty or unpredictable event, endogenous or exogenous to the supply chain, affecting one or more of the parties within the supply chain or its

business setting, thereby (negatively) influencing the achievement of business objectives.

It is necessary to say that one of the main risk sources is induced by human beings. The importance of risk management arises from the necessity to identify all the potential threats posed to supply chain continuity. It is necessary to translate the basic methodology of risk management into terms of SCM and to develop a framework that addresses the main threats. It is possible to understand that SCRM is the group of activities developed and performed by supply chain managers, encouraged to minimize and, in the best case, to neutralize the effects of these risks. Therefore, SCRM should be seen as an intersection of the risk management theory applied within the framework of SCM.

As stated in the definition above and shown in Figure 1, risks exist that are endogenous and exogenous to the supply chain. Exogenous risks are risks such as geographical, country or national, natural, and market risks. Market risks can be both exogenous and endogenous due to the fact that every supply chain member has an internal and an external customer.

Endogenous risks can be further subdivided into company and relationship risks. As can be deduced from above, risks can be allocated to more than one risk category. As a consequence, the term "risk" as such can have a different meaning depending on the area, company, country, sector, and so on. Supply chain risks can be controlled, avoided, or reduced, which includes sharing and transferring risk. The inventory risk of higher stocks, for example, can be avoided by using modular product design. This this method of complexity management allows storing less product parts, while offering the same number of variants to the customer. Several risks exist that can only be controlled by means of collaborative measures and incentives. Transparency, availability of information, and mutual trust are success factors for the effective anticipation of risks (Blecker, Kersten, Späth, & Bohn, 2005). Christopher (2003) analyzed the elements influencing risks in supply chains. In his vulnerability report, he identified four different levels at which risk drivers operate in supply chains:

- The first level, the risk drivers related to process and value streams, approaches the supply chain from an idealized integrated end-to-end perspective. From a purely process-based perspective, supply chain risks are principally the financial or commercial risks arising from poor quality, sub-optimal supply chain performance, demand volatility, and shifting marketplace requirements.

In reality, supply chains are rarely fixed, discrete, self-propelling, or self-protecting. The adoption of lean and agile practices (particularly JIT delivery) has made them increasingly reliant on the existence of a reliable, secure, and efficient communication, transport, and distribution infrastructure, thereby making supply chains increasingly vulnerable.

- The second level considers assets and infrastructure dependencies. It refers to the implications of loss (temporary or otherwise) of links, nodes, and other essential operating interfaces. To ensure that they continue to operate is likely to fall within

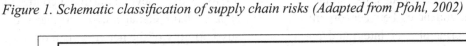

Figure 1. Schematic classification of supply chain risks (Adapted from Pfohl, 2002)

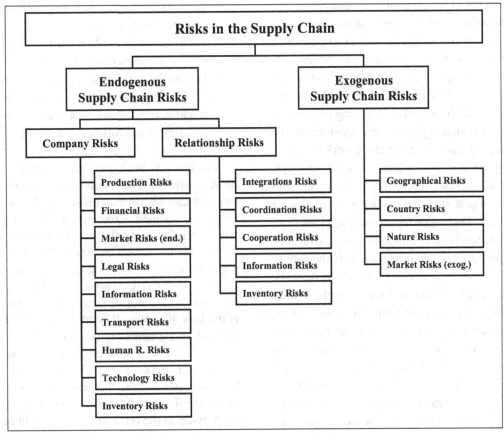

the responsibility of logistics, operations, IT, and human resource professionals. Facilities may house IT assets, which are nodes in the internal and interorganizational communications networks. Supply chain members are connected through nodes and links of national and international communications infrastructure and through the links and nodes of the transportation and distribution infrastructures. The links are, for example, roads, rail, shipping lanes, and flight paths, and nodes are rail stations, ports, and airports.

- The third level considers the organizational aspects that view supply chains as interorganizational networks. It moves supply chain vulnerability up to the level of business strategy and microeconomics. The links become trading relationships, particularly the power dependencies between organizations. The principles of integrated approaches to SCM (as set out in Level 1) rely on the premise that strong organizations will not abuse their position of power vis-à-vis weaker ones. Additionally, that information and risk will be shared selflessly for the good of all, within an enduring network of complementary trading relationships. While supply chain managers may work tirelessly to achieve this objective, other commercial interests, competitive pressures, and divergent strategic goals can work against them. Discretionary reconfigurations (e.g., outsourcing), as well as business failures or mergers and acquisitions within the supply chain or industry can all herald network instability at this and lower levels. Where dominant organizations have the power, capabilities, and the will to manage their supply chains in an open and collaborative way, "extended enterprises" will emerge. However, establishing and monitoring close cooperative partnering relationships is resource-intensive. Consequently, large

sophisticated customers have reduced the number of direct suppliers, often opting for single sourcing (usually by product line) as the lowest cost way to develop, manage, and monitor their supplier base. The downside of this is that it has given rise to one of the most widely recognized sources of supply chain risk—disruptions caused by the failure of a single source supplier.

- The fourth level considers environmental drivers. Factors for consideration are the political, economic, social, and technological elements of the operating and trading environment, as well as natural phenomenon—geological, meteorological, and pathological. All can affect a supply chain at each of the first three levels of the framework. The sources of risks emanating at this level are likely to be beyond the direct control of supply chain managers, nevertheless the susceptibility of the networks can often be assessed in advance, thus enabling informed decisions to be made regarding the merits of risk avoidance or mitigation strategies. For the further development of this chapter, Level 3, organizational, and interorganizational networks will be at the centre of the research in the following sections.

The impacts of supply chain disruptions can be very diverse. The magnitude of the negative impacts can be very decisive for the way the risks are managed. Creating an efficient supply chain, therefore, not only concerns cost-reduction to increase the return on assets (ROA), but also requires sensitive thinking about shortcomings and sources of risk. Another impact on supply chains resulting out of supply chain disruption is the loss of clients. It is common to think that the loss of a client only represents a loss of an order, but this can have bigger repercussions. It is extremely expensive to win an unhappy client back and, in addition, the negative publicity can be extremely harmful. Having the product in the right place, at the right time, at the right quality, and at the right price (4Rs) represents a core issue in market-oriented supply chain management. It is easier to win a new client than to recuperate the trust of an existing one. From this point of view, the effectiveness of the supply chain should avoid this market risk. The reason why financial risk management is probably the most profound risk management discipline is that not achieving financial targets set by management causes the worst outcome of a financial year in respect to a manager's salary or bonus. Therefore, one of the main objectives in a company is to increase the shareholder value. It is possible to see that the interaction between the different participants in the supply chain is a central issue in SCM. However, as shown for the management of financial risks, managers have the habit of not attending to a risk or its driver unless an incentive is at hand.

SCRM can only be implemented in a collaborative effort across the entire supply chain. An example for effects on supply chain performance due to the lack of coordination, where incentives can counteract inefficiencies, is the bullwhip effect. Chopra and Meindl (2004) show how the bullwhip effect increases manufacturing costs, inventory costs, replenishment lead time, transportation costs, shipping and receiving costs, and decreases the level of product availability and profitability of the entire supply chain. The barriers to coordination in the supply chain are among other incentive obstacles. These refer to the incentives offered to different stages or participants in the supply chain that lead to actions that increase variability and reduce total supply chain profits. These can be subdivided into local optimization within functions or stages of a supply chain and sales force incentives. Local optimization incentives focus only on the local strategy of a supply chain member, which do not optimize the total supply chain profits. Improperly structured sales force incentives are significant obstacles to the coordination in supply chains. In many companies, sales force incentives are based on the amount sold to the direct customer during

an evaluation period. The manufacturer measures only the quantity he sells to the distributor or retailers (sell-in), not the quantity sold to the end-consumer (sell-through). An incentive based on sell-in results in order variability being larger than the customer demand variability. In order to reduce the bullwhip effect and increase profitability, management should consider changing the incentives by aligning them with other supply chain members so that every member works toward maximizing total supply chain profit.

According to Chopra and Meindl (2004), there are three general groups of incentives to align objectives within a supply chain: aligning incentives across functions, pricing for coordination, and changing sales force incentives from sell-in to sell-through. The first involves coordinating the objectives of any function with the firm's overall objective. All facility, transportation, and inventory decisions should be evaluated based on their impact on profitability, not total or local costs. This helps to avoid situations like transportation managers making decisions lowering transportation costs but increasing overall supply chain costs at the same time.

It can be seen that the groups of incentives addressed above can have an impact on supply chain management, since they adhere to basic economic principles. However, most of them have not yet been implemented in industry, and for those that have been, it is not clear precisely which effects they had. Another aspect is that no incentive framework has yet been developed to counteract specific supply chain risks. In the following sections, models are developed whereby the mechanisms within supply chains can best be analyzed. It is important to stress that only models including all relevant variables can be used to ultimately deduct incentives needed to align objectives across functions and organizations in a supply chain, in order to optimize supply chain efficiency and counteract supply chain risks.

WHY MODEL SUPPLY CHAIN RISKS IN BUSINESS GAMES?

The aim of this chapter is, as mentioned, the analysis of the interorganizational sources of supply chain risks. Since a supply chain is a very complex system, the approach of modeling and simulating the object of investigation was chosen for this analysis. By simplifying the considered system, a model offers the possibility of elaborating effects and dependencies, which are foreclosed in the real system by many other factors. For analyzing different risks within a supply chain, it is necessary to be able to separate the several effects from each other for analyzing them one-by-one. Another important aspect for using a model and simulating a system is the chance to test strategies and observe their effects in a much shorter period of time than in reality. Also, risky strategies can be tested without fearing extreme or negative results. This aspect is, of course, decisive for analyzing risk management in a supply chain. No real supply chain would be changed according to a strategy that could be damaging to the supply chain performance.

For the concrete modeling of supply chains, many different approaches with different focuses exist. Since the "human factor" is a main cause for supply chain risks, this work focuses on that aspect. Therefore, an approach must be chosen that allows reproducing this non-deterministic human factor. Most models invented in the recent years are computer-based models (for a review of these models, see Chen [2004]). Since these deterministic programs do not allow reproduction of non-deterministic behavior, they are not suitable for the analysis in this work. That is why the approach of a manual business game was chosen for modeling and simulating supply chain risks. In this model, the non-determinism is realized via the human participants of the business game and their unpredictable decisions. The decisions the players have to make during the game correspond to the fundamental decisions in a company,

whereby the realistic behavior of a supply chain can be simulated.

The most famous manual business game on SCM is "The Beer Game" invented by MIT in the 1960s (Sterman, 1992). Since this report wants to focus not only on the dependencies and the business competition between the companies *within* a supply chain, but also *between* two supply chains, a new business game based on The Beer Game idea was developed.

DESCRIPTION OF THE MODEL

Compared to the MIT Beer Game, a main innovation was included in the developed business game—in the new game, two supply chains are competing with each other with the same product on the same market. The products that are manufactured by the supply chains are tables. The supply chains purchase from the same source, a "forest," by buying trees. At the end, both deliver to the same market, namely, the end-consumer, by selling complete tables. In between, there are three supply chain stations, which represent companies. These are a saw mill, a carpenter, and a dealer. The three stations of the two supply chains will be referred to as agents in the rest of this chapter, and are represented by one to three players each. The forest and the end-consumer are played by the supervisors of the game. As can be seen in Figure 2, each agent has a supplier upstream in the supply chain and a customer downstream in the supply chain.

This constellation of different companies was chosen because the interorganizational sources of risks are the focus of this work. From the game-theoretic approach, the business game was developed on two different game settings that will be analyzed later in this chapter. As can be seen in Figure 3, these are the "Dealer Game" and the "Internal Game."

The first approach contains the competition of the two supply chains against each other for a

Figure 2. Arrangement of the two supply chains

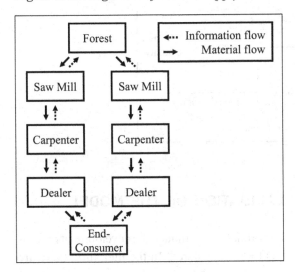

The parameters of the agents, which are relevant for a game-theoretic analysis, are chosen according to the interorganizational focus. In both games, the same inputs and outputs of the agents are identified as significant. These parameters are, as presented in Figure 4, the orders and deliveries, as well as the costs and revenues. Also, the inventory was taken into account, since ineffective stock represents a non-negligible risk of either non-availability of products or high capital lockup.

According to the identified parameters the business game was set on these characteristics as follows:

- The players are only allowed to communicate with each other by sending orders to their supplier and delivering goods to their customer. In each round the agents receive one order and one box with goods and send one of each. In the first ten rounds it takes two rounds until an order or a box reaches its destination. Later it is possible to shorten this time to one round.

maximal share of a fixed end-consumer demand. This game can be simplified by considering only the dealer and the end-consumer as agents. The second game setting analyses games within the supply chain, in which single agents compete in two-player games.

Figure 3. Game theoretic constellations in the supply chain game

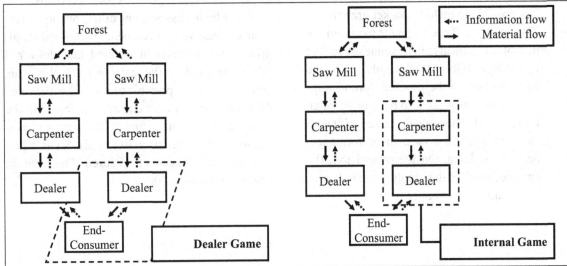

Figure 4. Main parameters of the agents

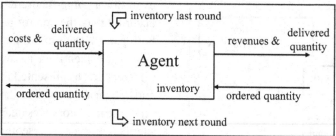

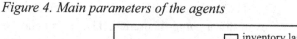

- As a core element of the game the agents set a price for their product, that is, one table or the material for one table, respectively. Each agent decides how many products he wants to order from its supplier. Only the forest and the end-consumer have different rules—the price the forest sets for the saw mill is fixed, and the order of the end-consumer depends on an arithmetical function. The function determines the quantity the end-consumer buys from the two dealers in relation to the price the dealers set. Another aspect is included in the function. The end-consumer sets a penalty for the next round, that is, he buys less tables when the dealers are not able to deliver as many tables as the end-consumer ordered. The whole amount of the bought tables is normally fixed, but it is possible to include market growth.
- The intention of each agent is to maximize its profit. The agent gains revenues by selling its products to its customer, subtracting the costs for buying the product from its supplier. Costs for stock also have to be taken into account. The profit of the agent is taken as an indicator for its own performance, on the one hand. On the other hand, the summed profit of the supply chain indicates the group's performance.

VALIDATION OF THE MODEL

For validating the model, the development process has to be considered. In the literature, there are two main possible approaches to developing a business model: the deductive logic and the inductive logic (Davis, 2005). Where the inductive model is developed from an empirical analysis of the reality and then generalizing and abstracting the parts of interest, the deductive model is based on a conceptual structure. Basic validated economic functions are combined modularly to generate a new model. In the case of SCRM, a deductive model is advantageous, because this approach allows the analyst to focus on the main points of interest. By designing a model based on validated modules, it is ensured that the model supports these effects and represents them correctly.

For a better assessment of the results, a reference game was developed. In this game, all prices and amounts of ordered and delivered tables are fixed on the starting level. With this construction, it is possible to prove that the rules do not promote or even enforce one result. In the considered case, all agents of both supply chains got the same profit after 30 rounds. So an equal treatment of all agents is ensured. This amount was normalized at 100%.

Since the agents that are closer to the end-consumer have the advantage of noticing changes of the market first, they are expected to profit by minimizing stock. That is why a "handicap" for the downstream agents was implemented by higher stock costs. As a result, when fixing all prices and amounts, the profits from Figure 5 will be reached.

SIMULATION OF THE SUPPLY CHAIN BY BUSINESS GAMES

On seven dates, the business game was played with different groups of undergraduate and graduate students under the supervision of the authors. These students were not involved in developing the game. In addition, they were not informed about the objectives of this research, and the game was communicated as a teaching instrument so that they should act independently without being influenced.

At each game, 6 to 12 persons took part, and 30 rounds were played. In the first two rounds, all prices and order amounts were fixed, in order to give the players the chance to get into the game. After the fourth round, a market growth was implemented, that is, the amount of tables bought by the end-consumer was increased.

As mentioned, the profits of the agents were used as an indicator for their performance. In Table 1, the result of each supply chain agent after 30 rounds is presented for the seven played games. For each game, the winner and the loser are marked by boldface.

From the results of the games, it is visible that, in most cases (five out of seven), the best and worst results were achieved in the same supply chain. Furthermore, the standard deviations in the right columns show that there are mainly two different cases of supply chain performance. The one is that the agents reach very similar results, that is, the supply chain has a very low standard deviation. This is reached, for example, for Supply Chain 1 in Game 1 or Game 2. In the other case, a high standard deviation occurred, that is, one agent with a very high result benefits from at least one other who achieved a very poor result. This clearly demonstrates two different strategies of working in a supply chain. One is the cooperative strategy,

Figure 5. Profit of the three agents after thirty rounds (Reference game with handicap)

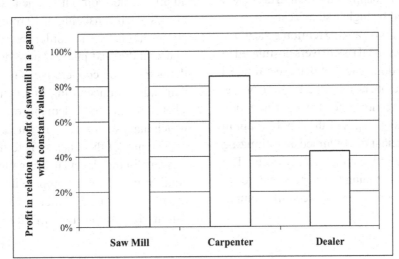

Table 1. Profits of supply chain agents after 30 rounds

	Supply Chain 1			Supply Chain 2			Standard Deviation SC 1	Standard Deviation SC 2
	Saw Mill 1	Carpenter 1	Dealer 1	Saw Mill 2	Carpenter 2	Dealer 2		
Game 1	152%	138%	121%	*199%*	*-29%*	151%	*16%*	120%
Game 2	95%	106%	77%	82%	*54%*	*269%*	*15%*	117%
Game 3	186%	227%	*434%*	*117%*	316%	388%	*133%*	141%
Game 4	*80%*	122%	*261%*	223%	146%	121%	95%	*53%*
Game 5	121%	129%	152%	*32%*	167%	*209%*	*16%*	92%
Game 6	92%	157%	*-19%*	72%	42%	*182%*	89%	*73%*
Game 7	53%	*96%*	28%	67%	34%	42%	34%	*17%*

where all agents try to benefit in equal terms. The other is the non-cooperative strategy, where each agent maximizes its own profit without caring about the others. In this case, higher revenues can be achieved than in the first case, however, normally, only for one agent and mostly for the agent closest to the end-consumer; in five out of seven cases, the dealer won the game. In Figure 6, the average profits for each kind of agent are calculated. It can be seen that the dealers, on average, gained approximately 50% higher profits than the saw mills or the carpenters. It has to be mentioned that this happened although the dealer was handicapped by higher stock costs.

The results of this passage reinforce the intra- and interorganizational risk drivers postulated in the previous section. The fact that the strongest supply chain members reap the highest profits shows that the incentives for local optimization within functions or stages of the supply chain in place are insufficient or not aimed at optimizing the performance of the entire supply chain. The importance of developing the right incentives to encourage the cooperation between the companies is given.

THE GAME-THEORETIC ANALYSIS OF SUPPLY CHAIN RISKS

Analyzed in a game-theoretic context, it is evident that the developed game is a static, multi-period game with time dependence. This is because all players make their decisions at the same time, over many periods. Thirty rounds were played in the analyzed games, and some decisions take more than one round to show consequence. Since the game can theoretically go on for more than the 30 rounds played, it is considered to be one with an infinite horizon. The game is subdivided into phases, each consisting of 10 rounds. After each phase, the players can confer about which strategy to use in the next phase. Therefore, we consider the game to be cooperative. The end-consumer demand is set according to a demand function. Therefore, the total demand of tables is fixed, which makes it a zero-sum game.

The aim of this chapter is to find an optimal strategy for the players in this game—a so-called equilibrium—and to compare it to the setting in the played game. Fudenberg and Tirole (1992) summarize: "a Nash equilibrium is a profile of strategies such that each player's strategy is an optimal response to the other buyers' strategies" (p. 11).

The implication of a Nash equilibrium for supply chain risk management (SCRM) is that the configuration of a supply chain is only then optimal to a specific supply chain participant, if it is favorable to all participants. The term "configuration" addresses the organizational and interorganizational constellations and the related risk drivers described in the beginning of this chapter.

The Nash equilibrium is defined by Nash (1950) as:

an n-tuple S_i^* is an equilibrium point if and only if for every i, $\pi_i\left(S_i^*\right) = \max_{all\ r_i}\left[\pi_i\left(S_i^*; r_i\right)\right]$. Thus an equilibrium point is an n-tuple S_i^* such that each player's mixed strategy maximizes his pay-off if the strategies of the others are held fixed. Thus each player's strategy is optimal against those of the others. (p. 3)

Subscripts in the definition are: π_i, which are the payoffs of the players i, following mixed strategies r_i. When the term n-tuple is used, we refer to a set of items that are each associated with a mixed strategy. A mixed strategy of a player i, in turn, is a collection of non-negative numbers, which have unit sum and are in one-to-one correspondence with the player's pure strategies.

In the supply chain game, two game settings exist, as shown in Figure 3. In the first, the two supply chains compete against each other, trying to maximize their respective share of the fixed customer demand. This game can be simplified by considering only the dealers as players, that is, an exogenous game constellation. The game shows a two-player game setup, similar to that described by Cachon and Netessine (2004). To simplify the analysis shown in the section "Static, Non-Repetitive Game Analysis," we assume the game to be a unique, single-period game, in which no time-dependency exists. This means that decisions in former games have no influence on decisions in the round analyzed. The aim is to evaluate whether or not a Nash equilibrium for dealer collusions exist. The initial assumption can be relaxed in the section "Exogenous, Infinite-Horizon, Inventory Game Analysis," where time dependency is introduced for a specific infinite-horizon game. Here, the aim will be to analyze which optimality conditions exist for a single dealer in a duopoly described by the

Figure 6. Average profits of the three kinds of agents

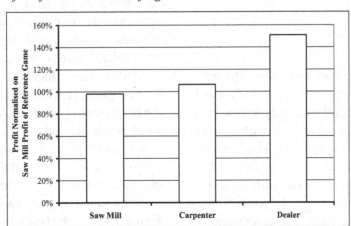

supply chain game. The third analysis considers endogenous games, in which single players compete in two-player games. These games are comparable to the inventory-games described by Netessine and Rudi (2003). They will be adjusted to this context in the section "Endogenous, Single Period, Inventory Game Analysis."

Static, Non-Repetitive Game Analysis

In essence, the two-player-game corresponds to the Newsvendor Game that Cachon and Netessine (2004) use as a basis for their analysis. As shown in Figure 7, the game is "symmetric and non-cooperative, which means that the players are indistinguishable, except for their names, and make decisions at the same time" (Morris, 1994, p. 59). The subscripts $i, j \in \{1; 2\}$ are used for the two players or dealers. The price the dealer demands this round is p_i, that of the last round is $\tilde{p}_i$. The pay-offs are π_i.

Every player decides on the price p_i of its product at the beginning of every round. The exogenous demand, symbolized by D_i, is then set according to the demand function of the customer. The price scenario, shown and discussed above, is inextricably intertwined with the following demand function:

$$D_i = \frac{\left(\frac{p_i + p_j}{2 p_i}\right)^3}{\left(\frac{p_i + p_j}{2 p_i}\right)^3 + \left(\frac{p_i + p_j}{2 p_j}\right)^3} ; \quad i, j \in \{1; 2\} \qquad (1)$$

If both players reduce their price, the total monetary market volume shrinks due to the fixed demand in tables within this duopoly, irrespective of the total budget. Conversely, the market grows when both decide to raise their price in equal amounts without changing the demand allocation. Market growth is indicated by the size of the letters in the matrix. The unit costs of the product are c_i and the unit revenues are r_i. The order quantity

of the dealer is given by Q_i. In the supply chain game, the products that Dealers 1 and 2 sell are substitutable. As a result, if the demanded price of Dealer 1 is too high, the customer simply buys from Dealer 2.

Each player wants to maximize payoffs by minimizing warehousing costs and maximizing earnings corresponding to demand. Deduced from the general optimization problem, this is a very strong assumption to make. However, relaxing this assumption would change the model to an extent as to make it irrelevant for use on the supply chain game model, where both dealers deliver to the same end-consumer. From the common Newsvendor Game, we arrive at the following optimization problem:

$$\max_{Q_i} \pi_i = \max_{Q_i} E_D \left[r_i \min(D_i, Q_i) - c_i Q_i \right] \qquad (2)$$

E_D marks the expected demand. Therefore, the function is a demand maximizing problem in which the variable order quantity Q_i needs to be optimized. In Figure 8, the schematic game setting in the analyzed game is presented.

A strategy in this game is optimal when the best response function in relation to the competitors demand is maximized. The best response function is defined by Cachon and Netessine (2004) as follows: "Given an n-player game, player i's best response (function) to the strategies y_i of the other players is the strategy y_{i-} that maximizes player i's payoff $\pi_i(y_i, y_i)$" (p. 17). The inventory level is the variable to be optimized by determining the corresponding order quantity Q_i. The ability of a dealer to deliver the exact amount of tables ordered (service reliability) only plays a role in the next games. Therefore, it is assumed here that the best response for the dealer is determined by its ability to maximize demand. Since demand is dependent on the price settings in relation to that of the competitor in this duopoly, the optimal price setting of a dealer is where his best response function reaches a local maximum. As Figure 9 shows, the best response for a dealer in

Figure 8. Game settings in the single period game

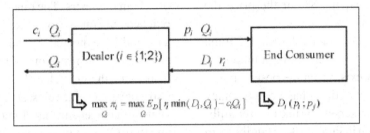

Figure 9. Best response of dealer's price settings in relation to the competitor

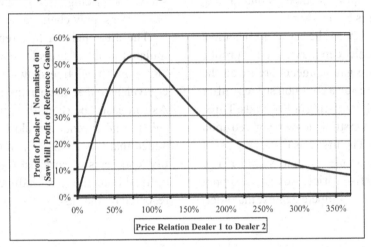

Figure 10. Best response functions of both dealers

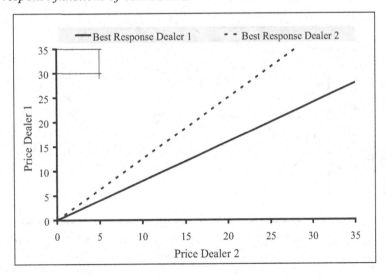

this duopolistic game setting would be to choose a price at approximately 78% of the price the competitor chooses.

According to the definitions of Nash (1950) and Fudenberg and Tirole (1992) above, a unique or multiple equilibria exist when the best response functions of the competitors have one or many intersections. Each intersection marks an equilibrium. As can be seen in Figure 10, no equilibrium exists for the duopoly under the assumption above and a single period analysis. Therefore, no ideal price setting can be found for every dealer to maximize his own profit without counteracting the objectives of his competitor.

Collusions might be an alternative arrangement by which every dealer can maximize his profits. In the supply chain game, agents are given the opportunity to agree on a common strategy after every game period, consisting of 10 rounds. Three variations of common strategies were agreed upon in our simulation. The first was that every agent orders the same quantities from its supplier. The second considered fixed prices, so that the supply chain can effectively compete against the other,

and the third was free competition among the supply chain members. The quantity agreement was reached only once. However, this strategy failed, as could be expected, because order quantities of the customer result out of the price set by the dealer and, therefore, hardly stay constant. This is a strategy that comes closest to the centralized inventory management model analyzed by Netessine and Rudi (2003). Further analysis of the strategy is abandoned here because it has no significance to the game. The second strategy was more relevant because it showed interesting results. Figure 11 shows the pricing strategy alternatives a dealer has in the supply chain game.

The area under a line represents the accumulated profit of a dealer over 10 rounds. The "Random Price" line shows the realistic pricing equivalent to that made in the supply chain game. As can easily be seen, this strategy amounts to suboptimal revenue developments. It might be added that this is the only of the four strategies that conforms to antitrust regulations. A more optimal outcome to an individual dealer is represented by the case where the two agree to take

Figure 11. Normalized profits of dealers

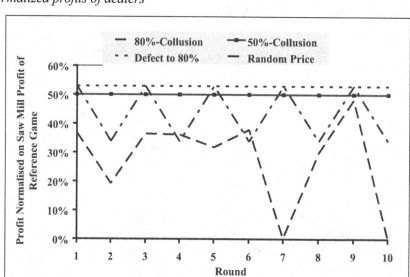

Figure 12. Average agent profits per round

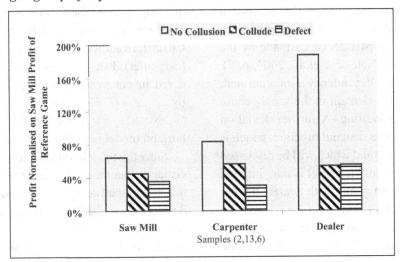

chances at offering their products at 80% of the other's price. Hence, oscillating revenues result, as the line "80%-Collusion" shows. In the next strategy, both agree to offer their products at the same price, which amounts to a 50% market share for both players. Another interesting observation is the strategy marked "Defect to 80%." This makes clear why this game has no equilibrium. A participant in collusion, as marked by 80% or 50%-Collusion, always has an incentive to defect by making use of his knowledge about the other's pricing strategy, even though it promises only slightly higher payoffs (compare Nash, 1950). However, when doing so, the competitor will soon realize that his competitor defected and go back to the "Random Price" strategy.

Figure 12 shows the realistic results gained from the first simulations with the supply chain game. The data analyzed only considers the games in which the players chose the advanced transportation and communication alternatives.

One would assume that profit and risk sharing among supply chain members, as propagated by modern SCM and SCRM theory, would ultimately increase joined accumulated profits. However,

the supply chain game indicates that it is of little advantage to any member. It must be added that the represented amount of simulations is not significant. However, it indicates that free competition is the better option for all agents. One might also add that other reasons for this result might be that important variables of real supply chains, like the importance of innovation out of R&D investments, are missing, and that the games in which supply chains colluded showed less market growth than those with free competition. Future simulations with the supply chain game will have to state whether the first assumptions are correct.

Exogenous, Infinite-Horizon, Inventory Game Analysis

As discussed, the infinite-horizon game is an extension of the single-period game, by introducing time dependency. Netessine, Rudi, and Wang (2004) discuss an inventory-competition model, which is aimed at deducting incentives to backorder. The setup is similar to what we described here, in that they define a duopolistic setup between two suppliers (retailers) competing for orders. However, several assumptions they make are relaxed in this game model. One is that they "assume that the first-choice demand does not depend on any past decisions made by the competing firms" (Netessine et al., 2004, p. 7). In this model, a time dependency is incorporated, which forms a core element in the supply chain games demand allocation. A further deviation marks the exogenous demand function, which is a modification of (1) and which will be discussed later. A restriction to this model is that, implied by the supply chain game, both dealers deliver to only one customer. This does have relevance to real supply chain constellations because there is an abundance of SMEs delivering to only one OEM.

The infinite-horizon model is given by the same subscripts as described in the previous section, "Static, Non-Repetitive Game Analysis." Enhancements to the model above are the periods $t = 1,...,n$ of observation, as indicated in Figure 13. The inventory of a dealer is given by $x_i^t = y_i^{t-1} - d_i^{t-1}$, where $x_i^t \geq 0$. The order quantity of the dealer is symbolized by Q_i^τ, where $\tau = t - (T_T + T_C)$ marks the time delay of deliveries. The time lag in the time dependency is therefore created by transport time, which is given by $T_T \in \{1; 2\}$ (rounds) and communication time by $T_C \in \{1; 2\}$ (rounds). An assumption for this game-theoretic model, predetermined by the supply chain game, is that the

dealer of Supply Chain 1 always orders an order quantity Q_i^τ from the carpenter of Supply Chain 1, who, in turn, buys from the saw mill of Supply Chain 1. In addition, we assume that the supplier (carpenter) always delivers the exact quantity ordered. Inventory replenishment is hence described by $y_i^t = x_i^t + Q_i^\tau$. Constraints to the subscripts are $Q_i^\tau \geq 0$ and $y_i^t \geq x_i^t$. Price per period in the infinite-horizon model is denoted by $p_i^t \geq 0$.

Since this model reduces the customer base of the dealers to one, the exogenous demand $D_i^t(p_i^t; p_j^t)$ denotes the total demand of the customer from both dealers as described by (1). Exogenous demand adheres to the constraint: $D_i^t \geq 0$. Total exogenous demand is fixed at $D^t \in \{20; 28\}$, which marks demand before and after "market growth" in round 4. Hence, total exogenous demand is given by $D^t = \overline{D}_i^t + \overline{D}_j^t$. In an infinite-horizon game, whether a dealer ran out of stock in the previous round also matters. This is why a penalty for non-delivery, given by ∂_i^t, is incorporated by $\overline{D}_i^t = \partial_i^t D_i^t$. The penalty has the following characteristics:

$$\partial_i^t(y_i^{t-1}; \overline{D}_i^{t-1}) = \frac{\min\left(y_i^{t-1}; \overline{D}_i^{t-1}\right)}{\overline{D}_i^{t-1}},$$

where $0 \leq \partial_i^t \leq 1$. The optimization condition aims at minimizing negative stock deviation or understocking. The inventory balance equation is:

Figure 13. Infinite horizon game constellation

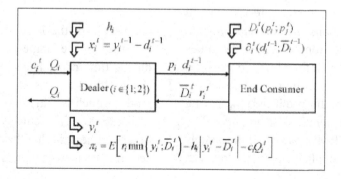

Box 1. Equation 3

$$\pi_i^t = E\left[r_i^t \min\left(y_i^t ; \overline{D}_i^t \right) - h_i \left| y_i^t - \overline{D}_i^t \right| - c_i^t Q_i^t \right]; \quad i \in \{1;2\}; \forall t = 1,...,n$$

Box 2. Equation 4

$$
\begin{aligned}
\pi_i(y_i^t > \overline{D}_i^t) &= E\sum_{t=1}^{\infty}\left[r_i^t \min\left(y_i^t ; \overline{D}_i^t \right) - h_i \left| y_i^t - \overline{D}_i^t \right| - c_i^t Q_i^t \right] \\
&= E\sum_{t=1}^{\infty}\left[r_i^t \min\left(y_i^t ; \overline{D}_i^t \right) - h_i \left| y_i^t - \overline{D}_i^t \right| - c_i^t y_i^t + c_i^t x_i^t \right] \\
&= E\left\{ \sum_{t=2}^{\infty}\left[r_i^t \min\left(y_i^t ; \overline{D}_i^t \right) - h_i \left| y_i^t - \overline{D}_i^t \right| - c_i^t y_i^t + c_i^{t-1}\left| y_i^{t-1} - \overline{D}_i^{t-1} \right| \right] \right\} \\
&\quad + E\left\{ r_i^1 \min\left(y_i^1 ; \overline{D}_i^1 \right) - h_i \left| y_i^1 - \overline{D}_i^1 \right| - c_i^1\left(y_i^1 - x_i^1 \right) \right\} \\
&= E\left\{ \sum_{t=2}^{\infty}\left[r_i^t \min\left(y_i^t ; \overline{D}_i^t \right) - h_i \left| y_i^t - \overline{D}_i^t \right| - c_i^t y_i^t + c_i^{t-1}\left| y_i^{t-1} - \overline{D}_i^{t-1} \right| \right] \right\} \\
&\quad + E\left\{ r_i^1 \min\left(y_i^1 ; \overline{D}_i^1 \right) - h_i \left| y_i^1 - \overline{D}_i^1 \right| - c_i^1 y_i^1 - c_i^1 x_i^1 \right\} \\
&= c_i^1 x_i^1 + E\sum_{t=1}^{\infty}\left[r_i^t \min\left(y_i^t ; \overline{D}_i^t \right) - h_i \left| y_i^t - \overline{D}_i^t \right| - c_i^t y_i^t + c_i^t \left| y_i^t - \overline{D}_i^t \right| \right] \\
&\quad i \in \{1;2\}, \forall t = 1,...,n
\end{aligned}
$$

$x_i^{t+1} = \left| y_i^t - \overline{D}_i^t \right|$. A profit maximizing dealer tries to turn over his total inventory once per round, whereby the delivery quantities would equal the inventory levels. When a dealer decides on his inventory level y_i^t for the period, his single-period expected net profit under the lost sale assumption is in correspondence with (2), given by Equation 3, shown in Box 1.

Thereby, it becomes a profit-maximizing problem, in which stock deviation from demand needs to be minimized. Corresponding to the last section, "Static, Non-Repetitive Game Analysis," cost and revenue parameters of the dealer are the unit costs c_i^t unit revenues r_i^t and unit inventory holding costs h_i. In analogy to Netessine et al. (2004), the total profit of the dealer over infinite periods, starting with initial inventories $x^1 \equiv (x_1^1 ; x_2^1)$ as is the case in the supply chain game, amounts to Equation 4, shown in Box 2.

To derive this result $Q_i^t = y_i^t - x_i^t$, and $c_i^t x_i^t = c_i^{t-1}\left| y_i^{t-1} - \overline{D}_i^{t-1} \right|$ for $t \geq 2$ are inserted. Further, we assume that the revenue $r_i^t \min(y_i^t ; \overline{D}_i^t)$ for $y_i^t > \overline{D}_i^t$ consists of the sold quantity $\left(r_i^t \cdot \overline{D}_i^t \right)$, from which opportunity costs $\left[r_i^t \cdot \left(y_i^t - \overline{D}_i^t \right) \right]$ are subtracted. Substituting the variable part of the optimization results to:

$$\pi_i(y_i^t > \overline{D}_i^t) = c_i x_i^1 + E\sum_{t=1}^{\infty} G_i^t\left(y_i^t \right) \quad i \in \{1;2\}; \forall t = 1,...,n$$

(5)

where

$$G_i^t\left(y_i^t \right) = \left(r_i^t - c_i^t \right)\overline{D}_i^t - \left(r_i^t - c_i^t \right)\left(\overline{D}_i^t - y_i^t \right) - \left(h_i + c_i^t \right)\left(y_i^t - \overline{D}_i^t \right)$$
$$i \in \{1;2\}; \forall t = 1,...,n$$

(6)

Now we introduce the notation $u_i^t = r_i^t - c_i^t$ for understocking costs or lost profit (opportunity costs), and $o_i^{\,t} = h_i + c_i^{\,t}$ for overstocking costs. The expected single-period net profit is therefore:

$$\pi_i^{\,t}(y_i^{\,t} > \overline{D}_i^{\,t}) = E\left[u_i^{\,t} \overline{D}_i^{\,t} - u_i^{\,t}\left(\overline{D}_i^{\,t} - y_i^{\,t} \right) - o_i^{\,t}\left(y_i^{\,t} - \overline{D}_i^{\,t} \right) \right]$$
$$i \in \{1;2\}; \forall\, t = 1,...,n$$

(7)

To determine the single-period profit-maximizing combination, the first derivative is made. Since demand is a function of the order level, the hidden derivate is given by:

$$\overline{D}'^{\,t}_i = \frac{\partial \overline{D}_i^{\,t}}{\partial y_i^{\,t}}.$$

It is assumed that the demand distribution $\overline{D}'^{\,t}_i$ can be approximated by a non-linear function with inventory-level dependency. The single-period derivative is shown in Equation 8.

$Br_i^{\,t}\left(\overline{D}_i^{\,t} < y_i^{\,t} \right)$ defines the best response of i and thereby the profit-maximizing point with the hidden variable dependencies of $y_i^{\,t}$. For $\dfrac{\partial \pi_i^{\,t}}{\partial y_i^{\,t}} = 0$ we get Equation 9.

It can be seen that the best response function consists of an endogenous part, consisting of the variables for unit costs and unit revenues $r_i^{\,t}$, and an exogenous part consisting of the quotient derivative of the non-linear demand distribution. Lippman and McCardle (1997) have demonstrated

in their Newsvendor Game that this Nash equilibrium exists. Netessine and Rudi (2003) show that this is a unique and globally stable equilibrium.

Re-introducing the notation $u_i^{\,t} = r_i^{\,t} - c_i^{\,t}$ for understocking cost or lost profit (opportunity cost), and $o_i^{\,t} = h_i + c_i^{\,t}$ for overstocking cost gives more insight into the optimality condition. See Equation 10.

Figure 14 schematically shows the path of the optimality condition (10). The profit function in the unique Nash equilibrium of this model shows a hyperbolic path and the unit costs function shows a linear path.

Both variables, unit costs $c_i^{\,t}$ and unit revenues $r_i^{\,t}$, span a three-dimensional plain, which results in a shift of the exogenous part of the best-response function. For further interpretation of this global Nash equilibrium, refer to the section, "Outcomes." The exogenous part is not considered in the graph and can only be incorporated once precise approximations can be made. Therefore, the graph only represents an idealized path with linear distribution.

Endogenous, Single-Period, Inventory Game Analysis

The supply chain game constellations analyzed up to now show that the main game variable rel-

Box 3. Equation 8

$$\frac{\partial \pi_i^{\,t}}{\partial y_i^{\,t}} = u_i^{\,t} \overline{D}'^{\,t}_i - \left[u_i^{\,t}\left(1 - \overline{D}'^{\,t}_i \right) + o_i^{\,t}\left(1 - \overline{D}'^{\,t}_i \right) \right] Br_i^{\,t}(\overline{D}_i^{\,t} < y_i^{\,t})$$

$$= u_i^{\,t} \overline{D}'^{\,t}_i - \left[\left(u_i^{\,t} + o_i^{\,t} \right)\left(1 - \overline{D}'^{\,t}_i \right) \right] Br_i^{\,t}(\overline{D}_i^{\,t} < y_i^{\,t})$$

Box 4. Equation 9

$$Br_i^{\,t}(\overline{D}_i^{\,t} < y_i^{\,t}) = C \cdot \frac{u_i^{\,t}}{u_i^{\,t} + o_i^{\,t}}; C = \frac{D_i'^{\,t}}{1 - D_i'^{\,t}} = const.; \quad i \in \{1;2\}; \forall\, t = 1,...,n.$$

Box 5. Equation 10

$$Br_i^t(\overline{D}_i^t < y_i^t) = C \cdot \frac{r_i^t - c_i^t}{r_i^t + h_i}; \; C = \frac{D_i''}{1 - D_i''} = const.; \quad i \in \{1;2\}; \; \forall \, t = 1,...,n.$$

Box 6. Equation 11

$$\pi_i(y_i; y_{i-}) = E\left[u_i D_i - u_i |D_i - y_i| - o_i |y_i - D_i|\right]$$
$$= E\left\{u_i D_i - \left[u_i(y_i - D_i) + o_i(y_i - D_i)\right]\right\}; \quad i \in \{1;...;n\}; \; D_i < y_i$$

evant for the optimization of a player's pay-offs is the inventory level of an agent i. Therefore, this section follows the same approach, analyzing the optimal inventory constellation of an agent i within the supply chain. For a model of the interactions within the supply chain as shown in Figure 3, two scenarios are given by Netessine and Rudi (2003). The first is a centralized inventory-management model, where the assumption is made that an overall inventory management is in place. The second is a decentralized-inventory model, in which every agent manages his own inventory. The experience made in the supply chain game shows that it is questionable how high the information connectivity must be to enable a centralized inventory management across the supply chain and to which extent supply chain members are prepared to give these decisions out of hand. The option of centralized inventory management was, therefore, abandoned in this section. The decentralized inventory-management model corresponds to that of Netessine and Rudi (2003). The optimal decision of agent i depends on the vector of inventory levels of the other agents in the same supply chain because one agent cannot substitute the product of its supplier against the product of an agent of the other supply chain. Staying with the notation of the analysis above, the inventory level of the agent is given by y_i and that of the other agents by y_{i-}. For simplicity of

the model, a single-period model is regarded; therefore, it does not contain time dependency. Demand D_i is then to a great extent influenced by the demand function given by (1). The function determines the demand of the dealer, which, in turn, is biased by the non-delivery penalty. An approximation of the demand distribution in this model D_i is given by a linear demand distribution function of the order quantity of the predecessor, which is a function of the inventory level of agent i. The expected profit of agent i in analogy to (4) is therefore given by Equation 11.

A game-theoretic situation arises where agent i will employ the best-response strategy $\tilde{y}_i$, which agent i plays to y_{i-} in an competitive environment. The equilibrium condition is therefore given by:

$$\pi_i(\tilde{y}_i; y_{i-}) = \max_{y_i} \pi_i(y_i; y_{i-}).$$

The best response will be denoted by $\tilde{y}_i \equiv Br_i(y_{i-})$. Given y_{i-}, it can be verified that π_i is concave in y_i. To obtain the best response, the first derivative of π_i with respect to y_i results in Equation 12. The best response under the condition that

$$D_i' = \frac{\partial D_i'}{\partial y_i} = const.$$

Box 7. Equation 12

$$\frac{\partial \pi_i}{\partial y_i} = u_i D_i' - \left[u_i \left(1 - D_i' \right) + o_i \left(1 - D_i' \right) \right] Br_i (D_i < y_i)$$

$$= u_i D_i' - \left[\left(u_i + o_i \right) \left(1 - D_i' \right) \right] Br_i (D_i < y_i); \quad i \in \{1; ...; n\}$$

Box 8. Equation 13

$$Br_i (D_i < y_i) = C \cdot \frac{u_i}{u_i + o_i}; \quad C = \frac{D_i'}{1 - D_i'} = const.; \quad i \in \{1; ...; n\}$$

Box 9. Equation 14

$$Br_i^t (\overline{D}_i^t < y_i^t) = C \cdot \frac{u_i^t}{u_i^t + o_i^t}; \quad C = \frac{D_i''^t}{1 - D_i''^t} = const.; \quad i \in \{1; 2\}; \forall t = 1, ..., n.$$

Box 10. Equation 15

$$Br_i (D_i < y_i) = C \cdot \frac{u_i}{u_i + o_i}; \quad C = \frac{D_i'}{1 - D_i'} = const.; \quad i \in \{1; ...; n\}$$

and $D_i' \geq 0$ is then characterized by Equation 13.

Interestingly, the result is the same as it was for the infinite horizon dealer game. This insinuates that the optimality condition of the exogenous game corresponds to that of the endogenous game. For the task of finding globally adequate incentives, this is a very valuable finding.

Outcomes

For the infinite-horizon game model, we have found a unique, globally stable, pure strategy Nash equilibrium, which is characterized by Equation 14, as was the case for the inventory game as in Equation 15.

As described above, first indications lead us to the assumption that demand for the dealer-game can be approximated by a non-linear function of higher order. Conversely, demand for the internal game can be approximated by a linear function. A comparison of these results shows that the internal best-response function then contains a numeric constant, whereas the dealer game's best response contains the above-named exogenous function of the order greater than zero. Since warehousing and product costs increase to the end of the supply chain, $h_{i\,endo} < h_{i\,exo}$, $c_{i\,endo}^t < c_{i\,exo}^t$ and $r_{i\,endo}^t < r_{i\,exo}^t$. Using the assumption that they differ in equal amounts, we can deduce that:

$$\frac{u_i}{u_i + o_i} \cong \frac{u_i^t}{u_i^t + o_i^t} \qquad (16)$$

If this holds, we can follow from (14) and (15), for a single period that:

$$Br_{exo} = Ext \cdot Br_{endo} \qquad (17)$$

Br_{exo} stands for the best response of the dealer game, and Br_{endo} for that of the inventory game. The term Ext in (17) is the time-dependant, non-linear factor, which characterizes a negative externality to the supply chain. Externalities are effects not directly reflected in the market. In the supply chain, it is the factor causing higher inventory levels upstream in the supply chain, without an equivalent remuneration (Pindyck & Rubinfeld, 1989). In this case, it amounts to the quotient of the endogenous and the exogenous parts of the best-response functions. Since the critical variable in the profit-optimization problem was that of inventory levels, the interpretation of these results shows that $0 < Ext < 1$. This implies that the externality naturally induces higher inventory levels for internal supply chain members in comparison to those members with access to the market. This finding corresponds to the supply chain game, where an extreme profit difference was noted in favor of the downstream supply chain, although the game settings were biased in favor of the upstream supply chain.

As mentioned before, literature in which game theory was applied to supply chain or logistics problems, as shown by Netessine et al. (2004), deducted equilibria for warehousing problems between two agents. Comparing these equilibria for the internal and external case in the researched game, we found that a natural disadvantage exists for upstream supply chain members, which induces a risk for all members. This pinpoints a barrier that in our mind can only be overcome by means of incentives. These need to fulfill two tasks: aligning supply chain objectives, and

eliminating the risk that defection is a feasible option for a single supply chain member.

FUTURE TRENDS

High inventory levels influence the cost reduction capabilities of a supply chain. Inefficient inventory management causes market price increases when overstocking occurs. On the other hand, understocking causes shipment quantity inaccuracies, a lack of supply availability, and has a negative impact on the volume mix requirements. All are supply risk characteristics as described by Zsidisin (2003) and are directly caused by the bullwhip effect. As we showed in the supply chain game, the bullwhip effect can only be mitigated up to a certain extent when implementing classical supply chain management measures such as improved communication and transportation infrastructure. As long as supply chain members follow different objectives, warehouse management or stocking along the supply chain will be inefficient and ineffective.

Chopra and Meindl (2004) identified three general categories of incentives for SCM by which common supply chain risk management objectives can be coordinated: aligning incentives across functions, pricing for coordination, and changing sales force incentives from sell-in to sell-through. The first involves coordinating the objectives of any function with the firm's overall objective. All facility, transportation, and inventory decisions should be evaluated based on their impact on profitability, not total or local costs. Pricing for coordination shows a model by which the market power of a manufacturer is regarded. If a manufacturer has no market power but large fixed costs associated with each lot, he should use lot-sized quantity discounts to achieve coordination for commodity products. Where the manufacturer has market power, he should introduce price discrimination by using two-part tariffs and volume discounts to help achieve coordination (Besanco, Dranove, Shanley, & Schaefer, 2004). Given demand uncertainty, manufacturers can use buy-back, revenue sharing, and quantity flexibility contracts to spur retailers to provide levels of product availability that maximize supply chain profits. Altering sales force incentives from sell-in to sell-through reduces the incentives for sales persons to push products to the retailer. Linking sales directly to the point-of-sale data can give supply chains a better planning horizon and considerably reduce variation of manufacturer sales compared to end-consumer demand (Blecker et al., 2005). Any such incentive has the potential to further reduce inefficiencies like the bullwhip effect.

As can be seen from our game results, supply chain inefficiencies caused by the bullwhip-effect had a negative impact on supply chains that did not collude. The game showed great standard deviations of revenue for these chains, where the dealers could react fastest to end-consumer demand fluctuations. Thereby, they gained the highest revenues. The game-theoretic models also show that Nash equilibrium exists for the non-cooperative settings. Therefore, the only options supply chain risk managers have to reduce the risk of supply chain members defecting is to impose high penalties on supply chain members who defect, which is not very realistic, or to create incentives, which shift the Nash equilibrium to a more favorable setting.

CONCLUSION

Competition among single companies is increasingly giving way to competition between supply chains. SCM has, therefore, gained increasing importance in corporate management. However, due to the nature of human interaction, the nonconformity of objectives fosters supply chain risks, which often jeopardize supply chain competitiveness. This stresses the necessity for new SCRM approaches in SCM. Such an approach can be an incentive framework whereby supply chain risk managers can mitigate organizational and interorganizational risk drivers. We have shown in a game, simulating interactions within and among organizations, how supply chain management techniques reach their boundaries when objectives are not aligned. To further analyze and pinpoint the drivers within these interactions, game-theoretic models of sections within and between the supply chains have been generated. These have shown that an external effect exists when comparing the Nash equilibria of the so-called inventory and dealer games. First indications exist that the externality is responsible for the profit gradient along the supply chain. If this is the case, incentives or an incentive framework can be developed to counteract this effect in SCRM.

The analysis of the supply chain game showed that a manual business game can simulate the complex circumstances of supply chains. With this, an excellent testing scenario has been developed on which the incentives could be simulated without unnecessarily risking unfavorable outcomes for entire supply chains or having to wait for a long time before the outcomes can be validated.

Contemporary SCM has paid little attention to the alignment capabilities of incentives. In addition, the risk potential of the nonalignment of supply chains has been neglected. Therefore, effective incentives can enable the alignment of decisions across the entire supply chain, by which the efficiency and service level of the entire supply chain can be maximized while optimizing profitability of all supply chain members. The importance of incentives, therefore, not only becomes an asset to SCM, but, in addition, SCRM gains a new field of research by extending organizational and interorganizational risk drivers by introducing the risk of the defection of single supply chain members when their objectives are not aligned with those of the entire supply chain.

ACKNOWLEDGMENT

We would like to thank Maik Brettschneider and Malte Müller for their tireless support in developing and executing the supply chain business game. In addition, we would like to thank Wendelin Groß for assisting us in the analysis.

REFERENCES

Besanco, D., Dranove, D., Shanley, M., & Schaefer, S. (2004). *Economics of strategy* (3rd ed.). New York: John Wiley.

Blecker, T., Kersten, W., Späth, H., & Bohn, M. (2005, April 5-6). Finding the optimal postponement approach for demand chain management. In *Proceedings of the 2nd European Forum on Market Driven Supply Chains: From Supply Chains to Demand Chains,* Milan, Italy (EIASM, pp. 1-26).

Brandenburger, A. M., & Nalebuff, B. J., (1997). *Co-opetition: A revolutionary mindset that combines competition and cooperation.* London: HarperCollins Business.

Cachon, G. P., & Netessine, S. (2004). Game theory in supply chain analysis. In D. Simchi-Levi, S. D. Wu, & Z. M. Shen (Eds.), *Handbook of quantitative supply chain analysis: Modeling in the e-business era* (pp. 13-65). Boston: Kluwer.

Chen, Z. L. (2004). Integrated production and distribution operations: Taxonomy, models, and review. In D. Simchi-Levi, S. D. Wu, & Z. M. Shen (Eds.), *Handbook of quantitative supply chain analysis: Modeling in the e-business era* (pp. 711-745). Boston: Kluwer.

Chopra, S., & Meindl, P. (2004). *Supply chain management: Strategy, planning, and operations, 2nd ed.*. Upper Saddle River, NJ: Pearson.

Christopher, M., (2003). *Creating resilient supply chains: A practical guide.* Cranfield, UK: Crown.

Christopher, M., (2004). *Logistics and supply chain management: Strategies for reducing cost and improving service* (6th ed.). London: Prentice Hall

Davis, D. (2005). *Business research for decision making* (6th ed.). Belmont, CA: Thomson.

Fudenberg, D. ,& Tirole, J. (1992). *Game theory.* Cambridge, MA: MIT Press.

Kaplan, R.S., & Norton, D.P. (1996). *The balanced scorecard: Translating strategy into action.* Boston: Harvard Business School Press.

Lippman. S. A., & McCardle, K. F. (1997). The competitive newsboy. *Operations Research, 45,* 54-65.

Morris, P. (1994). *Introduction to game theory.* New York: Springer.

Nash, J. (1950). *Non-cooperative games.* Doctoral dissertation, Princeton University, Princeton, NJ.

Netessine, S., & Rudi, N. (2003). Centralized and competitive inventory models with demand substitution. *Operations Research, 51*(2), 329-335.

Netessine, S., Rudi, N., & Wang, Y. (2004). *Inventory competitions and incentives to backorder.* Retrieved February 10, 2005, from http://www.netessine.com/

Pfohl, H.-C. (2002*). Risiko-und Chancenmanagement in der Supply Chain: Proaktiv—ganzheitlich—nachhaltig.* Berlin: Schmidt.

Pindyck, R. S., & Rubinfeld, L. R. (1989). *Microeconomics* (4th ed.). Upper Saddle River, NJ: Prentice Hall.

Simchi-Levi, D., Kaminsky, P., & Simchi-Levi, E. (2003). *Managing the supply chain: The definitive guide for the business professional.* New York: McGraw-Hill.

Sterman, J. D. (1992, October). Teaching takes off—Flight simulators for management education—"The beer game". *OR/MS Today*, 40-44. Retrieved February 21, 2005, from http://web.mit.edu/jsterman/www/SDG/beergame.html

Stock, J. R., & Lambert, D. M. (2001). *Strategic logistics management.* Boston: McGraw-Hill.

Zsidisin, G. A. (2003). Managerial perceptions of supply risk. *The Journal of Supply Chain Management, 33*(1), 14-25.

This work was previously published in Supply Chain Management: Issues in the New Era of Collaboration and Competition, edited by W.Y.C. Wang, M.S.H. Heng, and P.Y.K. Chau, pp. 355-387, copyright 2007 by IGI Publishing, formerly known as Idea Group Publishing (an imprint of IGI Global).

Section VI
Emerging Trends

Chapter XXII
The Future of Supply Chain Management:
Shifting from Logistics Driven to a Customer Driven Model

Ketan Vanjara
Microsoft, India

ABSTRACT

This chapter initiates the concept of a customer-centric model in supply chain systems. It discusses various constraints of present-day supply chain systems resulting from their roots being in logistics management and suggests an alternative next-level paradigm of a customer-centric matrix model. This chapter further demonstrates how this model would add value to the customer by taking the example of a healthcare information management system. The chapter also delves into the limitations of and anticipated issues and challenges in implementing the suggested model. Finally, the chapter hints at some broad directions for future research and action in the field. Emergent behavior is what happens when an interconnected system of relatively simple elements begins to self-organize to form a more intelligent and more adaptive higher-level system (Johnson, 2001).

INTRODUCTION

Supply chain systems have come a long way from their initial days when their sole purpose was to support the inventory management function in terms of controlling inventory carrying and fulfillment costs, while making inventory management more efficient and effective. However, as the roots of Supply Chain Management (SCM) lie in managing supplies or inputs to a process or an enterprise, most of the developments (solutions, tools, and technologies) in this field obviously have been around effective management of supply chain toward better, faster, and more cost-effective fulfillment of customer demand.

While this focus on logistics and inventory management has certainly helped business, it still falls short of making the best use of the current tools and technologies for businesses. In order to provide this SCM advantage to businesses, the next level of evolution for the concept of supply chain would be to focus on the needs of the ultimate consumer in contrast to the needs of interim customers (i.e., manufacturers) that are the present-day focus. This chapter seeks to explore the possibilities of elevating the focus of SCM from a logistics-driven model to the next level of customer-driven model, thereby enhancing the value delivered to the end customer. The issues and challenges expected in the process also are delved into.

The chapter reviews some of the latest literature available on SCM, describes various models of supply chain since its origin, enumerates the limitations of the existing supply chain model, and suggests a customer-centric model. Furthermore, it goes on to discuss the challenges in the implementation of this model and the constraints of this model that will have to be addressed. Supply and procurement of healthcare services as well as a health care information management software developed by the author for the creation and management of virtual healthcare communities in line with the suggested customer-centric model is used as an illustration throughout the chapter.

ORIGINS

As per one definition, SCM is the coordination of the demand and supply of products and services between a supplier's supplier and a customer's customer. It involves the flow of products, information, and money between the trading partners of a company's supply chain. The proactive improvement in the efficiency and effectiveness of the flow of goods, services, and knowledge across all stakeholders achieves the goal of reducing total costs and obtaining a competitive advantage for all parties.

Supply chain is the network of facilities (warehouses, factories, terminals, ports, stores, and homes), vehicles (trucks, trains, planes, and ocean vessels), and logistics information systems connected by an enterprise's suppliers' suppliers and its customers' customers. Supply chain flow is optimized when material, information, and money flow simultaneously in real time and without paper.[5]

SCM revolves around efficient integration of suppliers, manufacturers, warehouses, and stores. Other definitions are more comprehensive and detailed:

The challenge in supply chain integration is to co-ordinate activities across the supply chain encompassing these various players, whose systems are bound to be disparate right from the beginning. It is only with such integration that the enterprises can improve performance, reduce costs and increase their service levels to the end-user, the customer. These integration challenges are met not only by coordinating production, transportation, and inventory decisions but more generally by integrating the front-end of the supply chain, customer demand, to the back-end of the supply chain, the production and manufacturing portion of the supply chain. (Simchi-Levi et al., 2003)

As it can be seen from our discussion thus far and from the voluminous literature on supply chain, the focus is constantly on the network of facilities, logistics, supplies, and suppliers. This is due to two main reasons: (1) the origins of the concept of supply chain lie in logistics and in inventory. and (2) the supply chain is related mostly to manufacturing or tangible goods, and thereby, the developments in the services sector and in the knowledge economy are overlooked.

Some thoughts are emanating gradually on the use of supply chains for customer satisfaction. For instance, "efficient integration of suppliers, manufacturers, … so that enterprise can increase service level" (Simchi-Levi et al., 2003) and "maximize customer service and minimize cost of the same" (Frazelle, 2002). The closest one gets to customer focus is in the following statement:

[A] supply chain consists of all parties involved, directly or indirectly, in fulfilling a customer request. The supply chain not only includes the manufacturer and suppliers, but also transporters, warehouses, retailers and customers themselves ... the customer is an integral part of the supply chain. The primary purpose for the existence of any supply chain is to satisfy customer needs. (Chopra & Meindl, 2004)

However, most of the integration referred to in most SCM literature is the vertical integration of suppliers, manufacturers, distributors and other business partners for the ultimate purpose of customer consumption and satisfaction. Thus,

essentially, SCM has focused on vertical flow of goods and services toward order fulfillment, as described in Models A, B, and C in Figures 1, 2, and 3, respectively. But, as the delivery models of products and services become more complex (Model D), as shown in Figure 4, with the objective of fulfilling end-to-end requirements of a customer, supply chain systems will have to focus on integrating processes laterally, as well. The spread of such lateral processes across heterogeneous enterprises and geographical boundaries is becoming almost mandatory with the rapid globalization of enterprises, consequently adding to the challenge of managing supply chains.

MODEL A: Simple Vertical Model (1-1-1 Relationship)

This model is based on an enterprise with a single product, single supplier, and single customer. Such a scenario exists in the case of contractual outsourcing or certain niche industries, products, or markets. Here, an enterprise fulfills the demands of its customer by adding value to the inputs from its supplier. The only contribution made by SCM in this model is the control of inventory-carrying costs, if at all. This is only a marginal improvisation over JIT (just-in-time) inventory systems.

Figure 1. Simple vertical model (1-1-1 relationship)

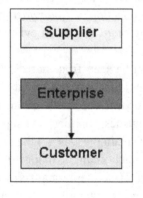

Figure 2. MODEL B: Simple vertical model (many-1-many relationships)

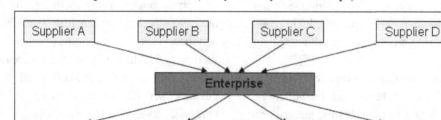

MODEL B: Simple Vertical Model (Many-1-Many Relationships)

In this model, the enterprise still has a single product and phase of production but has many suppliers and customers. Many of the enterprises that are creating and/or providing goods and services (e.g., component manufacturers for automobiles or home appliances, PCB fabs, etc.) would fall under this category. Here, an enterprise fulfills the requirements of its (many) customers by adding value to the inputs from its (many) suppliers. The contributions made by SCM in this model are more than just control of inventory carrying costs. SCM contributes to the overall inventory management of an enterprise, depending on the level of integration among the systems of the suppliers and the enterprise.

MODEL C: Complex Vertical Model (Many-Many-Many Relationships)

In this model, the enterprise has multiple products and phases of production and also has many suppliers and customers. A large number of enterprises that are creating and/or providing goods and services would fall under this category. This would include enterprises offering relatively complex products and services like white goods, home appliances, automobiles, IT and telecom equipment, real estate, banking, healthcare, and so forth.

Here, an enterprise either offers a variety of goods and/or services or has multiple phases of a complex production cycle that produces products to fulfill the requirements of its (many) customers by adding value to the inputs from its (many) suppliers. The contributions made by SCM in this model are enormous. A supply chain system in such a model is normally well-integrated with the inventory as well as with production planning and control systems of an enterprise and, thus, facilitates all the suppliers under the ambit of the SCM to support the inventory and PPC functions of the enterprise. Apart from controlling inventory-carrying and fulfillment costs, such an integrated approach also addresses issues related to timely deliveries (at different phases), quality of deliveries, exception handling, real-time changes in requirements, and so forth.

THE PROBLEM

While all the models mentioned earlier (A-C) contribute to customer satisfaction through reduced costs and faster deliveries, they add little direct value to the customer in terms of increased convenience, choice, or higher value for money. This is further compounded by the trends of globalization, restructuring of various industries, fragmentation of supply chain ownership, and the nature and structure of new industries evolving in the knowledge economy.

Figure 3. MODEL C: Complex vertical model (many-many-many relationships)

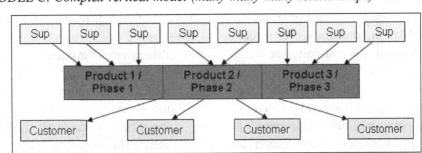

Figure 4. Healthcare services procurement by a patient

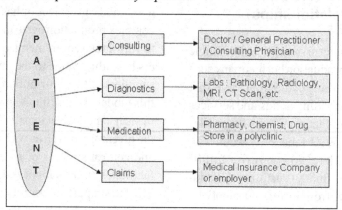

For a moment, let us step back to the physical world of goods and services as it existed a few decades ago. Taking the example of various services offered by governments to their citizens, a citizen had to go from pillar to post filling out various forms and documents for obtaining some service, and, after a few days if not weeks or months and a lot of agony, the citizen would get out of the bureaucratic maze with some positive result. This is quite akin to Model C with one major exception: the various stages of the process were not so efficiently integrated in case of a typical government organization.

To add to the convenience of their citizens, to introduce transparency into their work processes, and also to deliver faster positive results, many government organizations introduced the single-window system, whereby the end customer—the citizen—had to submit a set of documents only once at a window and collect deliverables in the form of some document, certificate, or money on a predetermined date or, sometimes, even instantaneously. As a result, the end customer could receive faster service with a lot of convenience. At the same time, the efficiency and effectiveness of various processes manned by specialist or expert bureaucrats was not compromised. It was either replaced with technology solutions or carried out in the back office without affecting the consumer.

Similar scenarios and examples exist today in services like travel and healthcare. The domain of healthcare services is replete with many of the issues and problems discussed earlier. For example, if a patient needs attention and requires the services of any of the healthcare service providers, at the very least, patients have to visit a doctor and a pharmacist. However, and more often than not, a number of visits to multiple service providers is required, especially if lab tests and diagnostic results are required. The prevailing bureaucratic governmental restrictions and the rigid health service practices add to the misery and suffering of patients by delaying their treatment. Typical stages of healthcare service procurement of a patient are shown in Figure 4.

As shown in Figure 4, the patient has to approach numerous service providers to get treated. Typically, the steps required are as follows:

- Patient visits the doctor.
- The doctor may suggest further diagnostic tests (the probability of this increases with the advancement of medical science).
- Patient goes to the respective laboratory for getting the diagnostic tests done.

- Patient visits the laboratory again to collect the diagnostic reports.
- Patient visits the doctor again with the diagnostic reports.
- The doctor prescribes medication to the patient.
- Patient visits the pharmacy to buy the medication.
- Patient approaches the insurance company or concerned agency for reimbursement of medical expenses. Alternatively, the medical agencies (like the physician) approach the insurance company for reimbursement.

It is clear from this example that it is quite an exercise to move people and documents all over the place, sometimes in circles, to access one important and critical service most people require continuously. This is true for most of the service sector industries.

The ERPs, CRMs, and SCMs of today's world need to integrate and elevate to provide a single-window solution to the end customer in various areas, especially the service sector. One way of doing this is to offer all the products and services related to a solution through a single enterprise—creating a Web-based single window. The government services department example can be extended here. One also can think of travel service firms offering all related services, like hotel bookings, car bookings, and so forth, or hospitals and healthcare polyclinics providing all the healthcare services in one place.

Figure 5. MODEL D: Matrix model (Many-many-many vertical and horizontal relationships spread across different enterprises or geographical locations)

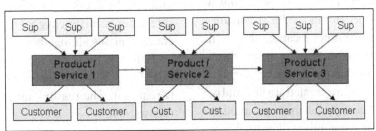

Figure 6. Application of matrix model in healthcare services provisioning

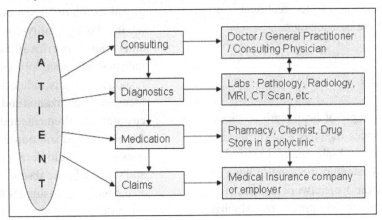

However, there are some significant limitations to this approach:

- Such an integration of services may not be possible in all domains.
- Integrated offering of all services may result in a loss of focus for an enterprise and thereby inhibit the enterprise from developing expertise in any field. As a result, the end customer may not get the best possible service, may get it at a premium, or both.
- The end customer does not get multiple options—if customers want to avail of the single-window convenience, they will have to hire a car through the same travel agent who books their tickets, although there could be better options elsewhere.
- Such a solution also creates a constraint of physical proximity, especially with respect to services like banking and healthcare. The consumer always has to visit or transact with a particular single-window service provider (e.g., a hospital). Thus, after procuring a product or service from a vendor, if consumers move to some other location, they will have no or limited access to the products and services of that particular vendor. For instance, after getting treated at a hospital or polyclinic, when a patient moves to another place, the patient not only will be unable to avail of the services provided by that hospital but also will not have his or her medical history to get faster and better treatment from a hospital at the new location.

THE SOLUTION

As seen in the example of healthcare services, solutions and services in today's world are offered by a chain of multiple enterprises within an industry, and customers personally have to navigate through a mesh of network to procure an end-to-end solution to their requirements, which is obviously not very convenient. Since the mesh of network is the cause of the problem, a corresponding solution ought to be network-based.

MODEL D: Matrix Model (Many-Many-Many Relationships Spread Across Different Enterprises/ Geographical Locations)

One way of offering the single-window solution to the end customer is by creating virtual communities (mesh of network) of service providers on the Web. These communities can share and exchange data on a need-to-know basis and provide the single-window advantage to the consumer without any of the limitations discussed earlier.

The introduction of a horizontal flow of supply chain in addition to a vertical flow is of major significance in the matrix model. This assumes greater importance when subset products or services of the same set are offered either by different business units of the same enterprise spread across different geographies or by different enterprises all together.

Before getting into more details of the solution, let us also harp upon why such a solution is required. The reasons for such a shift are as follows:

- The changing method of product or service provisioning is one reason. With the globalization of almost every industry and the increasing quality-consciousness of the consumer, it is critically important to any industry to respond appropriately. One major response of many industries has been their focus on specialization and customization of customer requirements and needs. With this, the end-to-end solution is provided to the consumer by multiple enterprises—physical and virtual. In the absence of a comprehensive solution, consumers have to approach more than one enterprise to fulfill their requirements. This is also known as multiple funnel delivery.

- With the fragmentation of supply chain ownership, it is becoming increasingly difficult for the consumer to get the best value for money in a convenient manner. If at all, the consumer is required to put in considerable effort to get good value.

- Intangibles occupy a prominent position in the consumption and commerce that happens worldwide today. The dynamics of commerce and the consumption of intangibles are quite different from those of tangibles. So are the supply chains. This, too, necessitates a different solution.

- With the growth of the Internet and other facilitating infrastructures, the customer expects 24/7 service based on a direct delivery model wherein services are delivered directly from the manufacturer or provider of services.

- Flexible pricing, product portfolio, promotions, and discrimination on service make the selection and procurement of a product or service a very complex decision for the consumer in the absence of an integrated solution.

- General expanse in the domain knowledge and increasing complexity in most domains of products and services add to the woes of the customer.

- An increasing number of alternatives in every sphere of products and services also compounds the problem.

All these and the primary requirement of providing the best value for money to the customer with utmost convenience create the need for a customer-centric SCM.

Virtual Communities

As mentioned earlier, the solution has to be network-based. A software solution created by the author for the formation and management of virtual communities for provisioning end-to-end healthcare services will be used as an example.

There are two potential solutions: (1) as mentioned earlier, hospitals and polyclinics (remember the single-window example); and (2) the creation of virtual communities of healthcare service providers, even globally.

While hospitals and polyclinics offer a viable solution, they are fraught with the limitations discussed earlier. Quite often, they also happen to be quite expensive. This necessitates the creation of a solution that would provide best services from distributed supply chains to the customer (here, the patient) with increased convenience.

The most compatible solution in such a scenario can be the creation of virtual communities of all the agencies involved in healthcare services provisioning. A virtual community is a collection of related individuals or organizations that connect with one another with the help of various communication media (e.g., the Internet) to fulfill a common objective or achieve a common goal. All are aware of different types of virtual communities like portals, newsgroups, chat groups, and so forth. However, most of them do not provide for transaction facility (if at all, it is permitted only within a closed user group), and most of them also are moderated or owned by an individual or an organization.

The virtual community proposed here is different on these two parameters. One, its primary function will be to facilitate transactions, and two; it will have shared moderation and ownership.

How will a virtual community help the customer?

- It becomes a one-stop shop for all the products and services in a particular segment.
- The customer can receive faster service.
- It is independent of location and, therefore, creates no physical proximity constraint. As the medical history of a patient is stored in the virtual space, a patient can obtain services

from almost any part of the world.

- It reduces unnecessary physical movement of the customer (here, the patient).
- Customers can avail of the best services from the service provider of their choice.
- It can be integrated with various data-capturing tools, including equipment like those used for self-diagnostics.

Applying the matrix model to healthcare services provisioning, the flow would look like Figure 6.

This model certainly will enhance the convenience of the patient, since now, the various service providers also are interconnected. A meshed solution as follows (Figure 7) will create the maximum impact.

The networked model interconnects all the service providers who, in turn, can interact with one another on a need-to-know basis. For instance, after a patient has gone through the diagnostic tests, they do not have to revisit the laboratories to collect the reports; these can be collected by the patient as well as the doctor over the Web. Similarly, the medication also can be delivered to a patient's home by the nearest pharmacy, based on the prescription posted by the doctor on the Web and subsequently collected or received by the pharmacist.

This substantially reduces the number of steps that a patient has to go through to get treated. In most of the cases, only two steps are required:

1. Patient visits the doctor for consultation.
2. Patient visits diagnostic labs for tests.

HOW DOES THE SOLUTION WORK?

In a virtual community, as the suppliers of all the interrelated products and services are interconnected logically, in spite of being separate geographically (in the form of different locations of the same enterprise) or legally (in the form of different enterprises), they are able to provide an end-to-end solution to the consumer faster and with enhanced convenience.

In the example of healthcare services, the core engine of virtual communities takes care of most of the steps. Here is how it works:

- Patient visits the doctor for consultation.
- If diagnostics are required, the doctor submits a prescription of tests to be conducted

Figure 8. High-level architecture of customer-centric model for supply of healthcare services

Figure 7. Networked model in health care services provisioning

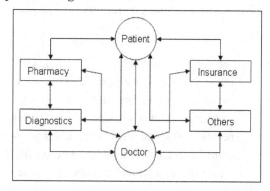

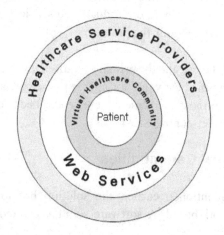

to the intelligent engine and database of the virtual community, where it is picked up by the diagnostic lab chosen by the patient. If diagnostic tests are not required, a prescription of medicines is submitted.

- Patient visits the diagnostic lab of its choice for conducting the tests.
- The lab pulls the test prescription from the database of the virtual community to conduct tests. Patients are not required to worry about the prescription.
- Diagnostic labs submit test reports to the same engine and database of the virtual community; where it is picked up by the doctor. The patient is spared a second visit to the lab.
- On receipt of test reports, the doctor submits a prescription of medicine. In most cases, patient will not have to visit the doctor again to obtain the prescription.
- The pharmacy of the patient's choice gets the prescription of the patient and manages to deliver the necessary medicines at the patient's doorstep. Again, this step does not require any movement on the part of the patient.
- Depending on the insurance plan, the doctor and/or patient can submit necessary documents electronically for claims processing and get paid by the insurance company directly into their bank account.

As all these steps happen over fiber (communication or Internet), the pace of transactions is much faster than physical movements of people and paper.

The availability of technologies like Web services and wireless networks not only make the solution feasible but make it even more capable.

The high-level architecture of such customer-centric model, wherein all the healthcare service providers can serve the patient by using the virtual healthcare community infrastructure through Web services, is shown in Figure 8.

BENEFITS OF A CUSTOMER-CENTRIC MODEL

A customer-centric model creates a win-win situation for all the stakeholders in the model. While it certainly benefits the customers and the suppliers involved in the model, it also creates some benefits at a higher level for the entire community. Some of the benefits generated by this model for various stakeholders are specified hereafter.

Generic Benefits

Greater value-add in the form of best price performance, procurement of end-to-end products and/or services, and greater customer convenience through provisioning of ease in the procurement of end-to-end products and services is the primary objective of the customer-driven model.

Be it supply of healthcare services or other services like travel, finance, and so forth, this enhanced supply chain model has certain inherent benefits for the customer as well as suppliers.

Benefits to Customers

- The community becomes a one-stop shop for all the interrelated products and services in a particular domain.
- The customer gets the best of both worlds—better and specialized services without the associated overheads of an integrated physical model.
- The customer also has the luxury of making choices among various service providers.
- There is no constraint of physical proximity. The customer can procure a product or service virtually anytime, anywhere.

Benefits to Suppliers

- Suppliers now can focus on their areas of specialization and yet offer their products and services at competitive prices to their customers.
- Depending on the nature of their product or service offering, suppliers need not be constrained by geographical proximity.
- In cases like pharmacies, suppliers can do away with physical stores altogether. Drugs can be shipped straight from their warehouse, based on prescriptions received.
- As participants of virtual community, suppliers can gain from mutual coordination and exchange of aggregated information

Benefits to Community

- The virtual community also creates quite a few extra benefits that can be shared by individual suppliers as well as customers. Such benefits are in the form of:
  - Creation of aggregated information and knowledge related to the industry.
  - Making the processes and workflows more efficient and effective, resulting into cost savings at individual entity levels.
  - Providing a platform to conduct industry-related research. For instance, medical schools and colleges as well as pharmaceutical companies can use the virtual healthcare community to conduct industry-specific research on aggregated data.

Thus, a customer-centric SCM would be beneficial to all the stakeholders in the supply chain. As mentioned earlier, the supplies, especially information supplies, in this model would flow vertically as well as horizontally. In the example of healthcare services, for instance, the diagnosis reports would flow vertically to the patient as well as horizontally to the doctor. Similarly, a prescription would flow vertically to the patient and horizontally to the pharmacy.

In addition to forward integration with ERPs, the existing supply chain systems need to incorporate the horizontal flow of information in order to facilitate the creation of such virtual communities and thereby enable enhanced customer satisfaction.

LIMITATIONS OF THE MODEL

Like any good solution, this one also comes with a set of its own limitations. Some of the limitations of this solution are as follows:

- As the model is heavily dependent on information and communication technologies, any interruption in the availability of these in the form of communication media like the Internet and so forth can cause disruption in providing basic services like healthcare. Many people on the east coast of the US experienced such an inconvenience due to major power outages during late 2003. This happened due to people's heavy reliance on electricity as the major source of energy.
- While the model would deliver better products and services to the customer faster and at a reasonable price, on the downside, it can have a sociological impact on persons for whom a personal visit to any product or service provider also creates an opportunity for social interaction. For instance, many of the older people in Australia have been objecting to the installation of ATMs that lead to closure of several bank branches. Though ATMs provide better and faster service 24/7, a personal visit to the bank for cash withdrawals or deposits is a far more important opportunity, especially for the retired and elderly, from a social interaction standpoint.

- In services like healthcare, such a heavily automated model also can lead to the creation of some information gaps. Repeated interactions with the patient provide the doctor with quite a bit of relevant information that cannot be obtained through a structured approach.

- Also, in services like healthcare, a relationship of mutual trust and faith between the patient and the doctor is of vital importance. As repeated interactions have a bearing on the depth and expanse of such a relationship, the technology-based solution certainly would hamper that.

ISSUES AND CHALLENGES

Coordination among various partners in a supply chain is a huge challenge even today in the present state of SCM solutions. With the increased complexity of the solution, more issues and challenges are expected to arise.

According to Chopra et al. (2004), over the past several decades, most firms have become less vertically integrated. As companies have shed non-core functions, they have been able to take advantage of supplier customer competencies that they did not have. This new ownership structure also has made managing the supply chain more difficult. With the chain broken into many owners and each having its own policies and interests, the chain is more difficult to coordinate. In their book, Chopra and Meindl (2004) go on to list the causes of difficulties in coordination as well as the impact of lack of coordination in integrated supply chain models.

The following are two points to be noted: (1) reducing vertical integration with the new ownership structure and (2) increased difficulty in coordination.

The customer-centric model proposes horizontal integration of broken supply chain ownerships at a much higher level and spread across geogra-

phies, potentially making it a global solution.

Some of the challenges that can be anticipated for the customer-centric supply chain management system are listed hereafter. Wherever possible, potential solutions to challenges also are mentioned, together with the issues.

- **Diversity:** The model is an attempt to provide a universal solution that is independent of geographical constraints. In other words, it seeks to provide a uniform solution to diverse environments. The diversity could be in the form of the following:

  - **Standards:** Different countries follow different standards and codes pertaining to various industries like healthcare. Addressing all of these in a single solution could be a major challenge. Some ways of making this happen can be through the adoption of standards like HIPAA (Health Insurance Portability and Accountability Act) of the US by various countries or cooperative creation and implementation of global standards under the aegis of a UN body like WHO (World Health Organization), and so forth.

  - **Laws:** Laws related to the conduct of various industries like healthcare are widely different in various countries. These also need to be aligned at a broad level in order for a universal solution to work. While this is very difficult and far-fetched, if all the countries in the world can sign charters and conventions on pollution control, IPRs and many such issues, and create a common legal framework at a higher level for the benefit of mankind (e.g., in the area of healthcare) this certainly can be made possible in the long term.

  - **Language:** A global solution also has to address the need of multiplicity of languages. This, though, is the least of problems, as quite a few solutions (from Microsoft Windows to small accounting packages like Quickbooks and MYOB) already have addressed this issue. Unicode-based solutions also can be considered to address this issue.

- **Creation of a Common Framework:** Given the diversity of laws, standards, and many other practices related to an industry, creation of a universal solution or a framework in itself would pose an enormous challenge. However, good news is that common global XML standards are emerging in most of the industries, from news to banking to healthcare to entertainment. In the healthcare sector, for instance, HL7 is almost a universally accepted standard, and most of the software solutions created for healthcare industry (no matter who creates them where) are HL7 compliant. In fact, the author and his team have created a common software framework of reusable components that can be used to construct a global solution for the healthcare industry.

- **Ownership and Control of Virtual Communities:** While the components of a supply chain have a broken ownership, the solution that ties them up needs to have some command and control structure. This, too, would be a challenge to reckon with. To address this, one either can fall back upon the proven model of managing the Internet and assigning IP addresses and domain names (Internet Corporation for Assigned Names and Numbers [ICANN]) or attempt to create a new model, based on the paradigm of ant colonies. An emergent system is smarter than the sum of its parts. There is no master planner or executive branch—the overall group creates the intelligence and adaptability. Randomness is a key component. Almost all emergent systems are networks or grids. They tend to be flatter and more horizontal. Experimentation is another key component (Exact Software, 2004).

- **Data Trusteeship and Use:** Needless to say, a software solution that facilitates and manages such virtual communities in any industry will also create large databases of immense value to the industry. However, as the aggregated data would belong to the community as a whole and not to any individual participant in the community, it has to be held and maintained under trusteeship in order to prevent any leakage or misuse. This responsibility also can be undertaken by the same body that owns and controls the virtual communities on a distributed or centralized basis.

- **Data Sharing:** Another challenge pertaining to data would be sharing it among different entities of the community on authorization by the owner of the data. An interesting paradigm shift that happens here is the split between the owner and the possessor of data. Taking the example of healthcare, a patient's data in the form of medical history are currently possessed as well as owned by the doctor. Therefore, whenever a patient moves from one place to another, there is a rare chance that the patient or the doctor at the new place will have access to historical medical records of the patient. However, the customer-centric model can shift the ownership of data to patients, who then can provide access to the doctor or medical institution of their choice.

- **Security and Privacy:** Since the solution depends on information and communication technology, it also is prone to the security and privacy threats faced by such networks. The threat is all the more perceptible, given the sensitivity of certain types of data, like financial data, medical records, and so forth. However, this is a manageable challenge, given the number of high-quality encryption solutions available now.

CONCLUSION

This chapter has initiated the concept of a customer-centric model in supply chain systems. The chapter also has discussed how the model can work and how it addresses various constraints of the existing, essentially vertical supply chain systems by putting forward a matrix model. Apart from the global trends in various industries and supply chain that necessitate such a paradigm shift, the chapter seeks to ascertain the high value addition of the customer-centric model and how it will enhance the present-day supply chains to the next level. It further has enumerated the limitations of the new model and the issues and challenges that are anticipated in implementing the customer-centric supply chain model. While discussing the issues and challenges, the author has attempted to suggest some potential solutions to the challenges. Finally, the chapter has provided some directions for future research and action.

THE FUTURE

As discussed earlier in this chapter and also noted in the literature surveyed, there is a definite shift from vertical integration to matrix relationships among various partners in the supply chain. This, in conjunction with globalization, specialization, and broken ownerships of various components of the supply chain, certainly creates a need for a paradigm shift in the models and solutions of supply chain management conceived and practiced so far. In the opinion of the author, whether this paradigm shift will happen in the future probably is not a question; when it will happen is worth speculating and preparing for.

In the years to come, one can expect more aggressive initiatives toward this paradigm shift. This also throws up multiple business and research opportunities in a completely new direction. Such opportunities will be created in both areas—the respective domains of various industries as well as the domain of information and communication technology. Given the wide scope of the suggested solution, there could be opportunities in the areas of international relations and creation of global standards, as well.

Some specific opportunities for the immediate future are the following:

- Creation of globally acceptable standards related to operations, transactions, workflow, and information flow in various industries, especially in those belonging to the knowledge economy.
- Creation of software components, frameworks, and libraries that can facilitate the implementation of a customer-centric supply chain management system.
- Innovating new concepts to address the challenges around data management and sharing.
- Conceptualization of management models for ownership and control of virtual communities.
- Creation of a legal framework that would govern the working virtual communities.

Finally, I believe that mankind has all the necessary knowledge, tools, and technologies to make this happen. Does it have the will in the larger interest of mankind? Will we do it? Let time answer these questions.

REFERENCES

Boeing SCOR case study. *Logistics of the Future*. Retrieved from *http://www.supply-chain.org/public/casestudiesboeing.asp*

Chopra, S., & Meindl, P. (2004). *Supply chain management:Strategy, planning, and operations*. Pearson.

Chorafas, D.N. (2001). *Integrating ERP, CRM, supply chain management and smart materials.* Averback.

Frazelle, E.H. (2002). *Supply chain strategy.* McGraw Hill

Hugos, M.H. (2002). *Essentials of supply chain management.* John Wiley & Sons.

Johnson, S. (2001). *Emergence—The connected lives of ants, brains, cities and software.* Touchstone.

Knolmayer, G., Mertens, P., & Zeier, A. (2002). *Supply chain management based on SAP sytems R/3 4.6, APO 3.0.* Springer.

Kubala, D. (2004). *Track, trace and control: The keys to collaborative supply chain execution.* Retrieved from *http://supplychain.ittoolbox. com/documents/document.asp?i=2632*

SCOR Basics. *http://www.supply-chain.org/public/scorbasics.asp*

Sengupta, S. (2004). The top ten supply chain mistakes. Retrieved from *http://www. manufacturing.net/scm/article/CA85844 .html?stt=%stt&pubdate= 7%2F1%2F2004*

Simchi-Levi, D., Kaminsky, P., & Simchi-Levi, E. (2003). *Managing the supply chain.* McGraw Hill.

Stadtler, H., & Kilger, C. (2002). *SCM and advanced planning: Concepts, models, software and case studies.* Springer.

Suresh, H. (2004). *E-enabled supply chain management.*

Value cycle management: A "non-linear" approach to supply chain management. (2004). Exact Software. Retrieved from *http://supplychain. ittoolbox.com/browse2.asp?c=WhitePaper&r=ht tp://hosteddocs.ittoolbox.com/VCMwpFinal.pdf*

This work was previously published in Global Integrated Supply Chain Systems, edited by Y. Lan and B. Unhelkar, pp. 48-66, copyright 2006 by Information Science Publishing (an imprint of IGI Global).

Chapter XXIII
Enterprise Resource Planning (ERP):
Past, Present and Future

Ronald E. McGaughey
University of Central Arkansas, USA

Angappa Gunasekaran
University of Massachusetts, Dartmouth, USA

ABSTRACT

Business needs have driven the design, development, and use of Enterprise Resource Planning (ERP) systems. Intra-enterprise integration was a driving force in the design, development, and use of early ERP systems, but increased globalization, intense competition, and technological change have shifted to focus to inter-enterprise integration. Current and evolving ERP systems thus reflect the expanded scope of integration, with greater emphasis on things like supply chain management and customer relationship management. This manuscript explores the evolution of ERP, the current status of ERP, and the future of ERP, with the objective of promoting relevant future research in this important area. If researchers hope to play a significant role in the design, development, and use of suitable ERP systems to meet evolving business needs, then their research should focus, at least in part, on the changing business environment, its impact on business needs, and the requirements for enterprise systems that meet those needs.

INTRODUCTION

Twenty years ago supplier relationship management was unique to the Japanese (those firms who embraced the JIT philosophy), China was still a slumbering economic giant, the Internet was largely for academics and scientists, and certainly not a consideration in business strategy; the very idea of a network of businesses working together as a virtual enterprise was almost like science fiction, and hardly anyone had a cell phone. The world has changed. The cold war is over and economic war is on. We have moved rapidly toward an intensely competitive, global economic environment. Countries like China and India are fast positioning themselves as key players and threatening the economic order that has existed for decades. Information technology (IT) is more sophisticated than ever, yet we still struggle with how to best use it in business, and on a personal level as well. E-commerce (B2B, B2C, C2C, G2C, and B2G) has become commonplace and M-commerce is not far behind, especially in Europe and Japan. This is the backdrop against which we will discuss the evolving enterprise information system. At this point we will call it ERP, but is should become evident in the course of reading this manuscript that ERP is a label that may no longer be appropriate.

In this article we define ERP and discuss the evolution of ERP, the current state of ERP, and the future of ERP. We will emphasize how the evolution of ERP was influenced by changing business needs and by evolving technology. We present a simple framework to explain that evolution. Some general directions for future research are indicated by our look at the past, present, and particularly the future of ERP.

ERP DEFINED

The ERP system is an information system that integrates business processes, with the aim of creating value and reducing costs by making the right information available to the right people at the right time to help them make good decisions in managing resources productively and proactively. An ERP is comprised of multi-module application software packages that serve and support multiple business functions (Sane, 2005). These large automated cross-functional systems are designed to bring about improved operational efficiency and effectiveness through integrating, streamlining, and improving fundamental back-office business processes. Traditional ERP

systems were called back-office systems because they involved activities and processes in which the customer and general public were not typically involved, at least not directly. Functions supported by ERP typically included accounting, manufacturing, human resource management, purchasing, inventory management, inbound and outbound logistics, marketing, finance, and, to some extent, engineering. The objective of traditional ERP systems in general was greater efficiency, and to a lesser extent effectiveness. Contemporary ERP systems have been designed to streamline and integrate operation processes and information flows within a company to promote synergy (Nikolopoulos, Metaxiotis, Lekatis, & Assimakopoulos, 2003) and greater organizational effectiveness. Many new ERP systems have moved beyond the backoffice to support front-office processes and activities. The goal of most firms implementing ERP is to replace diverse functional systems with a single integrated system that does it all faster, better, and cheaper. Unfortunately, the "business and technology integration technology in a box" has not entirely met expectations (Koch, 2005). While there are some success stories, many companies devote significant resources to their ERP effort only to find the payoff disappointing (Dalal, Kamath, Kolarik,& Sivaraman, 2003; Koch, 2005). Let us examine briefly how we have come to this point.

The Evolution of ERP

The origin of ERP can be traced back to materials requirement planning (MRP). While the concept of MRP was understood conceptually and discussed in the 1960s, it was not practical for commercial use. It was the availability of computing power (processing capability and storage capacity) that made commercial use of MRP possible and practical. While many early MRP systems were built in-house, often at great expense, MRP became one of the first off-the-shelf business applications (Orlicky, 1975). In essence,

MRP involves taking a master production schedule, inventory records, and a bill of materials and calculating time-phased material, component, and sub-assembly requirements, both gross and net. Note the term "calculating" was used rather than forecasting. With a realistic MPS, lead times that are known and predictable, accurate inventory records, and a current and correct BOM, it is possible to calculate material, component, and assembly requirements rather than forecast them. The shear volume of calculations necessary for MRP with multiple orders for even a few items made the use of computers essential. Initially, batch processing systems were used and regenerative MRP systems were the norm, where the plan would be updated periodically, often weekly. MRP employed a type of backward scheduling wherein lead times were used to work backwards from a due date to an order/start date. While the primary objective of MRP was to compute material requirements, the MRP system proved to be a useful scheduling tool. Order placement and order delivery were planned by the MRP system. Not only were orders for materials and components generated by a MRP system, but also production orders for manufacturing operations that used those materials and components to make higher-level items like sub assemblies and finished products. As MRP systems became popular and more and more companies were using them, practitioners, vendors, and researchers started to realize that the data and information produced by the MRP system in the course of material requirements planning and production scheduling could be augmented with additional data and meet other information needs. One of the earliest add-ons was the Capacity Requirements Planning module, which could be used in developing capacity plans to produce the master production schedule. Manpower planning and support for human resources management were incorporated into MRP. Distribution management capabilities were added. The enhanced MRP and its many modules provided data useful in the finan-cial planning of manufacturing operations, thus financial planning capabilities were added. Business needs, primarily for operational efficiency and, to a lesser extent, for greater effectiveness, and advancements in computer processing and storage technology brought about MRP and influenced its evolution. What started as an efficiency-oriented tool for production and inventory management had become a cross-functional information system serving diverse user groups.

A very important capability to evolve in MRP systems was the ability to close the loop (control loop). This was largely because of the development of real time (closed loop) MRP systems to replace regenerative MRP systems in response to the business need and improved computer technology—time-sharing rather than batch processing as the dominant mode of computer operation. On time-sharing mainframe systems, the MRP system could run 24/7 and update continuously. Use of the corporate mainframe that performed other important computing tasks for the organization was not practical for some companies because MRP consumed too many system resources. Subsequently, some opted to use mainframes (they were becoming smaller and cheaper, but increasing in processing speed and storage capability) or mini-computers (which could do more, faster than old mainframes) that could be dedicated to MRP. MRP could now respond to timely data fed into the system and produced by the system. This closed the control loop with timely feedback for decision making by incorporating current data from the factory floor, warehouse, vendors, transportation companies, and other internal and external sources, thus giving the MRP system the capability to provide current (almost real-time) information for better planning and control. These closed-loop systems better reflected the realities of the production floor, logistics, inventory, and more. It was this transformation of MRP into a planning and control tool for manufacturing by closing the loop, along with all the additional modules that did more than plan materials—they planned and controlled various production re-sources—that led to MRPII. Here, too, improved computer technology and the evolving business need for more accurate and timely information to support decision making and greater organizational effectiveness contributed to the evolution from MRP to MRPII.

The MRP in MRPII stands for manufacturing resource planning rather than materials requirements planning. The MRP system had evolved from a material requirements planning system to a planning and control system for resources in manufacturing operations—an enterprise information system for manufacturing. As time passed, MRPII systems became more widespread, and more sophisticated, particularly when used in manufacturing to support and complement computer integrated manufacturing (CIM). Databases started replacing traditional file systems, allowing for better systems integration and greater query capabilities to support decision makers, and the telecommunications network became an integral part of these systems in order to support communications between and coordination among system components that were sometimes geographically distributed, but still within the company. In that context, the label CIM II was used to describe early systems with capabilities now associated with ERP (Lope, 1992). The need for greater efficiency and effectiveness in back-office operations was not unique to manufacturing, but was also common to non-manufacturing operations. Companies in non-manufacturing sectors such as health care, financial services, aerospace, and the consumer goods sector started to use MRPII-like systems to manage critical resources, thus the M for manufacturing seemed not always to be appropriate. In the early 90s, these increasingly sophisticated back-office systems were more appropriately labeled enterprise resource planning systems (Nikolopoulos, Metaxiotis, Lekatis, & Assimakopoulos, 2003).

MRP II was mostly for automating the business processes within an organization, but ERP, while primarily for support of internal processes, started to support processes that spanned enterprise boundaries (the extended enterprise). While ERP systems originated to serve the information needs of manufacturing companies, they were not just for manufacturing anymore. Early ERP systems typically ran on mainframes like their predecessors, MRP and MRPII, but many migrated to client/server systems where, of course, networks were critical and distributed databases more common. The growth of ERP and the migration to client/server systems really got a boost from the Y2K scare. Many companies were convinced by vendors that they needed to replace older main-frame based systems, some ERP and some not, with systems using the newer client/server architecture. After all, since they were going to have to make so many changes in the old systems to make them Y2K compliant and avoid serious problems (this was what vendors and consultants often told them) they might as well bite the bullet and upgrade. Vendors and consultants benefited from the Y2K boost to ERP sales, as did some of their customers. Since Y2K, ERP systems have evolved rapidly, bringing us to the ERP systems of today. Present day ERP systems offer more and more capabilities and are becoming more affordable even for small-to-medium-sized enterprises.

ERP TODAY

As ERP systems continue to evolve, vendors like PeopleSoft (Conway, 2001) and Oracle (Green, 2003) are moving to an Internet-based architecture, in large part because of the ever-increasing importance of E-commerce and the globalization of business. Beyond that, perhaps the most salient trend in the continuing evolution of ERP is the focus on front-office applications and inter-organizational business processes. ERP is creeping out of the back office into the front and beyond the enterprise to customers, suppliers, and more in order to meet changing business needs. Front-office applications involve interaction with external constituents like customers, suppliers, partners, and more—hence the name front office because they are visible to "outsiders." Key players like Baal, Oracle, PeopleSoft, and SAP have incorporated advanced planning and scheduling (APS), sales force automation (SFA), customer relationship management (CRM), supply chain management (SCM), and e-commerce modules/capabilities into their systems, or repositioned their ERP systems as part of broader enterprise suites incorporating these and other modules/capabilities. ERP vendor products reflect the evolving business needs of clients and the capabilities of IT, perhaps most notably Internet-related technologies.

While some companies are expanding their ERP system capabilities (adding modules) and still calling them ERP systems, others have started to use catchy names like enterprise suite, E-commerce suite, and enterprise solutions to describe their solution clusters that include ERP among other modules/capabilities. Table 1 lists the various modules/capabilities (with modules deemed similar combined in cells) taken from the product descriptions of vendors like PeopleSoft, Oracle, J.D. Edwards, and SAP, who are major players in the ERP/enterprise systems market.

Perhaps, most notable about ERP today is that it is much more than manufacturing resource planning. ERP and ERP-like systems have become popular with non-manufacturing operations

Table 1. ERP modules

Modules
Enterprise Resource Planning (ERP)
Customer Relationship Management (CRM)
Asset Management Financial Management
Supplier Relationship Management (SRM) Business Collaboration
Inventory Management Order Processing
Data Warehouse Knowledge Warehouse Business Information Warehouse
Business Intelligence Analytics and Reporting Data Mining
E-Commerce Sales Management Field Service Management Retail Management
Facilities Management Maintenance Management
Warehouse Management Logistics Management Distribution Management
Project Management
Human Resource Management

like universities, hospitals, airlines, and more, where back-office efficiency is important and so, too, is front-office efficiency and effectiveness. In general, it is fair to say that today's ERP systems, or ERP-like systems, typically include, or will include (per vendor plans), modules/capabilities associated with front-office processes and activities. Alternatively, ERP modules are packaged with other modules that support front-office and back-office processes and activities, and nearly anything else that goes on within or between organizations and stakeholders. ERP proper (the back office system) has not become unimportant because back-office efficiency and effectiveness was, is, and will always be important. Today's focus, however, seems more to be external, as organizations look for ways to support and improve relationships and interactions with customers, suppliers, partners, and other stakeholders. While integration of internal functions is still important, and in many organizations still has not been achieved to a great extent, external integration seems now to be a primary focus. Progressive companies desire to do things—all things—faster, better, and cheaper (to be agile), and they want systems and tools that will improve competitiveness, increase profits, and help them not just to survive, but to prosper in the global economy. Today, that means working with suppliers, customers, and partners like never before. Vendors are using the latest technology to respond to these evolving business needs as evidenced in the products and services they offer. Will ERP be the all-encompassing system (with an updated name like ERPII) comprised of the many modules and capabilities mentioned, or will it be relegated to the status of a module in the enterprise system of the future?

ERP and the Future

New multi-enterprise business models like value collaboration networks, customer-centric networks that coordinate all players in the supply chain, are becoming popular as we enter the 21st century (Nattkemper, 2000). These new business models reflect an increased business focus on external integration. While no one can really predict the future of ERP very far into the future, current management concerns and emphasis, vendor plans, and the changing business and technological environments, provide some clues about the future of ERP. We turn our attention now to evolving business needs and technological changes that should shape the future of ERP.

E-commerce is arguably one of the most important developments in business in the last 50 years (it has been called the "Viagra" of business), and m-commerce is poised to take its place alongside or within the rapidly growing area of e-commerce. The Internet, intranets, and extranets have made e-commerce in its many forms (B2B, B2C, B2G, G2C, C2C, etc.) possible. Mobile and wireless technology are expected to make "always on" Internet and anytime/anywhere location-based services a reality, as well as a host of other capabilities we categorize as m-commerce. One can expect to see ERP geared more to the support of both e-commerce and m-commerce. Internet, mobile, and wireless technologies should figure prominently in new and improved system modules and capabilities (O'Brien, 2002; Sane, 2005; Bhattacharjee, Greenbaum, Johnson, Martin, Reddy, Ryan, et al., 2002). Vendors and their customers will find it necessary to make fairly broad, sweeping infrastructure changes to meet the demands of e-commerce and m-commerce (Bhattacharjee, Greenbaum, Johnson, Martin, Reddy, Ryan, et al., 2002; Higgins, 2005). Movement away from client-server systems to Internet-based architectures is likely. In fact, it has already started (Conway, 2001). New systems will have to incorporate existing and evolving standards and older systems will have to be adapted to existing and evolving standards, and that may make the transition a little uncomfortable and expensive for vendors and their customers. Perhaps the biggest business challenge with e-commerce, and even more so with m-commerce, is understanding how to use these new and evolving capabilities to serve the customer, work with suppliers and other business partners, and function internally. Businesses are just beginning to understand e-commerce and how it can be used to meet changing business needs as well as how it changes business needs, and now m-commerce poses a whole new challenge. It is a challenge for application vendors and for their clients. Back-office processes and activities and front-office processes and activities are being affected by e-commerce and will be affected by m-commerce. The strategic ramifications are significant as the Internet and mobile technology take a prominent place in the future of ERP systems. They will be key in meeting evolving business needs, and on the flip side, one can argue that the evolving technologies will give rise to new business needs.

The current business focus on process integration and external collaboration is a driving force for change that should continue for some time to come. Some businesses are attempting to transform themselves from traditional, vertically integrated organizations into multi-enterprise "recombinant entities" reliant on core competency-based strategies (Genovese, Bond, Zrimsek, & Frey, 2001). Integrated SCM and business networks will receive great emphasis, reinforcing the importance of IT support for cross-enterprise collaboration and inter-enterprise processes (Bhattacharjee, Greenbaum, Johnson, Martin, Reddy, Ryan, et al., 2002). Collaborative commerce (c-commerce) has become not only a popular buzzword, but also a capability businesses desire/need. c-Commerce is the label used to describe Internet-based (at least at present) electronic collaboration among businesses, typically supply chain partners, in support of inter-organizational processes that involve not just transactions, but also decision making, coordination, and control (Sane, 2005). ERP systems will have to support the required interactions and processes among and within business entities, and work with other systems/modules that do the

same. The back-office processes and activities of business network partners will not exist in a vacuum—many will overlap. There will be some need then for ERP processes to span organizational boundaries (some do at present), requiring a single shared inter-enterprise ERP system that will do it (we might call it a distributed ERP), or at least ERP systems that can communicate with and co-process (share/divide processing tasks) with other ERP systems—probably the most practical solution, at least in the near future. Middleware and enterprise portal technologies will likely play an important role in the integration of such modules and systems (Bhattacharjee, Greenbaum, Johnson, Martin, Reddy, Ryan, et al., 2002). In short, greater external integration that complements internal integration will be important in the future of ERP, as providers strive to enable companies to communicate and collaborate with other entities that comprise the extended enterprise (Bhattacharjee, Greenbaum, Johnson, Martin, Reddy, Ryan, et al., 2002). Internet-based technologies seem a necessary ingredient in this integrated, cross-enterprise ERP capability.

It is not uncommon now for companies to select only "suitable" modules rather than purchasing a complete packaged system, which may not be necessary given the core business processes of a company. That said, module capabilities and prices vary widely among vendors, and ERP is not cheap. Whether a company buys a "complete" solution or select modules, it still face several challenges with the development and implementation of ERP systems including: (i) the cost of the systems, (ii) alignment between information and business models, (iii) implementation issues (like integration, interoperability, and resistance to change), and (iv) post-implementation problems.

Web services are expected to play a prominent role in the future of ERP (O'Brien, 2002; ACW Team, 2004). Web services range from simple to complex, and they can incorporate other Web services. The capability of Web services to allow businesses to share data, applications, and processes across the Internet (O'Brien, 2002) may result in ERP systems of the future relying heavily on the service-oriented architecture, within which Web services are created and stored, providing the building blocks for programs and systems. Web service technology could put the focus where it belongs: on putting together the very best functional solution to automate a business process (Bhattacharjee, Greenbaum, Johnson, Martin, Reddy, Ryan, et al., 2002). The use of "best in breed" Web service-based solutions might be more palatable to businesses, since it might be easier and less risky to plug in a new Web service-based solution than replace or add on a new product module. A greater role for Web services is expected, and that, too, would heighten the importance of an Internet-based architecture to the future of ERP.

All from one, or best in breed? Reliance on a single vendor would seem best from a vendor's perspective, but it may not be best from the client's standpoint. While it may be advantageous to have only one proprietary product to install and operate, and a single contact point for problems, there are risks inherent in this approach. Switching cost can be substantial, and if a single vendor does not offer a module/solution needed by the client, then the client must develop it internally, do without it, or purchase it from another vendor. At any rate, the client may be faced with trying to get diverse products to work together, and the problems of doing so are well documented. The single source approach means an organization must place great faith in the vendor. So what about best in breed? That approach will be good if greater interoperability/integration among vendor products is achieved (Bhattacharjee, Greenbaum, Johnson, Martin, Reddy, Ryan, et al., 2002). There is a need for greater "out of the box" interoperability, thus a need for standards. Ideally, products will reach a level of standardization where software modules exhibit behavior similar to the plug-and-play hardware—you just plug in a new module, the system recognizes it, configures itself to accommodate

the new module, and eureka, it works! While this is much to hope for, increased standardization brought about by developments like the Service-oriented architecture might make this a reality, though probably not anytime soon. The fact that many are embracing standards for XML and more does give one some reason to hope, but whether the future of ERP software trends toward the single source or best in breed approach remains to be seen. Regardless of the direction, integration technologies will be important in the new breed of modular, but linked, enterprise applications. Middleware providers see a significant opportunity here in that their products facilitate module interaction. Increasingly, modules and or entire systems are provided by a new breed of vendors called application service providers (ASPs). These companies typically deliver their services via the Internet, and may become "the way" business partners integrate their systems—all partners could use the same ASP and the ASP systems would be the integrating force.

Data warehouses, data mining, and various analytic capabilities are needed in support of front-office and back-office processes and activities involved in CRM, SRM, SCM, field service nanagement, business collaboration, and more. Likewise, they are important in strategic management. Data warehouses are expected to play an important role in the future of ERP, either as a capability within ERP, or by working with the ERP system to exchange data needed to support related activities and processes. Ideally, the data warehouse would be integrated with all front-office, back-office, and strategic systems to the extent that it helps close loops by providing timely data to support decision making in any context. Knowledge management systems (KMS) endowed with neural networks and expert system capabilities should play a key role in decision making as they become more able to capture, model, and automate decision-making processes. Data warehouses and KMS should enable future ERP systems to support more automated business decision making (Strategic Systems of the Future, 1999; Bhattacharjee, Greenbaum, Johnson, Martin, Reddy, Ryan, et al., 2002). More automated decision making in both front-office and back-office systems should eliminate/minimize human variability and error, greatly increase decision speed, and hopefully improve decision quality. Business intelligence (BI) tools, offered by some vendors and planned by others, take data and transform it into information used in building knowledge that helps decision makers to make more "informed" decisions—no pun intended. Current business intelligence (BI) tools are largely designed to support strategic planning and control but will likely trickle down to lower-level decision makers, where their capabilities will be put to use in tactical and perhaps operational decision contexts. BI tools use data, typically from a data warehouse, along with data mining, analytic, statistical, query, reporting, forecasting, and decision support capabilities to support managerial planning and control. In combination with the data warehouse, KMS and BI should contribute to faster, better, and less costly (in terms of time and effort involved) decisions at all organizational levels.

At least in the near future, it appears that greater emphasis will be placed on front-office systems, as opposed to back-office systems, and sharing data, applications, and processes across the Internet (O'Brien, 2002). Back-office systems will not be unimportant, but they are more mature as a consequence of past emphasis, and many work quite well. Emphasis will be on more thorough integration of the modules that comprise back-office systems, integration of back-office systems with front-office and strategic systems, and integration of front-office, back-office, and strategic systems with the systems of other organizations. At present, greater organizational effectiveness in managing the entire supply chain all the way to the end customer is a priority in business. The greater emphasis on front-office functions and cross-enterprise communications, and collabo-

ration via the Internet, simply reflects changing business needs and priorities. A 2004 ITtoolbox survey of ERP users in Europe, North America, Asia, India, and elsewhere showed great interest in improved functionality and ease of integration and implementation (top motives for adding new modules or purchasing new ERP systems). Furthermore, the same survey showed greatest interest in modules for CRM, Data Warehousing, and SCM (top three on the list). The demand for specific modules/capabilities in particular shows that businesses are looking beyond the enterprise. This external focus is encouraging vendors to seize the moment by responding with the modules/systems that meet evolving business needs. The need to focus, not just on new front-office tools but also on strategy, will encourage greater vendor emphasis on tools like data warehouses and capabilities like business intelligence that support strategy development, implementation, and control.

The evolving environment of business suggests a direction for these comprehensive enterprise systems that would seem to make ERP less fitting as an appropriate label. The Gartner group has coined the term ERPII to describe their vision of the enterprise system of the future, with increased focus on the front office, strategy, and the Internet. ERPII is a business strategy and a set of collaborative operational and financial processes internally and beyond the enterprise (Zrimsek, 2002). Gartner projected that by 2005, ERPII will replace ERP as the key enabler of internal and inter-enterprise efficiency (Zrimsek, 2002). While the ERPII label may stick for a while, it is likely that ERP will be relegated to module/capability status, while a name more fitting for evolving inter-enterprise front office, back office, and strategic systems will replace the ERPII label, in much the same way that ERP replaced MRPII. Perhaps "enterprise systems" will be that new name, as it seems to be finding favor among vendors.

THE ERP EVOLUTION FRAMEWORK

This framework simply summarizes the evolution of ERP relating the stages in its evolution to business needs driving the evolution, as well as changes in technology. Table 2 presents the framework. As MRP evolved into MRPII, then ERP, and finally to ERPII (present state of ERP), the scope of the system expanded as organizational needs changed, largely in response to the changing dynamics of the competitive environment. As business has become increasingly global in nature, and cooperation among enterprises more

necessary for competitive reasons, systems have evolved to meet those needs. One can hardly ignore the technological changes that have taken place, because the current state of technology is a limiting factor in the design of systems to meet evolving business needs. From our examination of the evolution of ERP, we would conclude that the next stage of the evolution will come about and be shaped by the same forces that have shaped each stage, that being evolving business needs and advances in technology. The future of ERP systems seems destined to follow one of two courses: ERP will be relegated to the status of module within some broader system, or ERP will

Table 2. The evolution of ERP

System	Primary Business Need(s)	Scope	Enabling Technology
MRP	Efficiency	Inventory management and Production planning and control.	Mainframe computers, batch processing, traditional file systems.
MRPII	Efficiency, effectiveness and integration of manufacturing systems	Extending to the entire manufacturing firm (becoming cross-functional).	Mainframes and Mini computers, realtime (time sharing) processing, database management systems (relational)
ERP	Efficiency (primarily back office), effectiveness and integration of all organizational systems.	Entire organization (increasingly cross functional), both manufacturing and non-manufacturing operations.	Mainframes, Mini, and micro computers, Client server networks with distributed processing and distributed databases, Data warehousing and mining, knowledge management.
ERPII	Efficiency, effectiveness and integration within and among enterprises.	Entire organization extending to other organizations (cross-functional and cross-enterprise--partners, suppliers, customers, etc.).	Mainframes, Client Server systems, distributed computing, knowledge management, Internet technology (includes Web services, intranets and extranets).
IRP, Enterprise Systems, Enterprise Suite, or whatever label gains common acceptance.	Efficiency, effectiveness and integration within and among all relevant constituents (business, government, consumers, etc.) on a global scale.	Entire organization and its constituents (increasingly global) comprising supply chain from beginning to end as well as other industry and government constituents.	Internet, Web service Architecture, wireless networking, mobile wireless, knowledge management, grid computing, artificial intelligence.

evolve into that all-encompassing system, call it ERPII or something else, that contains most or all of the modules discussed herein. We expect the former as opposed to the latter will occur, with ERP (the traditional back office system) taking its place with MRP and MRPII. The functions ERP systems perform will remain important and necessary as have the functions of MRP and MRPII, but ERP will become part of something bigger, taking its place as an integral part of the enterprise system of the future. Whether that all-encompassing system is called ERPII, Interprise resource planning, enterprise suite, enterprise system, or a name that currently resides in the back of some vendor employee or researcher's mind, remains to be seen. One thing seems certain, the next stage in the evolution will hinge on the same forces shaping systems of the past—business need and technological change.

CONCLUSION

ERP has evolved over a long period of time. MRP gave way to MRPII, then MRPII to ERP, and finally ERP to ERPII. It seems quite likely that ERPII will give way to a new label. MRP still exists as will ERP, but most likely as a module, or capability rather than the label applied to an increasingly broad set of capabilities and modules that support the back-office, front-office, strategic planning and control, as well as integrating processes and activities across diverse enterprises comprising business networks. Whatever the name, current trends suggest certain characteristics which we can reasonably expect. This future system will have to support e-commerce and m-commerce, thus wireless technology, including but not limited to mobile, and the Internet will be key in the evolving architecture. An Internet-based architecture seems likely, and it may be a service-oriented architecture, wherein Web services are key, ASPs, or both. The increased emphasis on front-office systems and strategic planning and

control will likely influence new capabilities introduced by vendors for the next few years. Increased automation of decision making is to be expected with contributions from knowledge management and business intelligence systems fueled by advancements in the field of artificial intelligence. Greater interoperability of diverse systems and more thorough integration within and between enterprise systems is likely to remain a priority. An environment for applications much like the "plug and play" environment for hardware would make it easier for organizations to integrate their own systems and have their systems integrated with those of other organizations. Such an environment awaits greater standardization. This ideal "plug and play" environment would make it easier for firms to opt for a "best in breed" strategy for application/module acquisition as opposed to reliance on a single vendor for a complete package of front-office, back-office, and strategic systems. Moreover, such a development might move us closer to effective inter-organizational system integration and make fully integrated supply chain management a reality. Perhaps we might call the evolving system interprise resource planning to emphasize the inter-enterprise nature of these systems. Whatever they are called, it seems that what they will do goes far beyond what the enterprise resource planning (ERP) label would aptly describe, even when the "II" is appended.

From the discussion of ERP's future one can extrapolate certain desired capabilities for the enterprise systems of the future. Following is a list of desired/required capabilities:

- Facilitates an integrated supply chain
- Data transfer between modules is smooth and consistent
- Flexibility to support agile companies responding to dynamic business environment
- An architecture reflective of evolving enterprise models and evolving technology, like mobile wireless

- Database models/solutions support transaction-intensive applications (front office and back office), query intensive applications, and internal and external interaction with the database
- Systems take into account partnering enterprise characteristics like culture, language, technology level, standards, information flows, and provide flexibility to adapt as partnering relationships change
- Global vendor alliances to better meet needs of clients in any country
- Vendors and user companies adopt standards like XML, the Web service architecture, and evolving wireless standards with due consideration to global business requirements
- Greater flexibility and interoperability of modules, systems, and enterprises

For researchers and practitioners the advice is simple. There were two primary drivers in the evolution from MRP to MRPII, ERP, and finally ERPII. Those drivers were business need and technological change. Technological change made possible the development of systems to meet changing business needs. The needs may exist for a while before the technology can help meet them, and the technology can exist for a while before someone recognizes that it can be used to meet a current or evolving business need. In either case, the focus should be on monitoring business needs and monitoring technological change. Research that does both and is geared towards bringing the two together could make significant contributions to business. The Enterprise System of the future, whatever it is called, will be found at the convergence of business need and technological change. Perhaps researchers need to explore how we can do more to make that happen, rather than wait for it to happen and describe it as we have in this manuscript.

REFERENCES

ACW Team. (2004, August 23). SSA Global releases converged ERP with manufacturing capabilities, *Asia Computer Weekly*, 1.

Arinze, B., & Anandarajan, M. (2003). A framework for using OO mapping methods to rapidly configure ERP systems. Association for Computing Machinery. *Communications of the ACM, 46*(2), 61.

Bhattacharjee, D., Greenbaum, J., Johnson, R., Martin, M., Reddy, R., Ryan, H. L., et al.(2002). *Intelligent Enterprise, 5*(6) 28-33.

Conway, C. (2001, November 26).Top 20 visionaries:Comments of Craig Conway. *VARbusiness*, (1724), 35.

Dalal, N.P., Kamath, M., Kolarik, W.J., & Sivaraman, E. (2004). Toward an integrated framework for modeling enterprise resources.*Communications of the ACM, 47*(3), 83-87.

Davison, R.(2002). Cultural complications of ERP. Association for Computing Machinery. *Communications of the ACM, 45*(7), 109.

Genovese, Y., Bond, B.A., Zrimsek, B., & Frey, N.(2001). *The transition to ERP II: Meeting the challenges.* Retrieved July 7 from http://www.gartner.com/DisplayDocument?doc_dc=101237

Green, J. (2003). Responding to the challenge. *Canadian Transportation Logistics, 106*(8), 20-21.

Higgins, K.(2005, May 23). ERP goes on the road. *Information Week* (1040), 52-53.

Lee, J., Siau, K., & Hong, S. (2003). Enterprise integration with ERP and EAI. Association for Computing Machinery. *Communications of the ACM, 46*(2), 54.

Koch, C.(2004). *Koch's IT strategy: The ERP pickle.* Retrieved June 16, 2005 from http://www.cio.com/blog_view.html?CID=935

Kremers, M., & Dissel, H.V. (2000).ERP system migrations. Association for Computing Machinery. *Communications of the ACM, 43*(4), 52-56.

Kumar, K.,& Hillegersberg, J.V. (2000). ERP experiences and evolution. Association for Computing Machinery. *Communications of the ACM, 43*(4), 22-26.

Lope, P.F. (1992). CIMII: the integrated manufacturing enterprise. *Industrial Engineering, 24*, 43-45.

Markus, M.L., Tanis, C., & van Fenema, P.C. (2000). Multisite ERP implementations. Association for Computing Machinery. *Communications of the ACM, 43*(4), 42-46.

Nattkemper, J. (2000). An ERP evolution. *HP Professional, 14*(8), 12-15.

Nikolopoulos, K., Metaxiotis, K., Lekatis, N., & Assimakopoulos, V. (2003). Integrating industrial maintenance strategy into ERP. *Industrial Management + Data Systems, 103*, (3/4), 184-192.

O'Brien, J.M. (2002). J.D. Edwards follows 5 with ERP upgrade. *Computer Dealer News, 18*(12), 11.

Sane, V. (2005). *Enterprise resource planning overview*," Ezine articles. Retrieved July 2, 2005 , from http://ezinearticles.com/?Enterprise-Resource-Planning-Overview&id=37656

Scheer, A.-W., & Habermann, F.(2000). Making ERP a success. Association for Computing Machinery. *Communications of the ACM, 43*(4), 57-61.

Soh, C., Kien, S.S., & Yap, J.T. (2000). Cultural fits and misfits: Is ERP a universal solution. Association for Computing Machinery. *Communications of the ACM, 43*(4), 47-51.

Willcocks, L.P., & Stykes, R.(2000). The role of the CIO and IT function in ERP. Association for Computing Machinery. *Communications of the ACM, 43*(4), 32-38.

Zrimsek, B. (2002). *ERPII: The Boxed Set*. Retrieved July 7, 2005 from http://www.gartner.com/pages/story.php.id.2376.s.8.jsp.2004, ITtoolbox ERP Implementation Survey. Retrieved July 7, 2005 from http://supplychain.ittoolbox.com/research/survey.asp?survey=corioerp_survey&p=2

This work was previously published in International Journal of Enterprise Information Systems, Vol. 3, Issue 3, edited by A. Gunasekaran, pp. 23-35, copyright 2007 by IGI Publishing, formerly known as Idea Group Publishing (an imprint of IGI Global).

Chapter XXIV
A Multi–Agent Decision Support Architecture for Knowledge Representation and Exchange

Rahul Singh
University of North Carolina at Greensboro, USA

ABSTRACT

Organizations rely on knowledge-driven systems for delivering problem-specific knowledge over Internet-based distributed platforms to decision-makers. Recent advances in systems support for problem solving have seen increased use of artificial intelligence (AI) techniques for knowledge representation in multiple forms. This article presents an Intelligent Knowledge-based Multi-agent Decision Support Architecture" (IKMDSA) to illustrate how to represent and exchange domain-specific knowledge in XML-format through intelligent agents to create, exchange and use knowledge in decision support. IKMDSA integrates knowledge discovery and machine learning techniques for the creation of knowledge from organizational data; and knowledge repositories (KR) for its storage management and use by intelligent software agents in providing effective knowledge-driven decision support.

Implementation details of the architecture, its business implications and directions for further research are discussed.

INTRODUCTION

The importance of knowledge as an organizational asset that enables sustainable competitive advantage explains the increasing interest of organizations in KM. Many organizations are developing knowledge management systems (KMS) that are specifically designed to facilitate the sharing and integration of knowledge, as opposed to data or information, in decision support activities (Bolloju, Khalifa, & Turban, 2002). Decision support systems (DSS) are computer technology solutions used to support complex decision-making and problem solving (Shim, Warkentin, Courtney, Power, Sharda, & Carlsson, 2002). Organizations are becoming increasingly complex with emphasis on decentralized decision-making. Such changes create the need for DSS that focus on supporting problem solving activities on distributed platforms by providing problem specific data and knowledge to a decision maker anywhere, using Internet-based technologies. This trend necessitates enterprise DSS for effective decision-making with processes and facilities to support the use of knowledge management (KM).

Recent advances in systems support for problem solving and decision-making witness the increased use of artificial intelligence (AI) based techniques for knowledge representation (Goul, 2005; Whinston, 1997). Knowledge representation takes multiple forms including the incorporation of business rules, decision analytical models and models generated from the application of machine learning algorithms. Intelligent decision support systems (IDSS) incorporate intelligence in the form of knowledge about the problem domain, with knowledge representation to inform the decision process, facilitate problem solving and reduce the cognitive load of the decision maker. Weber and Aha (2003) identified requirements for organizational KMS where the central unit is a repository of knowledge artifacts collected from internal or external organizational sources. These KMS can vary based on the type of knowledge artifact stored, the scope and nature of the topic described and the orientation (Weber & Aha, 2003). Ba, Lang and Whinston (1997) enumerate the KM principles necessary to achieve intra-organizational knowledge bases as: (1) the use of corporate data to derive and create higher-level information and knowledge, (2) provision of tools to transform scattered data into meaningful business information. Knowledge repositories play a central and critical role in the storage, distribution and management of knowledge in an organization. Interestingly, Bolloju et. al. (2002) proposed an approach for integrating decision support and KM that facilitates knowledge conversion through suitable automated techniques to:

1. Apply knowledge discovery techniques (KDT) for knowledge externalization.
2. Employ repositories for storing externalized knowledge.
3. Extend KDT for supporting various types of knowledge conversions.

This article is motivated by these principles and attempts to develop and present an intelligent knowledge-based multi-agent architecture for knowledge-based decision support using eXtensible Markup Language (XML) related technologies for knowledge representation and knowledge exchange over distributed and heterogeneous platforms. The proposed architecture integrates DSS and KMS using XML as the medium for the representation and exchange of domain specific knowledge, and intelligent agents to facilitate the creation, exchanges and use of the knowledge in decision support activities. This is the primary contribution of this research to the existing body of knowledge in DSS, KMS and multi-agent research.

This research builds on existing bodies of knowledge in intelligent agents, KM, DSS and XML technology standards. Our research focuses on achieving a transparent translation between XML and Decision Trees through software agents. This creates the foundation for knowledge representation and exchange, through intelligent agents, to support decision-making activity for users of the system. We use a knowledge repository to store knowledge, captured in XML documents, that can used and shared by software agents within the multi-agent architecture. We call this architecture an *Intelligent Knowledge-based Multi-agent Decision Support Architecture* (IKMDSA). IKMDSA integrates KDT and knowledge repositories for storing externalized knowledge. It utilizes an intelligent multi-agent system with explanation facility to provide distributed decision support using Internet-based technologies. The implementation incorporates, and is built upon XML and its related technologies to achieve knowledge representation, storage and knowledge exchange among participating intelligent agents to deliver decision support to the user. The proposed IKMD-SA incorporates mechanisms whereby agents can provide distributed intelligent decision support by exchanging their knowledge using XML and its related set of standards. Implementation details of the implementation of the architecture and their implications for further research in this area by academics and practitioners are provided.

In the second section, we review relevant literature in intelligent agents and the role of decision trees in inductive learning and knowledge representation in terms of decision rules. In the third section, we discuss the role of XML in representing and facilitating knowledge exchange for intelligent agents. The fourth section provides a detailed description of the various components of the IKMDSA architecture and their inter-relationships in facilitating the creation, representation, exchange and use of domain specific knowledge for decision support tasks. In the fifth section, we provide a detailed description of the implementation of the architecture through the use of an illustrative example. The sixth section 6 includes a discussion of the implications of integrating KMS and DSS support in business, and the role of the proposed IKMDSA architecture. The seventh section concludes with limitations and future research directions.

LITERATURE REVIEW

Software Agents and Intelligent Decision Support Systems (IDSS)

An intelligent agent is "a computer system situated in some environment and that is capable of flexible autonomous action in this environment in order to meet its design objectives" (Jennings & Wooldridge, 1998). While the terms agents, software agents and intelligent agents are often used interchangeably in the literature, all agents do not necessarily have to be intelligent. Jennings and Wooldridge (1998) observe that agent-based systems are not necessarily intelligent, and require that an agent be flexible to be considered intelligent. Such flexibility in intelligent agent based systems requires that the agents should be: (Bradshaw, 1997; Jennings & Wooldridge, 1998)

- Cognizant of their environment and be *responsive* to changes therein.
- Reactive and proactive to opportunities in their environment.
- Autonomous in goal-directed behavior.
- Collaborative in their ability to interact with other agents in exhibiting the goal-oriented behavior.
- Adaptive in their ability to learn with experience.

Agent-based systems may consist of a single agent engaged in autonomous goal-oriented behavior, or multiple agents that work together to exhibit granular as well as overall goal directed behavior. The general multi-agent system is one in which the interoperation of separately developed and self-interested agents provide a service beyond the capability of any single agent model. Such mutli-agent systems provide a powerful abstraction that can be used to model systems where multiple entities, exhibiting self directed behaviors must coexist in a environment and achieve the system wide objective of the environment.

Intelligent agents are action-oriented abstractions in electronic systems entrusted to carry out various generic and specific goal-oriented actions on behalf of users. The agent abstraction manifests itself in the system as a representation of the user and performs necessary tasks on behalf of the user. This role may involve taking directions from the user on a need basis and advising and informing the user of alternatives and consequences (Whinston, 1997). The agent paradigm can support a range of decision making activity including information retrieval, generation of alternatives, preference order ranking of options and alternatives and supporting analysis of the alternative-goal relationships. In this respect, intelligent agents have come a long way from being digital scourers and static filters of information to active partners in information processing tasks. Such a shift has significant design implications on the abstractions used to model information systems, objects or agents, and on the architecture of information resources that are available to entities involved in the electronic system. Another implication is that knowledge must be available in formats that are conducive to its representation and manipulation by software applications, including software agents.

Decision Trees and IDSS

Models of decision problems provide analytical support to the decision maker by facilitating a greater understanding of the problem domain and allowing the decision maker to assess the utility of alternative decision paths with respect to achieving the objective of the decision task. Decision trees are a popular modeling technique with wide applicability to a variety of business problems (Sung, Chang, & Lee, 1999). The performance of a particular method in modeling human decisions is dependent on the conformance of the method with the decision makers' mental model of the decision problem (Kim, Chung, & Paradice, 1997). Simplicity of model representation is particularly relevant if the discovered explicit models are to be internalized by decision makers (Bolloju et al., 2002). Decision Trees represent a natural choice for IDSS whose goal is to generate decision paths that are easy to understand,

to explain and to convert to natural language (Sung et al., 1999). The choice of decision trees as the modeling methodology affords the ability to incorporate inductive learning in the IDSS. Decision trees are among the most commonly used inductive learning techniques used to learn patterns from data (Kudoh, Haraguchi, & Okubo, 2003; Takimoto & Maruoka, 2003). The ID3, C4.5, and SEE5 algorithms provide a formal method to create and model decision rules from categorical and continuous data (Quinlan, 1996; Sung et al., 1999) compared multiple machine learning techniques in predicting bankruptcies and found that the decision tree technique had the most interpretive power. In this research, the C4.5 (ID3) method is used due to the popularity of the algorithm (Kiang, 2003).

Additionally, decision trees solutions lend themselves to automatic generation of structured queries to extract pertinent data from organizational data repositories (Adriaans & Zantinge, 1996). This makes them particularly useful in providing insights and explanations for the nontechnical user (Apte & Weiss, 1997). Decision trees are especially suitable for decision problems that require the generation of human understandable decision rules based on a mix of classification of categorical and continuous data (Quinlan, 1996; Sung et al., 1999). They provide clear indication of the importance of individual data fields to the decision problem and are therefore useful in reducing the cognitive burden of the decision maker. It is clear that decision trees represent a powerful and easily interpretable technique for modeling business decisions that can be reduced to a rule-based form. The benefits of the technique highlighted above provide a strong basis for choosing decision trees as a component for intelligent DSS.

USING XML AND DECISION TREES FOR KNOWLEDGE REPRESENTATION AND EXCHANGE

XML and Document Type Definitions (DTDs)

Since the advent of the Internet, the World Wide Web has become very popular because of the simplicity provided by HTML for its usage and content presentation. HTML provides a fixed set of tags that are used to markup content (information) primarily for consumption by human beings. Despite its efficiency for presenting information in human readable format, HTML is very limited in extensibility and customization of markup tags and description of the data contained in those tags. This constraint limits the use of HTML by application software for information sharing in a distributed computing environment where application programs, including intelligent agents are expected to work with available data, rules and knowledge without human intervention.

The use of XML and its related set of standards, developed by the World Wide Web Consortium, (W3C http://www.w3c.org), have helped overcome some of these limitations. XML allows for the creation of custom tags that contain data from specific domains. XML is a meta-language that allows for the creation of languages that can be represented by customized XML tags. For example, a company in the furniture industry may develop customized tags for the representation of content to serve its business domain. By creating custom tags, the company can represent the data in a more meaningful and flexible way than it could using HTML. The company may also develop documents that represent business-rules using XML that can shared either with human agents or with software agents. Unambiguous understanding of the content of customized XML tags by interested parties requires description of both the content and structure of XML documents. This description

of structures in XML documents is provided by the XML schema which can be written following the set of standards called XML Schema and/or the Document Type Definition (DTD) language as adopted and standardized by the W3C. XML schema describes specific elements, their relationships and specific types of data that can be stored in each tag. XML documents can be validated and parsed by application software provided either the DTD or the XML Schema of the corresponding document is made available. XML parsers written in C, C++ or Java can process and validate XML documents (containing business rules and data) based on XML schemas written based on either the DTD or the XML Schema specification. Application software appropriate parser utilities are able to read and/or write to XML documents following the W3C standards and specification. This provides the foundation technology, built upon an agreed and accepted standard from W3C, for the capture, representation, exchange and storage of knowledge represented by business rules and related data in XML format that can be potentially used and shared by software agents.

Recent initiatives to develop technologies for the "Semantic Web" (Berners–Lee, Hendler, & Lassila, 2001) make the content of the Web unambiguously computer-interpretable, thus making it amenable to agent interoperability and automatic reasoning techniques (McIllraith, Son, & Zeng, 2001). Two important technologies for developing Semantic Web are already in place — XML and the resource description framework (RDF). The W3C developed the RDF as a standard for metadata to add a formal semantics to the Web, defined on top of XML, to provide a data model and syntax convention for representing the semantics of data in standardized interoperable manner (McIllraith, et al., 2001). The RDF working group also developed RDF Schema (RDFS), an object-oriented type system that can be effectively thought of as a minimal ontology modeling language. Recently, there have been several efforts to build on RDF and RDFS with more AI-inspired knowledge representation languages such as SHOE, DAML-ONT, OIL and DAML+OIL (Fensel, 1997). While these initiatives are extremely promising for agent interoperability and reasoning, they are at their early stages of development. In this article, we focus on the use of more mature and widely used and available standardized technologies such as XML and DTDs to represent knowledge. This approach, along with other initiatives, should allow researchers to develop intelligent agent-based systems that are both practical and viable for providing intelligent decision support to users in a business environment.

XML and Decision Trees for Knowledge Representation

The W3C XML specification allows for the creation of customized tags for content modeling. Customized tags are used to create data-centric content models and rule-based content models. Data-centric content models imply XML documents that have XML tags that contain data, for example from a database, and can be parsed by application software for processing in distributed computing environments. XML documents containing rule-based content models can be used for knowledge representation. XML tags can be created to represent rules and corresponding parameters. Software agents can then parse and read the rules in these XML documents for use in making intelligent decisions. Before making intelligent decisions, the software agents should be able to codify or represent their knowledge. Decision Trees and inductive learning algorithms such as ID3, C4.5 can be used by agents to develop the rule-based decision tree. This learned decision tree can be converted into an XML document with the corresponding use of a DTD. This XML document, containing the learned decision tree, forms the basis for knowledge representation and sharing with other software agents in the community. We demonstrate architecture for agent-based intelligent information systems to accomplish this.

XML and Decision Trees for Knowledge Representation and Exchange

Software agents for knowledge exchange and sharing in the agent community can exchange decision trees represented in XML documents. For example, a new agent can learn from the knowledge of the existing agents in the community by using the decision tree available in XML format in a knowledge repository. The existence of this knowledge repository allows knowledge to be stored and retrieved as needed basis by the agents and updated to reflect the new knowledge from various agents in the community. The explanatory power of decision trees from their ability to generate understandable rules and the provide clear indication of important fields for classification allows the incorporation of explanation facility, similar to expert systems, among the agents in this type of architecture (Sung et al., 1999). Moreover, explanation is essential to the interaction between users and knowledge-based systems (KBS), describing what a system does, how it works, and why its actions are appropriate (Mao & Benbasat, 2000). Among 87 KBS shell capabilities, users rated explanation facilities and the capability to customize explanations as the fourth and fifth most important factors, respectively (Stylianou, Madey, & Smith, 1992). Explanation can make KBS conclusions more acceptable (Ye & Johnson, 1995) and builds trust in a system. The ability of the agents to explain the decision rules used in the decision making process makes agents powerful tools to aid human agents in complex decision tasks. Such intelligent agent architecture, built around well-grounded and well-researched decision models along with standards-based widely available technologies (such as XML, DTDs), is a significant contribution to furthering research on agent-based distributed computing and DSS. In the following section, we present the details of IKMDSA and discuss its knowledge externalization, knowledge representation, knowledge management and knowledge delivery mechanism for decision support.

Integrated Intelligent Knowledge-Based Decision Support Architecture (IKMDSA)

A KMS has facilities to create, exchange, store and retrieve knowledge in an exchangeable and usable format for decision-making activity. IKMDSA utilizes ID3 algorithms to create knowledge from raw data to a decision tree representational form. A domain knowledge object represents information about a specific problem domain in IKMDSA. The domain knowledge object contains information about the characteristics of the various domain attributes important to the problem domain. The domain knowledge object describes the problem context and provides rules for making decisions in the problem context. The domain knowledge object represents the abstraction used for creating, exchanging and using modular knowledge objects in IKMDSA. IKMDSA uses intelligent software agents as the mechanism for encapsulation and exchange of knowledge between agents at the site of knowledge creation and the site of knowledge storage. Intelligent agents deliver knowledge to the user interface to support intelligent decision-making activity. The agent abstraction is built upon basic objects that take on additional behaviors, as required by its function (Shoham, 1993). Knowledge exchange and delivery in IKMDSA is facilitated through the exchange of the domain knowledge objects among intelligent agents. Figure 1 illustrates this basic building block of IKMDSA, where an agent has a composition relationship with the domain knowledge object, and thereby has access to knowledge in the form of standard XML document object model (DOM) objects.

Every agent can share its knowledge through the domain knowledge component by invoking its share knowledge behavior. The domain knowledge object contains behaviors to inform agents of the name of the problem domain, share information about the various domain attributes that are pertinent to the specific knowledge context, and share rules about making decisions for their specific problem domain. We use these core components to develop the functionality of IKMDSA to learn rules and domain attributes from raw data, create domain specific knowledge, share it with other agents and apply this knowledge in solving domain specific problems with a user. Once the attributes

Figure 1. Agents have access to domain knowledge objects that abstract domain specific knowledge

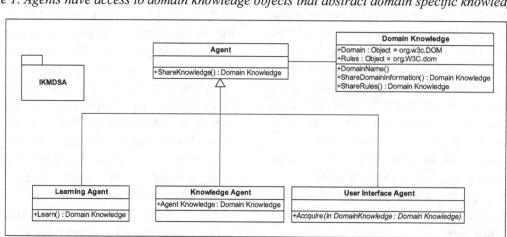

Figure 2. A schematic showing the generation, exchange, storage, retrieval and use of knowledge in IKMDSA

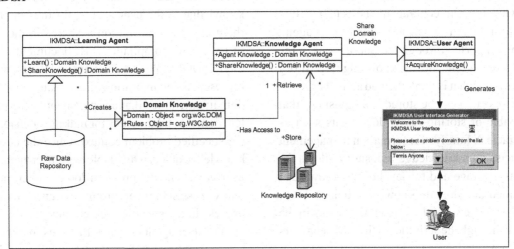

and domain rules are captured in the domain knowledge object, using standard XML DOM format, they can be exchanged between agents. Figure 2 provides a schematic of this activity sequence where knowledge is created from raw data and ultimately delivered in usable form to the decision maker.

Learning agents interact with a raw data repository and extract raw data used to generate domain specific knowledge. Our model does not specify the storage representation and the data contained in the repository may be of multiple representation formats including flat files, data stored as relational tables that can be extracted using multiple queries into a recordset, or raw data represented using XML documents. The learning agent extracts the raw data and applies machine learning algorithms to generate decision rules for the problem domain. The repository contains information about the context and syntactical representation of the information. This information provides the domain attributes pertinent to the decision problem. This generates domain specific knowledge in the form of domain attribute

information and rules for making decisions in the specific problem context. The system ensures that this knowledge is generated in a format conducive for sharing and use of the information across a distributed and heterogonous platform.

We use the domain knowledge object as the modular abstraction for knowledge representation and knowledge exchange facilitation in IKMDSA. Domain knowledge objects are made available to agents by the learning agent sharing the object with the knowledge agent. The knowledge agent manages the knowledge available in IKMDSA and allows for other agents in the system to know of, request and receive the domain knowledge in the system. The system utilizes the domain knowledge object as the modular knowledge abstraction for communication of knowledge across the multiple agents of the system. Therefore, when the domain knowledge object is shared with an agent of the system, the agent becomes aware of the problem context descriptions, in addition to the rules that govern decision-making in the specific problem context. The knowledge agent is also responsible for the maintaining the collection of domain knowledge available in the system through interactions with a knowledge repository. The Knowledge Agent contains methods to generate rules to support ad-hoc queries by the user agent. This is supported through the interactions of the Knowledge Agent with the knowledge repository of the system that is implemented as a set of XML documents that can be stored in a repository that is capable of storing XML documents such as the Oracle 9i family of information management products. This knowledge repository allows for the easy storage and retrieval of the knowledge contained in a domain knowledge object. Thus, the knowledge is available to all the agents in the system through the activities of the KM behaviors of the knowledge agent object. In this respect, the interactions among the agents in this system are modeled as collaborative interactions, where the agents in the multi-agent community work together to provide decision support and knowledge-based explanations of the decision problem domain to the user.

As shown in Figure 2, users of IKMDSA interact with the system through User Agents that are constantly aware of all domain knowledge contexts available to the system, through a list of names of the domain knowledge objects that is published and managed by the knowledge agent. This allows every user agent, and hence every user, to be aware of the entire problem space covered by the system. The user agent requests and receives the knowledge available for a specific problem domain by making a request to the knowledge agent, at the behest of the user. The knowledge agent, upon receiving this request, shares a domain knowledge object with the user agent, thereby making problem domain information and decision rules available to the user agent. The knowledge agents also serve as the means to service any ad-hoc queries that cannot be answered by the user interface agents, such as queries regarding knowledge parameters that are not available to the user interface agents. In such

cases, the Knowledge agent, with direct access to the knowledge repository can provide such knowledge to the user agents, for the benefit of the user. This information is shared in the form of two W3C compliant XML document object model (DOM) objects, Domain and Rules, which represent an enumeration and explanation of the domain attributes that are pertinent to the problem context and the rules for making decisions in the specified problem context. Once the domain knowledge object is available to the user agent, the user agent becomes problem domain aware and is ready to assist the user through a decision making process in the specific problem domain.

The user agent contains methods to generate a user-friendly interface to inform the user about problem domain attributes that are pertinent to the decision problem under consideration. The user interface offers explanations about each domain attribute and provides the user with contextual information on the different values that each domain attribute may take. This serves the purpose of informing the user and increasing their knowledge about the various factors that affect a decision in the problem domain under consideration. The user agent also contains methods to generate a decision making interface that allows a decision maker to consider and choose values for pertinent attributes. This selection process creates an instance of an observation that can be compared against the rules available to the user agent through the domain knowledge. The user interacts with the User Interface agent by asking question about the decision problem and receives responses containing decision alternatives and explanation of the choices made by the agent. This is achieved through parsing the decision rules based on the parameters supplied by the user. The agent compares the users' selections with the known rules and decides on the rule(s) that are fired for the given instance. These rules are formatted in a user-friendly format and made available to the user. This provides the user with a decision, given their selection of domain attributes and provides the user with explanations of the decisions made, given the selections made by the users.

The above sections provide a complete description of the process of knowledge creation, knowledge representation, knowledge exchange, KM and the use of the knowledge for decision making employed by IKMDSA. Figure 3 provides a schematic of this overall process. As shown in Figure 3, IKMDSA is designed for a distributed platform where the knowledge available to the agents in the system can be made available on an intranet and an Internet based platform by enclosing the domain knowledge objects in SOAP wrappers that enables the knowledge broker functions of the knowledge agent by making its knowledge available as a Web service.

IKMDSA consists of intelligent agents as discussed above that are able to provide intelligent decision support to the end-users. All of the agents in the architecture are FIPA compliant in terms of their requirements and behavior. The learning agents create knowledge from the raw data in a data repository, knowledge agents primarily acquire this knowledge from learning agents and manage this knowledge through a knowledge repository, while user agents help the users make decisions on specific problems using the knowledge contained in the decision trees. The exchange of knowledge between agents and between users and agents is achieved through sharing of content information using XML. The agents work on a distributed platform and enable the transfer of knowledge by exposing their public methods as Web Services

Figure 3. The intelligent knowledge-based multi-agent decision support architecture (IKMDSA)

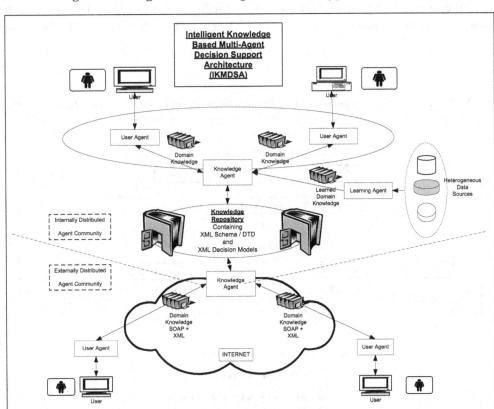

using SOAP and XML. The rule-based modular knowledge can be used and shared by agents. Capturing the modular knowledge in XML format also facilitates their storage in a knowledge repository - a repository that enables storage and retrieval of XML documents. The architecture allows for multiple knowledge repositories depending upon the problem domain. The benefits of such knowledge repositories are the historical capture of knowledge modules that are then shared among agents in the agent community. This minimizes the learning curve of newly created agents who are instantiated with the current knowledge that is available to the entire system. This is achieved in IKMDSA since agents have captured rule-based knowledge modules and have stored such knowledge modules in XML format in the knowledge repository for the benefit of the entire agent community and the system.

IKMDSA also provides a decision explanation facility to the end-users where agents are able to explain how they arrived at a particular decision. This has three important benefits:

- The end-user can understand how the decision was made by the software agent.
- The end-user can make a clear assessment of the viability of the decision.
- The end-user can learn about the problem domain by studying the decision paths used by the agent.

Agents are able to explain the rules and parameters that were used by the agent in arriving at the stated decision. This explanation facility is a natural extension of using decision trees in general for solving rule-based decision problems. Non-technical end-users are able to easily understand how a problem was solved using decision trees compared to other existing problem-solving methods such as neural networks, statistical and fuzzy logic-based systems (Sung et al., 1999). The IKMDSA architecture can provide intelligent distributed decision support that may be internal to the company and the other focusing on providing intelligent distributed decision support that may be external to the company. In the second case,

Figure 4. Decision Tree representation of the play tennis problem (adapted from Mitchell, 1997)

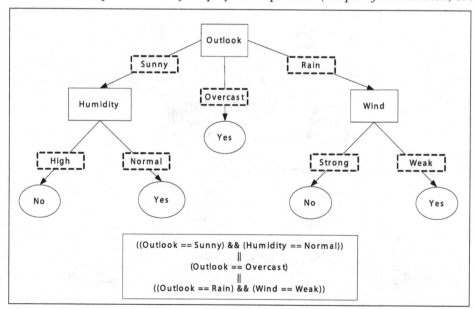

Figure 5. DTD for the representation of domain attribute in the play tennis problem

```
Domain.xsd   Domain.dtd*
<!-- DTD for Domain Attributes in the Play tennis Example -->
<!ELEMENT Context (DomainAttributes*)>
<!ATTLIST DomainContext  type CDATA #REQUIRED>
<!ELEMENT DomainAttribute(DomainAttributeName, nCategories, Category*)>
<!ELEMENT DomainAttributeName (#PCDATA)>
<!ELEMENT nCategories (#PCDATA)>
<!ELEMENT Caetgory (#PCDATA)>

Ready                                    Ln 4        Col 27
```

the proposed architecture incorporates the W3C Web Services architecture that uses the simple object access protocol (SOAP) and XML. The incorporation of this architecture creates a flexible means of exposing the services of the agents using the Web Services architecture by a company to its potential or existing global population of customers and suppliers.

Implementation of the IKMDSA Architecture and Illustrative Example

The problem domain selected for the initial proof of concept is the play tennis decision problem (Mitchell, 1997) using the ID3 decision tree method. The selection of the problem domain was due to it being widely adopted (Mitchell, 1997) to represent decision problems in the ID3 decision tree research and also for its simplicity in illustrating the proposed architecture. The decision problem for this problem domain is to decide whether, or not, to play tennis on a particular day based on climatic conditions such as the day's weather outlook, the level of humidity, the temperature, and the wind conditions. Figure 4 shows a schematic of the decision solutions un-

der consideration. The leaf nodes of the decision tree represent the final outcome of the decision of whether to play tennis on a certain day, based on what the weather is like. The problem is simple to understand; yet it illustrates the fundamental requirements of the system and provides an elegant way to test the various features of the agents and the architecture.

The end-user provides the existing weather condition to the user agent as input and the agent makes a decision and presents the decision to the end-user whether or not tennis can be played that particular day given the conditions entered by the user. The user is given information about each of the atmospheric conditions and their categories. These atmospheric conditions form the domain attributes for the play tennis problem and define the context specific information that is pertinent to this decision problem. The agent provides information on each domain attribute thereby informing the user through the process of selection of the attributes that are pertinent on any given day. The representation of the domain attributes generated by the agents shows the DTD and the XML files (see Figures 5 and 6) for the representation of information about the context of the problem domain. The XML representation

Figure 6. XML document showing domain attributes for the play tennis problem

Figure 7. The user interface presented to a user by the IKMDSA user agent

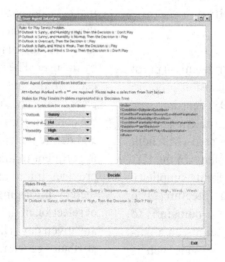

of the domain attributes is dynamically parsed by the user agent to generate a context specific user interface (as shown in Figure 7). This allows the user to make a decision about each pertinent domain attribute. After the user makes a selection from all the domain attributes, the user agent has enough information to make a decision about the problem domain. This is accomplished by parsing the set of domain rules that specify a final decision based on observations of domain attributes. As mentioned earlier, the user agent has access to an XML representation of domain rules about a given problem context, through the XML DOM object contained in the Domain Knowledge object for a decision problem. The structure for this set of rules is shown as a DTD in Figure 8, while Figure 9 shows the XML representation of the rules used by IKMDSA for the play tennis problem. The user agent parses these rules and identifies the rules that are fired for the given set of observations. These rules are then presented to the user in user-friendly format as explanation from the decision made by the user agent.

In the prototype implementation of the proposed IKMDSA architecture, we use the Java programming language to implement the agents as extensions of objects. The choice of Java was based upon the widely accepted advantage of Java providing portable code and XML providing portable data. In addition, we use Oracle 9i Database and Application Server platforms (http://www.oracle.com) to implement the knowledge repository and use the Sun Microsystems Java XML API toolkit to interface the agents with the XML repository. The decision tree implementation consists of tree nodes with branches for every category of the node variable. Each traversal from the root node of the decision tree to a leaf node leads to a separate decision path as illustrated in Figure 4. The agents contain methods to traverse the decision tree and obtain a decision path that can then be translated into an XML object and an XML document using a DTD file. These form the basis for the generation of decision alternatives and for the explanations of decisions by the agents. The agents are implemented as java beans and their explanations are available to the user through calls made to their public methods that are exposed as services, and presented to the user as dynamically generated web content by using Java Server Pages technology (http://java.sun.com/products/jsp/index.html).

Figure 8. DTD representation of the structure of rules

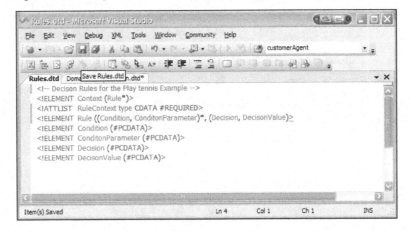

BUSINESS APPLICATION

Organizations are taking advantage of "data mining" techniques to leverage the vast amount of data to make better business decisions (Fan, Lu, Madnick, & Cheung, 2002; Padmanabhan & Tuzhilin, 1999). For example, data mining has been used for customer profiling in CRM and customer service support (Hui & Jha, 2000), credit card application approval, fraud detection, telecommunications network monitoring, market-based analysis (Fayyad, Piatetsky-Shapiro, & Smyth, 1996), healthcare quality assurance (Tsechansky, Pliskin, Rabinowitz, & Porath, 1999) and many other decision-making areas (Brachman, Khabaza, Kloesgen, Piatetsky-Shapiro, & Simoudis, 1996). There is a growing need to not only mine data for decision support, but also to externalize knowledge from enterprise data warehouses and data marts, to share such knowledge among end users through automated knowledge discovery and distribution system for effective decision support. In other words, there is an increasing need for the integration of KMS and DSS systems to meet the needs of the complex business decision situations. According to Bolloju et al. (2002) "Such integration is expected to enhance the quality of support provided by the system to decision makers and also to help in building up organizational memory and knowledge bases. The integration will result in decision support environments for the next generation" (p. 164). The proposed IKMDSA architecture illustrates such a next generation integrated KMS and DSS system. The detailed presentation of the implementation of the architecture is intended to further the research that combines multiple but related set of research streams such as data mining, automated knowledge discovery, knowledge representation and storage using XML, knowledge exchange among participating intelligent agents using knowledge context, and explanation facility (from expert systems research). The authors are currently extending the architecture in various business domains such as credit approval processing, bankruptcy prediction, electronic commerce and consumer behavior and Web mining.

Figure 9. Decision tree representation of the rule-based knowledge module for the play tennis problem in XML format

Emergent Internet technologies have significant impact on business processes of organizations operating in the digital economy. Realizing the potential benefits of emergent technologies is dependent on the effective sharing and use of business intelligence and process knowledge among business partners to provide accurate, relevant and timely information and knowledge. This requires system models to support and enable information integration, knowledge exchange and improved collaboration among business partners. Such systems must provide collaborating partners with intelligent knowledge management (KM) capabilities for seamless and transparent exchange of dynamic supply and demand information. Implementing and managing such integration over distributed and heterogeneous information platforms, such as the Internet, is a challenging task; yet, realizing this task can have significant benefits for organizations embracing such collaborations. An application of the IKMDSA for Collaborative Commerce to enable collaborative work in B2B e-Marketplaces would have significant benefits in developing information partnerships by creating the foundation for knowledge representation and exchange by intelligent agents that support collaborative work between business partners.

CONCLUSION, LIMITATIONS AND FUTURE DIRECTION FOR RESEARCH

In this research we have presented a methodology to represent modular, rule-based knowledge using the eXtensible Markup Language (XML) and the Document Type Definition (DTD) standards from the World Wide Web Consortium (W3C). Using this methodology, we have shown how such an approach can be used to create problem-specific knowledge modules that can easily be distributed over the Internet to support distributed IDSS design. Such an approach will facilitate intelligent decision support by providing the required knowledge representation and the decision analytical support. We had presented the conceptual architecture of such a distributed IDSS, and have provided details of the components of the architecture, including the agents involved and their interactions, the details of the knowledge representation and implementation of knowledge exchange through a distributed interface. We also provided indication of how such architecture might be used to support the user and how it might assume the role of an expert and provide explanations to the user, while retaining the benefits of an active DSS through extensible knowledge generation by incorporating machine learning algorithms. The example used in this article is simple, intuitive, and elegantly achieves its purpose of illustrating the use of the architecture while minimizing complications inherent to a more complex problem domain. We continue to do research on elaborating this architecture for a variety of problems that lend themselves to rule-based, inductive decision making with a need for user interactions and which benefit from greater understanding of the problem domain by the user.

The limitations of this research derive from the use of decision trees and inductive learning algorithms and techniques. The limitations inherent to decision trees and such techniques are also the limitation of this architecture. Therefore, further research needs to be conducted to understand how this architecture can be expanded to incorporate other types of learning and rule induction or rule creation to be shared and used by software agents. Despite this limitation, this research contributes significantly to the advancement of our understanding of how emerging technologies can be incorporated into intelligent agent-based architecture to enhance the value of such systems in distributed intelligent DSS that incorporates knowledge.

REFERENCES

Adriaans, P., & Zantinge, D. (1996). *Data mining.* Harlow, UK: Addison-Wesley.

Apte, C., & Weiss, S. (1997). Data mining with decision trees and decision rules. *Future Generation Computer Systems, 13,* 197-210.

Ba, S., Lang, K. R., & Whinston, A. B. (1997). Enterprise decision support using Intranet technology. *Decision Support Systems, 20*(2), 99-134.

Berners-Lee, T., Hendler, J., & Lassila, O. (2001). The Sematic Web. *Scientific American, 6(1),* 34-43.

Bolloju, N., Khalifa, M., & Turban, E. (2002). Integrating knowledge management into enterprise environments for the next generation decision support. *Decision Support Systems, 33,* 163-176.

Brachman, R., Khabaza, T., Kloesgen, W., Piatetsky-Shapiro, G., & Simoudis, E. (1996). Mining business databases. *Communications of ACM, 39*(11), 42-48.

Bradshaw, J. M. (1997). *Software agents.* Boston: MIT Press.

Fan, W., Lu, H., Madnick, S. E., & Cheung, D. (2002). DIRECT: A system for mining data value conversion rules from disparate data sources. *Decision Support Systems, 34,* 19-39.

Fayyad, U., Piatetsky-Shapiro, G., & Smyth, P. (1996). From data mining to knowledge discovery: An overview. In U. Fayyad, G. Piatetsky-Shapiro, P. Smyth & R. Uthurusamy (Eds.), *Advances in knowledge discovery and data mining* (pp. 1-36). Cambridge, MA: AAAI/MIT Press.

Fensel, D. (2000). The semantic Web and its languages. *IEEE Intelligent Systems, 15*(6), 67

Goul, M., & Corral, K. (in press). Enterprise model management and next generation decision support. *Decision Support Systems.*

Holsapple, C., & Singh, M. (2000). Toward a unified view of electronic commerce, electronic business, and collaborative commerce: A knowledge management approach. *Knowledge and Process Management, 7*(3), 159.

Hui, S., & Jha, G. (2000). Data mining for customer service support. *Information and Management, 38*(1), 1-14.

Jennings, N. R., & Wooldridge, M. (1998). *Agent technology: Foundations, applications, and markets.* London: Springer.

Kiang, M. Y. (2003 July). A comparative assessment of classification methods. *Decision Support Systems, 35*(4), 441-454.

Kim, C. N., Chung, H. M., & Paradice, D. B. (1997). Inductive modeling of expert decision making in loan evaluation: A decision strategy perspective. *Decision Support Systems, 21*(2), 83-98.

Kudoh, Y., Haraguchi, M., & Okubo, Y. (2003 January 27). Data abstractions for decision tree induction. *Theoretical Computer Science, 292*(2), 387-416.

Mao, J., & Benbasat, I. (2000). The use of explanations in knowledge-based systems: Cognitive perspectives and a process-tracing analysis. *Journal of Management Information Systems, 17*(2), 153-179.

McIlraith, S., Son, T. C., & Zeng, H. (2001March/April). Semantic Web services. *IEEE Intelligent Systems,* 46-53.

Mitchell, T. M. (1997). *Machine learning.* McGraw-Hill: New York.

Padmanabhan, B., & Tuzhilin, A. (1999). Unexpectedness as a measure of interestingness in knowledge discovery. *Decision Support Systems, 27,* 303-318.

Quinlan, J. R. (1996). Improved use of continuous attributes in C4.5. *Journal of Artificial Intelligence Research, 4,* 77-90.

Shim, J. P., Warkentin, M., Courtney, J. F., Power, D. J., Sharda, R., & Carlsson, C. (2002). Past, present, and future of decision support technology. *Decision Support Systems, 33*, 111-126.

Shoham, Y. (1993). Agent oriented programming. *Journal of Artificial Intelligence, 60*(1), 51-92.

Stylianou, A. C. Madey, G. R., & Smith, R. D. (1992). Selection criteria for expert systems shells: A socio-technical framework. *Communications of the ACM, 35*(10), 30-48.

Sung, T., Chang, N., & Lee, G. (1999). Dynamics of modeling in data mining: Interpretive approach to bankruptcy prediction. *Journal of Management Information Systems, 16*(1), 63-85.

Takimoto, E., & Maruoka, A. (2003 January 27). Top-down decision tree learning as information based booting. *Theoretical Computer Science, 292*(2), 447-464.

Tsechansky, M., Pliskin, N., Rabinowitz, G., & Porath, A. (1999). Mining relational patterns from multiple relational tables. *Decision Support Systems, 27*, 177-195.

Whinston, A. B. (1997). Intelligent agents as a basis for Decision Support Systems. *Decision Support Systems, 20*(1) pp.883-889.

Weber, R. O., & Aha, D. W. (2003). Intelligent delivery of military lessons learned. *Decision Support Systems, 34*(3), 287-304.

Ye, L. R., & Johnson, P. E. (1995 June). The impact of explanation facilities on user acceptance of expert systems advice. *MIS Quarterly, 19*(2), 157-172.

This work was previously published in International Journal of Intelligent Information Technologies, Vol. 3, Issue 1, edited by V. Sugumaran, pp. 37-60, copyright 2007 by IGI Publishing, formerly known as Idea Group Publishing (an imprint of IGI Global).

Chapter XXV
Mission–Critical Group Decision–Making:
Solving the Problem of Decision Preference Change in Group Decision–Making Using Markov Chain Model[1]

Huizhang Shen
Shanghai Jiaotong University, China

Jidi Zhao
University of New Brunswick, Canada

Wayne W. Huang
Ohio University, USA

ABSTRACT

Review on group decision support systems (GDSS) indicates that traditional GDSS are not specifically designed to support mission-critical group decision-making tasks that require group decision-making to be made effectively within short time. In addition, prior studies in the research literature have not considered group decision preference adjustment as a continuous process and neglected its impact on group decision-making. In reality, group members may dynamically change their decision preferences during group decision-making process. This dynamic adjustment of decision preferences may continue until a group reaches consensus on final decision. This article intends to address this neglected group decision-making research issue in the literature by proposing a new approach based on the Markov chain model. Furthermore, a new group decision weight allocation approach is also suggested. A real case example of New Orleans Hurricane Katrina is used to illustrate the usefulness and effectiveness of the proposed approaches. Finally, the article concludes with the discussion on the proposed approaches and presents directions for future research.

INTRODUCTION

Mission-critical events such as hurricanes, terrorist attacks, fires, and earthquakes require different governmental departments to work together to respond to those emerging crises and reach consensus quickly to make effective decisions within a short time period. Traditional group decision support systems (GDSS) have not specifically addressed this important issue in the research literature (Fjermestad & Hiltz 1999; Huang, 2003; Huang & Wei, 2000; Huang, Wei, & Lim, 2003; Tan, Wei, Huang, & Ng, 2000; Zigurs, DeSanctis, & Billingsley, 1991; Vogel, Martz, Nunamaker, Grohowski, & McGoff, 1990). A special type of GDSS, mission-critical GDSS (MC-GDSS), can be designed to support this group decision-making process.

Mission-critical group decision-making has some important characteristics that are different from conventional group decision-makings (Belardo & Wallace, 1989; Beroggi, Mendonça, & Wallace, 2003; Huang & Li, 2007; Limayem, Banerjee, & Ma, 2006; Mendonca, Beroggi, Gent, & Wallace, 2006; Wallace & DeBalogh, 1985): (1) decision-makers have to make nearly real-time decision. Decision-making on emergency response has to be made within a short time because of the nature of critical mission, (2) mission-critical decision-making problem is unstructured, fuzzy and unexpected in nature, and (3) information available to decision-makers is insufficient and not always accurate because complete information may not be collected in a short time, thus the decision makers can only rely on such incomplete information to making decisions. Therefore, conventional decision support approaches may not well solve decision problems of mission-critical events.

Prior research studies mission-critical decision-making from different perspectives. LaPorte and Consilini identify two emergency response patterns based on frequency and scene information respectively (LaPorte & Consilini, 1991). Ody

thinks that crisis decision-making task, one type of mission-critical decision-making tasks, consists of three segments, pre-incident identification of hazards, the use of agreed communications, and the introduction of a third party to promote the coordination of decision makers (Ody, 1995). Wilkenfeld, Kraus, Holley, and Harris design a decision support system, GENIE, and demonstrate the usefulness of GENIE to help decision makers maximize their objectives in a crisis negotiation. Experimental results show that GENIE users, as compared to non-users, are more likely to identify utility maximization as their primary objective and to achieve higher utility scores (Wilkenfeld, Kraus, Holley, & Harris, 1995). Papazoglou and Christou propose a method on optimization of the short-term emergency response to nuclear accidents, which seeks an optimum combination of protective actions in the presence of a multitude of conflicting objectives and under uncertainty (Papazoglou & Christou, 1997). Bar-Eli and Tractinsky explore psychological performance crises under time pressure towards the end of basketball games (Bar-Eli & Tractinsky, 2000). Zografos, Vasilakis, and Giannouli present a methodological and unified framework for developing a decision support system (DSS) for hazardous materials emergency response operations (Zografos, Vasilakis, & Giannouli, 2000). Weisaeth, Knudsen, and Tonnessen discuss how psychological stress disturbs decision making during technological crisis and disaster, at an operative level of emergency response and at the strategic and political level respectively (Weisaeth, Knudsen, & Tonnessen, 2002). Chen, Sharman, and Rao et al. develop a set of supporting design concepts and strategic principles for an architecture for a coordinated multi-incident emergency response system based upon emergency response system requirement analysis (Chen, Sharman, & Rao et al., 2005).

As Arrow points out, based on the construction of group preference, group decision-making is a procedure of synthesizing the preferences of each decision-maker in a group and sorting decision alternatives or choosing the best decision alternative from a decision alternative set (Arrow, 1963). Group decision preference relation of a group should satisfy five rational terms: preference axiom, impossible axiom, completeness, Pareto optimization, and non-autarchy (Arrow, 1963). Prior studies by Arrow (1963), Dyer (1979), Keeney (1975), and French (1986), and so forth, provide a theoretical foundation on group decision preference relation analysis in group decision-making research literature. Group decision preference is a function of individual preferences on group decision-making issues. Preference is a term originally coming from economics. In group decision-making research literature, it is used to represent decision-makers' partiality on value (Dyer & Sarin, 1979). The procedure of forming individual preference is a decision-maker's meta-synthetic thinking procedure of perceiving all the information relating to expectation, information, sensibility, creativity, and so on, which is a extremely complex procedure (Bordly & Wolff, 1981). Some prior studies try to explore these complicated issues from different angles, including Weighted Average Method, Bordly Multiplication (Bordly & Wolff, 1981), Bayesian Integration Method (Keeney & Kirkwood, 1975), Entropy Method (French, 1986), and Fuzzy Cluster Analysis (Dyer & Sarin, 1979). Generally speaking, a decision-making group's decision preference on decision alternative sets will change as decision-makers adjust their decision preferences after communicating with other group decision-makers through group interactions, which could lead to group decision-marking preference convergence.

In this article, how a group reaches decision consensus quickly and effectively in group decision-making on emergency response is focused on. Emergency response, as one type of mission-critical group decision scenario, requires an MC-GDSS to collect group members' decision-making choice preferences automatically and quickly determine a group's overall decision

choice preference. Further, group members may also dynamically change their decision preferences after seeing other group members' decision choice preferences during group decision-making process. This dynamic adjustment of decision preferences will continue until all the group members do not rectify their preferences. After a few rounds of group interactions with decision preference adjustment, group consensus may be reached on the group's final decision choice. Prior studies in the research literature have not considered the preference adjustment as a continuous procedure and neglected its impact on group decision-making. This article intends to address this important group decision-making research issue and proposes a new approach based on the Markov chain model.

In addition, one central element of group decision-making is decision weight. Prior main solutions to decision weight allocation in the research literature can be summarized. The first solution is the authority allocation method (Mallach, 2000). An authoritative decision maker allocates decision weight for each decision-maker, which may be biased. Another solution is the Nominal Group Technique (Potter & Balthazard, 2004; Shyur & Shih, 2006). Nominal Group Technique is a kind of anonymous survey which should be done for some rounds. Each member of a group endows weight to other decision members according to his/her own experience, value system, and personal judgment. The anonymous survey process will continue until all decision-making members' opinions converge. These two methods largely involve subjective judgment on decision weight allocation (Chen & Fu, 2005; Williams & Cookson, 2006), which is likely to lead to subjective biases as well. Other methods are based on forecasting each decision-maker's weight according to historical experience and data, such as entropy method and fuzzy cluster analysis (French, 1986), where two disadvantages exist. First, those require a lot of historical data, which is not easy to collect in reality. Second, the external environment of decision-making is changing fast. Therefore, historical successful experience may not provide a good indication for successful current and future decision-makings. This article proposes a new decision weight allocation approach, which can help address the problems of prior methods in terms of subjective biases and requiring substantial quantity of historical data.

The remainder of this article is organized as follows: The next section proposes a new decision weight allocation method. The third section presents a new approach to construct a Markov state transition matrix in group decision-making, addressing the neglected research issue of dynamically changed decision preference in the group decision-making process. A real case example of New Orleans Hurricane Katrina is used to illustrate the usefulness and effectiveness of the proposed approach. Finally, the article concludes with the discussion on the research results and presents directions for future research.

PROPOSING A NEW DECISION WEIGHT ALLOCATION APPROACH FOR MISSION-CRITICAL GROUP DECISION-MAKING

This section proposes a new decision weight allocation approach for mission-critical group decision-making. First, a group decision preference judgment matrix is defined, followed by a quantitative consistence indicator to measure decision-maker's decision consistence. Second, a clustering method to analyze the distances among decision preferences in a decision-making group is put forward. Finally, a decision weight is determined by both decision preference consistence indicator and decision preference distance indicator.

Group Decision Preference Judgment Matrix

In this article, the concept of preference utility value from economics literature to quantitatively represent preference, which describes preference direction or priority of a decision-maker is used. It would be difficult for a group member to accurately judge which decision choice is certainly the best among those alternative decision choices, especially for mission-critical problems. In reality, group decision-makers do pair wise comparisons *on each pair of two decision alternatives (or decision choices)* and give their decision preferences using fuzzy terms like "equal, a little better, better, much better, absolutely better." *Based upon this line of logic thinking, each decision-maker's preference utility value can be generated.* The definition of preference utility value $\theta_r(x^i, x^j)$ *and its quantificational values are given in Appendix A.1.*

Thus, according to the rth decision maker of a group, DM_r's pair wise comparison between each two alternatives on the set, we get a preference judgment matrix P_r. Apparently, it is a positive symmetrical matrix. Decision-makers only need to judge $s(s-1)/2$ times, which is equal to the amount of the elements of the upper or lower triangular matrix.

$$P_r = \begin{pmatrix} \theta_r(x^1,x^1) & \theta_r(x^1,x^2) & \cdots & \theta_r(x^1,x^s) \\ \theta_r(x^2,x^1) & \theta_r(x^2,x^2) & \cdots & \theta_r(x^2,x^s) \\ \cdots & \cdots & \cdots & \cdots \\ \theta_r(x^s,x^1) & \theta_r(x^s,x^2) & \cdots & \theta_r(x^s,x^s) \end{pmatrix} \quad (1)$$

Suppose there are l decision-makers, then there are l preference judging matrices altogether.

Decision Preference Consistence Indicator for a Preference Judgment Matrix

Although it is relatively easy for decision-makers to do pair wise comparisons and give the preference utility value, it may not be easy to derive sequential order of the decision alternatives from a preference judgment matrix. What is more, the derived order may often be self-contradictory. For example, analysis of a given preference judgment matrix may lead to a contradictory conclusion that A is more preferred than B, B is more preferred than C, and C is more preferred than A. This kind of contradiction indicates that a decision-maker may not always be consistent enough to make decision. As a result, a quantitative consistence indicator from AHP (Satty, 1988) is introduced to measure decision-maker's decision consistence. Let CI_r denote the rth decision maker DM_r's consistence indicator. The larger the indicator is, the worse the consistency of the preference judgment matrix becomes. Based on the theory of matrix, the preference utility value of DM_r on x^i, denoted by $\pi_r(x^i)$ can be derived and the consistence indicator from a matrix' characteristic vector and characteristic value, as illustrated in the Appendix A.2.

Clustering Analysis and Decision Preference Difference

Besides the individual carefulness measured by the consistence indicator, the differences among the individual preference and other's preferences (preference distance d_p) also play an important role in reaching consensus in group decision-making. As to an individual decision-maker, the larger the difference is, the extremer she is, and the less contribution she makes to the group consensus, and vice versa. In this section, firstly, a clustering method to classify the group decision-makers' preferences is introduced. Secondly, each decision-maker's preference distance to measure the extremenesses among the group members is

computed. The clustering method and the definition of preference distance (d_p) are illustrated in Appendix B. The Euclidean preference distance (d_p) between the preference utility value vector of DM_r on X and the specified cluster center shows the preference distance of the decision-maker under the average criteria. The smaller d_r is, the lower the decision-maker's preference distance is, and the more contributions the decision-maker makes to group consensus.

As to those clusters that only contain one element, the distances between the element and the cluster centers of all the other clusters are calculated and the minimum distance is chosen to represent the corresponding decision-maker's preference distance.

The Optimization of Decision Weight Allocation

The decision weight allocation for group decision-makers can be described as the following optimization problem.

$$\min F(w) = \sum_{r=1}^{l} [CI_r + d_r] w_r^2 \tag{2}$$

Subject to:

$$w_r \geq 0 \ (r = 1, 2, \cdots, l)$$

$$\sum_{r=1}^{l} w_r = 1$$

where $CI_r = (\frac{\lambda_{max}^{(r)}}{s-1} - \frac{s}{s-1})$ denotes the consistency degree of decision-maker DM_r and $\sqrt{\sum_{i=1}^{s} |\pi_r(x^k) - \pi(x^k)|^2} = d_r$ denotes that person's preference distance. Equation (2) shows that the higher an expert's consistency is, the lower her/his extremeness is and the larger weight she/he should be assigned. A solution of the decision weight vector assigned to a group of decision-makers, $W = (w_1, w_2, \cdots, w_s)$ is given in the appendix C. Thus we have:

$$w_r = \left. \frac{1}{}\middle/ [(CI_r + d_r) \bullet \sum_{r=1}^{l} \frac{1}{}\middle/ (CI_r + d_r)] \right.$$

This approach of allocating decision weighs has at least two advantages over traditional approaches. First, it is less subjectively biased because as the decision weight allocation is based on individuals' current objective decision information with less subjective factors. Second, the allocation approach may be more accurate because it considers both individuals' decision preferences and the differences between individual decision preferences and others' decision preferences of a group.

PROPOSING A MISSION-CRITICAL GROUP DECISION-MAKING SUPPORT APPROACH USING MARKOV CHAIN MODEL

This section proposes a mission-critical group decision-making approach to address the issue of the impact of dynamic decision-making preference change on group decision-making. More specifically, the Markov state transition matrix is used to determine the dynamic nature of group decision-making preference changes, decision-making convergence, and decision preference distance. The section on group decision-making and Markov chains presents how to construct this Markov state transition matrix. Based upon that, an optimal group decision-making choice can be generated.

Group Decision-Making and Markov Chains

After the t rounds adjustment, the preference utility values in all the rounds for decision-maker DM_r are:

$$\pi_r = \begin{cases} \pi_r^1(x^1) & \pi_r^1(x^2) & \cdots & \pi_r^1(x^s) \\ \pi_r^2(x^1) & \pi_r^2(x^2) & \cdots & \pi_r^2(x^s) \\ \cdots & \cdots & \cdots & \cdots \\ \pi_r^t(x^1) & \pi_r^t(x^2) & \cdots & \pi_r^t(x^s) \end{cases}.$$

In this matrix, each row stands for the preference utility value vector in each round. Comparing the kth row with the $(k+1)^{th}$ row ($\{k = 1, 2, \cdots, t\}$), if there exists $\pi_r^{k+1}(x^i) \downarrow \Leftrightarrow \pi_r^{k+1}(x^j) \uparrow$, the state variable $E_{ij} = E_{ij} + 1$ is set, which shows that the decision-maker has ever changed her/his preference from the alternative x^i to x^j. For each decision-maker, there are at most $t - 1$ times of adjustment. Packing all the adjustment for the group together, we have:

$$T_r = \begin{bmatrix} 1 - \sum_{j \neq 1} \frac{E_{1j}}{E_r} & \frac{E_{12}}{E_r} & \cdots\cdots & \frac{E_{1s}}{E_r} \\ \frac{E_{21}}{E_r} & 1 - \sum_{j \neq 2} \frac{E_{2j}}{E_r} & \cdots\cdots & \frac{E_{2s}}{E_r} \\ \cdots & \cdots & \cdots & \cdots \\ \frac{E_{s1}}{E_r} & \frac{E_{s2}}{E_r} & \cdots\cdots & 1 - \sum_{j \neq s} \frac{E_{sj}}{E_r} \end{bmatrix}$$

(3)

where T_r is the preference state transition matrix for decision-maker DM_r, E_{ij} denotes the preference transition times from x^i to x^j and $E_r = t - 1$ is the sample space for the state transition times.

For example, the preference utility value matrix for decision-maker DM_r is:

$$\Lambda_r = \begin{bmatrix} 0.1 & 0.3 & 0.2 & 0.4 \\ 0.2 & 0.2 & 0.3 & 0.3 \\ 0.2 & 0.3 & 0.2 & 0.3 \\ 0.2 & 0.4 & 0.2 & 0.2 \\ 0.3 & 0.3 & 0.2 & 0.2 \end{bmatrix}.$$

The first row of the matrix is the initial value and the sample space is $t - 1 = 5 - 1 = 4$.

Comparing the second row with the first row, we have $x^2 \rightarrow x^1, x^4 \rightarrow x^3$.

Comparing the third row with the second, we have $x^3 \rightarrow x^2$.

Comparing the fourth row with the third, we have $x^4 \rightarrow x^2$.

And, comparing the fifth row with the fourth, we have $x^2 \rightarrow x^1$.

According to Equation (9), we have the preference state transition matrix T_r for decision-maker DM_r is:

$$T_r = \begin{bmatrix} 1 & 0 & 0 & 0 \\ 0.5 & 0.5 & 0 & 0 \\ 0 & 0.25 & 0.75 & 0 \\ 0 & 0.25 & 0.25 & 0.5 \end{bmatrix}.$$

In this matrix, $\frac{E_{11}}{E_r} = 1$ shows that the decision-maker never changes her preference on x^1.

Define the overall state transition matrix of the decision-making group in the t rounds adjustment procedure as:

$$T = \frac{1}{l}\sum_{r=1}^{l} T_r. \tag{4}$$

In Appendix D, a review on discrete time Markov chains is given. It is also shown that the group decision-making procedure satisfies a Markov chain. Therefore, the Markov property can be used to predict adjustments of the decision-makers' preference.

Nine Implementation Steps of the Proposed Group Decision-Making Support Approach

The proposed approach for supporting mission-critical group decision-making works in following nine steps:

1. State a group decision-making problem and background information to each group member, including the mission-critical event, available information, constraints, decision alternatives, decision-making rules, the user handbook of a MC-GDSS that is being used, and so forth.

2. Each decision-maker gives her/his preference judgments between each two alternatives on the set of alternatives using the quantificational values given in Appendix A. The preference judgment values for decision-maker DM_r are presented in the matrix P_r. All the decision-makers can share their opinions, evidences, and explanations on the screen of the MC-GDSS system to support their view points.

3. Substituting the corresponding values into the approximate calculation algorithm presented in Appendix A yields the preference utility values for a decision-maker DM_r in the tth round, $\{\pi_r'(x^1), \pi_r'(x^2), \cdots, \pi_r'(x^s)\}$. As stated, the individual preference adjustment in group decision-making is a continuous procedure in which the decision-makers adjust their preference in each round respectively based on the communications among the group members. The continuous adjustments make group decisions converge gradually. The preference utility values vector $\{\pi_r'(x^1), \pi_r'(x^2), \cdots, \pi_r'(x^s)\}$ for the decision-maker is used for constructing the Markov state transition matrix in step (8).

4. With the preference values worked out in step (3), the preference utility values matrix Λ^t for the tth round are had. Using the Equation (-16), the preference distance d_{ij} between decision-maker DM_i and DM_j on X are had. Substituting these preference distances into Equation (17), the preference difference matrix D can be constucted. Furthermore, given $\varepsilon = \frac{\max d_{ij} - \min d_{ij}}{2}$, clustering analysis on the preference difference matrix D based on the definitions 3 and 4 can be done.

5. The MC-GDSS system displays the preference utility values and the clustering results on screen, which is a public communication space for group decision-makers to see and then maybe adjust their preferences. After that, members can go back to step (2) and begin another round of decision discussion with further preference judgment as well.

6. Repeat the above procedure from step (2) to step (5) for $t = 7 \pm 2$ times. The choice of $t = 7 \pm 2$ is based on two reasons. First, conventional Delphi method usually repeats more than four

times (Giunipero, Handfield, & Eltantawy, 2006; Lao, Dovrolis, & Sanadidi, 2006). Second, empirical research in psychology shows that 7 ± 2 is a common experienced value for human being's thinking-span (Myers, 2005; Murphy, Roodenrys, & Fox, 2006; Over, Hooge, & Erkelens, 2006). In addition, the value for t can also be determined by a group decision meeting organizer according to the meeting time limit and other factors.

7. Calculating the weight assigned to each decision-maker with the solution given in the appendix C yields the weight vector $W = (w_1, w_2, \cdots, w_s)$ for the group.

8. Constructing the Markov state transition matrix T using Equation (3) and (4) with the saved preference values $\{\pi_r'(x^1), \pi_r'(x^2), \cdots, \pi_r'(x^s)\}$.

9. Multiplying decision weight vector $W = (w_1, w_2, \cdots, w_s)$ by the preference matrix Λ in the last round, and then by the Markov state transition matrix T, we have Equation 5, seen in Box 1. Where $[x^1, x^2, \cdots, x^s]$ is the preference utility values vector on the decision alternative set X and $\max\{x^i\}$ ($i = 1, 2, \cdots, s$) is the final decision made by the group.

Here some points on this group decision-making support approach are clarified:

1. The nine steps of group decision-making only need some interactions between group decision-makers and a MC-GDSS system, without additional interactions of group decision meeting's organizer as in traditional group decision-making setting. In this way, decision-making process may be sped up, which is important to mission-critical decision-making tasks.

2. Each decision maker can share her/his opinion, present her/his explanation, and browse other's opinions anonymously or with her/his identity.

3. The clustering analysis result of individual decision preference values in each decision round is displayed in public screen and used as a reference for decision preference adjustment for the next decision round.

4. Every decision-maker is encouraged to adjust her/his preference based upon the clustering analysis result of the previous decision round. If each decision-maker sticks to her/his initial decision position and does not adjust her/his decision preference at all in following decision rounds, the group will never reach consensus and such group decision-making makes no sense, which should be stopped. Otherwise, after a few rounds of group interactions, it could be possible for

Box 1.

$$[w_1, w_2, \cdots, w_s] \begin{bmatrix} \pi_1(x^1) & \pi_1(x^2) & \cdots & \pi_1(x^s) \\ \pi_2(x^1) & \pi_2(x^2) & \cdots & \pi_2(x^s) \\ \cdots & \cdots & \cdots & \cdots \\ \pi_l(x^1) & \pi_l(x^2) & \cdots & \pi_l(x^s) \end{bmatrix} \begin{bmatrix} T_{11} & T_{12} & \cdots & T_{1s} \\ T_{21} & T_{22} & \cdots & T_{2s} \\ \cdots & \cdots & \cdots \\ T_{s1} & T_{s2} & \cdots & T_{ss} \end{bmatrix} = [x^1 \quad x^2 \quad \cdots \quad x^s]$$

$$(5)$$

a group to reach consensus and final group decision can be achieved.

A Real Case Illustrating the Usefulness and Effectiveness of the Proposed Approach

Background Information

1. New Orleans is the largest city of the state of Louisiana in the USA and the second largest American port next to New York City. It is located at the southeast part of the state of Louisiana and at the lower part of Mississippi River near the sea. The city is next to Pontchartrain Lake in its north. The city is around 950 square kilometers with a population of 500,000. Moreover, the Great New Orleans District has a population of 1180,000.

    In August 2005, Katrina, a category 5 hurricane called a "Perfect Hurricane" by meteorologists with its 280 kilometer-per-hour winds, lashed the city of New Orleans. New Orleans Mayor Ray Nagin of the city of New Orleans called for voluntary evacuation of the city's residents on August 27, 2005.

    On August 28, New Orleans Mayor Ray Nagin sent down a compelling order of all-out evacuation of the city's residents and provided 10 refuges for the city's remaining residents. The Louisiana Superdome is assigned as an island refuge.

    On August 29, Katrina made a landfall as a category 5 hurricane over the Gulf of Mexico and lashed Southern America. New Orleans's flood embankments could not withstand the ferocity of the hurricane and were breached at two sites. As a result, 80% of the city was flooded. In some parts of the city, the water continued to rise at a speed of one foot per hour.

Constraints

The New Orleans government assigned a 7000-people rescue army. For 700,000 refugees scattered in an area of 950 square kilometers, the rescuers were only one percent of the refugees.

The city was out of communication. Except the 10 refuges, the rescuers were not aware of the location or quantity of the refugees. The city was out of traffic transportation. The vehicles such as buses were not usable any more. Helicopters were the main transporters. Moreover, the city was out of clean water, power, and cooking. There have already appeared hostile looting and murders.

Decision Alternatives

x^1 (the first decision alternative for this mission-critical event): Search for the separated refugees. If the rescue is just in time, the death rate of the refugees can be reduced. Although people in refuges were besieged, they could be kept away from death.

x^2 (the second decision alternative for this mission-critical event): Evacuate those serious patients. Without clean water and power, they might die immediately.

x^3 (the third decision alternative for this mission-critical event): Evacuate people in refuges as there is no clean water, power, and cooking. Give up the search for separated refugees temporarily because they may not die in a reasonable time period.

x^4 (the fourth decision alternative for this mission-critical event): Arrest the looters in order to make the city safe, which can also help with the rescue work to be done in a safe context.

2. Assume that there are six decision-makers in the governmental rescue committee. Every decision-maker does pair wise judg-

ments and gives her/his preference judgment according to the quantitative values given in Table 1 of the first section. The initial preference judgment matrix is illustrated in Table 1.

3. Substituting the corresponding values into the approximate calculation algorithm presented in the appendix A, we have the preference utility values for a decision-maker DM_r in the tth round, $\{\pi_r^t(x^1), \pi_r^t(x^2), \cdots, \pi_r^t(x^o)\}$. The preference utility values for the six decision-makers in the first round are shown in Table 2.

4. With the preference utility values worked out in step (3), we have the preference utility values matrix Λ^t for the tth round. Using Equation (16), we have the preference distance d_{ij} between decision-maker DM_i and DM_j on X. Substituting these preference distances into Equation (17), the preference difference matrix D can be constructed.

The preference distances and the preference difference matrix are shown in Table 3.

Given $\varepsilon = \frac{\max d_{ij} - \min d_{ij}}{2}$, we have $\varepsilon^1 = 0.239$, as shown in Table 3 in bold font. Thus, we get $d_{31} \leq \varepsilon^1$, $d_{62} \leq \varepsilon^1$. According to the definitions 3 and 4, there are 4 clusters in this round, DM_1 and DM_3 belong to the same cluster in $\varepsilon^1 = 0.239$, so do the DM_2 and DM_6. DM_4 and DM_5 are independent clusters respectively. The cluster analysis result is shown in Figure 1. In Figure 1, the numbered black dots denote the current preference states of the decision-makers. The diameter of the circle is the clustering distance in this round, $\varepsilon^1 = 0.239$. All the dots that can be enclosed in a circle belong to a specific cluster, which shows that the decision-makers in the same cluster come to partial consensus in ε.

5. The preference judgment results can then feedback to all the decision-makers based

Table 1. Pair wise preference judgments and preference utility values on a set of alternatives

DM_1	x^1	x^2	x^3	x^4	π	CI	DM_2	x^1	x^2	x^3	x^4	π	CI
x^1	1.00	0.33	3.00	0.33	0.17		x^1	1.00	5.00	2.00	1.00	0.38	
x^2	3.00	1.00	2.00	1.00	0.36		x^2	0.20	1.00	1.00	0.50	0.12	
x^3	0.33	0.50	1.00	0.50	0.12		x^3	0.50	1.00	1.00	0.17	0.11	
x^4	3.00	1.00	2.00	1.00	0.35	0.097	x^4	1.00	2.00	6.00	1.00	0.39	0.087
DM_3	x^1	x^2	x^3	x^4	π	CI	DM_4	x^1	x^2	x^3	x^4	π	CI
x^1	1.00	0.33	2.00	0.20	0.13		x^1	1.00	5.00	3.00	2.00	0.50	
x^2	3.00	1.00	3.00	1.00	0.37		x^2	0.20	1.00	2.00	2.00	0.20	
x^3	0.50	0.33	1.00	0.50	0.12		x^3	0.33	0.50	1.00	0.33	0.10	
x^4	5.00	1.00	2.00	1.00	0.38	0.075	x^4	0.50	0.50	3.00	1.00	0.20	0.123
DM_5	x^1	x^2	x^3	x^4	π	CI	DM_6	x^1	x^2	x^3	x^4	π	CI
x^1	1.00	0.33	6.00	5.00	0.34		x^1	1.00	5.00	4.00	0.33	0.33	
x^2	3.00	1.00	5.00	3.00	0.48		x^2	0.20	1.00	0.50	0.33	0.09	
x^3	0.17	0.20	1.00	2.00	0.10		x^3	0.25	2.00	1.00	0.50	0.15	
x^4	0.20	0.33	0.50	1.00	0.08	0.139	x^4	3.00	3.00	2.00	1.00	0.43	0.132

Table 2. The preference value for every decision-maker in the first round

0.17	0.36	0.12	0.35
0.38	0.12	0.11	0.39
0.13	0.37	0.12	0.38
0.50	0.20	0.10	0.20
0.34	0.48	0.10	0.08
0.33	0.09	0.15	0.43

Table 3. Preference difference matrix in the first round

0					
0.313	0				
0.054	0.353	0			
0.393	0.245	0.446	0		
0.347	0.486	0.383	0.350	0	
0.321	**0.071**	0.354	0.307	0.532	0

upon the results as shown in Table 3 and Figure 1. Decision-makers can make adjustments after seeing the first round of deliberation. The group then begins another round of decision-making (i.e., repeating the decision-making process starting from step 2).

6. Repeat step (2) through step (5) for five times, t = 5.

7. Different preference difference matrices in each round are gotten. Here the difference matrix in the last round are only presented, as shown in Figure 2 and Table 4. The scales in Figure 1 and Figure 2 are the same.

DM_1 and DM_3 belong to the same cluster in ε^1 = 0.239, so do the DM_2 and DM_6. DM_4 and DM_5.

As shown in Figure 2, the clustering distance in the fifth round is ε^5 = 0.143. It can be seen that the individual preferences are clustered into three clusters. DM_1, DM_3 and DM_4 belong to the same cluster, DM_3 and DM_5 belong to the same cluster, and DM_2 and DM_6 belong to the same cluster. In Figure 2, the diameter of the larger circle is the clustering distance in the first round (ε^1 = 0.239). From this figure, it is easy to see that if we use this distance to cluster the individual preferences, five decision-makers have come to consensus in ε^1 = 0.239, that is, DM_1, DM_2, DM_3, DM_4, and DM_6. Thus the clustering distance is reduced gradually

in each round and shows the convergence of the group preference and the procedure of reaching consensus.

Substituting the values into the solution given in the appendix C yields the weight vector for the decision-making group W = (0.131 0.264 0.163 0.165 0.113 0.162).

8. Construct the Markov state transition matrix T using Equation (3) and (4) with the saved preference utility values $\{\pi_r^t(x^1), \pi_r^t(x^2), \cdots, \pi_r^t(x^s)\}$. In this example, if $\pi_r^k(x^i) - \pi_r^{k+1}(x^i) > 0.01$ and $\pi_r^{k+1}(x^j) - \pi_r^k(x^j) > 0.01$ occurs, it is

Figure 1. Clustering result of the individual preference utility values in the first round

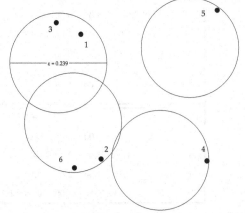

Table 4. Preference difference matrix in the fifth round

0					
0.155	0				
0.098	0.215	0			
0.079	0.145	**0.091**	0		
0.211	0.318	**0.115**	0.186	0	
0.155	**0.060**	0.236	0.168	0.346	0

Figure 2. Clustering result in the fifth round

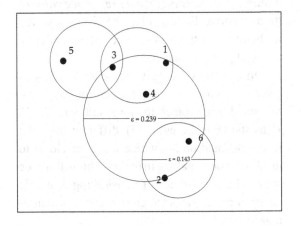

considered as an one time transition $\pi_r^{k+1}(x^i)\downarrow \Leftrightarrow \pi_r^{k+1}(x^j)\uparrow$, let the state variable $E_{ij} = E_{ij} + 1$, thus it indicates that the decision-maker DM_r transits from alternative x^i to alternative x^j for one time. The final preference state transition matrix is

$$T = \begin{bmatrix} 0.333 & 0.417 & 0.0417 & 0.208 \\ 0.125 & 0.875 & 0 & 0 \\ 0.083 & 0 & 0.917 & 0 \\ 0.292 & 0.333 & 0.083 & 0.292 \end{bmatrix}.$$

9. Multiply the weight vector $W = (w_1, w_2, \cdots, w_s)$ by the preference matrix Λ in the last round, and then by the Markov state transition matrix T, we have

$$\begin{bmatrix} 0.131 & 0.264 & 0.163 \\ 0.165 & 0.113 & 0.162 \end{bmatrix} \begin{bmatrix} 0.23 & 0.32 & 0.19 & 0.26 \\ 0.33 & 0.23 & 0.13 & 0.31 \\ 0.22 & 0.40 & 0.15 & 0.23 \\ 0.28 & 0.35 & 0.15 & 0.22 \\ 0.21 & 0.50 & 0.11 & 0.18 \\ 0.31 & 0.20 & 0.17 & 0.32 \end{bmatrix}$$

$$= [0.273 \quad 0.314 \quad 0.148 \quad 0.262]$$

(6)

$$\begin{bmatrix} 0.273 & 0.314 \\ 0.148 & 0.262 \end{bmatrix} \cdot \begin{bmatrix} 0.333 & 0.417 & 0.0417 & 0.208 \\ 0.125 & 0.875 & 0 & 0 \\ 0.083 & 0 & 0.917 & 0 \\ 0.292 & 0.333 & 0.083 & 0.292 \end{bmatrix}$$

$$= [0.219 \quad 0.476 \quad 0.169 \quad 0.133].$$

(7)

$[0.219 \quad 0.476 \quad 0.169 \quad 0.133]$ is the preference utility values vector on the set of alternatives X and the alternative x^2, corresponding to $\max\{x^i\}$ $(i = 1, 2, \cdots, s) = 0.476$, is the final alternative chosen by the decision-making group.

Comparing the result of Equation (6) with the result of (7), it can be seen that if the possible decision preference changes are not taken into account (the dynamic nature of group decision-making process), it will come to the static conclusion $x^2 R x^1 R x^4 R x^3$ as shown in Equation (6) (i.e., the preferred decision alternatives are determined in following sequential order: the most preferred decision alternative x^2, followed by the decision alternatives x^1, x^4, and x^3). This conclusion is drawn by traditional meta-synthetic approaches on group decision-making, that is, after decision weights for every decision-maker are assigned and fixed, the group preference value on each decision alternative is determined by the sum of each decision-maker's decision weight multiplied by her/his *current preference value* of the alternative. Finally, all alternatives are sorted in the order of their preference values to derive the final group decision.

On the other hand, if the possible decision preference changes are not taken into account, the conclusion comes to the result $x^2Rx^1R\,x^4R\,x^3$ as shown in Equation (7), different from the result of Equation (6), which would be closer to group decision-making in reality. This difference shows the importance of considering dynamic decision preference change into group decision-making model.

The decision difference between traditional methods and the currently proposed one may not always ensure a better group decision result, which will be further discussed.

Considering an ergodic Markov chaie, let T be a probability matrix. If there exists a $m(m > 1, m \in Z)$, which makes all the elements of T^m positive, T is called a normal stochastic matrix. A probability vector π must exist, which makes

$$\pi = \pi T \text{ and } \pi_j = \lim_{n\to\infty} T_{ij}^n \text{ for all } i \qquad (8)$$

The probability vector π is called the steady state vector for the state transition matrix T.

It is easy to show that the preference state transition matrix in our example is a normal stochastic

matrix. Thus there must exist a probability vector π, the steady state solution to the group decision-making problem on the alternative set. Therefore the following Equations are resolved.

$$\begin{cases} \pi = \pi T \\ \sum_{i=1}^{s} \pi_i = 1 \\ \pi_i > 0 \quad i = 1,\cdots,s \end{cases} \qquad (9)$$

or see Box 2.

We have

$$\pi = [0.161014988 \quad 0.663345006 \\ 0.128267958 \quad 0.047323744] \\ (11)$$

The result shown in Equation (11) represents the decision preference order $x^2Rx^1R\,x^4R\,x^3$, the same result derived from Equation (7). Note that now this conclusion in Equation (11) has nothing to do with the decision weight vector W and decision preference value matrix Λ in the last round, and only depends on the decision preference state transition matrix T.

Comparing the Equations (6), (7), and (11), several conclusions can be drawn:

1. The traditional meta-synthetic approaches on group decision-making, neglecting the

Box 2.

$$\begin{cases} [\pi_1 \quad \pi_2 \quad \pi_3 \quad \pi_4] = [\pi_1 \quad \pi_2 \quad \pi_3 \quad \pi_4] \begin{bmatrix} 0.333 & 0.417 & 0.0417 & 0.208 \\ 0.125 & 0.875 & 0 & 0 \\ 0.083 & 0 & 0.917 & 0 \\ 0.292 & 0.333 & 0.083 & 0.292 \end{bmatrix} \\ \pi_1 + \pi_2 + \pi_3 + \pi_4 = 1 \\ \pi_i > 0 \quad i = 1,\cdots,s \end{cases} \qquad (10)$$

dynamic nature of decision preference adjustments/changes of group decision-makers, can lead to the loss of important decision element/information for group decision-making.

2. The dynamic nature of decision preference adjustment/change is one important part of group decision-making process, which should not be neglected.

3. The conclusion drawn on Equation (11) merely depends on the Markov state transition matrix, not on the decision weight vector W and decision preference value matrix Λ in the last round. This shows that if there would be enough time for a group to continue group decision-making process, group consensus will be reached in the form as shown in Equation (11).

4. The static conclusion $x^2 R x^1 R x^4 R x^3$ derived from Equation (6) can be considered as a transient result that will change as group decision-making process proceeds.

5. The dynamic decision-making conclusion $x^2 R x^1 R x^4 R x^3$ derived from Equation (7) can be considered as a stationary result that includes the developing trend of group decision-making process. That is that, as group decision-making rounds continue ($t > 5 \rightarrow \infty$), group decision result will come to the conclusion as shown Equation (11), the same as being derived from Equation (7).

6. As a result, it is shown that the group decision-making steps based on the Markov Chain, can help a group derive decision conclusion, as shown by Equation (11), which could otherwise be achieved by a big number of (or even infinite) group decision-making rounds. Therefore, in mission-critical group decision-making situation with short response time, the proposed approach could help a group reach consensus on final group decision within a few decision-making rounds (usually 5~9 rounds), rather than a big number of decision-making rounds (or infinite decision-making rounds), which may lead to more efficient and effective group decision-making.

DISCUSSION AND FUTURE RESEARCH

Discussion and Implications

This study contributes to the research literature in three aspects. First, prior research does not consider group decision-making preference being dynamic, which would be fixed and not be changed in group decision-making process, neglecting its existence and its impact on group decision-making. The proposed approach in this article solves this problem using the Markov Chain model. Further, the proposed approach can automatically determine and present group decision-makers' decision preference distances as well as similar decision preference clusters they belong to, which clearly shows similar and different positions of group decision-makers on a given mission-critical decision-making task in its first round and subsequent decision-making rounds, which in turn may support group decision-makers in more effectively adjusting their decision preferences/positions to help reach group final decision more efficiently and effectively. This is very important to mission-critical decision-making tasks. Future studies can use empirical research methodologies to examine this research issue.

Second, the proposed group decision weight allocation approach solves the problems of traditional methods that require substantial historical decision data and largely involve subjective judgment.

Third, the proposed approach provides a solution to Coudorcet's group decision paradox. One commonly used group decision rule is group consensus or majority rule (Nunamaker, Briggs, Mittleman, Vogel, & Balthazard, 1997; Huang &

Wei, 1997; Huang, Wei, & Tan, 1999; Watson, DeSanctis, & Poole, 1988). When there are more than three decision alternatives, it may be possible to generate a group decision cyclic loop, which would be theoretically impossible to read a group consensus or majority rule (Coudorcet, 1785). For example, there are three decision-makers (DM_1, DM_2, DM_3) in a group and three alternatives (A, B, C). Table 5 shows possible decision results for each decision-maker.

It is so-called the Voting Paradox (also known as Condorcet's paradox) (Coudorcet, 1785; Deemen, 1999; Nanson, 1882), as shown in Figure 3.

Let the number of decision-makers in a group be l, P denotes the probability of generating group decision circular loop based on majority rule. Prior studies report the relationship between l and P,

as shown in Table 6 (Niem & Weisberg, 1968); but when l is large, the relationship between the number of alternatives s and P is shown in Table 7 (Niem & Weisberg, 1968).

In this research, each decision-maker's decision preference judgment matrix based on pair wise comparisons are had and the characteristic vector from AHP is introduced to derive the sequential order of decision alternatives of each decision-maker. When decision-makers do pair wise comparisons on decision alternatives, which leads to a group decision preference judgment matrix, this matrix might result in group decision cyclic loops. However, this matrix is only used for determining group decision-makers' decision weights, not for determining group's final decision. So it will not lead to Condorcet's paradox. When a group comes to the final group decision, a

Table 5. Decision result for each decisoin maker

Decision Maker	Preferences
DM_1	$A\ R_1\ B\ R_1\ C$
DM_2	$B\ R_2\ C\ R_2\ A$
DM_3	$C\ R_3\ A\ R_3\ B$

Figure 3. Voting paradox

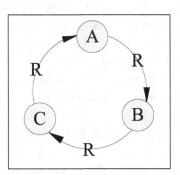

Table 6. Relationship between l and P

l	P
3	0.0556
9	0.078
15	0.082
25	0.0843
...	...
∞	0.0877

Table 7. Relationship between s and P

s	P
3	0.0877
9	0.4545
15	0.082
25	0.7297
...	...
∞	1

group decision cyclic loop can be avoided because the group decision sequential order of decision alternatives from a decision-maker are gotten based upon the calculation of the characteristic vector of her preference judgment matrix, not the preference judgment matrix itself. Therefore, the group decision-making approach proposed in this research can avoid the possibility of group decision circular loop, which provides a solution to Condorcet's paradox in group decision-making.

In practice, incorporating the proposed approaches to an existing GDSS system, the system may have a potential to help a group reach group decision consensus faster and more effectively, which can be especially important to mission-critical decision-making tasks. While global terrorism currently becomes one major threat to all the countries of the world, and while more globalized world economy would possibly lead to one country's major economic problem quickly becoming an emerging mission-critical problem of other countries within days or sometimes hours, many of those cross-border mission-critical problems would require group decision-makers to respond quickly and make decisions quickly. The proposed approach provides a possible solution to those mission-critical group decision-making problems that may be faced by both developed and developing countries. Field studies can be conducted to further investigate the effectiveness of such proposed GDSS systems in the future.

Research Limitation

It should be noted that not all the Markov state transition matrices in group decision-making process, based on the Markov chain approach, would surely be normal stochastic ones, which can be shown in the example.

If decision preference adjustment only runs for a few rounds, for example, $t < 5$, the overall state transition matrix for a group can be shown in the matrix T:

$$T = \begin{bmatrix} 1 & 0 & 0 & 0 \\ 0.5 & 0.5 & 0 & 0 \\ 0 & 0.25 & 0.75 & 0 \\ 0 & 0.25 & 0.25 & 0.5 \end{bmatrix}.$$

It is clear that T is not a normal stochastic matrix, and its steady state solution can not be resolved using Equation (9). In this case, group decision-making result can be conducted derived from Equation (7) instead of Equations (8) ~ (11). As a result, the proposed approach, though being efficient and effective in most cases, may not be so in all cases. Future research can look at this limitation and provide further improvement.

REFERENCES

Arrow, K. J. (1963). *Social choice and individual values*. New York: JohnWiley & Sons.

Bar-Eli, M., & Tractinsky, N. (2000). Criticality of game situations and decision making in basketball-an application of performance crisis perspective. *Psychology of Sport and Exercise, 1*, 27-39.

Belardo, S., & Wallace, W. A. (1989). Gaming as a means for evaluating decision support systems for emergency management response. In J. Sullivan & R. Newkirk (Eds.), *Simulation in emergency management and technology, simulation series* (pp. 113-117).

Beroggi, G. E. G., Mendonça, D., & Wallace, W. A. (2003). Operational sustainability management for the infrastructure: The case of emergency response. In A. Sage (Ed.), *Encyclopedia of life support systems*. Oxford, UK: EOLSS Publishers Co. Ltd.

Bordley, R. F., & Wolff, R. W. (1981). On the aggregation of individual probability estimates. *Management Science, 27*(8), 959-964.

Chen, R., Sharman, R., Rao, H. R., et al. (2005). Design principles of coordinated multi-incident emergency response systems. *Lecture Notes in Computer Science, 3495*, 81-93.

Chen, S. Y., Fu, G. T. (2005). Combining fuzzy iteration model with dynamic programming to solve multiobjective multistage decision making problems. *Fuzzy Sets and Systems, 152*(3), 499-512.

Condorcet, M. D. (1785). Essai sur l' Application de l' Analyse à la Probabilité des Décisions Renduesà la Plurali té des Voix. Paris: L'imprimerie Royale.

Deemen, A. V. (1999). *The probability of the paradox of voting for weak preference orderings, social choice and welfare.* Berlin: Springer.

Dyer, J. S., & Sarin, R. K. (1979). Group preference aggregation rules based on strength of preference. *Management Science, 25*(9), 22-34.

Fjermestad, J., & Hiltz, S. R. (1999). An assessment of group support systems experimental research: Methodology and results. *Journal of Management Information Systems, 15*(3), 7-150.

French, S. (1986). *Decision theory: An introduction to the mathematics of rationality.* Chichester: Ellis Harwood.

Giunipero, L., Handfield, R. B., & Eltantawy, R. (2006). Supply management's evolution: key skill sets for the supply manager of the future. *International Journal of Operations & Production Management, 26*(7), 822-844.

Huang, W. (2003). Impacts of GSS generic structures and task types on group communication process and outcome: Some expected and unexpected research findings. *Behavior & Information Technology, 22*(1), 17-29.

Huang, W., & Li, D. (2007). Opening up the black box in GSS research: explaining group decision outcome with group process. *Computers in Human Behavior, 23*(1), 58-78.

Huang, W., & Wei, K. K. (2000). An empirical investigation of effects of GSS and task type on social interactions from an influence perspective. *Journal of Management Information Systems, 17*(2), 181-206.

Huang, W., & Wei, K. K. (1997). Task as a moderator for the effects of group support systems on group influence processes. *European Journal of Information Systems, December 6,* 208-217.

Huang, W., Wei, K. K., & Lim, J. (2003). Using GSS to support global virtual team-building: A theoretical framework. *International Journal of Global Information Management, 11*(1), 72-89.

Huang, W., Wei, K.K., and Tan, C.Y. (1999). Compensating effects of GSS on group performance. *Information & Management, 35,* 195-202.

Huang, W., Wei, K. K., Watson, R. T., & Tan, C. Y. (2003). Supporting virtual team-building with a GSS: An empirical investigation. *Decision Support Systems, 34*(4), 359-367.

Keeney, R. L., & Kirkwood, C. W. (1975). Group decision making using cardinal social welfare functions. *Management Science, 22*(4), 430-437.

Lao, L., Dovrolis, C., & Sanadidi, M. Y. (2006). The probe gap model can underestimate the available bandwidth of multihop paths. *Computer Communication Review, 36*(5), 29-34.

LaPorte, T., & Consilini, N. (1991). Working in practice but not in theory: theoretical challenges of "High Reliability Organizations". *Journal of Public Administration Research and Theory, 1*(1), 19-47.

Limayem, M., Banerjee, P., & Ma, L. (2006). Impact of GDSS: Opening the black box. *Decision Support Systems, 42*(2), 945-957.

Mallach, E. G. (2000). *Decision support and data warehouse systems.* New York: McGraw-Hill.

Mendonca, D., Beroggi, G. E. G., Gent, D. V., & Wallace, W. A. (2006). Designing gaming simulations for the assessment of group decision support systems in emergency response. *Safety Science, 44* (6), 523-535.

Murphy, K., Roodenrys, S., & Fox, A. (2006). Event-related potential correlates of the word length effect in working memory. *Brain Research, 1112*, 179-190.

Myers, D. G. (2005). *Social psychology.* New York: McGraw-Hill.

Nanson, E. J. (1882). Methods of election, transactions and proceedings of the royal society of Victoria, Vol. 18.

Niemi, R. G., & Weisberg, H. F. (1968). A mathematical solution for the probability of the paradox of voting. *Behavioral Science, 13*, 317.

Nunamaker, J. F., Briggs, R. O., Mittleman, D. D., Vogel, D. R., & Balthazard, P. A. (1997). Lesssons from a dozen years of group support systems research: A discussion of lab and field findings. *Journal of Management Information Systems, 13*(3), 163-207.

Ody, K. (1995). Facilitating the "right" decision in crisis-Supporting the crisis decision maker through analysis of their needs. *Safety Science, 20*, 125-133.

Over, E. A. B., Hooge, I. T. C., & Erkelens, C. J. (2006). A quantitative measure for the uniformity of fixation density: The Voronoi method. *Behavior Research Methods, 38*(2), 251-261.

Papazoglou, I. A., & Christou, M. D. (1997). Decision support system for emergency response to major nuclear accidents. *Nuclear Technology, 118*(2), 97-122.

Potter, R. E., & Balthazard, P. (2004). The role of individual memory and attention processes during electronic brainstorming. *MIS Quarterly, 28*(4), 621-643.

Saaty, T. L. (1988). *What is the analytic hierarchy process?* New York: Springer-Verlag Inc.

Shyur, H. J., & Shih, H. S. (2006). A hybrid MCDM model for strategic vendor selection. *Mathematical and Computer Modeling, 44*(7-8), 749-761.

Tan, B., Wei, K. K., Huang, W., & Ng, G. N. (2000). A dialogue technical to enhance electronic communication in virtual teams. *IEEE Transactions on Professional Communication, 43*(2), 153-165.

Vogel, D. R., Martz, W. B., Nunamaker, J. F., Grohowski, R. B., & McGoff, C. (1990). Electronic meeting system experience at IBM. *Journal of Management Information Systems, 6*(3), 25-43.

Wallace, W. A., & DeBalogh, F. (1985). Decision support systems for disaster management. *Public Administration Review, 45*, 134-146.

Watson, R. T., DeSanctis, G., & Poole, M. S. (1988). Using a GDSS to facilitate group consensus: some intended and unintended consequences. *MIS Quarterly, 12*(3), 463-478.

Weisaeth, L., Knudsen, O., & Tonnessen, A. (2002). Technological disasters, crisis management and leadership stress. *Journal of Hazardous Materials, 93*, 33-45.

Wilkenfeld, J., Kraus, S., Holley, K. M., & Harris M. A. (1995). GENIE: A decision support system for crisis negotiations. *Decision Support Systems, 14*, 369-391.

Williams, A. H., & Cookson, R. A. (2006). Equity-efficiency trade-offs in health technology assessment. *International Journal of Technology Assessment in Health Care, 22*(1), 1-9.

Zigurs, I., DeSanctis, G., & Billingsley, J. (1991). Adoption patterns and attitudinal development in computer-supported meetings: An exploratory study with SAMM. *Journal of Management Information Systems, 7*(4), 51-70.

Zografos, K. G., Vasilakis, G. M., & Giannouli, I. M. (2000). Methodological framework for developing decision support systems (DSS) for hazardous materials emergency response operations. *Journal of Hazardous Materials*, *71*(1-3), 503-521.

ENDNOTE

[1] This work is supported by the National Science Foundation of China (NSFC) under Grant 70671066.

APPENDIX A

A.1 Definition of Preference Utility Value and a Set of its Quantificational Values

Let G denote a decision-making group, DM_r be the rth decision-maker of the group with l decision-makers, then $G = \{DM_r | r \in \Omega\}(\Omega = \{1, 2, \cdots, l\}, 2 \le l < +\infty)$. Let X be a set of alternatives, x^i be the ith alternative and there are s alternatives in the alternative set, then $X = \{x^i | i \in \Omega\}(\Omega = \{1, 2, \cdots, s\}, 2 \le s < +\infty)$.

Definition 1. Preference utility value $\theta_r(x^i, x^j)$: *Let* R_r *denote the preference relation of* DM_r *on X. Let* $x^i R_r x^j$ *denote that comparing* x^i *with* $x^i(x^i, x^j \in X)$, DM_r *tends to choose* x^i. *According to the needs of the decision-making, let* $\theta_r(x^i, x^j)$, *a real number, denote the quantificational difference of* DM_r's *preference degrees on the two alternatives* x^i *and* x^j.

Let's define the quantificational values of $\theta_r(x^i, x^j)$ as in Table 5.

$\theta_r(x^i, x^j)$	the signification to DM_r
1	x^i and x^j has equal preference degree
3	Compared with x^j, x^i is a little better
5	Compared with x^j, x^i is better
7	Compared with x^j, x^i is much better
9	Compared with x^j, x^i is absolutely better
2, 4, 6, 8	The middle state's corresponding utility values of the judgments
reciprocal	Compared x^j with x^i, the utility value of preference $\theta_r(x^j, x^i) = \dfrac{1}{\theta_r(x^i, x^j)}, \theta_r(x^i, x^i) = 1$

A.2 The Solving Process of the Consistence Indicator CI_r

From the theory of matrix, the Equation $(P_r - \lambda I)\pi^T = 0$ has at least one group of solutions, where π^T is the characteristic vector, λ is the characteristic value. An approximate calculation algorithm is given to get the maximal characteristic value $\lambda_{\max}^{(r)}$ and characteristic vector $\pi_r = (\pi_r(x^1), \pi_r(x^2), \cdots, \pi_r(x^s))$ of P_r in Appendix A.

1. Calculate the geometric mean of all the elements in each row of the matrix

$$\bar{\pi}_r(x^i) = \sqrt[s]{\prod_{j=1}^{s}\theta_r(x^i, x^j)} \quad i = 1, 2, \cdots, s \tag{12}$$

We have $\bar{\pi}_r = (\bar{\pi}_r(x^1), \bar{\pi}_r(x^2), \cdots, \bar{\pi}_r(x^s))$

2. Normalize $\bar{\pi}_r(x^i)$

$$\bar{\bar{\pi}}_r(x^i) = \frac{\bar{\pi}_r(x^i)}{\sum_{j=1}^{s}\bar{\pi}_r(x^j)} \quad i = 1, 2, \cdots, s \tag{13}$$

Then $\pi_r = (\pi_r(x^1), \pi_r(x^2), \cdots, \pi_r(x^s))$ is the approximate solution of the characteristic vector. We call $\pi_r(x^1)$ the preference utility value of DM_r on x^1. The set $\{\pi_r(x^1), \pi_r(x^2), \cdots, \pi_r(x^s)\}$ denotes the preference utility values set of DM_r on the set of alternatives.

3.   Calculate the maximal characteristic value $\lambda_{\max}^{(r)}$ of the matrix P_r

$$\lambda_{\max}^{(r)} = \sum_{i=1}^{s} \frac{(P_r \pi_r)_i}{s\pi_r(x^i)} \tag{14}$$

where $(P_r \pi_r)_i$ is the ith element of the vector $P_r \pi_r$.

The consistency test index CI from AHP is introduced (Saaty, 1988)

$$CI_r = \frac{\lambda_{\max}^{(r)} - s}{s-1} = \frac{\lambda_{\max}^{(r)}}{s-1} - \frac{s}{s-1} \tag{15}$$

Let CI_r denote the rth decision maker DM_r's preference judgment consistency. CI_r is an indicator to measure whether the decision maker's judgment is careful. The smaller CI_r is, the better it is. Especially, when $CI_r = 0$, the preference judgment matrix P_r is a complete consistency matrix, which represents the complete consistency of DM_r's preference judgment. However, when people do pair wise comparisons they cannot ensure their judgments are completely consistent because of the complexity of the objective reality and the limitation of human thoughts. There usually exists error of estimation which makes CI_r larger than 0. The larger CI_r is, the worse the consistency of P_r becomes.

APPENDIX B: CLUSTERING METHOD AND DEFINITION OF PREFERENCE DISTANCE

Packing all the preference values $\pi_r(x^i)$ ($1 \leq i \leq s$; $1 \leq r \leq l$) from the l decision-makers in the group, we have the $l \times s$ preference value matrix Λ

Definition 2. *The Euclidean preference distance between decision-maker DM_i and DM_j on a set of alternatives X is*

$$d_{ij} = \sqrt{\sum_{k=1}^{s} \left| \pi_i(x^k) - \pi_j(x^k) \right|^2}.$$

(16)

The Euclidean preference distance d_{ij} also denotes the difference of consensus between decision-maker DM_i and DM_j on X.

Packing the preference distances of all the l decision-makers, we have the $l \times l$ preference difference matrix,

$$D = \begin{bmatrix} 0 & & & & \\ d_{21} & 0 & & & \\ d_{31} & d_{32} & 0 & & \\ \cdots & \cdots & \cdots & 0 & \\ d_{l1} & d_{l2} & d_{l3} & \cdots & 0 \end{bmatrix}$$

(17)

where d_{ij} is nonnegative. The closer DM_i and DM_j are to each other, the smaller d_{ij} is. As $d_{ij} = d_{ij}$ and $d_{ij} = 0$, we have the matrix as shown in Equation (17).

Definition 3. *Let $C = \{c^\omega : \omega = 1, 2, \cdots, m\}$ be the preference cluster of the group G on a set of alternatives X, ε be the given clustering distance. If the distance between each two elements in c^ω satisfies the constraint $d_{ij} \leq \varepsilon \in c^\omega$, we call that c^ω is a cluster, that is, the sub-group comes to consensus in c^ω.*

Definition 4. *With respect to the decision-makers DM_i and DM_j, if $(d_{ij} \leq \varepsilon) \in c^\omega \subseteq C$, we call that DM_i and DM_j come to partial consensus in c^ω. As to $d_{rq} \leq \varepsilon^k \in c^k$, $(d_{ij} \leq \varepsilon^l) \in c^l$, if and only if $\varepsilon^k = \varepsilon^l = \varepsilon$ and $d_{ri} \leq \varepsilon$, $d_{rj} \leq \varepsilon$, $d_{iq} \leq \varepsilon$, $d_{jq} \leq \varepsilon$, we call $c^k = c^l$ is the same cluster.*

Example 1. *Suppose there is an initial preference utility value matrix as follows,*

$$\Lambda = \begin{bmatrix} 0.1 & 0.3 & 0.2 & 0.4 \\ 0.2 & 0.4 & 0.1 & 0.3 \\ 0.3 & 0.1 & 0.4 & 0.2 \\ 0.4 & 0.2 & 0.3 & 0.1 \\ 0.3 & 0.3 & 0.3 & 0.1 \\ 0.2 & 0.2 & 0.2 & 0.4 \end{bmatrix}.$$

(18)

Substituting the values into Equation (16), the consensus difference matrix (the preference difference matrix) as follows is had,

$$d = \begin{bmatrix} 0 & & & & & \\ 0.2 & 0 & & & & \\ 0.4 & 0.447 & 0 & & & \\ 0.447 & 0.4 & 0.2 & 0 & & \\ 0.374 & 0.316 & 0.245 & 0.141 & 0 & \\ 0.141 & 0.245 & 0.316 & 0.374 & 0.346 & 0 \end{bmatrix}.$$

(19)

1. Given $\varepsilon^1 \leq 0.15$ thus $d_{61} = d_{54} = 0.141 \leq \varepsilon^1$

The results DM_1, $DM_6 \in c^1$ and DM_4, $DM_5 \in c^2$ can be had. Although $d_{61} = d_{54} \leq \varepsilon^1$, $\min\{d_{65}, d_{64}, d_{51}, d_{41}\} = 0.346 > \varepsilon^1$ thus c^1, c^2 are not the same cluster according to Definition 4 and the two clusters come to partial consensus separately. DM_2 and DM_3 have not come to consensus with others as shown in Figure 3.

Figure 3.

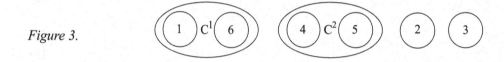

2. Given $\varepsilon^2 \leq 0.2$, we have $d_{21} = d_{43} = 0.2 \leq \varepsilon^2$ and $d_{61} = d_{54} = 0.141 \leq \varepsilon^1$, that is, DM_1, $DM_2 \in c^3$ and DM_3, $DM_4 \in c^4$ come to consensus respectively based on the consensus of DM_1, $DM_6 \in c^1$ and DM_4, $DM_5 \in c^2$. Here c^3 and c^4 are not the same cluster, as shown in Figure 4.

Figure 4.

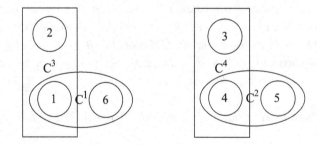

3. Given $\varepsilon^3 \leq 0.25$, we have $d_{61} = d_{54} = 0.141 \leq \varepsilon^1$, $d_{21} = d_{43} = 0.2 \leq \varepsilon^2$, and $d_{62} = d_{53} = 0.245 \leq \varepsilon^3$, that is, DM_1, DM_2, $DM_6 \in c^5$ come to consensus in c^5 and DM_3, DM_4, $DM_5 \in c^6$ come to consensus in c^6 as shown in Figure 5.

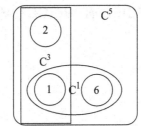 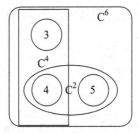

Figure 5.

Assume k clusters are being sought after clustering with given ε and there are $\hat{l}$ elements in one of the k clusters, c^{ω}.

Definition 5. *To those clusters that have more than 2 elements, that is, $2 \leq \hat{l} \leq s$, the cluster center is defined as*

$$\hat{\pi} = \frac{1}{\hat{l}} \sum_{i=1}^{\hat{l}} \pi_i .$$

(20)

The Euclidean distance of preference between a decision-maker DM_r and the specified cluster center is then defined as

$$d_r = \sqrt{\sum_{k=1}^{s} \left| \pi_r(x^k) - \hat{\pi}(x^k) \right|^2} .$$

(21)

APPENDIX C: A SOLUTION OF THE DECISION WEIGHT VECTOR

Construct the Lagrange function for the optimization model,

$$L(w,\xi) = \sum_{r=1}^{l} [(\frac{\lambda_{max}^{(r)}}{s-1} - \frac{s}{s-1}) + \sqrt{\sum_{k=1}^{s}(\pi_r(x^k) - \hat{\pi}(x^k))^2}]w_r^2 + 2\xi(\sum_{r=1}^{l} w_r - 1). \tag{22}$$

From the first-order condition of Equation (24), we have

$$\begin{cases} \frac{\partial L}{\partial w_r} = 2[(\frac{\lambda_{max}^{(r)}}{s-1} - \frac{s}{s-1}) + \sqrt{\sum_{k=1}^{s}(\pi_r(x^k) - \hat{\pi}(x^k))^2}]w_r + 2\xi = 0 \\ \frac{\partial L}{\partial \xi} = \sum_{r=1}^{l} w_r - 1 = 0 \end{cases}$$

which implies that

$$\begin{cases} w_r = \dfrac{-\xi}{[(\frac{\lambda_{max}^{(r)}}{s-1} - \frac{s}{s-1}) + \sqrt{\sum_{k=1}^{s}(\pi_r(x^k) - \hat{\pi}(x^k))^2}]} \tag{23} \\ \sum_{r=1}^{l} w_r = 1 \tag{24} \end{cases}$$

Thus, we have

$$\begin{cases} \xi = -\dfrac{1}{\sum_{r=1}^{l} 1 \Big/ [(\frac{\lambda_{max}^{(r)}}{s-1} - \frac{s}{s-1}) + \sqrt{\sum_{k=1}^{s}(\pi_r(x^k) - \hat{\pi}(x^k))^2}]} \tag{25} \\ w_r = \dfrac{1}{[(\frac{\lambda_{max}^{(r)}}{s-1} - \frac{s}{s-1}) + \sqrt{\sum_{k=1}^{s}(\pi_r(x^k) - \hat{\pi}(x^k))^2}] \bullet \sum_{r=1}^{l} 1 \Big/ [(\frac{\lambda_{max}^{(r)}}{s-1} - \frac{s}{s-1}) + \sqrt{\sum_{k=1}^{s}(\pi_r(x^k) - \hat{\pi}(x^k))^2}]} \tag{26} \end{cases}$$

From Equation (26), the decision weight vector assigned to a group of decision-makers, $W = (w_1, w_2, \cdots, w_s)$ can be derived.

414

APPENDIX D: DISCRETE TIME MARKOV CHAINS AND MARKOV PROPERTY OF THE GROUP DECISION-MAKING PROCEDURE

A sequence of random variables $\{E_n\}$ is called a Markov chain if it has the Markov property:

$$T\{E_{n+1} = j \mid E_n = i, E_{n-1} = i_{n-1}, ..., E_0 = i_0\} = T\{E_{n+1} = j \mid E_n = i\}$$
$$T_{ij} = T\{E_{n+1} = j \mid E_n = i\} \tag{27}$$

Here, E_i is an event and T_{ij} is the probability to transit from state i to state j of the event. The property is called Memoryless. In other words, "Future" is independent of "Past" given "Present." Here the transition probabilities T_{ij} satisfy

$$T_{ij} \geq 0, \quad \sum_{j=0}^{\infty} T_{ij} = 1.$$

The Chapman-Kolmogorov Equation for a discrete-time Markov chain is as follows: If the distribution at time t_n is $\pi^{(n)}$, then the distribution at time t_{n+1} is given by

$$\pi^{(n+1)} \tag{28}$$

Because each decision-maker in the group independently puts forward her/his preference judgment matrix, the preference state E^r of decision-maker DM_r is independent of other decision-makers and the future preference state E_{n+1}^r is independent of other states except the current state E_n^r, thus the group decision-making procedure satisfies Equation (27).

Obviously, the transition probabilities T_{ij} constructed from Equation (3) satisfy

$$T_{ij} \geq 0, \quad \sum_{j=0}^{\infty} T_{ij} = 1.$$

Equation (4) shows that the overall state transition probabilities matrix is the mean value of the matrices of transition probabilities of each decision-maker, thus the group property is implied in the individual properties.

Therefore, the Chapman-Kolmogorov Equations, Equation (28) can be used to get $\pi^{(n+1)}$ at "time" t_{n+1} from $\pi^{(n)}$ at "time" t_n.

This work was previously published in Journal of Global Information Management, Vol. 16, Issue 2, edited by Felix B. Tan, pp. 35-57, copyright 2008 by IGI Publishing, formerly known as Idea Group Publishing (an imprint of IGI Global).

Index